Law, Liberty, and Parliament:
Selected Essays on the Writings of
Sir Edward Coke

Sir Edward Coke

Law, Liberty, and Parliament

SELECTED ESSAYS
ON THE WRITINGS OF
SIR EDWARD COKE

Edited and with an
Introduction
by Allen D. Boyer

Liberty Fund
INDIANAPOLIS

Introduction © 2004 Liberty Fund, Inc.
All rights reserved
Printed in the United States of America

08   07   06   05   04   C   5   4   3   2   1
08   07   06   05   04   P   5   4   3   2   1

Cover art: Engraved portrait of Sir Edward Coke by R. White.
Courtesy of Allen D. Boyer.
Frontispiece: Engraved portrait of Lord Chief Justice
Sir Edward Coke, by Simon van der Passe, ca. 1618–20.
Courtesy of Sir John Baker.

Library of Congress Cataloging-in-Publication Data
Law, liberty, and parliament:
selected essays on the writings of Sir Edward Coke
edited and with an introduction by Allen D. Boyer.
p.   cm.
Includes bibliographical references and index.
ISBN 0-86597-425-X (hard: alk. paper)
ISBN 0-86597-426-8 (paper: alk. paper)
1. Coke, Edward, Sir, 1552–1634.
2. Law—England—History.
KD621.C64L39   2004
349.42—dc22   2003058932

Liberty Fund, Inc.
8335 Allison Pointe Trail, Suite 300
Indianapolis, Indiana 46250-1684

Contents

❧ ❧ ❧

Introduction *vii*

Editor's Note *xv*

Introduction to Coke's "Commentary on Littleton"
THOMAS G. BARNES
1

Writing the Law
RICHARD HELGERSON
26

The Place of *Slade's Case* in the History of Contract
A. W. B. SIMPSON
70

Sir Edward Coke and the Interpretation of Lawful Allegiance in
Seventeenth-Century England
DAVID MARTIN JONES
86

Sir Edward Coke (1552–1634): His Theory of "Artificial Reason" as a
Context for Modern Basic Legal Theory
JOHN UNDERWOOD LEWIS
107

Further Reflections on "Artificial Reason"
CHARLES M. GRAY
121

Against Common Right and Reason:
The College of Physicians v. Dr. Thomas Bonham
HAROLD J. COOK
127

Bonham's Case and Judicial Review

THEODORE F. T. PLUCKNETT

150

The "Economic Liberalism" of Sir Edward Coke

BARBARA MALAMENT

186

Sir Edward Coke, Ciceronianus: Classical Rhetoric and
the Common Law Tradition

ALLEN D. BOYER

224

The Common Lawyers and the Chancery: 1616

SIR JOHN BAKER

254

The Crown and the Courts in England, 1603–1625

W. J. JONES

282

The Procedure of the House of Commons Against
Patents and Monopolies, 1621–1624

ELIZABETH READ FOSTER

302

The Origins of the Petition of Right Reconsidered

J. A. GUY

328

Coke's Note-Books and the Sources of His *Reports*

SIR JOHN BAKER

357

Index

387

Introduction

❧ ❧ ❧

Sir Edward Coke was born in the village of Mileham, Norfolk, on February 1, 1552. His family belonged to the minor gentry. His father was Robert Coke, a lawyer attached to Lincoln's Inn. His mother, Winifred, owned lawbooks, a fact that suggests she was a remarkable woman.

In 1567, at age fifteen, Coke enrolled at Trinity College, Cambridge, leaving in 1570 without taking a degree. On January 21, 1571, a date he carefully recorded, Coke arrived in London and enrolled at Clifford's Inn. In 1572 he moved on to the Inner Temple and began attending the courts in Westminster. Coke was called to the bar in April 1578.

In 1579 Coke argued his first case in the King's Bench, and won by out-researching his opponent. Edward, Lord Cromwell, had sued a parson for defamation, but Coke showed that the plaintiff's case was based not on the Latin text of the statute, but on a badly translated Law French abridgement. Soon afterward, Coke's role in arguing *Shelley's Case* (1581) brought him wider acclaim. *Shelley's Case* featured anomalous facts, an ingenious new reading of black-letter conveyancing formulae, and a prominent family bitterly divided over religion. Coke orchestrated an energetic, brilliant defensive action and then celebrated the victory by circulating manuscript copies of his arguments —his first published case-report.

During the 1580s and 1590s, Coke became one of the most prominent lawyers in England. The great cases in which he participated, usually winning his point, were many. In *Chudleigh's Case* (1594), Coke argued that the Statute of Uses flatly made all transfers "to use" subject to the rules on similar transfers made at law. In *Slade's Case* (1602), Coke argued successfully that a plaintiff seeking payment for an unkept promise to pay money should be allowed to sue in assumpsit, rather than being required to bring an action for debt. This decision helped make assumpsit actions synonymous with contract claims and opened the door more broadly to jury trials. Professional advancement followed. Coke became recorder of Coventry in 1585, of Norwich in 1586, of

London in 1592. He was made solicitor general (June 1592) and attorney general (April 1594), appointments he owed to the support of the Cecil family. During the Parliament of 1593, Coke served as speaker of the Commons. As a government prosecutor, Coke took part in the treason prosecutions of Elizabeth's last decade. In early 1601 he presented the case that sent the Earl of Essex to the scaffold. After the accession of James I, who knighted him in May 1603, Coke continued to serve as attorney general. He prosecuted Sir Walter Ralegh (the bitterest proceeding of his career). The winter of 1605–1606 saw him investigating the Gunpowder Plot.

Coke was appointed chief justice of the Court of Common Pleas in June 1606. He was appointed chief justice of the King's Bench in October 1613 and was dismissed from the bench in November 1616. His tenure on these courts was a turbulent period, marked by friction with King James I and two archbishops of Canterbury, Richard Bancroft and George Abbot.

Throughout the reign of James, as during Elizabeth's years on the throne, the Puritan believers of England faced prosecution by Anglican bishops and by the Court of High Commission. In its proceedings, the High Commission questioned defendants under oath, often forcing them to choose between incriminating themselves or committing perjury. (This was the notorious "ex officio oath," so called because it was used in proceedings initiated directly by the commission.) The commission also meted out fines and prison terms.

Skillfully seeking every legal advantage, the Puritans sued in common-law courts for writs of prohibition, orders enjoining such prosecutions. Their lawyers argued that the commission's powers to interrogate, fine, and imprison were invalid, simply because these powers were set forth only in letters patent issued by the crown—not by the statute that established the commission. Effectively, such arguments suggested that the royal prerogative was limited by what Parliament enacted, and they tended to align Puritan defendants, the House of Commons, and common-law judges against the crown and the Anglican hierarchy. Rather than relentlessly pursuing conflict, Coke emphasized the need to limit the High Commission to serious, "enormous" cases and to prevent misuse of the power to compel self-incrimination. Nonetheless, when compared with other judges, Coke circumscribed the High Commission's jurisdiction more closely. In *Fuller's Case* (1607), Coke wrote that "when there is any question concerning what power or jurisdiction belongs to ecclesiastical judges . . . the determination of this belongs to the judges of the common law."

In November 1608, when King James personally tried to resolve the feuds among his judges and churchmen, the controversy reached its highest pitch. James informed the common-law judges that he planned to decide the dispute between his courts of law and the tribunals of the church he headed; the judges were all his servants, he explained, and accordingly he could withdraw cases from their consideration and decide them himself. In reply, Coke asserted that the king lacked the professional training necessary to serve as a judge. He wrote that he had told James "that God had endowed His Majesty with excellent science, and great endowments of nature; but his Majesty was not learned in the laws of his realm of England . . . which law is an act which requires long study and experience, before that a man can attain to the cognizance of it." The king reportedly "fell into that high indignation as the like was never known in him, looking and speaking fiercely with bended fist, offering to strike him, etc., which the Lord Coke perceiving fell flat on all four; humbly beseeching his majesty to take compassion on him and to pardon him." James continued to rage, until Robert Cecil intervened.

The controversy faded out, leaving the chief justice with the reputation of a man who sought out explosive confrontations. Yet Coke was not constantly at odds with the crown; nor was Coke the only judge who infuriated James; nor was he the only judge whom James bullied or suspended. Coke was frequently willing to favor the crown. *The Prince's Case* (1606) allowed James to recover many crown estates that had been cheaply sold during Elizabeth's last years. In *Calvin's Case* (1608), Coke and the judges finessed a delicate political issue, whether James's Scottish subjects possessed the rights of English subjects. However confrontational the course that Coke steered as chief justice, the confrontations are not the entire story.

In 1613, against his own will, Coke was advanced to the King's Bench. For more than a century, a quarrel had smoldered between King's Bench and Chancery. King's Bench judges had asserted that chancellors could not interfere with the finality of judgments given by courts of law, while chancellors had claimed that they could mitigate harsh law-court judgments even after those judgments had been handed down (effectively allowing someone who had lost in the law courts to appeal yet again to chancery). In a trio of controversial cases, *Heath v. Ridley* (1614), *Glanvill v. Courtney* (1614), and *The Case of Magdalene College* (1615), Coke and Lord Chancellor Ellesmere sparred over such issues.

In the same period, Coke stirred up other enmities. In 1614, during the Addled Parliament, he reversed precedent and kept the judges from advising the House of Lords on points of law. Prohibitions were issued routinely to the Admiralty, to the Council of the North and the Council of the Marches, and to other prerogative courts. In *Bagg's Case* (1615), Coke announced that the King's Bench had the authority "to correct all lesser authorities in the realm," a claim that could be stretched to cover even Chancery.

In the spring of 1616, a case pitting common-law rights against episcopal privilege—a decision reported as *Colt v. Glover,* or as *The Case of Commendams*—finally brought matters to a head. King James had supplemented the bishop of Coventry and Lichfield's income with the profits of an additional rectory, only to see a landowner challenge his action. James wrote to the judges, stating that the case concerned his power to govern the church and asking that they stay proceedings until he decided whether further consultation between judges and churchmen was required. The judges unanimously replied, in a letter probably drafted by Coke, that the king's letter was "contrary to law" and that "our oath in express words is that in case any letter comes to us contrary to law that we do nothing by such letters, but certify your Majesty thereof, and go forth to do the law." James summoned the judges. He tore up their letter and demanded of each judge whether he now would obey any future royal order. All the judges save Coke backed down. Asked what he would do, Coke answered, "When that case should be, he would do that [which] should be fit for a judge to do."

In late June, Coke was suspended from his privy council seat, charged with showing contempt for the Chancery and the crown. Meantime, James ordered, Coke was not to ride on the summer assize circuit. Instead, he was to censor his own law reports, "wherein (as his majesty is informed) there be many exorbitant and extravagant opinions set down and published for positive and good law." When Coke refused to recant, the king finally acted. On November 16, 1616, Coke was removed from the bench. It was said, John Chamberlain wrote, that "four p's" had overthrown the chief justice, "that is, pride, prohibitions, praemunire, and prerogative."

Within a few months, Coke had bought back royal favor. He arranged a match between his daughter Frances and the duke of Buckingham's older brother. This brought Coke a return to his seat on the Privy Council, although he never returned to judicial office. The cost was a scandal—an armed clash

between his servants and the servants of his wife, who opposed the match—
and final marital estrangement.

Coke traced the source of law to custom and judicial wisdom rather than to
royal command. He gave mythic dimensions to the common law by tracing
legal doctrines into dim antiquity. More importantly, Coke defined law as the
"artificial reason" of the judges, a professional consensus based on training and
experience. "Reason is the life of the law," he wrote, "nay the common law
itself is nothing else but reason; which is to be understood of an artificial perfection of reason, gotten by long study, observation and experience, and not
of every man's natural reason."

   "Nothing that is contrary to reason, is consonant to law," Coke wrote. While
such assertions dated back to Bracton, Coke and his colleagues pursued the
principle with newfound energy. Coke asserted that judges found law and
did not make it, but he clearly preferred reform by judicial action to reform
by legislation. He argued that legal traditions were rich enough to solve any
question facing a court. As lawyer and as judge—in cases such as *Davenant v.
Hurdis* (1598), *Tooley's Case* (1613), and the notable *Taylors of Ipswich* (1614)—
Coke supported artisans seeking to follow their trades over opposition from
craft guilds.

   In 1610, in *Bonham's Case,* Coke laid the foundations for judicial review of
legislation, allowing judges to strike down statutes. "It appears in our books,"
Coke wrote, "that in many cases, the common law will control acts of Parliament, and sometimes adjudge them to be utterly void; for when an act of
Parliament is against common right and reason, or repugnant, or impossible
to be performed, the common law will control it, and adjudge such act to be
void."

Absent from the House of Commons for nearly three decades, Coke returned
for four parliaments in the 1620s. In these assemblies, he figured as one of the
Commons' most prominent leaders. Always an oracle, he ended as somewhat
of a statesman, moving into opposition to the crown.

   In the Parliament of 1621, Coke attacked abuses within the legal system. The
Commons showed a vogue for impeaching state officers; Coke supported this
effort by supplying precedents and conducting crucial hearings. The Commons began by attacking corrupt monopolists and then turned upon the man

who had approved their patents, Lord Chancellor Sir Francis Bacon. Coke headed the committee that investigated Bacon and fended off compromises that might have saved his rival.

In late December, after Coke and the Commons had asserted the right to debate and legislate on all matters concerning the commonwealth, the king retaliated. Coke was arrested and James dissolved the Parliament. Coke was removed from the Privy Council and spent most of 1622 in confinement, initially in the Tower, later under house arrest.

In the Parliament of 1624, Coke seemed temporarily chastened. Complaints were once more aired, but this time hopefully. The session was a short-lived interlude in the worsening relationship between the Commons and the crown. The Parliament of 1625, the first convened by Charles I, saw a sea change in Coke's role. No longer was he the tireless legislator who analyzed the details of bills. Instead, linked with opposition figures, he pressed a series of initiatives uncongenial to the new king—criticizing his foreign policy, challenging his decisions on religion, and hesitating to grant financial support.

The Parliament of 1628 was Coke's most memorable. The duke of Buckingham—once James's favorite, now Charles's favorite—had recklessly brought on wars with both France and Spain. This had led, in turn, to new crises at home: fears of taxation without parliamentary consent, the institution of martial law, and the royal power to imprison without cause shown. Coke was now the crown's most prominent critic. "Other Parliaments had been concerned with particular liberties," Conrad Russell has written, such as purveyance and customs duties and monopolies, but it was this Parliament "which first saw these liberties as collectively threatened by a threat to the ideal which held them all together, the rule of law." The metaphors Coke employed in his speeches to the Commons—that no man was tenant at will for his liberties, or that if a lord could not imprison a villein without cause, no king could imprison a freeman without cause—provided an ideology that closely associated liberty and property.

Coke led the Commons in rejecting compromise. "I know that prerogative is part of the law," Coke cautioned, "but sovereign power is no parliamentary word: in my opinion, it weakens Magna Carta. . . . Magna Carta is such a fellow that he will have no sovereign." When Charles warned the Commons that he would veto any bill that did more than reconfirm Magna Carta, Coke responded by suggesting that the Commons present exactly such a measure— the Petition of Right, something more than a list of grievances, if less than an actual bill of rights. In June 1628, when the king returned an evasive answer and announced his intention to prorogue Parliament, Coke played a final, pivotal role. On June 6, in highly dramatic circumstances, he named Buckingham as "the grievance of grievances" and "the cause of all our miseries." With the favorite under attack, Charles backed down. On June 7, 1628, the king assented to the Petition.

This was Coke's last venture into public life. He retired to his mansion at Stoke Poges, where he apparently worked to complete his *Institutes*. In August 1634, while the old man lay dying, the king's men ransacked both Coke's study at Stoke and his files at the Inner Temple. Coke died late on the evening of September 3, 1634. His papers vanished for seven years, until the Long Parliament voted that they be returned to his heir and published.

In his lifetime, Coke published eleven volumes of judicial decisions, known to lawyers simply as "the *Reports,*" and his massive *Book of Entries* (1614). The value of these collections, as a working reference for the bar, has never been gainsaid. Sir Francis Bacon wrote: "Had it not been for Sir Edward Coke's reports (which, though they may have errors, and some peremptory and extra-judicial resolutions more than are warranted, yet they contain infinite good decisions and rulings over of cases), the law, by this time, had been almost like a ship without ballast."

In 1628 the old judge published his masterwork, the *Commentary upon Littleton,* known ever thereafter as "Coke on Littleton." The book ostensibly presents Coke's glosses on the text of the *Tenures* of Sir Thomas Littleton, a treatise on the law of real property. In fact, however, Coke's glosses range broadly across the law of his day. *Coke on Littleton* was the first volume of Coke's four *Institutes of the Laws of England.* The *Second Institute* covers thirty-nine statutes of significance, beginning with Magna Carta. The *Third Institute* covers criminal law. The *Fourth Institute* was a treatise on structural constitutional law and the powers of the various government bodies existing in England—legislative, administrative, ecclesiastical, collegiate, metropolitan, even baronial. After Coke's death, some of his other works found their way into print: treatises on bail and mainprise, treatises on copyhold tenures, and two additional collections of cases.

Wherever the common law has been applied, Coke's influence has been monumental. As legal historian William Holdsworth noted, Coke's works have been to the common law what Shakespeare has been to literature, and the King James Bible to religion. He is the earliest judge whose decisions are still routinely cited by practicing lawyers, the jurisprudent to whose writings one turns for a statement of what the common law held on any given topic. His discussion of a phrase from Magna Carta, *nisi legem terrae,* is one of the earliest commentaries to give a deeply constitutional resonance to the phrase "due process of law." For his defense of liberties and property rights, for his assertion of judicial independence, for his active, careful role in adjusting law to the demands of litigants and the interests of society, few figures have deserved more honor.

                                                            Allen D. Boyer

Editor's Note

❧ ❧ ❧

The essays collected here were published on two different continents and over a span of more than seventy years. Only as necessary has any standardization of usage, style, spelling, or form been applied, except that references are uniformly presented in footnote form. In certain pieces, occasional notes and cross-references that would have directed the reader to pages or sections not included in the present volume have been silently deleted.

Introduction to Coke's "Commentary on Littleton"

THOMAS G. BARNES

❧ ❧ ❧

Having playfully suggested in the *Notes* to the first volume of Coke upon Littleton that Littleton's motto might just as well have been "One Law and One Book," the Editor must reveal at the outset that the tomb of Littleton's great commentator, Sir Edward Coke, carries a Latin inscription exalting the deceased as *Duodecem Liberorum [et] Tredecim Librorum Pater,* Father of Twelve Children and Thirteen Books. One begs the question of how accurate the number of children is, but thirteen books was dead-on for the eleven volumes of *Reports* published in Coke's lifetime, his *Book of Entries* (1614), and his *First Institutes,* Coke upon Littleton (1628).[1] Supposing that by modern American academic standards Coke has published more than enough not to have perished, Littleton also could hardly have been denied tenure on the grounds of the quality of his one book. But these considerations are less relevant than to contrast the real motto of Littleton—*Ung Dieu et Ung Roy,* One God and One King—with the motto chosen by Coke at his call at serjeant-at-law a day before going to the Common Pleas: *Lex Est Tutissima Cassis,* Law is the Safest Helmet.[2] Littleton's motto reflected the conventional Catholic piety of the twilight of the Middle Ages and asserted a fervent, even prayerful monarchism that had marked relevance in the England of the Wars of the Roses. Coke's England of 1606 was no longer Catholic (and God need not be tolled since He was Protestant if not Anglican and certainly English). A century of

1. Catherine Drinker Bowen, *The Lion and the Throne* (Boston, 1956), p. 535.
2. *Ibid.,* p. 280. Mrs. Bowen translated "Cassis" as shield, which is much too free a rendering; this is not the worst bit of literary license in the book.

strong Tudor monarchy had banished the specter of rival royal houses engaged in civil war for a crown hanging on a bush; and indeed, instead had raised the specter of a monarch so strong as to be fearsome if not restrained by the Law. If perhaps this is to invest retrospectively too much portentousness in Coke's motto, there is no doubt that it was a perfect and complete statement of his guiding principle, his singular devotion to the primacy of the law.

Reference to "helmet" strikes the right note of bellicosity in Coke. Throughout his life and long career as advocate, judge, councillor and parliamentarian he was a fighter, toughly adversarial, aggressive, never wont to lose a case by faint prosecution. Like the true soldier, he was courageous under fire, resilient in defeat, and magnanimous (only) in victory. But "helmet" also bespeaks a certain defensiveness—it is a device of protection rather than a weapon. *Justitia* in European iconography has always been represented holding scales in one hand and a sword in the other (whether she is blindfolded or not varies); she never wears a helmet. Perhaps in Coke's day she needed one. Justice fared poorly in an age of assertive, absolutist monarchs, and as she needed protection so was her law the armor of the liberties of the monarch's subjects. If this was not all that apparent to Coke in June 1606, when he basked in the favor of King James I, who had rewarded his servant's fourteen years as counsellearned by elevation to the chief justiceship of the Common Pleas, it would become evident enough a decade later when the servant was driven from the bench as if he were a treasonous clerk.

Edward Coke came from an old and modestly well-to-do gentle family in Norfolk. Born in 1552 at his father's manor house at Mileham, he was the only boy among seven sisters. Schooling at Norwich was liberating if nothing else. In fact it was a great deal more, for there he acquired a mastery of Latin grammar and rhetoric that got him into Trinity College, Cambridge, in 1567 and never deserted him. Coke's reputation for learning owed a great deal to his Latinity, in an age when education meant a command of that language above all else. The rhetoric of Latin was the foundation of his logic; its grammar, vocabulary, and syntax the mortar, stone, and chisel of those finely wrought Latin maxims that he tossed off with abandon to embellish his obiter dicta and lend them an antiquity and authority that seduced his contemporaries and corrupted his successors; its philology and etymology the foundation of his grasp of English and Law French and the source of his legal-historicism. Absent his Latinity, Coke might have been easier reading, but his written corpus would have been much reduced in substance and lessened in persuasiveness. Cambridge, which he would always revere as alma mater, made no mistake in conferring upon him by grace after only three and one-half years the degree master of arts, for it recognized in the young man destined for the lawyer's, not the parson's, robe a true son and disciple of scholastic learning.

Coke was of the last generation of English barristers who as a matter of course would pass a year or two at one of the inferior Inns of Chancery before going on to an Inn of Court. The commendable justification for such a sojourn was that the fledgling barrister would learn something about the chirographic and procedural, the clerical and "paper" side of the law before proceeding to the superior Inn to learn the law. The denizens of the Inns of Chancery were court clerks and attorneys, clearly inferior in professional function and also — almost by necessary deduction — inferior in social status to the advocate-barristers who peopled the Inns of Court. Increasing definition of the distinction in status (rather than in function) in Elizabethan England impelled the governing barristers of the Inns of Court, the "benchers," to exclude the attorneys from their "company" and to confine them to the Inns of Chancery satellite to every Inn of Court. The benchers were acting not only from their own somewhat inflated self-esteem but also responding to the reality that the sons of noblemen and gentlemen flocking to the Inns of Court for a year or two introduction to the common law would not tolerate rubbing elbows with their social inferiors or be prepared to admit that they could learn anything useful from them. Therefore, the clerks and attorneys were to keep their place in the Inns of Chancery and *real* gentlemen maintain their exclusivity in the Inns of Court. What was lost to the future barrister was intimacy with the entire adjective dimension of the law, an immediate comprehension of how and even why so much of the law was process rather than substance. In a sense, young Edward Coke was lucky in a way his successors would not be. His year at Clifford's Inn, following Cambridge and before entering the Inner Temple in 1572, reinforced his almost medieval scholastic bent, enabled him to perceive the law from the bottom up, and taught him all of the method and some of the skills of the legal draftsman. In short, the year at Clifford's Inn formed Coke in an institutional frame and a pedagogy that more closely resembled the world of Justice Sir Thomas Littleton a century earlier than it did the world of Chief Justice Sir Edward Coke less than a half century later.

In his six years' studentship at the Inner Temple — he was admitted in April 1572 and called to the bar in April 1578 — Coke progressed rapidly through the exercises: moots, which were exceptionally long and complicated at the Inner Temple; simple "case-putting"; attendance at Readings (twice-yearly lectures on statutes); residence; court-sitting. In the twilight of his career, Coke would deprecate the value of the Readings as "long, obscure, and intricate, full of new conceits, liker rather to riddles than lectures, which when they are opened they vanish away like smoke" [I *Institutes,* fol. 280.b.]. One supposes that he excepted from this harsh judgment his own Readings, one at Lyon's Inn in 1579 and the other at the Middle Temple in 1592![3] Of the dozen Readers young Coke should have heard at the Temple, three were to become Serjeants-at-Law and two of these judges, the most eminent being Edmund Anderson, Chief Justice of the Common Pleas, 1582–1605. It is difficult to believe that he did not find their efforts intellectually rewarding. Yet his own experience as a student at the Temple gave point to the convention that the informal activities at the Inns were as much a feature of legal education as the formal exercises. Tradition has it that sometime during his last year before call, Coke led a student rebellion against the Inn's cook for the poor food served in hall! He drafted a Latin bill of particulars against the cook, arguing that the cook in his malfeasance had breached his engagement with the Inn (and its students), and he presented the case personally before the benchers to the admiration of his fellows and the favorable notice of his superiors. The records of the Inn are silent as to the outcome, indeed, silent as to whether the incident actually occurred.[4] But henceforth, thanks to the so-called "*Cook's Case,*" there would be no end of puns on the name of Edward Coke—pronounced by his contemporaries "cook." Few, though, surpassed that of his inveterate foe and rival, Francis Bacon: too many Cokes spoil the law.

Coke's early rise in the profession was meteoric. The Readership at Lyon's Inn a year after his call was a rare, perhaps unique honor for one of such short continuance at the bar. He soon enjoyed a large practice, of a mixed sort, well rooted in his East Anglican home counties of Norfolk and Suffolk. Within a decade of call this practice had expanded so much as to place him in the front rank of leaders, men who were widely sought after as advocates and counselors, enjoying practices that were genuinely national rather than merely regional. His appointment in 1586 as recorder of Norwich in his native county—that

---

3. The Lyon's Inn reading, which is extant, was on 27 Edw. 1. Statute de Finibus (1299); the Inner Temple reading, which was discontinued after the fifth lecture because of the plague, was on the Statute of Uses (1536). No longer extant, it would have been interesting to compare it with Francis Bacon's reading on the same statute.

4. *Calendar of Inner Temple Records,* I. F. A. Inderwick, ed. (London, 1896).

is, as counsel to the urban corporation and judge of its criminal courts—was a belated recognition of his regional reputation; the year before, he had become recorder of Coventry in the West Midlands, a clear mark of his national reputation a bare seven years after his call.

Coke early gained a reputation as a masterful conveyancer. His well-noted-up copy of Littleton served him well. Conveyancing tested the legal learning and the creative skills of the lawyer, to say nothing of his prophetic capacity since so many conveyancing devices crashed in flames when litigated. Coke's years as practicer corresponded with the heyday of extravagant, even bizarre interests in property created by pushing the Statute of Uses beyond the extremes of logic to allow legal interests to be created that were in complete defiance of the rules of the limitations of estates at common law. Most of these interests were in furtherance of the settlement of landed estates, and a good many of them raised the threat of perpetuities.

Coke patently did not like perpetuities: he reported, with ill-concealed glee, a number of the cases in which the courts averted the threat by judicial surgery. The contingent remainder was the first culprit. No sooner had that interest been fully accepted, in *Colthirst v. Bejushin* (1550),[5] than the peril of perpetuities was perceived, and the courts turned to cutting back the contingent remainder. This surgery was largely completed in *Shelley's Case,* decided the year after Coke's call and reported by him.[6] But perpetuities was like the hydra-headed monster. *Shelley's Case* notwithstanding, if the contingent remainder was created by way of uses, it could be a valid legal interest by action of the Statute of Uses and by virtue of the fact that the courts were prepared to accept limitations by way of uses that they would not accept by way of limitations at law. Not until *Chudleigh's Case* (1595) was the danger of such perpetuities by way of uses housebroken, by the simple expedient of holding that the legislative intent of the Statute of Uses was to make limitations by way of uses subject to the rules governing estates at common law. Somewhere in between, as contingent remainders were successively bridled, the courts managed to curb the ingenious device creating a settlement in perpetuity by a succession of life estates in remainder, in *Lovelace v. Lovelace* (1558).[7]

Coke lived, practiced, and reported in these exciting (from the real property

5. Plowden, 2.

6. 1 Co.Rep., 88b (1579). *Shelley* is reported also by Dyer, Moore, and Anderson, and of the four reports, Coke's is patently the least reliable—but the most frequently cited!

7. Chudleigh, 1 Co.Rep., 113b; *Lovelace,* see A. W. B. Simpson's excellent treatment of this and the other leading cases in his *An Introduction to the History of the Land Law* (Oxford, 1961), ch. IX.

lawyer's vantage point) times, and his practice, like those of his less eminent conveyancer-contemporaries, was built high on the fast footwork necessary to keep at least one step ahead of the courts and one step away from crashing instruments. He wrought well. A conveyancer's form-book in its fifth edition in 1683 contains an exquisite settlement drawn sometime between 1584 and 1592 for Henry, Ninth Baron Scrope, by a number of counsel *inter alios* Edward Coke.[8] This device's longevity owed all to the fact that it was limited by way of two life estates, which put it outside of the strictures against contingent remainders, successive life estates, and even the (post-1620) legal executory devise as devices creating perpetuities. In fact the Scrope settlement epitomized the modest, cautious device of two lives, which proved a thoroughly workable means to effect settlement without raising the specter of perpetuities. It was also the foundation of the brilliant device of Orlando Bridgman in the midseventeenth century, the "strict settlement," which passed muster of Lord Nottingham's rule of perpetuities in the *Duke of Norfolk's Case* (1681) and served the landed aristocracy of England well for just two centuries until the Settled Land Act of 1882 made all settled land alienable.[9]

The leading advocate and (conveyancing) prophet received honor in his own land when the Inner Temple made him a bencher in 1590 and called him reader in 1592. In 1592–1593 he also entered upon a higher career on a greater stage, with a vengeance. He was created Solicitor-General, the number two law officer of the Crown, made recorder of London, a post that almost invariably went to a barrister high in regal favor, and named Speaker of the House of Commons in the Parliament of 1593. This last was also a mark of royal favor, the role of the Speaker being to maintain the monarch's interests in the House. He had sat only once before, as MP for a Suffolk borough in the previous Parliament of 1589; in 1593 he was returned as one of the two Norfolk county MPs, a sign of the esteem in which the Queen's great minister, Lord Burghley, held Coke. As Speaker he presided over a hot session, during which the House and the Queen clashed over Parliamentary meddling in ecclesiastical matters, a role strenuously denied the Commons by the Supreme Governor of the Church of England, Elizabeth I. His skill in serving both the jealous master that was

8. J. H., *The Compleat Clerk,* 5th ed. (London, 1683), pp. 369–386; from the names of the counsel and other internal evidence the date of this settlement and its provenance can be established.
9. 3 Chan.Cas., 1 and 2 Swanson, 454. Strict settlement can still be used both to settle land consensually and to settle the profits from the alienation of the land. The great agricultural depression of the 1870s gutted many large estates, and what the free market did not do then, death duties have done since to destroy the landed estate and hence strict settlement.

the House and his even more jealous mistress the Queen damped down the controversy. His reward came exactly one year after Parliament ended: he was appointed Attorney-General on 10 April 1594. In doing good to Master Coke, the Queen did well for herself; obtaining as her chief legal counsel the inestimable services of a barrister already accounted the finest lawyer of the day.

The attorney-generalship was a mixed blessing for the politically ambitious lawyer desirous of judicial office. Since the beginning of the Tudor epoch in 1485, there had been sixteen holders of that office before Coke. Six had gone to the bench, four as Chief Baron of the Exchequer, one as Chief Justice of the Common Pleas, and one as Chief Justice of the King's Bench (the last being John Popham, CJKB, 1592–1607). Three had become Master of the Rolls, the second judgeship in Chancery. The remainder had not been promoted. The problem was that Elizabeth had a positive liking to keep her Attorney-General in place for a long time. Her father, Henry VIII, had not had an Attorney-General who lasted longer than six years; her grandfather, Henry VII, had had only two Attorneys-General, and the last had died in office after twenty-one years' arduous service. Elizabeth was in this, as in so much else, more her grandfather's scioness than her father's. Her first Attorney-General, Gilbert Gerrard, appears to have had the longest tenure of any in history, twenty-two years, before becoming Master of the Rolls. John Popham had succeeded him and served eleven years. Only Thomas Egerton, in the office from 1592 to 1594 before becoming Master of the Rolls, had enjoyed fast promotion; in 1596 he became Lord Chancellor and held that office for a near-record twenty-one years. Coke served for twelve years, three of them under Elizabeth's successor, the first Stuart king, James I.

In becoming Attorney-General, a Tudor lawyer gave up the chance of becoming a Sergeant-at-Law and thereby to practice in Common Pleas (Sergeants alone had audience there) and to enjoy the fairly steady odds of about one in five or one in six of becoming a judge of one of the three common-law courts. He had at best a vague *spes successionis* to a chief justiceship, at worst to the Rolls, given a vacancy. In terms of income from fees, the office was not inferior in profit to that of a Sergeant's practice and usually was worth more. The Attorney-General was not barred from private practice; rather, the office attracted clients as none other did. The greatest drawback might well be the work entailed in it. The Attorney-General was required to appear in all prosecutions brought for the Crown in Star Chamber, all major prosecutions in King's Bench, all cases enforcing regal rights in the Exchequer, and prosecutions in great matters of state before any court. He was also involved in criminal investigation touching important matters, requiring his presence at interrogations of suspects (sometimes by torture). He drafted proclamations, pardons, and Crown bills for Parliament. He was constantly called upon for legal advice to the Crown, opinions on points of law, and drawing cases to be put to the judges for advisory opinion. He represented the Crown's interests in such rudimentary appeals as the law allowed. He also attended the House of Lords during the Parliament in an advisory capacity. He enjoyed considerable procedural privileges in all judicial proceedings and he was accorded precedence over all other barristers. But he worked hard for such advantages as the office brought, including a larger private clientele, which he dared not favor over his official duties under threat of losing his office.

Coke's tenure of a dozen years proved particularly onerous. It was a period of great commotion, marked by growing political and religious divisiveness, acts of subversion of church and state, deadly threats to the monarch's person, and dissension in the principal organ of state, the Privy Council. Parliament became the focus for all ills, and because of the necessity to raise money for a sea war against Spain and civil war in Ireland, it became almost a routine institution. High taxes, markets on the Continent closed by war, and a succession of crop failures brought want and economic dislocation, creating a threatening undercurrent of unrest. Attorney-General Coke was called upon to step up the prosecution of Roman Catholic priests to a traitor's death and to bring to the harsh justice of the age plotters against the Queen's life, including her own physician. More ominous were the first prosecutions resulting in death for Protestant sectaries since the Catholic "Bloody Mary" in the 1550s. As Attorney-General, Coke managed the prosecution in three of the greatest state trials in England's history: the trial of the Earl of Essex and his followers for the coup d'état attempted in 1601; the trial of Sir Walter Raleigh and supposed coconspirators to kill King James and put the King's comely cousin, Arabella Stuart, on the throne shortly after James's accession; the trial of the Catholic fanatics who in 1605 attempted the most spectacular stroke of political terrorism in history, to blow up the King and the entire Parliament with gunpowder. These celebrated cases were only the tip of an iceberg of trials in which Coke prosecuted for the safety of the King and realm. Coke's vigorousness and harshness in prosecution were remarked upon by his contemporaries only as manifestations of remarkable patriotism and loyalty to his monarch. Victorian Englishmen, who knew neither war nor treason, permitted themselves the luxury of roundly condemning Coke for his choleric severity. Our age might be better disposed to understanding him.

In 1605, the first chief justiceship (that of the Common Pleas) to open since Coke became Attorney-General fell vacant with Edmund Anderson's death. It was filled by another ancient Templar, Francis Gawdy. Coke's disappointment ended when Gawdy died less than a year later. In June 1606, Coke was made Sergeant—a requisite, though in his case pro forma, step to the bench—and a day later Chief Justice of the Common Pleas. At fifty-four he was aged by contemporary standards. He had buried one wife (Bridget Paston, who had brought him an old fortune, died in 1598), and he might well have wished he could bury the second, a harridan he had married after less than six months' mourning for Bridget. His second wife, Lady Elizabeth Hatton, had been the young, high-spirited widow of an elderly knight; her grandfather, Lord Burgh-ley, had he lived the few months required to see Elizabeth marry Coke, would have approved, if for no other reason than that Coke had beaten Francis Bacon to the widow. Elizabeth was given to histrionics and vile temper tantrums. Selfish, demanding, a prodigal spender, she gave Coke a daughter, denied him peace, sued him in Star Chamber, deserted him and stripped his house of its furnishings, and having outlived him spoke a venomous epitaph of him, "We shall never see his like again, praises be to God."[10] The scandal and indignity visited upon Coke by this unfortunate union placed him at considerable dis-advantage at critical points in his judicial career. It eroded his reputation for integrity, pushed him to excesses in conduct, and played into the hands of his enemy, Francis Bacon. Bacon never forgot Coke's preferment over him for the Attorney-Generalship or Coke's success in winning the widow Hatton and her fortune that Bacon desperately needed. Whatever else led to two great falls by Chief Justice Coke, Bacon's enmity contributed mightily to working them.

The rapidity with which Coke as Chief Justice of the Common Pleas as-sumed an adversarial, even hostile stance toward regal policy has puzzled generations of scholars. As Attorney-General he had been the quintessential "King's man," advancing the Crown's cause. As CJCP, Coke repeatedly took positions that appeared inimical to the Crown interest. The explanation must be complex, if for no other reason than that Coke was a complex man. What can be largely excluded from consideration at the outset is the notion that the

10. British Library; Harleian MS. 7193, fol. 16.

explanation lies in some external factors, in regal policies or regal ambitions, in some changes in royal personnel that both signaled and effected basic changes in direction of government. If we look for the explanation in some seismic change in royal policy to which Coke responded, we will not find it. James I and his political and legal advisers did not even gradually forsake goodness for evil, let alone suddenly clamp down on previous practices or previous liberties. Rather, the explanation must be sought in Coke himself, in the context of his learning and of his role.

The first thing that must be noticed (and which is easily overlooked) is that Coke was the first judge of Common Pleas in almost a century who had never practiced in that court as an advocate. He had been a Sergeant for only a day, and this lack of experience markedly distinguished him from his predecessors and his three brother judges on the court. That is not to say that he was ignorant of what went on in Common Pleas; his *Reports,* containing cases there before he joined its bench, indicates that he was intellectually familiar with its doctrine and even its procedures, and well aware of the nature of its peculiar and limited jurisdiction (largely to party-and-party property litigation). What he lacked was immersion in "the course of the court." Coke would have been the last to have disparaged the importance of that experience; he recognized "the course of the court" as the true foundation of precedent to be followed by the court.[11] He did not, though, think like a Common Pleas jurist; he was untouched by the tradition of the court, and consequently was impatient of the experientially imposed intellectual and sentimental limitations on the way a Common Pleas jurist thought.

Coke came to Common Pleas, then, fully formed. Moreover, his experience at bar had been gained in two courts where the common law was undergoing the most rapid development: King's Bench and Star Chamber. In great part, that development meant rapidly expanding jurisdiction. In the short expanse of Coke's career the King's Bench had acquired a wide and growing jurisdiction in civil actions; during his tenure as Attorney-General, Star Chamber, ostensibly a court of criminal jurisdiction, became even more openly a tribunal for obtaining civil remedy.[12] Indeed, in the case of the latter, Coke had him-

---

11. Coke, CJKB, and Hobart, CJCP, on reference from Star Chamber in *Proctor's Case* (1614), rendered opinion that the question posed "must be determined by the precedents of the Court of Star-Chamber," 12 Co.Rep., 118, at 118. For a treatment of precedent in this sense, see T. G. Barnes, "A Cheshire Seductress, Precedent, and a 'Sore Blow' to Star Chamber," *On the Laws and Customs of England: Essays in Honor of Samuel E. Thorne,* M. S. Arnold, et al., eds. (Chapel Hill, 1981), pp. 363–79.

12. T. G. Barnes, "Star Chamber Litigants and Their Counsel, 1596–1641," *Legal Records and the Historian,* J. H. Baker, ed. (London, 1978), pp. 11–12.

self played a large part. The development also meant an increasing emphasis on precedent as the basis for legal change. Here, a fine line must be drawn if we are not to misunderstand Coke's view of precedent and its relationship to the law. One of his more striking maxims makes clear his meaning:

> New adjudication does not make new law, but makes plain the old; adjudication is the *dictum* [saying] of law, and by adjudication law which was before hidden is newly revealed.[13]

The law existed, it was not created by the court—only statute could make new law. Therefore, "legal change" as Coke understood it was the process and result of revelation. There was an analogy: the fact of theological revelation as the medieval Church had practiced it. Coke, ever the schoolman, was even better aware of the analogy than the larger society of which he was a part and which was deeply imbued with the intellectual tradition of its Christian civilization.

The existence of the law revealed by adjudication was not a discouragement of judicial activism. On the contrary, it invited it by reassuring the judge that he need not let go the old in pursuit of the new, the established for the novel, the real for the merely theoretical. The notion was a license for judicial activism. Coke was, above all else, an activist. As a judge he was a judicial activist.

What was a judicial activist to do on a court that was mired in the most exquisitely sophisticated doctrinal construct of the most fully fashioned body of substantive law (property) the age knew? He could, according to the lights of that artificial reason of law that Coke posited as the jurist's method, refine the law to broad jurisprudential policy ends in order to suit the existing corpus of law to new requirements. Coke certainly did just this in his seven years on the Common Pleas bench, as his own *Reports* testify, carrying his brethren with him in most instances and ignoring them in favor of his own position when they differed with him. But there was something else the judicial activist could do, especially if he enjoyed the latitude for individual initiative in procedural matters that the presidency of the court afforded him (and him alone). He could, indeed would, feel himself bound to maintain and expand the jurisdiction of the court against all other tribunals. This, too, Chief Justice Coke certainly did, by dusting off an old common-law writ that had already been used against the ecclesiastical courts and had elicited episcopal complaint before Coke took his seat on the bench: prohibition. Coke used prohibition

---

13. *Novum judicium non dat jus novum, sed declarat antiquum, judicium est juris dictum et per judicium jus est noviter revelation quod diu fuit velatum,* 10 Co.Rep., 42; Editor's translation.

with a hitherto unknown prodigality and broadened scope. The writ could be directed against any court, secular or ecclesiastical, and the parties and their counsel in litigation in the court to prevent the continuance of a case that the court issuing the prohibition claimed was not within the other court's jurisdiction. During Coke's tenure as CJCP, most of the shower of prohibitions loosed by him fell upon the ecclesiastical courts because of their determination to maintain jurisdiction over cases for tithes. But prohibitions were also directed to Chancery, Requests, Wards & Liveries, the regional Councils in Wales and the North, the High Court of Admiralty, and a number of other jurisdictions. Two major jurisdictions were excepted—King's Bench and Star Chamber—for a number of reasons that can't be gone into here, but including Coke's residual reverence for those courts and how they were refining the law to proper ends *pro bono publico.*

Prohibitions brought Coke into confrontation with all those vested interests represented in the courts to which they were directed, not least the litigants. Coke made powerful enemies, including Lord Chancellor Egerton, archbishops, and other officers of state, and his enemies were closer to the King than Coke was. Prohibitions became a standing grievance against Coke at virtually every level of English polity. With reason, for they could be seen as mere dog-in-the-manger attempts to acquire more business for Common Pleas and profit for its judges; as a restrictive practice on the freewheeling, wide open, unregulated forum chasing that characterized litigation at the time; and as a pernicious device to unsettle the harmony and untune the balance of judicature. This is not to question the motives of Coke, which were doubtless of the highest even when apparently to baser ends. It is to explain why he was no sooner on the bench than he had stirred up opposition to his own person and fallen afoul of the ultimate arbiter of judicial propriety and ultimate loser if judicature fell warring within itself, the King.

More than a court's business and jurisdiction lay behind Coke's activism. He took an exalted view of the role of the judiciary, based upon his historical perception of the institution's antiquity, its integrity in the civil polity, and its responsibility for the maintenance of its charge, the law. In 1600 a reporter for the Star Chamber noted: "A sayinge of Mr. Atturnie [Coke] often used by him in his arguments, that it is his duetie to informe ther lordships of the trueth and state of the cause and then that the judgement is thers."[14] Judg-

14. Inner Temple Library: Petyt MS. 511, vol. 13, fol. 131v.

ment imposed a unique burden upon the judge, one not shared by counsel whose "duetie" was to open the truth of the matter so far as he was able. And as Attorney-General Coke acknowledged, even his client—the monarch—did not share the burden of judgment if he was before the court in a legal way. Coke understood perfectly the adversarial dialectic of the law. For all of his prerogative and privileges, despite his immunity to prosecution and suit by others, admitting him to be the fount of justice, when the King was at law he was substantially on the same footing as any other party. He was to be heard, but judgment was the judge's. Here was the point of friction between Coke and James I. For James saw the judge as merely his delegate, with revocable powers, an adviser whose counsel was to be accepted or rejected as the principal willed. James would not interfere with the ordinary course of judicature. But when he believed a vital interest of the Crown was at stake in law, he expected his judges to advise him and not to forget their office as his delegates.

Had it not been for a practice of long standing (from at least the middle years of Elizabeth's reign) much expanded by James I, Chief Justice Coke and his profligacy with prohibitions would have been merely a nuisance, albeit a painful one. What caused Coke to become increasingly perceived of by the King and his ministers as a real threat was the attitude he struck with respect to advisory opinions elicited from the judges by royal command. At the outset Coke did not object to the procedure, but he early showed himself prickly toward regal interests in such matters. In 1607, James and the Council conferred with all the judges on the validity of prohibitions upon the complaint of the clergy. Coke spoke for his brethren in upholding the legality of prohibitions. But he went further, speaking only for himself, in answering James's claim to be able to decide such matters himself. Coke told the King that though the law was reason and the King had natural reason, he could not personally exercise judicature because he did not have "artificial reason" of the law that came only by study. James exploded: then he would be *under* the law? Coke's rejoinder became legendary. He cited Bracton's immortal axiom that the King was under God and the law (ignoring the likelihood that Bracton meant natural law, not the common law). Two years later there was a second confrontation between James and the judges over prohibitions, which ended with a frightened Coke on his knees if not his face before an outraged monarch.

In these instances and in others, Coke had acted responsibly and in a way supported by custom and precedent, even if he sometimes spoke rashly. But in 1608 Coke seconded Chief Justice Thomas Fleming of the King's Bench in objecting to the entire procedure of advisory opinions. The issue touched whether the four English counties bordering Wales were within the jurisdiction of the Council of the Marches of Wales. At a Privy Council meeting at which eleven of the twelve judges were present, Fleming spoke for them all in refusing to deliver their opinions, on the ground that the judges were to deliver opinions only "as the causes and the cases fell out before them judicially between partie and partie. . . ."[15] At that point, James himself, with the Prince of Wales in tow, entered the chamber and launched into a warm disquisition on the power of the King in judicature. He ended by putting the question himself. In the ensuing row, growing from the continued obstinacy of the judges, Coke argued that whether the four counties were intended within the Statute of Wales was a question of fact that had to go to a jury, not a question of law. James replied, correctly, that it was a question of law and the judges should decide it (so far was his "artificial reason" sound). The conference broke up with an angry King, tearful judges, and no opinion rendered.

If Coke's law was bad, his and Fleming's proposition that advisory opinions were wrong was untenable. Coke as Attorney-General and Fleming as Solicitor-General (1595–1604) had both drafted briefs to put such questions to the judges for advisory opinions. Their position in the Wales matter had a future. In 1615, Coke, who had replaced Fleming as Chief Justice of the King's Bench upon the latter's death two years before, raised an objection to advisory opinions in the case of the Reverend Edmund Peacham for treason. This time, it was directed primarily against advisory opinions elicited by polling the judges singly, as being without precedent. This argument would not wash though it was a refined one addressing a genuine threat to judicial integrity, for polled separately even the toughest judge might cravenly yield. As early as his first year on the bench Coke and the then Chief Justice of the King's Bench had given opinions on impositions without consultation with the other judges. In 1611 Coke had refused to give his personal opinion on the validity of proclamations as legal instruments without consulting the other judges; only when all the judges had been brought together were opinions rendered by Coke and his brethren. He would not win the next round. In *Peacham's Case* the other judges deserted Coke. His obstinacy was added to the long list of demerits that brought about his final fall in 1616.

Coke's removal from Common Pleas to King's Bench in 1613 constituted a

---

15. Huntington Library: Ellesmere MS. 1763, "Pro Marchiis Walliae," 3 Nov. 1608.

fall in all but name, a veritable kick upstairs. A judge's profits from litigation in King's Bench were considerably less than in Common Pleas, and Coke took a major financial loss. It was also perceived popularly as a rebuke. Coke wept. Bacon, who had suggested the ploy, was gleeful. In fact, he and the King had made a mistake, for Coke was capable of greater mischief on a grander stage in King's Bench, where the criminal cases touched the Crown directly, than in Common Pleas. To soften the blow Coke was made a Privy Councillor; this also increased his potential for being troublesome.

If the King thought the boot would be admonitory he was soon disabused. In Star Chamber a few months later, Coke came close to inflicting a "sore blow"—as the King put it—on that court.[16] *Peacham's Case* in the next year was followed by a cause célèbre between King's Bench and Chancery, Coke and Ellesmere, over Chancery's entertainment of a kind of appeal from judgment in the King's Bench. Coke fetched from his bag of historical relics the ancient action of praemunire, triable in King's Bench, to threaten Chancery. Praemunire had lain unused since Henry VIII had menaced the entire clergy of England with it to pry them away from Rome at the beginning of the Reformation. Coke's threat spurred the King to an extraordinary sitting in Star Chamber in 1616. He lectured the judiciary on their duty, reproved Coke obliquely, cataloged the King's Bench's attacks on other courts, and settled jurisdictions by a Solomonic threatening to cut at least one Chief Justice in two. In the trials of the King's favorite, the Earl of Somerset, his lady, and their conspirators for murdering by poison the lady's lover, Coke hinted darkly at a wider scandal, winning the enmity of James, who was already mortified by the affair. And finally, in the famous *Case of Commendams* (1616), touching the King's right to permit a clergyman to hold more than one ecclesiastical charge, Coke alone among the twelve judges refused categorically to promise obedience to the King's will in such matters in the future. As eleven judges knelt in humiliating obeisance to the King, Coke stood upright. To color the King's determination to break Coke, his *Reports* were searched by the King's counsel-learned for points derogatory of royal prerogative, and upon Coke's spirited defense of the few items with which they taxed him, he was sacked as Chief Justice on 10 November 1616. He was only the first judicial martyr in early Stuart England. Charles I would, with varying severity, punish a Chief Baron, a Chief Justice of the King's Bench, and a Chief Justice of Common

16. Barnes, "Cheshire Seductress," pp. 379–82.

Pleas on one or another pretext, for one or another reason. In 1640, an outraged opposition in Parliament would exact their revenge on the King's "evil judges" by impeaching those who had supported Ship Money on appeal in 1638.

With Coke's fall his official career was eclipsed. It was not, however, entirely finished. Because he was considered a financial genius by no less a man than his foe Bacon, he was readmitted to the Privy Council within a year of his fall. Without parliamentary supply in almost a decade, the royal revenues were reduced and the King was reluctant to call Parliament again to revive them. Coke's role as financial wizard gave a renewed outlet for his activism, and one which very nearly restored him fully to royal favor. Coke's contribution was characteristic of him and quite in keeping with his wonted judicial activism. We cannot be sure that he suggested the brilliant move of prosecuting whole-sale wealthy miscreants in order to raise revenue from their fines or by allowing them to compound for their fines. We do know that as a Privy Councillor in Star Chamber and giving judgment early by virtue of his lowly precedence, he generally cast the fines that would be imposed. These were enormous: Dowager Countess of Shrewsbury £20,000 (1618); Earl and Countess of Suffolk (for his peculation as Lord Treasurer) £30,000 (1619); Secretary of State Sir Thomas Lake and relatives for libel £16,666 (1619); thirteen Low Country merchants for exporting gold and silver, £136,333 (1619) — altogether amounting to exactly one-quarter of the total sum of Star Chamber fines estreated between 1596 and the court's abolition in 1641. While not even the greatest part of these fines were collected, they were effectively used to persuade others to make fiscal peace with the Exchequer. Coke had the considerable satisfaction of settling some old personal and political scores in these cases. Suffolk and Lake had been among his chief enemies in the Council. Their fall was brought about by the rise of the King's new favorite, George Villiers, Duke of Buckingham; Coke's fortunes rose with the new favorite's, and he assured himself of Buckingham's favor by forcibly abducting his youngest daughter from Lady Hatton's house and marrying the girl to Buckingham's older brother.

Financial shifts did not avail to provide adequate revenue, and in 1621 James was compelled to summon Parliament for the first time in seven years, to provide funds for the conduct of a costly and contradictory foreign policy. Sir Edward Coke, a loyal Privy Councillor, was returned as MP for a borough in the King's control. Whatever hopes James had that Coke would be in the vanguard of those directing and defending royal policy in the Commons were dashed from the start. Coke found again a forum worthy of his talents, his learning, and his activism, but not one in which these attributes would be as much appreciated or as much needed by the King as by the growing opposition to his policy. This is not to depict Coke as a weathervane or a mercenary. On the contrary, what he saw at stake in the Parliament of 1621 was the preservation of the integrity of the law against the encroachments of the King's ministers bent upon wrong, even pernicious policies and prepared to subvert the law to the end of effecting those policies. The grievances of the King's subjects were to be redressed in a legal way, under protection of the law, in a preservation of the subjects' liberties, by the "High Court of Parliament."

"The High Court of Parliament" was not quite entirely the confection of Coke, but it relied for its substantiation as anything more than a notional fiction upon the torturous and tortured history propounded by that oracle of the law. His developed brief can be easily consulted as, appropriately, Chapter One, "Of the High and Most Honourable Court of Parliament," in his *Fourth Institutes.* Coke upon Littleton, *First Institutes,* Sect. 164, contains Coke's long disquisition on "this high court of parliament" with its "so transcendent" jurisdiction, tracing its history back to Anglo-Saxon times. No matter that Coke confused apples and oranges in finding a history as early as the ninth century for an institution that began in the midthirteenth. No matter that its strictly judicial function was something less than a consistent and even development, and was greater at its origins than since, that it had lapsed and been revived to lapse again and be revived again as a modest instrument of appeal. The faint fire could be stoked up to white-hot heat, and in the Parliament of 1621 Coke blew hardest on the embers. He was rewarded by the emergence of an institution that, having revived impeachment, turned it on a hapless, obscure, Catholic lawyer in Wales, crushed monopolists, broke the Attorney-General, and finally dragged down Lord Chancellor Bacon. In the next Parliament, 1624, impeachment ousted Lord Treasurer Middlesex, and in the early Parliaments of Charles I later in the decade only dissolution saved the King's great favorite and chief minister, the Duke of Buckingham, from destruction. And none stood higher in that "High Court" than Sir Edward Coke. None was busier in patiently explaining the law, passionately urging action or restraining rashness, managing, cajoling, arguing, discoursing, debating.

For his pains in 1621, Coke was with a few other prominent leaders of the opposition committed to the Tower for some months. In 1624, he enjoyed the rare favor of Prince Charles and Buckingham as they countered James's pacifism and took England to war with Spain, with Parliament cheering them on (and voting modest supply, for the first time in fifteen years, to conduct the war). In the Parliaments of 1621 and 1624 it is fair to say that Coke was the most influential man in the Commons. In the first Parliament of Charles I, 1625, though he had to share that honor with two others, his influence as the *jurisperitus* of the "High Court" was still dominant. In 1626 he was prevented from sitting in Parliament by being made sheriff, a fate that befell other opposition stars. He came back into his own with the first session of the Parliament of 1628. The "Petition of Right," a unique instrument raised to safeguard the subjects' liberties and to redress grievances, reluctantly consented to by Charles, was above all others' his creation.

In the second session of the Parliament of 1628 Coke was silent though he remained in the House as the reassuring presence of its legal oracle. Coke was not the only prominent opposition leader of the 1620s who withdrew from center stage in this session as hotter, more radical men raised an ominous specter. But one suspects he had a singular motive for his silence. Parliament might be a "High Court," but it was also a political organ responding to other imperatives than the cool judgment of the "artificial reason" of the law. Parliament had begun to manifest a taste for power that seemed to beg the limitations of law.

This was Coke's last Parliament. There would not be another for eleven years as Charles embarked on his "Personal Rule." On 3 September 1634, Coke died, in his eighty-third year. His passing did not go unnoticed in high places. As he lay dying at Stoke Pogis, Secretary Windebank, in execution of the King and Council's warrant, quietly searched through and carried off his papers, an action replicated in his chambers at the Inner Temple shortly after his death. Nothing treasonable or seditious, nothing that, had it reached the public, would have shaken the kingdom to its foundations was discovered. Probably no corpse in England's history was ever so posthumously terrifying as that of Sir Edward Coke. The King paid him a high honor.

Coke was secure in his reputation among his contemporaries, in the fears of his King and in the love of his fellow MPs, in the admiration of lawyers for his legal learning displayed in the *Reports,* in the respect of clerks of courts for his helpful and practical little *Book of Entries* and among those students for whom he undertook his *First Institutes* to bring them all of Littleton's lore and more of his own. Perhaps most significantly he was famed among the widest range of his countrymen for his stalwart defense of their liberties under law and the maintenance of the supremacy of the law that assured them liberty. When the revolution that Coke could not have imagined—but which would have sorrowed him to see had he lived so long—overtook the nation and destroyed or maimed all its institutions, he was revered as a hero by those mere artificers, the Levellers, who sought a new order with a broader franchise for a continuous Parliament. At the same time Hobbes condemned Coke for his medieval obscurantism and the irrationality of his belief that law was custom and not the command of Leviathan—a man can also be exalted for the enemies he makes as much as by the friends he keeps. Coke's renown went far beyond his partisans. It touched such old adversaries as the Roman lawyer, Sir Julius Caesar, whom he had bombarded with prohibitions to the Court of Requests, but who remembered Coke's kindness in admitting him to the Inner Temple. Coke's fellow Norfolkman, the Reverend Thomas Fuller, the uncritical admirer of the legion he deemed worthy of inclusion in his secular hagiography, managed (despite himself) to achieve truth to the measure of his hyperbole in his epitaph of Coke: "His works will last to be admired whilst Fame hath a trumpet left her, and any breath to blow therein."[17]

Coke is one of those rare figures of genuinely major historical importance who has fared worse at the hands of his subsequent admirers than at those of his contemporary detractors. His contemporaries not only knew him better but they certainly better knew the age in which he acted, the constraints under which he acted, the objectives for which he acted. Coke was a complex man—but he was not complicated, and his historiographers have worked arduously to demonstrate that he was. Indeed, the term "historiographer"—as distinct from biographer—is the clue to understanding the incubus that bears down Coke's subsequent reputation. It is often remarked that Coke has never found a decent biographer. True. Virtually all biography of seventeenth-century figures (the most notable exception is Oliver Cromwell) is difficult. In Coke's case, thanks to the fact that most of his papers disappeared, not least because of the King's paranoia, the task is made yet more difficult. But the problem is compounded in its difficulty by the fact that Coke has been required by historians, ancient and modern, to serve as a symbol of something begun and not yet completed. In short, he has been robbed of eternal sleep, of the mere mortality that permits blissful oblivion for lesser men. We are like Charles I, less fearful, but still apprehensive of what Coke's cadaver can do, what it still means, what it still signifies.

The Whig historians, who flourished in the eighteenth and nineteenth cen-

17. Thomas Fuller, *The Worthies of England,* II (London, 1682), p. 452.

turies and stood enamored of the rise of Parliament, the emergence of the
rule of law, the achievement of liberties of speech and association and religious observance, and the evolution—not too fast—of democratic government, saw Coke as the harbinger or protoepitome of all those developments.
Therefore, Coke being beastly to Raleigh or the Jesuit Father Carnet, abducting his daughter of fourteen to marry her to a sybaritic courtier, or loosing
a diatribe of xenophobic anti-Hispanicism in Parliament in 1621 demanded
some explanation, even justification, sufficient not to detract from his "good
qualities" or to embarrass the sensibilities of his later admirers. Such morally
judgmental history is, of course, frowned on today and no longer practiced
(one supposes). Recent historians tend, however, to fall into a similar trap in
seeking to understand Coke. Fifty years ago, Coke was hailed as an early exponent of "economic liberalism," a precursor of Adam Smith and the emergence
of nineteenth-century capitalist doctrine.[18] In the 1970s, two admirable works
devoted entirely to Coke appeared. One, by a French scholar, argued that Coke
must be seen as a precursor of Locke and Montesquieu and accorded him a
place in the history of antiabsolutist political theory just a step behind them.[19]
What was intended as a handsome compliment is in fact the grossest flattery:
Coke was a political theorist in the sense that anyone who can think straight, is
involved in politics, and has had recorded what he said in the political process
is a political theorist. He might rank with Locke as a significant Englishman of
their century, but Locke owed virtually nothing to Coke, whose vaunting of
the law's primacy constituted in Locke's view as great a peril to the working and
preservation of civil government as monarchical absolutism. The other work,
by an American scholar, credited Coke with development of "constitutional
positions" that would permit English law to adapt to "new social and economic conditions."[20] There is merit in the suggestion of the interpretation—
but it presupposes an understanding of constitutionalism on Coke's part that
could not have emerged until after one bloody revolution and another blood-
less one in seventeenth-century England. Not even Coke was capable of such
perspicacity.

18. Donald O. Wagner, "Coke and the Rise of Economic Liberalism," *Econ. Hist. Rev.,* 1st ser. 6 (1935),
30–44, and "The Common Law and Free Enterprise: An Early Case of Monopoly," *Econ. Hist. Rev.,* 1st
ser. 7 (1937), 217–20. Barbara Malament, "The 'Economic Liberalism' of Sir Edward Coke," 76 *Yale Law
Journ.* (1966–1967), 1321–58 [reprinted here on p. 186], convincingly demolishes Wagner's thesis, and those
of his disciples' variations on that theme.
19. Jean Beauté, *Un grand juriste anglais: Sir Edward Coke, 1552–1634, ses idées politiques et constitutionelles*
(Paris, 1975).
20. Stephen D. White, *Sir Edward Coke and the "Grievances of the Commonwealth," 1621–1628* (Chapel
Hill, 1979), p. 23.

There is little evidence that Coke had a coherently thought out "constitutional position" beyond that traditional understanding of English polity from the late Middle Ages called mixed monarchy. Significantly, both sides in the struggle between King and Parliament in the 1620s and into the 1640s (though not beyond) agreed that England was a mixed monarchy. Simply put, mixed monarchy was consensual governance by the King and the estates—the latter being the clergy, the nobility, and the commonalty, represented in Parliament. Agreement was essential, compromise the means to obtain it, and the law the regulator of relations within the mix. Not surprisingly, Coke devoted much of his attention to the last element, both when he was judge and afterward as parliamentarian. For Coke the law was a substitute for constitutionalism, and he was wont to stress the regulator as mediator when King and estates fell out. He had plenty of opportunity to urge this in the 1620s. He did not like either the word or the concept "sovereign," since it suggested not a mixture of equals but a hierarchy of unequals. Yet in standing against the King's apparent lust for sovereignty he was not unaware that Parliament was drifting toward a counterassertion suspiciously like sovereignty. Consequently he exalted the role of law, which as mediator could function only if its primacy was accepted by both King and estates as binding upon them severally and jointly. He had no doctrine of separation of powers, judicial review, or other such later constitutional ideas. But Coke cast the function of the law in civil polity to a higher plane than any other of his contemporaries in the political struggles of the age, and thanks to his posthumous fame as the common law's greatest oracle he influenced a later generation of lawyers to believe that the law was an essential "power" in a constitution raised on the separation of powers.

Coke's saving grace as jurist and politician was an almost perfervid ignoring of the future. He appears less to have been negligent of it than to have dreaded it. He seldom alluded to it, let alone dwelt upon it, save in the most immediate (never in the distant) future. He was not particularly comfortable thinking about the present. In fact, he preferred the past, always the distant past, of the Year Books, of Magna Charta, or Edward I. In the debate on the Petition of Right in May 1628, in taking strong exception to a clause added by the Lords saving the King's "sovereign power," Coke thundered,

> I know that prerogative is part of the law, but "Sovereign Power" is no parliamentary word. In my opinion it weakens Magna Charta, and all the statutes; for they are absolute, without any saving of "Sovereign Power"; and should we now add it, we shall weaken the foundation of the law, and then the building must

needs fall. Take we heed what we yield unto: Magna Charta is such a fellow, that he will have no "Sovereign." [21]

The old man must be taken at his word: Magna Charta was a living person to him.

Coke's past-mindedness differed from that which the modern historian seeks to inculcate in his student. His was all anachronism, the past living in the present; we attempt to see the past on its own terms rather than on ours. We fail repeatedly. Coke, never having tried for the simple reason that our sublime sensitivity is the product of nineteenth-century German positivism, could only succeed in his endeavor. He did. The result was determinative of the future of whole areas of the common law. This was not because he planned it that way, but because his contemporary authority among lawyers was such as to convince them that his vision of the living past as present was the law. As the historian is struck by certain great events into which all the past appears to have flowed and out of which all the future issued—the Reformation of the sixteenth century and the French Revolution of the late eighteenth century are such—so he sees something of the same phenomenon in the common law with Coke as aperture.

Coke upon Littleton effected just such a convergence-divergence for the law of property. Coke not only updated Littleton, he made Littleton's terse sections the foundation for all subsequent property law to Coke's own day. There was no need to go behind Coke—Littleton was to be found there, a kind of groom to Coke. One result, and an immediate one, was an almost instantaneous stopping of recourse to the Year Books by lawyers. There was no need to do so: Lord Coke had done it. Judge Littleton was there to bear witness to the completeness of Coke's compilation, and those Latin maxims with their ring of authenticity not only lent credence to the effort but supplied the point in a short, sharp sentence of a few elegant Latin words. Perhaps it never occurred to lawyers to question how there could have been so much Latinity in the "book-law" of medieval England written in Law-French. It didn't matter. Even if the spuriousness (in the sense that Coke made them up, not that they falsely represented the law) was perceived, the maxims were a pithy summation of the law. No wonder that even today, in a popular handbook of maxims for lawyers, of the 1100 maxims given, just half are directly ascribed to Coke's works.[22]

21. *Parliamentary History,* II (London, 1807), col. 357.
22. *Latin for Lawyers,* 3d ed. (London, 1960).

Coke was quite prepared not only to make up maxims but also to fashion the doctrine behind them. An eminent medievalist, Samuel E. Thorne, has given us a rule of thumb by which to put ourselves on guard if not to detect when Coke was up to creating law:

> [I]t is well to remember that sentences beginning "For it is an ancient maxim of the common law," followed by one of Coke's spurious Latin maxims, which he could manufacture to fit any occasion and provide with an air of authentic antiquity, are apt to introduce a new departure. Sentences such as "And by these differences and reasons you will better understand your books," or "And so the doubts and diversities in the books well resolved," likewise indicate new law. If I may formulate a theorem of my own, I advance this—the longer the list of authorities reconciled, the greater the divergence from the cases cited.[23]

Professor Thorne points out that such new departures were small and often very technical. It should also be observed that Coke probably believed that in most cases he was not creating anew but merely enunciating law that was there, though hidden or wanting explicit evidence to establish it. The process in his mind was a matter of discovery, not fabrication.

What Coke did for property law in the *First Institutes* he undertook to do for other branches in the succeeding three, which he managed to complete but understandably, because of their political sensitivity, did not publish in his lifetime. None of the latter three *Institutes* attained the bulk, comprehensiveness, or profundity of Coke upon Littleton; the commentary on Littleton was a lifetime's labor and an exposition of the law that Coke had worked with from his earliest days at the Temple. The *Second Institutes,* on Magna Charta and the statutes, was polemically inspired, and its unevenness of treatment from one statute to another was dictated less by the importance of the statute to the law than to the contemporary political concerns of Coke's later years. The *Third Institutes,* on the criminal law, suffered severely from the author's past-mindedness and his tendency to concentrate on treason and felony to the reduction of the growing (in number and importance) misdemeanors that were adjusting criminal law to the repression of more sophisticated crime in a more complex society. The *Fourth Institutes* was the best ordered and the most evenly executed of the *Institutes,* demonstrating powers of organization and sustained argumentation that eluded Coke in everything else he wrote. Because it was descriptive of the courts of his day, it had a much shorter useful life

23. Samuel E. Thorne, "Sir Edward Coke, 1552–1952," Selden Society Lecture (London, 1957), p. 7.

than the three other *Institutes*. It was the hottest politically, since it bore down heavily and caustically on the ecclesiastical and non-common-law courts.

The *Reports* had extraordinary contemporary impact. They appeared to contain all the requisite case law from 1572 (when Coke entered the Inner Temple) to 1616 (when he was sacked as CJKB). They were, in fact, a monument to Coke's career and in critical points in important cases better represented what he thought the law to be than what the court said it was. That they were often rambling and sometimes so opaque as to be virtually incomprehensible mattered less than the fact that they bore the stamp of authenticity of Coke's reputation and his authoritative assertion. They were ampler than either Dyer's or Plowden's reports earlier, though lacking in the systematic method Plowden employed in his *Commentaries*. They generally set out the pleadings in a case — a pedagogical device, since Coke put great emphasis on a student learning sound pleading. More often than not, especially in the earlier cases, Coke was at pains to advance general propositions of law, emphasizing the substantive matter of the case and providing analysis of it. In part they became the model for all subsequent reporting. And they were probably the most frequently cited and most often argued-over reports the law has known. Their "authority" was not seriously questioned until well into the nineteenth century, and even then the courts found it both difficult and inconvenient to deny their authority. While uncritical admiration for them disappeared, they remained part of every learned lawyer's armory of argument until this century.

If Coke remained the legal oracle in his own country by virtue of the *Institutes,* especially Coke upon Littleton, and the *Reports,* he became the founding father of the common law in England's American colonies. On 11 November 1647, the General Court of the Massachusetts Bay Colony ordered that "to the end we may have the better light for making & proceedings about lawes, that there shalbe . . . procured for the use of the Courte from time to time" two copies each of Coke's *First* and *Second Institutes,* Coke's *Reports* (I–II), Coke's *Book of Entries,* Michael Dalton's *Country Justice,* and John Rastell's *Les Termes de la Ley*.[24] For more than a century thereafter generations of fledgling lawyers in all the colonies wrestled with Coke upon Littleton to learn the land law, resonated to Coke's encomium of that "fellow" who "will have no 'Sovereign'" in the *Second Institutes,* and sacked the *Reports* for all the case law they could find. Thomas Jefferson, studying the law under George Wythe in the 1760s,

24. *Records of the Governor and Company of the Massachusetts Bay in New England,* II. N. B. Shurtleff, ed. (Boston, 1853), p. 212.

took more readily to the *Institutes* than might have been expected of one of his fastidious reading habits. Coke's history was a curative against David Hume's *History of England* and its Tory revisionism of the Whig Triumph, and we can guess that Jefferson's detestation of Hume commended Coke to him all the more. John Adams found it difficult to conduct a case in Boston without some reference to Coke. In 1774 when Adams, under the pseudonym "Novanglus," asserted that Parliament had no authority over the colonies and that each was a separate realm under the King with its own independent legislature, he started from Coke's *Institutes.* His fellow Bostonian James Otis, in arguing against writs of assistance, raised his whole case on Coke's perverse assertion in *Bonham's Case* that the courts would control acts of Parliament even to the extent of voiding them.[25] Yet it fell to a nonlawyer, a single-minded foe of British rule over the colonies, a Harvard-trained rabblerouser, Sam Adams, to recruit the spectral oracle to the Patriot cause whether willing or not, whether indeed he could be made to speak for it or merely stood mute: "whether Lord Coke has expressed it or not . . . an act of parliament made against Magna Charta in violation of its essential parts, is void."[26] Of such boundless assertions and fungible authorities are revolutions made. Beg the question as to what extent Coke fell in behind Citizen Sam—scores of others of our Founding Fathers had no doubt which side he was on and none questioned the magnitude of the aid he gave them.

25. 8 Co.Rep., 121a (1610).
26. Quoted in H. T. Colbourn, *The Lamp of Experience* (New York, 1965), p. 75.

Writing the Law

RICHARD HELGERSON

☙ ☙ ☙

Some thirty years before Roger Ascham attacked English rime, another humanist made a similar attack on English law. "Who is so blind," Thomas Starkey wrote in his *Dialogue Between Pole and Lupset* (1529–32), "that seeth not the great shame to our nation, the great infamy and rot that remaineth in us, to be governed by the laws given to us of such a barbarous nation as the Normans be?" Again English practice is condemned as medieval and barbarous. And again the solution is radical extirpation and replacement. "All," writes Starkey, "by . . . one remedy should be amended and correct, if we might induce the heads of our country to admit the same: that is, to receive the civil law of the Romans, the which is now the common law almost of all Christian nations."[1] As Roman verse would repair the barbarism of English poetry, so Roman law will cure the infamy and rot of English law.

Since the twelfth century, Roman civil law, the body of law that in late antiquity was instituted, digested, and codified by order of the Emperor Justinian, had been "received" as the common law of most parts of Europe. Roman law was taught in the universities and gradually came to be practiced in the courts. Though some early English jurists, Bracton most notable among them, studied this newly recovered Roman law and brought Roman ideas to the discussion of English law, England resisted the reception. Neither the procedure nor the substance of English law bore the Roman stamp. Its leading spokesmen were not university professors but serjeants-at-law; its prime source was not a written text but unwritten precedent; its language was not Latin but law French. In all these respects, English law seemed from Starkey's human-

"Writing the Law" is reprinted from Richard Helgerson, *Forms of Nationhood: The Elizabethan Writing of England* (Chicago: University of Chicago Press, 1992), chap. 2. Reprinted with permission of Richard Helgerson and the University of Chicago Press.

1. Thomas Starkey, *A Dialogue Between Reginald Pole and Thomas Lupset,* edited by Kathleen M. Burton (London: Chatto and Windus, 1948), pp. 174–75.

ist perspective repellently uncouth: "full of much controversy," "of small authority," lacking all "stable ground." Clearly, this whole farrago of "barbarous customs and ordinance" would best be "wiped away" and replaced with that "which we call the very civil law . . . the most ancient and noble monument of the Romans' prudence and policy" (p. 175).

Starkey's advice was not followed. Indeed, it may not have been heard. Unlike Ascham's *Schoolmaster,* the *Dialogue Between Pole and Lupset* was not published until the nineteenth century and seems even in manuscript never to have reached its intended recipient, King Henry VIII.[2] All the same, in our own century, the few paragraphs Starkey devoted to the need for legal reform have been much cited. A celebrated legal historian, F. W. Maitland, is responsible for this attention. In 1901, in his famous Rede Lecture, *English Law and the Renaissance,* Maitland presented Starkey's views as evidence of a serious threat to the continuity of English law. In the second quarter of the sixteenth century, the common law of England was, according to Maitland, experiencing a crisis that made a reception of the sort Starkey recommended a distinct possibility. The institutional machinery for it was in place. Newly endowed professorships of civil law at both Oxford and Cambridge were there to train the necessary legal practitioners, while existing courts, like Star Chamber, Chancery, and Requests, could have served as a scene for a decisive expansion of their activity, as similar courts had already done in the German and Scottish receptions. There were, moreover, indications that the life of the common law was, as Maitland put it, "by no means lusty."[3] The yearbooks, which for centuries had provided an account of current Westminster practice, ceased publication in 1535; in 1547 "divers students of the common laws" appealed formally to the privy council, claiming that the old laws were being set aside in favor of the "law civil"; and a decade later one observer reported that King's Bench and Common Pleas, the principal courts of the common law, had so little business that the lawyers just

2. See G. R. Elton, "Reform by Statute: Thomas Starkey's *Dialogue* and Thomas Cromwell's Policy," *Proceedings of the British Academy* 54 (1968): 165–88. While arguing against Henry's having received the *Dialogue,* which he considers incomplete, Elton does present evidence that even in this form it circulated among Cromwell's supporters and may have had an effect on some Cromwellian legislation. In dismissing the usual understanding that Starkey "advocated the simple replacement of the common law by the civil law of Rome" as a misreading, Elton is, however, himself guilty of misreading. The *Dialogue* does advocate that replacement, though it also advocates codification of existing English law as a less satisfactory but still desirable solution to the uncertainty characteristic of legal practice in England. That the suggestion of codification should arise from a Romanist critique of English law is itself highly significant. It is from the "Roman" point of view that the unwritten character of English law seems most objectionable.

3. Frederic William Maitland, *English Law and the Renaissance* (Cambridge: Cambridge Univ. Press, 1901), p. 22.

stood and "looked about them" (p. 82). The menace was of course averted. The common law regained its former vigor, and no reception occurred. But the fear (or the hope) of its occurrence was not wholly groundless.

Or so Maitland claimed. In the nearly nine decades since he wrote, that claim has been subjected to much scrutiny and much criticism, criticism so severe as to have been characterized as successful demolition. Starkey, say the critics, was an unrepresentative figure out of touch with the English legal community, and he may, in any case, not have meant what he seemed to be saying. Yearbook-style reporting continued unabated in manuscript. Common-law business experienced no significant decline, and there was no great increase in civilian practice. The continuity of English law was, in short, never threatened.[4]

Sweeping as this rejection would seem to be (and not all the critics would agree with all its points), it nevertheless shares with Maitland's original thesis a powerful set of assumptions. English law and the course of English legal history are fundamentally unlike their counterparts elsewhere in Europe. Germany, Scotland, France, Italy, Spain, Portugal, and Holland all received Roman civil law. England didn't. England's law is homegrown, continuous, insular, and unique. Law elsewhere is borrowed, shared, historically broken. In their legal institutions, foreigners are thus doubly foreign: foreign to themselves as well as to the English. No wonder that even on the continent few writers in Maitland's time could be found willing to give "a hearty good word for the reception" (p. 8). It had meant their own national undoing. Thus, whether one agrees with Maitland that the English themselves barely escaped a similarly disastrous self-alienation or with his critics that the threat was never particularly great, a happy celebration of English difference seems well justified.

Maitland himself cogently defined the ideological basis of this widespread agreement. "We have all of us," he remarked, "been nationalists of late. Cosmopolitanism can afford to await its turn" (p. 8). Perhaps that turn has now

---

4. Among the most prominent critics of Maitland's thesis are W. S. Holdsworth, *A History of English Law,* 16 vols. (London: Methuen, 1903–66), 4.252–85; G. R. Elton, "The Political Creed of Thomas Cromwell," *Transactions of the Royal Historical Society,* 5th series, 6 (1956): 78, and "Reform by Statute," pp. 176–77; H. E. Bell, *Maitland: A Critical Examination and Assessment* (Cambridge, Mass.: Harvard Univ. Press, 1965), pp. 130–37; and S. E. Thorne, "English Law and the Renaissance," in *La Storia del Diritto nel Quadro delle Scienze Storiche* (Florence: L. S. Olschki, 1966), pp. 437–45. Reinterpretations and positive reevaluations of Maitland's argument have been proposed by W. H. Dunham in a review of Bell's *Maitland, Yale Law Journal* 75 (1966): 1059–64, and Dafydd Jenkins, "English Law and the Renaissance—Eighty Years On: In Defence of Maitland," *Journal of Legal History* 2 (1981): 107–42.

arrived. In what must be the most radically unsettling reassessment of Mait-land's thesis, J. H. Baker has recently argued that medieval law did not survive in sixteenth-century England and that there was no reception, as such, on the continent.[5] Maitland's initial question—how and why did England resist the reception that overwhelmed the rest of Europe?—was based on a misunder-standing of both the English and the continental situation. England did not resist and the continent did not succumb, at least not to a formal reception. Instead, both underwent much the same process of fundamental change. "In point of detail the English story could not be more different from continental legal history. But in the shift of emphasis from *doctrine* (or common learning) to *jurisprudence* (or judge-made law) the similarity is striking" (p. 59). Both English and continental lawyers paid far more attention to decided cases, par-ticularly to cases decided in the newly strengthened central courts, at the end of the century than they did at its beginning, and both paid less attention to common reason and erudition. The vaunted difference of English law from law on the continent is thus less profound than it is usually made to seem. Not only do both systems have a history marked by significant discontinuity, they have, if we believe Baker, much the same history.

In discussions of Maitland's thesis, Baker's cosmopolitanism stands out as extraordinarily rare. But anticipations of it can easily be found elsewhere in the development of English legal scholarship. In the 1610s, precisely at a time when claims of the uniqueness and antiquity of English law were being pressed with particular intensity, the lawyer and antiquary John Selden argued that the differences had been much exaggerated. Like Baker, Selden denied that the continent had experienced anything like a full reception. Contrary to the usual English assumption that "the supreme and governing law of every other Christian state (saving England and Ireland) . . . [is] the old Roman imperial law of Justinian," he insisted that "no nation in the world is governed by [that law]." "Doubtless," he continued, "custom hath made some parts of the im-perials to be received for law in all places where they have been studied, as even in England also," but that only means that they have become part of the local law. England is thus not unique in its uniqueness. "Every Christian state hath its own common laws, as this kingdom hath."[6] Nor can the English boast of

---

5. J. H. Baker, "English Law and the Renaissance," *Cambridge Law Journal* 44 (1985): 46–61. This essay has been reprinted in Baker, *The Legal Profession and the Common Law: Historical Essays* (London: Hamble-don Press, 1986), pp. 461–76.

6. John Selden, *The Historie of Tithes* (1618), pp. 478 and 480. The following quotation concerning the

the greater antiquity or more perfect continuity of their law. "All laws in general are equally ancient. All were grounded upon nature, and no nation was that out of it took not their grounds; and nature being the same in all, the beginning of all laws must be the same." Though this last does not much resemble Baker's argument, it does have a similar effect. It minimizes difference and suggests that English and continental law have equivalent, if not identical, histories.

Why then, if a "cosmopolitan" account of English legal history has been available for nearly as long as a "nationalist" one, does Baker's rejection of Maitland seem so novel, novel even with respect to Baker's own previous work, since just a few years earlier he had concluded another examination of Maitland's thesis with the "nationalist" opinion that "parallels with the continent seem to be neither close nor instructive"?[7] Is it simply that the differences are obvious and inescapable, while the likenesses are deep and difficult to ferret out? To some extent this is surely the case. The various civil law systems of continental Europe have more in common with one another than any of them has with the English legal system, and that shared similarity is in large part owing to a greater dependence on the authority of Roman civil law. In this sense, the continental reception and the English failure to undergo such a reception are historical realities that cannot be denied. But those realities can themselves function to mask ideological engagements. That Baker has moved toward a "cosmopolitan" understanding of English legal history at a time when England itself has been moving toward greater participation in the European Community is no more surprising than Selden's move in the opposite direction when legal cosmopolitanism appeared a threat to the parliamentary interest he supported.[8] The most carefully researched and disinterested legal history is, like any other history, strongly inclined to tell the story its author and the audience for which he writes want to hear.[9] And for a very long time the favored story has been one of essential difference.

---

equal antiquity of all systems of law comes from Selden's 1616 edition of Fortescue's *De Laudibus Legum Angliae*, sig. C1. For a careful discussion of these texts and Selden's other early writings, see Paul Christianson, "Young John Selden and the Ancient Constitution, ca. 1610–18," *Proceedings of the American Philosophical Society* 128 (1984): 271–315.

7. J. H. Baker, *The Reports of John Spelman*, 2 vols. (London: Selden Society, 1978), 2.50.

8. Further evidence of the growing cosmopolitanism that marks the difference between Baker's two assessments of Maitland is furnished by Gino Gorla and Luigi Moccia, "A 'Revisiting' of the Comparison Between 'Continental Law' and 'English Law' (16th to 19th Century)" and Luigi Moccia, "English Attitudes to the 'Civil Law,'" *Journal of Legal History* 2 (1981): 143–56 and 157–68. Daniel R. Coquillette's articles, cited in note 22 below, are also symptomatic of this shift.

9. Despite my introductory declaration of having been surprised by evidence that, in at least one in-

The telling of that differentiating story seems to have begun late in the fourteenth century with John Wycliffe's *De Officio Regis* (1379), and it was strongly seconded a century later by Sir John Fortescue in his *De Laudibus Legum Angliae* (1470), where the political implications of legal difference are made explicit.[10] In a passage to which I alluded at the end of the last chapter, Fortescue distinguished between what he called the *dominium politicum et regale* characteristic of England and the continental (particularly French) *dominium regale*. Where in England the king had no power to change the laws without gaining the assent of the whole realm represented in parliament, the French monarch's will was absolute. Empowered by the Justinianic maxim *Quod principi placuit legis habet vigorem* ("What has pleased the prince has the force of law"), civil law kings might easily degenerate into tyranny. English common law provided a barrier against such degeneration and thus served to maintain the liberty of the subject. Seen this way, England's legal difference seemed a proper cause for rejoicing, a legitimate source of national pride.

And so it was to remain, by most accounts, for centuries—indeed so it is still today. But difference can as easily cause anxiety as pride. We have already encountered one notable instance of such anxiety in Spenser's lament: "Why a God's name may not we, as else the Greeks, have the kingdom of our own language?" For Spenser, England's difference was a mark of inferiority, a sign of insufficient civility. Some such fear troubles even Fortescue's *De Laudibus*. It was, after all, the "glorious fame" of Roman law and the possibility that an English prince beguiled by that fame might wish to impose Roman law on his people that made Fortescue's defense of English law necessary. And with the spread of humanist ideas in the next century that need increased. Starkey's complaint and his proposal may have had no influence whatsoever. But they are nevertheless symptoms of a crisis no less significant than the one Maitland identified. Even if Maitland's critics are right that English law was in no danger of being replaced by Roman law, English law *was* in danger of being replaced by a "Romanized" version of itself. Indeed, that is what happened. England did not receive Roman law. But it did receive a Roman idea of the law, or rather a Roman idea of the form in which the law should present itself.

Starkey argues for this lesser reception as well as for the greater. If England

---

stance, forced me to tell a story I did not want to tell, this inclination has no doubt shaped the present book in ways that are quite beyond my knowing but that will be retrospectively visible should any sufficiently distant future reader care to look. The authorial "I" is multiply constituted and wants contradictory things.

10. Maitland, *English Law*, pp. 10 and 52–53. See also H. D. Hazeltine's preface to Sir John Fortescue, *De Laudibus Legum Anglie*, edited by S. B. Chrimes (Cambridge: Cambridge Univ. Press, 1942), p. xvii.

is not to receive Roman law, it should at the very least "use the same remedy that Justinian did in the law of the Romans." It should gather the law and cause it "to be written . . . in our mother tongue, or else put into the Latin" (p. 174). A few years later, Richard Morison, who had been at Oxford and Padua with Starkey and who, like Starkey, had entered the service of Thomas Cromwell, presented the king with a *Discourse Touching the Reformation of the Laws of England* (1535) in which he proposed "to attempt if the common laws of this your realm that now be unwritten might be written; that now be dispersed and uncertain might be gathered together and made certain; that now be in no tongue might be reduced into the Latin tongue."[11] And Morison too takes as his model for this reforming enterprise the work of Justinian. "This thing, though it be hard, as all noble things be, yet is it not impossible. The laws which now we call civil, before the Emperor Justinian's time were as much dispersed and as far out of order as ours be" (pp. 440–41). What the Romans did the English can and should do. They should write the law, produce an English equivalent of the *Corpus Juris Civilis*. Not only would such a book remedy the law's confusion and uncertainty, it would stand as a mark of civility, a mark of England's freedom from barbarism.

Neither Starkey nor Morison ever produced such a book. Morison tried but with little success. Starkey did not even try. Nor did anyone else of their generation. They identified a need but were unable to satisfy it. In this they resemble Ascham, who called for a classicizing reform of English verse but failed to accomplish that reform himself. Spenser, Sidney, and their contemporaries responded to Ascham's call, struggled to provide England with the missing quantitative meter, and ended by producing an art of English poetry equivalent to, though distinct from, the ancient art, one that justified itself in Daniel's *Defense of Rime* by association with English law. In the law itself, there could, however, be no comparable answer to Starkey's call, no completion of Morison's aborted project, for the obvious reason that the work of Starkey and Morison, unlike Ascham's *Schoolmaster,* remained unknown. Younger men, men of precisely the age of Sidney and Spenser, did nevertheless manage to reconceive the "Romanizing" project that had preoccupied their Henrician predecessors, and they brought it to a conclusion that was both as successful and as far removed from the original ambition as was the Elizabethan erection of barbarous rime into a distinguished "native" art of poetry.

11. Quoted by S. E. Thorne, "English Law," p. 440. See also Elton's discussion of Morison in "Reform by Statute," pp. 177–80.

The most conspicuous of these younger men was then and still remains Sir Edward Coke. Born in 1552, the same year as Spenser, Coke provided in his *Reports* (1600–1615), his *Book of Entries* (1614), and his *Institutes* (1628–44) something of a *Corpus Juris* for England. To identify Coke as the chief "Romanizer" of English common law may, however, seem little short of absurd. No less likely candidate for such a distinction seems imaginable than this man whose mind, in the memorable phrase of J. G. A. Pocock, "was as nearly insular as a human being's could be."[12] Yet I would contend that Coke's very insularity, his myopic insistence on the uninterrupted Englishness of English law, was the product of a constant sense of legal and national difference, a persistent awareness of a rival system of law against which English law had to defend and define itself. Coke was insular not by ignorance but by ideological necessity. His insularity was part of a self-presentational strategy. Furthermore, neither that insularity nor the cosmopolitan awareness that underlay and enabled it were his alone, though in him both reached extraordinary proportions and led to no less extraordinary results. Both were shared by his generation, the generation of lawyers and legal scholars born between the midcentury and the mid-1560s. Coke's massive legal writings were just one manifestation of a common, age-based project, a project that began to emerge in the last years of Elizabeth, was powerfully shaped by the conflicts of James's reign, and produced its most enduring monument, Coke's own *Institutes,* only after Charles had become king.

Though there are real differences between English law and the law practiced elsewhere in Europe and real similarities between the history of English law and the histories of those other legal systems, neither the nationalist nor the cosmopolitan position is simply a matter of getting the facts right. Each is ideologically motivated, and each depends on the other (even if only as a signifying absence) to be a position at all. So in the sixteenth and early seventeenth centuries, the project, anticipated by Starkey and Morison and realized by Coke and his generation, of writing English law derived both its inspiration and its cogency from its Roman and continental rival. Nor was the rivalry only between domestic law and a foreign counterpart, for the civil law had its schools, its professors, its practitioners, and its courts in England. In law,

---

12. J. G. A. Pocock, *The Ancient Constitution and the Feudal Law* (1957; enlarged ed. Cambridge: Cambridge Univ. Press, 1987), p. 56. On the more general issue of the insularity of English legal scholarship in this period, see Donald R. Kelley, "History, English Law and the Renaissance," *Past and Present* 65 (1974): 24–51. A criticism of Kelley's argument by Christopher Brooks and Kevin Sharpe can be found, together with Kelley's response, in *Past and Present* 72 (1976): 133–46.

as in other areas, national consolidation had a double face. It turned inward to find out and eliminate those practices and those institutions that failed to reflect back its own unitary image, and it turned outward to declare its defining difference—*and* to assure itself that such difference was not so different that it would be taken as a sign of backwardness or barbarity. And what I here express in this abstract personification, this figure of a nationalist Janus, was for Coke and his contemporaries a matter of immediate and lived experience. Their own individual interest and identity, the interest and identity of the professional community (or communities) to which they belonged, the interest and identity of the nation they were helping (for whatever reason) to construct depended on the meanings they succeeded in attaching to their activities. And those meanings depended in turn on the play of differences in a system of signifying relations—a *langue,* as a Saussurian might say, to enable their *paroles.*

What then did it mean in Coke's generation to write the law? This question has no simple answer. There was a general agreement that such writing was needed and an equally general understanding that it must in some way be related to Justinian's writing of Roman law. In this agreement and understanding, Starkey and Morison shared. But the particular situation of the Elizabethans differed considerably from that of Starkey and Morison, and individual Elizabethans were differently situated from one another.[13] From these differences in situation came differences in their sense of how the writing should be carried out and whose interests should be served by it. Differences in training and practice between common lawyers and civilians, jurisdictional conflicts between common-law courts, civil-law courts, and courts of equity, questions of royal prerogative and parliamentary privilege, more particular issues like the proposed union of Scotland and England, personal antagonisms and ambitions: all these served to divide Coke and his legal contemporaries from one another and to make their writing of the law a counter in their personal, political, and professional disputes. Nor did the struggle end with the death of this generation and the posthumous publication in the 1640s of the final three volumes of Coke's *Institutes.* Controversy continued for centuries as the products of their joint undertaking were variously appropriated, anno-

13. The enormous increase in litigation during Elizabeth's reign no doubt gave greater urgency in the later period to the sense that England's law needed reform. See C. W. Brooks, "Litigants and Attorneys in the King's Bench and Common Pleas, 1560–1640," in *Legal Records and the Historian,* edited by J. H. Baker (London: Royal Historical Society, 1978), pp. 41–59.

tated, emulated, revised, criticized, or replaced by their English and American successors.

In the discussion that follows, I will not often be able to look forward to these subsequent developments. Nor will I have much chance to look across the Channel at the similar projects that were going on there. But some awareness of later and distant events is necessary if we are not to construe the meaning of the Elizabethan enterprise too narrowly. For that enterprise reaches back through the early sixteenth-century humanists to late antiquity and beyond and forward even to our own day, and it has many parallels in the other emerging nation-states of early modern Europe. To give equal attention to this broad range of related activities would be to miss the specificity of the Elizabethan experience. But to neglect the broader range would result in a no less serious distortion. It would be to mistake the dialect of sixteenth- and early seventeenth-century legal discourse in England for a self-enclosed and self-sufficient language. The accent and inflections of Coke's project, even some of its essential vocabulary and syntax, may have belonged to him and his generation alone, but its deep structure made it part of a language spoken wherever national self-representation and the Roman legal tradition converged.

Plans for an English *Corpus Juris*

Members of the same generation do not necessarily like each other. Nor do they always agree. Edward Coke's most persistent antagonist was a lawyer just nine years his junior: Francis Bacon. Rivals in the 1590s for the post of solicitor general, for the attorney-generalship, and for the hand of Lady Hatton (all of which Coke got), their mutual scorn flared up in an Exchequer proceeding in 1601. As Bacon told the story to Robert Cecil, Coke "kindled" at an apparently slighting motion Bacon had made. "Mr. Bacon," Coke is supposed to have said, "if you have any tooth against me, pluck it out, for it will do you more hurt than all the teeth in your head will do you good." Bacon answered coldly: "Mr. Attorney, I respect you. I fear you not. And the less you speak of your own greatness, the more I will think of it." The exchange continued in much the same vein, Coke declining "to stand upon terms of greatness" toward Bacon, who, he said, was "less than little, less than the least," and Bacon insisting that Coke "not depress me so far, for I have been your better, and may be again, when it please the queen." At this Coke spoke, as Bacon put it, "neither I nor himself could tell what, as if he had been born attorney general; and in the end bade me not meddle with the queen's business, but with mine own."[14]

Anger, animosity, and injured pride are not all that finds expression here, though they are obvious enough. The exchange also foreshadows an ideological break that would soon separate the two men, if it hadn't already. For Bacon, all status depended on the queen. The son of a man the queen had appointed lord keeper, he had once been Coke's better. With Coke as attorney general, that ranking was reversed but might change again "when it please the queen." Coke, on the other hand, is made to speak as if he thought his greatness his own, "as if he had been born attorney general."

Bacon no doubt misrepresents Coke, who could on occasion show a keen awareness of his dependence on royal favor. And, in writing to the queen's principal secretary, Bacon may also have had reason to misrepresent himself. But seen in the light of the continuing relation between the two men, Bacon's dramatic rendering of their confrontation seems prophetically true. Over the course of the next two decades, he and Coke would repeatedly differ in situations where royal prerogative and the common law—in Coke's view, the subject's most precious birthright—were in conflict. In 1613, as King James's solicitor general and with the express intent of weakening Coke and recovering "that strength to the king's prerogative which it hath had in times past and which is due unto it" (11.381), Bacon got Coke transferred from the Court of Common Pleas to the less crucial Court of King's Bench. In the next few years, with Bacon now attorney general, he and Coke clashed over Peacham's Case, the Case of Commendams, and the Case *De Rege Inconsulto,* all of which pitted the king's prerogative against judicial freedom. Then in 1616, as a result of these conflicts, Bacon succeeded in having Coke removed from the privy council and dismissed as chief justice. From this triumph, Bacon's fortunes continued to rise, as he assumed in turn the posts of lord keeper and lord chancellor, until in 1621 a strong common-law parliament, led by Edward Coke, found Bacon guilty of accepting bribes and impeached him.

Which is ultimately superior, the king or the law? Whatever else was at stake in these various confrontations, this was a question that ran through all of them. In their actions and institutional commitments, Bacon and Coke con-

---

14. *The Works of Francis Bacon,* edited by James Spedding, 14 vols. (London: Longmans, 1857–74), 10.3. Volumes 8–14 of this edition are often cited as volumes 1–7 of *The Letters and Life of Francis Bacon.* I have not followed this practice.

sistently took opposite sides. Bacon favored the king; Coke, the law. Yet with regard to that great project of writing the law, the project which produced as its most significant accomplishments Coke's *Reports* and *Institutes,* even these antagonists agreed. If Coke wrote English law in such a way as to answer the objections that humanists like Starkey had directed at it, Bacon foresaw and defined that need. From 1593, when in his first reported parliamentary speech he called for an abridgment of the laws and statutes of the realm, to the 1620s, when he included an "Example of a Treatise on Universal Justice" in his *De Augmentis Scientiarum* (1623), Bacon made the writing of the law the single most important and most prominently reiterated element in his program for civic reform.[15] Like Starkey, he considered the uncertainty of English law its greatest defect and, again like Starkey, he presented Justinian's redaction of Roman law as the exemplary remedy for such a failing. He never attacks English law for its barbarousness. By the 1590s such outright condemnation was no longer possible, particularly for a common lawyer like Bacon. Nor does he urge a reception of Roman law. That too had passed beyond the verge of even hypothetical possibility. But he does recommend "a general amendment of the state of [the] laws" and a reduction of them "to more brevity and certainty" (7.316) that in all but the smallest details adheres to the Justinianic program.

What that program stood for in Bacon's mind was first a certain formal order and then a certain conception of authority. Following Justinian's *Corpus Juris,* Bacon recommended that the two main bodies of English law, common law and statute law, be separately reduced and recompiled, for "this," he says, "was the plan followed by Trebonianus"—Justinian's chief assistant—"in the *Digest* and *Code*" (5.100). He then urged that this "heroic" (10.336) two-part work be surrounded with a set of auxiliary books: "institutions; a treatise *de regulis juris;* and a better book *de verborum significationibus,* or terms of the law" (13.70). Like the *Digest* and *Code,* each of these has its counterpart in Justinian's *Corpus Juris.* The *Institutes* is one of the four major parts of the *Cor-*

15. The following passages, which I have arranged in approximate chronological order, provide a good idea of both the persistence and the character of Bacon's ideas concerning the writing of English law: "Opening of Speech on Motion for Supply" (8.213–14); *Gesta Grayorum* (8.339–40); *Maxims of the Law* (7.313–87), *The Advancement of Learning* (3.475–76); "A Preparation Toward the Union of Laws" (7.731–43); "A Speech . . . [on] a Motion Concerning the Union of Laws" (10.336); "Commentarius" (11.74 and 94); "Letter to King James" (13.59–60); "A Memorial Touching the Review of Penal Laws and the Amendment of the Common Law" (12.84–86); "Proposition . . . Touching the Compiling and Amendment of the Laws of England" (13.61–71); *Advertisement Touching an Holy War* (7.14); and *De Augmentis Scientiarum* (5.88–110). Despite extraordinary personal and historical changes from the 1590s to the 1620s, Bacon's views on this topic remained remarkably consistent, so consistent that I have felt free to draw on various passages in summarizing his views without regard for chronology.

pus, while *De Verborum Significatione* and *De Regulis Juris* are the two last titles in the *Digest.* In describing what such books should be like, Bacon obviously had these Roman models in mind. Institutes, to take only the example most relevant to our consideration of Coke, should, he advised, "be arranged in a clear and perspicuous order," should "run through the whole private law," and should not "touch . . . the public law" (5.105), all characteristics of Justinian's *Institutes.*[16] But form was not the only thing Bacon derived from his Roman model. He also drew on that model for a conception of authority and its appropriate expression. From first to last, Bacon imagined the writing (or rewriting) of the law as belonging essentially to the monarch.[17] The formal order he seeks derives from monarchic authority. As Justinian "wrote" Roman law, so Elizabeth or James should "write" the law of England. Unless an English monarch would play Justinian, Bacon could not be the English Tribonian he clearly aspired to be. Without a royal author the law could not be written. No other source of authority was imaginable.

   This combination of formal adherence to the pattern of the *Corpus Juris* and

16. Bacon's interest in the institute as the crucial genre for the writing of national law was widely shared in early modern Europe. There have been a number of valuable surveys of this literature: Klaus Luig, "The Institutes of National Law in the Seventeenth and Eighteenth Centuries," *Juridical Review* n.s. 17 (1972): 193–226; Alan Watson, *The Making of the Civil Law* (Cambridge, Mass.: Harvard Univ. Press, 1981), pp. 62–82, and "Justinian's Institutes and Some English Counterparts," *Studies in Justinian's Institutes,* edited by P. G. Stein and A. D. E. Lewis (London: Sweet and Maxwell, 1983), pp. 181–86; F. H. Lawson, "Institutes," *Festschrift für Imre Zajtay,* edited by R. H. Graveson et al. (Tübingen: Mohr, 1982), pp. 333–55; John W. Cairns, "Blackstone, an English Institutist: Legal Literature and the Rise of the Nation State," *Oxford Journal of Legal Studies* 4 (1984): 318–60; and the introduction to *Justinian's Institutes,* edited by Peter Birks and Grant McLeod (Ithaca, New York: Cornell Univ. Press, 1987), pp. 7–26. See also A. W. B. Simpson's discussion of institutional writing in relation to other forms of legal literature in "The Rise and Fall of the Legal Treatise: Legal Principles and the Forms of Legal Literature," *University of Chicago Law Review* 48 (1981): 632–79.

17. In his first parliamentary speech in 1593, Bacon claimed that "nothing should tend more to the eternal praise of her majesty" (8.214) than a general abridgment of the law, and he was still saying much the same thing under a new monarch more than twenty years later. "After I had thought of many things," he wrote to King James in 1616, "I could find, in my judgment, none more proper for your majesty as a master, nor for me as a workman, than the reducing and recompiling of the laws of England" (13.62). Such "lawgivers" as Justinian, to whom he regularly points as the most obvious example, stand only behind "founders of estates" in the "degrees of sovereign honor." They are *principes perpetui,* for they continue to rule "after their decease in their laws" (13.64). It is to this eminence that he urged first Elizabeth and then James to aspire. With few exceptions, all the texts in which Bacon argued for the rewriting of the law—his *Maxims,* his *Advancement of Learning,* his "Preparation Toward the Union of Laws," his "Memorial Touching the Review of Penal Laws," his "Proposition Touching the Amendment of the Laws," and his *De Augmentis Scientiarum*—were addressed to the monarch. Even in his private notes, he thought of the king as his eventual audience: "Persuad. the k. in glory, *Aurea condet saecula.* New laws to be compounded and collected; lawgiver *perpetuis princeps*" (11.73–74). And when he slipped his familiar plea for a rewriting of the law into the script of the revels he prepared for the "readers and ancients" of Gray's Inn, he directed it to a fictional Prince of Purpoole (8.339–40). With the support of the monarch, who is the "soul of the law" (8.313), his project would prosper. Without that authorizing support, it had neither hope nor meaning.

an association of the writing of the law with monarchic (or imperial) power recurs with some regularity in the Bacon-Coke generation. In 1613, Henry Finch, a collaborator of Bacon's on a commission whose charge was to reduce "concurrent statutes . . . to one clear and uniform law" (13.71), published a book of his own that W. S. Holdsworth has called "the most complete and best institutional book before Blackstone."[18] This book, Finch's *Nomotechnia* (1613), later Englished as *Law, or a Discourse Thereof* (1627), began with a dedication to King James, based its organizational scheme on Justinian's *Institutes,* and devoted a portion of every chapter to what one historian has called an "obsequious" consideration of the relevant function of royal prerogative.[19] Still more obviously devoted both to Justinian and to the king was John Cowell, whose law dictionary, *The Interpreter* (1607), stirred up a storm of parliamentary opposition by its uncompromising advocacy of royal absolutism and whose *Institutes of English Law* (1605) follows the order of Justinian's *Institutes* chapter by chapter.[20] Others—William Fulbecke, Lodowick Lloyd, Sir John Hayward, and Sir John Dodderidge—while they did not go as far as Bacon, Finch, or Cowell in the project of writing English law according to the Roman pattern, did nevertheless argue that the two systems were amenable to such reduction to a common order. And when they were not asserting the similarity of the two laws, English lawyers of this generation agonized over the differences between them. In 1588, Abraham Fraunce could, for example, worry about the familiar charge that "the civil law . . . is both in itself more constant and philosophical [than the common law] and also by Justinian more methodically . . . put down."[21] Two decades later, Sir Thomas Ridley gave new point to such worry with his highly laudatory *View of the Civil and Ecclesiastical Law* (1607). King James's open admiration for this *View* moved Coke "from thence to prophesy the decay of the common law."[22] No one of this

18. W. S. Holdsworth, *A History of English Law,* 16 vols. (London: Methuen, 1903–66), 5.399.

19. Wilfred Prest, "The Dialectical Origins of Finch's *Law*," *Cambridge Law Journal* 36 (1977): 343. On the relation between Finch and Justinian, see Alan Watson, "Justinian's Institutes and Some English Counterparts," *Studies in Justinian's Institutes,* edited by P. G. Stein and A. D. E. Lewis (London: Sweet and Maxwell, 1983), pp. 181–86.

20. On the *Interpreter* affair, see J. P. Sommerville, *Politics and Ideology in England, 1603–1640* (London: Longman, 1986), pp. 121–27. The more general opposition between absolutist and common-law notions of rule that figures largely in this chapter is a principal subject of Sommerville's valuable book.

21. Abraham Fraunce, *The Lawiers Logike* (1588), sig. ¶¶1–1ᵛ.

22. Quoted by Brian P. Levack, *The Civil Lawyers in England, 1603–1641: A Political Study* (Oxford: Clarendon Press, 1973), p. 123. For an excellent discussion of civilian attitudes toward the common law, see Levack's chapter on "The Laws of England," pp. 122–57. The contribution of civilians to English legal thought has been surveyed in a series of articles by Daniel R. Coquillette. Particularly relevant to the con-

generation, including Ridley, called for the kind of reception Starkey had proposed in the 1530s. But their work as a whole testifies to a pervasive insecurity regarding the stability and authority of English law and an equally pervasive sense that the appropriate remedy was to write that law in accordance with the Roman model. To that extent they were all partisans of an English reception.

But could even so limited a reception be undertaken without substantive alteration? Wouldn't the very nature of both English law and the English state be affected? "The common law of England is," as Bacon several times notes, "no text law, but the substance of it consisteth in the series and succession of judicial acts from time to time which have been set down in the books we term yearbooks or reports" (12.85). He does not wish to alter this fundamental character. That would, he says, be "to cast the law into a new mold"—a "perilous innovation" (13.67). But whatever he may claim to the contrary, wouldn't that be the result of his reform? In England, the chief example of text law was statute, law enacted by the king-in-parliament. If, as he intends, Bacon's proposed registering and recompiling of the common law is itself accomplished by the same king-in-parliament, won't its product be statute law? The chief foreign example of text law, Roman civil law, was made text law through just such a process of registration and recompilation. "Justinian the emperor," wrote Bacon, "by commissions directed to divers persons learned in the laws, reduced the Roman laws from vastness of volume and a labyrinth of uncertainties unto that course of the civil law which is now in use" (13.66). This is how Justinian became the Roman lawgiver, how Elizabeth or James might become an English lawgiver.

Bacon continues to differentiate between *lex scripta* and *lex non scripta,* between "text law" and "customs well registered," but in the light of his project the difference is increasingly hard to see. When customs are registered at the king's behest, they become text law and the king becomes their author. In his *True Law of Free Monarchies* (1598), King James based his own claim to absolute sovereignty on just such an act of royal authorship: "kings were the authors and makers of the laws, and not the laws of the king."[23] Whether the law is authored by a conquering monarch, as James here imagines, or re-

cerns of this chapter are the first two articles in the series: "Legal Ideology and Incorporation I: The English Civilian Writers, 1523–1607" and "Legal Ideology and Incorporation II: Sir Thomas Ridley, Charles Molloy, and the Literary Battle for the Law Merchant, 1607–1616," *Boston University Law Review* 61 (1981): 1–89 and 315–71.

23. *The Political Works of James I,* edited by Charles Howard McIlwain (Cambridge, Mass.: Harvard Univ. Press, 1918), p. 62.

authored, as Bacon recommends, by a king who has inherited his crown by due descent, the effect is much the same. Absolute royal prerogative is expressed and confirmed. And the loser is always the judge. Instead of those "judicial acts," which Bacon identified as the source of English common law, royal acts now make the law. "Leave not the law to the pleasure of the judge," James told parliament in 1607, "but let your laws be looked into" — by which he clearly intended just such an "amending and polishing" as Bacon had been urging on him, "for," as James said, "I desire not the abolishing of the laws, but only the cleaning and sweeping off the rust of them" (p. 293).

Always there, lurking about the edge of consciousness, was the menacing stigma of barbarism. Set against all others, Finch claimed, English law holds its head as high "as cypresses among the pliant shrubs" ("quantum lenta solent inter viburna cupressi"). To any sixteenth-century grammar school boy, these words would have had a special resonance. They are taken from Virgil's *Eclogues,* where they celebrate the superiority of Rome.[24] Rome's erstwhile eminence, Finch seems to be saying, is now England's. But then comes the familiar complaint. "Among the innumerable men trained in this august discipline [of English law], no one has yet arisen to supply an excellence of method to match its excellence of matter." The law lies "damaged" and "fragmented" in "a more than Anaxagorean confusion." Describing English law as an "ancient palace that hitherto hath been accounted (howsoever substantial) yet but dark and melancholy" and announcing his own project of "gaining some comfortable lights and prospects toward the beautifying of this ancient palace," Cowell expresses a similar view.[25] Gothic buildings are dark and melancholy. Light and prospect belong to the newer classicizing architecture. Both Finch and Cowell bring us once again to the verge of a reception. What is "damaged," "fragmented," "dark," and "melancholy" in English law is uniquely its own and must be sacrificed. When legal reform has done its reordering and opened its neoclassical "lights and prospects," the remaining substance will be essentially Roman. In all but detail, the *Corpus Juris Communis Anglicani* Bacon, Finch, and Cowell envision will be indistinguishable from Justinian's *Corpus Juris Civilis.* And the consequences of that likeness will be more than aesthetic. To imitate the self-presentational form of Roman law is not only to escape barbarism; it is also to adopt something like the imperial order of

24. Henry Finch, *Nomotexnia* (1613), sig. ¶iii[v]. I am grateful to G. W. Pigman for directing my attention to the echo from Virgil.

25. John Cowell, *The Interpreter* (1607), sig. *3.

the Roman state. That is the program Bacon and Cowell were urging, one in which Finch's *Nomotechnia* and Cowell's *Institutes* participate.

But for all the importance of Bacon's various programmatic statements, of Finch and Cowell's institutional writings, of the lesser contributions of Fraunce, Fulbecke, Dodderidge, and the rest, theirs were not, even in their own generation, the works that made it possible for Englishmen to feel that their law had been written in an authoritatively satisfying way. That role fell rather to the work of Bacon's great rival, Sir Edward Coke, a man who ignored Finch, called Cowell "Doctor Cowheel," and stood firmly against the absolutist conception of royal prerogative that seemed to Bacon, Finch, Cowell, and the others an intrinsic part of their project. If Ridley's *View* with its detailed and eulogistic description of the *Corpus Juris,* if Cowell's books and Bacon's schemes seemed threats to the common law and particularly to that preeminence that Coke felt the law should exercise over even the king's prerogative, then those threats would have to be answered in something like their own terms: by a writing of the law. This is what Coke did. But he did it in a way that altered the fundamental understanding of what such writing meant, by writing against writing.

Reporting the Unwritten Law

Late in his life, Coke made a catalog of his extensive library. Among the books he listed were Bacon's *Instauratio Magna,* Fulbecke's *Parallels,* Cowell's *Interpreter,* Ridley's *View,* and no less than eight different editions of various parts of the *Corpus Juris.* He did not list either Finch's *Nomotechnia* or Cowell's *Institutiones,* but a copy of the former survives with his other books at Holkham House and the latter is quoted in the catalog itself.[26] Passing from books on the laws of England to those on the civil law, Coke recalls Cowell's assertion of the similarity between the two systems: "Dr. Cowell in his *Institutions of the Laws of England* . . . saith that 'the principles of both . . . are the same, the definitions and divisions of things are the same, the rules plainly agree, the statutes are similar; they differ only in idiom and method.'"[27] Clearly Coke had been

26. W. O. Hassall, *A Catalogue of the Library of Sir Edward Coke* (New Haven, Conn.: Yale Univ. Press, 1950), nos. 422, 435–39, 445, 459, 461, 464, 466, 469, 486–91, and 745. For Finch's *Nomotechnia,* see p. xxii n. 56.

27. Hassall, *Catalogue,* p. 38.

attending to what his contemporaries were writing and thinking. But, as one might expect, he did not approve of everything he saw. On the title page of Bacon's *Instauratio Magna,* he wrote, "It deserveth not to be read in schools, / But to be fraughted in the ship of fools," to which he added in Latin: "You purpose to reconstruct the teaching of wise men of old. Reconstruct first our laws and justice." [28]

Bacon's judgment of Coke was more generous. "Had it not been for Sir Edward Coke's *Reports,*" he wrote James in 1616, "the law by this time had been almost like a ship without ballast." But a few pages later he uses the same image for "the treatise *de regulis juris*" on which he was himself engaged. "I hold it of all other things the most important to the health, as I may term it, and good institutions of any laws. It is indeed like the ballast of a ship, to keep all upright and stable." And not many lines go by before the implicit comparison is made explicit. "I do assure your majesty, I am in good hope that when Sir Edward Coke's *Reports* and my *Rules and Decisions* shall come to posterity, there will be (whatsoever is now thought) question who was the greater lawyer" (13.65 and 70). [29] In Bacon's cosmopolitan philosophizing, Coke saw only folly. For Coke, Bacon stood outside the legal pale. His *Instauratio Magna* contributed nothing to the restoration of English law. Bacon himself drew the line differently. Both he and Coke are within it. They compete in the common enterprise of ballasting the ship of English law. But underlying the difference in their judgment of one another was a shared sense of need. They agreed that "to reconstruct our laws and justice" — "instaurare leges justiciamque" — was a task of great urgency.

Bacon identified Coke's *Reports* as part of this undertaking. That Coke also saw his *Reports* this way puts a distance between those reports and all previous books of the same sort. When Coke began publishing reports in 1600, the shelf to which they would naturally be added contained some fifteen printed volumes: nine volumes of collected yearbooks, the abridgments of Fitzherbert and Brooke in three volumes, two volumes of Plowden's reports, and one volume of reports left by Sir James Dyer. In addition, many lawyers would have had a few volumes of manuscript reports (Coke had at least sixteen), whether

28. Catherine Drinker Bowen describes this volume in *The Lion and the Throne: The Life and Times of Sir Edward Coke* (Boston: Little, Brown, 1956), pp. 424 and 549–50. I adopt Bowen's translation of Coke's Latin. For the original, see Hassall, *Catalogue,* no. 745.

29. Peter Stein discusses Bacon's *Maxims* in relation to the Roman tradition in *Regulae Juris: From Juristic Rules to Legal Maxims* (Edinburgh: Edinburgh Univ. Press, 1966), pp. 170–76.

of their own composition or copied from the work of others.[30] But in all this material, nothing would have presented itself as a response to the humanist critique of English law. Rather than defending the law, these books were its unreflective products. Yearbooks, abridgments, and reports supplied a record, a more reliable record than that provided by memory and oral transmission, of what had happened in court, what pleadings had been used, and what decisions had been reached. But they said nothing of the relation of English law to other legal systems, nor did they address any but an immediate and professional audience.

Coke's work as a reporter began in this narrow tradition. From 1572, when at the age of twenty he entered the Middle Temple, he regularly attended court proceedings in Westminster Hall. And from 1581, he kept a careful record of the many cases he observed. Assembled in seven fat notebooks (the first alone filled 900 octavo leaves), these manuscript reports were a principal source of Coke's vast legal erudition.[31] As such, they performed to an extraordinary degree the quite ordinary function of such literature. They helped make the reporter himself a more able lawyer. But by 1600, when he published his first volume of reports, Coke began to have a new idea of what they could do. No longer were reports merely a convenient aid to memory. They now had a polemical purpose as well. They provided a defense and illustration of the English legal system itself, a defense against precisely those threats represented by the humanist interest in Roman law.

The recourse to print was itself a sign of this change. Prior to Coke's, only Plowden's reports had been printed in their author's lifetime, and Plowden felt compelled to apologize for the innovation. He allowed it only to prevent a pirated and defective edition. Coke too expressed some reluctance about committing his work to print, but he did so in a preface that was otherwise devoted to the importance of writing. Without written and published yearbooks, "the opinions, censures, and judgments" of past judges would have been "long sithence wasted and worn away with the worm of oblivion," and with them the certainty of the law itself would have been lost. "For," he continued, "I have often observed that for want of a true and certain report, the case that hath

30. The printed reports are surveyed by Theodore F. T. Plucknett, "The Genesis of Coke's Reports," *Cornell Law Quarterly* 27 (1942): 190–213. For a discussion of both manuscript and printed reports, see L. W. Abbott, *Law Reporting in England, 1485–1585* (London: Athlone Press, 1973).
31. J. H. Baker describes the three extant manuscripts and speculates concerning the contents of the other four in "Coke's Note-Books and the Sources of his Reports," *The Legal Profession and the Common Law,* pp. 177–204.

been adjudged standing upon the rack of many running reports (especially of such as understood not the state of the question) hath been so diversely drawn out as many times the true parts of the case have been disordered and disjointed and most commonly the right reason and rule of the judges utterly mistaken."[32] Coke objected not only to the fallibility of "slippery memory" but also to the anonymity and vagary of the common-law manuscript culture, to what he called "wandering and masterless reports." Fixed in print and authored by the queen's attorney general, his work was meant to remedy this defect.

In this first preface, Coke made no direct reference to any competing legal system. Nor did he insist on the particularity of English law. But from the opening sentences of his second preface of 1602, the vigorous defense of English law against all rivals became his constant theme. "Of all laws," he insisted, the common laws of England "are most equal and most certain, of greatest antiquity and least delay, and most beneficial and easy to be observed." Had he simply taken the standard humanist complaints and reversed them, Coke could hardly have produced a more blindly partisan claim. Equality, certainty, antiquity, efficiency, and accessibility were the very qualities others attributed to the written law of Rome, qualities they found sadly lacking in England's unwritten law. Coke denied all that. Though he admitted that the Romans may "justly . . . boast of their civil laws," he argued that even they recognized the superiority of English law. Had they not thought it superior, they would have changed it during the centuries when they occupied ancient Britain. But this they didn't do, for the law now practiced in England is the same that Brutus brought from Troy a millennium before the Roman invasion.

Even among Coke's contemporaries, this fantastic historical claim was widely rejected. "Hyperbolical praise," Hayward called it, praise of a sort "now out of season, as never suitable but with artless times."[33] Less artless notions were widely available. Many agreed with Starkey that English law descended from the Normans. Others attributed its essential features to the Saxons. And still others, Hayward among them, thought it of mixed origin, mingling Roman, Saxon, Danish, and Norman elements. But Coke's assertion, though he argued for it at length in subsequent prefaces, was less a matter of historical

32. I quote Coke's *Reports* by volume and signature from the following first editions: 1 (1600); 2 (1602); 3 (1602); 4 (1604); 5 (1605); 6 (1607); 7 (1608); 8 (1611); 9 (1613); 10 (1614); and 11 (1615). The present quotation is from 1. ❧ iii–iii^v.

33. Sir John Hayward, *A Treatise of Union of the Two Realmes of England and Scotland* (1604), sig. C2.

truth than of polemical necessity. One way to escape the charge of medieval barbarism was to claim an origin well before the arrival of the barbarians, an origin that reached back to "time out of mind." Nor was this merely a matter of establishing the superiority of English law through its superiority of age. The immemorial character of that law also made it proof against royal encroachment.

Already in his second preface, written and published while Elizabeth was still queen, Coke praised "the ancient law of England" for its independence from monarchic will. Against English government by law, he set "the tyranny of other nations wherein powerful will and pleasure stands for law and reason. . . . In other kingdoms the laws seem to govern, but the judges had rather misconster law and do injustice than displease the king's humor" (2.¶iv^v–v). With James's arrival on the throne of England, the threat to the law's independence became more immediate, and Coke's warnings became proportionally more precise. The preface to his fourth volume of reports, the first published under James, is a sermon against legal innovation. The correcting of old laws is dangerous; the making of new ones, more dangerous still. Even the digesting and expounding of the law has its perils. Two particular events prompted Coke's concern. One was a conversation with the new king in which James complained of the uncertainty of English law. The other was a royal command that the penal statutes be abridged and digested. Coke warmly applauds the king's initiative in both instances, but he hedges his applause with such reminders and such qualifications that James might well have doubted his sincerity. His description of the king's complaints leads to this quotation from Bracton: "The king is under no man, but only God and the law, for the law makes the king. Therefore let the king attribute that to the law which from the law he hath received, to wit, power and dominion. For where will and not law doth sway, there is no king" (4.Bv). And his discussion of the command ends in a series of potentially disabling cautions. "Certain statutes concerning the administration of justice . . . are," Coke writes, "so woven into the common law . . . as it will be no small danger to alter or change them." And as for bringing the common law itself "into a better method," he doubts "much of the fruit of that labor" (4.Biii^v).

This last set of objections speaks directly to the project of writing English law on which not only James but also Bacon, Finch, Cowell, and many others were already engaged. Undertaken "in the high court of parliament" and limited to penal statutes ("with such caution as is beforesaid"), such writing, Coke is willing to acknowledge, would be "an honorable, profitable, and commendable work for the whole commonwealth" (4.Biii^v). But then it immediately reminds him—the lack of any transition is striking—of another project, one far more closely in keeping with the true spirit of English law and far better calculated to answer the complaints that have been directed at it: his own. "This fourth part of my *Reports*," he writes,

> doth concern the true sense and exposition of the laws in divers and many cases never adjudged or resolved before, which for that they may in my opinion tend to the general quiet and benefit of many, the only end (God knoweth) of the edition of them, I thought it a part of my great duty that I owe to the commonwealth not to keep them private, but being withal both encouraged and in a manner thereunto enforced to publish and communicate them to all, wherein my comfort and contentation is great, both in respect of your singular and favorable approbation of my former labors, as for that I (knowing my own weakness) have one great advantage of many famous and excellent men that have taken upon them the great and painful labor of writing. For they to give their works the more authority and credit have much used the figure *prosopopeia* in feigning divers princes and others of high authority, excellent wisdom, profound learning, and long experience to speak such sentences, rules, and conclusions as they intended and desired for the common good to have obeyed and observed. . . . But I without figure or feigning do report and publish the very true resolutions, sentences, and judgments of the reverend judges and sages of the law themselves. (4.Biii^v–iv)

Coming immediately after Coke's discussion of the king's intended redaction of the penal laws, this passage inevitably suggests a relationship—perhaps a rivalry—between the two projects. Both involve writing the law; both are meant to secure "the general quiet and benefit of many"; both claim to serve the commonwealth. But the two differ in ways that make one a bulwark of the law, the other a threat to it.

So long as the common law was left untouched, Coke did not oppose a redigesting of the penal statutes. But he was clearly worried that reform would not stop there. For more than a decade, Bacon had been proposing that all English law, common law as well as statute law, be brought "into a better method." In James, England now had a king who was reacting favorably to such suggestions, a king who had already ordered that the work be begun, a king who showed neither sympathy for nor understanding of the judge-centered law that for Coke was the very mark of the English nation. Such a menace could not be left without a response. Indeed, the shape of a response had already emerged. If James and Bacon thought the law needed writing, Coke had his own way of writing it. Instead of digests, abridgments, and methodical rearrangements, he presented reports. "For," he said, "I hold him not discrete that will *sectari rivulos* when he may *petere fontes*"—"that will follow rivulets when he may seek out sources" (4.Biii^v). An abridgment leads away from the law; a report reveals its very source. "The reporting of particular cases or examples is," he insists in one of his later prefaces, "the most perspicuous course of teaching the right rule and reason of the law, for so did almighty God himself when he delivered by Moses his judicial laws. . . . And the glossographers, to illustrate the rule of the civil law, do often reduce the rule into a case" (6.¶vi). Not even Coke can resist the temptation to draw authority from the civil law, but he does so to legitimate a quite un-Roman literary mode.

And why should his avoidance of *prosopopeia* be a matter for such ardent self-congratulation? Perhaps because *prosopopeia* is the figure adopted in the most famous of all legal abridgments, Justinian's *Institutes*—"which," as Coke elsewhere remarks, "Justinian assumeth to himself, although it were composed by others" (8.diii^v). Coke was as eager not to make the king speak the law as Justinian, Tribonian, and such English followers of theirs as James and Bacon were to make him its speaker. *Rex est lex loquens.* Against this Roman maxim favored by James and his supporters and represented by the literary fiction of Justinian's *Institutes,* Coke and his *Reports* reply, *Judex est lex loquens.*[34] The law speaks not through the king but through "the very true resolutions, sentences, and judgments of the reverend judges and sages of the law themselves, who for their authority, wisdom, learning, and experience are to be honored, reverenced, and believed" (4.Biv). Coke does not deny that English law is the king's. But it is the king's only as the kingdom is his, by due and lawful inheritance; it is not his to make or to alter.

What most provoked Coke's royalist opponents was not the omission of a kingly speaker from his *Reports.* The genre did not, after all, invite such an intrusion. What bothered them was rather the inescapable presence of another voice, that of Sir Edward Coke himself. "Let not the judges . . . meddle with

34. James cited the maxim *rex est lex loquens* in his parliamentary speech of 1607 (*Political Works,* pp. 291 and 299). The maxim was also used by Lord Chancellor Ellesmere, who attributes it specifically to "some grave and notable writers of the civil law" (*A Complete Collection of State Trials,* edited by T. B. Howell, 21 vols. [London: Longman, 1816], 2.693). For Coke's *judex est lex loquens,* see 7.biv.

the reports," wrote Bacon in the *De Augmentis,* "lest from being too fond of their own opinions, and relying on their own authority, they exceed the province of a reporter" (5.104), and in an earlier memorandum he left no doubt what judge he had in mind. "Great judges," he told the king, "are unfit persons to be reporters, for they have either too little leisure or too much authority, as may appear by [the reports of Dyer and Coke], whereof that of my Lord Dyer is but a kind of notebook, and those of my Lord Coke's hold too much *de proprio*" (12.86). But it was Bacon's elder collaborator, the lord chancellor Thomas Egerton, who reacted with greatest outrage to Coke's *de proprio.* "That your lordship is *lex loquens,*" he scribbled angrily on a draft of his "Observations upon the Lord Coke's *Reports,*" "out of whose mouth like oracles proceed laws to posterity, that as you are Lycurgus in prescribing laws for the commonwealth, so you will be a means in protecting literature for their necessary use; that as you are *a lato* in counseling for the good of all, so you will be a Hercules in defending that which is for the good of all." [35] In Egerton's view, Coke had not merely exceeded the province of a reporter, he had usurped the place of the king. He, not James, is the *lex loquens* in his *Reports,* the English Lycurgus and Hercules.

The individual reports, in which Coke offends, according to Egerton, by "scattering or sowing his own conceits almost in every case" (p. 297), provide one scene for this usurpation. But another is furnished by the often expansive prefaces that from 1600 to 1615 head all eleven volumes. These prefaces were as much a departure from generic precedent as was Coke's deliberate resort to print. Unlike the prefaces that introduce the earlier reports of Plowden and Dyer, these constitute a running defense of England's native legal system, an extended occasional and polemical discussion of the nature, sources, and proper acquisition of the common law. And here, still more obviously than in the reports themselves, Coke speaks in his own person and out of his own authority. He lists the law's essential features and asserts their immemorial history; he describes the ancient and modern books of the common law; he discovers the law's hidden coherence and warns against alteration; he praises not only the law itself but all its institutions, texts, and practitioners; [36] he dis-

---

35. In Louis A. Knafla, *Law and Politics in Jacobean England: The Tracts of Lord Chancellor Ellesmere* (Cambridge: Cambridge Univ. Press, 1977), p. 190.

36. As examples of Coke's hyperbolical praise of all legal things English, consider the following: he calls the Inns of Court "the most famous university for profession of law only . . . that is in the world" (3.Div^v), Littleton's *Tenures* "a work of as absolute perfection . . . as any book that I have known written

misses the testimony of chronicle history and the authority in legal matters generally of anyone but common lawyers; he defines the constitutional relationships of the king, parliament, and the law; he claims primacy in jurisdiction for the common law and its courts over all other law and all other courts; and he insists repeatedly on the importance of true reports. So wide-ranging and so influential were these prefaces, that it would not be too much to say that in them Coke transformed a largely unreflective cultural practice into an ideological weapon. If he did not quite invent English law, he did invest it with a new polemical meaning. And in doing so, he won for himself in sober fact a position not unlike the one Egerton sarcastically attributed to him. He came to be known as the supreme oracle of English law.

The English-speaking world divides the study of legal history between two distinguishable scholarly communities. In one are those trained as lawyers and affiliated with schools of law; in the other, those trained as historians and located in departments of history. Coke's *Reports* have been differently appropriated by each. The law-school scholars have concentrated on the substance of the reported cases and on the mode of their reporting; the mainline historians have been more interested in the prefaces and the constitutional ideas they express. Each emphasis has its blindspot. Where the lawyers regard Coke's prefaces as a charming but largely negligible adjunct to the real legal stuff of his *Reports,* the historians treat his ideas as though they had no textual embodiment at all.[37] From neither point of view can one appreciate the representational force of Coke's amphibious literary form. The law-French cases address a purely professional audience and insert themselves into a textual sequence that stretches from the yearbooks, through the printed reports of Plowden and Dyer, down to the court reports of our own time. The prefaces, printed in both Latin and English but not in law French, speak to a broader English and even continental readership and belong rather in the company of books like Fortescue's *De Laudibus,* Christopher St. Germain's *Doctor and Student* (1530), or Sir Thomas Smith's *De Republica Anglorum* (1565). Coke's great accomplishment was to bring the two together, to make the characteristic court-centered form of English legal literature the vehicle for a description and defense of English law. The special authority of each was thus made to support the other. Here,

---

in any human learning" (10.div^v–v), English lawyers nonpareils of "honesty, gravity, and integrity" (2.¶v), and English law "the most ancient and best inheritance that the subjects of this realm have" (5.Avi).

37. The essays of Plucknett and Baker cited in notes 30 and 31 above illustrate the lawyers' emphasis; the intellectual historians' emphasis can be found in Pocock's *Ancient Constitution,* pp. 30–69, and Sommerville's *Politics and Ideology,* pp. 86–111.

on the one hand, were the sages of the law, advocates and judges, debating and deciding the great leading cases—467 of them in all—that had been heard in the various English courts for a period of some thirty-five years. And here, on the other hand, was Sir Edward Coke, attorney general, chief justice of Common Pleas, chief justice of the King's Bench, a man who had been in constant attendance at Westminster Hall for those thirty-five years and more, introducing the law and explaining its special place in the life of England's commonwealth. These were working books, books that every common lawyer needed to own and consult. But they were also ideal figurations of the legal community and the nation—books that told not only how the law functioned and what the courts had decided but also what England was and what part lawyers had in the making of its identity.

This potent combination of polemical preface and reported proceedings found a highly significant imitator just as the last of Coke's eleven volumes was appearing. In 1615, Sir John Davies, the king's attorney general for Ireland, published his *Irish Reports* with a lengthy "preface dedicatory" addressed to the lord chancellor. Coke's prefaces were never dedicatory. He deliberately avoided any reliance on patronage. The authority of his books derives from the law alone—and from their author's special relationship to it. And had Coke dedicated one of his books, it would certainly not have been to Thomas Egerton. But despite Davies' participation in a social and political circuit that by 1615 was openly hostile to Coke, his book draws on the energy released by Coke's coupling of prefaces and reports, and it makes still more explicit the meaning of that literary exploit.

In Davies' account, reports are so intrinsic to the common law, to the English *jus non scriptum,* that one could hardly survive without the other. Thus, though no reports remain from the twelfth or thirteenth centuries, Davies assumes that they must once have existed, for Glanville and Bracton "affirm that the law of England was *jus non scriptum* in their times."[38] "Reports are but comments or interpretations upon the text of the common law, which text was never originally written, but hath ever been preserved in the memory of men, though no man's memory can reach to the original thereof" (sig. *1^{v}–2). Reports put in writing what is always and forever unwritten. They are a form of writing that denies the supremacy of the written, that forbids access to an identifiable origin or author, whether king, parliament, or judge. The unwritten law that reports represent is "connatural to the nation," made by

38. Sir John Davies, *Le Primer Report des Cases . . . en Ireland* (1615), sig. *1^{v}.

the English people "out of their own wisdom and experience . . . not begging or borrowing the form of a commonwealth either from Rome or from Greece as all the other nations of Europe have done" (sig. *2ᵛ). Of all systems of law, it is "the most perfect and most excellent and without comparison the best to make and preserve a commonwealth . . . far more apt and agreeable than the civil or canon law or any other written law in the world besides, howsoever some of our own countrymen, who are *cives in aliena republica et hospites in sua,* may perhaps affirm the contrary" (sig. *2–2ᵛ).

Davies thus joins Coke in giving the lie to Starkey and all his humanist descendants. What the humanists read as a sign of England's barbaric inferiority is in fact the mark of its constitutional superiority. But this answer depends for its credibility on a written text, the reports to which it is attached. If the common law of England truly has "more certainty in the rules and maxims, more coherence in the parts thereof, [and] more harmony of reason in it" (sig. *2ᵛ) than does any other human law, the evidence is to be found in the proceedings of its courts as recorded in texts such as these. In Coke's *Reports* and in Davies', the writing that Starkey, Morison, Bacon, Finch, Cowell, and the others demanded is accomplished. But it is a writing against writing, a writing in defense of the unwritten, a writing that opposes any institute, digest, or code, one that opposes even the written laws of England itself, "namely our statutes or acts of parliament" (sig. *2). It is, furthermore, a writing that in English and Latin prefaces addresses those unlearned in the law only to tell them of that which they cannot understand, the impenetrably written/unwritten law-French reports that fill the greater part of the volume they hold in their hands. As such, this writing preserves the special prerogative of the professional community in whose collective memory the unwritten law resides, making that community "connatural," as Davies says of the law itself, "to the nation."

The Form of Coke's *Institutes*

In the preface to his second volume of *Reports,* Coke praised Elizabeth for never interfering with the law. "Bless God for Queen Elizabeth," he wrote, "whose continual charge to her justices . . . is that for no commandment under the great or privy seal, writs or letters, common right be disturbed or delayed and, if any such commandment (upon untrue surmises) should come, that the justices of her laws should not therefore cease to do right in any point"

(2.¶v). King James failed to exercise the same restraint. In 1616, he sent order by Francis Bacon, then his attorney general, to the twelve common-law judges that they should halt proceedings in what has since come to be known as the Case of Commendams. Before taking any further action, they were to consult with the king himself. Under Coke's leadership, the judges refused. Their oath of office forbad them, they said, to respect such an order. They were then summoned before the king and coerced into submission. Eleven acquiesced. Only Coke resisted. Asked how he would respond to a future royal directive, he answered, "When the time shall come, I shall do that which will become a judge."[39]

This answer did not please the king. Within a month Coke was suspended from the privy council, forbidden to ride circuit, and ordered to revise his *Reports,* "wherein, as his majesty is informed, be many extravagant and exorbitant opinions set down and published for positive and good law." Behind this last demand stood a detailed and highly critical set of "observations" on Coke's *Reports* written by Lord Chancellor Egerton. These charged that Coke had "purposely labored to derogate much from the rights of the church and the dignity of churchmen and to disesteem and weaken the power of the king in the ancient use of his prerogative, to traduce or else to cut short the jurisdiction of all other courts but of that court wherein he himself doth sit, and in the cases of [the] subject sometimes to report them otherwise than they were adjudged."[40] Coke's own opinion of his work was quite different. After several months, he announced that he could find in all eleven volumes only five trivial errors, none of which touched any of the great issues that were exercising the king, the chancellor, and the attorney general.[41] This last act of defiance brought swift retribution. "For certain causes now moving us," the king commanded, "we will that you shall be no longer chief justice."

Coke never again sat on the bench of an English court of law. Nor did he publish any further reports.[42] He did not, however, abandon all hope of royal

39. Bowen, *The Lion and the Throne,* p. 378. The first and last quotations in the next paragraph also come from Bowen, pp. 379 and 388.

40. Knafla, *Law and Politics in Jacobean England,* p. 297. The conflict in 1616 between Egerton's Court of Chancery and Coke's common law jurisdiction has been expertly surveyed by J. H. Baker in "The Common Lawyers and the Chancery: 1616," *The Legal Profession and the Common Law,* pp. 205–29.

41. Six months after Coke's fall, Bacon was still expressing concern over the *Reports.* "I did call upon the judges' committee also," he wrote Buckingham in May of 1617, "for the proceeding in the purging of Sir Edward Coke's *Reports,* which I see they go on with seriously" (13.199).

42. Two additional volumes appeared posthumously in 1658 and 1659, but these were not prepared for publication by Coke, contain only cases heard prior to the loss of his judicial position, and include no authorial preface.

preferment. Instead, in one of the ugliest episodes of his life, he reingratiated himself with the king by forcing his daughter to marry Sir John Villiers, the elder brother of the king's new favorite, the earl of Buckingham. As a result, Coke was returned to the privy council, where he proved sufficiently amenable to be chosen for a parliamentary seat under royal control. But once in parliament, he caused the crown no less annoyance than he had as a judge. Indeed, so objectionable was his behavior in the parliament of 1621 that he was dismissed from the council and briefly imprisoned on a charge of treason. He returned to parliament in 1624 and supported the policies of Prince Charles and Buckingham. But in 1625, in Charles's first parliament, he renewed the attack, and in the parliament of 1628, at the age of seventy-six, he took a leading part in promoting the petition of right. "Shall I," he demanded early in the debate leading to the petition, "be made a tenant-at-will for my liberties, having property in my own house but not liberty in my person? There is no such tenure in all Littleton! . . . It is a maxim, *the common law hath admeasured the king's prerogative,* that in no case it can prejudice the inheritance of the subjects. It is against law that men should be committed and no cause shown. I would not speak this, but that I hope my gracious king will hear of it. Yet it is not I, Edward Coke, that speaks it but the records that speak it."[43]

As his parliamentary colleagues would have known, no man could say with greater authority than Coke what was or was not in Littleton. At just about the time that he made this speech, his own massive commentary on Littleton's *Tenures,* the first part of his *Institutes of the Laws of England* (1628), appeared in print. After a lapse of thirteen years, the years that had passed since the publication of his last volume of *Reports,* Coke thus returned to the job of writing English law. But the form of this new writing was significantly unlike that of his *Reports.* By its title this work proclaimed its affinity with Justinian's writing of Roman law. Here, as if in belated recognition of the need defined by Starkey, Morison, Bacon, Finch, and Cowell, was a comprehensive introduction to the common law of England—not merely a collection of cases, nor even the kind of general defense found in the earlier prefaces, but a genuine institutional work. Even the four-part organization, which Coke announces, though only the first part was immediately available, might be taken as allud-

43. Bowen, *The Lion and the Throne,* p. 484. Bowen seems to have assembled this "speech," which accurately represents things Coke said even though he may never have produced this particular string of words as a single utterance, out of a variety of sources. See, for example, the different reports of Coke's interventions in the House of Commons on March 29, 1628, in *Commons Debates 1628,* edited by Robert C. Johnson and Maija Jansson Cole, 3 vols. (New Haven: Yale Univ. Press, 1977), 2.187–209.

ing to the four books of Justinian's *Institutes*. But in every other way the two are strikingly unlike. If Coke, whom Selden in this same year called the "great *monarcha juris*," wrote institutes of the laws of England, as the emperor Justinian had written institutes of Roman law, he did so in the name of principles like those embodied in his *Reports* and his parliamentary speeches, principles inimical to royal lawgiving. And for that purpose he invented an institutional method so foreign to that of Justinian and his legion of followers that it has often seemed no method at all.

Systematic organization—what Bacon called "clear and perspicuous order" (5.105)—is the mark of Justinian's *Institutes*. Following the example of the second-century *Institutes* of Gaius, Justinian (or rather his law-writing commissioners, Tribonian, Theophilus, and Dorotheus) divided the law into three large categories: the law of persons, the law of things, and the law of actions. This division was itself highly significant. But underlying and preceding it was another still more fundamental division, one that Bacon notices when he says that an institutional work should "run through the whole private law" but should not "touch . . . the public law" (5.105). With the exception of a brief final chapter on criminal trials, public law has no place in Justinian's *Institutes*. The imperial state is responsible for the book's existence. Its every word is said to proceed "from the emperor's lips." But from within the book the constitutional order of the state, though pervasively present, is invisible. In this organizational scheme power flows only one way. The public creates and sustains the private. The private has no effect on the public. Here the "maxim" Coke produced for the parliament of 1628—"the common law hath admeasured the king's prerogative"—would be unthinkable. Not only is there no common law, but such law as there is provides no access to the imperial prerogative. From the perspective of Justinian's *Institutes,* the emperor's prerogative remains immeasurable for the simple reason that it is kept almost completely out of sight. And the glimpses one does get of it—the prefatory announcement that the *Institutes* themselves have been composed "with our authority and at our instigation" and the famous declaration in the second chapter that "what has pleased the prince has the force of law"—hardly invite further question.[44] By dividing the public from the private and making only the latter the subject of the basic introductory book by which Roman lawyers were initiated into their profession, Justinian defines the proper sphere of their activity. They are to concern themselves with "the well-being of individuals," as that well-being

---

44. *Justinian's Institutes,* translated by Birks and McLeod, pp. 33 and 36.

has been established by imperial rule. They are not to interfere with "the organization of the Roman state."

The publication and reception of Coke's *Institutes* would seem to have been governed by a similar division. The work as a whole was written in four parts, three of which—the second part "containing the exposition of many ancient and other statutes," the third part "concerning high treason and other pleas of the crown and criminal causes," and the fourth part "concerning the jurisdiction of the courts"—deal in obvious and important ways with public law. In these volumes, Coke addresses issues that have no equivalent in Justinian's *Institutes,* such matters as the ancient liberties of Englishmen, the laws protecting the person and power of the king, the function of the various English courts, beginning with the high court of parliament. But none of these volumes was printed in Coke's lifetime, and none has been reprinted as often or read as intensively as part 1, the commentary on Littleton, the one part that does limit itself to private law. Royal intervention was responsible for the delayed appearance of the last three volumes. Hearing that Coke was about to "set forth" a book in 1631, King Charles ordered that it be suppressed. "The king fears," wrote Lord Holland to Secretary Dorchester, "somewhat may be to the prejudice of his prerogative, for [Coke] is held too great an oracle amongst the people, and they may be misled by anything that carries such an authority as all things that he either speaks or writes."[45] And a few days before Coke's death in 1634 the king had the dying oracle's manuscripts seized. Seven years later parliament arranged for their release and publication.[46] But even after parts 2, 3, and 4 appeared, they failed to attain the professional centrality of *Coke on Littleton*. While they each had seven editions, *Coke on Littleton* went through at least nineteen, plus numerous synopses, abridgments, and rearrangements. Whether by royal allowance or professional choice, the first part was the only one that truly functioned as an institutional work. For two and a half centuries, it alone, unaccompanied by the other three parts, provided both English and American lawyers with a basic introduction to the common law.

The frame of Coke's *First Institute* was provided by Littleton's *Tenures* (1482), a work that on its own account had already been compared to Justinian's *Institutes.* In a passage Coke twice quotes, William Camden said that "the students of the common law are no less beholding" to Littleton's *Tenures* "than

45. *Calendar of State Papers, Domestic, 1629–1631* (London: Longman, 1860), p. 490.
46. Baker, "Coke's Note-Books," pp. 196–98.

the civilians to Justinian's *Institutes*."[47] Like Justinian's book, Littleton's is perspicuously ordered, confined to private law, and free from learned citation. It presents just one part of the law, the part that dominated the practice of most lawyers, clearly and on its own authority. But these apparent similarities conceal large and significant differences. Justinian's *Institutes* draws its authority from an emperor whose word is law. Littleton has only his own authority as a judge, a judge who here speaks not from the bench but privately to his son, for whose instruction his book was written. Justinian's *Institutes* is the law. Littleton's *Tenures* (and eventually Coke's commentary with it) came to be regarded as law, but it refuses to make such a claim itself. "And know, my son," Littleton writes in the epilogue to his book, "that I would not have thee believe that all which I have said in these books is law, for I will not presume to take this upon me."[48] For Littleton, as for Coke after him, the law itself is always elsewhere. Nor is this the only difference between the English book and the Roman. The order and coverage of Littleton's *Tenures* are strikingly unlike those of Justinian's *Institutes*. Instead of Justinian's division into persons, things, and actions, Littleton divides his book into estates in land, tenures and services, and other legal characteristics of landed estates. Littleton's attention is thus confined almost entirely to land law, to real property, a subject that in Justinian has no independent identity—as persons, things, and actions have none in Littleton.

If Littleton's *Tenures* was regarded merely as a treatise on medieval land law, its narrowness of focus would be of no great consequence. But when it was made, as Coke and the legal profession made it, the foundation for an English institute, for the book that would introduce Englishmen to the legal order under which they lived, then the consequences of its peculiar limitations were significant indeed. Consider the difference between a book that begins, as Justinian's does, by defining law and justice in broad and abstract terms and one whose opening words are: "Tenant in fee simple is he which hath lands or tenements to hold to him and his heirs forever" (1.1a). In Littleton, abstract justice is never mentioned and persons, Justinian's next subject, emerge only as tenants, whether in fee simple, fee tail, or dower, for life or years, at will

---

47. *Reports* 10.dv, and *Institutes* 1.¶3ᵛ. Except where otherwise indicated, I quote Coke's *Institutes* from the following editions: Part 1 (1628); part 2 (1642); part 3 (1644); and part 4 (1644). For all of part 1, except the preface, I quote leaf rather than signature numbers, with "a" for recto and "b" for verso. These leaf numbers from the first edition supply the standard reference system for subsequent editions.

48. *Institutes* 1.394b.

or by copy. No wonder learned foreigners thought the book barbarous.[49] But out of its hard and narrow rules of tenancy, Coke constructed a defense of English liberties against the encroachment of royal absolutism. "Shall I have estate in my land and be tenant-at-will for my liberty? Littleton never discovered that!"[50] In a statement like this, ownership of landed property—and in Coke's account tenancy takes a long step toward outright ownership—becomes the basis for and a type of the liberty of the subject. And Littleton's *Tenures,* the book that tells all about such ownership, becomes a notable work of *public* law, one capable of measuring, as Coke put it, the king's prerogative.

Simply by reprinting Littleton's *Tenures* under the new title of *The First Part of the Institutes of the Laws of England,* Coke made an important statement. He said to any who would advocate court-sponsored legal reform, as Bacon, Cowell, and James had done, that English law had already been written and that its writing, far from being an expression of royal power, demonstrated the limits of that power. But Coke was unwilling to leave it at that. In addition to reprinting and translating Littleton's *Tenures,* he commented on it at extraordinary length. *Coke on Littleton* is set forth in three parallel columns, one for Littleton's original law French, one for Coke's English translation, and one for Coke's commentary. But most often the commentary, though printed in smaller type, runs past the other two, spilling around the bottom of the other columns to fill many extra lines and even many extra pages. Nor is the commentary Coke's only addition. Down the margins, so thickly crowded on many pages as to constitute an independent fourth column, are references to a wide variety of sources. Together, this commentary and these references not only greatly augment the length of Littleton's *Tenures.* They change its ideological character and the experience of reading it.

In his *Irish Reports,* Sir John Davies had made the lack of any significant commentary on Littleton a sign of the certainty of English law. Mocking the civil law for its "gloss upon gloss and book upon book," Davies pointed to the English difference. "Of the professors of our law, whoever yet hath made any gloss or interpretation upon our Master Littleton, though into that little

---

49. In his article on Littleton in *The Interpreter,* John Cowell quoted the French civilian François Hotman's opinion of the *Tenures* as "confused, clumsy, and ridiculous." According to Cowell, English law generally was equally subject to scorn. It "has hardly escaped," he wrote, "among foreigners the blame of barbarism" (*Institutiones Juris Anglicani* [1605], sig. A4).

50. The two versions of this remark that I have here combined read: "I shall have estate in my land, and be tenant at will for my liberty. Littleton never discovered that," and "Shall I be tenant for life of my land and at will for my liberty?" *Commons Debates 1628,* pp. 195 and 209.

book of his he hath reduced the principal grounds of the common law with exceeding great judgment and authority and with singular method and order?"[51] Coke violated that reserve. He wrapped Littleton's spare text in a thick garb of commentary, to which subsequent English jurists—Chief Justice Hale, Lord Chancellor Nottingham, Francis Hargrave, and Charles Butler—have added still further layers. One effect of this continuing labor of commentary has been, as Davies' remark suggests it would be, to make English law more nearly resemble the text-law of the Roman tradition, particularly as that tradition appeared in the *mos italicus* of the glossators and post-glossators. Seen this way, Coke becomes an English Azo or Bartolus. His own copy of Justinian's *Institutes* with the glosses of Azo's student Franciscus Accursius—a copy that contains many marginalia in Coke's own hand—belongs to this type.[52] The resemblance would thus not have been lost on him, even if he forgot Davies. Dressed in Coke's commentary, Littleton became fit company for the glossators' Justinian Coke knew best.

But the other effect Davies predicted, the introduction of the uncertainty characteristic of the civil law, was specifically denied by Coke. In the preface to his *Second Institute,* in a passage that clearly recalls Davies, Coke distinguished between his commentaries and those of the civilians. "Upon the text of the civil law," he wrote, "there be so many glosses and interpretations and again upon those so many commentaries, and all these written by doctors of equal degree and authority, and therein so many diversities of opinions, as they do rather increase than resolve doubts and incertainties." So far Coke agreed with Davies. But his own commentaries, though similar in appearance, were not liable to the same charge. "The difference then between those glosses and commentaries and this which we publish is that their glosses and commentaries are written by doctors, which be advocates, and so in a manner private interpretations, and our expositions or commentaries . . . are the resolutions of judges in courts of justice in judicial courses of proceeding, either related and reported in our books or extant in judicial records or in both, and therefore being collected together shall (as we conceive) produce certainty, the mother and nurse of repose and quietness" (2.A6ᵛ). From Starkey on, certainty was the great desideratum, the mark of civility over barbarism. In claiming that his commentaries attain that certainty, while those of the civilians do not, Coke

51. Davies, *Le Primer Report,* sig. *4ᵛ–5.
52. Hassall, *Catalogue,* no. 469. I have not seen this volume, which was published in Lyon in 1559, but I have seen the presumably similar 1555 Geneva edition with Accursius' glosses.

responds in a particularly pointed way to the humanist critique. The unwritten law of England, the law of the judges and the courts, is not less civilized than the imperial law of Rome. It is more civilized—more civilized because more certain.

Coke's departure from the civilians was, however, also a departure from Littleton. As J. H. Baker has remarked, "Littleton relied on reason and common learning, and disdained to cite precedents."[53] Coke cited them in such profusion and at such length that his *Institutes* seem at times almost a continuation of his *Reports*. The *doctrine* (to use Baker's term) which supplied Littleton's authority, as it supplied the authority of the medieval civilians, was thus replaced by *jurisprudence,* by law decided in court. In this process, the law became less writable even as it was written. For all his modest disclaimers, Littleton set down the law as he understood it to be. The law for him was a purely synchronic system. It existed only in the present. Where it came from, whether or how it had changed, what cases it may or may not have been applied to—these were matters of no concern to him. A book, whose systematically ordered sentences were all equally present, could thus readily contain the law.[54] Coke's thickly layered work says something quite different. In it, Littleton himself becomes a figure of the past. The law dates back to time out of mind, but it has been revealed in many cases, many statutes, and many books, of which Littleton's is only one. Commenting on Littleton's first paragraph—a commentary that fills nearly eighteen tightly printed folio pages—Coke ranges from *Domesday Book, Magna Carta,* Bracton, Britton, and Fleta to his own *Reports.* He cites dozens of cases and a still more numerous array of statutes. From this perspective, the law seems rather a diachronic practice than a synchronic system. Always faithful to itself, it can nevertheless not be fully apprehended in any one schematic representation.

Rivaling the praise for Coke's vast learning that echoes down the centuries are complaints about his obscurity and want of method. Lord Keeper North said that *Coke on Littleton* "is the confusion of a student and breeds more disorder in his brains than any other book"; Blackstone called it "greatly defective

---

53. Baker, "English Law and the Renaissance," p. 59.
54. The many branching diagrams that later readers (Coke among them) have produced to describe the contents of Littleton's *Tenures* are testimony to its systematic, synchronic quality. Ideally, it can all be seen at once. No comparable representation of Coke's commentary would be possible. Instead of systematizing, it disrupts system, introducing dimensions that a diagram cannot show. For a collection of branching diagrams based on Littleton, see *The First Part of the Institutes of the Laws of England,* 2 vols. (Philadelphia: Robert H. Small, 1853), 1.xli and xliii–lx.

in method"; and Sir James Stephens thought the defect Coke's: "A more disorderly mind . . . would be impossible to find."[55] It is certain that anyone
coming to Coke's *First Institutes* with expectations formed by reading Justinian
or Blackstone—or even Littleton—will be bewildered and dismayed. Topic
follows topic with no apparent order and often with only the smallest suggestion from Littleton's text. The single phrase "maxim in law" from a section concerning an uncle's inheriting from his nephew leads to a definition of *maxim,*
a discussion of the particular maxim in question, a list of twenty-two "foun-
tains" from which Littleton derives "his proofs and arguments in these three
books," and another list of fifteen bodies of English law, from the *lex coronae*
to "the laws of the east, west, and middle Marches, which are now abrogated"
(1.11a–b). Juries are discussed in a chapter on rents, parliament under tenure in
burgage, the king's prerogative under socage, and *Magna Carta* under knight's
service. Some word in Littleton usually sets Coke off on these digressions, but
anticipating what chapter will prompt what topic is virtually impossible. Who,
for example, would think of looking for a defense of ancient readings in a chapter on releases or a discussion of justices of assize in one on continual claim?
In the *First Institutes,* as Coke published it, the only way to find these passages
and hundreds of others like them is to read straight through. No acquaintance
with Littleton will tell where in the commentary a particular subject can be
found.

Coke himself foresaw this difficulty. "I had once intended," he wrote, "for
the ease of our student, to have made a table of these *Institutes.*" But he decided against it. "When I consider that tables and abridgments are most profitable to them that make them, I have left that work to every studious reader"
(1.395a).[56] Behind this apparently offhand refusal is a theory that shapes all
Coke's writing. "Reason," he remarked in commenting on the chapter from
Littleton concerning frankalmoign, "is the life of the law; nay, the common
law is itself nothing else but reason." But this reason neither is nor should be
immediately accessible to all. For this is not "every man's natural reason." It
is rather "an artificial perfection of reason, gotten by long study, observation,
and experience," a quality proper to the law and to those who have immersed

---

55. Roger North, *The Lives of the Norths,* 3 vols. (London: Henry Colburn, 1826), 1.21n. William Blackstone, *Commentaries on the Laws of England,* 4 vols. (1765–69; facs. rpt. Chicago: Univ. of Chicago Press,
1979), 1.73. And Holdsworth, *A History of English Law,* 5.482 n1.

56. Coke's reluctance in this regard was quickly violated. "The undeniable importunity of some espe-
cial friends" pushed the printer into supplying a "table" to the *First Institute* as early as its second edition
in 1629, just a year after the first. See the note to that effect on the title page to the second edition.

themselves in it. "If all the reason that is dispersed into so many several heads were united into one, yet could he not make such a law as the law of England is, because by many successions of ages it hath been fined and refined by an infinite number of grave and learned men, and by long experience grown to such a perfection for the government of this realm as the old rule may be justly verified of it, *Neminem opportet esse sapientiorem legibus:* No man (out of his own private reason) ought to be wiser than the law, which is the perfection of reason" (1.97b).

Coke's "no man" had, as Thomas Hobbes noticed, one particular man in sight: the king.[57] Kings did not make the law—Coke's "grave and learned men" are obviously lawyers and judges—nor are kings fit to interpret or apply it. This, according to his own report, is what Coke told King James to his face. Sometime early in his reign (the precise date is unclear), in support of a claim that he might decide cases in person, James is supposed to have said that "he thought the law was founded on reason, and that he and others had reason as well as the judges." Coke's answer, an answer that he may or may not actually have given but that he certainly wanted to be thought to have given, closely resembles what he was later to write in his *Institutes*. "True it was," he claimed to have said, "that God had endowed his majesty with excellent science and great endowments of nature. But his majesty was not learned in the laws of his realm of England, and causes which concern the life or inheritance, or goods, or fortunes of his subjects. They are not to be decided by natural reason, but by the artificial reason and judgment of law, which law is an act which requires long study and experience before that a man can attain to the cognisance of

57. Thomas Hobbes, *A Dialogue Between a Philosopher and a Student of the Common Laws of England,* in *The English Works,* edited by Sir William Moleworth, 11 vols. (London: Bohn and Longman, 1939–45), 6.14–15. In response to the lawyer, who quotes this passage from Coke, the philosopher (obviously Hobbes himself) says: "Do you think this to be good doctrine? Though it be true that no man is born with the use of reason, yet all men may grow up to it as well as lawyers; and when they have applied their reason to the laws (which were laws before they studied them, or else it was not law they studied) may be as fit for and capable of judicature as Sir Edward Coke himself, who, whether he had more or less use of reason, was not thereby a judge, but because the king made him so. And whereas he says, that a man who should have as much reason as is dispersed in so many several heads could not make such a law as this law of England is, if one should ask him who made the law of England, would he say a succession of English lawyers or judges made it, or rather a succession of kings? And that upon their own reason, either solely, or with the advice of the lords and commons in parliament, without the judges or other professors of the law? You see therefore that the king's reason, be it more or less, is that *anima legis,* that *summa lex,* whereof Sir Edward Coke speaketh, and not the reason, learning, and wisdom of the judges. But you may see that quite through his *Institutes of Law* he often takes occasion to magnify the learning of the lawyers, whom he perpetually termeth the sages of the parliament or of the king's council. Therefore, unless you say otherwise, I say that the king's reason, when it is publicly upon advice and deliberation declared, is that *anima legis;* and that *summa ratio* and that equity, which all agree to be the law of reason, is all that is or ever was law in England since it became Christian, besides the Bible."

it; and that law was the golden metewand and measure to try the causes of the subjects; and which protected his majesty in safety and peace." At this reply, the king was "greatly offended" and said "that then he should be under the law, which was treason to affirm." To which Coke quoted Bracton: "The king must not be under any man but only under God and the law."[58]

One way of keeping the king under the law was to preserve the distinction between natural and artificial reason, to write the law according to a method governed by the latter rather than the former. In adopting Ramistic logic for his *Nomotechnia,* Finch violated this distinction, as Justinian did in reducing Roman law to "perspicuous order." Both make the artificial reason of the law accessible to the natural reason of princes and other laymen. Coke's commentary makes no such concession. Though Coke himself points to "Littleton's arguments logically drawn *a divisione*" (1.235b) and says that lawyers should study logic, the effect of his own book is to keep whatever rational order the law may have hidden, to preserve something of the oral even in the midst of a written and printed text. Coke was enough a man of his time to admit that various branches of the law can be logically diagrammed, that individual maxims can be written, that terms can be defined and legal relations described, that cases can be cited and the reasons governing them can be set forth. But, for him, the law's fundamental coherence, its reason, resides only in the mind of the diligent and experienced *artifex,* the well-trained lawyer.

In Coke's work, this lawyerly perception of coherence takes on an almost mystical quality.[59] "The knowledge of the law is," he wrote in commenting on Littleton's chapter "Of Escuage," "like a deep well, out of which each man draweth according to the strength of his understanding. He that reacheth deepest, he seeth the amiable and admirable secrets of the law, wherein, I assure you, the sages of the law in former times . . . have had the deepest reach" (1.71a). And elsewhere he suggests that ideally the lawyer should so merge with

58. From the posthumous *Twelfth Reports,* quoted by Roland G. Usher in "James I and Sir Edward Coke," *English Historical Review* 18 (1903): 664. Usher casts considerable doubt on the accuracy of Coke's account but none at all on the fact that Coke would have wanted to be known as having said something like this to the king.

59. Compare *Reports* 3.Cii, where Coke talks of the "coherence and concordance" that emerges from the yearbooks and concludes from this that "without question *lex orta est cum mente divina,* and this admirable unity and consent in such diversity of things proceed from God, the fountain and founder of all good laws and constitutions." In knowing the laws of England, the lawyer knows the mind of God. Thus to say that the king is under God and the law are, for all practical purposes, one. For a discussion of Coke's notion of artificial reason, see Charles Gray, "Reason, Authority, and Imagination: The Jurisprudence of Sir Edward Coke," in *Culture and Politics: From Puritanism to the Enlightenment,* edited by Perez Zagorin (Berkeley: Univ. of California Press, 1980), pp. 25–66.

the law that its mind and his will be one. *"Ratio est anima legis.* For then are we said to know the law when we apprehend the reason of the law, that is, when we bring the reason of the law so to our own reason that we perfectly understand it as our own; and then, and never before, we have such an excellent and inseparable property and ownership therein as we can neither lose it nor any man take it from us" (1.394b).

Property no man can take from us, a self identified with the legal order of the nation, artificial reason beyond the reach of lay understanding: these are the products of professional study as Coke presents it. But more than that, they are meant to arise in a quite specific way from the experience of his book, arise as a result of its deliberate want of method. More perspicuous orderings are merely misleading. They pretend that the whole can be perceived apart from the multiplicity of particulars that constitutes it. Coke disagrees. Though he sometimes talks of making the student's way easy and of opening the law to "any of the nobility and gentry of this realm or of any other estate or profession whatsoever," he realizes that frustration and confusion will often be the reader's first experience. "And albeit the reader shall not at any one day (do what he can) reach to the meaning of our author or of our commentaries, yet let him no way discourage himself, but proceed, for on some other day, in some other place, that doubt will be cleared" (1.¶¶4–4^v). Breaking through to a larger, more complete understanding is the experience Coke promises the diligent reader.[60] But until one has taken the arduous and twisting path that leads to that summit, to what Coke calls the *summa ratio* (1.97b), one must simply accept the visionary promise on faith. Borrowing from Roman law, James talked often of the *arcana imperii,* the secrets of state, that were reserved to the king alone.[61] As Coke presents (and represents) it, the common law has its own *arcana, arcana* that would exclude the king even from the judgment seat in his own Court of Star Chamber, where an empty throne and

60. That "breaking through" was in fact the experience of reading Coke is suggested by the advice Jeremiah Gridley gave the young John Adams. "You must conquer the *Institutes.* The road to science is much easier now than it was when I set out; I began with *Coke Littleton* and broke through" (Bowen, *The Lion and the Throne,* p. 514).

61. See, for example, James's 1616 speech in Star Chamber where he insisted that "the absolute prerogative of the crown . . . is no subject for the tongue of a lawyer." Elsewhere in the same speech, James denied the countervailing secrecy of the law. "Though the laws be in many places obscure and not so well known to the multitude as to you," he said to his judges, "and that there are many parts that come not into ordinary practice, which are known to you because you can find out the reason thereof by books and precedents, yet know this, that your interpretations must always be subject to common sense and reason"—by which he clearly meant subject to him. "For," as he continued, "I will never trust any interpretation that agreeth not with my common sense and reason, and true logic; for *Ratio est anima legis* in all human laws without exception" (*Political Works,* pp. 333 and 332).

cloth of state awaited him, and empower rather a professional community of learned lawyers. Not merely the product of a disorderly mind, Coke's lack of method was both politically motivated and politically effective. It allowed him to write the law without weakening its oppositional prerogative, allowed him to produce what was in effect a writing against the written, a writing against the Roman imperial tradition and all that it stood for.

The idea of writing the law in a book of institutes belonged to Justinian and imperial Rome. And the idea that England needed such a book came from the combined influences of Renaissance humanism and national consolidation. In succumbing to those ideas, Coke joined a movement that was strong not only in his own generation but that was to find numerous adherents throughout Europe for the next two hundred years. Thus broadly considered, his *Institutes* is a profoundly cosmopolitan work. But in abandoning Justinian's model for a scheme of his own devising, one that better represented the particularity of England and of English law, he took a distinctly nationalist stand. He made insularity the sign not of barbaric inferiority but of political freedom, and in so doing he wrote the nation, albeit from a limited polemical and professional perspective, even as he wrote the law.[62]

Uncouth Learning and Professional Pride

Two statements from another nation and a much later time suggest the power and persistence of Coke's work and the continuance of the system of differ-

---

62. In this section I have respected King Charles's censorship and the legal profession's choice and have concentrated only on Coke's *First Institute*. Looking across the sections that head Coke's four volumes, we can, however, see form expressing itself in another way, one that both reinforces and complicates what we have already noticed. Part 1 begins with fee simple, the strongest claim on real property recognized by English common law; part 2, with *Magna Carta*, the earliest of the statutes Coke discusses and the most important; part 3, with "the highest and most heinous crime of high treason" (3.B2); and part 4, with "the high and most honorable court of parliament" (4.B2). The strongest, the earliest, the most heinous, and the most honorable: these are each the supreme exemplars of the categories to which they belong. And each, in one way or another, implicates the king. All land derives ultimately from the king. There is in England no allodial land, no land held outright by anyone but the king. He alone could be said not to be a tenant. In similar manner, "all liberties," including those set forth in *Magna Carta*, "at the first were derived from the crown" (2.B3). As for high treason, it concerns the king directly—his life, his lineage, his seals and coin, his chief officers, and his peace. And the king sits in parliament, summons it into session, and prorogues it at will. In each case, the supreme legal exemplar depends on the supremacy of the crown. But in each the crown is also limited. The king cannot reclaim the lands or liberties that derive from him. The law of treason protects both the king and the subject. No offense but those named in the statute of 25 Edward III can be punished as treason. And parliament must pass any new law for it to take effect. The king cannot legislate on his own. If the order of Coke's *Institutes*, both the order of its four volumes with respect to one another and the order of the materials in each, represents the order of the state, it is an order under law.

ences within which its meaning was originally generated. The first comes from Thomas Jefferson, writing to James Madison in 1826.

> You will recollect that before the Revolution, *Coke Littleton* was the universal elementary book of law students, and a sounder Whig never wrote, nor of profounder learning in the orthodox doctrines of the British constitution, or in what were called English liberties. You remember also that our lawyers were then all Whigs. But when his black-letter text and uncouth but cunning learning got out of fashion, and the honied Mansfieldism of Blackstone became the student's hornbook, from that moment, that profession (the nursery of our congress) began to slide into Toryism, and nearly all the young brood of lawyers now are of that hue.[63]

The second comes from a Jeffersonian judge, George Sharswood of Philadelphia, addressing the publishers of the first American edition of *Coke on Littleton* in 1854.

> I have been much gratified by the examination of your elegant edition of *Coke upon Littleton,* with Hargrave and Butler's notes. It is highly creditable to your enterprise as a publisher. The work itself is one which cannot be too highly prized, or too earnestly recommended to the diligent study of all who wish to be well grounded in legal principles. For myself, I agree with Mr. Butler in the opinion that "he is the best lawyer, who best understands *Coke upon Littleton.*"
>
> My judgment is altogether in favor of the use of the book in its original form, and not as presented in Thomas's *Coke.* It may be that the original wants method; but the life and spirit of it are lost when it is hacked to pieces to be refitted together upon a new and different skeleton. Lord Coke was deeply imbued with the love of his profession, and one of the advantages derived from the study of his works is that somewhat the same spirit is insensibly transferred to his readers.[64]

Two hundred and twenty-six years after its original publication, in a country that had severed its ties with England more than seven decades before, *Coke on Littleton* was still in competition not only with Blackstone's *Commentaries* but also with a rearrangement of itself for the place of "student's hornbook."

But behind the competition with Blackstone and Thomas was the old com-

---

63. Thomas Jefferson quoted by Julian S. Waterman in "Thomas Jefferson and Blackstone's Commentaries," *Illinois Law Review* 27 (1933): 635.

64. George Sharswood quoted on an advertising sheet in *The First Part of the Institutes of the Laws of England,* 2 vols. (Philadelphia: Robert H. Small, 1853).

petition with Justinian. As many scholars have noticed, Blackstone's *Commentaries* takes much of its analytic frame from Justinian. And Thomas's rearrangement of Coke, which agrees with Blackstone almost chapter for chapter, does the same.[65] The division of persons, things, and actions can clearly be discerned in both. And what doesn't come from Justinian, an overarching binary division into rights and wrongs, comes from Finch's original ordering of his *Nomotechnia.* These structural influences were variously mediated by such books as Sir Matthew Hale's *Analysis of the Law* (1713) and Thomas Wood's *New Institute of the Imperial or Civil Law* (1704) and *Institute of the Laws of England* (1720), but they nevertheless remain obvious. The perspicuous ordering that for Bacon was the mark of an institutional work thus had in the eighteenth and nineteenth centuries the same prime exemplars as when Bacon wrote. But more interesting still, the opposition between these orderly institutes and Coke's cunningly unmethodical book persisted, and the significance of that opposition remained much the same. In Jefferson's view, Coke's "uncouth" learning was the vehicle for a political position that he called "Whig" and that he opposed to the "Toryism" of Blackstone's "honied" *Commentaries.* For Sharswood, not politics (at least not explicitly) but rather professional pride was at stake. *Coke on Littleton,* unlike Thomas's rearrangement, filled lawyers with the love of their profession. And since Thomas boasted that he had retained every word of *Coke on Littleton,* the form of the original, not its content, must have produced this effect.

Intimately linked to one another in the reception of Coke's writings, even at so great a remove as nineteenth-century America, politics, professional pride, and literary form were also linked at their inception. Whether in his *Institutes* or his *Reports,* Coke associated England's "ancient constitution," a constitution that subordinated executive power to the common law, with a particular way of writing the law. In the case of the *Reports,* that association was easy and obvious. Reports, like the yearbooks before them, provided a "natural" record of the unwritten law. They remain tied by their very form to the courts and their proceedings. Institutes have a different history and a different set of formal allegiances. They belong to the *Corpus* of a written law and emanate

---

65. J. H. Thomas, *A Systematic Arrangement of Lord Coke's First Institute* (Philadelphia: Robert H. Small, 1827). On Blackstone's similarity to Justinian, see Cairns, "Blackstone, an English Institutist." The political ideology of Blackstone's *Commentaries* and its relation to the book's formal arrangement has been discussed by Duncan Kennedy, "The Structure of Blackstone's Commentaries," *Buffalo Law Review* 28 (1979): 205–382. Kennedy's important article neglects the intertextual associations of Blackstone's organizational scheme with Justinian and his successors.

from the emperor. In both respects they would seem antagonistic to the legal and constitutional values Coke supported. Only the sense of a severe menace directed at the common law, a menace associated with both the civil law and the monarch, could explain the production of a book like his. To preserve the common law and make it a power in the political and professional struggles that engaged him, Coke had both to write it and to write it in a form that could claim at least some affiliation with the Roman imperial model. To that extent he too was *civis in aliena republica et hospes in sua*. Such self-estrangement is endemic to national self-writing. Not even the arch-insular Coke could avoid it. But he did nevertheless so successfully attenuate his alienation and the inescapable Roman affiliation that went with it that one could set his *Institutes* not only in the line of Justinian and his progeny, including eventually Blackstone and Thomas, but also and more obviously against them. Coke made his *Institutes* bear an anti-institutional, anti-monarchic, anti-Roman ideology, an ideology that left the king, the very font of the law for the civilians, looking like a foreigner in his own country—a task no doubt made easier for Coke by the fact that King James *was* a foreigner.

Coke's defense of English law has much in common with Daniel's defense of English rime. Both respond to humanist attacks; both repel expressions of sovereign power; both celebrate immemorial custom; and both turn the Renaissance against itself. Coke's position could not, however, be claimed as still another version of Gothic, at least not as he presented it. In his view, English law was originally Trojan, and its first written form in Britain was Greek. But this historical myth was the most vulnerable part of his work and the least essential. Many of his contemporaries rejected it, and within a very few years the rejection was universal. Instead his readers took him as a kind of Goth— "uncouth," as Jefferson put it—a defender of ancient Saxon liberties, a man who said that he would "derive from the conqueror as little as [he] could" (3Inst.B1^v). Overriding and informing these particular oppositions of Trojan and Roman, Goth and Greek, Saxon and Norman, was for Coke, as for Daniel, the fundamental opposition of self and other, English and foreign. Not only was the common law "appropriated to this kingdom of England as most fit and apt for the government thereof," it had "no dependency upon any foreign law whatsoever" (2Inst.D1^v). Like rime, the common law was quintessentially English, a sign of unity snatched from the play of difference: *e duobus unum*. And as Daniel and Spenser glorified poets, so Coke glorified lawyers. They were the alchemists whose minds held the secret of this national quintessence. Individual self-assertion (still more marked in Coke than in Spenser or Daniel), communal self-assertion, and national self-assertion once again depend both on one another and on the formal characteristics of a certain body of writing. For Coke and the many English and American lawyers who have been formed by his work, reports and institutes have been more than mere generic categories. They have been ways of constituting identity, ways of being in the world.

The Place of *Slade's Case* in the History of Contract

A. W. B. SIMPSON

❧ ❧ ❧

The results of *Slade's Case* are well known, and no decision in the books is re-garded as being more important in the history of parole contracts. In this article the circumstances leading up to the decision will be examined rather than the decision itself, except in so far as it seems arguable that a re-examination of the previous history of *indebitatus assumpsit* will enable the case to be better interpreted than has been usual in the past. Now the action of *indebitatus assumpsit* has always fitted unhappily into a general theory of contract, and the reasoning which lay behind this peculiar form of action has caused not a little difficulty.[1] This has not been eased by the brevity of the reports of many of the cases upon the subject. The orthodox story is this.[2] The action of debt upon a simple contract was unsatisfactory; it involved precise pleading, besides being hampered by the archaic wager of law, and it did not lie against executors. About the middle of the sixteenth century lawyers began to devise a method of escape by using the action of *assumpsit,* and by 1558 they had succeeded.[3] The creditor brought an action of *assumpsit,* and declared that the defendant was indebted to him in a certain sum, and, being so indebted, made a sub-sequent promise to pay the same sum; for breach of this subsequent promise the plaintiff brought his action. In the King's Bench the judges were prepared to treat this subsequent promise as a mere fiction, and so did not allow it to be traversed by the defendant; the judges of the Common Pleas, however, re-

"The Place of *Slade's Case* in the History of Contract" is reprinted from the *Law Quarterly Review* 74 (July 1958): 381–96. Reprinted by permission of A. W. B. Simpson and Sweet and Maxwell.

1. *E.g.,* Milsom, "Not Doing Is No Trespass," 1954, *Camb.L.J.,* 105.
2. Established by Ames, *Lectures in Legal History,* Lect. XIV, pp. 147 *et seq.*
3. Ames thought that the development must have occurred before the death of Brooke, the author of the *Abridgement;* for his reasons see *Lectures in Legal History,* p. 146.

jected the fiction and only allowed the action if the subsequent promise had actually been made. In 1585 a new Court of Exchequer Chamber was set up to hear error from the King's Bench,[4] and in this court the Common Pleas judges had a majority vote, the King's Bench judges being excluded. This court habitually reversed the judgments of the King's Bench in cases of *indebitatus assumpsit,* following the Common Pleas view of the law, but the King's Bench stuck to its guns, with the result that there was an unseemly conflict between the courts. This conflict was finally resolved in *Slade's Case* in 1602[5] by the old informal Court of Exchequer Chamber, which included the King's Bench judges, deciding in favor of the practice of the King's Bench. Soon afterward it was settled by *Pinchon's Case* (1612)[6] that *indebitatus assumpsit* lay against the debtor's executors; here once again the progressive King's Bench triumphed. These two cases allowed *assumpsit* to become coterminous with debt on a contract. *Slade's Case* is, however, allowed a peculiar importance: not only did it resolve the conflict between the courts but it also settled the rule that purely executory bilateral contracts were enforceable — that a promise against a promise created an enforceable agreement.[7] Thus *Slade's Case* is not only important in the history of *indebitatus assumpsit* but is also relevant to the development of special *assumpsit*. Holdsworth wrote,

> It was *Slade's Case* which fixed the character of the action of *assumpsit;* for, as we have seen, it enabled it to absorb the greater part of the sphere occupied by the action of debt, and to become a remedy for purely executory contracts.[8]

Now the orthodox view, well established as it is, seems to the writer to correspond somewhat inexactly with the available evidence in a number of points; though in part supportable it stands in need of correction in detail. If the resulting picture of the relationship between *debt sur contract* and *indebitatus assumpsit* is not so neatly composed as has been thought in the past this may be because the law of the sixteenth century was confused and capable of rapid change in a way which becomes impossible when the doctrine of precedent and the availability of organized reports have laid their steadying hands upon the courts.

4. 27 Eliz. I. c. 8.
5. 4 Rep. 92a, Yelverton 20, Moore 433, 667, and see Bodleian MS. Rawl.C. 720, f. 42a.
6. 9 Rep. 86b.
7. *E.g.,* Kiralfy, *The Action on the Case,* p. 184; *The English Legal System,* 2nd ed., p. 69; Potter, *Historical Introduction to English Law,* 3rd ed., p. 455; Holdsworth, *A History of English Law,* Vol. III, p. 445.
8. Holdsworth, *A History of English Law,* Vol. III, p. 451.

Although the development of the action on the case is largely the story of the old remedies being superseded by new, nevertheless the courts in the sixteenth century clung to the principle that no single state of affairs should give rise to two separate causes of action. Alternative remedies were not merely discouraged; they were regarded as forbidden by law.[9] This was the legal theory of the time, and it had somehow to be squared with the brute fact that the courts were prepared to allow the supersession of old remedies by new. The line of reasoning which allowed *indebitatus assumpsit* to overcome debt was based upon the judges' readiness to allow pleaders to rely upon distinctions between the two forms of action, and the causes of action upon which they were founded, which were fine and artificial. This process did not begin in the middle of the sixteenth century, but much earlier, in the *Case of the Sale of Barley* in 1505.[10] Here the buyer of barley brought an action on the case against a seller who had failed to deliver, instead of an action of debt, which would have been the old action appropriate to the situation.[11] The pleading device employed in 1505 to distinguish the cause of action in case from that in debt was that of describing the act of which the plaintiff complained as a conversion of the barley, rather than a mere failure to deliver, and to allege that the defendant had undertaken (*super se assumpsit*) to deliver the barley simply as a means of showing why the conversion was a wrongful act. Upon the better view this device failed, for the plaintiff had no property in the barley, and could not therefore complain if it had been converted. In *Pickering* v. *Thoroughgood* (1533)[12] the facts were substantially similar, there being a sale of malt to the plaintiff with part payment of the price. The seller failed to deliver. Here again debt would seem to have been the appropriate action, but the plaintiff experimented with case. Perhaps warned by the report of the case in 1505, by then probably in circulation, he abandoned the conversion device, and alleged that the defendant "bargained and sold to the plaintiff forty quarters of malt . . . and assumed and promised to deliver it accordingly"; there was no allegation

9. *Aston's Case* (1585) Dyer 250b, *in margine*, cited by Kiralfy, *The Action on the Case*, p. 164, represents the one exception to this principle in the sixteenth century, but the decision was doubted—see *Cantrel* v. *Church* (1601) Cro.Eliz. 845. It must be noted that *Aston's Case* first appeared in print in Treby's edition of Dyer in 1688. In *Wade* v. *Braunch* (1596) 2 And. 53 the rule that case only lies where there is no other remedy is based upon the Statute of Westminster II, c. 24.

10. Y.B. Mich. 20 Hen. VII, f. 8, pl. 18; Keilway, 69 and 77. For the record see Kiralfy, *A Source Book of English Law*, p. 150, *sub nom. Orwell* v. *Mortoft*. No judgment has been found by Kiralfy.

11. The goods were unascertained, so no property could pass.

12. *Spelman's Reports* (M.S.). The original is, of course, in law french. The case is in two MSS.: B. M. Harg. 388, f. 67b and Camb.U.L. Gg.LL. 5, f. 30a. On these reports see a note in (1956) 72 *L.Q.R.* at p. 334.

of any *subsequent* promise. The King's Bench allowed the action to succeed,[13] the defendant having moved in arrest of judgment, "that this action did not lie, because an action of debt lay, and where a general action lies, there in the same case a special action on the case does not lie." The court was thus forced to distinguish the respective causes of action. Spelman J. said,

> And as for the fact that he could have an action of debt, this makes no difference, for the action [of debt] is based on the debt and the *detinet,* but this action is based on the other's tort—that is on the breach of promise.

With this reasoning Fitzjames C.J. and Coningsby J. agreed,

> It seems that the action lies, and it is at the election of the plaintiff to choose one action or the other, for they are based upon different points as Spelman has said.

To Portman J. the distinction between the causes of action appeared too refined, and he dissented upon the ground that,

> . . . the promise is part of the covenant, and all one, and no act done by the defendant, but solely the non-delivery, for which detinue[14] lies.

Now it must be noted that although in this case the action of *assumpsit* was allowed in place of an action of debt for unascertained goods, yet the same reasoning would apply to allowing *assumpsit* in place of debt for money due,[15] for in both cases the form of action superseded would be the same. So far as the King's Bench was concerned it seems clear that *assumpsit* was allowed in such cases from 1533 onwards. The last doubt upon the point is found earlier, in 1521, when the Yearbook reporter regards it as unsettled, and says so in a note. The case to which the note is appended[16] allows *assumpsit* to lie against a debtor's executors, and it might well be thought that *a fortiori* it ought to lie against a living debtor. This view is not, however, to be found in the early cases upon the topic; the feeling appears to have been that, since *debt sur contract* did not lie against executors *assumpsit* ought to lie to fill a gap in the law,

---

13. The case also raised the difficulty over the actionability of non-feasance, which was still unsettled at this date.

14. More properly debt, but there is some confusion in terminology over the appropriate action for unascertained goods, as also over the buyer's action for specific goods sold. See Fitzherbert, *New Natura Brevium* (ed. 1677), p. 263.

15. Examples in modern times of *indebitatus assumpsit* for goods are cited by Ames, *op. cit.,* p. 89.

16. Y.B. Pasch. 12 Hen. VIII, f. 11, pl. 3.

but that if the debtor was alive, it ought not, because there was no gap to fill. We then have *Pickering* v. *Thoroughgood* in 1533 and thereafter the evidence of Brooke's *Abridgement*. Brooke, abridging *Jordan's Case* (1536)[17] notes that *assumpsit* will lie in place of debt. The Yearbook report of the case he purports to abridge hardly goes this far, for on one view of the facts debt would not have lain in any case; the other point of view, expressed by Spelman and Port JJ. was that *assumpsit* was being brought in lieu of an action of debt, which would have lain equally well upon the facts, and their reasoning can well be regarded as supporting the proposition that *assumpsit* lay generally against living debtors. Another case in Brooke's *Abridgement,* dated 1542,[18] makes it certain that by then actions of *assumpsit* in place of actions of debt were entertained, for it lays down that a recovery in debt bars recovery in *assumpsit* for the same sum, and vice versa, a ruling which shows that the fourth resolution in *Slade's Case* embodied a rule known to the King's Bench since the middle of the century. In both these cases which have been cited from Brooke it is noticeable that he calls his reader's attention to the fact that the cases were in the King's Bench, and we may well infer that in his time the practice of the Common Pleas was different, the action not being allowed there. Similarly, the King's Bench since 1521, under the influence of the progressive Fineux C.J., allowed *assumpsit* against executors,[19] whereas the Common Pleas did not.[20]

The next step was for the Common Pleas to allow *indebitatus assumpsit*. This appears to have been taken by 1573.[21] No doubt the underlying motive behind the change was the fear of the Common Pleas judges that they would otherwise lose business. Thereafter, so the orthodox account goes, both the courts allowed the action, but the Common Pleas treated the subsequent promise as a fact, the King's Bench as a fiction. To this accepted account of the divergence several objections may be raised.

17. Y.B. Mich. 27 Hen. VIII, f. 24, pl. 3; Brooke, *Accion sur le Case* 5. Mr. Fifoot, *History and Sources of the Common Law,* p. 353n., dates the case 1528 on the basis of what is, in fact, a printer's error in the vulgate edition of the Yearbooks, and also because a Brooke appears as a judge in the case; the only possible Brooke is Richard Brooke, but he died in 1529, and so Mr. Fifoot thinks that the case must be earlier than this. There are, however, objections to this solution. Richard Brooke was a judge of the Common Pleas, whereas *Jordan's Case* is in the King's Bench; furthermore, Spelman appears to be a judge in the case, and he was not raised to the Bench until 1531. The only possible solution appears to be to accept 1536 as the date of the case, and to treat "Brooke" as a mistake, perhaps, for Luke, who was a King's Bench judge from 1532 to 1544. The only surviving Yearbook MS. (now in the Library of Congress) dates the case 1536 and has the same error. Spelman's MS. Reports contain the case (Harg. 388, f. 97a) and also date it 1536.
18. Brooke, Abr. *Accion sur le Case,* 105.
19. Y.B. Pasch. 12 Hen. VIII, f. 11, pl. 3.
20. Brooke, Abr. *Accion sur le Case,* 106, note (1546), Y.B. 27 Hen. VIII, f. 23, pl. 21.
21. *Edwards* v. *Burre* (1573) Dalison 104.

In the first place it is clear that the plaintiff's cause of action in *assumpsit* is breach of promise. There is, however, only one case in the reports which ever holds that the promise in *indebitatus assumpsit* must be made subsequently to the incurring of the debt. This case is in 1572, reported in Dalison.[22] The plaintiff, suing in the King's Bench declared "*quod cum defendens indebitatus fuisset al pl. pro duodecim denarijs solutis Assumpsit solvere. . . .*" Manwood *arguendo* objected (*inter alia*) that the plaintiff should have said "*quod postea assumpsit.*"[23] This objection was sustained by Catlin C.J., Whiddon and Southcote JJ. Now this case stands on its own in so far as it treats the allegation that the promise is subsequent as being essential. In earlier cases,[24] and in the pleading precedents in Rastell's *Book of Entries*,[25] published in 1566, there is no hint of this idea. In later cases the position is not so clear. There are cases where the promise of the defendant is alleged to have been made subsequently, but no indication that this was regarded as essential,[26] and of course such allegations may have been factually true and not mere pleading forms. In *Slade's Case,* though this point seems to have been overlooked, the special promise is expressly alleged to have been made contemporaneously,[27] and in none of the reports is the point discussed. It seems proper, therefore, to regard the decision in 1572 as representing an innovation; in the absence of a fuller report the reason behind this innovation must be treated as obscure. It seems wrong, however, as some writers have done,[28] to attribute any great importance to the subsequent promise, or to go further and relate the whole basis upon which *indebitatus assumpsit* was allowed into the law to so ephemeral a doctrine, which certainly played no part in the early development of the new action. Mr. Mil-

22. *Anon.,* Dalison 84.

23. The same notion is implied in Manwood's account of the doctrine of consideration offered *arguendo* in *Manwood* v. *Burston* (1587) 2 Leon. 203. There is no indication in the report that the court agreed with him. In *Sidenham* v. *Worlington* (1585) 2 Leon. 224 in the Common Pleas Periam J. says that the allegation of a subsequent promise is usual, but not that it is essential.

24. *Pickering* v. *Thoroughgood* (1533), Brooke, Abr. *Accion sur le Case* 5; *Jordan's Case,* Y.B. 27 Hen. VIII, f. 24, pl. 3; *Edwards* v. *Burre* (1572) Dalison 104.

25. Rastell, *Entries,* f. 4a, 1 and 2.

26. *E.g., Hinson* v. *Burridge* (1594) Moo. 701.

27. For the pleadings, see 4 Rep. 91. The Latin goes ". . . *in consideratione quod idem Johēs adtunc et ibidem . . . barganizasset et vendidisset . . . super se assumpsit et adtunc et ibidem fideliter promisit. . . .*" The tense of "*barganizasset et vendidisset*" ("had bargained and sold") conflicts, it is true, with the twice repeated "*adtunc et ibidem*" ("then and there") and is presumably chosen to establish the necessary causal connection between bargain (the consideration) and promise. The pleadings, read as a whole, are thought to maintain the proposition in the text. The pleading form referred to in the Anonymous Case of 1572 involves the word "*postea,*" and it may be that pleaders, in omitting "*postea*" and substituting "*adtunc et ibidem*" forgot to alter the tense.

28. Milsom, *op. cit.,* at p. 111; Ames, *op. cit.*

som,[29] perplexed by the relationship between *indebitatus assumpsit* and the doctrine of consideration, suggests that it is the forbearance by the creditor from suing for his debt which is the consideration for the promise to pay, and thus manages to fit *indebitatus assumpsit* into a "detriment" notion of consideration, a feat which had hitherto defied ingenuity. Mr. Milsom's argument is nowhere to be found in the cases, and is indeed denied in the one case where something like it makes a momentary appearance. In *Gill* v. *Harewood* (1587)[30] the plaintiff alleged that the defendant was indebted to him, and in consideration that the plaintiff should forbear to sue him in debt for a little time the defendant promised to pay the debt. The facts having been found in favor of the plaintiff the defendant moved in arrest of judgment that no consideration was shown, since no precise time for forbearance was limited, but merely "*parvum tempus.*" The court rejected this argument, "for the debt in itself is a sufficient consideration." Furthermore Mr. Milsom's argument is based upon the supposition that the promise to pay had to be a subsequent promise, and seeks to explain why this subsequent promise was sufficient to exclude the action of debt, whereas, as has been argued, it seems that the subsequent promise was not (except in one case long after the establishment of the *indebitatus* action) regarded as necessary at all. Now it may be, as Mr. Milsom says,[31] that "To say that by the middle of the sixteenth century *assumpsit* had become a purely contractual action, and that a debt precedent was accepted as a sufficient consideration, is an unsatisfactory restatement. . . ." Yet the cases consistently do say that the debt itself is the consideration,[32] and the explanation for this is not at all difficult to follow so long as we realize that "consideration" only means "reason." If I buy goods from John Doe and thus make a contract with him, upon which debt will lie against me, this is a very good reason why I should then and there or later promise to pay him the price of the goods. The courts in the sixteenth century, once they had adopted the idea that there must be a reason for every actionable *assumpsit,* did not at first trouble themselves too much over an analysis of the various reasons which the

29. Milsom, *op. cit.,* at p. 112.

30. 1 Leonard 61. There are a number of cases where the plaintiff, instead of suing in *indebitatus assumpsit,* brought special *assumpsit,* and alleged a forbearance to sue specifically as consideration for a promise to pay a sum of money owed; such cases fall into a class of their own. Examples are *Linghill* v. *Broughton* (1616) Moo. 853; *Hog* v. *Block* (1589) Moo. 685; *Sackford* v. *Phillips* (1594) Moo. 689. The alternative pleading forms are clearly distinguished in *Austin* v. *Bewley* (1620) Cro.Jac. 549.

31. Milsom, *op. cit.,* at p. 112.

32. *E.g., Gill* v. *Harewood,* "the debt itself is a sufficient consideration"; the point is well brought out by Gawdy *arguendo* in *Hughes* v. *Rowbotham* (1593) Poph. 30. See also *Anon.* (1582) Godbolt 13; *Smith* v. *Johnson* (1600) Moo. 601.

law allowed; such an analysis was undertaken after the reasons themselves had become established.[33] Indeed, *indebitatus assumpsit* was allowed long before anybody had begun to talk about the need for consideration, and in 1587 it was said in the Common Pleas in *Whorwood* v. *Gybbons*[34] "that it is a common course in actions upon the case against him by whom the debt is due, to declare without any words *in consideratione*"; as Anderson C.J. said in another case, "there is no necessity to be so curious in the consideration, for that is not traversable."[35]

A second objection to the currently accepted account of the difference in practice between the courts is that the basis of the dispute between the court of King's Bench and the court of Common Pleas is not as clearly defined as has been supposed. The difference has been expressed in terms of pleading, by saying that the Common Pleas allowed the special promise to be traversed whilst the King's Bench did not.[36] This is certainly incorrect. If the defendant wished to deny the promise he pleaded the general issue — *non assumpsit* — and the case then went to the jury.[37] The jury could be directed to find a special verdict, but if they were not directed to do so, or did not do so, they could only find for or against the plaintiff generally. The practice of the courts in allowing special verdicts was therefore crucial in determining whether the special promise was a fiction or not. The *locus classicus* upon the difference of practice is *Edwards* v. *Burre* (1573) where Wray J. explained the then state of the law. He said that in the King's Bench proof of the debt is sufficient, "car le dette est assumption en ley." The reason is that the common law does not allow a man to have an action on the case if another action is available;[38] presumably the King's Bench judges thought that the implied promise sufficiently distinguished the causes of action. Wray J.'s distinction is supported by an obscure case in the Common Pleas in 1586,[39] where Periam J. states the rule for that

33. *E.g.,* by Manwood *arguendo* in *Manwood* v. *Burston* (1587) and by Coke *arguendo* in *Stone* v. *Wythipol* (1593) Cro.Eliz. 126.

34. Gouldsborough 48.

35. *Brown* v. *Garbrey* (1588) Goulds. 94. His statement is not quite correct; it was traversable specially if executory. Anderson C.J. was reproving Coke, who had firm views upon the need for finding a unity in the various "considerations" recognized by law.

36. *E.g.,* Fifoot, *op. cit.,* 359; Plucknett, *op. cit.,* 608. The implication of these writers is that some sort of special traverse was possible in the Common Pleas.

37. This is obvious since the defendant is denying the *assumpsit*. This is the general issue, and was the plea in *Slade's Case*. Clearly both courts had to allow the general issue to be pleaded; any other course of action would have been absurd.

38. Dalison 104.

39. *Anon.,* Godbolt 98. The report goes, "A bargains with B for twenty loads of wood, and B promises to deliver them at D. If he fail an action upon the case lieth. But Periam Justice said, that upon a simple

court. The case is concerned with an action on the case in lieu of an action of debt for unascertained goods sold. About this date we find actions of *indebitatus assumpsit* allowed in that court.[40] Now it has always been assumed that the practice of the Common Pleas (and therefore the law applied in the court of Exchequer Chamber set up in 1585) remained constant up to *Slade's Case* upon the principle stated by Wray J. in 1573. This assumption seems open to doubt, and the evidence seems to show that toward the end of the sixteenth century the Common Pleas judges determined to destroy *indebitatus assumpsit* entirely, and completely rejected this form of action. Such a swing of judicial opinion is not without parallel at this time, and cannot be rejected as *a priori* unlikely,[41] and the cases tell in its favor.

When the new court of Exchequer Chamber was set up by statute in 1585[42] the hearing of writs of error from the King's Bench became the concern of the judges of the Common Pleas and those Barons of the Exchequer who were of the degree of the coif. The machinery of the new court as at first established was unsatisfactory and was altered in 1587;[43] thereafter the Common Pleas judges were able to control the law administered in the King's Bench. They had the monopoly of the action of debt, and where before 1585 they had to ape the evasions of the action permitted in the King's Bench they could now prevent those evasions entirely. Upon a writ of error only the record came up for review, and in an action for *indebitatus assumpsit* if the defendant pleaded *non assumpsit* and the King's Bench judges did not permit a special verdict to be found, the Exchequer Chamber could not overrule the King's Bench upon the ground that the promise was fictitious, for this fact would not appear on the record.[44] By refusing to allow special verdicts the King's Bench could indeed prevent the point upon which they differed from the Common Pleas ever coming before the Exchequer Chamber. The Common Pleas could only restore their jurisdiction by destroying *indebitatus assumpsit* completely and this they were prepared to do. Thus, in the reported Exchequer Chamber cases on *indebitatus assumpsit* we find that the ground upon which the King's

---

contract for wood upon an implicative promise an action upon the case doth not lie. Rodes Justice, If by failure of performance the plaintiff be damnified to such a sum; this action lieth."

40. *E.g., Gill* v. *Harewood* (1587), *Anon.* (1586) Godbolt 98, *Whorwood* v. *Gybbons* (1587).

41. Compare the vacillations in the law of property at this time.

42. 27 Eliz. 1, c. 8.

43. 31 Eliz. 1, c. 1.

44. Thus, the court could direct the jurors that if they found the debt proved they *must* find for the plaintiff. This is what Wray J. did in *Edwards* v. *Burre* (1573) Dal. 104.

Bench was overruled is always the same—that in the circumstances disclosed on the record debt and not *assumpsit* is the proper form of action.[45] In none of these cases is there any discussion of express or implied promises to pay, nor of refusals to allow evidence to be tendered against the promise alleged. The Exchequer Chamber simply enforced in all its rigor the rule against duplicity of remedies, and refused to split hairs about the respective causes of action in debt and in *indebitatus assumpsit*. They were able to do this because the record in the *indebitatus* action was bound to disclose an enforceable debt, and no pleading trick could avoid this.

This was not the only sphere in which the Common Pleas judges asserted their new power. They also habitually reversed the King's Bench when it allowed *assumpsit* to lie against executors.[46] Out of this conflict there seemed to be no escape for the King's Bench except by way of capitulation, had it not been for the fact that the old Exchequer Chamber, in which all the judges and Barons of the degree of the coif sat, was still in existence, and it was before all the judges, sitting in Sergeants' Inn, that *Slade's Case* was brought for argument. How this clever move was engineered is not known, and it is difficult to disentangle the various stages in that case from the reports. Apparently it was argued twice in the Exchequer Chamber, once in 1597 and again in 1600, besides being discussed on several occasions.[47] Judgment was finally given for the plaintiff in the King's Bench in 1602. After the first argument judgment was apparently declared in favor of the defendant, but presumably not enrolled.[48] The second argument led to a change of view in favor of the plaintiff, and in the end he succeeded. The case was treated by contemporaries as having deliberately changed the law,[49] and we must now attempt to discover what precisely this change in the law was.

Perhaps it will be as well to dispose first of all of the notion that the case

45. *Paramour* v. *Payne* (1595) Moo. 703 (a plea of *non assumpsit* with the jury finding for the plaintiff); *Maylard* v. *Kester* (1598) Moo. 711; *Turges* v. *Beacher* (1595) Moo. 694 (*semble* the same plea and verdict as *Paramour* v. *Payne*). Compare *Hinson* v. *Burridge* (1594) where judgment was affirmed because debt was not available in the circumstances. This constant overruling of the King's Bench may have encouraged the device of bringing special *assumpsit* and alleging as consideration a forbearance to sue by the creditor. See the cases cited in note 30 above.

46. *Matthew* v. *Matthew* (1595) Moo. 702; *Hughes* v. *Rowbotham* (1593) Popham 30; *Pyne* v. *Hide* (1601) Goulds. 154; *Stubbings* v. *Rotheram* (1595) Cro.Eliz. 454; *Serle* v. *Rosse* (1596) Cro.Eliz. 459.

47. *Slade's Case* is reported in Coke's *Reports,* Vol. IV, at 92a, in Yelverton at 20, and twice in Moore, at pp. 433 and 667. These reports supplement each other considerably. Coke's argument for the plaintiff *in banc* is reported in Bodleian MS. Rawl.C. 720, Mich. 43–44 Eliz., pl. 21, f. 42a; presumably this argument was tendered in reply to a motion in arrest of judgment.

48. Moo. 433.

49. See *Pinchon's Case,* 9 Rep. 86b, at 88b.

decided anything about mutual promises and their enforceability.[50] The consideration which was alleged in support of the promise of payment in the case was the bargain and sale of the wheat growing on the defendant's land—this bargain and sale had been completed before the moment when action was brought, and the consideration alleged was therefore executed. There was no question in *Slade's Case* of there being "a promise for a promise." It is true that the contract of sale was in one sense executory—it had not been performed by either party—but it was not the seller's promise to deliver the goods, but the contract of sale itself, which had been made, which was the consideration alleged; the implied promise of payment was therefore supported by an executed consideration. Since the promise implied, and the contract, were alleged to have arisen at one and the same moment, the consideration was not past.[51]

Once this is appreciated the famous statement that "every contract executory imports in itself an *assumpsit*"[52] can be given an intelligible meaning. Contract in the sixteenth century and early seventeenth is not synonymous with agreement; it means (*inter alia*) "a situation where debt lies"—for example a bargain and sale or a loan of money is a contract. The dictum, translated out of the contemporary jargon, means that wherever a situation has arisen where the writ of debt *sur contract* would lie against a person, and that person has not paid the debt ("executory") an *assumpsit* to pay the money will be implied. Now it may seem that this gives a banal meaning to "executory" for clearly, one might say, nobody can sue in *assumpsit* for a debt if the debt has been paid. The point is, however, that in *indebitatus assumpsit* the plaintiff sues not for the debt but for unliquidated damages,[53] and the implied promise might well be held to survive the payment of the debt, allowing the creditor to sue for damages (say for late payment) after the debt had been paid in full. The insistence that the contract must be executory is linked closely to the rule that a judgment in an action of debt bars *assumpsit* for the same sum, and the rule (embodied in the fourth resolution in *Slade's Case*) that in *indebitatus assumpsit* not only damages but the debt itself may be recovered.

The rule that mutual promises are consideration for each other belongs

---

50. The idea that it did has today become dogma. See Holdsworth, H.E.L. III, 445; Kiralfy, *The English Legal System*, 69; *The Action on the Case*, 184.

51. On *indebitatus assumpsit* and the rule as to past consideration, see below.

52. This is a quotation from *Norwood* v. *Read* (1558) Plowden 180, a case not at all concerned with mutual promises.

53. The difference might be considerable. The debt in *Slade's Case* was £16, but the damage amounted to 40 marks.

wholly to the sphere of special *assumpsit* and has no relevance to the *indebitatus* action; conversely *Slade's Case* has no relevance to special *assumpsit*. There has been much confusion over this. For *indebitatus assumpsit* to lie the defendant must be indebted; the existence of a simple contract debt depends upon the receipt of a *quid pro quo* and not upon the furnishing of consideration. Normally this means that there must be an actual receipt of a tangible benefit by the defendant, as would be the case in a contract of loan. The contract of sale of specific goods is the one apparent exception to this rule, and *indebitatus assumpsit* lay not only on a sale and delivery but also on a bargain and sale. This is because a bargain and sale had been admitted as a contract, though performed on neither side, in the fifteenth century,[54] upon the fictional basis that the "property" passed at once to the bargainee when the goods were bargained and sold, although the goods had not yet been delivered; the bargainee obtained, in the "property," a *quid pro quo*. The reason why an executory agreement for sale was enforceable by writ of debt was not the fact that there had been mutual promises. Indeed, *indebitatus assumpsit* for the price of goods sold and delivered stands upon exactly the same ground as *indebitatus assumpsit* for the price of goods bargained and sold; nothing turns upon the fact that in one case the sale has been performed on one side and in the other it has not. Thus, the development of the entirely unrelated doctrine that a promise is a good consideration for a counter promise takes place without any reference to *Slade's Case*. The sixteenth-century cases upon the point are well known;[55] Dr. Kiralfy has suggested that the enforceability of mutual promises was only admitted in the King's Bench.[56] It is true that the earliest case which clearly shows that the Common Pleas accepted the doctrine is in 1615,[57] yet the rule seems to have been admitted in that court in 1578,[58] though the leading cases on the subject are certainly King's Bench cases. In no case on the point is the action of *indebitatus assumpsit* and its limitations treated as being material.

What then was decided in *Slade's Case?* First, that *indebitatus assumpsit* was a permissible form of action, and that the objection that debt lay in the same circumstances was no longer to be regarded as important. This represents, of course, a complete rejection of the very recent decisions of the statutory court

54. See Fifoot, *op. cit.,* 228.
55. See Fifoot, *op. cit.,* pp. 399 and 400, and the cases there cited: he maintains that the enforceability of mutual promises was accepted by 1558.
56. Kiralfy, *The Action on the Case,* 184.
57. *Nichols* v. *Rainbred* (1615) Hobart 88.
58. *West* v. *Stowel* (1578) 2 Leon. 154.

of Exchequer Chamber, and can only be viewed as an astonishing act of judicial legislation, which fully accounts for the attitude of later lawyers to the decision. No attempt was made in *Slade's Case* to draw refined distinctions between the causes of action in debt and *assumpsit,* as had been done earlier; the rule that no two actions should lie on a single state of facts was entirely abrogated. Thus, Coke's report says,

> It was resolved, That every Contract executory imports in itself an *Assumpsit,* for when one agrees to pay Money, or to deliver any Thing, thereby he assumes or promises to pay, or deliver it. . . .[59]

Assumpsit and Debt were in future to be true alternative remedies. This aspect of the case is made clearer by a consideration of Coke's argument for the plaintiff *in banc.*[60] The major point at issue in the case, in his view, was whether or not Case lay in the circumstances; this he treated as turning upon the problem of alternative remedies. His entire argument upon this point was directed toward showing that alternative remedies were—and, indeed, always had been—a commonplace of the law. This argument could be given a certain degree of plausibility, for the distinctions drawn by earlier courts between the precise causes of action which gave rise to competing forms of action were fine and subtle, and were introduced to square legal theory with the reality as it would appear to a layman, which was that election between remedies was permitted. Authorities were mustered by Coke to illustrate his thesis—as an example we may take the well-known *Surgeon's Case* (1370).[61] Coke cited this and added that an Appeal of Mayhem would also have lain in the circumstances: thus the case supports him. This is, of course, a mere perversion of authority; for our purposes its importance lies in the fact that it shows Coke in full attack upon the doctrine which forbade duplicity of remedies, and thus illustrates the fundamental issue raised by *Slade's Case.*[62]

What is extremely curious is the survival after this decision of the distinction between *indebitatus assumpsit* and special *assumpsit.* Before *Slade's Case*

59. 4 Rep. ff. 94a and 94b.
60. Bodleian MS. Rawl.C. 720, f. 42a.
61. Y.B. Mich. 43 Edw. III, f. 33, pl. 38.
62. The other cases cited by Coke were:— Y.B. Trin. 12 Ric. II, pl. 5 (Ames, *Foundation,* p. 7); Y.B. Pasch. 21 Hen. VI, f. 55, pl. 12; Y.B. Mich. 12 Edw. IV, f. 13, pl. 9; Y.B. Mich. 2 Ric. III, f. 14, pl. 39; Y.B. Trin. 13 Hen. VII, f. 26, pl. 4; Y.B. Pasch. 14 Hen. VIII, f. 31, pl. 8; Y.B. Mich. 27 Hen. VIII, f. 24, pl. 3; *Core's Case* (1536) Dyer 20a; Brooke Abr. *Accion sur le Case* 105 (1542); *Pecke* v. *Redman* (1556) Dyer 113a; Brooke Abr. *Accion sur le Case* 108 (1558); *Andrew* v. *Boughey* (1552) Dyer 75a; *Norwood* v. *Read* (1558) Plowden 180; *Hunt* v. *Bate* (1568) Dyer 272a.

the promise alleged was said to have been supported by the debt as consideration,[63] and in the case itself the pleadings treat the debt as consideration. In the body of the report, however, Coke changes ground and treats the seller's promise to deliver the goods as consideration for the promise to pay[64]—incorrectly as the pleadings stand; in doing so Coke perhaps intentionally was suggesting a possible simplification of the law, for this way of looking at the matter assimilates the two branches of *assumpsit*. After *Slade's Case* this development did take place, and the pleadings in *Pinchon's Case*,[65] which concerned a loan, treat the delivery of the money to the borrower and not the existence of the contract of loan as the consideration for the promise to repay. This is how we look at the matter today, and we recognize no difference in principle between suing on a sale for a failure to pay the price of goods, and suing on a building contract for failure to build. Yet until the forms of action were abolished the distinction between *indebitatus assumpsit* and special *assumpsit* was irrationally maintained upon the odd basis that in *indebitatus assumpsit* the promise was an implied promise, a doctrine assumed to have been hallowed by *Slade's Case*. In fact it is not to be found in that case at all, if we are using the term "implied" to suggest that the promise is some sort of fictional promise akin to some of the implied promises of modern contract and quasi contract. *Slade's Case,* as Coke reports it, denies the distinction between agreement and "undertaking" (*assumpsit*), or promise, and says that when A agrees to deliver a horse he thereby assumes or promises to deliver it; there is no need to imply a promise or undertaking because one has, in fact, been given. This point formed the subject-matter of the second part of Coke's argument for the plaintiff *in banc.* He said,

> The other matter which deserves no discussion is this. If this action should be maintained, there being an agreement to pay and not a promise, [then] every agreement is a promise, as was agreed in the case of Norwood and Reade that on every executory agreement a man will have an action on the case. For [an agreement] amounts to a promise.[66]

This again is how we treat an agreement today for the purposes of the law of contract, and we are, of course, prepared to infer agreement from conduct,

63. See above.
64. 4 Rep., ff. 94a and 94b.
65. Coke's "Entries," *Action sur le Case* 1. An earlier example of the use of special *assumpsit* instead of *indebitatus assumpsit* is *Mackerell v. Bachelor* (1601) Goulds. 168.
66. Bodleian MS. Rawl.C. 720, f. 43a.

since persons do not in practice make their promises in formal language or use terms of art in their daily affairs, in spite of the curious recent opinion of the Court of Appeal which implies the contrary.[67] When today a promise inferred from conduct or loosely expressed words is enforced we do not think of it as an implied promise in any fictional sense. The survival of the two forms of *assumpsit* has never been satisfactorily explained. It may be suggested, however, that it was caused by the reintroduction of the practice of alleging a subsequent promise instead of a contemporaneous one; this became the recognized form of pleading in the common counts.[68] This practice was assisted by a decision in 1617, *Hodge* v. *Vavisour*,[69] where a subsequent promise was alleged, and it was argued that a precedent debt was a past consideration, and so bad. The court, for no very good reason, held the consideration good, and thereafter the habit of declaring on a subsequent promise became inveterate. The subsequent promise had to be implied in the full sense that it was a doctrinal fiction (except in the rarest instances), whereas a contemporaneous promise would either be express or implied in the narrow sense of being deducible from words and conduct at the time of the agreement. In this way it seems was the unification of the law of contract prevented.

Finally, the other rulings in the case must be noted. Popham C.J., in delivering the judges' opinion, laid down that in future *assumpsit* would not lie against executors;[70] the decision in *Norwood* v. *Read* (1558),[71] repeatedly overruled, as we have seen in the Exchequer Chamber set up in 1585, was now, *obiter,* overruled in the old Exchequer Chamber as well by all the judges, who thus took upon themselves the task of declaring the law in the abstract. This ruling gives to *Slade's Case* the character of a compromise between the courts rather than a simple triumph for the King's Bench. *Assumpsit* was in future to occupy only the area formerly covered by debt *sur contract*,[72] and no more. *Pinchon's Case* in 1612[73] reversed this opinion and allowed executors to be sued;[74]

---

67. *Oscar Chess, Ltd.* v. *Williams* [1957] 1 W.L.R. 370. The citation of *Chandelor* v. *Lopus* (1603) Cro.Jac. 4 in support of this decision seems to the writer, with great respect, to be valuable only as an example of the undesirability of using old cases decided upon pleading points no longer relevant to the modern law as if they established a rule for contemporary decision.

68. See Chitty on *Pleading,* 2nd ed., p. 48, 7th ed., Vol. II, p. 34, Smith's *Leading Cases,* 13th ed., Vol. I, p. 635.

69. 3 Bulstrode 222.

70. Yelverton 20. This ruling is ignored in Coke's *Report*.

71. Plowden 180.

72. Which did not lie against executors.

73. 9 Rep. 86b.

74. In later cases an attempt was made to limit the rule in *Pinchon's Case* to actions of *assumpsit* against

it can hardly be represented as "an attempt to reopen the decision in *Norwood* v. *Read*,"[75] for in 1612 the burden lay not upon the critics but upon the
defenders of that discredited decision, and its re-establishment was again an
act of naked judicial legislation.[76] The court also ruled in *Slade's Case* that in
indebitatus assumpsit the *causa debendi* must be pleaded; a general "*indebitatus
assumpsit solvere*" was insufficient. This ruling shows that the judges, in allowing the supersession of debt, were at pains to ensure that defendants in the
newer action would not be surprised in court through its looser pleading. The
other rulings in the case are too well known to need mention here.

The consequences of *Slade's Case* were various and important, but they lie
outside the scope of this article. I have sought to show that the issues involved
in the case were more important than writers have previously suggested, but
not to show the consequences of their resolution in the way chosen by the
judges in 1602. The results of this new look at the antecedents of the case
seem to suggest that its status as a leading decision is greater than has been
supposed. It will be wise to end this article upon a cautionary note by drawing attention to the fact that the cases used as authorities are frequently brief
and cryptic, and where Coke is concerned deliberately polished; furthermore,
tracking down the relevant cases is a chancy undertaking, and one cannot be
certain that a relevant authority has not been overlooked, for the indexes to
the old reports are often deficient. As a result the conclusions advanced here
can only be tentative.

---

debtors. This failed. See *Sanders* v. *Esterby* (1617) Cro.Jac. 417; *Bersford* v. *Woodroff* (1616) Cro.Jac. 404;
Clark v. *Thomson* (1621) Cro.Jac. 571; *Fawcet* v. *Charter* (1624) Cro.Jac. 662.

75. Fifoot, *op. cit.,* 360.
76. No arguments were heard. See the report in Cro.Jac. 294.

Sir Edward Coke and the Interpretation of Lawful Allegiance in Seventeenth-Century England

DAVID MARTIN JONES

ఞ ఞ ఞ

I

A problem for the seventeenth-century Englishman was the nature of the allegiance he owed to the state. What allegiance was, how it was declared, to whom it was due and how it was limited, were questions that perennially troubled Englishmen. In the course of the century defenders of the authority of the lawful hereditary monarchy in church and state evolved the dominant theory of allegiance, namely that all subjects were by oath in law and conscience obligated to the monarch who was, of course, placed on his throne by God. At moments of crisis in the century, however, factious elements in the state challenged the crucial act on which this whole theory was based: they challenged the state's use of loyalty oaths and treated allegiance as a relationship of mutual dependence between ruler and ruled. Little of this argument about the nature of political obligation can be understood unless it is recognized that central to all debate on this issue was a concern for precedent and tradition. Members of the seventeenth-century political nation,[1] in assessing the loyalty they owed the lawful monarch, treated as authoritative proofs derived from history (ideally English), law (ideally English common law) and the Bible.

"Sir Edward Coke and the Interpretation of Lawful Allegiance in Seventeenth-Century England" is reprinted from the *History of Political Thought* 7, no. 2 (summer 1986): 321–40. Reprinted by permission of David Martin Jones and Imprint Academic.

1. The political nation constituted roughly two percent of the population, see for instance Ivan Roots, *The Great Rebellion 1642–1660* (London, 1966), p. 1. It was representatives of the political nation that sat in parliament and administered the machinery of government in the localities. It was to this nation that the managers of the English state in the seventeenth century looked for whole-hearted support. This paper explores the attitude of this nation to the problem of allegiance.

J. P. Kenyon, in his essay "The Revolution of 1688: Resistance and Contract,"[2] has shown that the English approach to political thought was strictly legalistic and historical, "roughly speaking oldest was best."[3] It was the antecedents of a particular doctrine that established its validity. Innovative schemes of government, new modeling of the state, the abstract speculations of a Hobbes, Harrington or Locke had little appeal to the conservative legal-mindedness of the English governing classes. This tendency became even more pronounced after the traumas of the Interregnum.

In the political controversies that raged in the 1640s and even in the 1680s, as Europe moved toward rationalism, the English political nation paid particular attention to the law and constitution of the realm in order to demonstrate that a theory of allegiance was legitimate. A theory of allegiance, if it was to have any credibility for the English political nation, in fact had to offer an interpretation of English law, English history and the obligations of conscience.[4] However, not only was the problem of allegiance debated in these terms, Englishmen also paid careful attention and attached great importance to the recognized English authorities on these subjects.

In considering their legal and constitutional obligations, members of the seventeenth-century English political nation considered the writings of Sir Edward Coke seminal. Seventeenth-century pamphlet writers came to view Coke as the "great oracle" of the common law tradition because he had performed the crucial service of filtering this tradition for seventeenth-century consumption. Commentators upon the lawful duty of allegiance frequently referred to the great medieval English lawyers—to Bracton, Glanvill, Fortescue and Littleton—but they received this legal tradition and these authorities, to a very large extent, through the commentaries and reports of Coke. How, we may ask, did the common law tradition affect the perception of allegiance in seventeenth-century England? An adequate answer to this question must further consider Coke's ascendancy within this tradition and the way in which his lucubrations were interpreted in those years of crisis when loyalty was a subject of constant speculation and debate.

2. J. P. Kenyon, "The Revolution of 1688: Resistance and Contract," in *Historical Perspectives: Studies in English Political Thought and Society,* ed. N. McKendrick (London, 1974).

3. *Ibid.,* p. 56.

4. The question of allegiance necessarily involved a moral dimension because nearly everyone agreed that all power derived from God. Moreover, the oath that confirmed the allegiance owed by all subjects to the lawful superior involved the religious bond of conscience. Most seventeenth-century discussion of allegiance is consequently conducted along lines suggested by developments in English casuistry. See, for instance, J. M. Wallace, *Destiny His Choice: The Loyalism of Andrew Marvell* (Cambridge, 1968), Ch. 1.

II

At least from the time of Fortescue's *De Laudibus Legum Angliae* English law-yers had attempted to legitimize the particular laws of different nations by reference "not to reason and the knowledge of universals, but to antiquity and usage."[5] By this reasoning the common law of England could be proved better than that of other nations precisely because it was oldest. J. G. A. Pocock, who has contributed greatly to our understanding of the common law tradi-tion,[6] considers that the English governing class had always been deeply aware of an "ancient constitution."[7] However that may be, the *doctrine* of the an-cient constitution did not receive its classical formulation until the early seven-teenth century. Not surprisingly it was largely the product of common law-yers. The doctrine assumed that English common law was "common custom, originating in the usages of the people and declared, interpreted and applied in the courts."[8] Moreover, as all custom was by definition immemorial, any declaration of law constituted a declaration "that its content had been usage since time immemorial."[9] These assumptions, J. G. A. Pocock contends, were now made the framework of an historical theory "based on record, axiom and judgement," which contained "at every turn the presumption that law was immemorial."[10]

Legal history, as understood by common lawyers, thus became a series of declarations about the immemoriality of the law. The doctrine of the com-mon law and ancient constitution achieved widespread popularity amongst the English political nation at the start of the seventeenth century and it was Sir Edward Coke who gave this doctrine its most satisfactory formulation. For Coke, the common law that the King's judges declared, was a distillation of common custom, itself unwritten and immemorial. "It embodies the wisdom of generations, as a result not of philosophical reflection, but of the accu-mulations and refinements of experience."[11] The law represented an artificial

---

5. J. G. A. Pocock, *The Machiavellian Moment* (Princeton, 1975), p. 14.
6. In a series of books and articles, see particularly: J. G. A. Pocock, *The Ancient Constitution and the Feudal Law: A Study of English Historical Thought in the Seventeenth Century* (Cambridge, 1957), and J. G. A. Pocock, *Politics, Language and Time: Essays in Political Thought and History* (London, 1972).
7. The idea emerged notably during the conflict between York and Lancaster in the fifteenth century.
8. Pocock, *Politics, Language and Time,* p. 209.
9. *Ibid.*
10. *Ibid.* Pocock argues that: "It therefore became possible to believe that the whole framework of En-glish Law and (when that term came into use) the "constitution"—meaning the power of applying and declaring the law—had existed from the obscure beginnings of English history, from a time earlier than the earliest historical evidences."
11. Pocock, *The Ancient Constitution,* p. 35.

reason which, in the decision of the judge, recalled the knowledge of many generations of men, each decision based "on the experience of those before and tested by the experience of those after." Consequently, it was wiser than any individual, even the King.[12]

This then was the myth of the ancient constitution. Lawyers accordingly took everything in the records of the common law to be immemorial and they took every piece of evidence in those records as a declaration of what was already immemorial.[13] The belief in the ancient constitution obviously had a considerable impact on a society whose political thinking was largely dominated by legal considerations. It was not, as Pocock shows, the creation of one man. However, Coke "did more than any other man to summarize it and make it authoritative."[14]

The immemorial law and ancient constitution of the realm necessarily dominated the thinking of the English political nation about allegiance, and Coke's commentaries on the law as it affected that duty were consequently imbued with authority by later generations. Thus, when in the course of the century alterations to government occurred, requiring a corresponding change in allegiance on the part of the subject, attempts were made both to justify and also to reject the change in allegiance on the basis of criteria deduced from Coke and the ancient constitution.

In 1642 parliament had justified its resistance to Charles I on the grounds that the ancient constitution preserved a balanced mixture of monarchy, aristocracy and democracy and that the people's representative had the constitutional right to resist the disequilibrating activities of a potential tyrant. Indeed, there was such a consensus amongst the political nation that many Royalists agreed that the constitution was mixed; what they disagreed with was parliament's resistance. The complexities of this disbelief were such that many who fought on the parliamentary side in the Civil War refused to submit to the authority of the English Commonwealth after 1649 because regicide had destroyed the ingredients of the constitutional mixture.[15]

---

12. *Ibid.*

13. The doctrine involved a paradox. As Pocock points out if the idea that the law is custom implies anything it is that the law is in constant adaptation and change, yet the fact is that the lawyers, holding that the law was custom, came to believe that the common law and with it the ancient constitution had always been what they were now, that they were immemorial. *Ibid.,* p. 36.

14. J. G. A. Pocock, *The Ancient Constitution and the Feudal Law* (Cambridge, 1957), pp. 36–37. Sir Edward Coke (1552–1634) was successively Attorney-General, 1593; Chief Justice of Common Pleas, 1606; Chief Justice of Kings Bench, 1613; disgraced, 1616; and a problematic MP up to 1628.

15. M. J. Mendle discusses the general belief in a mixed, monarchical constitution in "Politics and Political Thought," in *The Origins of the English Civil War,* ed. Conrad Russell (London, 1978). See also

Again, in 1689, arguments derived from legal and constitutional precedent
were used to justify the transfer of authority from James II to William and
Mary. Those who favoured this change maintained that it was constitutionally justified and validated a concomitant change in the allegiance of subjects. Nevertheless, the Non-Jurors who refused to swear allegiance to the new
regime argued that the ancient constitution supported their stance.

It could be argued that perhaps too much attention has been paid by historians of ideas to the philosophical arguments about allegiance that occurred
in the course of the seventeenth century. This has occasioned the neglect of
the much more influential legal arguments of which Sir Edward Coke was the
great exemplar. It is to these arguments that we now turn. In the remainder of
this paper I shall discuss what common lawyers like Coke understood to be
the nature and extent of lawful allegiance, and how Coke's writings on allegiance were interpreted by later seventeenth-century pamphleteers in order to
justify opposed views of the allegiance required by the law and constitution of
the realm.

III

The two major sources of Coke's interpretation of the law as it affected allegiance were contained in "Calvin's Case," published in the seventh volume of
his legal *Reports,* and in his account of homage, fealty and the law relating to
High Treason in the *Institutes,* largely published after his death.[16]

Calvin's case was brought before the Chief Justices of the realm sitting in
the Exchequer Chamber in 1608 in order to clarify the law as it affected allegiance. The state regarded the findings of the judges in this case to be so important that a number of those involved in the case felt constrained to publish
an account of the proceedings.[17] Yet by far the most influential report of the

W. Lamont, *Marginal Prynne* (London, 1963), for an excellent discussion of one who supported parliament
in 1642, but who refused to submit to the Rump's unconstitutional rule after 1649.

16. Sir Edward Coke, "Calvin's Case," in *The Reports of Sir Edward Coke Kt., Late Lord Chief Justice of
England . . . of divers Resolutions and Judgments given upon solemn arguments . . . and the reasons and causes
of the said Resolutions and Judgments* (London, 1658). Sir Edward's report of Calvin's case also appears in
W. Cobbett, *et al., Cobbett's Complete Collection of State Trials and Proceedings for High Treason . . . from
the earliest period to the present time,* Vol. 2 (London, 1809), cols. 607 ff. (hereafter *State Trials*). Sir Edward
Coke, *The Institutes of the Laws of England* (5 vols., London, 1817). *The first part of the Institutes or a commentary upon Littleton. The second part containing the exposition of many ancient and other statutes. The third
part concerning High Treason and other pleas of the crown. The fourth part concerning the jurisdiction of courts.*

17. See W. Cobbett, "The case of the Postnati, or the union of the realm of Scotland with England,"

case for those concerned about the lawful interpretation of allegiance was that published by Sir Edward Coke.

In his exordium to Calvin's case Coke characteristically stressed that the decision the judges reached was based on English law and precedent. The judges consulted "no strange histories, cited no foreign laws [and] produced no alien precedents and that for two causes":[18] firstly, because the laws of England were "copious in this point" and secondly, because Coke believed that a decision that vitally affected (amongst other things) freehold and inheritance in England, should only be decided by the laws of the realm.

Coke reported that the judges defined allegiance as "a true and faithful obedience of the subject due to his sovereign."[19] This "ligeance and obedience" was, the judges declared, "an incident inseperable to every subject: for as soon as he is born he owes by birthright ligeance and obedience to his sovereign."[20] With a characteristic seventeenth-century flair for analogy, Coke averred that "as the ligatures or strings do knit together the joints of all the parts of the body, so doth ligeance join together the sovereign and all his subjects."[21]

The judges believed that every subject owed his sovereign a natural allegiance by the fact of his birthright and the protection and security that the sovereign afforded. The king was a "natural liege lord and his people natural liege subjects."[22] The actual form that this allegiance took could, however, be prescribed by the "municipal laws of the kingdom." In England, the municipal laws had ordained that an oath represented the best method of confirming the allegiance that a subject naturally owed his sovereign: "the municipal laws of the realm have prescribed the order and form of it; and this [is] to be done upon oath at the torn or leet."[23] The subject, therefore, owed the crown a natural allegiance which the law required him to demonstrate by oath at the local

---

in *State Trials,* cols. 559 ff. Cobbett included the reports of Mr. Serjeant Moore, Sir Francis Bacon's speech as counsel for Calvin and Lord Chancellor Ellesmere's speech in the Exchequer Chamber. See also L. A. Knafla, *Law and Politics in Jacobean England* (Cambridge, 1977). In Calvin's case, the eponymous Scot complained that he had been disseised of his free tenement in Haggerston, Shoreditch. The defendants pleaded that Calvin was an alien born in Scotland. Hence the question whether the "postnati," that is persons born in Scotland after the accession of James I to the throne of England, were to be treated as aliens born in Scotland or as subjects, was brought before the courts. A case that so vitally affected the nature of the allegiance owed to the crown was referred to the Exchequer Chamber and heard before the twelve Chief Justices of the realm. See W. Holdsworth, *A History of the English Law* (London, 1926), Vol. 9, p. 77 ff.

18. Sir Edward Coke's report of Calvin's case in *State Trials,* col. 612.

19. *Ibid.,* col. 613.

20. *Ibid.,* cols. 613–14.

21. *Ibid.*

22. *Ibid.,* col. 616.

23. *Ibid.,* col. 615.

court.[24] Coke recognized that allegiance could not be considered as beginning with the oath sworn in the court leet, "for many men owe true allegiance that never were sworn in a leet."[25]

The judges thus took cognizance of two main categories of allegiance:[26] natural allegiance determined by birthright; and legal allegiance described in an oath prescribed by the laws of the realm. Indeed, that natural allegiance should have a legal form seemed to the judges fundamental to the ancient constitution of the realm. In his report of Calvin's case Coke examined in detail the origin and development of the feudal oath of allegiance, still sworn by all subjects in the local courts administered by the Justices of the Peace, but by the first decade of the seventeenth century largely superseded by the more detailed oaths of Allegiance and Supremacy introduced by parliament since 1560.[27]

By the feudal oath of allegiance which Coke found in the legal writings attributed to the thirteenth-century Bishop John Britton,[28] the subject swore to:

> be true and faithful to our sovereign lord king and his heirs, and truth and faith
> shall bear of life and member and terrene honour, and you shall neither know or
> hear of any ill or damage intended unto him that you shall not defend.[29]

The judges averred that this oath contained five excellent qualities: it was, "indefinite and without limit"; it enjoined two excellent qualities, to be true and faithful; it obliged the subject to his sovereign lord the king and his heirs; it

24. From about the eleventh century all English subjects were expected to swear allegiance to the crown. This duty was performed at the local court when a subject reached twelve years of age. The court leet was "a royal police court co-ordinate with the sheriff's tourn . . . in the one the local lord's steward is judge, in the other the sheriff." F. W. Maitland, "Leet and Tourn," in *Selected Historical Essays of F. W. Maitland,* ed. Helen M. Cam (Cambridge, 1957), p. 41. In the seventeenth century it was the job of the Justices of the Peace to exact this oath during their local court sessions. See *The Booke of the Justice of the Peace* (London, 1560), p. 86, and John Kitchin, *Le Court Leete, et le Court Baron* (London, 1613), pp. 46–48.

25. *State Trials,* col. 614.

26. At least these were the two most important categories. The judges also discussed two lesser categories of allegiance: by acquisition or denization; and "ligeantia localis" which applied to foreign visitors for the duration of their stay in England, *ibid.,* cols. 615–18.

27. The oath of Supremacy (1560) required from all office-holders in church and state a declaration that the crown was supreme in all causes, "ecclesiastical as well as temporal." The oath of Allegiance (1606) could be required of any subject who was not of noble birth. It required an acknowledgment of the crown's temporal capacity and the denial of any external power of deposition. These state oaths were much more specific in the details of the allegiance required by the crown from its subjects. See G. W. Prothero, *Select Statutes and Other Constitutional Documents of the Reign of Elizabeth and James* (Oxford, 1913).

28. John Britton, Bishop of Hereford, *The Treatise on English Law Formerly Attributed to John Britton Based on Henricus de Bracton's De Legibus et Consuetudinibus Angliae,* cited by Coke, *State Trials,* col. 618. See also, F. M. Nichols, *Britton: On the Laws of England* (2 vols., Oxford, 1865).

29. *State Trials,* col. 618.

required faith and honor on the part of the subject until "the letting out of the last drop of our dearest hearts blood"; finally it was binding in all places, "he that is sworn to the king for his ligeance . . . is to be true and faithful to the king and if he be once sworn for his ligeance, he shall not be sworn again during his life."[30]

Although Britton's oath was feudal, Coke linked it to yet more ancient oaths. In fact he found proof that its roots lay in the miasmic Arthurian origins of the English Empire.[31] By establishing a mythopoeic framework within which the feudal oath of Britton's day operated Coke provided the recent oaths of supremacy and allegiance with a valuable source of legitimation. Despite their modernity Coke, by linking them to the feudal oath of loyalty, had contrived a niche for these state oaths in the ancient constitution and the immemorial past.

Having made these important observations about legal allegiance the judges continued their investigation by providing future generations with a description of the scope of a subject's allegiance. The judges decided that "ligeance and faith and truth, are qualities of the mind and soul of man and cannot be circumscribed within the predicament of ubi."[32] The point the judges wished to make was that the allegiance owed by the subject was not solely territorial in character. Allegiance, they maintained, had a personal as well as a geographical dimension. In other words the "ligeance of the subject was of as great an extent and latitude as the royal power and protection of the crown and e converso."[33] As power and protection drew the subject's allegiance it followed that this allegiance could not be geographically limited. As the king's power and protection "extendeth out of England" the allegiance that necessarily followed it "cannot be local or confined within the bounds thereof."[34]

However, it was a maxim of the law that the king possessed two capacities, or bodies: one political, the other personal. The personal capacity represented the king's natural body, "descended of the blood royal of the realm . . . and is subject to death, infirmity and such like."[35] The political capacity was framed by the "policy of men." It had developed in medieval jurisprudence to avoid

30. *Ibid.*
31. Coke found traces of the feudal oath of allegiance in the laws of Edward the Confessor which he believed had Arthurian antecedents, *ibid.*, cols. 618–19.
32. *Ibid.*, col. 619.
33. *Ibid.*
34. *Ibid.*, col. 623.
35. *Ibid.*, col. 624.

a number of constitutional difficulties.[36] In this capacity the king represented an immortal corporation. In the opinion of the judges it endowed the person of the king with these "perfections: that the king in law shall never be said to be within age; that his blood shall never be corrupted; and that if he were attainted before, the very assumption of the crown purgeth it . . . that his body in law shall be said to be as it were immortal; for there is no death of the king in law, but a demise as it is termed."[37]

In 1608 the judges had to decide to which capacity of the king allegiance was due. In making this decision they were mindful of the fact that the concept of the political capacity had been used by the Despensers in the fourteenth century to legitimate their resistance to the person of King Edward II. Hugh Despenser contended that the subject's oath of allegiance bound him not to the king's person, but to the king as an embodiment of the kingdom and its law. In other words, this unofficial theory of allegiance maintained that if the monarch substituted his personal whim for the immemorial law the subject was bound by his oath to the political capacity to resist the king's person. "Homage," in the Despenser view, "and oath of the subject is more by reason of the crown than by reason of the person of the king. So that if the king doth not guide himself by reason in right of the crown, his lieges are bound by their oath to the crown to remove the king."[38]

The judges in Calvin's case, however, unequivocally maintained that allegiance was due to the person of the king and not to the political capacity, "or to his crown or kingdom distinct from his natural capacity."[39] The judges produced a number of reasons for their interpretation of allegiance. The oath that every subject was presumed by law to have taken to the king was sworn to the natural body. It was, the judges felt, impossible to take an oath to an invisible corporation. In all indictments of treason it was assumed that the king's person had been compassed with death. Lastly, because (the judges argued) the king held the kingdom by virtue of his inherent birthright, by "descent from

---

36. The politic capacity served a number of useful purposes administratively, and avoided the possibility of an Interregnum, *ibid.,* col. 628; and Bacon's speech as counsel for Calvin, *ibid.,* col. 597.

37. *Ibid.*

38. Bacon, *ibid.,* col. 559. The paucity of parliamentary political theory at the start of the Long Parliament was such that opposition MPs revived the Despenser view in an attempt to legitimate their resistance to the King. From 1642 onwards a number of parliamentary pamphleteers argued that parliament represented the political capacity of the crown while the king's person was in the seditious hands of his "wicked" counsellors. See for instance, "A Declaration of the Lords and Commons in Parliament . . . May, 1642," in S. R. Gardiner, *The Constitutional Documents of the Puritan Revolution 1625–60* (Oxford, 1979), pp. 256–58; and Samuel Clarke, *England's Covenant Lawful . . .* (London, 1643), p. 15.

39. *State Trials,* col. 624.

the blood royal whereupon succession doth attend," allegiance must be due to the royal blood.[40]

In the opinion of the judges, then, the laws of England declared that the natural allegiance owed by the subject must be due to the person of the king who received his title by inherent birthright. The judges condemned the Despenser treason, and Coke described it as "a damnable and damned opinion."[41] For special purposes the law had made the king a body politic, but allegiance was due to "our natural liege sovereign descended of the blood royal of the kings of this realm, omni, soli, et semper."[42]

In order to place the problem of allegiance beyond all doubt the judges decided that the allegiance owed by all subjects was not only natural, due to the person of the king and the form of it prescribed by law, it was also dictated by the law of nature which was immutable, preceded all law and formed part of the law of England.

The judges' decision to place the origins of allegiance outside the province of human law was crucial. Human laws might be changed but that which was according to nature was unalterable. Coke reported that the "obedience of the inferior to the superior, of the subject to the sovereign was due by the law of nature many thousand years before any law of man was made; which ligeance or obedience . . . could not be altered; therefore, it remaineth still due by the law of nature."[43] For the judges in Calvin's case it was, in fact, between sovereignty and allegiance that laws were "begotton."[44] The judges argued that if a people were conquered, allegiance to the conqueror had to be established before any laws were passed.[45] Allegiance had a legal form, the oath, but the duty itself was before all laws. Consequently, the judges concluded, it continued and was "in vigour where laws are suspended and have lost their force."

Thus the judges in Calvin's case found that allegiance of a subject to a sovereign was natural and based on the protection and security that the sovereign gave. This allegiance in England had a legal form, the oath, which the subject swore to the person of the king. The king achieved the throne by virtue of inherent birthright. The judges further acknowledged that the oath and the law

40. *Ibid.*, col. 625.
41. The Despenser treason was declared such by the first parliament of Edward III, see *ibid.*, col. 627.
42. *Ibid.*, col. 628.
43. *Ibid.*, col. 652.
44. So said Bacon in his speech for Calvin, *ibid.*, col. 576. Coke expressed analogous sentiments, *ibid.*, col. 652.
45. *Ibid.*, see also cols. 629–30.

of nature from which it derived intended that the subject's allegiance should
be unalterable.

It would seem that so comprehensive a treatment of allegiance locked Englishmen into an infrangible loyalty. Yet it remains to be seen if Coke altered
or modified his view of lawful allegiance in any of his later writings upon the
law and constitution of the realm. In fact, in his discourse on the statute of
treason in the third part of his *Institutes of the Laws of England,* Coke developed one of the assertions made by the judges in Calvin's case—that there is
a mutual bond between a king and his subjects based on their obedience and
his protection. "As the subject oweth to the king his true and faithful ligeance
and so the sovereign is to govern and protect his subjects,"[46] was one of the
conditions of allegiance noted by the judges in Calvin's case. In his *Institutes,*
Coke discussed this condition placed upon a subject's allegiance especially as
it was affected by Sir Edward's reading of the 1495 Statute of Treason (11 H.
7, c. 1), the so-called "de facto" act.

The 1495 statute maintained that no subject should suffer as a result of performing his duty of allegiance: "no manner of person . . . that attend upon
the king and sovereign lord of this land for the time being in his person and
do him true and faithful service of allegiance . . . that for the same deed and
true service of allegiance . . . they be in no wise convict or attaint of high treason."[47] In his *Institutes* Coke assumed that this statute applied only to the king
in actual possession of the crown and kingdom. In a statement often quoted
by seventeenth-century proponents of the doctrine of "defactoism" Coke asserted that:

> For if there be a King in possession although he be *rex de facto et non de jure,*
> yet is he *signior le roy* within the purview of this statute and the other that hath
> right and is out of possession is not within this act. Nay if treason be committed
> against a *king de facto et non de jure* and after the king *de jure* cometh to the crown
> he shall punish the treason due to the king *de facto,* and a pardon granted by a
> king *de jure* that is not also *de facto* is void.[48]

46. *Ibid.,* col. 614.
47. G. R. Elton, *The Tudor Constitution: Documents and Commentary* (Cambridge, 1960), pp. 4–5.
48. The four parts of *The Institutes of the Laws of England* were produced at various dates in the course
of the seventeenth century: *Part I or a Commentary upon Littleton,* 1628; *The Second Part of the Institutes of
the Laws of England containing the exposition of many Ancient and other Statutes,* 1644; *The Third Part of the
Institutes: Concerning High Treason and other Pleas of the Crown,* 1644; and *The Fourth Part of the Institutes:
Concerning the Jurisdiction of Courts,* 1644.

In his *Institutes,* Coke modified the judgment he and his fellow judges reached in Calvin's case. Although the judges had referred to the fact that allegiance and protection were mutual bonds, "duplex et reciproci ligamen,"[49] they had also held that allegiance was due to the person of the king, that the king was legitimate or "de jure" by his inherent birthright, and that allegiance due to the legitimate king could not be altered. In his *Institutes,* however, Coke felt that allegiance bore a strict relationship to possession. Consequently the subject owed loyalty to the "seignior le roy" in actual occupation of the throne, whether or not he had a legitimate claim to it. Instead of possession being one of a number of factors to be considered when allegiance was under discussion, it now became the governing principle of allegiance.[50]

IV

Coke in his commentaries upon the common law as it affected the duty of allegiance had provided a variety of material useful to pamphleteers working in the crisis years of the 1640s and 1680s. This paper, however, will only consider the uses made of Coke's legal writings during the constitutional crisis of 1689, when parliament required subjects to take new oaths of allegiance to William and Mary, despite the fact that James II was alive but not in actual occupation of the throne. How then did those who defended the revolutionary settlement and also those who rejected the new settlement use Coke's observations on the immemorial law and ancient constitution to defend their particular contemporary standpoint?

As it becomes increasingly apparent[51] that radical Whig contractual theories of the relationship between ruler and ruled had little appeal to the conservative-minded apologists for the settlement of 1689, so also it would seem that most defenders of the revolution looked to support that defense by reference to the law and ancient constitution of the kingdom. This was certainly true of the Anglican establishment which conformed to the new settlement in church

---

49. *State Trials,* col. 614.

50. Interestingly, the *Institutes* were not published until the civil war when the Long Parliament issued them in 1644. Coke's views on the treason statute were used by the defactoists of the 1650s to defend their allegiance to the "unlawful" power of the Commonwealth and Protectorate. See Wallace, *Destiny,* and John Hall, *The True Cavalier examined by his principles and found not guilty of schism or sedition* (London, 1656), p. 120.

51. See for instance Kenyon, *Historical Perspectives,* pp. 43–69.

and state but nevertheless wished to establish the fact that James's desertion of the realm and the concomitant enthronement of William was constitutionally permissable.

Defenders of the revolution of 1689 were not slow to avail themselves of Coke's treatment of the 1495 treason statute in order to legitimize their submission to William and Mary and to swear new oaths of loyalty to the King and Queen which parliament required. In general the plethora of pamphlets published between 1689 and 1693 that advised loyalty to William and Mary argued that allegiance should only respect possession. In other words, the subject's loyalty should be performed to the actual occupant of the English throne.[52] Daniel Whitby, a "polemical divine," asserted that:

> Allegiance is such a thing that no man may owe to more than one lord. It is the duty that no man owes or by the law should pay, but to his sovereign who in an imperial kingdom can be but one. By the law of the land I am bound to yield obedience to him who is in possession of the land whether he has rightful possession or not.[53]

This position was lawful, the pamphleteers of 1689 argued, because it was defended in the treason statute of 1495 and because the "oracle of the law" (Coke) had ruled that that statute treated allegiance as due only to the king in possession. Influential Anglican supporters of submission to the Williamite cause, like Edward Stillingfleet and William Sherlock, adopted Coke's interpretation of the statute of treason.[54] Toward the end of his *The case of the allegiance,* Sherlock embarked on a prolonged defense of Coke's ruling on the 1495 Statute against the objections propounded by a fictitious Non-Juror.[55]

---

52. For the purposes of this paper discussion is confined to a number of pamphlets published between 1689 and 1691. Their arguments are widely repeated elsewhere. The effective cause of the controversy was *An Act for the abrogating of the Oaths of Supremacy and Allegiance, and appointing other oaths* (1 William and Mary c. VIII). This act removed the Elizabethan oath of Supremacy (1560) and the Jacobean oath of Allegiance (1606) from the statute book and introduced new, much briefer oaths of Allegiance and Supremacy to William and Mary. Failure to take the oaths by 1 August 1689 brought suspension from office ecclesiastical as well as civil, see C. F. Mullet, "Religion, Politics and Oaths in the Glorious Revolution," *Review of Politics* (1948), p. 464.

53. Daniel Whitby, *Considerations humbly offered for taking the oaths of allegiance to King William and Queen Mary* (London, 1689), pp. 3–4. See also *Dictionary of National Biography,* ed. S. Lee, Vol. LXI (1900), p. 28.

54. Edward Stillingfleet was the Bishop of Worcester and contributed *A Discourse Concerning the Unreasonableness of a New Separation . . .* to the controversy in October 1689. William Sherlock was a more controversial figure; he initially refused the oaths of allegiance to William and Mary but later changed his mind. He was appointed Dean of St. Paul's in 1690.

55. The Non-Jurors were those office-holders in church and state who refused to transfer their allegiance from James to William and Mary. They were mainly Anglican churchmen who formed a Non-Juring

Sherlock averred that the oaths of allegiance to William had to be taken in the sense that "courts of justice or learned judges and lawyers give of them, tho we must abide by their judgements when it comes to be tried whether we have broken or kept these laws." [56] Oaths of allegiance, Sherlock felt, were legal oaths, the terms and extent of which were controlled by law and parliament.

In other words, the oaths of allegiance sworn to kings should be judged according to legal and political considerations rather than the potentially more exacting standards set by religion and conscience.[57] The Juring Anglican Tories [58] maintained that subjects ought to swear allegiance to William because constitutional law and its greatest interpreter, Coke, had always defended submission to the king in possession. Such a stance could be further supported by reference to English constitutional history, notably the precedents set during the internecine struggles between the Houses of York and Lancaster in the fifteenth century.

Nevertheless, Sherlock argued that such an approach to allegiance did not undermine the hereditary nature of the English monarchy. Eristically he maintained that the English monarchy was hereditary, but that the possession of the throne could change hands. "The most that can be said," he wrote, "is that when any particular family, by the providence of God and the consent and submission of the people is placed in the throne of right the crown ought to descend to the heir of that family."[59] However, if God's providence altered the succession then allegiance must be paid to the king in possession. In the opinion of lawyers who were best suited to interpret the components of the constitution, England was, Sherlock contended, an "hereditary monarchy with this reserve; of paying allegiance to the king in possession when the legal heir cannot obtain his right."[60]

Daniel Whitby evidently agreed with the stance adopted by fellow Juring Anglicans like Stillingfleet and later by Sherlock, but he attempted to use evi-

---

church in the 1690s. For a discussion of the Non-Jurors see L. M. Hawkins, *Allegiance in Church and State: The Problem of the Nonjurors in the English Revolution* (London, 1928).

56. William Sherlock, *The case of the allegiance due to sovereign powers stated and resolved according to scripture and reason and the principles of the church of England* (London, 2nd edn., 1691).

57. The Jurors also defended their submission to William and Mary on moral grounds. However, they were happier when treating allegiance and the oaths as a matter of law rather than conscience.

58. Those Anglicans who believed they acted constitutionally when they swore allegiance to William and Mary.

59. Sherlock, *The case of the allegiance due to sovereign powers*, p. 57.

60. *Ibid.*

dence drawn from Coke's *Reports* to justify loyalty to the new regime. Interestingly, he employed arguments promulgated by Coke in his report of Calvin's case to justify taking the new oaths of allegiance to William. This attempt, however, ran into severe difficulties when Whitby invoked the notion of the king's "politic capacity" to support his case. When another person becomes "king regnant in possession," Whitby maintained that:

> He [the legitimate king] is legally dead for that time, his political capacity being then separated from the natural person of the king, then must the subjects of England be from their allegiance to him for that time; for though ligeance is due, as was resolved in Calvin's case, to the natural person of the king and not to the political capacity only, yet it is only due to the natural person of the king when it is accompanied with his political capacity for otherwise he could never divest himself of it.[61]

Indeed, this was precisely the type of treatment of the two capacities of the king that the judges, by tying allegiance to the person of the king, had hoped to make impossible.

Whitby also blurred the distinction made by the judges in Calvin's case between natural and legal allegiance to suit his defense of the new oaths. At one point he professed that the subject could swear lawful allegiance to William and Mary, and yet not compromise his natural loyalty to James, a truly creative interpretation of the judges' remarks in Calvin's case.[62] Several pages on, Whitby contradicts this assertion by remarking that legal allegiance is in fact a mere confirmation of natural allegiance. Nevertheless, he felt that although the judges in Calvin's case had declared allegiance to the lawful king natural, natural allegiance itself was not "immutable and indispensable."[63] He based this precept on his radical treatment of the laws of nature, some of whose rules were more binding than others:

> When it is said natural allegiance is due by law of nature it is a law of nature such that does not oblige in all circumstances . . . this law ceases when circumstances cease—when power of protecting, governing and preserving cease without my fault and I can have them from another only on condition of allegiance.[64]

61. Whitby, *Considerations humbly offered*, p. 9.
62. *Ibid.*, p. 17.
63. *Ibid.*, p. 20. This is the opposite of Coke's opinion expressed in Calvin's case, see *State Trials*, col. 630.
64. Whitby, *Considerations humbly offered*, p. 23.

Natural allegiance, Whitby concluded, was based on government and protection and must follow the king in possession:

> When we have lost our governor de jure, and he is out of possession, that we should have government, and we cannot have it but from the king de facto; there must be a necessity that we should yield obedience or allegiance to him.[65]

This pamphlet in fact illustrates the difficulties that some Jurors had with the problem of allegiance to a "de facto" authority.

Daniel Whitby justified submission to King William for the "time being" by creating an implausible distinction between legal and natural allegiance. Other pamphleteers with a better grasp of the nostrums that supported the ancient constitution were more circumspect in their attempts to modify the distinction the judges had drawn between natural and legal allegiance. One anonymous author[66] augmented the nuances in allegiance detected by the judges. The pamphleteer who wrote this *Vindication* argued that the word allegiance was capable of a variety of interpretations. In its weakest form, and the one this writer felt the framers of the new oaths intended, allegiance meant "only such subjection and obedience as is agreeable to the laws."[67] Law was on the side of the king actually in possession. The allegiance sworn to William, moreover, did not conflict with the allegiance sworn to James, as all the subject was performing in both cases was obedience according to the law. The oath to James only implied "legal obedience."[68]

The most telling use of this differentiation between types of allegiance was made by Sherlock. Sherlock asserted that the law of nature dictated the formation of government and society for the general benefit of mankind. Yet nowhere did it decree that a particular king should reign, or form of government prevail.[69] Natural allegiance was due, therefore, to the king in actual administration of government, whether or not that king derived his title from Noah and the patriarchs or was descended from a usurper. It was due to all kings settled in government *per se* and "for that reason to the Prince who governs."[70] Consequently, the form that allegiance took in particular countries,

---

65. *Ibid.*, p. 24.

66. *A vindication of those who have taken the new oath of allegiance to King William and Queen Mary upon principles agreeable to the doctrines of the church of England in a letter to a noble lord* (London, 6 November 1689).

67. *Ibid.*, p. 8.

68. *Ibid.*

69. Sherlock, *The case of the allegiance due to sovereign powers,* p. 28, see also pp. 37–40.

70. *Ibid.*, p. 28.

that is legal allegiance, was mutable. Legal allegiance and the legal oaths which confirmed that allegiance were "due only by law and therefore can oblige no further than human laws do, which must always give way to the law of God."[71] Natural allegiance, Sherlock argued, always took precedence over legal allegiance. The legal allegiance sworn to the king really assumed that the king was in actual possession of the throne. It meant, in fact, no more than to maintain and defend him in possession of the throne, but it did not imply a duty to restore the king to the throne after he had lost or deserted it.

Juring writers in 1689 thus tried to make the revolution conform to the requirements of constitutional law as depicted in Calvin's case and in Coke's *Institutes.* In general they emphasized Coke's treatment of allegiance in the *Institutes* to strengthen their contention that all subjects owed allegiance to the king in possession. When, however, they attempted to incorporate in their books and pamphlets evidence taken from the judgment reached in Calvin's case, they plunged into constitutional difficulty. The judges in Calvin's case had argued that natural allegiance was due to the lawful king descended from the blood royal of the realm, and that although there was a distinction between natural and legal allegiance the latter was essentially a confirmation of the former.[72] The Juring pamphleteers of 1689 put this distinction to a purpose for which it was not intended; they used it to justify their submission to a "de facto" ruler. The one Juring writer who did use this distinction effectively, Sherlock, amputated it from its original context. Sherlock stressed that all allegiance depended on possession. In the Jurors' interpretation of the constitution right would ultimately have to give way to might.

The Non-Jurors, who refused to swear loyalty to the new monarchy of William and Mary, were not slow in condemning the construction that the Jurors had placed on the law as it affected allegiance. Non-Jurors like Theophilius Downes, Charles Leslie and Henry Dodwell looked to past constitutional precedent to show that those who defended the new oaths of allegiance were misguided. The more cynical Non-Jurors like Leslie observed how convenient it was for the Jurors to find that the constitution could be adapted to the requirements of the new monarchy. Pragmatism and expediency appeared more important considerations for the Juror than the more difficult option of following conscience and honor.[73]

71. *Ibid.*
72. *State Trials,* cols. 614, 652.
73. This was the view of Charles Leslie, see for instance his *The Constitution, laws and government of England vindicated in a letter to the Reverend Mr. William Higden* (London, 1709).

The Non-Jurors vigorously denied the Jurors' interpretation of allegiance. Downes,[74] for one, oppugned the view that allegiances could possess varying and apparently contradictory senses. Study of the ancient constitution and its exponents, Cotton, Spelman and Coke, indicated that allegiance derived from the feudal notion of "ligeance." The reason that subjects of the realm were called liegemen of the king was, Downes opined, because of "their persons being under his jurisdiction and protection."[75]

In his argument for unalterable allegiance to the person of the king, based upon the propositions established in Calvin's case, Downes tried to show that allegiance was a positive duty of obedience to be performed at all times to the legitimate monarch whether or not he was in actual possession of the throne. The two types of allegiance that the judges distinguished in Calvin's case were complementary and not contradictory and, Downes believed, always imparted "an obligation to defend our sovereign's crown and dignity, to the utmost of our power, against all persons whatsoever, without any exception; and never to give any assistance or support, to any of his enemies against him."[76] Allegiance, Downes argued, could never be a neutral or negative quality. It required the actual support and assistance of the liegeman: "By true and faithful obedience . . . must be understood all those positive duties of fidelity and obedience which every subject owes his sovereign by virtue of his allegiance."[77]

Allegiance, Downes contended, was a duty that could be borne only to one master. It was impossible for a subject to maintain allegiance to two opposing sovereigns, adherence to one necessarily involved treason to the other. The common law of the realm as established in Calvin's case nowhere obliged men to "cross and contradictory obligations,"[78] and:

> as for those subtle distinctions between a higher and lower kind of allegiance; an allegiance due to a king *de facto,* and another at the same time to a king *de jure;* an absolute and a conditionate, an active and an unactive; a reserving and un-reserving allegiance. I say . . . *ubi lex non distinguit ibi non distinguendum est.*[79]

The fact that allegiance had a legal form, the oath, did not mean that allegiance was circumscribed by the law. It was only called legal allegiance because

---

74. Theophilius Downes (of Balliol College), *A discourse concerning the signification of allegiance as it is to be understood in the new oath of allegiance* (London, 1690).

75. *Ibid.,* p. 7.

76. *Ibid.,* p. 9.

77. *Ibid.,* p. 12.

78. *Ibid.,* p. 13.

79. *Ibid.*

"the law required it of every subject upon oath and had prescribed the form and manner of it."[80] This positive duty of allegiance, Downes asserted, was universally due by all laws, and the oath was exacted from subjects only to confirm that which was due by natural, divine and human law.[81] "The security of the sovereign power," Downes wrote, "being of such vast importance to the preservation of peace and justice, and even to the very being of law, and political society . . . the wisdom of the law has thought it necessary to tie all those obligations faster by the sacred bond of a religious oath."[82]

Allegiance was an essential duty of the subject and subjects had always been required by the ancient constitution to perform an active and unreserved fidelity to the legitimate monarch.[83] In order to emphasize this point Downes quoted the five "excellent things" found by the judges in Calvin's case in the old feudal oath of allegiance. Downes reiterated Coke's view that that oath conveyed an allegiance "neither circumscribed by time nor place, it is unconditionate and unreserved."[84] The oath exacted "an active vigorous loyalty, exacting all that is in the sphere of moral possibility," not a "lazy, passive allegiance" that required nothing but submission.[85]

By basing his conception of allegiance on the ruling given by the judges in Calvin's case, Downes could further argue that allegiance was due only to the king's person and not to his crown or kingdom distinct from his "natural capacity." Legal allegiance was therefore inseparable from the person of the king and a confirmation of the allegiance all subjects owed naturally. Downes again followed Coke's report of Calvin's case in adding that the law of nature that dictated the necessity of allegiance was incompatible with change and alteration. Natural reason had indicated the need for government and taught men the necessity of contributing their actual assistance to the preservation of society and, consequently, to the sovereign power essential to its continuation. In Downes's opinion both the constitution and the commentaries of its most illustrious interpreter clearly showed that the oath of allegiance confirmed an antecedent and unalterable natural allegiance due to the lawful hereditary monarch.

It is a curious fact that while Downes's treatise made no mention of Coke's

80. *Ibid.*
81. *Ibid.*
82. *Ibid.*
83. *Ibid.*
84. *Ibid.*, p. 14.
85. *Ibid.*, p. 18.

views on the treason statute of 1495 other, less reticent, Non-Jurors did not avoid this problem. Charles Leslie, in fact, bitterly criticized Coke's interpretation of allegiance expressed in the *Institutes*. Leslie dismissed the *Institutes* as a spiteful response by Coke to his disgrace at court.[86] In an effort to liberate the laws and government of England from the deliberate misconception of the Jurors, Leslie maintained that the principle of possession, once accepted, effectively subverted the immemorial constitution. The principle of possession rendered all other constitutional considerations irrelevant. It meant that "there remains no other principle in the world, no right, no wrong, no just or unjust, no proof, no examination, no trial."[87] Possession as a justification for the exercise of authority undermined the idea of law and reduced all government to the precept "let us take whatever is uppermost, be it right or wrong!"[88]

Leslie further argued that the favorite historical evidence adduced by the defactoists of 1689 to support their submission to William — the fifteenth-century dynastic struggle between York and Lancaster — actually disproved their contention that authority was based upon possession. York and Lancaster fought so bitterly because they considered right to be on their respective sides:

> Both York and Lancaster did pretend to be next in blood to the crown and so to have the right. But neither of them thought this right could be extinguished by possession, for each of them fought against the other who had got into possession, and set up his "de jure" against the other's "de facto." Could any of them think that de facto and de jure were the same, or that the right was extinguished by possession?[89]

In their treatment both of law and history the Jurors, therefore, had purposely misrepresented and misinterpreted the nature of the ancient constitution. Non-Jurors like Leslie believed that when the law mentioned possession it referred only to a just and lawful possession, not to an arbitrary usurpation.

---

86. Charles Leslie observed that the publication of the *Reports* occurred whilst Coke was still a Chief Justice. The *Institutes*, however, were largely written after his disgrace in 1616. Leslie inferred that after that date Coke was not so favorably disposed to tying allegiance to an indefeasible hereditary right. Leslie, *The Constitution*.

87. *Ibid.,* pp. 75–76.

88. *Ibid.,* p. 52.

89. *Ibid.,* p. 28.

V

Thus, in 1689, both Non-Jurors and Jurors used the ancient constitution and Coke's commentaries upon it selectively, to support their different viewpoints. Those who supported the new regime of King William and Queen Mary had to establish that their assumption of sovereign power was not revolutionary and, above all, had not altered the nature of the constitution. The Non-Jurors who claimed an indefeasible loyalty to the hereditary monarchy found ample justification for their stance in legal judgments like that given in Calvin's case. The problem for the Jurors who tried to use the received body of legal and constitutional ideas to justify the alteration in government was that these ideas were not intended to legitimate change and upheaval.[90] On the other hand, the problem for the Non-Jurors was that they possessed convincing arguments but little support. Moreover, in any preoccupation of this kind with allegiance, being right, but clearly irrelevant, had the long-term effect of discrediting their right. As the new regime became legitimized by time, the Non-Jurors became a disgruntled irrelevance.

90. See Pocock, *Politics, Language and Time,* pp. 209–11.

Sir Edward Coke (1552–1634): His Theory of "Artificial Reason" as a Context for Modern Basic Legal Theory

JOHN UNDERWOOD LEWIS

❧ ❧ ❧

When legal historians attempt to fix the dividing line between medieval and modern theories of law they usually look to the writings of Sir Edward Coke.[1] In his work are to be found both an exposition of English law as it was in his day and the bold outlines of a new jurisprudence that, because of the political pressure brought upon jurists by the conflict between Parliament and Crown over the nature and limitations of prerogative, was forced into existence. In Coke's work, remarked Dean Pound, are to be found the outlines of every point of modern law;[2] and the influence on Anglo-American law of his commentary on the Magna Carta in the second part of his *Institutes* continues to be felt to this day. Except for that commentary—and for the legislation of Edward I—little had been done up to the seventeenth century to forge a system of legal precepts resting upon authoritative texts.

Before Coke had finished, however, this situation had changed radically. His dictum in *Bonham's Case*[3] that "the common law will control acts of parliament, and sometimes adjudge them to be utterly void . . . when . . . against common right and reason" became in the years to follow the single most im-

---

"Sir Edward Coke (1552–1633): His Theory of 'Artificial Reason,'" is reprinted from the *Law Quarterly Review* 84 (July 1968): 330–42. Reprinted by permission of Sweet and Maxwell.

1. *E.g.,* Holdsworth, *Some Makers of English Law* (Cambridge, 1966), VI; *Hist. of English Law* (London, 1924), V., p. 423 *et seq.;* Lévy-Ullmann, *English Legal Tradition* (London, 1935), pp. 142 *et seq.,* 228 *et seq.;* Thorne, "Sir Edward Coke," Selden Soc. Lect. (London, 1957), p. 5 *et seq.*

2. Pound and Plucknett, *Hist. and System of the Common Law* (Rochester, 1927, 3rd ed.), p. 300.

3. (1610) 8 Co.Rep. 114a at 117b–118b.

portant source in English law for the concept of judicial review.[4] It reflects, to give a specific example, the view that the law is the sole source of governmental powers and implies the doctrine that the existence or non-existence of a power is a matter of law, not of fact. This in turn implies that the courts could and should determine whether certain alleged powers exist and to mark off their limits. Such doctrine was inherent in all the seventeenth-century cases on prerogative, as the *Proclamation Case* clearly shows.[5] The Septennial Acts of 1730, in which the courts were forbidden to overrule legislative enactments, in part diminished this doctrine by strengthening the tendency to make parliamentary legislation superior to adjudication; but the notion that previously established common law interpreted by the courts in the light of "reason" is superior to all other was continually expressed until about 1760.[6] Not even then, however, was the test of "reasonableness" to which *Bonham* refers done away with; nor has it ever ceased to function. "Due process of law," for example, applies in America, if not in England, to substantive rather than merely procedural law; and such law is said there to violate "due process" precisely in so far as it is unreasonable.[7]

This "reasonable" element in law of which Coke wrote, and which is the focal point for legal historians seeking to understand how a relatively smooth transition was made possible at the end of the Tudor period from a legal world that saw little parliamentary activity in the making of law to one that saw much, is also of interest to the legal philosopher. He wants to understand the nature of law itself and to explain why and under what conditions men have an obligation to obey it; and when he runs into the claim that law, to be law, must be "reasonable" he knows that he has come across a definition and theory of law in which intellect rather than the Sovereign's will holds an exalted place. This is exactly what Coke thought. "Law," he wrote, "is perfect reason, which commands those things that are proper and necessary and which prohibits contrary things";[8] and the mere fact that it might have been willed by an authority to be law was in his view relatively unessential to its

---

4. Smith, "Dr. Bonham's Case and the Modern Significance of Lord Coke's Influence," 41 Wash.L.R. 297 at 313.

5. (1611) 12 Co.Rep. 74 at 75.

6. Corwin, "The Establishment of Judicial Review," 9 Mich.L.R. 102 at 104. Plucknett puts the "technical end" of the courts' check by "reason" on parliamentary legislation at 1688 (the Revolution): "*Bonham's Case* and Judicial Review," 40 Harvard L.R. 30 at 53.

7. Goodhart, "Law of the Land," *Magna Carta Essays* (Charlottesville, Va., 1966), p. 38 *et seq.*

8. Inst. I. (Thomas, ed. London, 1818), Vol. I, p. 15; folio paging 319b.

nature and, in the last analysis, beside the point in explaining why men ought to obey it.[9]

This sounds to us like strange doctrine. For it is common knowledge today that Parliament could at any time, simply by the exercise of its sovereign power, reduce the phrase "supremacy of law" to mere words;[10] and to those who are accustomed to looking at the nature of law through the eyes of Austin, Coke's conception of law is either unintelligible or, at best, woefully inadequate. Sovereign will fails even to gain mention, much less predominance, in his definition. Then too, his idea that the "reasonableness" of law is somehow the source of its binding force is quite out of step with the powerful movement in English jurisprudence to think of legal obligation as created by some social fact—such as the "social contract" described by Locke or the "habitual obedience" to the Sovereign pointed to by Austin or, simply, the "recognition" of the law's validity that Professor Hart has singled out.

Any attempt to understand Coke's conception of law from the standpoint of nineteenth- or twentieth-century analytical jurisprudence, however, is self-defeating. Nor should this be surprising. Definitions of law in terms of sovereign will and the theories of its binding force entailed by them made a relatively late appearance in the history of jurisprudence—certainly long after Coke's time. The fact that Hobbes held such doctrine demands that this statement be qualified, of course, but it is true to say that for the most part the "command theory" of law was foreign to medieval and early modern thought.[11] Indeed, even the idea that law could be something consciously made was seldom held; it was conceived of, rather, as a body of declared custom that had been authoritatively approved.[12] This notion carried well into the Tudor period. There were, it is true, instances in which law was thought to be made rather than declared, and this is evidenced by *Chudleigh's Case* in 1589.[13] But such cases are exceptions, not the rule. It was not until the nineteenth century that command theories of law could even begin either from the standpoint of

9. In contrast to his near contemporaries Bodin (1530–96) and Hobbes (1588–1679). See below, p. 113 *et seq.*

10. Wade, "The Basis of Legal Sovereignty" [1955] *Cambridge Law Journal* 172 at 196. McIlwain, "Sovereignty in the Present World," 1950 *History* (N.S.) 1 at 9 *et seq.; cf.* Gough, *Fundamental Law in English Const. Hist.* (Oxford, 1961), p. 211 *et seq.*

11. Goodhart, "An Apology for Jurisprudence," *Interpretations of Modern Legal Philosophies* (N.Y., 1947), pp. 283, 284.

12. von Mehren, "The Judicial Conception of Legislation," *ibid.* at p. 751.

13. 1 Co.Rep. 113b at 131a.

doctrine or in relation to the working of law to hold their own in the battle over whether law is more accurately and illuminatingly defined in terms of reason or sovereign will.[14]

This question of whether law itself is a product of reason or of will is still being disputed. So is the question of whether the source of men's obligation to obey it resides primarily in the maker's will or in the content of the law he makes.[15] For this reason an examination of Coke's definition of law is of more than historical interest. In spite of this, the only full assessment of it seems to have been made by Hobbes.[16] Sir Matthew Hale's reply to Hobbes' critique could, perhaps, be said to constitute an exception here,[17] but his abilities are thought by some to have been better exercised in legal history and common law than in jurisprudence. Lévy-Ullmann claims, for example, that when Hobbes transferred the topic of law from the legal to the philosophical domain, Hale lost his way.[18] It might be remarked, though, that perhaps the fault for this lay not with Hale, but with Coke. His First *Institute,* which is his commentary on Littleton's *Tenures* and in which the bulk of his basic theory of law is to be found, is in Holdsworth's words a "legal encyclopaedia arranged on no plan except that suggested by the words and sentences of Littleton."[19] It is more rather than less difficult to read than Littleton's bare text.

The effort to read Coke, however, should be made. For in the history of jurisprudence since the thirteenth century, thinking about the nature of law has polarized around two basically incompatible points of view, and Coke holds a "pure" version of one of them. According to the first, law is portrayed as an act of will that derives its binding force from the threat of sanction; in the other it is held to be a rational ordinance or directive judgment, commanding obedience to itself primarily because what it directs the citizens to do is reasonable and in that sense just. As can be seen from a glance at Coke's definition of law as "perfect reason," he adopts this latter position. He did not, however, hold it in order to defend the typically continental but un-English doctrine that municipal laws contrary to the Laws of Nature have no binding

---

14. *Cf.* Lewis, *Mediaeval Political Ideas* (London, 1954), p. 1; Brecht, *Political Theory* (Princeton, 1959), p. 138 *et seq.*

15. *E.g.,* the Hart-Fuller exchange in 71 Harvard L.R.; Hughes, "The Existence of a Legal System," 35 N.Y.Univ.L.R. 1001; Shuman, *Legal Positivism* (Detroit, 1963), Chaps. 1, 4–6.

16. "Dialogue of the Common Laws," *Works* (Molesworth, ed., 1840), VI, p. 25 *et seq.*

17. (1609–76). Hale's rebuttal is printed in full: Holdsworth, H.E.L. V, p. 500 *et seq.*

18. *Op. cit.* p. 229. But Holdsworth disagrees: H.E.L. V, p. 478 *et seq.*

19. *Makers,* p. 123.

force. Before dealing with this point in detail, the political context in which his idea of law was operative is relevant.

Coke's major contribution to the political and historical development of law lay in his insistence upon preserving the medieval idea of the supremacy of law during an age when "political speculation was tending to assert the necessity of the supremacy of a sovereign person or body, which was above the law. . . ."[20] The Stuarts' notion of the divine right to rule was, of course, instrumental in strengthening this tendency; and the precise issue Coke faced was over royal prerogative—whether it could be controlled by Parliament and what, if any, its limits were. In so far as this was an issue over sovereignty it was between the "high court of Parliament" and the King.[21] But, because Coke thought that the powers of Parliament were, or should be, identically those of the common law,[22] the issue in which he was involved can also be described as the "conflict between the royal prerogative and the common law."[23]

It is this identification of parliamentary jurisdiction with the authority of the common law that makes his definition of law so important not only to the historian who wants to understand the relation that was thought to exist in the seventeenth century between common law and "fundamental law," or to the political theorist who seeks a way critically to discuss the problem of whether or how limitations can be placed on sovereign rule; it is also important to the legal philosopher. For he can look to Coke's definition of law to gain an insight into what, ideally at least, law is, and then use that ideal, much, for example, as Bentham did in his own way with the principle of utility, to evaluate the aims and content of legislation. Coke's own utilization of common law for this purpose is perhaps nowhere more clearly shown than in *Rowles* v. *Mason* (1612).[24] The common law, he declared, "corrects, allows, and disallows both Statute Law and Custom, for if there be repugnancy in a statute, or unreasonableness in Custom, the Common Law disallows and rejects it. . . ." His aim here is clear: it was to keep the law up to date; and to this end, says Holdsworth, he adapted "medieval common law—envisaged as such primarily through the Magna Carta—to the needs of his own newly emerging society."[25]

20. *Ibid.* at p. 126.
21. Gough, p. 48 *et seq.*
22. 2 Co.Inst. 626. *Cf.* Thorne, "Courts of Record and Sir Edward Coke," 2 U. Toronto L.J. 24 at 48 *et seq.*
23. Goodhart, *op. cit.*, n. 7 *supra*, p. 42.
24. (1612) 2 Brownl. 198 (C. B.).
25. *Sources and Lit. of English Law* (Oxford, 1925), p. 140.

Coke's definition of law as "perfect reason, which commands those things that are proper and necessary, and which prohibits contrary things" has been one of the most persisting and fruitful definitions of law that has ever been given, and parallels those set down by, for example, Cicero, Aristotle, Bracton, Gerson, Grotius, Aquinas and Hooker.[26] Nor is it an outmoded view; for some writers today such as Fuller, Hall and Davitt, S. J., remain in one way or another faithful to it.[27] There is, however, an ambiguity in Coke's version that prompts a question. What does he mean when he says that law is "perfect reason"? Does he mean, as Aquinas for instance did, that law is an "ordinance of reason,"[28] a directive judgment that guides men in their choice of means to be used in the attainment of social goals?[29] It is difficult to say; for when Coke defines law in terms of reason he seems to be referring to its *reasonableness* rather than, as Aquinas did, to its being essentially a rule or principle of human action. Lending support to this interpretation is the fact that when he comments on Littleton's use of the word "rule" he says it means "maxim" or "principle" or "axiom."[30] But a principle in law is not thought by Coke to be a starting-point for action, a directive judgment that orders means to ends in the sphere of human activity. It is conceived of, rather, as a starting-point "from which many *cases* have their . . . beginning."[31] What he seems to be concerned with here, in other words, is the internal logical consistency of English law as a system and not, primarily, with a defense of the notion that a law should be defined in terms of reason rather than will because, being essentially a directive, its creation depends upon the maker's intellectual perception of factual, objective relationships between means and ends, relationships that are neither formally dependent upon nor constituted by an act of will. To look at Coke's work this way helps to explain why he makes such statements as "ancient principles of law ought not be disputed."[32]

However, if it is the law's reasonableness rather than its characteristic of

26. *Cf.* Thomas' ed. of Inst. I (Vol. I, p. 15; folio 319b), where Suarez is also listed. But for Suarez law is "the act of a just and right will . . .": De Leg. I, p. 5, n. 26.

27. Fuller, *op. cit., The Law in Quest of Itself* (Boston, 1966), pp. 1–43; *The Morality of Law* (N. Haven, 1964), Chaps. 1, 3; Davitt, *The Elements of Law* (Boston, 1959), Pt. 2; Hall, *Living Law* (Indianapolis, 1949), Chaps. 1, 2; *Studies in Jurisprudence* (N.Y., 1958), Chaps. 1–3. Davitt refuses to push his theory to the point of holding without qualification that "an unjust law is no law" (*Elements*, p. 82 *et seq.*). Perhaps unfortunately, Fuller takes the contrary view. See below, p. 119.

28. *Summa Theol.,* pp. 1–2, 90, 4c.

29. *Ibid.* at p. 90, 1c. *Cf.* Davitt, "Law as Means to End—Thomas Aquinas," 14 Vanderbilt L.R. 65.

30. Inst. I, p. 17 (11a).

31. *Ibid.* at p. 17 (34a); italics mine.

32. *Ibid.*

being a directive judgment that is foremost in Coke's mind, a new question arises. Hobbes was the first to ask it, and it was meant to strike at the heart of Coke's theory of law. If the quality of being reasonable is the hallmark of good laws, why could not ordinary men formulate them just as easily as lawyers? "Though it be true," Hobbes says, "that no man is born with the use of reason, yet all men may grow up to it as well as lawyers; and when they have applied their reason to the laws . . . may be as fit for and capable of judicature as Sir Edward Coke himself."[33] This criticism of Coke miscarries somewhat, perhaps because the purely analytical vantage-point from which he levelled it prevented him from appreciating fully the fact that Coke had selected a definition of law that could serve both to settle the problem of royal prerogative (not, admittedly, in a way that was satisfactory to the Crown), and to impose some semblance of order upon a legal system that was quickly coming apart at the seams. It does have the merit, however, of forcing into the open the need to determine exactly what Coke means when he says that reason constitutes the essence of law.

In order to accomplish this it is necessary to refer again to the fact that until the Tudor period law was thought of as "declared" rather than consciously made. Only God, it was supposed, could make real law—which He then embodied in custom. This outlook was operative only in relation to substantive law, of course, not to procedural law; for, indeed, it was by the use of writs that the common law was centralized and developed by the King, and for centuries legal treatises themselves were nothing more than collections of writs with a few added comments.[34] By 1550, however, parliamentary activity in making law was intensified; and because Parliament was then essentially a "high court," the need for a system of *stare decisis* was fast becoming pressing. This is nowhere better verified, perhaps, than in *Wimbish* v. *Tailbois*,[35] which dealt with the Statute of Uses enacted by the Parliaments of Henry VIII. In it the court was faced with the unhappy task of reconciling the conflicting notions that rights in property were static and that Parliament had the power to interfere with private rights. It was only the tendency to look at enacted law in such cases in terms of reason and equity that prevented English law from losing what little systematic character it possessed. Then, within the two decades that followed 1569, this tendency was made irreversible; for in that year Bracton

33. *Works,* VI, p. 14.
34. Harding, *Social Hist. of English Law* (London, 1966), p. 195 *et seq.*
35. (1550) 1 Pl. 38 at 54–60 (C.B.).

was printed. He had said three centuries earlier that "the law makes the King," and that "there is no king where will rules and not the law"[36] and this time what he said found acceptance. In *Ratcliff's Case,*[37] for example, the common law was said to rest upon the law of God, while in *Harbert's Case*[38] it was held to be in keeping with the "perfection of reason." During this same period the common law was also being referred to as "fundamental law."

In order to reconcile the often-times conflicting directions in which customary and enacted law were moving, however, it was not enough simply to rely upon "reason and equity" in individual, isolated cases as they came before the Bench. What was demanded in these circumstances at the end of the sixteenth century if English law was to exist as a unified system was a technique of binding precedents. Somehow, someone had to find a principle that could be used to survey the vast array of judicial "examples" that had been accumulating since early medieval times and that would enable jurists to select those that could serve as broad precedents. Coke provided it. His definition of law as "perfect reason" became the standard against which the facts of law were measured. It was the core of his theory of precedent, and he used it to forge an aggressive, internally consistent common law that could—and did—serve as a powerful weapon against royal prerogative.[39] That he may have employed his standard in radically unhistorical ways, as instanced by the "precedents" he called upon in *Bonham,* is in the last analysis unimportant here. What he wanted to do, what he thought needed to be done, was to make Parliament the judicial body of pre-eminence that it had been in the fourteenth century: to make it the highest court in the realm and the "very apex of the common law."[40] From *Bonham* on, then, the test of "reasonableness" became supreme; and the move in *Nichols* v. *Nichols* (1576)[41] towards firmly establishing the principle that "it is the office of the judges to expound the words of an act of parliament so that they may agree with equity and good conscience" was finally completed.

In order to understand why Coke's definition of law was able to serve as the technical instrument for building a system of *stare decisis* and to see why it was able to unite the aims of Parliament with those of the common law as

---

36. *De Legibus,* fo. 107.
37. (1592) 3 Co.Rep. 37 at 40a.
38. (1586) 3 Co.Rep. 11b at 13b.
39. Harding, pp. 204, 214, 223.
40. Thorne, "Courts of Record," p. 48 *et seq.*
41. (1576) 2 Pl. 477 at 487.

it was then understood, it is necessary to analyse in some detail his concept of "reasonableness." After all, the thesis that "reason" should guide the making and interpreting of law had been presented and defended at least as early as Bracton. There must, one suspects, have been something unusual about Coke's conception of it. There was; and the sense in which it was can readily be seen in the light of the brief historical sketch just drawn of the events and thinking about law that preceded his own definition of it.

When Coke used the terms "reason" and "reasonable" to define law he did so not so much in order to make the point, as some medievals did, that law is a body of directive judgments that serve to guide certain kinds of social activity, but in order to provide a principle that could give English law an internal consistency. To this the following point can now be added: when Coke asserted that the essence of law is "reason" he was not referring, as Hobbes clearly seems to have thought, to the reasoning that is engaged in by just anyone. In his theory of law it is not a question of whether the man in the street is able to reason about legal matters as well as a Chief Justice can; for when he wrote that *nihil quod est contra rationem est licitum,*[42] this was not to be understood as referring to every man's "natural" reason but to that *legitima ratio,* which he described as the result of long study, observation and experience. This is borne out by the following text:

> Reason is the life of the law, nay, the common law itself is nothing else but reason; which is to be understood of an artificial perfection of reason, gotten by long study . . . , and not of every man's natural reason. . . . This legal reason *est summa ratio.* And therefore if all the reason that is dispersed into many several heads were united into one, yet could he not make such a law as the law of England is; because by many successions of ages, it hath been . . . refined by an infinite number of grave and learned men, and by long experience grown to such a perfection for the government of this realm, as the old rule may be justly verified of it, *Neminem opportet esse sapientiorem legibus:* no man (out of his own private reason) ought to be wiser than the law, which is the perfection of reason.[43]

This text sheds light back upon the dictum in *Bonham* that when parliamentary legislation is "against common right and reason" the established common law will control it. Indeed, so exalted was Coke's opinion of common law that he equated it even with the Law of Nature, with the law of reason. "Funda-

42. Inst. I, p. 19, (97b).
43. *Ibid.* at p. 1 (97b); Coke's parentheses.

mental law," "reasonableness" and the common law are thus not only unified but identified; and although this may be shocking to those who see in his work the continuation of the traditional notion of natural law displayed in the works of medieval thinkers and in Saint Germain's *Dialogues Between the Doctor and the Student* (*c.* 1581), the words are Coke's:

> . . . the jurisdiction of [the Court of Star Chamber] dealeth not with any offence, that is not *malum in se,* against the common law, or *malum prohibitum,* against some statute.[44]

That Coke does not use the concept of "reason" the way the medievals did, however, and that, unlike them, he does not equate "fundamental law" with the orthodox sense of "higher" or "natural" law ought not be surprising. For whereas the basic disputes in legal theory during the Middle Ages centered upon the related psychological questions of whether man's rational power has a primacy over his will in the performance of practical activities such as law-making and of whether the natural law is based upon divine reason or God's expressed will, the problems that Coke had to grapple with were of an altogether different nature. The political events of his time had brought the issue of royal prerogative to a head while the rapidly increasing quantity of legislation enacted by Parliament sharply intensified the need to find a way of reconciling it with previously accepted custom. To these difficulties Coke's insistence upon the supremacy of law, coupled with the maxim that law is "perfect reason," brought a brilliant solution. By its application he was able to translate medieval common law into modern without forcing a break between the two. "Coke's books," Maitland wrote in a personal letter to Holdsworth, "are the great dividing line, and we are hardly out of the Middle Age till he has dogmatized its results."[45] He remolded the medieval common law in such a way that "it was made fit to bear rule in the modern English state."[46]

This is not to say, however, that Coke's notion of law is free of shortcomings. His view that law is to be defined in terms of "perfect reason," while sound in theory, may in practice be both deceptive and dangerous. For rules that are true in the abstract may turn out to be false in concrete situations.[47] This is especially true when, as in Coke's case, principles of law are understood to be

---

44. Inst. IV, p. 63.
45. Holdsworth, *Makers,* p. 129.
46. *Ibid.* at p. 132.
47. *Cf.* Sir William Jones, *Essay on the Law of Bailments* (1781), p. 60. Sir William's reference is not to Coke himself but to the position generally.

indisputable axioms[48] from which particular laws are to be deduced with certitude. Furthermore, his basic theory of law is conservative in the extreme and can, if mishandled, lead to a situation in which the law loses touch with social reality. With the economic and political explosions of the nineteenth century that is what happened; and it took a Bentham to come to grips with the fact.

The point has now been reached where it is possible to determine Coke's place in the history of basic legal theory. Many editors of readings in jurisprudence have already attempted to do this, of course; and when they came to Coke they often listed him among those writers for whom law is a product of reason rather than will. His definition of law as "perfect reason commanding those things that are proper and necessary" has been grouped with the definitions of men such as Cicero, Bracton, Aquinas and Hooker. But to place him this way can be misleading, and for two reasons. First, although it is true that Coke does hold in common with writers such as Aquinas and Hooker the view that law is a product of the law maker's intellect rather than will, he does so for a reason quite different from theirs. When someone such as Aquinas, for example, says that law is a work of reason he does so because he thinks that the primary function of law is to guide or direct men to act in ways necessary for attaining or preserving the "common good" and that what those ways are can be determined only by the law maker's reasoned judgments, not by mere fiat.[49] For Coke, on the other hand, law is a work of reason in this sense, that it is the nature of law to be reasonable; and the test of its reasonableness, he thinks, is its ability to withstand the test of time.

Secondly, Coke's concept of law entails a theory about the nature of legal obligation that is markedly different from that held by a writer like Aquinas. According to Aquinas, the obligation men have to obey a law is a moral one.[50] A law is meant to make clear to those subject to it what means will lead them to the "common good"; and once perceiving that relationship of means to end they ought freely to act accordingly.[51] Because Coke does not consider law in these terms, however, he does not think this way. In his view, the obligation men have to obey a law stems from its "reasonableness"; and whether the law in question is reasonable is to be determined by whether or not it conforms to

48. Inst. I, p. 16 (67a).
49. *Summa Theol.*, pp. 1–2, 90, 1 and 4; and p. 99, 1.
50. *Ibid.* at pp. 1–2, 96, 4. This does not mean that for Aquinas moral obligation is legal obligation, nor that there is no distinction between the two. It means that there is no such thing as "purely penal" laws. *Cf.* Davitt, *Elements*, p. 191 *et seq.*
51. For a detailed consideration see *ibid.* at p. 78 *et seq.*

settled opinion. "The wisdom of the judges and sages of the law," he wrote, "have always suppressed new and subtle inventions in derogation of the common law. And therefore the judges say . . . we will not change the law which always hath been used."[52]

After Coke's time, his conception of law moved through history in the thought of men such as Lord Mansfield (1705–93), whose decisions as Chief Justice of the Court of King's Bench ensured the continuity of the common law's development amidst the gigantic changes wrought by the Industrial Revolution and the ideas of Bentham, even as Coke's own work guaranteed its continuity during the age of the Renaissance and Reformation and of the great inception of Roman law into the English system.[53] A statute, Mansfield argued in *Omychund* v. *Barker* (1744), "can seldom take in all cases, therefore the common law that works itself pure by rules drawn from the fountain of justice is for this reason superior to an Act of Parliament";[54] and his continual references to notions like "eternal justice," as in *Towers* v. *Barnett* (1786),[55] were, as Winfield suggests, high-minded ways of talking about "what is reasonable."[56] The lasting influence of this principle was concretely attested to by Lord Wright in the *Fibrosa* case (1942):

> . . . any civilised system of law is bound to provide remedies for cases of what has been called unjust enrichment or unjust benefit, that is, to prevent a man from retaining . . . some benefit . . . which it is against conscience that he should keep. . . . The standard of what is against conscience in this context has become more or less . . . defined, but in substance the juristic concept remains as Lord Mansfield left it.[57]

Although the concept of "reasonableness" has continued to play a powerful role in English law, it has never had a single meaning. The attempt to show how wide its variety of meanings is would be beyond the scope of this paper,[58] but at least two of the ways it has been defined should be mentioned. The first, best expressed perhaps by Sir Frederick Pollock, is that "what is reasonable" refers to "an ideal standard, which . . . is none other than that general consent of right minded and rightly informed men which our ancestors in the pro-

---

52. Inst. I, p. 21 (282b).
53. Holdsworth, *Makers,* p. 175.
54. *Ibid.* at p. 166.
55. 1 Term Rep. 133 at 134.
56. Winfield, *Law of Quasi-Contracts* (1952), p. 20.
57. *Fibrosa Spolka Akcyjna* v. *Fairbairn Lawson Combe Barbour Ltd.* [1943] A.C. 32 at 61, 63.
58. See Winfield, "Ethics in English Case Law," 45 Harvard L.R. 112 at 125.

fession called reason. . . . In modern terms, we say that the duty of the court is to keep the rules of law in harmony with the enlightened common sense of the nation."[59] Pollock's emphasis here upon "enlightened common sense" and "right-minded and rightly informed men" brings his formulation of the standard quite close to Coke's, with its stress upon "perfect reason." In the second definition, the standard of "reasonableness" is taken to be simply what the average member of the community thinks is reasonable. An instance of this use is found in *Barker* v. *Herbert* (1911),[60] where it was stated that the common law "is, or ought to be, the common sense of the community." Whenever "reasonableness" is understood in this way, however, it is usually necessary to determine what the common sense of the community is before any decisions can be handed down; and in the attempt to do this it is, significantly, often necessary to tighten or restrict the standard itself. Thus in *Donoghue* v. *Stevenson* (1932),[61] the key decision in our day regarding the question whether the manufacturer of an article is under a duty to third persons to take "reasonable care" to see that his article is free from harmful defects, Lord Atkin contracted "*general* public sentiment" to "*sound* common sense."[62] With this contraction of the standard we are brought back to Pollock's view—and to Coke's.

Even more illustrative of the importance of "reasonableness" to English law than the fact that it has actually been employed by the courts is the further fact that directions for its use have been included in a number of statutes. The Adoption Act 1950,[63] for example, and the Variation of Trusts Act 1958[64] show this quite clearly. To say, however, that most laws are reasonable, at least in intention, is not to imply that it is logically impossible to define law in terms of sovereign will—as Fuller, for example, seems to hold.[65] That such definitions were formulated in Coke's own time by Bodin, and by Hobbes, who directly criticized Coke, is evidence enough for this; and the evidence is strengthened when the names of Bentham, Austin and, in our own day, Kelsen are added to the list.

There are, however, two ways in which Coke's definition of law and those similar to it can be seen to be superior to those given in terms of sovereign will. In the first place, whereas definitions in terms of "reasonableness" are

59. "Judicial Caution and Valour" (1929) 45 L.Q.R. 293 at 294.
60. [1911] 2 K.B. 633 at 644.
61. [1932] A.C. 562.
62. [1932] A.C. at p. 599; italics mine.
63. s. 5 (2).
64. s. 1 (1).
65. In, *e.g.*, The Morality of Law, p. 123 *et seq.*

able on their own merits to provide a basis upon which the courts can work toward equitable decisions and the enhancement of truly human interests,[66] definitions in terms of sovereign will are not. In order to show how worthwhile social goals can be reached, or indeed, even whether there are any such goals, such definitions must look to some principle—as, for example, the notion of utility—lying outside and not logically entailed by their content. In a definition like Coke's, however, the values of fairness and justice either comprise the very meaning or "reasonableness" in law or are properties that flow from it.

Secondly, a definition of law in terms of "reasonableness" is better able than a voluntaristic one of giving a realistic account of legal obligation. The proposition that a man ought to obey a law because what it directs him to do is reasonable can readily be seen to be more defensible than the view that his obligation flows from a sovereign will; for when the reason given for obedience to a law is simply the ruler's wish that it be obeyed, what ought to be done in the legal order comes to be equated with what is enforceable. This is, of course, the "bad man" theory of law; and while it may explain why bad men do in fact obey laws, it cannot by itself explain why they ought to. Nor, more importantly, can it explain why good men obey them.

If pursued to the end, these questions about the nature of law and legal obligation can be seen to be ultimately extra-legal: they can be answered fully only if the conceptions of man and human society which they presuppose as their framework are made explicit. For law is made by men to serve them; their nature determines its purpose. Once its purpose has been determined according to the demands of man's nature, however, it is the law, not men, that ought to be sovereign. Sir Edward Coke saw this more clearly than most.

66. Dowrick, *Justice According to English Common Lawyers* (London, 1961), p. 29.

Further Reflections on "Artificial Reason"

CHARLES M. GRAY

☙ ☙ ☙

One property gained by intense training in English law (besides sharpening of common intellectual faculties and stored-up knowledge of rules, cases, research methods, etc.) is an "aesthetic" feel for the system that operates as a control on stock responses. An initiate possessed of this property will sometimes be disposed to resolve first-impression cases in a different way than an exemplary lay reasoner (whether a better way is perhaps a hard question). Here the ordinary modern use of "art" may be a guide: A lawyer is an "artist," not only in the sense that he has a *techne* or skill, and not only in the sense that he deals primarily with man-made or "artificial" law that cannot be known by deduction from universal truths, but also in the sense that long acquaintance with a certain type of artifact has given him a refined sense of "what fits," of what response is correct on an unexpected occasion. Analogously, I daresay if you asked me to choose among a number of alternative bars of music to follow some I had just heard, I would not make the same choice—within a limited range of subtlety—as a jury of symphony players. I would probably avoid crude errors, such as choosing a snatch of Sousa to continue a Beethoven quartet. But offered several plausible answers, I daresay I would not be able to tell the difference, and in effect would decide by tossing a coin, or else I would pick something too obvious—not necessarily something disastrously cacophonous, but not what the experts would agree is most truly consonant with what went before.

Let us look at just one of Coke's examples. There was a rule that if A disseises B and dies, and A's heir enters, B may not reenter on A's heir, but is

"Further Reflections on 'Artificial Reason'" is reprinted from Perez Zagorin, ed., *Culture and Politics from Puritanism to the Enlightenment* (Berkeley: University of California Press, 1980). © 1980 The Regents of the University of California. Reprinted by permission.

driven to his writ of entry—i.e., must sue to recover the land, or assume the plaintiff's role in a trial of the title. An exception to this rule held that B does not lose his right of reentry if he makes continual claim—i.e., does enough (whatever exactly counts) to avoid the appearance of acquiescing in the disseisin. A further exception held that B does not lose his right of reentry if he is abroad in the king's service when he is disseised, even though he has not made continual claim. The idea, obviously, is that somebody overseas does not have a fair chance to know that he has been disseised and thus to exercise the option of continual claim. His being abroad, moreover, is not of his own choice, but pursuant to duty. Therefore it cannot be objected that in going abroad he undertakes the risk of being damaged while he is away. In addition, the law ought to show a certain bias in favor of good soldiers off fighting the king's wars. As between two innocent parties—an heir who has entered on his ancestor's apparent property and an old soldier disseised by the other party's ancestor—it is fair enough to tip the balance toward the old soldier.

Now comes the case of someone disseised when he is abroad on his own business. The right answer is that this man is to be treated like the old soldier: he may reenter on the disseisor's heir even though he has not made continual claim. Obviously he is somewhat in the same case as the old soldier and somewhat not. He cannot have made continual claim as easily as someone at home. However, he can be said to have incurred the risk by going abroad voluntarily. He will not suffer a terrible loss if we hold against him. He will only suffer the necessity of bringing suit to recover his own, if it is his own. There is no policy reason, analogous to "veteran's benefit," to favor him.

This is the kind of situation in which I suspect Coke of thinking that the layman is likely to jump the wrong way, not from lack of intelligence or of a clear enough appreciation for the *basic* equities, but from a lack of refined sense for what "feels right" in the whole setting of English law. The layman may be too inclined to "toss a coin" or to see the choice as "tragic" or trivial, a matter of throwing a certain inconvenience onto one or the other of two parties, neither of whom is morally blameworthy. Or the layman may be too inclined to the "gross" solution of favoring the mainline rule: on the whole, the law makes people bring suit when they wait around until their disseisors die. It makes some exceptions, but the best policy is usually not to make exceptions if it can be helped. It can be helped here on *cessante ratione* grounds. Since the special considerations applying to old soldiers don't apply here, it is better not to analogize the cases.

Now, perhaps the lay solution is less than a disaster. If the law went that way it would probably not quarrel with the law of nature or lose its right to hold up its head in foreign company. The solution is not disastrous, just a little inartistic. Why? Well, the "sensitive" approach is to emphasize the way in which the old soldier's case and the foreign traveler's *are* alike—neither can easily make continual claim. But isn't that just an arbitrary choice of which aspect to emphasize?

Here we reach the interesting touches in Coke's analysis. He classifies the sensitive argument in this case as the argument *ab impossibile,* and considers it related to more obvious instances, as where the law does not enforce self-imposed duties impossible of performance: The foreign traveler *can't* make continual claim, so don't hold it against him when he doesn't. Part of the point depends on a relationship with more obvious instances: isn't it a little jarring to hold that people need not perform promises that turn out to be impossible for reasons beyond their control, and at the same time to hit a man who might have helped himself by making continual claim but couldn't? Is it coherent to throw the risk on the foreign traveler in our case and yet not to make promisors insurers against acts of God? The spirit of the approach begins to emerge: The "artist" will look beyond the immediate context, to coherence with more remote areas of the legal system. The right answer must harmonize with chords the lay judge will not hear.

Another step increases the subtlety. Coke recognizes that "impossibility" is slippery. Sometimes when we talk about the impossible in law, we refer, not to what is literally impossible, but to what it is unfair to expect, including what it is unfair to expect people to anticipate when they make contracts or go on vacations in Paris. With this in mind, the foreign traveler's side in our case will seem to weaken. It is not literally impossible in every case for a disseisee visiting in France to find out about the disseisin and hurry home in time to make continual claim. People in England may have equally good hardluck stories— as if I am disseised in Yorkshire while lying sick at Brighton—but we don't excuse them on grounds of impossibility. In most cases, if foreign travelers left their affairs at home in reliable hands they would find out about disseisins in reasonable time. The law might stretch a point as to what counts as continual claim; for instance, if a man asks his friends to inform him of disseisins and, being informed, takes steps as quickly as possible, we'll say he has done as much as need be to make continual claim. But why be sorry for someone who has tarried abroad for ten years and wanders home to find his affairs in a mess? Why treat him like old soldiers, who, though they may find out about disseisins, really can't take steps to protect themselves, at least not without unthinkable violation of duty? So the pendulum seems to be swinging back to the "vulgar" solution.

But then the artist thinks of something more remote. It so happens that English law holds it impossible for juries to find events alleged to have taken place abroad. Plainly, this is legal impossibility, not realistic impossibility. Juries proceeding on evidence obviously can make reasonable judgments about whether something happened in France. But by presumption of law they "cannot"—a presumption reflecting the ancient theory of the jury. It would be incoherent for the law to presume that juries are as incapable of determining foreign facts as blind men of seeing, and yet for it to take note of the realistic possibility that visitors to France are not hopelessly incapable of keeping informed about their interests in England and getting home fast when they are in danger. If English law is blind to France in one respect, so—for the sake of artistic coherence—must it be in others. If juries cannot conclude from the testimony of twelve bishops that a contract was made in France, the law must say that for all it knows there are no post offices in France, and all sojourners in that country are stuck in insuperable mud.

Needless to say, one man's art is another man's silliness. I think, however, that the example is of the type of several others in Coke. If one wants to use general everyday language about the example, one might say that a spirit of "generosity" can be picked up from the study of a lot of English legal rules and situations—a tendency not to insist on formalisms, on various kinds of "strictness," on rules that disable from doing what comes naturally, at least when people haven't a sporting chance to avoid them. Such a tendency might reflect the same contingent "national character" that Sir Thomas Smith, for example (in his *De Republica Anglorum*), invoked to account for various features of English law: The English are a rustic, active race, and a "generous" one. (This includes shadows of older senses of generous, not just "liberal"/"lenient," but "magnanimous," "possessed by a kind of carelessness that is both aristocratical and rural.") Folks that get disseised are inclined to go out and take it back. There are good reasons for restraining them if they wait too long and propose to dispossess someone who personally did them no offence, but strict insistence on that hasn't worked out. Exceptions have been made in a generous spirit, the national character has been yielded to. Yielding to that is not unlike yielding to *pudor,* giving way to notions of decency or becomingness which, as a rude but chaste people, we are sensitive to. (Compare the argument *ab inconvenienti* in Coke: A woman doing homage shall not say "I become your woman." The onlookers would blush, hearing a lady say that to a man not her husband.) Nor are these cases unlike giving way to Nature, as in the examples in Calvin's Case. The law has better taste than to fight Nature. Knowing when Art should make way for Nature is itself Art, perhaps the highest kind.

A somewhat different sort of case is illustrated under Coke's argument ab utile. (Note the heading, but watch that "utile," for the main point may be that while the law respects utilitarian considerations in their place, it avoids the vulgar temptation to focus on them too narrowly.) Take the undisputed rule that I cannot convey Blackacre in fee with a condition of reentry if the feoffee alienates Blackacre. The natural man will tend to suppose that this is simply a rule favoring trade and limiting the dead hand. In truth, it has those purposes even primarily, but they are not *all* it involves. Suppose the case comes along where A conveys Blackacre to B in fee on condition that B not alienate Whiteacre. A lay judge will probably latch onto the social policy behind the first, undisputed rule and hold that the condition in the new case is void. It seems essentially the same sort of thing—an attempt by use of conditions to tie up land and prevent people from trading freely with their own. But the lay judge will be wrong. The prohibition on attaching a condition against alienating Blackacre to a conveyance of Blackacre in fee involves an elusive non-utilitarian idea that does not apply to the Whiteacre case. The idea is hard to express. It is not clearly a moral idea, though it is allied with a certain order of moral ideas (those that try to locate the wrongness of some acts—such as not keeping promises—in an affinity with self-contradictoriness). Roughly, it is "repugnant" (i.e., self-contradictory) to use your freedom to divest yourself of all interest in a tenement and *in the same breath* to try to prevent someone else from doing the same *with respect to the same tenement.* That has an affinity with saying "I give you a fee but I don't" = "I, having an alienable interest, propose to put you in my place, retaining no reversionary interest to myself, yet I do not propose to put you fully in my place, because I do not mean for you to have an alienable estate." Talking that way is represented as a mixture of unintelligible speech and wickedness, though to natural reason it is not especially unintelligible, and if it is wicked it is only because a free-alienation policy is useful, and that as much for Whiteacre as for Blackacre.

I do not suggest that this is defensible thinking, and I daresay that it was sometimes imposed on Coke by the need to save the phenomena. My only suggestion is that he found it convincing. Generalizing, he believed that it is too easy for the layman to suppose that practical or policy reasons explain rules that are actually explicable in part by what I can only call "funny sensibilities"—nearly incommunicable feelings that *are* rather like trained-instinctive canons of suitability in the fine arts. "It just won't do"—which isn't to say for a moment that policy reasons aren't at least 90 percent of why it won't. But the other 10 percent . . . Perhaps long study, not of law, but of common law real property would instill in any normal person a kind of aesthetic, an aptitude for funny sensibilities—precisely the sense that understanding the practical purposes of the rules and the everyday moral judgments behind them is, by and large, the way to right results, and yet that there is a residue where the only explanation is the poetry of the system. For that residue, the justification for "in tune" decisions is not so much their intrinsic virtue as a presumptive interest in not untuning the system as a whole and starting a process like cosmic decay. Remember that real property was the heart of legal learning in Coke's day, and that it was Littleton's elementary introduction to that subject which he considered "the most perfect and absolute work that was ever written in any humane science."

Against Common Right and Reason:
The College of Physicians v. Dr. Thomas Bonham

HAROLD J. COOK

✿ ✿ ✿

From the last decade of the sixteenth century well into the middle of the seventeenth, the London College of Physicians attempted to enforce its juridical authority over medical practitioners in London. One part of that story is known to historians because of the declaration made against the College in favor of the unlicensed Dr. Thomas Bonham by Chief Justice Sir Edward Coke—a declaration that has caused many to wonder whether Coke meant to introduce the principle of judicial review of Acts of Parliament. Discussions of Bonham's case have largely confined themselves to attempting to reconstruct Coke's opinion and its possible common law implications from reports of his declaration, both printed and manuscript, and from the ways in which others took his meaning. Yet the record allows us to examine the political and institutional context of Bonham's case as well. When that is done, Coke's view stands out clearly as an exception to all precedents in the case. He viewed the College of Physicians as acting like a monopoly when it should rather have been a sort of fraternity; in fact, the College had no exact institutional parallel in England. Coke also ignored the interpretations of the College's authority established both by the court of King's Bench and by a conference of royal judges, precedents not mentioned by Coke but clearly in his mind as he struggled to find a way to do justice despite the evident law of the land.

Although the institutional and judicial history of Bonham's case is not part of the reports of the case in Common Pleas, it is crucial to our understanding of the issues. Knowing this background to the case helps to explain why

"Against Common Right and Reason: *The College of Physicians v. Dr. Thomas Bonham*" is reprinted from the *American Journal of Legal History* 29 (1985): 301–22. Reprinted by permission of Harold J. Cook and the *American Journal of Legal History.*

Coke avoided the apparently simple issues at stake, introducing instead an argument about the drafting of the College's charter that some have interpreted as a "constitutional" position. It helps to remind us that Coke in fact argued not about statutes, but about royal charters (although in this case one further authorized by statute). It also helps to show that although probably not meant to be a general statement about common law courts overturning Acts of Parliament, Coke's declaration was indeed full of political implications, in part because it concerned such a unique institution, the College of Physicians.

The historiographical debate over the meaning of Chief Justice Coke's opinion in Bonham's case can be summarized briefly. According to the printed record, in 1610 Coke declared that because the College of Physicians was both judge and prosecuting body in cases brought before it, the Parliamentary Acts confirming its statutory authority were "void." As one part of a much larger report, Coke wrote that "the censors cannot [at the same time] be judges, ministers, and parties" to a decision. Since Coke believed that a statute ratifying a charter in which a person or corporation could judge their own cases in law must be "contradictory," he went on to say that "it appears in our books, that in many cases, the common law will controul Acts of Parliament, and sometimes adjudge them to be utterly void: for when an Act of Parliament is against common right and reason, or repugnant, or impossible to be performed, the common law will controul it, and adjudge such Act to be void. . . ."[1] In other words, the College itself was without authority to punish unlicensed medical practitioners despite the Parliamentary Acts granted to it.

Some have tended to argue that Coke's words indicate that he believed that the courts of common law could exercise judicial review over Acts of Parliament—a position familiar to citizens of the United States but unacceptable in the British system of government, in which Parliament is supreme.[2] Others, most notably Samuel Thorne, have argued that Coke's remark was not intended to serve as an interpretation of the English constitution, but rather was derived from Coke's reading of statutory law precedents; he merely declared that a statute providing one thing and at the same time its opposite was a contradictory statute, "repugnant," and hence null and void.[3] Most recently, Charles Gray has compared manuscript reports of the case and the

1. "Dr. Bonham's Case," 8 Co. Rep. 107a–121a, 77 Eng. Rep.
2. T. F. T. Plucknett, "Bonham's Case and Judicial Review," *Harv. L. Rev.* 40 (1926): 30–70; Raoul Berger, "*Doctor Bonham's Case:* Statutory Construction or Constitutional Theory?," *U. Pa. L. Rev.* 117 (1969): 521–45.
3. S. E. Thorne, "Dr. Bonham's Case," *L. Q. Rev.* 54 (1938): 543–52.

other printed version[4] to Coke's words given in his *Reports*. Gray has concluded that Coke used a statutory construction in his spoken opinion, but later expanded the wording for the printed text to make a constitutional point: a point that some people nearly contemporary to the 1610 decision took seriously.[5] The importance of Coke's declaration in the American colonies of the 1760s is recognized by all historians who have commented on it;[6] but its immediate historical context has not yet been fully explored. Before returning to Bonham's case, therefore, let us see what can be known about the reasons for the trial.

The College of Physicians was a unique institution in early modern England. Chartered in 1518 under Cardinal Wolsey's Chancellorship, the College was formed around three humanistically-trained royal physicians and three London physicians, all with academic doctorates of medicine. Very few M.D.'s inhabited England until after the mid-sixteenth century, and those few academic physicians who were English had been almost entirely trained abroad. Therefore, according to the preamble of the College's charter, Henry VIII's express desire in forming the College was to encourage medical learning—to encourage the new Italian medical humanism of his royal physicians.[7]

Throughout the early modern period the College of Physicians remained a small and academically elite group of English M.D.'s despite the fact that increasing numbers of Englishmen were earning M.D.'s in the English and Continental universities. In 1606, when Doctor Bonham came into view, there were only twenty-four Fellows of the College allowed, with the four royal physicians as "supernumerary" Fellows. To enter, one had to be British (the formerly "English" requirement having been changed in order to admit John Craige, one of James I's royal physicians and a Scot), to have taken an M.D. at a university, and to have undergone a three-part Latin examination in medical theory administered by the President and Censors with a following interview with each of the Fellows at their homes, afterwards being voted up or down by the whole College. If the statutory number of Fellows was full, the successful applicant for a place would become a Candidate, normally the most senior Candidate being raised to the first vacant Fellowship. In part, then, the

---

4. "College of Physicians' Case," 2 Brownl. and Golds. 255–66, 123 Eng. Rep.

5. Charles M. Gray, "Bonham's Case Reviewed," *Proc. Am. Phil. Soc.* 116 (1972): 35–58.

6. See Bernard Bailyn, *The Ideological Origins of the American Revolution* (Cambridge, Mass.: Harvard Univ. Press, 1967), 177.

7. George N. Clark, *A History of the Royal College of Physicians of London* (Oxford: Clarendon Press, 1964), 56–60.

College of Physicians resembled an academically-rooted fraternity.[8] But because it was chartered, with regulatory power over others, it was not simply a fraternity like the Inns of Court or the "College" of Doctors' Commons.

Part of the reason it seems an odd corporation institutionally is that the College was also an odd corporation juridically. By an Act of Parliament confirming their charter passed during the reign of Henry VIII the College had gained the right to sit as a court itself in order to judge all other practitioners: to admit those academically qualified to membership, to grant licenses to those without academic qualifications but proven practical experience, and to punish those practicing badly and without their license. A statute of Queen Mary's first Parliament also allowed the officers of the College to imprison offenders and to keep them there at their pleasure.[9] The juridical authority of the College thus flew in the face of the common law assumption that to practice medicine one needed only the consent of the patient.[10] Moreover, the College's powers of medical licensing overlapped with those of the bishops to grant licenses to physicians and surgeons,[11] and with the universities' ability to issue licenses for the practice of physic and surgery (something in addition to their power to grant degrees).

Thus, although several Continental, especially Italian, colleges of physicians existed as models for Henry VIII's English imitation,[12] when established in England the College of Physicians looked a rather strange beast institutionally. The College was not affiliated with a university nor a municipality as colleges of physicians so often were on the Continent. It was neither a joint-stock company, nor a group centered around a royal patent to have the sole right to produce or vend some particular commodity; both of these kinds of economic monopolies were later institutional innovations. The closest contemporary economic parallel would appear to be the great "regulated" company,

---

8. For more details on the internal structure of the College of Physicians, see chap. 2, Harold J. Cook, *The Decline of the Old Medical Regime in Stuart London* (Ithaca, N.Y.: Cornell University Press, 1986).

9. 14 & 15 Hen. 8, c. 5; 32 Hen. 8, c. 40; 1 Mariae, St. 2, c. 9.

10. The only exception to this was that "if one which is no physician or surgeon [i.e., one who is not licensed by Church, guild, or university] . . . will take a cure upon him, and his patient dieth under his hand, this hath been holden to be a felonie," Christopher Merrett, *A Collection of Acts of Parliament, Charters, Trials at Law and Judges Opinions* (London, 1660), 66. Sir Edward Coke held the same view. Coke, *The Fourth Part of the Institutes of the Laws of England* (London, 1648), 251.

11. 3 Hen. 8, c. 11.

12. G. Whitteridge, "Some Italian Precursors of the Royal College of Physicians," *J. Royal College of Physicians London* 12 (1977): 67–80; Charles Webster, "Thomas Linacre and the Foundation of the College of Physicians," in *Essays on the Life and Work of Thomas Linacre c. 1460–1524,* ed. Francis Maddison, Margaret Pelling, and Charles Webster (Oxford: Clarendon Press, 1977), 198–222.

the Merchant Adventurers: only members had a right to exercise their mystery, but could do so individually only as long as they obeyed the rules of the group. Perhaps more pertinently, founded around a core of Court servants it was somewhat like the College of Arms, which had incorporated the heralds in 1483/4 by a grant of Richard III, or to the defunct corporation of royal minstrels founded by Edward IV in 1469, that prohibited all minstrels from practicing their art publicly anywhere in England (except the county palatine of Chester) unless they had been admitted to the minstrel's body by vote of the members.[13] From the beginning, the College of Physicians was a creation imitating Continental institutions but in a constitutional no-man's land, having statutory authority but in fact being linked closely to the royal Court; and as the Crown's authority waxed and waned, so too did that of the College.

Since the College was so closely associated with the Court, it is not perhaps surprising that its actual power to act upon its authority grew in the later 1580s as the Elizabethan regime became more assertive. The College of Physicians obtained the blessings of the Crown for reviving its juridical powers (dormant since the early 1570s) by entering into an arrangement with Sir Francis Walsingham in 1588.[14] During the 1590s the College began to prosecute a significant number of surgeons, among others, who were by statute limited to practicing on outward ailments only, by the use of external remedies alone. The Barber-Surgeon's Company had been warned by letter in 1595 against allowing its members to practice internal medicine.[15] But two surgeons who had been offenders of the physicians' privileges and imprisoned by the College, Roger Jenkins and Simon Read, tried to fight the College's authority by bringing their complaints to Chief Justice Popham in 1602, the year in which Dr. Thomas Bonham returns to the written record.

Jenkins had long refused to obey the College's juridical authority. His medical practice had been brought to the attention of the College as early as 1596, the year after the College's written warning to the surgeons. He was found guilty by the College in August of practicing illicitly, fined 20s., and forced to sign a bond for £20 never to practice internal medicine thereafter. In December of 1596, however, he was back before the College, first denying that he had practiced or was practicing medicine, and then promising not to do so again.

13. A. Wagner, *The Heralds of England* (London: HMSO, 1967), 130–31.
14. Mentioned in the *Annals of the College of Physicians,* vol. III: 70a. My thanks to the officers and Fellows of the Royal College of Physicians for permission to quote from documents in their archives.
15. Ibid., II: 115b–116a.

In March and August of 1597 he came before the College yet again, on the second occasion giving a bond doubling the first not to practice again. The College brought him up on charges another time in April of 1599; he confessed once more to having practiced, was fined 50s., and was told to render his previous bond of £40 on pain of being imprisoned. He appeared again in June and December of 1600, and in July of 1601.[16]

Read first came to the attention of the College in the summer of 1601, having practiced medicine badly on the wife of Richard Cuckston of Westminster. After an examination in English (the proceedings were otherwise in Latin), the College Censors declared him completely ignorant and unlearned, and so fined him £5 (the maximum under the statute for one month's illicit practice) and imprisoning him until he paid. On 7 August he was released on two conditions after a letter from the Lady Howard was sent on his behalf: on the condition that he free from prison two poor men he had locked up for fictitious debts (a not uncommon method for medical practitioners to recover unpaid fees), and that he give a signed money bond never to practice in London again.[17]

When Jenkins and Read came before the College yet another time during the winter of 1601–1602, and when Jenkins defied the College, declaring that he would exercise the art of healing as he saw fit when the need arose, the President and Censors of the College ordered them both imprisoned.[18] From mid-February until early April the two surgeons remained in prison, but they also retained a lawyer.[19] He entered on their behalf a writ of *corpus cum causa* (a form of *habeas corpus*) before Chief Justice Popham, complaining of severity and injustice. Popham in turn granted them temporary freedom until their case could be heard.

The hearing took place on 8 April. After listening to the officers of the College, the prisoners' counselor at law, and the two prisoners themselves, Popham decided eight points:

1. First, there is no sufficient license without the Colledge seale.

2. No Surgeon, as a surgeon, may Practise Phisick, no, not for any disease, though it be the great Pox.

---

16. Ibid., 120b, 125a, 127b, 139b, 145a, 147a–b, 150b.
17. Ibid., 150a, 151a.
18. Ibid.
19. The fact that the two secured a lawyer suggests that they were helped by the Barber-Surgeon's Company.

3. That the Authoritie of the Colledge, is strong and sufficient to commyt to Pryson.

4. That the Censure of the Colledge, rysing from lesser Mulctes to greater, was equall and reasonable.

5. That it were fit, to set [to] Phisitions Bills, the day of the mooneth and the Patientes name.

6. That the Lord Cheef Justice cannot bayle or deliver the College Prysoner: but is by lawe to deliver him up to the College Censure.

7. That a free man of London, may lawfully be imprysoned by the Colledge.

8. That no man, though never so learned a Phisition, or doctor may Practise in London, or within seaven myles, without the Colledge Lycence.

The pleased officers of the College, finding all their powers upheld, returned a letter of thanks to Popham.[20]

As it happens, Thomas Bonham publicly associated himself with a well-known surgeon in the same year as Popham's decision—with William Clowes the elder, one of the most prominent surgeons of London (and elected a Warden of the Barber-Surgeon's Company in 1594). Clowes published a book in 1602 on the King's Evil, giving advice to surgeons on how to cure it "artificially," including the administration of internal medicines, and illustrating those practices with case histories.[21] He therefore gave suggestions to other surgeons for curing a disease with internal medicines in the same year that the full statutory authority of the College of Physicians to prohibit all others' internal medical practices was found to be sound. Bonham appears as "in Medic: Doct." in the signature to a Latin poem written in praise of Clowes's book. Bonham's association with Clowes in 1602 is significant, for his relations with the London surgeons steadily strengthened just as the College of Physicians was trying to bring them to heel.

Bonham probably associated himself with the surgeons because they were an important group of practitioners from whom he could learn some medicine and from whom he could get referrals as he tried to build up his own practice. Probably still somewhat new to London, he would have needed all the help

20. *Annals,* II: 155b–157a. Read was freed from prison and his fine was remitted on 5 May by the intervention of the Bishop of London (ibid., 158a). Jenkins was later released, perhaps because he paid his fine, for he continued to be brought before the College on complaints in later years.

21. William Clowes, *A right frutefull and approoved treatise, for the artificiall cure of that malady called in Latin Struma, and in English the Evill, cured by the Kinges and Queenes of England* (London, 1602).

he could find.[22] According to the records of Cambridge University, Bonham had matriculated a sizar at St. John's College during the Easter term of 1581. If he had matriculated at the usual age of between sixteen and eighteen he would have been born between 1563 and 1565. As a sizar, he probably came from a relatively humble family. He had earned a Bachelor's degree in 1584–1585 (which he took the trouble to incorporate at Oxford in the same year) and had stayed on for a Master's degree, which he completed in 1588.[23] We then lose track of him, but it is probable that like other well-educated men without means who sought employment outside the church he took up medical practice.[24] In all likelihood he went through the seven years additional study necessary for an M.D. at Cambridge, since the College of Physicians did not contest his claim to the degree in later years, and since he later incorporated an M.D. at Oxford. Although curiously there seems to be no record of Cambridge rewarding him with a medical doctorate, it is probable that he took the degree there, perhaps in the mid-1590s. In all likelihood, at some point between taking the M.D. and associating himself with Clowes in 1602, Bonham had moved to the metropolis to try to make his way in the best medical market in the realm.

Bonham also publicly associated himself with the Barber-Surgeon's Company in their next attempt to gain the right to administer internal remedies; he signed their petition to Parliament at the beginning of 1605.[25] But the College of Physicians immediately gathered support to stop the petition from having any effect, and the quick prorogation of James's first Parliament postponed the Barber-Surgeon's hopes.[26]

Since the College now clearly had the upper hand institutionally and continued to prosecute unlicensed practitioners, Bonham apparently decided that the better part of valor was to join the College—as it turned out, an unfortunate decision. On 6 December 1605, now about forty years old, he presented himself to the Censors for examination preceding membership. He did not answer the Censors' questions to their satisfaction, however, being told to

22. On the question of how practitioners, including physicians, attempted to set up their practices, see chap. 1, *Decline of the Old Medical Regime.*
23. Joseph Foster, *Alumni Oxonienses* (Oxford: Parker & Co., 1891–1892); John and J. A. Venn, *Alumni Cantabrigienses* (Cambridge: Univ. Press, 1924–1927).
24. The relationship between the cure of souls and medical practice has been pointed out most strongly by Charles Webster; see, for example, his "English Medical Reformers of the Puritan Revolution: A Background to the 'Society of Chymical Physitians,'" *Ambix* 14 (1967): 21–22.
25. Charles Goodall, *The Royal College of Physicians of London Founded and Established by Law* (London, 1684), 361.
26. *Annals,* II: 180b, 181b, 182a.

study more diligently and to return at the next general meeting of the College. After missing several meetings, Bonham returned on 14 April, but his replies to questions this time were "not pertinent." Moreover, because he had practiced without membership in or license of the College, the Censors fined him £5, to be paid by the next meeting of the *comitia censorum,* and threatened him with imprisonment if he did not meet that obligation. In the meantime, he was told to abstain from his livelihood. Bonham ignored this verdict—after all, he had been practicing in London for several years. He did not return to the College for reexamination either. But now that he had been noticed by the officers of the College, they would not ignore him. On 3 October 1606 they put on record the fact that he was continuing to practice contrary to the College's statutes and Acts and despite several summonses to appear. Bonham was to be arrested and fined £10.[27]

One month later, on 7 November, Bonham appeared before the *comitia censorum* of the College, but with a lawyer in tow (Dr. Smith). The College President, Henry Atkins, undoubtedly speaking in Latin, repeated Bonham's history of disobedience over the past year, and then asked if he had come to make satisfaction or to be examined again. Bonham could have swallowed his pride and agreed to be reexamined. Instead, he put on his hat and said that he practiced and would continue to practice without seeking the permission of the College and without obeying the President, since they had no power over graduates of the universities—a point that his lawyer elaborated by so interpreting various clauses of the Acts governing the College. But because the law was clearly in their favor (as shown by the eighth point of Popham's decision), the President and Censors sent Bonham to Newgate prison to be held at their pleasure for contempt. Within a week, however, Bonham's lawyer had entered a writ of *habeas corpus* before the court of Common Pleas, which freed him on 13 November.[28]

The fact that Bonham was freed on *habeas corpus* by the new Chief Justice of the Common Pleas worried the officers of the College. Jenkins and Read four years before had not been freed by Popham; in fact, he had declared that the "Lord Cheef Justice cannot bayle or deliver the College Prysoner." Since that case the College had been keenly cultivating Lord Chancellor Ellesmere as well as Popham and other officers of the Crown.[29] But Sir Edward Coke

27. Ibid., 185b, 188b, 190a.
28. Ibid., 190a, 191a.
29. Ibid., 185b–187a.

is nowhere mentioned in the contemporary records of the College. The fact that Bonham had a lawyer, and that the lawyer knew to go to the Chief Justice of Common Pleas with the *habeas corpus,* also suggests that the Barber-Surgeon's Company was helping Bonham. Coke's use of *habeas corpus* against the jurisdictions of inferior courts (and later against superior courts) greatly annoyed other Crown officers.[30] If Coke continued to free prisoners locked up by the College, the effectiveness of the College's regulation would be greatly impaired.

The College therefore took action to reiterate its juridical authority by appealing to the Crown's law officers. After a delay in the spring to stop another Barber-Surgeon's petition to the Parliament for the right to administer internal remedies,[31] the College officers met with a committee of judges. They gathered on 1 May at the home of Lord Chancellor Ellesmere. In addition to Ellesmere himself, Sir John Popham, Sir Thomas Fleming (Chief Baron of the Exchequer), two other judges from the court of King's Bench (Williams and Tamfield), and two judges from the court of Common Pleas (Walmesley and Warburton) attended.[32] Notably, Coke was not invited.

Those judges present at Ellesmere's heard, examined, and resolved a series of questions. Among their unanimous decisions, two spoke to the general issues of the Bonham matter:

> It was resolved by all that practized or coulde practise pfisice oyther in London or within the compass of seven miles of the same must submitt them selves to the examinacion of the President and Colledge as they be required thereunto by their authoritie notwithstanding anye patent allowance or priviledge given them in Oxford or Cambridge either by their degree or otherwise.
>
> They all resolved that, for not well doeing useing or practising the facultie or arte of physike or for disobedience or contempte donne and committed against anye ordynaunce made by the colledge . . . they may committ the offenders without bayle or mayneprise. . . .[33]

The clear support of these judges encouraged the College officers to gather more evidence in order to move against Bonham yet again, this time in the

---

30. J. H. Baker, *An Introduction to English Legal History,* 2d ed. (London: Butterworths, 1979), 124, 127; idem, "The Common Lawyers and the Chancery: 1616," *The Irish Jurist,* n.s., 4 (1969): 368–98; cf. Charles M. Gray, "The Boundaries of the Equitable Function," *Am. J. of Legal Hist.* 20 (1976): 192–226.

31. *Annals,* II:193a; *Historical Account of Proceedings Between the College of Physicians and Surgeons* (London, 1690), 4.

32. *Annals,* II:193b.

33. "Opinions of Lord Chancellor and Judges on Question re Charter of College of Physicians, 1607" (R.C.P., 2020/3); also printed in Merrett, *A Collection of Acts of Parliament,* 116–21.

common law courts. The members of the College were asked to remember when Bonham had practiced—undoubtedly to inform their lawyer.[34] The College also pursued additional testimony from others against Bonham.

The most important new evidence against Bonham in 1608 came in regard to the practice of one Mrs. Paine of Aldersgate Street. In November of 1607, she had been complained of to the College Censors on two occasions for bad practice. When Mrs. Paine came to answer the charges on 22 December, she said that she did all her practice on the advice and authority of Dr. Bonham. When she returned with Bonham on another occasion, Bonham vigorously denied having anything to do with Paine's practice, and stressed that there was no business arrangement between them. One of those who testified against Paine, however, claimed that Paine had often said that she never did anything without Bonham's assistance.[35]

In Trinity term of 1608, the College of Physicians sued Bonham in King's Bench for twelve months' illicit practice—the year since the judges had given their opinions—at £5 per month, or £60, a considerable sum. Moreover, the College's case was argued not by their own lawyer but by Attorney General Hobart.[36]

Bonham's continued harassment by the College both sitting as a court itself and taking matters to the court of King's Bench led him to counterattack. In addition to retaining counsel to plead his case before King's Bench, Bonham returned to Chief Justice Coke's court. It was during the Michaelmas (autumn) term of 1608 that Bonham brought suit for £100 damages against the College for trespass against his person and wrongful imprisonment, claiming that the College "with force of arms [vi et armis] . . . took and imprisoned" him "against the law and custom of this kingdom of England."[37] Also, Bonham hired as his attorney a man named Richard Coke. This Richard Coke was not a brother or descendant of Sir Edward's, but it is possible that he belonged to a collateral line of descent.[38]

The legal arguments in Common Pleas were fairly straightforward. The law-

---

34. *Annals,* II:194b.

35. *Annals,* 6 Nov. and 27 Nov., 4 Dec. and 22 Dec. 1607; 8 Jan., 5 Feb., and 1 July 1608.

36. Sir George N. Clark was aware of some proceedings in King's Bench but does not give a coherent picture of these events: Clark, *History of the Royal College,* 212–13. R. S. Roberts also reports this case in a somewhat less confused manner, citing K.B.C.R.R., 1403, rot. 299–299d: Roberts, "The London Apothecaries and Medical Practice in Tudor and Stuart England" (Ph.D. diss., Univ. of London, 1964), 133–39. More recently, Charles Gray has discovered a manuscript report of the case, summarized in his "Bonham's Case Reviewed," 41.

37. Coke, "Bonham's Case," 106b.

38. Coke, "Bonham's Case," 107a; Charles Warburton James, *Chief Justice Coke: His Family and Descendants at Holkham* (New York: Charles Scribner's Sons, 1929).

yer for the College of Physicians argued that the Act of 1540 "intends, that none shall practice here but those which are most learned and expert, more than ordinary."[39] The King had felt it necessary to take particular care for the health of the people of London since it "is the heart of the kingdom." According to the Act, therefore, the College could punish for "doing and using" physic without its license (illicit practice) as well as for "ill using" physic (malpractice). The Act of 1553 also gave the College undoubted authority to imprison offenders.[40] The law was clear and explicit.

To this, Bonham's lawyer replied by arguing about the intention of the law. The College's acts and charters were intended to prevent bad practice or the practice of impostors. Being a medical graduate of Cambridge, Bonham was one of the "grave and learned" men whom the Acts sought to encourage. The fact that he possessed a university degree, therefore, ought to exempt him from the College's jurisdiction.

Moreover, to the objection that not every M.D. was a "learned and grave" man as intended by the statute, Bonham's lawyer answered that "all their study [in the texts at university] is practice." He also argued that having become a "doctor" meant having been judged capable of teaching:

> and when a man brings with him the ensign of doctrine, there is no reason that he should be examined again, for then if thou will not allow of him, he shall not be allowed, though he be a learned and grave man, and it is not the intent of the King to make a monopoly of this practice.

Therefore, Bonham's lawyer concluded, the Act "doth not inhibit a doctor to practice, but [only] punisheth him for ill using, exercising, and making [of physic]"—it could punish an M.D. for malpractice but not for illicit practice. In other words, he argued, the College could imprison the "empiric and impostor" for illicit practice, but not a learned doctor such as Bonham.

After hearing these arguments, the court of Common Pleas adjourned the case for consideration. Nevertheless, the case against Bonham in the court of King's Bench proceeded, with Attorney General Hobart leading the College's charge. About 3 February 1609, they handed down their verdict: Bonham had been found guilty of illicit practice for one year, being fined £60. As Chief Justice Fleming said, "'the case had been long pending'" and "'there

---

39. 32 Hen. 8, c. 40, read as an extension of 14 & 15 Hen. 8, c. 5. Here and below I follow the arguments of the lawyers, reported in 2 Brownl. and Golds. 255–60, confirmed in summary by Coke, "Bonham's Case," 107a–113b.

40. 1 Mariae, St. 2, c. 9.

is not any great difficulty in it that requires argument by the bench'" (since matters had been settled by the judges in 1607).[41] The College sent a delegation of thanks to the Lord Chancellor, the Chief Justice, the other four judges (Fenner, Williams, Yelverton, and Croke), the serjeant of the law, the Attorney and Solicitor Generals, and all others who had helped the College.[42] Bonham, probably unable to pay the fine, was sent to prison. A month later, his alleged accomplice, Mrs. Paine, was also fined £10 by the College and imprisoned.[43]

Bonham nevertheless tried to help himself in several ways. The suit against the College in Common Pleas was still pending, and Bonham refused to drop it. He also became a freeman of the Barber-Surgeon's Company.[44] Moreover, he got the Archbishop of Canterbury to intercede on his behalf with the College. Archbishop Bancroft wrote the College a letter, dated 3 October, protesting against their obstinacy in holding a learned man in prison:

> Whereas one Dr. Bonham, Dr of physicke, a man (as I have bene enformed) very
> well learned in the Greek and Latin tongue, having taken his degree in the Universitie of Cambridge with good commendacion, hath ben upon differences and
> suits betwixt yow and him committed to prison, and there deteyned for diverse
> monthes, to his great impoverishment and discredit (a course seldome held either
> by yow, or your predecessors with that severity, especially against a man of his
> reputation) these are to desire yow to have some better consideration of him, and
> to shew him what charitable favour yow may for his release. Otherwise I shall
> be driven (for the respect I beare unto his good partes) to move the Lordes in
> his behalfe, who I suppose will not approve of such your extremity used towards
> him, and may perhaps thinke so large an authority to be ill bestowed upon men
> that can use it with no better moderation, And so not doubting of your good
> consideration of the premisses I commit yow to God. . . .

To this ominous letter the College responded by sending a delegation to speak with the Archbishop. They explained that their proceedings were legal, that they conformed to the decision of the judges, and that it was Bonham who was obstinate. If he would agree to drop his suit before Coke, they would free him from prison. In the end, they persuaded the Archbishop, who agreed that

41. Quoted in Gray, "Bonham's Case Reviewed," 41; also see the exemplification of recovery against Dr. Bonham in King's Bench, 13 Feb. 6 Jacobi, given in Goodall, *The Royal College of Physicians*, 166–77.
42. *Annals,* III:1a.
43. 3 Mar. 1609.
44. Roberts, "The London Apothecaries," 133–39.

unless Bonham submitted himself to the College and dropped his suit, "he would be unworthy of forgiveness and undeserving of friendship or favor."[45]

But Bonham did not drop his suit. A year after his imprisonment by King's Bench, in the winter (Hilary term) of 1610, his case before the Common Pleas was finally decided, and in a close three to two decision went against the College, allowing him to go free. Chief Justice Coke and Justice Daniel (neither of whom had been present at the judges' meeting in 1607) found against the College on all points. Justices Walmesley and Foster sided with the College on all points—Walmesley had been at Ellesmere's. But according to the College of Physicians there was a swing vote: Justice Warburton, who had also been present at the meeting of 1607. Warburton apparently decided on the basis of disliking Bonham's imprisonment rather than other points of law.[46] The college was fined £40—in effect reducing Bonham's fine in King's Bench to £20.

Walmesley gave the minority opinion for the College, an opinion that probably represents something like the argument made at Ellesmere's.[47] He argued that since the statute was in the negative ("no person" could exercise the practice of physic, etc.), only one verdict could be made: no one could oppose the College's licensing authority. Walmesley also glossed the preamble to the College's charter as conveying to the College a paternalistic duty of the King:

> It is the office of a King to survey his subjects, and he is a physician to cure their maladies, and to remove leprosies amongst them, and also to remove all fumes and smells, which may offend or be prejudicial to their health . . . and so if a man be not right in his wits, the King is to have the protection and government of him, lest he being infirm, waste or consume his lands or goods;[48] and it is not sufficient for him that his subjects live, but that they should live happily; and [he] discharges not his office, if his subjects live a life, but [only] if they live and flourish; and he hath cure as well of their bodies as of their lands and goods for health for the body is as necessary as virtue to the mind. . . .

Therefore, the King had delegated this responsibility for his subjects' health to the College of Physicians by giving them the ability to restrict who prac-

45. *Annals,* III: 4b.

46. Ibid., 6a.

47. The arguments of Walmesley given here are from 2 Brownl. and Golds. 260–62.

48. A statute on the King's prerogative in the late thirteenth century allowed the King to take permanent wardship of the "natural fool" (*fatuus naturalis*) and trusteeship in cases of temporary loss of mental capacity (*non compos mentis*): Michael Donnelly, *Managing the Mind* (New York: Tavistock, 1983), 70–71.

ticed. None could practice without the College's permission, not excepting university graduates in medicine.

Moreover, Bonham had given an "absurd and contemptuous answer . . . that he would not be ruled nor directed by [the College] (being grave and learned men), and for that . . . he was worthily punished and committed; for it should be a vain law if it did not provide punishment for them that offend against that." To the College and its licentiates people committed their lives, and so for the good health of all in London, the College had obtained from Henry VIII the "power to make laws" governing physic, a power of Parliament, "for those which are so learned may be trusted with anything." Therefore, the College had the right to hold a court and to commit "as any other court may for a contempt of common right, without act of Parliament." It was, in short, better to trust and to give police powers to the grave and learned men of the College than to trust a university "where a man may have his degree by grace without merits."[49]

Walmesley believed that only "grave and learned" men ought to practice physic, and that such men had to be found by some expert and learned body since the universities could not always be relied upon to turn out such men. For this reason, Henry VIII had established the College of Physicians and had given it the power to select only the most learned and virtuous physicians. In doing so, he had delegated a part of his prerogative power to the College. Thus the College could not only police others, but fine and imprison those who were in contempt of its authority, for otherwise the powers delegated to it by the King would be nothing. Like other corporate bodies, the College of Physicians had the right to sit as a court in order to judge and punish those who infringed upon its jurisdiction, especially since these were grants stemming from the prerogatives of the Crown; and Walmesley declared against Bonham, agreeing with the other judges' opinions of 1607 and with the decision in King's Bench of 1609.

But Chief Justice Coke read the intentions of the law differently than Walmesley. Coke was both more precise in his reading of the statutes, less impressed with the physicians of the College as a group to be trusted with the juridical power to choose and govern learned men, and less deferential to the Crown's prerogative to create monopolies.

Coke began by quoting Galen. *Ubi philosophia definit, ibi medicine incipit*

---

49. The English universities could, if they chose, grant degrees "by grace" to those who had not undergone the full course of study.

("where philosophy ends, there medicine begins"): there was nothing certain in medical matters. Coke read the College's chartered authority not as giving it the duty and ability to determine the fit and the unfit for medical practice, but as consisting of two separate powers contained in two clauses. The first clause concerned illicit practice; the College could fine a practitioner 100s. for every month of practice without the license of the College.[50] Whether that practice was good or bad was immaterial. The second clause (empowering the Censors to enforce the first clause) specified that the College could also imprison a practitioner—stating that they could do so for "not well doing, using, or practicing" physic (as the judges had translated "*non bene exequend' faciend' et utend' illa*" in 1607).[51] Coke considered these two sentences as treating of separate issues rather than viewing the second as an authorization to punish for the behavior specified in the first. The one, he thought, concerned illicit practice, the other malpractice; the first allowed a fine, the second imprisonment. Coke also clearly stated that he did not believe practice without the College's license to be the same thing as malpractice. In other words, Coke made a much clearer distinction than had previously been done between illicit practice and malpractice.

The implication Coke drew from distinguishing between these two clauses —between illicit practice and malpractice—was that the College's judgment of someone as unfit for certification was not the same as finding him guilty of malpractice. A practitioner who did not have the moral status of a grave and learned man as affirmed by the College might still not commit malpractice. Coke therefore declared that according to his reading of the clauses in the charter Bonham could be fined for illicit practice, but the College had no power to imprison him for that fine *nor* for contempt, the College having the power to imprison for malpractice only. This reading considerably circumscribed the College's power.

Coke went even further, fundamentally doubting whether the first clause

---

50. ". . . nemo in dicta Civitate aut per septem Miliaria in circuitu ejusdem exerceat dictam facultatem nisi ad hoc per dict' Presidentem & Comunitatem . . . sub pena Centum Solidorum pro quolibet mensa quo non admissus eandem facultatem. . . ." *The Statutes of the Realm,* vol. 4, (1819), 213 (abbreviations expanded).

51. The President and Censors "habeant [haberent] supervisum et scrutinium, correctionem et gubernationem omnium et singulorum dicte Civitatis Medicorum, . . . ac punitionem eorumdem pro delictis suis in non bene exequend' faciend' et utend' illa. . . . [:] Ita quod punicio hujusmodi [eorundem] medicorum utentium dicta facultate Medicine [medicinae] sic in praemissis deliquentium per Fines Amerciamenta & Imprisonamenta Corporum suorum, et per alias vias rationabiles & congruas exequatur [exequeretur]." The words in brackets are Coke's alterations of the text; in other passages he consistently changes the first person plural (e.g., "nostris") to the third person singular (e.g., "suis"), in both pronouns and verbs, when quoting the royal authorization.

itself could be considered valid. Since he read it as granting the College authority to fine unlicensed practitioners who competed with them, he made the published statement since argued by historians:

> The censors cannot be judges, ministers, and parties. . . . And it appears in our books, that in many cases, the common law will controul Acts of Parliament, and sometimes adjudge them to be utterly void: for when an Act of Parliament is against common right and reason, or repugnant, or impossible to be performed, the common law will controul it, and adjudge such Act to be void.[52]

Containing a clause that provided for an absurdity—that the College would be both judge and party to a case—the charter of the College confirmed by Parliamentary Act was therefore invalid. According to Charles Gray, the manuscript reports differ slightly but significantly on the words used, indicating that originally Coke had in mind a "construal" rather than a "voiding" of the statute, although both printed versions use the word "void."[53] At any rate, Coke used his reading of the College's charter to overthrow the College's authority to fine unlicensed medical practitioners.

As for the second clause, Coke allowed that the College could fine and imprison someone for malpractice, but here, too, he gave a novel opinion; he declared that the courts of common law could "traverse," or themselves decide the facts established in the Censor's judgments.[54] In saying this, Coke stated that justices could decide the issue of whether medical practice was good or not. The College was not to be the only expert judge of medical practice—or rather, any judge with a university education could find whether a medical case had been handled correctly or not. In deciding this, Coke held to what most graduates of an English university would have thought, for as Charles Webster and Margaret Pelling have pointed out, medicine was taught in the arts faculties of Cambridge and Oxford, and so most young men would have picked up some smattering of medical knowledge during their years there, so often refusing to acknowledge the physicians as a wholly separate body of experts.[55] (It should also be said that most members of the public had strong and independent views of medical practice in early modern England.)[56] Thus,

52. Coke, "Bonham's Case," 118a.
53. Gray, "Bonham's Case Reviewed," 42–44; Gray therefore supports Thorne's view of Coke's original meaning.
54. 2 Brownl. and Golds. 265–66.
55. Pelling and Webster, "Medical Practitioners," in *Health, Medicine and Mortality in the Sixteenth Century,* ed. Webster (Cambridge Univ. Press, 1979), 203.
56. The literature of medical criticism by the laity is large, but for one example of some contempo-

the College was not just to lose its supervision of medical licensing, it was not even to be the arbiter of medical practices.

Coke's decision was therefore consistent with many of his other decisions. He upheld the special nature of the reasoning of judges learned in the common law, and thus their ability to oversee the decisions of all lower courts, not allowing any special "experts" to decide matters.[57] He denied that such bodies as the College had the right to fine and imprison without supervision, something that would have made them courts of record.[58] And he denied the right of corporate bodies to be judge and party in matters touching its "monopoly," something he soon argued against in many other cases involving the rights of Englishmen to live by their skills.[59] In doing so, he voided a "monopoly" granted by royal charter, although further authorized by Parliament, as he soon did in other cases.[60] As Gray has noticed, Coke's precedents in Bonham's case all derived from previous declarations against royal patents.[61]

It will also be noticed that in arriving at his decision Coke did not meet the issue at hand head on.[62] Bonham's lawyer had argued that the medical graduates of the universities were to be excepted from the College's jurisdiction. Although Coke clearly sympathized with the nature of the complaint, it was an impossible defense given the explicit nature of the statutes. Moreover, every interpretation previously placed upon the statutes went against Bonham's lawyer. So Coke had to reach for a more fundamental argument.

raries' opinions of London doctors, see "Let Closestoole and Chamberpot Choose Out a Doctor" (1607), ed. Dorothy M. Schullian, *J. Hist. Medicine* 33 (1978): 409–16. Also see ibid., and chap. 1, *Decline of the Old Medical Regime.*

57. It is well known that Coke had firm ideas about the special nature of judicial reasoning; for two recent views of what he meant, see John U. Lewis, "Sir Edward Coke (1552–1633): His Theory of 'Artificial Reason' as a Context for Modern Basic Legal Theory," *L.Q. Rev.* 84 (1968): 330–42; Charles Gray, "Reason, Authority, and Imagination: The Jurisprudence of Sir Edward Coke," in *Culture and Politics from Puritanism to the Enlightenment,* ed. Perez Zagorin (Berkeley: Univ. of California Press, 1980), 25–66.

58. S. E. Thorne, "Courts of Record and Sir Edward Coke," *Univ. of Toronto L.J.* 2 (1937–8): 24–49.

59. I owe many thoughts about contemporary views of the rights of Englishmen to use their labor to David Sacks. Also see D. O. Wagner, "Coke and the Rise of Economic Liberalism," *Econ. Hist. Rev.* 6 (1935–6): 30–44; idem, "The Common Law and Free Enterprise," ibid. 7 (1936–7): 217–20; Elizabeth Read Foster, "The Procedure of the House of Commons Against Patents and Monopolies, 1621–1624," in *Conflict in Stuart England: Essays in Honour of Wallace Notestein,* ed. William A. Aiken and Basil D. Henning (London: Jonathan Cape, 1960), 57–85; Christopher Hill, *Intellectual Origins of the English Revolution* (Oxford: Clarendon Press, 1965), 225–65; Barbara Malament, "The 'Economic Liberalism' of Sir Edward Coke," *Yale L.J.* 76 (1967): 1321–58; David Little, *Religion, Order, and Law* (New York: Torchbooks, 1969), 167–217; J. H. Hexter, "Property, Monopoly, and Shakespeare's *Richard II*," in *Culture and Politics,* 1–24; and Stephen White, *Sir Edward Coke and "The Grievances of the Commonwealth," 1621–1628* (Chapel Hill: Univ. of N. Carolina Press, 1979), 86–141.

60. White, *Sir Edward Coke,* 136–41. As White points out, the question was not so much whether monopolies were good or bad as what constituted a "monopoly," 118–19.

61. Gray, "Bonham's Case Reviewed," 44–46.

62. Ibid., 41.

In doing so, he had to ignore the statement in the Parliamentary Act declaring that

> All and every Graunte Articles and other thyng conteigned and specified in the said lettres patentes be approved graunted ratefied and confermed in this present parliament and clerely auctorised and admytted by the same, good laufull and avaylable to your said body corporate and their Successours for ever in as ample and large manner as may be taken thought and construed by the same.[63]

Such a declaration would seem to require a judge to interpret the statute in a broad rather than a narrow manner.

It would thus appear that Coke's view of the case stemmed from a sense that an injustice had been done in creating a corporation with powers such as the College rather than from a view of either statutory precedent or natural law theory.[64] As in Walmesley's opinion, at the root of Coke's judgment lay firm views about the moral character of the College's authority. Coke's views seem to have been very like those of Archbishop Bancroft, who had protested against the imprisoning of a university man. Coke, before delivering his opinion on the two points of illicit practice and malpractice, spoke about the universities of Cambridge and Oxford as being higher than the College of Physicians, just as a father is higher than his children, or a fountain is higher than the small rivers that descend from it. Coke believed that it ought to be presumed that the universities turned out men who were profound, sad, discreet, and learned, thus giving them the right to practice physic without having those virtues confirmed by the College's examination.[65] The moral authority of an educated physician counted for more than his narrow expertise, which any judge could inspect in cases of malpractice.

This issue between Walmesley and Coke was perhaps the most important in the regulation of medicine in the seventeenth century, and clearly touched on ideas of the order of the kingdom. All the judges agreed that only grave and learned men should practice physic. But Coke felt that the grant of a medical degree by Cambridge certified Bonham to be grave and learned. No other

---

63. 14 & 15 Hen. 8, c. 5.

64. Cf. Thorne, "Dr. Bonham's Case," 549.

65. 2 Brownl. and Golds., 264. Also see the slightly different revision of Coke's words given in Gray, "Bonham's Case Reviewed," 39–40. It may be worth noting that the only objection William Prynne has to Coke's decision in Bonham's case is that Coke placed Cambridge before Oxford, which Prynne (as an Oxford man) believes should be reversed: Prynne, *Brief Animadversions on, Amendments of, and Additional Explanatory Records to, the Fourth Part of the Institutes of the Lawes of England . . . by . . . Coke* (London, 1669), 155–74.

institution ought to have to pass on a physician's qualifications, especially one that would be both party and judge in cases of illicit practice. The College might be chartered to judge malpractice; but medicine contained no mysteries impenetrable to any educated man, and so common law courts could traverse the College's decisions in malpractice cases. There was no good reason for College of Physicians' coercive activities, especially in cases of unlicensed practice alone. By implication, Coke did not believe that the King's prerogative powers entitled him to transfer the power to decide on the merits of particular physicians from the universities to the College. On the other hand, Walmesley, and probably the other judges present at Ellesmere's in 1607, believed that Henry VIII had established a body of the most learned and grave practitioners in London. They, and not the universities, where degrees could be obtained by grace or royal mandate, ought to pass on a physician's moral and medical abilities. Moreover, it should be presumed that any practitioner in contempt of them ought to be punished, as anyone should be punished who was contemptuous of any other properly constituted authority.

But Coke had dug deeply into the few and tenuous precedents available to him in order to find some authority for a fundamentally different view of the College of Physicians that would allow him to free Bonham from prison. Perhaps not surprisingly, he seems to have seen the College as a strange combination of two kinds of bodies: an economic monopoly and a learned fraternity. As a learned fraternity, he had no dispute with the College's charter. But as an economic monopoly, he found no justification for a small group of learned physicians trying to restrict the practices of others, particularly university-trained physicians. His construction of the charter's clauses, dividing the penalties for illicit practice from those for malpractice, was stretching a point, but it allowed Warburton to vote with Coke and Daniels that Bonham had been unfairly imprisoned.[66]

Because the law was so clear Coke had to doubt its validity, and because of who had earlier decided in favor of the College's authority, that was a political issue. He probably meant to overturn a royal patent when it seemed unjust rather than to argue for common law jurisdiction over Acts of Parliament; in this case the patent just happened to have been confirmed by an Act. But behind this particular patent stood most of the royal judges, stiffened by Ellesmere. If not a "constitutional" position in the sense in which it is usually

66. Gray, "Bonham's Case Reviewed," 41; Thorne, "Dr. Bonham's Case."

interpreted, Coke's decision does reflect conflicting views of the power of the English courts to contradict decisions of the Crown.

Given the background to Coke's decision, one can well understand why Lord Chancellor Ellesmere and King James were furious with it. King James, on the advice of that great governmental rationalizer, Sir Francis Bacon, together with Ellesmere, immediately called Coke's opinion into question.[67] Because it did get at points about who was to administer the law other judges used Bonham's case to attempt to nullify other statutes as well.[68] Coke's apparent meaning also explains why Bonham's case could be used to strengthen arguments in favor of free trade.[69] The specific directions Coke gave the College concerning how to proceed in future cases, including the keeping of better records, provided a loose framework for later legal actions by the College of Physicians, and were cited in other cases.[70] But it must also be noted that after the Restoration Coke's declaration in Bonham's case was explicitly found to provide no precedents for other common law cases brought by the College of Physicians, since the College was found to be indeed a court of record.[71]

As for Bonham himself, he incorporated his M.D. at Oxford in the summer of 1611, giving him all the rights and privileges of an Oxford graduate. Three years later, he was admitted to Gray's Inn. But he also apparently continued to practice medicine as a member of the Barber-Surgeon's Company. On 8 July 1614 the surgeon George Perin was accused of illicit practice by the College, and he threw the blame on Dr. Bonham, as Mrs. Paine had years before. A few years later, Bonham was one of the two men to whom Thomas Bretnor dedicated his translation and enlargement of a book on the medical uses of opium. He signed a petition of the Barber-Surgeon's against the new charter of the College of Physicians in 1621. He served as an assistant in the Barber-Surgeon's Company, and apparently sponsored surgical experiments in his home. In the

67. Berger, "Doctor Bonham's Case," 540–51; Plucknett, "Bonham's Case," 49–52.

68. Gray, "Bonham's Case Reviewed," 51–57.

69. William Shepheard, *Of Corporations, Fraternities, and Guilds* (London, 1659), 88–89. My thanks to Joseph Biancalana for this reference.

70. "Doctor Alphonso, and the Colledge of Physitians in London" (1614), 2 Bulstrode 259, 80 Eng. Rep.

71. "Colledge of Phisitians and Cooper or Hubert" (1675), 3 Keble 588, 84 Eng. Rep.; "Dr. Groenvelt v. Dr. Burwell et al." (1699), 1 Ld. Ray. 454–72, 91 Eng. Rep. It should be pointed out, however, that Coke stood by his opinion of the College during his tenure on the bench and later; see his declarations in "The Corporation of Physicians, Against Dr. Tenant" (1613), 2 Bulstrode 185–86, 80 Eng. Rep.; and "Doctor Alphonso, and the Colledge of Physitians of London" (1614), 2 Bulstrode 259. Coke drew the reader's attention to his report of Bonham's case when he wrote of the institution of the College in his *Fourth Part of the Institutes,* 251–52. Twenty years later, William Prynne made no additions or objections to Coke's remarks in his *Brief Animadversions on . . . the Fourth Part of the Institutes,* 155–74.

late 1620s, in London, in his early sixties, he died, survived by a servant in medicine and surgery, Edward Poeton, who edited and published Bonham's well-respected papers on medical practice in 1630. As a footnote, it might be added that even years after his 1609 trial in King's Bench, a squabble was going on at Court over who was to receive that half of his fine due the King.[72]

Thus, before we place too much weight on the words Coke used in his declarations alone (or the words of other judges, for that matter), we ought to examine the precise contexts of those opinions. Coke does not direct our attention to the previous decisions in Bonham's case because they so clearly tend in another direction than his. These other views of the issues in the case by other judges help us to understand why so careful a student of the law, if also a person so firm in his convictions of justice, was forced to decide an issue in a way that was interpreted in his own time as a "constitutional" innovation despite his apparent intentions.

In a period that saw cases like *Bates*'s (or the "case of impositions," 1606), few judges could see their way clear to opposing extensions and delegations of the royal prerogative.[73] Many new social and economic needs could in fact be most efficiently met by extending the authority of the Crown.[74] But in a period also rife with debate over royal patents, it is perhaps not surprising that Coke saw the College's activities against Bonham as being like other economic monopolies: as infringing upon the right of an Englishman (in this case a university graduate) to exercise his skill and learning. Coke was one of the few judges who did find ways to opposing extensions and delegations of the prerogative that seemed unjust, even if he sometimes had to stretch his points. It may be well to remember in these days when more and more historical interpretations of the civil war argue about the novelties of the royal government that not all innovations were monarchical.

72. Foster, *Alumni Oxonienses;* Venn and Venn, *Alumni Cantabrigienses;* Joseph Foster, ed., *The Register of Admissions to Gray's Inn, 1521–1889* (London: Hansard Publ. Union, 1889), vol. I, 135; Angelo Sala, *Opiologia: Or, A Treatise concerning the Nature, properties, true preparation and safe use and Administration of Opium,* trans. and enlarged by Thomas Bretnor (1618), sigs. A2v–A3v (this "chemical" preparation had obvious uses to surgeons not only as a medicine but as a pain killer); Clark, *History of the Royal College,* 214; Alexander Read, *Treatise on the First Part of Surgery* (1634), 231, quoted in George Parker, *The Early History of Surgery in Great Britain* (London: A. and C. Black, 1920), 107; Thomas Bonham, *The Chyurgians closet; or, an Antidotarie chyrurgicall* (1630); S.P. 14/94/216.
73. Also see J. H. Baker, "New Light on *Slade's Case,*" *Cambridge L. J.* 29 (1971): 51–67, 213–36.
74. See, for example, the "constitutional" problems raised when the work of the Commissions of the Sewers were extended to meet new and real needs, an example given in L. L. Jaffe and E. G. Henderson, "Judicial Review and the Rule of Law: Historical Origins," *Law Quarterly Rev.* 72 (1956): 348–50; also see J. P. Dawson, "The Privy Council and Private Law in the Tudor and Stuart Periods," *Mich. L. Rev.* 48 (1950): 393–428; 627–56.

The context and outcome of Bonham's case also remind us that decisions in courts were not the whole of the law in early modern England. All but three of the royal judges maintained the College's authority, and only two of those three fundamentally doubted the laws on medical practice. The College also had many friends at the royal court. Within a short time of Bonham's case, the College of Physicians regained its juridical confidence and acted as if Coke had never uttered a word. Practitioners such as Bonham did finally get the medical statutes overturned in the courts under the Commonwealth (again in Common Pleas), only to have them return to force as the Crown again gathered strength in the later 1670s.[75] Behind Bonham's case lie important issues about medical regulation by the College of Physicians in the early seventeenth century, issues of a political if not a constitutional nature.

75. For more on the legal vicissitudes of the College of Physicians in the seventeenth century, see *Decline of the Old Medical Regime in Stuart London.*

Bonham's Case and Judicial Review

THEODORE F. T. PLUCKNETT

❧ ❧ ❧

I

By an old and universal custom the reports of Sir Edward Coke are referred to simply as "The *Reports,*" and no more striking tribute could be paid to their unique position in our legal literature. Partly, no doubt, this is due to their didactic character, combining as they do the elements of report, treatise, legal history and general criticism, thus becoming not only a repertory of decisions for the practitioner, but also a textbook for the advanced student, who finds in them elaborate discussions of every branch of English law. That alone would have made these eleven volumes a truly remarkable achievement, but for their own age they possessed yet another aspect, which must here receive our attention. Their author was something more than a lawyer with an extraordinary knowledge of the arcana of the common law; more, too, than an antiquary of great distinction, even in an age of such amazingly erudite scholars as William Prynne, John Selden and Sir Robert Cotton; for to all this he added the character of political philosopher. Urged by a presentiment of the coming conflict of Crown and Parliament, he felt the necessity of curbing the rising arrogance of both, and looked back upon his country's legal history to find the means. This instinctive appeal to history for guidance was characteristic, and the choice of a legal rather than any other solution was amply justified by the remarkable continuity and stability of English law during the vicissitudes of the seventeenth century. His attitude is aptly expressed in one of his own picturesque phrases: "Let us now peruse our ancient authors," he wrote, "for out of the old fields must come the new corne."[1] So it

"*Bonham's Case* and Judicial Review" is reprinted, with permission, from the *Harvard Law Review* 40 (1926): 30–70. © 1926 by the Harvard Law Review Association.

1. 4 *Co. Inst.* 109.

was in this spirit that he labored at the ancient patrimony of his profession, those short, thick folios of black-letter Year Books,[2] and from their forbidding mass of obsolescent technicalities raised a harvest of political theory which was destined to be the food of far-distant states to which he had never given a thought.

The solution which Coke found was in the idea of a fundamental law which limited Crown and Parliament indifferently. What that law was, its nature and its contents, were questions as difficult as they were insistent—and, as subsequent events showed, capable of surprising solutions. The nearest we find to an explicit definition of this fundamental law is the assertion of the paramount law of "reason." For the rest, the common lawyer's "reason" is left in as much uncertainty as he himself ascribed to the Chancellor's equity.[3] Moreover, Coke was prepared to advance medieval precedent for his theory, and in so doing has drawn upon his head the criticisms of later investigators. Just as these criticisms are, from the point of view of modern scholarship, it is only fair to the Chief Justice to insist that his view of history was not ours, and that it is only by the standard of his own day that a true evaluation of his learning and intellectual honesty can be formed. Although it must be confessed that even then he cannot be found altogether faultless, yet it is believed that a sufficient explanation will be found to establish his *bona fides*. His doctrine is certainly based largely upon medieval precedents and the extent to which they justify it is an interesting subject for investigation. But if we reach a different estimate from his of the Year Book authority for his dogma, this must not be taken as necessarily involving a severe censure of Coke. He himself has told us that though the fields are old, the corn is new.

His theory reaches its final expression in *The Case of the College of Physicians,* commonly called *Dr. Bonham's Case,* of which we have two reports, one by Coke himself, who presided at the trial as Chief Justice of the Common Pleas;[4] the other by Brownlow, who was present at the later stages of the case in his capacity of Prothonotary of the court.[5] Brownlow reports earlier proceedings than Coke, while the latter naturally preserves his own judgment at greater length. Taken together, the two sources enable us to reconstruct the

2. The collected uniform edition associated with the name of Sergeant Maynard did not appear until nearly half a century after the death of Coke.

3. For "reason," see Sir Frederick Pollock, "History of the Law of Nature," in *Essays in the Law* (1922) 157.

4. 8 Co. 114a (C. P. 1610); the pleadings are at f. 107a.

5. 2 Brownl. 255 (C. P. 1610).

arguments in the case with considerable detail and fair certainty, although as we shall see later, the accuracy of Coke's reports has been attacked.[6]

In April, 1606,[7] Thomas Bonham was summoned to appear before the President and Censors of the Royal College of Physicians, who examined him, and finding that he was deficient in medical science, imposed upon him a fine of a hundred shillings and forbade him under pain of imprisonment to practice physic until he had been admitted by the College. Bonham continued to practice, however, and in October was resummoned. This time he defaulted, and was sentenced in his absence to a fine of ten pounds, and a warrant was issued for his arrest. Early in November he appeared and refused to submit to reexamination, on the grounds that he was a Doctor of Medicine of the University of Cambridge, and that the Royal College of Physicians had therefore no jurisdiction over him. Thereupon the Censors (without the President) committed him to prison in the Counter of Fleet Street, whither he was conveyed by the servants of the President and Censors. Bonham now brought an action for false imprisonment against the leading members of the Royal College of Physicians.

The pleadings of the defendants set forth that letters patent dated 10 Hen. VIII had incorporated them as the Royal College of Physicians, with powers to fine practitioners in London who were not admitted by them, and further general powers to govern all the physicians in London and district with fine and imprisonment—in all cases one-half of the fine was to go to the King, and one-half to the College. This patent was confirmed by the statute 14 & 15 Hen. VIII, c. 5, which in turn was confirmed by the statute 1 Mar. c. 9, with the addition of a general command to all gaolers to keep such persons as the President and College shall commit to them, without bail or mainprise. It was in pursuance of these statutory powers that the College claimed to have committed Dr. Bonham.

Protracted argument followed, particularly on the question whether graduates of the universities were under the jurisdiction of the Royal College,[8] for as Sergeant Doddridge argued, "the Statutes of this Realm have always had great respect to the Graduates of the Universities, and it is not without cause," he adds sympathetically, "for *Sudavit & Alsit,* and hath no other reward than this Degree which is Doctor."[9] The details of these discussions, which lasted

6. *Infra,* p. 168.
7. 8 Co. 115a.
8. *Ibid.* 116a; 2 Brownl. 256–57.
9. 2 Brownl. 258.

for several terms, need not detain us, for finally the case came up for a formal argument among the judges themselves. In the course of the lengthy disputes which took place upon the bench, we find an interesting confession of faith in Tudor paternalism by Walmesley, who deduced from the preamble of the letters patent that: "it is the Office of a King to survey his Subjects, and he is a Physician to cure their Maladies, and to remove Leprosies amongst them, and also to remove all fumes and smells, which may offend or be prejudicial to their health, as it appears by the several Writs in these several Cases provided, and so if a man be not right in his Wits, the King is to have the Protection and Government of him . . ."[10]—a notable example of a new political theory being read into the venerable texts of the *Registrum Brevium*. Walmesley, indeed, could not see any possibility of objection to a despotism so enlightened. "It is a marvellous thing," he asserted, "that when good Laws shall be made for our Health and Wealth also, yet we will so pinch upon them, that we will not be tryed by men of Experience, Practice and Learning, but by the University, where a man may have his Degree by grace without merit, and so for these Reasons he concluded that this Action is not maintainable."[11]

Then came the judgment of the Chief Justice, Sir Edward Coke.[12] He took up the challenge of Justice Walmesley, and delivered a glowing eulogy upon the University of Cambridge, of which he was later to become Lord High Steward, while of the Crown he used an extravagant form of words almost certainly adapted from the famous claim of Richard II to bear the law in his breast: "the King hath had extraordinary care for the health of his Subjects. *Rex enim omnes artes censetur habere in scrinio pectoris sui.*"[13]

He then rehearsed the whole history of the case, and with the concurrence of Warburton and Daniel,[14] concentrated his attention upon two points which he regarded as decisive in support of the action. In the first place, the College did not possess the powers they claimed over unlicensed (as distinct from incompetent) practitioners; and secondly, even if they did, they had not pursued them aright. It is the fourth of the five reasons adduced in support of the former of these propositions that has since become so famous.[15] He points out

---

10. *Ibid.* 260. The care of the public health is still ascribed to the Crown as *medicus regni.* (1909) 25 *L. Q. Rev* 291. We very probably have here a minor result of the Reformation—the Crown succeeds the Church as supervisor of the medical profession.

11. *Ibid.* 262.

12. 8 Co. 116b; 2 Brownl. 262.

13. 8 Co. 116b; 2 Brownl. 264.

14. As to this, see *infra,* p. 169.

15. 8 Co. 118a; 2 Brownl. 265.

that the Royal College of Physicians were to receive one-half of all the fines, and are therefore not only judges, but also parties in any case that comes before them, and it is an established maxim of common law that no man can be judge in his own case.[16] "And it appears in our books that in many cases the common law will controul acts of parliament and sometimes adjudge them to be utterly void: for when an act of parliament is against common right or reason, or repugnant[17] or impossible to be performed, the common law will controul it and adjudge such act to be void";—words which challenged both Crown and Parliament, and provoked controversies which have continued to our own day. We shall have to consider how far the authorities cited by Coke support this contention; what light recent researches into early Year Book law have thrown upon the subject; the reception accorded to the doctrine by contemporaries; its gradual abandonment in England; and its results in America.

II

The first of these questions has already received some attention, and the significance of *Tregor's Case*,[18] which is one of Coke's principal authorities, has been the subject of considerable discussion. It will be sufficient to summarize here the results which have been reached by the present writer in an earlier study.[19] In the first place, Coke has seriously misquoted the Year Book thus: "Herle saith some statutes are made *against law and right,* which those who made them *perceiving,* would not put them into execution." The italicized words are interpolations by Coke which do not appear in the original, and introduce an idea of some superior "right" which Herle certainly did not entertain.

---

16. For more than a dozen exceptions to this maxim, see 2 Rolle, *Abridgment* 93 and the numerous citations in Quincy, 525 (Mass. 1865). One of the cases cited by Coke has the following: "*Rolf:* I will tell you a fable. Once upon a time there was a Pope who had committed a great offence, and the Cardinals came to him and said *Peccasti,* and he said, *Judica me.* And they said *Non possumus quia caput es ecclesiae; judica teipsum.* And the Pope said *Judico me cremari,* and he was burnt. And in this case he was his own judge, and afterwards he was a Saint. So it is not inconvenient for a man to be his own judge." Y. B. Hil. 8 Hen. VI, 6. The reference must be to Saint Marcellinus, but the story here is not quite the same as that in general circulation. His legend appears in the Breviary, where his feast is April 26. See the notes by Sir Frederick Pollock in (1895) 10 *Eng. Hist. Rev.* 293, 536.

17. The meaning of repugnant is not clear; it would almost seem that it meant no more than distasteful to the court; there is no evidence to show what Coke meant by it precisely. In United States v. Cantril, 4 Cranch, 167 (U. S. 1807), it is used in the peculiar sense of "self-contradictory." Elsewhere Coke uses it in the sense of "contrary to common law." 1 *Co. Inst.* 206b; *cf.* Sullivan v. Adams, 3 Gray, 476 (Mass. 1855).

18. Y. B. Pasch. 8 Edw. III, 26.

19. Plucknett, *Statutes and Their Interpretation in the 14th Century* (1922) 68–70.

The only meaning which Herle's words can reasonably be made to bear is that sometimes the legislator has repented of a hasty piece of work and has been content to allow it to become a dead letter. Secondly, whoever reads the whole of Herle's remarks can see that he did not regard the statute then under discussion as falling within this category; on the contrary, he suggested a perfectly obvious and straightforward interpretation of it, in which Hilary concurred. It cannot be denied that Coke's first authority is far from convincing.

His second instance is the anonymous case printed by Fitzherbert from an inedited Year Book as *Cessavit* 42, which also has been discussed elsewhere.[20] It goes much further to support his thesis than does *Tregor's Case,* and recent discoveries have increased its historical value. In the *Graunde Abridgement* of Fitzherbert it occupies but two lines, and they not altogether intelligible, but in Coke's telling the story gains an aunt and a niece as well as considerable clarity—all derived from an unspecified and unidentified source. However, even in the form in which it appears in Fitzherbert, it is plain that the judgment was in complete accordance with that in an earlier case, *Copper v. Gederings,*[21] which is much more fully reported, and for our knowledge of which we are indebted to the Year Books of the Selden Society. The details of the earlier case need not detain us here: suffice it to say that the Statute of Westminster the Second enacted that the right of action in *Cessavit* should descend from a lord to his heir; but when an heir brought his writ, Chief Justice Bereford refused to maintain it, on the ground that if the action were allowed, certain general principles of the common law would be disturbed. It is true that upon several occasions Bereford had the hardihood to embody his own distinctly original views upon legal problems in his judgments,[22] but in this case the same decision was given half a century later in the case *Cessavit* 42 quoted by Coke, and was duly enshrined in the books of authority as the final law upon the subject.[23] Here then is no mere caprice of one particular judge but a *catena* of authorities extending from the middle of the fourteenth century down to Coke's own day. The statement of Sir Frederick Pollock[24] that "no

---

20. *Ibid.* 66.

21. Y. B. 3 Edw. II, 105. All three of the MSS. report the case as in the text, but as the record has not been clearly identified, there may be some doubt as to exactly what happened. Even assuming that Maitland found the correct record, there is no great inconsistency. The plaintiff may well have sought leave to retire from the writ in view of an inevitable judgment that the action was not maintainable.

22. Plucknett, *op. cit. supra* note 19, at 129–31.

23. *Natura Brevium* (1553) clvii *d;* Fitzherbert, *Natura Brevium* (Hale's ed. 1755) 209; *cf.* 2 Co. *Inst.* 402, 460.

24. Pollock, *First Book of Jurisprudence* (3d ed. 1911) 264.

case is known, in fact, in which an English court of justice has openly taken on itself to overrule or disregard the plain meaning of an Act of Parliament" must be taken subject to this exception (and others will appear later), which the publication of the Selden Society's Year Books has brought to light. The courts in these cases did undoubtedly "disregard the plain meaning of an Act of Parliament"; but in telling the story Lord Coke has made the important addition of the words "because it would be against common right and reason, the common law adjudges the said act of parliament as to that point void." There is no such judgment as this in the report; the statute is not held void; it is just ignored. To this fact Coke has really added an explanation and a theory all his own — an addition that was to be of immense importance in subsequent history.

The third great precedent cited by Coke is another case in Fitzherbert— *Annuitie* 41. A better report, however, is translated below[25] from the earlier and very rare *Abridgment* of Statham, where it appears as *Annuitie* 11. The Statute of Carlisle, first put forth in 1305 and finally enacted in 1307, had much to say of ecclesiastical affairs, and notably of a legal problem which had long been prominent in the courts. Many of the smaller religious houses did not possess common seals, but contented themselves with the personal seal of their head. Thus questions inevitably arose as to whether a particular document under an abbot's seal was his personal deed binding only himself, or the deed of the ecclesiastical corporation of which he was the head. To do away with this fruitful source of confusion the statute orders all such religious houses to have a common seal for their corporate acts, and (unless such is the case already) to place this seal in the custody of the prior and four worthiest brethren who shall keep it secured under the abbot's private seal, so that the abbot cannot use it without the knowledge of the convent. By this means it was hoped that the presence of the conventual seal would be an infallible proof of the concur-

---

25. "Pasch. 27 Hen. VI. One Rous brought annuity against an abbot and showed a deed of annuity made by the abbot's predecessor and sealed with the convent seal, which annuity was of certain bread, beer, robes and other things &c. *Pole.* The Statute of Carlisle said of Cistercians and Premonstratensians and Austens who have convent and common Seal, that the common seal shall be in the keeping of the prior (who is under the abbot) and four others, the wisest of the house; and that any deed sealed with the common seal which is not in such custody shall be void. And we tell you that at the time when this deed was sealed, the seal was out of their custody, and the opinion of the Court was that this statute is void for it is impertinent to be observed, for the seal being in their custody, the abbot cannot seal anything with it, for when it is in the abbot's hands it is *ipso facto* out of their custody. And if it were observed, every common seal would be defeated by a simple surmise which cannot be tried &c. *Vide, quia bene debate et plusours excepcions pris al ple &c.*"

Miss Klingelsmith in 1 *Statham* (1915) 114, has followed the traditional view and translated "impertinent" by "impossible."

rence of the convent in the act of its head. Was this statute in direct conflict with Church law? The general idea that temporal regulations could be made specifying the mode of authentication required to give validity to the temporal acts of spiritual bodies is reasonable enough, and one can heartily sympathize with the common lawyers' fervent desire to devise a means of knowing exactly when an act was that of the corporation, and when it was only the personal act of its head. But the means adopted involved grave interference with the internal economy of ecclesiastical bodies, which was already the subject of ca-nonical legislation. The Church's law placed the custody of the common seal in the hands of the head alone, and afforded as yet no effective means of ensur-ing the concurrence of the members in the act of their sovereign.[26] However, we find in 1366 that in his visitation of a priory which had suffered from an autocratic head, the Bishop of Lichfield ordered that the common seal should be kept in a chest with three locks, one for the prior and the others for two canons to be elected by the whole house.[27] This is clearly in the spirit of the Statute of Carlisle, but it seems to have been not the normal arrangement but a special discipline for a spendthrift abbot. Canon law still charged the head of a house with the duty of keeping and honestly using the common seal, and inasmuch as the statute professed to relieve him of this duty, it was certainly trespassing upon ecclesiastical territory.[28] If the statute could have simply in-sisted upon conventual acts bearing the conventual seal, there would probably have been little trouble, but it went further and proceeded to invalidate acts bearing even the conventual seal if it had not been kept in the custody of the prior and four brethren as laid down in the act. This was a necessary step, and the intention was clearly to modify the rigor of the statute and to protect con-

26. "Unusquisque [prelatus] per se illud [*sc.* sigillum] custodiat, vel uni soli de cuius fide confidat cus-todiendum committat, qui etiam iuret quod illud fideliter custodiet, nec ad sigillandum aliquid alicui concedet nec ipse etiam aliquid sigillet inde ex quo possit praejudicium alicui generari, nisi quid dominus eius prius legerit et viderit diligenter et sic praeceperit sigillari." *Const. Ottonis* (1679) 69 (enacted in 1236). The delegation of the seal here contemplated is that which was customarily made to officials who relieved their principals of much routine work, and is quite distinct from the compulsory delegation of the seal to subordinates in order to ensure their constitutional control over their head.

27. *Stretton's Second Register* (8 Salt Soc. Collections (n. s.) 1905) 114. At an earlier period the Pope him-self might prescribe such an arrangement where the case necessitated it: Innocent III, for example, imposed it upon the spendthrift abbot of Bourgueil in 1198: "praecipimus etiam ut duo fratres bonae vitae et maturae aetatis sigillum capituli custodiant nec ideo aliquid nisi de communi assensu sigillent." *Register I,* ep. 311 (Migne, *Patrologia Latina,* CCXIV, 271).

28. It is interesting to note that a similar device was in use (voluntarily, it would seem) in some lay communities; for example Coventry in 1424 kept its common seal in a bag which in turn was sealed by four citizens, while in 1421 the common seal was kept in the common chest of which the mayor and three others held one key each—the number of keys rising to five by 1445. *Coventry Leet Book* (1867) 22, 73, 218. Probably the sealed bag was kept within the common pyx.

vents against abbots who applied the conventual seal without the knowledge of their convent.

Nevertheless this provision was obviously impossible to work, unless, perhaps, the close and cordial cooperation of the Church could have been secured,[29] and the common law courts were therefore still in the same dilemma of having to settle disputes between abbots and their convents without being able to impose any regulations upon them, or to obtain any reliable facts as to their participation or otherwise in acts which purported to be conventual.

This difficulty is clearly brought out in the case before us, which arose in 1449 — over a hundred and forty years after the passing of the statute. A convent invoked the aid of the statute to defeat a deed charging them with an annuity, on the ground that at the time the deed was made their common seal was not in the proper custody specified in the act. The opinion of the court was twofold. There was the famous piece of dialectic which demonstrated that the statute could not be obeyed, for if the seal was kept by the prior and four brethren, how could the abbot use it at all? This was followed by the more convincing reason that if the latter part of the statute was to be applied, a convent could virtually avoid any of its acts by simply alleging that the seal was not in the proper custody — a fact that the lay courts had no satisfactory means of trying.

Several points require attention. First, we are told of no judgment, but only the "opinion" of the court, and this does not necessarily mean more than that the reporter believed that the court inclined to one side rather than the other. Judgment is not reported and may never have taken place. Secondly, we do find the word "void" used of a statute, though it is unfortunate that we have no access to any document earlier than about forty years after the event, and that the arguments, which we know were very full and interesting, are no longer extant. Thirdly, Mr. Brinton Coxe's conjecture[30] that the decision was influenced by considerations of canon law is less convincing (although the statute certainly was an interference in purely ecclesiastical matters), since it was the abbey which sought to maintain the validity of the statute, and the lay judges who held that it was void. Finally, the excuse given by the judges for their opinion is not the impossibility of applying the act, as stated by Coke[31] and

---

29. Where a convent alleged that an act had been sealed "furtively" without their knowledge or consent, canon law permitted the sworn evidence of the brethren to be taken: c. 5, X. 2. 19. (1187–1191).

30. Coxe, *Judicial Power and Unconstitutional Legislation* (1893) 158.

31. 2 *Co. Inst.* 587–88.

Blackstone;[32] for the court still had spirit enough to call the statute "impertinent," although it is very significant that it was thought prudent to accompany this with a piece of ratiocination making out a superficial impossibility. The inference is irresistible; the court was feeling distinctly nervous at such a step, even if only expressed in a mere opinion, and the contrast with the earlier cases in which statutes were brushed aside without apology and almost without comment, is very striking.

How far, then, is the case authority for the thesis which Coke builds upon it? In the first place, there are the very serious objections that the report is scanty and only tells of the debate upon one point, although we know that many other questions were raised and discussed in the case. Consequently it becomes all the more necessary to insist that the passage that we have in the *Abridgment* is not a judgment, but what the reporter believes to be the "opinion" of the court on this one point that happened to interest him. Probably no judgment was given at that hearing, but only an adjournment to a later term, by which time the court may well have changed its opinion, or counsel have shifted their arguments to other and less controversial grounds—a frequent occurrence in Year Book cases. In the report as we have it there is no discussion whatever of the proposition that the statute was void, but merely Pole's plea, immediately followed by the court's opinion. In view of this drastic suppression of the arguments *pro* and *contra,* which we know were numerous, it would be very hazardous to assume that we can accurately reconstruct the court's sentiments upon the subject, seeing that all information as to the divergent points of view of the various counsel, which is equally necessary for a correct interpretation of the case, is completely lost. In addition to this it is impossible to tell what weight (if any) this point had in determining the court's judgment (if such there was), for other points were debated. Historically, therefore, the case contains far too many unknown factors to be used with any degree of confidence or safety.

But this was manifestly not the point of view from which Sir Edward Coke and most of his contemporaries would have regarded the case; and so it is only fair that we should try to divest ourselves for a moment of the critical habits of the modern historian, and see the case as it would have appeared to a seventeenth century lawyer. It is printed clearly and intelligibly in a famous and authoritative folio, with all the pomp and circumstance of Law-French and

32. 1 *Bl. Comm.* 91.

black-letter. The text is therefore assumed to be satisfactory enough. True, we have only an "opinion"; but since it has been in the abridgments for over a century, the "ancients and sages" of the law surely must have valued it highly. It may certainly be presumed to have the approbation of that much respected judge, Sir Anthony Fitzherbert, who set it there; consequently its authority is undeniably high. As for the subject matter and the actual grounds for the decision, they are brief enough to be quoted *verbatim;* and so one can shift the burden of interpreting them on to the learned reader, who at least cannot deny that "the opinion of the Court was that the statute is void." The diversity of the reasons assigned for the decision is more apparent than real, for our old lawyer will refuse to admit that the dialectic we speak of so slightingly is not a very palpable difficulty—even something of the same nature as the well-nigh impossibility of trying the issue so confidently authorized in the act. The word "impertinent" is not so clear as it might be, but broadly speaking, "impossible" seems to get the meaning well enough. Treated in this way, the case takes a rather different aspect, and if we say, as we surely must, that it is much less convincing to us than to Coke, we must also add that the difference is due to the centuries which separate us from his age and thought.

The last case to which Chief Justice Coke gives extended notice, approaches the problem from a different angle. In early Year Book days the king was "prerogative." That is to say, there was a certain point beyond which the ordinary law of the land did not apply to him—in much the same way, for example, (though to a much less extent) as "one cannot use the law of the land in all its points against a merchant."[33] What will happen then if a statute conflicts with this prerogative character of the Crown?

Such a situation arose out of the vast overturning of legal titles due to the suppression of religious houses and chantries at the Reformation. In consequence of various statutes large numbers of landed properties were deemed to be in the seisin of the Crown, and remained in that condition until they were granted out to subjects by royal letters patent. Many of these lands were subject to complicated incidents and obligations which the statutes attempted to adjust. For example, many lands not only supported their ecclesiastical owners, but had also been subjected to various rent charges and rents sec, payable to laymen who were in no way connected with religious foundations. Clearly these people should not be made to lose their incomes merely because the lands upon which they were secured had been confiscated; so the act explicitly

33. Bereford, C. J., in Y. B. 4 Edw. II, 154.

provides that such rents shall be saved to all manner of persons. Consequently the seisin of the king, and that of his patentee if the lands had been granted out, made no difference, and rents of this class were duly paid by the king and those deriving title from him. So far there was no difficulty. But some of the lands were subject to a peculiar burden known as rent service, and here complications arose. Rent service is a rent reserved at the time of making a feoffment, and is due to a lord from his tenant in virtue of their feudal relationship and the fealty which it involved. It is not a charge, but a feudal service, and the lord can exact it by distress (even though there be no clause of distress in the feoffment to authorize it), for although the land is held by the tenant in demesne, yet it is also held by the lord in service, and a lord can distrain within his own fee. When land subject to this type of rent came into the king's hands, it suffered a change. The king is prerogative and cannot stoop to perform services to any man, and therefore these rent services are extinguished immediately the lands come into the king's seisin. The statute for the suppression of the chantries, however, in its endeavor to be as just as possible, contained a general saving of all peoples' rights to rents (including rent services) due from chantry lands.[34] Here, then, is a conflict between the prerogative and the statute; the one extinguishes these rents, and the other protects them. Which shall prevail? A group of Elizabethan cases which Lord Coke cites[35] gives us the answer. The first is anonymous, but dated 1572.[36] The report is brief: "*Memorandum,* That it was resolved by the opinion of the Court in the Bench, That the seigniory and tenure of obit land, or chantry land, is extinct by the possession of the King, by the act of 1 E. 6. [c. 14] notwithstanding the saving in the act; *propter absurditatem* &c." So we have here yet another sort of defect which has been suggested as fatal to an act of Parliament; to "impertinence" and, apparently, impossibility, we must now add absurdity. At first sight the decision sounds drastic, but the report goes on to explain that even if the tenure is extinguished (and of course it can never be revived afterward), nevertheless the rent services which were part of the tenure can still be exacted by the lord from the king's grantee by means of distress and avowry. The situation is curious: the court, greatly daring, refuses to recognize the express words of the statute in favor of rent services, and roundly declares them extinct *non obstante* the act; but what it takes away with one hand, it prudently restores with the other, for it con-

---

34. (1547) 1 Edw. VI, c. 14, § 17. At the suppression of the monasteries, this concession was deliberately refused, not only to rent services, but also to rents sec. (1539) 31 Hen. VIII, c. 13, § 4.

35. 8 Co. 118b.

36. 3 Dyer, 313 (K. B. 1572).

cedes that the quondam lord—we may no longer call him lord after the king's seisin—may still exact his rent by way of distress. In fact, the court's temerity had no practical result whatever beyond the change of one single word, as we may learn from *Strowd's Case,*[37] in which the matter was finally settled thus:

> If a man has lands which were once parcel of the possessions of a chantry, and which came to the King under the Statute of Dissolution at the time of the dissolution, and were formerly held of someone else by rent and fealty [*i.e.,* by rent service] or by service which is chivalry, the King's patentee shall now hold the tenements according to the patent [*i.e.,* of the King] and not of the former lord and his heirs, and by the services by which they were anciently held, save that the same rent that was formerly rent service, he shall pay as a rent charge distrainable of common right only by the said person who was formerly lord and his heirs. And thus was the saving in the said statute expounded by the Justices of the Common Bench.

The question is now displayed in its right proportions. The decision is identical with that in the anonymous case which we have just mentioned, but without the rhetoric. The ostentatious judgment "notwithstanding the saving in the act" is now reduced to its proper place as being merely an expounding of the statute. The act saves these rents, and so did both of the judgments. The only difference was that the statute still called them rent services, although the judges, for technical reasons bordering upon pedantry, preferred to call them rent charges. In the former case the court adopted this terminology with a pretentious flourish; in the second, it soberly described its action as simply exposition.

One need only quote the words of Coke in this connection to show clearly how much he has magnified the importance of these cases: "So the statute of 1 E. 6. c. 14 gives chauntries, &c. to the King, saving to the donor, &c. all such rents, services, &c. and the common law controuls it, and adjudges it void as to services, and the donor shall have the rent, as a rentseck, distrainable of common right, for it would be against common right and reason that the King should hold of any, or do service to any of his subjects, 14 Eliz. Dyer 313. and so it was adjudged in . . . Strowd's case."[38] Nowhere does Coke's dogma of a controlling common law appear in the reports of these cases, and the voidance of the statute on those grounds is certainly not "adjudged in Strowd's case."

37. 1 And. 45 (C. P. 1575); 3 Leon. 58 (C. P. 1575); 4 Leon. 40 (C. P. 1575).
38. 8 Co. 118b.

Finally, Sir Edward Coke concludes this portion of his argument with an imaginary case: "So if any act of parliament gives to any to hold, or to have cognisance of all manner of pleas arising before him in his manor of D., yet he shall hold no plea to which he himself is party; for as hath been said, *iniquum est aliquem suae rei esse judicem.*" [39] His argument began with the proposition that letters patent could not make a man judge in his own case, and as a result of the subsequent discussion, he reached the position that an act of Parliament of this nature was equally ineffective.

We have now taken Coke's authorities as he presents them, and it remains, first, to assess the value of his arguments from the point of view of contemporary scholarship. *Tregor's Case* proves nothing; *Cessavit* 42, on the other hand, is a strong precedent in his favor; *Annuitie* 41 would have looked strong also, although it is, in fact, of doubtful import; while *Strowd's Case* is valueless. To his fellow justices, therefore, Coke was able to present a fairly convincing case in which the weak points were by no means obvious to an uncritical mind, while there was at least one clear and incontestable precedent in his favor. If, however, we apply modern scholarship to the problem, and make use of sources which were not available in his day, the result is rather different. As we have already indicated, the facts alleged by the Chief Justice can even be confirmed in some cases by newly published Year Books; but on the other hand, the theory which he believed to be their legal foundation must be credited to his own political thought rather than to that of his medieval predecessors upon the Common Bench. In discussing *Copper v. Gederings,* which anticipated the judgment in *Cessavit* 42, we pointed out that although the court deprived an heir of a right of action explicitly granted to him by a statute, because such an action if allowed would seriously disturb the general law on such matters, yet the court did not inquire into the authority of the statute, nor even the conflict of it and the common law. It simply quashed the writ on a plea to the action. The constitutional question was never discussed, nor even raised. The nature of statutes was not questioned, and there is certainly not the faintest suggestion of declaring a statute void. The judges did indeed prefer in this case to follow the common law rather than the statute, but they tell us nothing of their inherent right to "control" legislation in its name. A few more instances are extant of this strange habit of quietly ignoring a statute without assigning

---

39. This "manor of D." is, of course, none other than the manor of Dale which figures so often in the imaginary cases propounded by common lawyers. Corwin, *The Doctrine of Judicial Review* (1914) 69, however, finds a new precedent in this "case arising in the manor of Dales [*sic*] where it was held" etc.

any constitutional grounds for doing so, or specifying what powers the court claimed to possess in that behalf, and they have already been discussed elsewhere.[40] Finally it must be insisted that these cases are comparatively early, and are not to be found in the later Year Books. Coke's work is therefore in the nature of an antiquarian revival of obsolescent law with a view to applying it to current needs, an attitude toward history which was characteristic of the age, and which can be illustrated from the controversial literature of all parties.

It may be of interest to examine here a few other cases which have been alleged in support of the theory by Sir Edward Coke in other parts of his *Reports*—for *Dr. Bonham's Case* is not the only place where these high powers are attributed to the common law judges.

We will begin with the famous *Sheriff of Northumberland's Case*[41] which figures largely in the arguments of *Calvin's Case*[42] and later in *Godden v. Hales*,[43] and which has not yet been thoroughly examined. There is a short note upon the case by Coke,[44] but the fullest treatment of it is from the pen of his life-long rival, Lord Bacon, in his *Maxims, regula* xix.[45] These maxims were apparently written earlier than 1597 although they were not published until 1630; so there is a possibility of their being known to Coke while he was preparing what we have preserved to us as the twelfth part of his *Reports*. Lord Bacon's remarks are as follows:

> So if there be a statute made "that no sheriff shall continue in his office above a year, and if any patent be made to the contrary it shall be void; and if there be any *clausula non obstante* contained in such patent to dispense with the present act, that such clause also shall be void;" yet nevertheless a patent of a sheriff's office made by the king for term of life, with a *non obstante,* will be good in law, contrary to such statute which pretendeth to exclude *non obstantes:* and the reason is, because it is an inseparable prerogative of the crown to dispense with politic statutes, and of that kind; and then the derogatory clause hurteth not.

Reference to the Year Book shows clearly enough that some such case arose, but we are told most definitely that "forasmuch as this was the first time, the

40. Plucknett, *op. cit. supra* note 19, at 60, 66–71.
41. Y. B. Mich. 2 Hen. VII, 20.
42. 7 Co. 1a, 14a (C. P. 1608).
43. 2 Shower, *475 (K. B. 1686) (reported more fully in Bacon, *Abridgment,* tit. *Prerogative,* D7).
44. 12 Co. 18.
45. 7 Bacon, *Works* (Spedding ed. 1879) 369–72.

Justices, Sergeants, and King's Attorney agreed that they should study the matter well, and then be heard; and what they said counted for nothing, since they wished to retain their freedom to say what they liked, and to consider what they had said up till now as nothing." With these words the report concludes and nothing is known of the later history of the case. There is, moreover, in Brook's *Abridgment* another report of the case[46] which is still more emphatic; "and the matter was let drop on this day and nothing was adjudged," we there read. There could hardly be a more explicit warning against using it as a precedent, or regarding it as adjudging or deciding upon any point of law; and yet in defiance of this disclaimer in the report itself, we find it quoted in *Calvin's Case* as "agreed." It was all to no use that the authority of the case was afterward denied, for in *Godden v. Hales* the court apparently felt that if there was no such decision in *The Sheriff's Case* there ought to have been, and so they proceeded to raise the case posthumously to the dignity of a precedent after the lapse of two hundred years by adjudging "that the case of sheriffs in the second year of *Henry the Seventh,* was law, and always taken as law."[47] So much, then, for the authority of the case. As for the substance of the arguments reported in the Year Book, still further comments will have to be passed. As both Coke and Bacon remark the report alleged that the statutes 28 Edw. III, c. 7, and 42 Edw. III, c. 5, forbid any sheriff from serving more than a year in his office, even if his patent should contain a clause *non obstante* this present act; and that Henry Percy claimed to hold office under such a patent appointing him Sheriff of Northumberland for life notwithstanding the statute. There are two facts which are very material to the discussion, but which do not figure in the Year Book report at all. The first is that the statutes quoted contain no such provision forbidding clauses of *non obstante.* The second is that this provision does occur in another statute, *viz.* 23 Hen. VI, c. 7, which is not mentioned in the arguments, but this very act contains also an express saving of the rights of those sheriffs who held office for life. Percy's patent is therefore perfectly valid under the statute.[48] We may suggest a reason why the novel debate in the Year Book was never resumed; when the judges and sergeants and the king's attorney eventually "studied the matter well" they must have discovered the existence of this statute of Henry VI and the saving it contained in favor of

46. Tit. *Patentes,* 109.
47. 2 Shower, *478.
48. Percy was sheriff until the death of Richard III when he was superseded by Sir Robert Maners; he was restored in 1488—immediately after this case—when he rendered accounts from the beginning of the reign, including the whole of Maners' term.

shrievalties in fee. Once this statute was found, further argument became un-necessary. Finally it will be observed that the situation discussed by Coke and Bacon of a patent attempting to dispense with a statute although the statute itself forbids it, did not arise in this case at all.

The Prior of Castle Acre v. The Dean of St. Stephen's[49] is sometimes quoted as an example of the limitation of the powers of the legislature. The case is much too complicated for full treatment here, but the material point is that a priory which was "parson" of a church was suppressed and vested in the Crown by virtue of an act of Parliament. Did the Crown thereby become "parson" of the church? Chief Justice Frowyke summed up after protracted argument:

> As for the other matter, whether the king can be parson by the Act of Parliament, as I see it, it is not a great matter to argue, for I have never seen that a temporal man can be parson without the agreement of the Supreme Head. And in all the cases which have been put, *sc.* of benefices in Wales and benefices which laymen have in their own use,[50] I have seen the matter, and the king had them by the assent and agreement of the Supreme Head. So a temporal act without the assent of the Supreme Head cannot make the king parson.

At the end of the report we find a significant "*Quaere*" which becomes all the more explicable when one remembers the words of Justice Kingsmill who had said, "We cannot make any temporal man by our law to have spiritual juris-diction, for no one can do this save the Supreme Head," and that the Act of Supremacy was less than thirty years ahead. From our point of view, however, the case is less important, for the fact that a statute could not operate in the ecclesiastical sphere proves no more than does the fact that it could not operate in any other foreign jurisdiction.

III

Such then were the grounds upon which Coke built his imposing theory. We must now describe the reception which his contemporaries accorded it. For the time being, Coke was dominant, and consequently we find his point of

---

49. Y. B. Hil. 21 Hen. VII, 1–5.
50. Coningsby had argued that "infants and laymen can and do hold prebends which have no cure of souls, and so the King can be parson, as any layman can, for there is an endowed vicarage with the cure of souls"; and the King has divers benefices in Wales which are continually in his hands.

view expressed repeatedly in the courts. True it is that Bacon was influential enough to secure the promotion of his rival to the more dignified but less lucrative post of Chief Justice of the King's Bench on the death of Sir Thomas Fleming in 1613, yet his successor in the Common Pleas, Sir Henry Hobart, was a staunch upholder of Coke's view of the common law, as may be seen in *Day v. Savadge*.[51] Savadge, on behalf of the City of London, had exacted certain wharf-dues from Day, although the latter claimed that by the custom of the City he was not liable. The issue reached was that there was no such custom, and the question arose as to how its existence could be tried. The City claimed the ancient privilege, confirmed to them, it was alleged, by a statute of 7 Ric. II,[52] which authorized their Recorder, by word of mouth, to declare what were the customs of the City—to which it was objected that such a procedure would make them judge in their own case. The judgment of Chief Justice Hobart dealt with a number of points, and in discussing the so-called statute he declared that "even an Act of Parliament made against Natural Equity, as to make a Man Judge in his own Cause, is void in itself, for *Jura naturae sunt immutabilia* and they are *leges legum*."[53] A noteworthy feature of the case, which is reported by the Chief Justice himself, is that no authorities are cited for the proposition that an act of Parliament against natural equity is void, and that no reference whatever is made to *Bonham's Case* as establishing it. Clearly, then, in Hobart's opinion, the truth of its doctrine was beyond dispute, and although it was already possible to refer to Coke's report of *Bonham's Case,* which was published in 1611, it is highly probable that Hobart's natural caution warned him against too open a tribute to one whose fortunes had already begun to decline.

That Hobart was a thorough believer in Coke's doctrine, however, can be seen just as plainly in his judgment in *Lord Sheffield v. Ratcliffe*[54] where he claims wide power of judicial review: "if you ask me, then, by what rule the judges guided themselves in this diverse exposition of the self same word and sentence? I answer, it was by that liberty and authority that judges have over laws, especially over statute laws, according to reason and best convenience,

51. Hobart, 85 (K. B. 1614).
52. There is room for discussion as to the exact nature of this confirmation; for our purposes, however, the question is immaterial, for the court undoubtedly believed that it was dealing with a true statute. See *Historical Charters and Constitutional Documents of the City of London* (1884) xxviii–xxx, 70–73, 314.
53. This is a rather serious misquotation of Bracton, f. 4, who had written that "jura enim naturalia dicuntur immutabilia quia non possunt ex toto abrogari vel auferri; potuit tamen eis derogari vel detrahi in specie vel in parte."
54. Hobart, 334a, 346 (K. B. 1615).

to mould them to the truest and best use. . . ."[55] Coke had claimed that the common law was fundamental, and it was an inevitable corollary of this theorem that the bench, as the sole repository of this common law, should regard itself as thereby endowed with authority to treat statutes with the widest discretion. It is impossible to deny that Hobart's doctrine is implicit in that of his predecessor.

Coke's removal to the King's Bench in 1613 was the prelude to still sterner measures, in view of the fact that he was soon to give still more offense; in June, 1616, he was suspended from his office and ordered to "correct" his *Reports*. In the following October there was a schedule of five questions which were put to the Chief Justice by the King, apparently on the suggestion of Bacon and the Solicitor-General, Yelverton, the fourth of which demanded an explanation of the dictum in *Bonham's Case* that the common law will control acts of Parliament. Coke's written reply is preserved for us,[56] and shows his complete confidence in the historical basis of his theory. "The words of my report do not import any new opinion," he wrote, "but only a relation of such authorities of law, as had been adjudged and resolved in former times, and were cited in the argument of Bonham's case; and therefore the words of my book are these; 'It appeareth in our books, that in many cases the common law shall control acts of parliament, and sometimes adjudge them to be utterly void,'" (quoting the long passage from his report containing the mediaeval precedents which we have already considered in detail), "which cases being cited in the argument of this case," he continued, "and I finding them truly vouched, I reported them in this case, as my part was, and had no other meaning than so far as those particular cases there cited do extend unto." Here as elsewhere Coke refused to acknowledge any substantial error in his writings, and boldly met his accusers by repeating the offending passages word by word as he first wrote them. He had been suspended from office some months earlier and commanded to correct his *Reports,* but the only defects he would acknowledge were a few trifling slips which he protested were extremely few, considering the magnitude of his work.[57]

An even more serious attack upon the judgment in *Bonham's Case* has been

---

55. These words were quoted by General Varnum in the course of his argument in Trevett v. Weeden. See *infra*, p. 181.

56. 6 Bacon, *Works* (1803 ed.) 405.

57. But in at least one case Coke has been found guilty of reporting exactly the opposite of the actual decision in a case. Wallace, *Reporters* (4th ed. 1882) 174; *cf.* Beale, Southcott v. Bennett (1899) 13 *Harv. L. Rev.* 43.

attributed to the Chancellor, Lord Ellesmere, who, it is said, prepared a set of criticisms upon the *Reports* which remained in manuscript until the early part of the eighteenth century.[58] Besides accusing the Chief Justice of trampling upon the Act of Parliament of 14 and 15 Hen. VIII, "having no precedent before him, but many judgments against him," it is further alleged that this was "in triumph of himself, being accompanied by the opinion of one Judge only for the matter in law, where three other Judges were against him." In his report Coke claims the concurrence of Justices Warburton and Daniel, and also the extra-judicial support of Sir Thomas Fleming, Chief Justice of the King's Bench;[59] while Sergeant Hill in a manuscript note in his copy of Ellesmere acquits Coke of this charge on the independent evidence of Brownlow, who implies that Coke had a majority on the bench.[60] It would seem that the Royalist party did not regard this point as easy to establish, for it does not appear in the list of five objections which Coke was ordered to meet. It is very significant, too, that even Lord Ellesmere in his address to Chief Justice Montagu, commending those judges who do not declare statutes void for being contrary to reason and common right, makes one exception—"I speak not of impossibilities or direct repugnances."[61]

Upon the fall of Coke, his doctrine naturally suffered an eclipse, which, however, was not total, for we find Justice Berkeley announcing "that in some cases the Judges were above an act of Parliament."[62] Experiments were indeed made during the Commonwealth, notably in the *Instrument of Government,*[63] in the direction of establishing a fundamental law, but with little success. It was not until the Restoration that we find it again in the reports, and then it is strangely twisted to the advantage of the Crown. In the famous case of *Godden v. Hales,*[64] it was argued whether the Crown had the prerogative of dispensing with "laws of government," for, said Sergeant Glanvil, "there's a great Distinction between the Laws of Property and those of Government"—and if we would express in one compendious sentence the difference of outlook between modern and medieval political thought, it would be hard to improve

---

58. *The Lord Chancellor Egerton's Observations on the Lord Coke's Reports.* London folio, n. d. [?1710—British Museum Catalogue]. For its authorship, see 5 Holdsworth, *History of English Law* (1924) 478 n. 1; (1920) 36 *L. Q. Rev.* 4.

59. 8 Co. 117a, 121a.

60. This note is printed in 4 Co. (Thomas and Frazer ed. 1826) 375, n. c.

61. Moore, 828 (K. B. 1616).

62. 2 [James Grant], *Law and Lawyers* (1840) 212.

63. See Jenks, *Constitutional Experiments of the Commonwealth* (1890).

64. 2 Shower, *475 (K. B. 1686); Bacon, *Abridgment,* tit. *Prerogative,* D7.

upon this. To the middle ages they were all one.[65] Sir Thomas Powys "urged that the King's Prerogative was, and is as much the Law of England as any Statute." Much was made of the *Sheriff of Northumberland's Case*[66] although Northey vigorously denied its authority. Finally the "Lord Chief Justice took time to consider of it, and spake with the other Judges, and three or four Days after, declared that he and all the Judges (except *Street* and *Powell,* who doubted) were of opinion, that the kings of *England* were absolute sovereigns; that the laws were the king's laws; that the king had a power to dispense with any of the laws of government as he saw necessity for it; that he was sole judge of that necessity; that no act of Parliament could take away that power; that this was such a law; that the case of sheriffs in the second year of *Henry the Seventh,* was law, and always taken as law; and that it was a much stronger case than this; and therefore gave judgment for the defendant." The prerogative is undoubtedly part of the common law of the land, and if statutes cannot alter the fundamental law, then surely the prerogative is beyond their reach. Coke's doctrine is already bearing strange fruit. The fact that the decision has ever since been the subject of severe condemnation on political grounds must not be allowed to obscure the legal and historical basis for it. In the words of Mr. Brinton Coxe:[67]

> According to now prevalent American ideas, if the constitution of England had been written, and such a prerogative right had been constitutional, the court ought to have done precisely what it did. Moreover, had the decision been one in favour of a popular right instead of a prerogative right, the assertion of a judicial competency of deciding a questioned statute to be contrary to binding right, might have been, perhaps, very differently regarded. . . .
>
> Trevett *v.* Weeden[68] was a case in which a statute, made under an *unwritten* constitution, and destroying the popular right of trial by jury, was judicially rejected as unconstitutional and therefore void. In the interests of popular rights, an American court flatly refused to obey a clearly worded statute. Godden *v.* Hales was a case in which an English court, also proceeding under an *unwritten* constitution, did likewise in the interests of royal prerogative.

---

65. Compare Bacon's observation quoted *supra,* p. 164; and for examples of the medieval attitude toward public law, see Plucknett, "The Lancastrian Constitution," in *Tudor Studies Presented to A. F. Pollard* (1924) 163 *et seq.*

66. Discussed *supra,* p. 164.

67. Coxe, *op. cit supra* note 30, at 166–67.

68. This famous Rhode Island case will be discussed *infra,* p. 181.

However much the judgment may be esteemed as a striking application of Coke's theory, there is no denying that politically it created an intolerable situation, from which there was no escape save by the Revolution settlement safeguarded by Section XII of the Bill of Rights. As a practical issue in English constitutional law, the Revolution of 1688 marks the abandonment of the doctrine of *Bonham's Case,* and the realization of the futility of seeking permanence in a legal system which was suffering change as inevitable as it was radical. The attempt to check the divergent careers of Crown and Parliament by subjecting them both to the dead hand of the ancient common law, only revealed the disconcerting fact that the Crown had everything to gain by an appeal to antiquity, and that it was the common law itself, of which the prerogative was a part, which was the source of offense. The so-called vacillation of Coke himself must be attributed much more to this inherent weakness in his position, than to insincerity or lack of courage. Even believers in Coke's dogma, had they seen the events of James II's reign and the Revolution, could hardly have escaped confessing that the sovereignty of Parliament was more tolerable than a fundamental law of which the Stuart prerogative was so legitimate a portion.

In its earlier stages, the exponents of the theory did not define their "fundamental law" any too closely, and sometimes we find it described as a controlling common law, sometimes as reason, sometimes as natural equity. The Revolution showed that the common law was a dangerous basis to select: the Bill of Rights, moreover, had boldly overthrown several portions of it, and had created a situation which was virtually an *impasse* on any other theory than that of a supreme legislature, for there was no possible middle course between James II and William III, between the inalienable, irreducible and unalterable prerogative, and the statutory Bill of Rights which abolished notable portions of it. Nevertheless, people continued to argue that the legislature was limited by reason, or perhaps even, by natural equity, and it is in this form that we find the last traces of the influence of *Dr. Bonham's Case* in England.

In the *City of London v. Wood,*[69] the City sued in the Court of the Mayor and Aldermen against Wood for a fine due to them under a London by-law for refusing the office of sheriff, the by-law in question specifying that the fine may be exacted in any City court of record. It was argued *inter alia* that this

69. 12 Mod. *669 (Mayor's Court, 1701).

was bad, as they were judge in their own case, and on these and other grounds the judgment was reversed on error. The judgment of Lord Chief Justice Holt shows clearly how perplexed he was by the questions involved in this position. "So in this case it is plain," he observed,[70] "he is guilty of a wrong in not obeying the act of common council, for it is a law in *London;* and every by-law is a law, and as obligatory to all persons bound by it, that is, within its jurisdiction, as any act of parliament, only with this difference, that a by-law is liable to have its validity brought in question, but an act of parliament is not; but when a by-law is once adjudged to be a good and reasonable by-law, it is to all intents as binding to those that it extends to as an act of parliament can be." But this perfectly sound modern doctrine is accompanied by a reminiscence of pre-Revolution teaching: "But THE TRUE GREAT POINT is, that the court is held before the mayor and aldermen, and the action brought in the names of the mayor and commonalty; . . . and this cannot be by the rules of any law whatever, for it is against all laws that the same person should be party and judge in the same cause. . . . And what my Lord *Coke* says in Dr. *Bonham's Case* in his 8. *Co.* is far from any extravagancy, for it is a very reasonable and true saying, That if an act of parliament should ordain that the same person should be party and judge, or, which is the same thing, judge in his own cause, it would be a void act of parliament; for it is impossible that one should be judge and party, for the judge is to determine between party and party, or between the government and the party; and an act of parliament can do no wrong, though it may do several things that look pretty odd; for it may discharge one from his allegiance to the government he lives under, and restore him to the state of nature; but it cannot make one that lives under a government judge and party. An act of parliament may not make adultery lawful, that is, it cannot make it lawful for *A.* to lie with the wife of *B.* but it may make the wife of *A.* to be the wife of *B.* and dissolve her marriage with *A.*" In the course of the fourteen folio pages which this judgment occupies, then, Lord Holt wavers helplessly between two incompatible opinions. Thus he assures us that the validity of an act of Parliament cannot be questioned; but that all the same, it may be void if it enacts an "impossibility"[71] — that is to say, something contrary to the axioms of natural justice in all laws; that acts can certainly "do several things that look pretty odd," although, finally, it is to be believed that they can do no

---

70. *Ibid.* *678, *687.

71. For this peculiar use of "impossible" in the sense of "unbecoming," compare the "impertinent" of Annuitie 41, *supra* note 25.

wrong![72] Such is the sad state of wreckage to which Lord Coke's stately theory had been reduced after the successive hurricanes of the Great Rebellion and the Glorious Revolution.

Only fragments remain. In *The King v. Inhabitants of Cumberland*,[73] an indictment had been found against the county for not having repaired a bridge, and was removed into the Court of King's Bench by *certiorari* at the instance of the prosecutor. The defendants objected to this procedure as the statute 1 Ann. c. 18, § 5, enacted that such matters were to be determined in the counties where they arose and not elsewhere, "'and that no presentment or indictment for not repairing such bridges . . . shall be removed by *certiorari* out of the said county into any other court.'" No statute could be clearer, but this is what Lord Chief Justice Kenyon said about it: "The words of this act of parliament are very general: but if in the construction we were to read them in their full extent, it would introduce a solecism in the law; for it must be remembered that in these cases the defendants are the inhabitants of a county, and if the indictment cannot be removed by *certiorari,* and a suggestion entered on the record that the inhabitants of the county are interested in order to have the trial elsewhere, the indictment must be tried by the very persons who are parties in the cause. This, I believe, would be an anomalous case in the law of *England.* However, this question does not rest on that general observation. If this were *res integra,* we should consider whether the extensive words of this statute ought not to be narrowed in their construction, in order to arrive at that point, which is the object of all laws, the attainment of justice." The Chief Justice then went on to examine a long series of precedents where *certiorari* had issued and not been challenged—some of these cases being only one year after the statute. "Therefore on the authority of all these cases," he proceeded, "whatever might have been our opinion if it had been *res integra,* (though in forming an opinion for the first time on the subject we should have been anxious for reasons of substantial justice to have controlled the extensive operation of the general words of the statute of *Anne,*) we are of opinion that the *certiorari* was properly issued." Briefly stated, although Lord Kenyon contemplated the possibility of having to consider whether the principle of *Bonham's Case* might not be applicable, yet he was obviously glad of the opportunity for avoiding such a

72. It may be remarked that 12 Mod. is not very highly estimated as an example of law reporting; see Wallace, *Reporters* (4th ed. 1882) 355–56, 389–90. A few years earlier, Holt had declared it to be the judges' daily task to "construe and expound Acts of Parliament, and adjudge them to be void." King v. Earl of Banbury, Skin. 517, 527 (K. B. 1695).

73. 6 T. R. 194, 195, 197 (K. B. 1795).

delicate discussion by sheltering behind the long series of precedents which he enumerates to the length of two folio pages. Indeed, Lord Kenyon had availed himself of the same device only a few years earlier in *Leigh v. Kent*[74] when he refused to make absolute a rule to stay proceedings against a clergyman for non-residence, on the objection that an affidavit had not first been filed that the offense was in the county where the proceedings were brought, this being the requirement of the statute, 21 Jac. I, c. 4. His judgment, in which Justices Buller and Grose concurred, was that "I think no such affidavit is necessary; it has never been usual to take that step. And though, where the words of an act of parliament are plain, it cannot be repealed by *non-user,* yet where there has been a series of practice, without any exception, it goes a great way to explain them where there is any ambiguity." In short, the courts reserve the right tacitly to ignore a statute, if they can show that it has never been followed.[75] A very similar case on a different statute is that of *Stewart v. Lawton*[76] where Sergeant Cross objected to the statute 8 Ann. c. 9, that it required the plaintiff to be examined on oath in his own case—which (at that date) was "repugnant to common right" within the meaning of the rule in *Bonham's Case,* which he quoted at length. Without definitely accepting or denying this proposition, Justice Park based his judgment on that of Lord Kenyon in *Leigh v. Kent,* for here, too, the custom had been not to comply with the act.

It is worthy of note that about this time the courts were prepared to treat statutes with scant respect, but without giving any constitutional justification, in a manner which forcibly recalls the early fourteenth century. A striking example was when the mere deposit of deeds was held to operate as an equitable mortgage in *Russel v. Russel*[77] in the teeth of the Statute of Frauds which required all such transactions to be in writing and signed, the decision following an earlier experiment in that direction[78] and becoming in turn the source of a considerable line of development.[79]

---

74. 3 T. R. 362 (K. B. 1789).

75. For traces of such a doctrine in the fourteenth century, see Plucknett, *op. cit. supra* note 19, at 143–44; *cf.* Quincy, 51 (Mass. 1865). Another remarkable example of this strange notion occurs in 1287. The Statute of Gloucester, c. 3, had recognized a form of action, but when a party tried to use it, his opponent pleaded that "although the statute is as the plaintiff says, yet so far there has never been issued out of the king's chancery a writ of entry upon the statute; and he prays judgment." Judgment was accordingly given that the plaintiff had no remedy by a writ of entry and must bring a writ of right. *Chester County Court Rolls* (Chetham Soc. 1925) 75, no. 196.

76. 1 Bing. 374 (C. P. 1823).

77. 1 Bro. C. C. 269 (1783).

78. Hales v. Van Berchem, 2 Vern. *618 (Ch. 1708).

79. See *Ex parte* Coming, 9 Ves. 117 (Ch. 1803), and 2 White and Tudor, *Leading Cases in Equity* (8th

Long before this, however, we begin to find cases in which Coke's dogma was openly questioned in the courts. Thus in *The Duchess of Hamilton's Case*[80] we have the words of Sir Thomas Powys who argued that "in *Day* and *Savage* in Hobart, 87 it is indeed said that an Act of Parliament may be void from its first Creation, as an Act against Natural Equity; for *Jura Naturae sunt immutabilia, sunt leges legum*.[81] But this must be a very clear Case, and Judges will strain hard rather than interpret an Act void *ab initio*." It is significant that even the application of Coke's principle is now to be decently veiled under the cloak of "interpretation."

A decisive step in the destruction of the theory was taken in *Parish of Great Charte v. Parish of Kennington*,[82] when it was held that although it was a good principle that a man should not be judge and party, yet if a situation arose in which the only competent judge assigned by statute was interested in the dispute, he could, and ought to proceed notwithstanding. The principle of this judgment was affirmed in *Grand Junction Canal Co. v. Dimes*[83] by Lord Langdale, Master of the Rolls, in spite of the citation by counsel of such cases as *City of London v. Wood, Day v. Savadge,* and *Bonham's Case.* Moreover, judgments become more emphatic as the nineteenth century proceeds: "It is contrary to the general rule of law, not only in this country, but in every other, to make a person judge in his own cause," said Mr. Justice Blackburn in 1866, ". . . though the Legislature can, and, no doubt, in a proper case would, depart from that general rule," requiring, however, that the intention be clearly expressed.[84] Finally, in 1871 we have a categorical denial of Coke's principle. "I would observe," said Mr. Justice Willes,[85] "as to these Acts of Parliament, that they are the law of this land; and we do not sit here as a court of appeal from parliament. It was once said, — I think in Hobart (1), — that, if an Act of Parliament were to create a man judge in his own case, the Court might disregard it.[86] That dictum, however, stands as a warning, rather than an authority to be followed. We sit here as servants of the Queen and the legislature. Are we

---

ed. 1912) 86. At times the government connived at the judicial abrogation of legislation which was found to be imprudent, according to Lord Kenyon in Smith v. Armourers Co., 1 Peake, 148 (K. B. 1792).

80. 10 Mod. 115 (C. P. 1712).

81. We have remarked above, p. 167, on this misquotation from Bracton; here (with an additional error) it is, moreover, distinguished in a marginal note as "*Maxim* in Law."

82. 2 Strange, 1173 (K. B. 1742).

83. 12 Beav. 63, 77 (Rolls Court, 1849).

84. Mersey Docks Trustees v. Gibbs, L. R. 1 H. L. 93, 110 (1866).

85. Lee v. Bude & Torrington Junction Ry., L. R. 6 C. P. 576, 582 (1871).

86. The allusion is to Day v. Savadge, *supra* note 51.

to act as regents over what is done by parliament with the consent of Queen, lords and commons? I deny that any such authority exists. . . . The proceedings here are judicial, not autocratic, which they would be if we could make laws instead of administering them."

Such, then, is the history of the origin, growth, decline, and fall of Chief Justice Coke's doctrine in the English courts of law. But we cannot leave this portion of the subject without a reference to the celebrated passage in Blackstone[87] upon the matter.

> Lastly, acts of parliament that are impossible[88] to be performed are of no validity; and if there arise out of them collaterally any absurd consequences, manifestly contradictory to common reason, they are, with regard to those collateral consequences void. I lay down the rule with these restrictions; though I know it is generally laid down more largely, that acts of parliament contrary to reason are void. But if the parliament will positively enact a thing to be done which is unreasonable, I know of no power that can control it: and the examples usually alledged in support of this sense of the rule do none of them prove, that where the main object of a statute is unreasonable the judges are at liberty to reject it; for that were to set the judicial power above that of the legislature, which would be subversive of all government. But where some collateral matter arises out of the general words, and happens to be unreasonable; there the judges are in decency to conclude that this consequence was not foreseen by the parliament, and therefore they are at liberty to expound the statute by equity, and only *quoad hoc* disregard it. Thus if an act of parliament gives a man power to try all causes, that arise within his manor of Dale; yet, if a cause should arise in which he himself is party, the act is construed not to extend to that, because it is unreasonable that any man should determine his own quarrel. But, if we could conceive it possible for the parliament to enact, that he should try as well his own causes as those of other persons, there is no court that has power to defeat the legislature, when couched in such evident and express words, as leave no doubt whether it was the intent of the legislature or no.

From what has been shown in the earlier portions of this paper, it will be evident that Blackstone underestimates the historical strength of Coke's doctrine, but his conclusion is typical of the best judicial opinion, expressed in such

87. 1 *Bl. Comm.* (1st ed. 1765) 91.
88. Note that this "impossible" is really the "impertinent" of Annuitie 41.

cases as *The Duchess of Hamilton's Case,*[89] *Great Charte v. Kennington,*[90] *Mersey Docks Trustees v. Gibbs,*[91] and others.

The text we have quoted above is from the first edition of the *Commentaries,* 4to, Oxford, 1765, and remained unaltered until the ninth edition. There is an interesting note, said to be in Blackstone's own hand, in the margin of a copy of the eighth edition, published in 1778, which makes the third sentence read, "But if parliament will positively enact a thing to be done which is unreasonable, I know of no power *in the ordinary forms of the Constitution that is vested with authority* to control it." The ninth and all the later editions have this modification. Quincy suggests[92] that the alteration shows that the great commentator had changed his opinion in favor of the theory of judicial review, in consequence of American precedents. This is not very likely, while it may be doubted whether the verbal change necessarily implies any great change of opinion. If it really is significant, however, it will be necessary to stress the fact that the wording is extremely vague, and if taken literally might contain serious implications. For example, if this power is not in the "ordinary forms" of the constitution, where else could it be? Can it be supposed that the constitution contains extraordinary forms for emergency use, whose existence is in the nature of a state secret? Or does the sentence contain a veiled reference to such means as were used in America against the Stamp Act? Perhaps it might be helpful to recall the Revolution of 1688, the conduct of which would have been impossible under the "ordinary forms of the constitution"; but even so, there is little profit to be gained by attempting to describe a revolution in terms of constitutional law. The simplest explanation seems to be that the word "ordinary" must not be interpreted too strictly, and that all Blackstone means to imply is that such an act is subject to no control save that of force, whether actually armed, or simply the moral force of public resentment, and that the legal mechanism of the constitution alone is powerless to remedy the situation.

89. *Supra* note 80.
90. *Supra* note 82.
91. *Supra* note 84.
92. Quincy, 526 (Mass. 1865).

IV

It now remains to describe briefly the career of the doctrine in America. Settlers naturally carry with them the main outlines of their native law, and it is perfectly natural that there should have been some vague acquaintance with the common law in New England, although all of them did not view their legal inheritance with equal enthusiasm. Some had gone forth partly with the intention of erecting a theocracy based not on the common law but on the Bible, and in such communities professional lawyers were long under a cloud, their functions being performed by preachers and laymen administering the Scriptures and common sense.[93] With the economic and political growth of the colony, it became necessary to adopt a more refined system of law to meet the requirements of their prospering classes of landowners and merchants. Then it was that the common law began to revive, and its theoretical application to the colonies as laid down in their charters came to be something more than merely nominal. It is a significant sign of the new tendency that we find the General Court of Massachusetts in 1647 ordering two copies to be bought of *Coke upon Littleton,* Coke's *Reports, Coke upon Magna Carta,* the *Book of Entries,* the *New Terms of the Law,* and Dalton's *Justice of the Peace,*[94] while in the year before they had set out in parallel columns[95] their own laws and the "fundamental and common lawes and customes of England" to show that they were keeping as closely as possible to the system of the parent country.

In due course we begin to see the results of this step. Justice Symonds of Boston, Massachusetts (some time later a Deputy Governor), became an open admirer of the common law of England and in the long and ambitious judgment which he rendered in *Giddings v. Browne*[96] we have the first clear example of an act of legislature being invalidated by the judiciary in America. The town meeting had voted £100 toward providing a house for Mr. Cobbet, a minister, and the present case arose out of Browne's refusal to pay. Symonds held that "it is against a fundamentall law in nature to be compelled to pay that which

93. See in general Reinsch, "The English Common Law in the Early American Colonies," 1 *Select Essays in Anglo-American Legal History* (1907) 367. The Puritan element must not be exaggerated; nor was it present in all the colonies.

94. Hilkey, *Legal Development in Colonial Massachusetts* (37 *Columbia Univ. Studies,* No. 2, 1910) 66.

95. 1 *Hutchinson Papers* (Prince Soc. 1865) 197–247. Since the above was written, an entirely new construction has been placed upon this document by Mr. Richard B. Morris who has made the first critical examination of it in his article, "Massachusetts and the Common Law: The Declaration of 1646" (1926) 31 *Am. Hist. Rev.* 443–53.

96. 2 *Hutchinson Papers* (Prince Soc. 1865) 1–15.

others doe give." That positive law cannot prevail against fundamental law, he supports with passages drawn from Finch[97] and Dalton, and some hearsay precedents in Ipswich and Weymouth.

Political events also directed the colonists' attention toward the English common law, which they came to regard as the palladium of their civil liberties. The vigorous rule of Andros in 1688 set Bostonians thinking about *Habeas Corpus,* while at the same time the abrogation of their charter by James II provoked an outspoken claim to independence, in support of which they were said[98] to "hold forth a law book, & quote the Authority of the Lord Cook to Justifie their setting up for themselves; pleading the possession of 60 years against the right of the Crown."

It was two generations later that Coke's influence bore its most important results, however. His name and authority were used freely in *Paxton's Case*[99] by Otis in his indecisive attack upon writs of assistance but still more so in an even greater cause. The disaffection caused by the Stamp Act very early took a legal complexion: ". . . our friends to liberty take the advantage of a maxim they find in Lord Coke that an Act of Parliament against Magna Carta or the peculiar rights of Englishmen is *ipso facto* void," wrote Lieutenant-Governor Hutchinson, on 12th Sept., 1765.[100] "This, taken in the latitude the people are often enough disposed to take it, must be fatal to all government, and it seems to have determined great part of the colony to oppose the execution of the act with force. . . ." A popular demonstration led to the resignation of the only officer who had authority to sell the stamps which the act required to be affixed to most legal documents; thereby producing an additional complication, as we learn from the Governor-historian Hutchinson's "Summary of the Disorders in the Massachusetts Province proceeding from an Apprehension that the Act of Parliament called the Stamp Act deprives the People of their Natural Rights."[101] He relates that "A committee [of the Assembly] at this sitting [25 Sept., 1765] had reported certain resolves, and among others, one that all courts should do business without stamps and that their proceedings should

---

97. Finch, *Law, or, A Discourse Thereof* (1627) 74, develops the proposition that "Common Law [is] nothing els but common reason," and that positive laws contrary to it as void, as are those contrary to the law of nature. The first edition appeared in 1613 under the title Νομοτεχνια.

98. "An Account of the Colonys and Provinces of New England in general, More particularly of that of the Massachusetts," printed from MS. Lambeth 841 in Perry, *Papers Relating to the History of the Church in Massachusetts* (1873) 39, 42.

99. Quincy, 51, 401 (Mass. 1761, published in 1865).

100. 26 MS. *Archives of Massachusetts,* ff. 153–54 (preserved in the State House, Boston).

101. *Ibid.* ff. 180, 183.

be valid to all intents and purposes, but the house having spent several days upon it, dropped it. . . . The reason given for their resolve, and since given by the people in general for going on with business without stamps is this, that the stamp officer has resigned and no stamps to be had; but upon further consideration and the many arguments used in the publick prints to support the doctrine, the prevailing reason at this time is, that the Act of Parliament is against Magna Charta and the natural rights of Englishmen, and therefore according to Lord Coke null and void."

The popular and lay view of the legal situation was so firmly held that the judges were in due course asked for an authoritative statement. As it was out of term, they were able to postpone their decision for a time, during which period researches were made and an anxious correspondence conducted between Hutchinson and the distinguished Massachusetts Justice, John Cushing, on the situation created by the practical impossibility of getting stamps. "I have been well informed,"[102] wrote Cushing to the Lieutenant-Governor on February 9, 1766, "that Mr. Gridley[103] the beginning of November last was fully of opinion the Court could not proceed on civil matters, but since, on searching authority, judges we ought to proceed. What he has found I know not, and am doubtful whether he can find any in point. It's true, it is said, an Act of Parliament against natural equity is void. It will be disputed whether this is such an Act. It seems to me the main question here is whether an Act which cannot be carried into execution should stop the course of justice, and that the Judges are more confined than with respect to an obsolete Act. If we admit evidence unstamped *ex necessitate,* Query if it can be said we do wrong." As the months went by Cushing's opinions became more settled, and we find him writing to John Adams, "I can tell the grand jury the nullity of Acts of Parliament, but must leave you to prove it by the more powerful arguments of the *jus gladii divinum,* a power not peculiar to kings and ministers"; to which Adams replied,[104] "You have my hearty concurrence in telling the jury the nullity of Acts of Parliament, whether we can prove it by the *jus gladii,* or not. I am determined to die of that opinion, let the *jus gladii* say what it will."

The *jus gladii* spoke with no uncertain voice, but still there remained something to be said when finally arms yielded place to the toga; the Congress had resolved in 1774[105] "that the respective colonies are entitled to the common

---

102. 25 *ibid.* f. 55.
103. Jeremiah Gridley was twice Attorney-General.
104. 9 Adams, *Works* (1854) 390–91.
105. 1 *Journals of the Continental Congress* (1904) 69.

law of England,"—a statement which their founders would have hesitated to make—and it remained to decide how much weight to allow it in their legal system. From this time onward Coke's influence is obvious, and the practice of judicial invalidation of acts for unconstitutionality, which had begun in colonial days,[106] steadily grew. In *Robin et al. v. Hardaway et al.*[107] several persons of Indian descent attempted to vindicate their freedom in spite of a statute of 1682 (and others) which reduced them to slavery. The plaintiffs' arguments were eloquent. "All acts of legislature apparently contrary to right and justice are, in our laws, and must be in the nature of things, considered as void. The laws of nature are the laws of God, whose authority can be superseded by no power on earth. A legislature must not obstruct our obedience to Him from Whose punishments they cannot protect us. All human constitutions which contradict His laws, we are in conscience bound to disobey. Such have been the adjudications of our courts of justice. And cited 8 Co. 118a *Bonham's Case.* Hob. 87.[108] 7 Co. 14 *Calvin's Case.*" The defense was learned; Puffendorf was used to prove that slavery was a part of the law of nature, and the dicta of Coke were matched by the words of Blackstone which we have already discussed.[109] This issue, however, was not argued to a decision, for the court eventually found that the obnoxious statute had been repealed in 1705. Nevertheless, the arguments throw considerable light upon the legal thought of the period.

In 1786 there followed the much-discussed case of *Trevett v. Weeden*[110] in the Superior Court of Rhode Island. An act of the legislature had imposed penalties on all who refused to take the state's paper money at its face value, empowering any justice of the Superior Court or the Court of Common Pleas, to try offenders summarily without jury. Upon Weeden being so tried on the information of Trevett, Major-General Varnum, for the defense, argued that as the act took away trial by jury, it was contrary to Magna Carta and fundamental rights.[111] We will not follow the learned advocate's lengthy disquisition on English history from Egbert to date; as may be expected, he often quotes "that great oracle of the law, Lord Coke," holds that the act is "repugnant and impossible," for the judges cannot proceed "without any jury . . . according

106. See Colden's protest, July 5, 1759, in *New York Historical Society Collections* (1869) 204.

107. Jeff. 109 (Va. 1772).

108. This is Day v. Savadge, *supra,* p. 167.

109. 1 *Bl. Comm.* 91; Puffendorf, Vattel, and Blackstone were all very widely read in America at this time.

110. No report, save the pamphlet by Varnum (Providence, 1786) who was counsel for the defense. The record is in 10 *Records of the State of Rhode Island* (1865) 219.

111. It should be observed that at this date Rhode Island had no written state constitution, beyond the old charter of Charles II (1663).

to the law of the land" as the act commands, and exhorts the judges to exercise their inherent powers over legislation, as had been done in the reports of
Hobart, Plowden, and Coke—with the theoretical support of Vattel.[112] The
question of paper money was highly controversial, and it is doubtless in view
of their difficult position, faced as they were by a determined legislature supported by the public which was in a state of intense excitement, that the court
gave a judgment which has never since ceased to puzzle commentators. Two
views are possible. One, expressed by Stiness,[113] emphasizes the fact that in
form the court's judgment was simply that they had no jurisdiction to try the
case, as they were not the special court erected *ad hoc* by the statute. This is
certainly the judgment on the record, but there was much more in it than this.
Legally, Stiness' view is incontestable, but politically there is more to be said
for the conclusion of Cooley who claims that the judgment held the act to be
unconstitutional and void.[114] We do not know what was said from the bench,
but according to contemporary newspapers[115] three judges declared the act
unconstitutional, one doubted the court's jurisdiction, and the Chief Justice
expressed no opinion save that in his judgment as it appears on the record.
While it is true that judgment was given solely on the question of jurisdiction,
as Stiness contends, it is nevertheless true that a majority of the bench had expressed the view that the act was void. The reason for the court's taking refuge
in this technicality was soon made plain by subsequent events. The judges were
immediately summoned to appear before the General Assembly "to assign the
reasons and grounds of their judgment in adjudging an act of this Assembly
unconstitutional, and therefore void."[116] The Assembly, then, knew very well
the true grounds for the decision; but the judges brought the record with them
showing that their judgment was on the point of jurisdiction. The device was
successful, and the baffled Assembly had to discharge the judges as no criminal charge was laid against them, voting, however, that "no satisfactory reasons
have been rendered by them for their judgment." As a legal precedent, the case
proves nothing, but as a fact in the history of political thought in America,
Trevett v. Weeden is striking testimony to the strength of the Coke tradition.

112. 1 Vattel, *Le Droit des Gens, ou Principes de la Loi Naturelle* (1758) iii, § 34.
113. Stiness, "The Struggle for Judicial Supremacy," in 3 Field, *State of Rhode Island and Providence
Plantations at the End of the Century* (1902) 107 *et seq.*
114. Cooley, *Constitutional Limitations* (1903) 229; but not void as against the charter, nor does the charter expressly give jury trial as there supposed. For a full and recent discussion of the political environment
of the case, which employs much interesting evidence drawn from contemporary newspapers, see Charles
Warren, "Earliest Cases of Judicial Review of State Legislation by Federal Courts" (1922) 32 *Yale L. J.* 15.
115. Quoted by Stiness, *op. cit. supra* note 113, at 108.
116. 10 *Records of the State of Rhode Island* (1865) 218.

A few years later a similar doctrine was applied under curious circumstances in the South Carolina case of *Bowman v. Middleton*.[117] Eighty years previous to this litigation two families had disputed the boundaries of their respective lands, and an act of the legislature[118] in 1712 had settled the matter by laying down the bounds and confirming the inheritance to the younger sons of one of the contestants who had died intestate. The court held that no title could pass under this act which was "against common right and *magna carta* . . . That the act was, therefore *ipso facto* void," and "That no length of time could give it validity." The reasons for its voidance were that it deprived the one family of its property without judicial proceedings or trial by jury, and deprived the eldest son of the other family of his inheritance, again without trial by jury, inasmuch as the land was partitioned among his brothers—this latter point bearing upon the important attempt made by the colonists to abolish primogeniture.[119]

The adoption of the practice of setting up written state constitutions was soon to render Coke's doctrine unnecessary. Common right is vague at the best, and cannot compare with a well-drawn constitution as a check upon legislative action. The fundamental nature of written constitutions was foreshadowed in the states,[120] where Vattel's teaching had tremendous influence, and was laid down in the Supreme Court of the United States by Marshall's famous and much discussed judgment in *Marbury v. Madison*.[121] But Massachusetts has long remained partial to the doctrine learned from Lord Coke in her colonial days, and in 1826,[122] and again in 1850,[123] her courts have mentioned with approval the old English cases in which it is embodied.[124]

---

117. 1 Bay, 252 (S. C. 1792).

118. For the interpretation of such private acts, see 2 *Bl. Comm.* 346, and *cf.* Campbell's Case, 2 Bland, 209, 232 (Md. 1829).

119. Important constitutional points were involved, which, however, do not bear directly on our subject. The main cases are discussed in Hazeltine, *Appeals from Colonial Courts to the King in Council* (7 *Brown Univ. Historical Seminary Papers,* 1896), and Andrews, "The Connecticut Intestacy Laws" (1894) 3 *Yale Review,* 261. It has been held that the common law of inheritance has never prevailed in Connecticut. Campbell's Appeal, 64 Conn. 277, 290, 29 Atl. 494, 495 (1894).

120. In Holmes v. Walton, 4 Halst. 444 (N. J. 1780), (see A. W. Scott, "Holmes vs. Walton: The New Jersey Precedent" (1898) 4 *Am. Hist. Rev.* 456); Den v. Singleton, 1 Martin, 42 (N. C. 1787); Kamper v. Hawkins, 1 Va. Cas. 20 (1793). For an able demonstration that the idea of judicial review was quite familiar to the framers and ratifiers of the Constitution, see Beard, *The Supreme Court and the Constitution* (1912).

121. 1 Cranch, 137 (U. S. 1803).

122. Commonwealth v. Worcester, 3 Pick. 461, 472 (Mass. 1826).

123. William v. Robinson, 6 Cush. 330 (Mass. 1850). Both cases approve of City of London v. Wood, *supra* note 69.

124. For the theory that there is an unwritten as well as a written constitution, at the present day, see McClain, "Unwritten Constitutions in the United States" (1902) 15 *Harv. L. Rev.* 531.

V

This is a long story, and all the time Sir Edward Coke plays a dominating part. He took the practice of the fourteenth century—an age when courts and statutes were still something of a novelty—and filled it with a new spirit, the product of his own genius. The result was really a new doctrine although fortified, he honestly believed, with incontestable precedents from the middle ages; for he knew well that without such support it would have availed nothing, although with it, there was a possibility that the new theory might prevent the imminent strife between Crown and Parliament. His personal defects alone could not have sufficed to discredit so remarkable a contribution to political science. Indeed, his views were shared even by the cautious Hobart, who later succeeded in winning the respect of republicans as well as royalists. The weakness lay in the theory itself, first, because its medieval basis was always open to dispute, and so it was possible to support the vague feeling that it was a novelty by showing that its roots in the past were not as deep as its partisans alleged. The extent to which the theory was a novelty may be judged from the fact that both its supporters and its opponents did not realize the implications of treating the common law as fundamental; but surely, if the common law had always been fundamental, then the prerogative lawyers would have obtained the judgment in *Godden v. Hales* long before 1686. Coke deserves our respect for the originality of his contribution to the political problem of his day, but it proved too strange and too uncertain to serve his purpose.

Secondly, the Revolution alone could finally settle the problem. The march of events had led Englishmen to look to Parliament and not to the Crown as the embodiment of their national life. Apparently opportunist and fickle, Parliament had nevertheless led the nation in its search for the *via media* and had reflected the varying moods of the people. The nation felt that the political pressure of public opinion expressed through Parliament was a more certain safeguard than the operation of judicial institutions, admirably though they had worked during most of the Stuart conflict. The rise of popular government therefore naturally brought with it the sovereignty of Parliament. Nevertheless, Coke's teaching was not altogether vain. His learning and prestige had made enough disciples on the bench to familiarize lawyers with the outlines of his thought, and eventually the strangeness wore off until it became evident that the new thought could be grafted on to the common law. The Revolution came only just in time to prevent the conversion, and to make it finally clear that there was no place for it in English constitutional law. But the common law was not confined within the four seas. In the American colonies the Revolution meant something different. Parliament was not their hero but a distant and unsympathetic body in whose deliberations they had no part. When it aroused their resentment, therefore, it was natural to remember the teaching of the great Chief Justice, which had not been faced with the problem of the Revolution settlement in American minds. The sovereignty of Parliament was by no means so obvious an implication of the Revolution to people who had not lived in London during the critical years from 1685 to 1688. It is a cardinal fact that to the eighteenth-century American the doctrine of a fundamental common law was familiar, and regarded as quite consistent with the common law scheme of things. Finally there came the reception of Vattel's theoretical discussions which coincided so nearly with the less elegant but equally fruitful dicta from the English judge. It was due not only to that doctrine, but also to the firm faith that "what my Lord Coke says in Bonham's Case is far from any extravagancy" that we owe the bold experiment of making a written constitution which should have judges and a court for its guardians.

The "Economic Liberalism" of
Sir Edward Coke

BARBARA MALAMENT

❧ ❧ ❧

Sir Edward Coke, master of the turbulent political and legal arenas of early Stuart England, ranks among his country's most influential jurists. Recent historiography has given him an additional role of special significance. His career is now considered a prism through which we may see the impending triumph of industrial capitalism and its ideological handmaiden, classical economic liberalism. Cast as spokesman for a burgeoning class of entrepreneurs, he is held to have served them through a broad attack on monopolies and the intricate regulatory structure of the Tudor state and to have reshaped the common law in conscious anticipation of *laissez-faire* precepts.

But Coke's career did not in fact fit this heuristic construct. He was not among the venturesome merchants and manufacturers of his age (1552–1634), and he was fickle in his regard for their interests. His opposition to monopolies was selective; he challenged neither the fundamentals of the prevailing regulatory structure nor the paternalistic ideas which supported it. In some instances his arguments resembled those of economic liberals. But always his underlying principles were as alien to the early nineteenth century as they were familiar to the sixteenth.

Those who have missed the distinctly Tudor cast of Coke's thinking have been either lawyers interested in establishing common law sanction for modern anti-trust theory[1] or historians seeking an ideological explanation for the origin of the Civil Wars. Long convinced that these wars arose over divergent definitions of English liberties or the respective authority of Parliament

"The 'Economic Liberalism' of Sir Edward Coke" is reprinted by permission of The Yale Law Journal Company and William S. Hein Company from the *Yale Law Journal* 76 (1967): 1321–58.

1. Coke's views were cited, for example, in one of the most famous American anti-trust cases, *Standard Oil Co. v. United States,* 221 U.S. 1, 51, 54 (1911). In this case, the company's interpretation of the early common law would seem to be the more accurate. See pp. 210–23 *infra.*

and Crown, historians traditionally[2] advanced a political interpretation of the protest against monopolies. It went something like this: statutory proscription of monopolies constituted the first invasion of the King's absolute prerogative.[3] It was effected by Coke and his "patriot" friends, who were known defenders of Parliament's jurisdiction in matters of taxation. Since the Crown received considerable sums of money in return for its favors, what Coke and his friends must have wanted was to remove the threat of royal financial independence. Though generally plausible,[4] this traditional analysis became suspect after the 1930's when historians began reinterpreting the struggles between Court and Country. Once they had settled upon an economic interpretation, historians found in the opposition to monopolies a suggestion[5] that Coke and the parliamentarians were early advocates of *laissez-faire.*

This suggestion threatens now to become dogmatic assertion. Yet even proponents of the *laissez-faire* thesis differ significantly among themselves. Ephraim Lipson,[6] Eli Heckscher,[7] and John N. Nef,[8] for example, cautiously

2. For one important exception to the standard political argument, see 4 D. Hume, *History of England* 394 (rev. ed. 1850). As an early partisan of *laissez-faire,* Hume traced the origins of that theory back to the monopoly controversy and argued that the House of Commons had attempted to "give liberty to the trading part of the nation."

3. Following Fortescue, most Englishmen believed theirs to be a *dominium politicum et regale* in which the Crown had a discretionary prerogative to act on the advice of its counsellors and also an inherent and absolute prerogative in matters such as defense and foreign affairs. Exclusive trade privileges originated in an effort to encourage self-sufficiency and to make England's international position more secure, hence the Crown claimed an absolute right to grant such privileges—a right which Parliament challenged directly by enacting the Statute of Monopolies in 1623, 21 Jac. 1, c. 3. For a lucid and exceptionally good discussion of why Coke and the parliamentarians did not realize the radical implications of their action and of the extraordinary consensus in theory, see M. Judson, *The Crisis of the Constitution* (1949).

4. It could not explain, however, Coke's repugnance to monopolies prior to his break with the Court. Nor could it explain why adherents of the Court Party such as Lionel Cranfield and even Francis Bacon urged reform from above—the abrogation of certain odious monopolies by the King. For Cranfield's views, see D. Willson, *The Privy Councillors in the House of Commons, 1604–1629,* at 45 (1940); for Bacon's views, see "Advice to Sir George Villiers" in 2 *The Works of Bacon* 375, 385 (1841), where he describes monopolies as "cankers of all trading" and urges that they not be admitted "under specious colours of public good."

5. It is possible to interpret the Civil Wars as an economic conflict yet not ascribe to the partisans different economic theories. This is what Lawrence Stone, Trevor-Roper and R. H. Tawney have done, however tacitly, in their discussions of the gentry. As to monopolies, William H. Price has discussed the economic grievances regarding exclusive patents without deducing an ideological framework. See Price, "English Patents of Monopoly," 1 *Harv. Econ. Studies* 70 (1913). And insofar as any differences of theory did exist, George Unwin suggested that they arose not because of any peculiar foresight or modernity but simply because merchants tended to prosper under freer conditions of trade than did manufacturers. Unwin's suggestion was hardly new and could not explain why so many of the protests against monopolies originated from unemployed craftsmen as opposed to thwarted merchants. But by revealing the conflict in mercantile and industrial interests and by enabling historians to assess how Court policy more nearly favored the latter, Unwin's study helped explain the merchants' impatience under the early Stuarts. See G. Unwin, *Industrial Organization in the Sixteenth and Seventeenth Centuries* (1904).

6. 3 E. Lipson, *The Economic History of England,* especially at 283 (1931).

7. 1 E. Heckscher, *Mercantilism* 291–94 (M. Shapiro trans. 1935).

8. J. Nef, *Industry and Government in France and England,* 42 (1962).

suggested that Coke's views provided a link between mercantilist and classical economic theory. They pointed to his "aversion" to statutes regulating the
terms of enclosure and apprenticeship and his narrow construction of their
provisions, the ability of later litigants to cite his opinions when contesting
modern forms of trade restraint, and the rhetoric of "free trade" which accompanied his denunciation of monopolies. Yet they confined themselves to the
long-range implications of Coke's views. Nowhere did they ascribe to Coke a
conscious anticipation of *laissez-faire*.

The more extreme position was adopted first by Donald O. Wagner,[9] who
argued that monopolies were not inconsistent with prevailing legal theory,
that Coke deliberately distorted precedent in order to hold them unlawful.
His argument was then endorsed by Christopher Hill,[10] who believed that a
"liberal" Coke would reinforce his general interpretation of the early Stuart
period. Having politicized Tawney's thesis[11] of an emergent capitalist ethos by
linking Puritans, parliamentarians and merchants, and having concluded that
their opposition to the Court was motivated by the latter's policy of industrial regulation, Hill placed Coke among the enterprising and the individualistic. Through Hill's interpretation, Coke became the ally of the Puritans, the
spokesman who created common law sanction for their *laissez-faire* demands.

I

The facts of Coke's life, however, weaken Hill's general thesis. In a career of 60
years, Sir Edward spent nearly 40 attached to the Court as Solicitor and Attorney General, Chief Justice of the Court of Common Pleas and of the King's
Bench.[12] By birth, he was a country gentleman from Norfolk; by devotion, an
Anglican;[13] by conviction, a social conservative. Like many of his contempo-

---

9. Wagner, "Coke and the Rise of Economic Liberalism," 6 *Econ. Hist. Rev.* 30 (1935). See also Wagner,
"The Common Law and Free Enterprise: An Early Case of Monopoly," 7 *Econ. Hist. Rev.* 217 (1937). In
both articles, Wagner was attempting to refute R. H. Tawney's proposition that the common law had an
inherent bias in favor of economic individualism. See Tawney, *Introduction* to T. Wilson, *A Discourse upon
Usury* (1958).

10. Hill tentatively endorsed Wagner's findings in C. Hill, *Puritanism and Revolution* 28 (1964). Then,
after further research, he elaborated upon Wagner's thesis. C. Hill, *Intellectual Origins of the English Revolution* 225–65 (1965).

11. This famous thesis first appeared in R. H. Tawney, *Religion and the Rise of Capitalism* (1926).

12. The dates of these appointments were 1592, 1593/94, 1606 and 1613 respectively.

13. "In his old age he agreed with the Puritans, but he continued to support the Established Church."
1 J. Campbell, *The Lives of the Chief Justices of England* 353 (1873). Coke's early views—his opinion of the
Puritan demands at Hampton Court (1604), the Commons' *Apology* of that same year, or even their Peti-

raries, he disapproved of inferiors who sought to rise through the legal profession. At an assembly of benchers of the Inner Temple held in February of 1601 Coke, then Attorney General, ordered that "none hereafter shall be admitted into this House . . . but only such as shall be of good parentage and of no evil behaviour. . . ."[14] Presumably, "good parentage" included country gentlemen, for at the time Coke himself was both getting rich and climbing the social ladder. In his private practice, he had acquired many lucrative retainers. He had married an heiress, and upon her death in 1598 he married another. Coke became so wealthy that in 1601 he was able to entertain Queen Elizabeth at Stoke Poges. When he died he left some 99 estates and, according to Samuel Thorne,[15] twice that number had passed through his hands.

To the extent that Coke was willing to engage in land speculation, he perhaps demonstrated a form of "capitalist spirit." But when it came to more modern undertakings in trade or industry, Coke showed remarkable skepticism. For one thing, he doubted the remunerative possibilities of manufacturing, so much of which was in the hands of monopolists. In his famous *Charge* to the Norwich Assizes delivered in 1607, Coke expressed his dislike of the monopolist and further observed that he

> for the most part useth at a deare rate to pay for his foolishnes: For some of that profession have bene so wise, to sell twentie, thirtie, or perhaps fortie pound land a yeare, and bestow most part of the money in purchasing of a Monopolie: Thereby to anoy and hinder the whole Publicke Weale for his owne privat benefit: In which course he so well thriveth, as that by toyling some short time, either in *Starch, Vineger,* or *Aquavitae,* he doth in the end thereby purchase to himselfe an absolute beggerie, and for my owne part, their purposes and practices considered, I can wish unto them no better happinesse.[16]

---

tion of 1610—are unknown. Apart from his resistance to Church demands for the co-ordinate jurisdiction of ecclesiastical and secular courts (which reflected a jealous regard for the common law rather than anti-Anglican sentiment), Coke seems to have expressed himself on religious issues only after 1621. In that year he strongly demanded the stricter enforcement of recusancy laws, a position he again took in 1625.

The question is whether anti-Papist, anti-Arminian fears unaccompanied by any (known) sympathy for Calvinism justify calling Coke a "Puritan." Many loyal Anglicans shared his fears; and on the basis of his denunciation of Dr. Montague in 1625 it would seem that Coke's main concern was Elizabethan in its political emphasis on state unity and security as opposed to theology. It should also be recalled that even in the debates leading to the Petition of Right in 1628 Coke's great contribution was political and not religious. H. Hulme, *The Life of Sir John Eliot* 186–93 (1957). Coke was in no sense obsessed by religious questions. He was not devout in his personal life but continued his nominal allegiance to the Anglican Church.

14. 1 *A Calendar of the Inner Temple Records* 439 (F. Inderwick ed. 1896).

15. Thorne, "Tudor Social Transformation and Legal Change," 26 *N.Y.U.L. Rev.* 10, 13 (1951).

16. *The Lord Coke, His Speech and Charge,* at Hb (1607). The speech was piratically published by one Robert Pricket with, according to Coke, many errors and omissions. Preface to 7 Co. Rep.

Nor did Coke have any confidence in trading concerns. Though an honorary member of the Spanish Company[17] and, in his capacity as Attorney General, one of the draftsmen of the charter of the Virginia Company,[18] he seems to have invested in neither.[19] He had been in his 30's when the trade depression following 1586 set in,[20] old enough to appreciate the precariousness of commerce and to confirm his habit of investing in land.

In this habit, Coke distinguished himself from many of his legal colleagues. Perhaps because so much of their practice was in London, there seems to have been great temptation for them to invest in the trading companies which were likewise centered there. Oliver St. John was involved in the Providence Island Scheme;[21] Sir Edwin Sandys, Sir Thomas Roe, John Selden and Sir John Popham all had connections with the Virginia Company.[22] All were or became staunch opponents of monopolies, at least the monopolies of others. As early as 1607, Coke had come to share their views, but apparently not their economic interests.

Even in his strictly legal capacity, Coke was not particularly sensitive to commercial needs. Despite the increasing interest in problems of joint-stock ownership, negotiable instruments, commercial contracts, debt and insurance, he devoted no special attention to them in his writings. The first of his *Institutes* dealt with land tenure, the second with various statutes, the third with criminal law, and the fourth with the jurisdiction of different courts. Taken together,[23] the *Institutes* come to over two thousand pages, only one of which treats of bankruptcy and only one of forfeiture. Commercial contracts as such are not even mentioned.

It might be objected that Coke set out to elucidate the laws of England, and that with the exception of the usury and bankruptcy statutes, these laws did not relate to business needs. But in the *Institutes* the descriptive and the

17. He seems to have been admitted in return for helping draft the Company's charter of 1604. A. Friis, *Alderman Cockayne's Project* 157, 158 (1917).

18. F. Maitland, *English Law and the Renaissance* 31 (1901).

19. I am very much indebted to Professor Theodore K. Rabb of Harvard University for assistance on this point.

20. According to Lawrence Stone, the conclusions of W. R. Scott as to the decay of trade at this time must still be considered valid. See Stone, "State Control in Sixteenth-Century England," 17 *Econ. Hist. Rev.* 103, 108 (1947).

21. J. Hexter, *The Reign of King Pym* 77–84 (1941). Throughout chapter four, the familial and financial ties of many important Puritans are explained.

22. C. Bedwell, *A Brief History of the Middle Temple* 41–48 (1909).

23. The first part of the *Institutes of the Laws of England* was published in 1628, the second in 1642, the third and fourth in 1644. [The parts of work are hereinafter cited as 1–4 *Inst.,* to the pagination of the original editions.]

prescriptive were joined. Had Coke wanted to make a point of commercial problems, he might easily have done so. His colleagues may also have lacked foresight and failed to distinguish between business and municipal corporations[24] or between negotiable instruments and promissory notes,[25] but this simply indicates that Coke was no more modern in outlook than they. When legal historians speak of Coke as a "transitional" figure attempting to adapt old common law forms to modern needs, they are referring primarily to his treatment of land tenure.

Those who go further do so on the basis of cases which Coke did not decide.[26] He has been credited, for example, with the decision in *Slade's Case*[27] which facilitated the enforcement of contracts. Until the mid-sixteenth century, claims for liquidated damages had to be sued under a writ of debt. The procedure hampered recovery, since it permitted a wager of law[28] and demanded greatly detailed pleading. Plaintiffs much preferred the action of assumpsit, which was allowed by courts only if the defendant had expressly promised to repay his debt. *Slade's Case* held that the mere existence of a debt implied a promise to repay and that this implication sufficed to ground an action in assumpsit. The decision marked an advance in the adaptation of old common law forms to commercial convenience. But Coke was not responsible for it. In 1602 he was Attorney General, not Chief Justice of the King's Bench.

When appointed to the bench, Coke did have an opportunity further to adapt the law to commercial changes. The courts were in great need of general principles to help determine the validity of consideration given to the defendant in cases arising from a writ of assumpsit. The formulation of such principles would have avoided a series of narrow or absurd decisions and aided the

24. Williston, "The History of the Law of Business Corporations before 1800," 3 *Select Essays in Anglo-American Legal History* 195, 204 (1909).

25. Inland bills of exchange apparently were not in common use until at least the 1650's. Cranch, "Promissory Notes Before and After Lord Holt," *id.* at 72, 79.

26. They assume that merely because Coke reported a case he helped arrive at its decision. This must have been Fifoot's assumption when he credited Coke with the decision in *Slade's Case*. See C. Fifoot, *The English Law and Its Background* (1932). But Coke began taking notes on cases he heard argued from the time of his call to the bar (1578) and began publishing them in 1600, long before he was raised to the bench. Most of the cases reported were decided by other justices. And although Coke elaborated upon the decisions he reported, only at times did he indicate his approval by calling the reader's attention to their importance either in his comments "To the Reader" or within the cases themselves. The existence of such clear affirmation would seem to be essential, therefore, when ascribing to Coke the views embodied in cases he did not decide. He may have accepted the decisions in all cases as law, but this does not mean that he himself would have arrived at the same conclusion.

27. 4 Co. Rep. 91, 76 Eng. Rep. 1072 (K.B. 1602).

28. Thorne, *supra* note 15, at 19–20. If neighbors (usually twelve) swore on behalf of the defendant, the plaintiff could not succeed.

judicial enforcement of contracts. But Coke accepted the existing analytical framework, deficient as it was.[29] At times, through his penchant for historic technicalities or through inadvertence,[30] he even thwarted the needs of commerce. In 1612, for example, he still insisted that the validity of incorporations depended upon the correct stipulation of name and place in the letters patent.[31]

Indeed, the common law possessed no fund of commercial wisdom. Commercial law was a distinct and separate body because medieval merchants had demanded a more expeditious treatment of their problems than the common law courts provided. They used the staple courts, courts of fairs and boroughs.[32] After the decay of these courts in the sixteenth century, they turned to the Admiralty and to other courts of equity whose procedure was not burdened by rigid forms of action and whose decisions were based on customary trade usages compiled in the law merchant.[33] This provoked a reaction among defenders of the common law and led to attempts to arrogate the jurisdiction of the courts of equity. Competition with Chancery had brought about the improvements in the action of assumpsit mentioned before.[34] But merchants seem to have thought these improvements in common law forms insufficient. Both the Chancery and the Admiralty survived the Civil Wars even though they were prerogative courts.

That they survived was due to no support from Coke, for he continued the earlier attempts to arrogate equity jurisdiction to the common law. His attacks on Chancery are notorious, but at least he enjoyed the support of those who, like Selden, believed that "equity is a roguish thing."[35] When he persisted in attacking the Admiralty, however, Coke stood alone. Not since 1575 had the common lawyers challenged this court whose jurisdiction Queen Elizabeth

29. On the need for formulating general principles see C. Fifoot, *supra* note 26, at 150, which seems to be the clearest account of early contract law. Coke's failure to think beyond his contemporaries may be seen in *Mallory v. Lane,* Cro. Jac. 342, 79 Eng. Rep. 292 (Ex. 1614), and *Therne v. Fuller,* Cro. Jac. 396, 78 Eng. Rep. 338 (K.B. 1615).

30. Coke reported the dictum in *Pinnel's Case,* 5 Co. Rep. 117, 77 Eng. Rep. 237 (C.P. 1602), in a manner that made it seem, on anything but the most careful reading, a rule of law, thus enabling courts in the late nineteenth century and even now to insist that partial payment of a debt was no consideration for a promise to forego the balance, but that the offer of something different, however disproportionate in value, would suffice.

31. See Coke's report of *The Case of Sutton's Hospital,* 10 Co. Rep. 23, 77 Eng. Rep. 960 (K.B. 1612).

32. 4 *Inst.* *237; C. Fifoot, *supra* note 26, at 104.

33. Burdick, "Contributions of the Law Merchant to the Common Law," 3 *Select Essays in Anglo-American Legal History* 34, 35–39 (1909).

34. *Id.* 41.

35. Quoted in Tudsbery, "The Law Merchant and the Common Law," 24 *L.Q. Rev.* 392, 400 (1918).

had upheld in cases arising upon the seas, in foreign ports and even at home if the dispute involved denizen and foreign merchants.[36] Coke deliberately misconstrued her settlement and in 1610 he sought to stay the Admiralty's proceedings. He invented a transparent legal fiction to the effect that contracts between merchants, denizen and foreign, were made in the English port regardless of where they were actually made,[37] and then asserted common law jurisdiction over all cases involving merchants which arose in England. The Fourth Part of his *Institutes,* published posthumously, contained a bitter attack on the Admiralty.[38]

This attack evoked equally bitter responses from spokesmen for the mercantile interest.[39] Godolphin, Zouch, and Prynne[40] all defended the jurisdiction of the Court of Admiralty. Support for this court was so great that it was not until after the Restoration that the common law obtained a monopoly of commercial litigation.[41] At that time, the common law courts were compelled to adopt the rules of the law merchant for lack of any adequate precedent of their own.[42] Nothing necessitated this incorporation except jurisdictional rivalry. In the long run merchants gained little; in the short run, they suffered great inconveniences, inconveniences which did not at all trouble Sir Edward Coke. He believed, no doubt, that politically the defence of the common law was in the interest of the merchants since they shared many grievances against the Crown.[43] Yet when the interests of the merchants and the common law courts diverged, he favored the courts and with no apparent hesitation.

36. W. Prynne, *Brief Animadversions on, Amendments of, and Additional Explanatory Records to the Fourth Part of the Institutes of the Laws of England Concerning the Jurisdiction of Courts* 99 (1669).

37. *Id.* 95–98.

38. 4 *Inst.* *134–47.

39. For a detailed discussion of the Admiralty Court, see Brian Levack's unpublished study, Department of History, Yale University.

40. See generally J. Godolphin, *A View of the Admiral Jurisdiction* (1661); R. Zouch, *Jurisdiction of the Admiralty* (1669); and W. Prynne, *supra* note 36. In stressing the distinction between the law merchant and the common law and the need of merchants for speedy, certain remedies, Prynne quoted Selden's *Mare Clausum (The Right and Dominion of the Sea),* which appeared in 1618. W. Prynne, *supra* note 36, at 94–95. This is not to say that the remedies afforded by the Admiralty were ideal. They were not, and occasional complaints such as that of Sir Arthur Ingram could be heard. The point here is that the Admiralty provided the best legal assistance to merchants available in seventeenth-century England.

41. 5 W. Holdsworth, *History of English Law* 143 (1924).

42. Tudsbery, *supra* note 35, at 398–400.

43. Coke also shared many grievances with the Puritans, grievances which were coincidental. See generally J. Eusden, *Puritans, Lawyers, and Politics in Early Seventeenth-Century England* (1958).

II

Coke resembled the Puritan merchants in neither his priorities nor his interests and background. Nor did he share their alleged predilection for *laissez-faire*. In Commons he supported many statutes of "mercantilist" nature; on the bench he construed all such statutes in accordance with the rules of his day. Coke's decisions may have been narrow, but not because he sought deliberately to weaken judicial enforcement of regulatory legislation. Unlike economic liberals, he had no wish to dismantle the paternal structure of the sixteenth and seventeenth centuries. From Lord Burghley,[44] Coke had acquired a profound admiration for Tudor legislation, an admiration which survived even his break with the following (Stuart) Court.

That break occurred in 1621, shortly after the general election in which Coke was returned to Parliament.[45] A serious trade crisis then existed, so much of the debate concerned proposals to repair the economy. Coke's advice was frequently sought, and he now was under no constraint to endorse the official policy of regulation. Indeed, his personal pique at having been by-passed in the selection of a new Lord Chancellor might easily have inspired an indiscriminate opposition to any policy proposed by the King. Coke's political views had altered markedly as a consequence of his new allegiance to Parliament. Whereas he had previously accorded the Crown a wide range of discretionary authority to regulate customs duties by proclamation[46] and to order impositions,[47] Coke now denied such prerogatives. But no new thoughts on eco-

44. C. Read, *Lord Burghley and Queen Elizabeth* 586 n. 26 (1960). Because Lord Burghley (William Cecil) was in some sense the architect of Tudor paternalism, his association with Coke is of special importance.

45. Many historians date Coke's break from June 30, 1616 when he was sequestered from the Council Table and forbidden to ride summer circuit as a Justice of Assize, *Acts of the Privy Council of England, 1615–1616,* at 649 (1925). In that year, he was called before the Council to explain his *Reports* and on November 16 he was removed from his position as Chief Justice of the King's Bench. Nevertheless, Coke himself seems not to have regarded the events of 1616 as marking an irrevocable breach with James. He thought of nothing but recovering himself from disgrace and immediately began making arrangements for the marriage of his daughter to Sir John Villiers, the older brother of the Duke of Buckingham. The marriage arranged, Coke was restored to the Privy Council on April 1, 1617. *Acts of the Privy Council of England, 1616–17,* at 216 (1927). In 1621 he was listed as one of the Privy Councillors in the House of Commons and when Parliament opened, James expected him to cooperate with the Court Party. See D. Willson, *supra* note 4, at 89. The final break came in 1621, after the election and after Coke was by-passed in the selection of a new Lord Chancellor.

46. 276 *State Papers Domestic, Elizabeth, 1598–1601,* at 521.

47. Coke supported the decision in *Bate's Case* in 1606, but said nothing to the effect that the King's discretion was unconfined. 278 *State Papers Domestic, Charles I, 1634,* at 351. For another issue on which Coke altered his views, see 5 W. Holdsworth, *History of English Law* 450 (1924), and note that this eminent

nomic policy accompanied his redefinition of royal authority. Coke conceded to Parliament those powers he denied to the Crown.

Certainly, his approach to foreign commerce was free of *laissez-faire* notions.[48] At the beginning of the session in 1621, Sir Edwin Sandys, reporting for the Committee Concerning the Decay of Trade of which he was chairman, listed scarcity of coin as the chief cause of the trade depression.[49] Coke agreed with his diagnosis and enumerated seven reasons for the scarcity.[50] Included in his analysis were the license of the East India Company to transport bullion, the unfavorable balance of trade, and the nature of the trade that was pursued. Displaying a medieval attitude toward luxury, Coke complained that too much commerce with France dealt in "wines and lace, and such like trifles." Tobacco too, was considered a luxury and as Sandys noted,[51] most of England's trade with Spain was absorbed by the importation of tobacco. Why not, he suggested, forbid the expenditure of so much money abroad by compelling the purchase of tobacco from the colonies. As a shareholder in the Virginia Company, Sandys naturally wished to create a monopoly for that Company and also suggested that the growth of tobacco in England be proscribed.[52] Coke thought that the growing of tobacco at home would help the farmers,[53] but he did go along with the proposal to forbid the import of Spanish tobacco.[54]

His greatest concern, however, was with England's staple commodity, cloth. In the early part of the seventeenth century, the production of finished cloth

---

historian believed that although Coke departed from certain of his former political opinions, "his outlook was always that of a statesman of the latter part of the Tudor period." *Id.* 456.

48. Coke's protectionist bias was revealed many more times than suggested above. He requested, for example, stronger penalties against the export of iron and copper and prayed that timber too might not be transported. 3 *Inst.* *97. The export of these metals, necessary for England's defense and economic self-sufficiency, had previously been prohibited. See Statute of Staples, 27 Edw. 3, c. 3 (1353); 33 Hen. 8, c. 7 (1541); 2 & 3 Edw. 6, c. 37 (1548). Thus, by upholding the existing statutes, Coke was upholding traditional tenets of economic policy. And even when he appeared to endorse free trade, Coke invoked very traditional arguments. On May 17, 1621, when a bill was introduced "to prohibit the importation of corn," he opposed it saying: "If we bar the importation of corn when it aboundeth, we shall not have it imported when we lack it. I never yet heard that a bill was ever before preferred in Parliament against the importation of corn, and I love to follow ancient precedents," 1 J. Campbell, *supra* note 13, at 322. The export of corn had been prohibited because Tudor statesmen wished to guarantee an adequate food supply at home. To prohibit the import of corn would have endangered that supply so Coke opposed the bill.

49. 1 *Parliamentary History* 1196–97 (March 1, 1621).

50. *Id.* 1195 (Feb. 26, 1621).

51. *Id.* 1196 (Feb. 27, 1621).

52. 3 *Commons Debates*, 1621, at 8 (W. Notestein, F. Relf & H. Simpson eds. 1935).

53. *Id.*

54. 1 *Journals of the House of Commons* 581 (April 18, 1621).

had declined and it was widely thought that this decline was related to the practice of exporting unfinished cloth and importing finished cloth. Since the reign of Edward III, the Crown had attempted to eliminate this practice and to encourage the domestic industry by prohibiting the import of all cloth.[55] Elizabeth too, sought to enforce this policy, but like her predecessors, she was compelled to abandon it for want of adequate domestic dyeing and finishing skill. As an alternative policy, she set about encouraging the export of finished cloth[56] and extended the privileges of the great trading companies. The most important of these was the Merchant Adventurers Company, to which she granted the exclusive right to export to Upper Germany and France as well as to the Low Countries.[57] Because of the concentration of its trade in London, its exclusive admission policies, its high prices and its practice of "cloth stretching," the Company became most unpopular. Sir Edward decried these practices.[58] But above all, he objected to the export of unfinished cloth.[59]

In the hope of aiding the unemployed clothiers and of increasing the revenue of the State by eliminating the need to import finished cloth,[60] Coke went so far as to embrace the ill-starred project of Alderman Cockayne, who founded a new company to export only finished cloth.[61] The project ended in disaster, with other nations retaliating by prohibiting the import of English cloth. By that time Coke had withdrawn his support because of the nature of the Company.[62] But he persisted in his aim of encouraging home industry. In 1621, when the Shrewsbury drapers' local monopoly of the Welsh cloth trade was thrown open, Coke helped ensure that their cloth had to be finished be-

55. 11 Edw. 3, c. 3 (1337).
56. 8 Eliz. 1, c. 6 (1565).
57. C. Lucas, *The Beginnings of English Overseas Enterprise* 79 (1917). This was the Charter of 1564.
58. A. Friis, *supra* note 17, at 244.
59. See Coke's memorandum of December 18, 1613 in "Sir Julius Caesar's Notes from the Privy Council Meetings Relating to Alderman Cockayne's Project," *id.*, app. D, at 458. Throughout his writings, Coke made many references to the virtue of encouraging home industry either by prohibiting the import of clothes finished abroad or the export of unfinished English cloth. 2 *Inst.* *41.
60. These were the same arguments used by Cockayne on behalf of his project. 3 E. Lipson, *supra* note 6, at 374–75.
61. Only three of James's Privy Councillors supported his decision to endorse the project and the most enthusiastic among them was Coke. A. Friis, *supra* note 17, at 26. According to this account, Coke endorsed the project for opportunistic reasons and was made a councillor as a token of James's gratitude. But Coke's position here was perfectly consistent with the views he expressed after breaking with the Court and besides, Coke withdrew his support of the project in January, 1616, when he was neither resigned nor determined to lose favor.
62. *Id.* 467; 86 *State Papers Domestic, James I, 1615–1616,* at 358 (March 27, 1616).

fore being sold.[63] And in 1624, he advised that the export of wool be made a felony.[64] Sir Edward was not averse to the regulation of foreign trade. He only insisted that Parliament do the regulating.[65]

This constitutional issue of who was to do the regulating never arose with regard to domestic trade: Tudor monarchs had judiciously requested parliamentary sanction for their economic policies. They received such sanction because of the consensus regarding the need to maintain full employment, a proper wage and price structure, a sufficient amount of land under tillage and fair trade practices. Tranquility, too, was an accepted goal of economic policy[66] because the Tudors assumed a conflict among private interests and the need artificially to maintain harmony.[67] In the sixteenth century, England had only just recovered from years of internecine strife and lacked the policy system necessary to quell food and land riots. The enforcement agents were informers,[68] Justices of the Peace and Councillors, whose inefficiency made essential the prevention of unrest. Prevention and paternalism went hand in hand with a multitude of regulations designed to remove potential grievances. According to Tudor habits of thought, to challenge these regulations would be to challenge the entire underpinning of the social fabric.

This is precisely what advocates of the *laissez-faire* thesis suggest Coke hoped to do, a contention which must be examined in detail. Take, for example, Coke's attitude toward the enclosure laws which prohibited the conversion of farm land to pasturage. In 1607, he proceeded against rioters who had tried to force down enclosures.[69] But Coke seems to have recognized the validity of the protest and, two years later, led a commission "towards reforming depopulation, converting tillage into pasturage, and preventing decay of husbandry."[70]

---

63. T. Mendenhall, *The Shrewsbury Drapers and the Welsh Wool Trade in the XVI and XVII Centuries* 176 (1953).

64. 1 *Journals of the House of Commons* 678 (March 6, 1623).

65. "That no Commodity can be banished, but by Act of Parliament." 1 *Journal of the House of Commons* 581 (April 18, 1621). See also 3 *Inst.* *181–85.

66. Fear of disorder helps to explain Star Chamber jurisdiction over semi-criminal problems not covered by common law courts, *e.g.,* prices, trade control and enclosures. A. Pollard, *Wolsey* 77 (1929).

67. The body politic ideal so much admired in Coke's day ought properly to have led to an assumption of harmony among private interests and also among private and public. Yet as so often happens, the self-image of the Tudors was basically prescriptive. When it came to legislating or pointing out wrongs, Coke and his contemporaries fully recognized the gap between theory and practice and it was perhaps that recognition which allowed for movement in a society whose ideal was static.

68. On the importance of informers see Beresford, "The Common Informer, the Penal Statutes and Economic Regulation," 10 *Econ. Hist. Rev.* (2d ser.) 221 (1957).

69. 28 *State Papers Domestic, James I, 1603–1610,* at 373 (Sept. 1607).

70. *Id.* 541 (Sept. 2, 1609).

At that time he was still a Crown servant. Yet even in 1624 he believed that the Tudor enactments which applied to the 25 midland counties most affected by the conversion of land should remain in force.[71] Enclosure by agreement might be all right, provided it did not lead to depopulation and did not involve the conversion to pasturage. "Agriculture or Tillage," Coke wrote, "is of great account in Law, as being very profitable for the Commonwealth. . . ."[72]

So great was the fear of food shortage that the Tudors sought to encourage husbandry by artificially supporting the price of corn[73] as well as by prohibiting the conversion of arable land. At the same time, they frowned on individual attempts to raise prices for the sake of private gain. Regulation was to be national and it was to provide for the common good. The "Preamble" to a statute enacted in 1552 decried, for example, the increase in the price of goods necessary for men's subsistence due to the practices of those who minded "only their own lure without respect of the Commonwealth, to the great damage, impoverishing and disquieting of his majesty's subjects."[74] That was the "Preamble" to the great declaratory act against forestalling and the related offences of regrating and engrossing: the purchase of merchandise, victuals and other commodities on their way to market for the purpose of restricting supply, the reselling of commodities brought to and purchased in the same market at a higher price, and the purchase of corn or grain, butter or cheese, fish or other

---

71. See 3 *Inst.* *204; Beresford, "Habitation vs. Improvement: The Debate on Enclosure by Agreement," in *Essays on the Economic and Social History of Tudor and Stuart England* 40–66 (F. Fisher ed. 1961).

72. 1 *Inst.* *85b. Coke's concern for tillage and also tenurial rights probably explains why he reported *Tyrringham's Case,* 4 Co. Rep. 36b, 76 Eng. Rep. 973 (K.B. 1584), so favorably. The plaintiff in the case was a farmer of a landlord in Northamptonshire who had purchased a house, land and part of the meadow and commons belonging to a neighboring estate. Prior to the sale, that part of the commons had been used by the tenant of the original landlord for pasturage, but the new landlord forbade the tenant to graze his cattle. When the tenant chased out the cattle of the new landlord's farmer, the farmer brought an action for trespass. The case was very complicated because the defendant needed pasture land to graze the cattle he used to till his land. The question confronting the King's Bench, therefore, was whether as a condition of his socage tenure, the pasturage was appurtenant to his husbandry. A long dictum followed the court's decision in favor of the defendant as to the benefit of maintaining land in tillage. In the court's words, or better, in Coke's, "the common law prefers arable land before all other." If the defendant were forbidden to use the commons, he would be forced to convert land now used for tillage into pasture. Parliament had made excellent statutes to keep up the price of corn and thereby to encourage husbandry, but these would be ineffectual if men were compelled to convert arable land. It is reasonable to attribute these views to Coke even though he did not decide the case, because in his "Comment to the Reader" Coke explained how important and wise a decision he thought it was and obviously interpolated his own policy considerations within the text of his report.

73. See note 72 *supra.* For an opposite view of Tudor policy see Letwin, "The English Common Law Concerning Monopolies," 21 *U. Chi. L. Rev.* 355, 367–68 (1954), where Letwin suggests that low prices were the object of laws against forestalling and engrossing. What he seems to forget is that these became statutory offenses in times of scarcity when prices were already high and the object was to prevent famine and profiteering.

74. 5 & 6 Edw. 6, c. 14 (1552).

dead victuals with the intent of reselling. Statutes prohibiting these crimes, as they were considered, date back to the thirteenth century and were passed periodically until late in the eighteenth.[75] Usually, they were enacted in times of great scarcity[76] and then remained in force after the immediate crisis. The offences they defined were already indictable at common law, but the statutes also assigned punishments to be enforced by the courts.

Coke's first experience with the statutes against forestalling and engrossing seems to have come in 1598, when he was Attorney General. In that year, he attended a conference of all the justices, who decided that any "merchant, subject, or stranger, bringing victuals or merchandize into this realme, may sell them in grosse: but that vendee cannot sell them againe in grosse, for then he is an ingrosser . . . and may be indicted thereof at the common law, as for an offence that is *malum in se*."[77] At first appearance, Coke and the justices were making an exception for foreign traders and restricting the purview of the Statute of 1552. Yet that Statute specifically excluded persons transporting "things imported from beyond the seas," and this exception was upheld by 13 Eliz. 1, c. 25. Parliament had recognised that the initial sale by importers could be in gross and sought only to proscribe intermediate sales among middlemen.

If Parliament's intent was clear on this question, it was not too obvious which items were to be subsumed under the general category of "victuals." Certain commodities such as corn were mentioned specifically, but the statute of 1552 made no attempt to enumerate all "victuals." Instead it was left to the courts to determine. Their guideline was the "Preamble" to the statute, which stressed goods necessary for subsistence. Salt clearly fell into that category,[78] but fruit did not. At least that is what Coke and the other justices resolved in *Baron v. Boys*.[79] The Exchequer had already excepted fruit,[80] so Coke and his colleagues were in no way departing from precedent. Nor were they revealing an "aversion" to the statute. Coke himself tried at least four cases in-

75. In 1772, the statute of Edward VI was repealed by 12 Geo. 3, c. 71, but badgers, engrossers, forestallers and regrators remained indictable at common law. Only in 1844 with the enactment of 7 & 8 Vict., c. 24, were the offences of forestalling, regrating and engrossing entirely abolished. W. Sanderson, *Restraint of Trade in English Law* 97–98 (1926).

76. For a good summary of the laws against forestalling, see Jones, "Historical Development of the Law of Business Competition," 35 *Yale L.J.* 905, 906–20 (1926).

77. 3 *Inst.* *196. An offence that was *malum in se* was against the law of nature or the law of God and thus even the King could not dispense with a statute proscribing such an evil. Birdsall, "*Non Obstante—* A Study of the Dispensing Power of English Kings," in *Essays in History and Political Theory in Honor of Charles Howard McIlwain* 56 (1936).

78. 3 *Inst.* *195–96.

79. 13 Co. Rep. 18, 77 Eng. Rep. 1429 (Ex. 1608).

80. Braddon v. Bowen, Cro. Jac. 214, 79 Eng. Rep. 187 (Ex. 1608).

volving forestallers and engrossers. One he dismissed on technical grounds,[81] the other three he decided against the defendants.[82] In the Third Part of his *Institutes*[83] Coke devoted a chapter to explaining the laws and seems fully to have approved of them.

Coke appears to have been similarly sympathetic to the single most extensive regulatory enactment of the period. Passed in 1563, the Statute of Artificers[84] regulated entrance into given trades, provided full employment to craftsmen, and guaranteed the quality of the skill. It sought to "banish idleness, advance husbandry, and yield unto the hired person, both in time of scarcity, and in the time of plenty, a convenient proportion of wages."[85] Justices of the Peace were empowered to fix wages and for the first time a national apprenticeship requirement was imposed.[86] Regulations were so detailed that any one at all inclined toward "free trade" would have found them intolerable.

But Coke fully endorsed the Statute of Artificers. As Chief Justice of the Common Pleas, he was expected to deliver a charge to the assizes at the beginning of each term of the law courts and to draw up a list of articles for presentment. Whether his list differed from his predecessor's is difficult to say.[87] But at Norwich he asked that the constables of each hundred see that "All masters be presented that . . . give greater wages than shall be set down by the justices of the peace" and that they "inquire into and present masters who turn away servants before the time for which retained, for that thereby many become rogues and idle persons."[88] That was in 1607. In the 1630's, he still believed that the many statutes made for the "punishment of riots, unlawful assemblies, . . . excessive taking of wages contrary to the statutes of labourers and

81. King & Goldesborow v. Whider, 2 Bulst. 317, 80 Eng. Rep. 1152 (K.B. 1614). For the difficulty common informers encountered in trying to produce admissible evidence, see Dewey, "The Common-Law Background of Antitrust Policy," 41 *Va. L. Rev.* 759, 763 n. 13 (1955).

82. Suckerman & Coates v. Warner, 2 Bulst. 248, 80 Eng. Rep. 1097 (K.B. 1614); R. v. Davies, 1 Rolle 11, 81 Eng. Rep. 291 (K.B. 1614); R. v. Wray, 1 Rolle 194, 81 Eng. Rep. 426 (K.B. 1615). See generally W. Illingworth, *An Inquiry into the Laws, Ancient and Modern, Respecting Forestalling, Regrating and Ingrossing* (1800).

83. 3 *Inst.* *194–97.

84. 5 Eliz. 1, c. 4 (1562).

85. *Id.,* preamble.

86. The apprenticeship clauses were not part of the original bill; they were added through the initiative of the Commons. For new insight into the formulation of the Statute see S. Bindoff, *The Making of the Statute of Artificers, Elizabethan Government and Society,* especially at 68–79 (1961). Until 1563 apprenticeship regulation had been left to guild towns, whose assistance in enforcing the new statute was still required by the administrative weaknesses of the Tudor state. But the Statute of Artificers did mark a decisive step toward national uniformity and control, and indeed most of Coke's criticism of guilds was directed against ordinances which were either more stringent than the new Statute or which conflicted with other of the newly formulated national policies.

87. M. Davies, *The Enforcement of English Apprenticeship, 1563–1642,* at 232 (1956).

88. *The Lord Coke, His Speech and Charge* (1607); 276 *State Papers Domestic, Elizabeth, 1598–1601,* at 519.

artificers" were "good statutes" whose lack of enforcement was to the "great let of the common law, and wealth of this land. . . ."[89]

Coke's performance on the bench, however, is more controversial. Prior to the Restoration, there were very few cases in which the question of apprenticeship even arose. Coke decided two of them while Chief Justice of the King's Bench. The more famous was *The Taylors of Ipswich Case*[90] which involved the relationship between a guild ordinance and the Statute of Artificers. The Merchant Taylors had required that their permission be obtained to exercise a trade after the prospective craftsmen had completed their apprenticeship. The defendant, a private tailor to a "freeman of Ipswich," refused to clear with the society, which then brought suit. Coke found that the Statute did not apply to domestic servants, but this was no more than a dictum. The defendant had in fact been properly apprenticed. Coke never addressed himself to the validity of the apprenticeship regulations because the point in issue was whether or not the Merchant Taylors might compel fully apprenticed craftsmen to obtain their permission to practice their trade. The Taylors' charter granted them the right to pass by-laws so that the question was the validity of the particular ordinance.[91]

Coke decided that it was not valid because the Merchant Taylors' ordinance tended to create a monopoly and violated the "liberty and freedom of the subject." This was after *The Case of Monopolies*[92] had been decided, and Coke had the solid weight of precedent behind him. Citing this case, he explained that the law forbade no man to exercise the trade for which he was qualified. Idleness was abhorred by the law because it was "the mother of all evil, . . . and especially in young men, who ought in their youth . . . to learn lawful sciences and trades, which are profitable to the Commonwealth."[93] What Coke objected to was not the statute but the possibility that a man qualified to work under the act might be prevented from doing so by a guild. Even Heckscher

89. 4 *Inst.* *40.
90. 11 Co. Rep. 53, 77 Eng. Rep. 1218 (K.B. 1614).
91. The "new monarchy" had asserted itself over chartered towns and other corporate bodies; The Ordinances of Corporations Act, 19 Hen. 7, c. 7 (1503), bestowed on judges the power to abrogate new guild ordinances made without their consent. See W. Cunningham, *The Growth of English Industry and Commerce* 26 n. 2 (1907). Most accounts fail to distinguish between Coke's censure of a particular ordinance and an institution itself. To censure the former may have signified a weakening of the power of corporate bodies but it was perfectly consistent with contemporary practice as suggested by the statute mentioned above. Significantly, Coke did not challenge the charters of properly incorporated bodies and generally reflected the Tudors' ambivalent attitude—their desire for national control but recognition of administrative problems which still gave great importance to pluralist groups.
92. 11 Co. Rep. 84b, 77 Eng. Rep. 1260 (K.B. 1602).
93. 11 Co. Rep. at 53b, 77 Eng. Rep. at 1219.

recognized the weakness of basing his estimate of Coke as a free trader on this case, and relied on Coke's narrow construction in the second of the two cases he decided.

That was *Tooley's* (or *Tolley's*) *Case*[94] in which the defendant, a Londoner, had taken up the work of an upholsterer after serving his apprenticeship as a wool packer. He was prosecuted by the Crown because the Statute of Artificers provided that a man must be apprenticed to the specific trade he practiced. The statute had not, however, enumerated the trades which came under its scope. Each section covered different trades and the section on apprenticeship was very vague: "None shall set up, occupy, use or exercise any craft, mystery or occupation, now used or occupied within the realm of *England* or *Wales;* except he shall have been brought up therein seven years at least as an apprentice."[95] In a dictum, Coke said the provision did not cover upholstering because it was neither a "trade nor a mystery and did not require any skill."

According to Heckscher,[96] this was the first time the courts had ever excluded a craft: Coke was using immoderate discretion to narrow the scope of the statute because he had an "aversion" to apprenticeship regulation. This interpretation would seem to be incorrect. The occupation of buying and selling had been excluded twice in different decisions.[97] More important, it had been excluded on the ground that it required no special skill, precisely the ground on which Coke excluded upholstering. He and the other justices[98] considered the maintenance of a certain standard of skill among craftsmen the basis for the apprenticeship rule; hence employments requiring no training seemed outside the scope of the Statute.

Even if Heckscher were correct and Coke was the first to construe a trade as being outside the statute, it would not at all follow that he opposed apprentice-

94. 2 Bulst. 186, 80 Eng. Rep. 1055 (K.B. 1613).

95. 5 Eliz. 1, c. 4, § 31 (1562).

96. 1 E. Heckscher, *Mercantilism* 292 (M. Shapiro trans. 1935).

97. In 1580 judgment was given in the Exchequer upon an information against a clothier, that the statutory "exercising a trade" was not applicable to the buying of unfinished cloth and its later sale by the buyer after being put out for finishing. In 1600 the occupation of costermonger was said to be exempt. These decisions are cited in M. Davies, *The Enforcement of English Apprenticeship* 241 (1956). Generally, the judicial interpretation of the Statute was far from being so uniformly unfavorable as has been supposed. Derry, "The Enforcement of a Seven Years' Apprenticeship Under the Statute of Artificers," in 4 *Abstracts of Dissertations for the Degree of Doctor of Philosophy for the University of Oxford* 10–11 (1931). Indeed, there is evidence to suggest that the Statute was still enforced at the end of the seventeenth century. Letwin, *supra* note 73, at 364–65.

98. And also other commentators on the statute. For although section xxiv explicitly mentioned manual occupations, within ten years after the statute passed, an unsigned "Memorandum" ascribed the apprenticeship regulation to the need to maintain skill as well as the need to restrict the number of artificers. The "Memorandum" is published in 1 *Tudor Economic Documents* 353–63 (R. H. Tawney & E. Power eds. 1924).

ship regulation. As Thorne has shown, the sixteenth century witnessed a general trend toward curtailment of judicial supplementation of statutes which had nothing to do with economic policy.[99] As the number and importance of statutory enactments increased, so too did the narrowness with which the courts interpreted the words of Parliament. A more modern awareness of legislative competence was leading the courts to restrict their discretion and apply the intention of the legislature. In the Statute of Artificers, as in the Statute against Forestallers, Parliament's intention was stated in general terms and it was up to the courts to determine which trades fell within their scope. A negative decision with regard to a particular trade need not, therefore, imply any bias.

Coke's central concern in *Tooley's Case* was neither *laissez-faire* nor the unskilled nature of the upholstering trade. The issue of skill arose because it was in the indictment and because it constituted one of the arguments of the defense counsel. But the gravamen of the argument was the privilege of London.[100] The statute had stipulated that a man must be apprenticed to the specific trade he practiced. The custom of London permitted freemen who had been apprenticed to any trade to practice any other. London was an incorporated city, the validity of whose customs had been recognized by royal charter and confirmed by Parliament. Section 33 of the statute explicitly excluded the City from its scope. Coke found for Tooley because he was a Londoner, and not because Coke had an "aversion" to the statute.

III

On the basis of his attitude toward the three most important Tudor regulations, it can hardly be said that Coke departed from contemporary legal and economic opinion. He supported paternalistic measures, using his judicial authority to uphold their provisions and purposes. Advocates of the *laissez-faire*

99. See his brilliant *Introduction* to T. Egerton, *A Discourse upon the Exposicion & Understandinge of Statutes* (Thorne ed. 1942). Holdsworth explains that in the Tudor-Stuart period, dismissals of prosecutions of all types of cases for seemingly minor inaccuracies in the indictment were frequent. 4 W. Holdsworth, *History of English Law* 531 (1924).

100. Unlike civilian lawyers who opposed municipal corporations on the ground that they impugned the sovereignty of the state, Coke and the common lawyers usually defended the privileges of the City and other incorporated towns. See 2 *Inst.* *20; *The Chamberlain of London's Case,* 5 Co. Rep. 62b, 79 Eng. Rep. 150 (K.B. 1590); Clearwork v. Constable, Cro. Eliz. 110, 78 Eng. Rep. 367 (K.B. 1588); Waggoner v. Fish, 2 Brownl. & Golds. 284, 123 Eng. Rep. 944 (C.P. 1610) (also reported as *The Case of the City of London,* 8 Co. Rep. 121b, 77 Eng. Rep. 658 (K.B. 1610)).

thesis were quite mistaken in suggesting a deliberate attempt to weaken enforcement of statutory regulations. And they were also mistaken in suggesting a deliberate distortion of precedent when dealing with cases of monopoly. According to Wagner,[101] Sir Edward undermined a tolerance of restrictive practices long established at common law; his economic liberalism led him to introduce novel anti-monopoly notions into his decisions. But Coke dealt fairly with precedent and insofar as he made any contribution to the legal underpinnings of capitalism, it was to modify the blanket proscription of all contracts in restraint of trade.

Since the fifteenth century, courts had refused to enforce contracts in which one party promised not to practice his trade.[102] In *Colgate v. Bacheler,* which was decided two years before *The Case of Monopolies,* the King's Bench still found that "to prohibit or restrain any to use a lawful trade at any time, or at any place" is against public policy and unenforceable.[103] Coke was the first to modify this doctrine and he did so in *Rogers v. Parrey.*[104] The case involved the validity of a promise made by the defendant to the effect that in consideration of so much paid to him by the plaintiff, he would not exercise his trade as joiner in London for twenty-one years. The defendant had not abided by his promise and was being sued. Coke found for the plaintiff, thus upholding a contract made in restraint of trade.

Proponents of the *laissez-faire* thesis could have used the decision in *Rogers v. Parrey* to their advantage,[105] for the sanctity of contract and right to eliminate competition through voluntary agreement were vital aids in the growth of modern capitalism. Courts in the nineteenth century[106] used Coke's rea-

---

101. See note 9 *supra.*

102. R. Wilberforce, A. Campbell & N. Elles, *The Law of Restrictive Trade Practices and Monopolies* 39–55 and *passim* (1957) [hereinafter cited as Wilberforce].

103. Cro. Eliz. 872, 78 Eng. Rep. 1097 (K.B. 1601).

104. 2 Bulst. 136, 80 Eng. Rep. 1012 (K.B. 1613). The more decisive departure from precedent, however, was *Broad v. Jollyfe,* Cro. Jac. 596, 79 Eng. Rep. 509 (K.B. 1619).

105. But only to a certain extent—because Coke actually decided the case on the narrow basis of contract law, finding for the plaintiff on the sole ground that the consideration he had offered the defendant was sufficient. In the important conflicting precedent, *Dyer's Case,* Y.B. 2 Hen. 5, 5B (1414), the defendant's bond that he would not practice his trade was not enforced. But there was no consideration at all for Dyer's bond, and later cases and commentators have argued that the case is simply part of the early evolution of the doctrine of consideration. Mitchell v. Reynolds, 1 P. Wms. 181, 24 Eng. Rep. 347 (Ch. 1711) (Lord Macclesfield); Letwin, *supra* note 73, at 373–74. Besides, insofar as the case raised questions of policy, Coke agreed that a man cannot bind himself not to use his trade generally as Dyer had done for that would deprive him of his livelihood. The only reasonable restraint he might voluntarily accept was not to exercise his trade for "a time certain, and in a place certain," Rogers v. Parrey, 2 Bulst. 136, 80 Eng. Rep. 1012, 1013 (K.B. 1613).

106. See, e.g., Mitchell v. Reynolds, 1 P. Wms. 181, 24 Eng. Rep. 347 (Ch. 1711); Maxim-Nordenfelt Ammunition Co. v. Nordenfelt, [1894] A.C. 535.

soning to uphold contracts more restrictive than that in *Rogers v. Parrey.* Yet the decision was ignored by Wagner who wanted to demonstrate the radical implications of Coke's attack on monopolies and not Coke's contribution to the growth of modern trusts.

That Coke did attack some[107] monopolies is certain. Whether his attack necessarily represented a departure from precedent or whether the common law had an inherent bias against trade restraint has aroused great controversy. In the seventeenth century, "monopoly" meant both private acts of hoarding and exclusive trade privileges bestowed by the Crown.[108] No precise precedent existed for the second of these forms because it was not until 1601 that royal patents became actionable at common law.[109] Cases involving the Crown prerogative had previously come before the Star Chamber and Privy Council; only the popular and parliamentary outcry induced Elizabeth to concede common law jurisdiction. Private monopolies, however, had long been void[110] and centuries of case-law could be applied to royal monopolies. So too, could the broad policy of full employment: royal privileges were exclusive and prevented craftsmen in monopolized trades from working. Most important, Coke and other litigants could cite evidence of long-standing government antipathy to restrictive guild practices. Guild ordinances which fixed prices at extortionate levels or lowered quality or excluded an unreasonable proportion of applicants had nearly always been unlawful.[111]

---

107. For the very limited nature of Coke's attack, see pp. 216–23 *infra.*

108. 6 *Oxford English Dictionary* 624 (1933).

109. See Elizabeth's "Golden Speech," delivered on November 20, 1601, in Price, *supra* note 5, app. K. Wagner thought the absence of precise precedent indicated previous common law acquiescence in monopolies and therefore deduced a departure in policy from *The Case of Monopolies.*

110. See p. 210 *infra.*

111. For complaints against restrictive guild practices, see Jones, "Historical Development of the Law of Business Competition," 35 *Yale L.J.* 906, 922–30 (1926), and Kellet, "The Breakdown of Guild and Corporation Control over the Handicraft and Retail Trade in London," 10 *Econ. Hist. Rev.* (2d Ser.) 381–83 (1958).

William L. Letwin, perhaps the ablest proponent of the view that the common law effected a *volte face* in order to void trade restraints in the seventeenth century, cited only one example of prior acquiescence in "unfree" trade: *The Case of the Archbishop of York,* in which a court upheld the custom of the Archbishop's manor at Ripon that no one should operate a dyeing house there without the Archbishop's license. See Letwin, *supra* note 73, at 373. But this case involved rights attached to a manor bestowed by the King and to have decided otherwise would have meant challenging the Crown's prerogative and the Archbishop's privilege. Thus the decision testifies more to the state of political opinion in medieval England and to the power of the Church than to the common law attitude toward trade restriction.

In fact, by the fourteenth century, English courts were already invalidating guild ordinances, apparently on the basis of early statutes. Examples of early decisions against particular guild ordinances may be found in Jones, *supra,* at 928. Statutes prohibiting agreements to fix the terms of employment go back as far as 1300. Wilberforce, *supra* note 102, at 65. But not even Coke claimed these statutes were declaratory of the common law. R. Wright, *The Law of Criminal Conspiracies and Agreements* 40 (1891). There were, of course, cases

Decisions involving guild restraints provided excellent precedent by which
to void monopolies, even though the common law had never been granted
jurisdiction over actual charters.[112] The problem was the paucity of such decisions: the privilege of judging ordinances had been conceded only recently[113]
and litigation never really arose until after the guilds had declined and after
they had resorted to practices which were a travesty of their purpose.[114] This
was in the very late sixteenth and early seventeenth centuries when there was a
spate of cases. The most important, *Davenant v. Hurdis,*[115] concerned the validity of a by-law which required members of the Merchant Taylors to employ
cloth-making brethren on at least half their cloth or pay a forfeit. The plaintiff, Davenant, had refused to comply with the by-law and when distrained for
the forfeit brought an action in trespass. Sir Edward was his counsel; Francis
Moore[116] represented the Company.

Coke's basic claim was that the by-law tended to create a monopoly. If members could be compelled to employ cloth-making brethren on half their cloth,
then eventually they might be required to employ brethren on all of it. Other
members would then be put at the mercy of the cloth workers of the Company
and cloth workers outside would be put out of work and compelled to subsist

---

in which guild privileges were upheld. But these were tried in the prerogative courts. H. Fox, *Monopolies
and Patents* 21 n. 6 (1949).

   In dealing with guild restrictions, Coke and his contemporaries could not invoke the doctrine of conspiracy in restraint of trade because until 1721 combinations of workers to raise wages or otherwise to alter
the conditions of employment were not held to be criminal conspiracies at common law. Bryan, "The Development of the English Law of Conspiracy," 27 *Johns Hopkins University Studies in Historical and Political
Science* 257–58 (1909).

   112. That is, no court could invalidate a guild charter in the same way the court voided an industrial
patent in 1603, and no *exact* precedent existed because of limited common law jurisdiction over institutions
having royal sanction.

   113. See note 91 *supra* as to when even the ordinances become actionable at common law.

   114. Guilds were originally meant to regulate trade whereas in their decline they resorted to restrictive
practices. The distinction between regulation and restriction may seem unsound and imprecise today but
it had a very real meaning in the sixteenth and seventeenth centuries. It was the difference between setting
just as opposed to extortionate prices; between enforcing standards of quality as opposed to adulterating
goods. And most important, it was the difference between harmonious government in a trade and acrimonious dissension caused by the exclusion of many who sought membership and training in the craft of their
choice.

   115. Moore 576, 72 Eng. Rep. 769 (K.B. 1598). Coke did not report this case except within the context
of his discussion of monopolies in *The Case of Monopolies,* 11 Co. Rep. 84, 86, 77 Eng. Rep. 1260, 1263 (K.B.
1602), and 2 *Inst.* *48.
   Other cases were *Norris v. Staps,* Hobart 210, 80 Eng. Rep. 357 (K.B. 1616), and *The Tailors of Ipswich
Case,* 11 Co. Rep. 53, 77 Eng. Rep. 1218 (K.B. 1614). See also Kellet, *supra* note 111, at 381–95.

   116. That Francis Moore represented the Merchant Tailors notwithstanding his opposition to monopolies in the Parliament of 1597 suggests the apolitical nature of the adversary system even in the sixteenth
century. Coke was then Attorney General but seems to have argued the case in a private capacity. The fact
of his defense of Davenant in itself proves nothing of his attitude toward monopolies. But the arguments
he used in 1599 were precisely those later used by Coke's adversary in *The Case of Monopolies.*

on relief. To deprive a skilled craftsman of the right to practice his trade, Coke said, was to deprive him of the "liberty of the subject."[117] In support of his argument, he cited a dictate from the civil law,[118] and a number of cases in which by-laws or patents had been held valid because they were for the public good:

> a regulation that all ships must harbor in one port and no other, a grant by the King giving a skilled foreigner the sole right to make sailing canvas, and another giving a skilled projector exclusive right to drain lands, a by-law that all cloth sold in London must first be inspected and passed at Blackwell Hall, a by-law of St. Albans requiring each inhabitant to pay a contribution toward cleaning the town, and by-laws for the maintenance of bridges, walls, and similar public works.[119]

According to Wagner,[120] Coke's argument was weak and the King's Bench accepted it only because Chief Justice Popham was himself opposed to monopolies and because Francis Moore, counsel for the defendant, conceded that the ordinance of the Merchant Taylors would be void if it did in fact create a monopoly. But their unanimous refusal to defend a monopoly suggests a consensus about the prior state of the law. And if Coke had anticipated serious resistance to his argument, he might have cited the few early decisions against guild restrictions. Instead, he counterposed regulations made in the public interest with the ordinance of the Merchant Taylors. The cases which he cited[121] affirmed the right of municipal corporations to make laws which carried out local customs provided they were consonant with law and reason.[122] The test of reason was the public interest, which in *Davenant v. Hurdis* Coke construed to mean full employment of skilled craftsmen. This definition, being perfectly consistent with Tudor policy and with the prevailing view of employment as one of the inherent rights of Englishmen,[123] did not require elaboration.

117. *The Case of Monopolies*, 11 Co. Rep. 84b, 86b, 77 Eng. Rep. 1260, 1263 (K.B. 1602).

118. Moore at 580, 72 Eng. Rep. at 771.

119. Letwin, *supra* note 73, at 361.

120. Wagner, "The Common Law and Free Enterprise: An Early Case of Monopoly," 7 *Econ. Hist. Rev.* 217, 218 (1937).

121. The last three by-laws cited by Coke (see text accompanying note 119 *supra*) were upheld in these cases respectively: *The Chamberlain of London's Case*, 5 Co. Rep. 62b, 77 Eng. Rep. 150 (K.B. 1590); *Clark's Case*, 5 Co. Rep. 64, 77 Eng. Rep. 152 (C.P. 1595); and *Jeffrey's Case*, 5 Co. Rep. 66b, 77 Eng. Rep. 155 (C.P. 1590).

122. See *The Case of the City of London*, 8 Co. Rep. 121b, 77 Eng. Rep. 658 (K.B. 1609).

123. M. Judson, *The Crisis of the Constitution* 37 (1949).

Nevertheless, it received elaboration four years later when the King's Bench for the first time tried and voided royal patents. *The Case of Monopolies*[124] arose on an action brought by Edward Darcy against T. Allen for infringing his privilege to make, import[125] and sell playing cards. The patent had been granted in August of 1598 and thereafter the plaintiff, a Groom of the Privy Council, had had difficulty enforcing it.[126] The Council does not seem to have been able to help him, so that when Elizabeth opened her patents to the scrutiny of the common law, he immediately took advantage of the opportunity to prosecute. The litigation was carried on until Easter term, 1603, when the decision was handed down.

Virtually every account credits Coke with that decision. But in 1603 Coke was Solicitor General and, like the other legal officer of the Crown, the Attorney General, he was obliged to defend the contested patent. The decision in *The Case of Monopolies* was not Coke's own and even if it were it would in no way demonstrate his distortion of precedent.

According to Coke's report,[127] the King's Bench cited *Davenant v. Hurdis* and general statements of principle to void monopolies—statements from Fortescue,[128] the Bible,[129] and a decision in the reign of Henry IV to the effect that royal grants must not burden the subject.[130] The decision in *The Case of Monopolies,* however, rested principally on an appeal to traditional values and public policy of the common law. The court held that all trades furnishing employment to subjects, thus preventing idleness, were of value to the Commonwealth and an exclusive grant to exercise such a trade was against the

124. 11 Co. Rep. 84, 77 Eng. Rep. 1260 (K.B. 1602); Darcy v. Allen, Moore 672, 72 Eng. Rep. 830 (K.B. 1602).

125. Darcy had been granted two distinct patents: one for the exclusive sale and production of playing cards, and one for the exclusive right to import such cards. The court's opposition to the latter was to the use of the royal dispensing power to nullify acts of Parliament and is not referred to in this discussion.

126. For the repeated complaints made by Darcy, see 31 *Acts of the Privy Council, 1600–1601* (n.s.), 55–56 (1906), and 32 *Acts of the Privy Council, 1601–1604* (n.s.) 132–33, 237, 501 (1907).

127. Coke reported *The Case of Monopolies* twelve years after it was decided. In his discussion, he made it very clear that he supported the decision for the defendant by calling the readers' attention to the "glorious preamble and pretence of this odious monopoly." 11 Co. Rep. 84b, 88b, 77 Eng. Rep. 1260, 1266 (K.B. 1602).

128. Wagner observed that Coke's references to chapter 26 of Fortescue's *De Laudibus Legum Angliae* were incorrect, but that in chapter 85 of his *Third Institutes,* Coke correctly cited chapters 35 and 36. The second of these chapters urged that every inhabitant "is at his full liberty to use and enjoy whatever his farm produceth." Wagner, "Coke and the Rise of Economic Liberalism," 6 *Econ. Hist. Rev.* 36 n. 1 (1935).

129. "No man shall take the nether or the upper millstone to pledge: for he taketh a *man's* life to pledge." *Deut.* 24:6. Coke concluded that scripture showed that "a man's trade is accounted his life, because it maintaineth his life; and therefore the monopolist that taketh away a man's trade, taketh away his life and therefore is so much the more odious. . . ." 3 *Inst.* *181.

130. *The Case of Monopolies,* 11 Co. Rep. 84b, 86, 77 Eng. Rep. 1260, 1262 (K.B. 1602).

liberty and benefit of the subject; that monopolies were not only prejudicial to the traders excluded but also to the public generally because of their three inseparable incidents: the raising of prices, the deterioration of quality of the goods and the impoverishment of excluded trades.

Technically, the law in question was statutory. But most of the statutes cited were declaratory of the common law. In Coke's words, "admission and allowance of the justices ought to be holden for law."[131] Difficulties arose when the courts had long decided a matter in one way and Parliament then legislated in another.[132] But the problem did not arise here and no one challenged the validity of statutory citations.

One of the more important was the Statute of Labourers, 25 Edw. 3 (1350). It had been enacted because the shortage of labor created by the Black Death put great inflationary pressure on wages and King Edward wished to restore them to their original level. But in addition to fixing wages, the statute compelled all those "able in body and under the age of sixty" to work. Like the Statute of Artificers which Coke also reported, it sought to enforce full employment. Both of these enactments imposed an obligation to work, and it would seem that the "libertye" or right to work upheld by *Davenant v. Hurdis* and *The Case of Monopolies* actually derives from this obligation. If public policy required that all be usefully employed, then certain privileged individuals could not be permitted to deprive others of their trade. The statutes created the obligation; the courts upheld the right. Monopolies led to unemployment and were therefore void at common law.

Monopolies also raised prices arbitrarily. Apart from the new political problem of royal sanction, many laws forbade private attempts to manipulate the market. Coke could draw upon 27 Edw. 3, c. 11 and later acts which prohibited the forestalling of wine and other victuals or wares. Cases involving the infringement of these statutes came before the Star Chamber and the Council. But as the statutes were declaratory, local courts helped to enforce them and so did the courts of common law.[133] A case reported in one of the books of Assize,

---

131. 2 *Inst.* *399 and the table on "laws" following.

132. In the 1620's, Coke fully acknowledged the competence of Parliament to legislate contrary to the common law. See, e.g., 4 *Inst.* *14. But he warned that statutes which flew in the face of custom would not last very long. 4 *Inst.* *31.

133. 4 W. Holdsworth, *History of English Law* 377 (1922). Coke cited to the reign of Edward III very frequently because it was then that the first real efforts at national regulation were made and because the statutes of that reign bore a marked resemblance to those of Elizabeth's. Moreover, Coke wanted precedents from as far back in time as possible. The *Year Books* date from Edward I but the sixteenth century edition which Coke used started only with the reign of Edward III. W. Holdsworth, *Sources and Literature of English Law* 75–79 (1925).

for example, spoke of a Lombard indicted in London for various offences, including "practicing by words to enhance the price of merchandise."[134] It was argued on his behalf that, as his words had not had the intended effect and no damage had been done, he had committed no offence. His plea was overruled, however. As in *The Case of Monopolies,* the court sought no actual evidence of the inseparable incidents to forestalling or monopolies.[135]

The application of the statutes against forestalling and engrossing had always been narrow. But Coke might have noted any number of cases on behalf of the common law's bias against attempts by individuals to manipulate prices. That he did not do so suggests that Coke (and the court whose decision he was reporting) assumed the parallel between the offences of engrossing and forestalling and monopolies would be obvious to his contemporaries. It was obvious to a complainant in 1587[136] and also to Coke's arch-enemy, Bacon, who wrote: "Monopoly and engrossing differ only in this, that the first is by patent from the King, the other by act of the subject, between party and party; but both are equally injurious to trade and the freedom of the subject, and therefore equally restrained by the common law."[137]

Thus by citing the offences of forestalling and engrossing Coke was appealing to trade restraints generally recognized as analogous to royal monopolies. So far from distorting precedent or arbitrarily imposing his own views, Coke drew upon the common law bias against individual forms of trade intervention and applied it to exclusive privileges conferred by the Crown. His logic was valid; his citations apposite. Anything "liberal" in his opposition to monopolies had likewise been present in ideas or judgments handed down for many centuries.

IV

Two "liberal" elements did appear in the indictment of monopolies: the rhetoric of "free trade" and the belief in open markets implicit in demands that prices not be manipulated or artificially controlled. Both elements encouraged

---

134. 43 Assizes pl. 38 *as cited in* 4 W. Holdsworth, *History of English Law* 376 (1922).

135. Mason, "Monopoly in Law and Economics," 47 *Yale L.J.* 34, 38 (1937).

136. See 2 *Tudor Economic Documents* 260 (R. H. Tawney & E. Power eds. 1924).

137. Bacon's statement in his *Abridgement* is quoted in H. Fox, *Monopolies and Patents* 21 n. 6 (1949). For further information regarding the relationship between forestalling and monopolies, see V. Mund, *Open Markets: An Essential of Free Enterprise* 44–45 (1948).

historians in their estimate of Coke as a proponent of *laissez-faire*. But studied in context, both show him to have been very much a man of his age. "Free trade" had a specific political meaning and involved no rejection of the State; the belief in open markets was a medieval legacy, underpinned by considerations foreign to classical economics.

Instead of looking forward to a competitive and unregulated system of enterprise, Coke looked back to the ideal of the body politic with its emphasis on public good over private gain. This ideal pervaded much of Tudor thought, transmitting the scholastics' distrust of middlemen and speculators as well as the medieval notion of monopoly as a simple act of hoarding or price fixing.[138] Coke's notion was very similar, for apart from royal patents, he knew no more sophisticated form of trade restraint. In the sixteenth and seventeenth centuries, no enterprise was of sufficient size independently[139] to corner the market. Size did not enter into the prevailing definition of monopoly[140] and problems of efficiency and market division never even arose.[141] The grounds for censuring monopolies were therefore what they had always been: fear of fraud and the pursuit of "excessive" gain. However tacitly,[142] Coke believed that prices should be determined justly[143] where all could observe the true weight and quality of an item. Secretiveness seemed to bespeak dishonesty, hence the desire for "open" markets.

Based on moral precept rather than an abstract theory of competitive price determination, Coke's belief in open markets implied no understanding of *laissez-faire*. He came to this belief from assumptions tangibly different from those of economic liberals, and he accorded the State a positive and beneficent role they denied it. Whereas "liberals" were confident that markets might best be kept open without regulation and therefore urged the repeal of engrossing and forestalling laws,[144] Coke upheld those

138. The term "monopoly" originally covered all pacts by which merchants set prices and created artificial scarcities. De Roover, "Monopoly Theory Prior to Adam Smith: A Revision," 65 *Q.J. Econ.* 492, 498–511 (1951).

139. That is, without the sanction of royal protection.

140. See 21 Jac. 1, c. 3 (1623); Bork, "The Rule of Reason and the Per Se Concept: Price Fixing and Market Division I," 74 *Yale L.J.* 775, 783 (1965).

141. For the most part, the problem of collusive agreements to fix prices did not arise either; forestalling and engrossing were acts by one man without a partner.

142. It must be remembered that Coke never presented his ideas on economic policy in any coherent form and that, like his contemporaries, he did not compartmentalize economic, social and political theory.

143. The emphasis here is on the "justness" of prices, so that in time of economic crisis or shortage, Coke supported the right to set prices nationally. The real question in the sixteenth century was which institution ought to have final judgment as to price level—guilds, corporations, courts or Council.

144. Of the important classical theorists, Adam Smith was most concerned about these laws, for they

laws,[145] convinced that if ever trade were left free individuals would selfishly try to impose restraints. He welcomed State efforts to prevent monopolies, just as he had welcomed State efforts to maintain full employment and an adequate supply of food.

It was the head of state, however, who created the most odious monopolies of all. Exclusive as well as restrictive, royal grants of privilege aroused great protest. And because that protest was directed against a form of central intervention, it found expression in peculiarly modern rhetoric. A cry went up for trade free of royal privileges. It was supposed to have been silenced by Elizabeth's concession of common law jurisdiction. But it was not silenced and in his report of *The Case of Monopolies,* Coke upheld the right of Englishmen to "freedom of trade and traffic."

In view of his support for the major enactments of Tudor paternalism, it must be clear that "free trade" meant something rather different to Coke than to economic liberals. Implying no rejection of parliamentary regulation, it meant in fact trade free from arbitrary and exclusive privileges *bestowed by the Crown.* It was a political argument; Coke's citations in this section of his report of *The Case of Monopolies*[146] all involved efforts of the Crown to by-pass Parliament. Many of those efforts had as little to do with restrictive privileges as with unregulated trade. Wagner thought them entirely irrelevant and indeed he called Coke a legal liar.[147] But Wagner mistakenly evaluated Coke's citations in terms of preconceived, modern notions of free trade.

Coke cited,[148] for example, 9 Edw. 3, c. 1 & 2 which provided that

---

were still in force when he wrote. He compared the fear of engrossing and forestalling "to the popular terrors and suspicions of witchcraft," observing that the statute of Edward VI "by prohibiting as much as possible any middle man from coming between the grower and the consumer, endeavored to annihilate a trade, of which the free exercise is not only the best palliative of the inconveniences of a dearth but the best preventative of that calamity." He attributed the enactment of the law to popular odium against the trader and the tendency in time of scarcity to impute distress to the avarice of the corn merchant; he attacked the law as preventing the proper division of labor and imposing injurious restraints on trade. See A. Smith, *The Wealth of Nations,* bk. IV, ch. 5 (1937).

145. See p. 199 *supra.*

146. The "free trade" argument constituted only one section of the indictment of monopolies.

147. This charge runs throughout Wagner's discussion of *The Case of Monopolies* in "Coke and the Rise of Economic Liberalism," 6 *Econ. Hist. Rev.* 30, 38–42 (1935).

Wagner's difficulty was in part Coke's fault because many of the cases or statutory citations bearing on the "free trade" argument were not mentioned until Coke wrote his *Institutes* at which time he was more daring in his political views than when he reported *The Case of Monopolies.* Many of the citations discussed above appeared only in the *Institutes* where their relevance specifically to "free trade" is not always clear.

On the other hand, Wagner ignored Coke's injunction to interpret statutes according to the intention of their authors. "The rehearsal or preamble of [a] statute," Coke said, "is a good means to find out the meaning of the statute, and as it were a key to open the understanding thereof." 1 *Inst.* *79. Had Wagner followed Coke's injunction, he might have found more logic to the citations than he did.

148. *The Case of Monopolies,* 11 Co. Rep. 84b, 88, 77 Eng. Rep. 1260, 1265 (K.B. 1602). Wagner was

all Merchants, Strangers and Denizens, and all other and every of them . . . that will buy or sell Corn, Wines, . . . Flesh, Fish . . . and all other things vendible, from whence soever they come by Foreigners or Denizens, *at what Place soever it be, City, Borough, Town, Port of the Sea, Fair, Market,* or elsewhere within the Realm, *Within franchise or without,* may freely without Interruption sell them to what Persons it shall please them. . . . (Emphasis added.)

This statute was confirmed, as Coke went on to note, by 25 Edw. 3, c. 2.[149] Both seemingly enacted complete freedom of commerce. But the reason Coke cited them was because they were to be observed notwithstanding any charter or letter patent of the King to the contrary. That this was his reason is suggested not only by the context of the citations, but by his following reference to article 18 of Magna Carta.

According to his own discussion of the Charter,[150] article 18 dealt with the procedure to be followed in attaching the personal estates of Crown servants who were also Crown debtors. Specifically, it provided that

If any that holdeth of us lay-fee do die, and our sheriff or bailiff do shew our letters patent of our summon for debt, which the dead man did owe to us; it shall be lawful to our sheriff or bailiff to attach and inroll all the goods and chattels of the dead, being found in the said fee . . . *to the value of the same debt.* . . . (Emphasis added.)

The King had previously attached the whole of the decedent's estate, or as much as he could, not just the equivalent amount owed.[151] Thus article 18 limited the use of the King's letters patent.

Coke also cited articles 29 and 30 of Magna Carta.[152] The former was the "due process" provision, significant because it forbade the King arbitrarily to seize a man's goods, and restricted his prerogative powers. Article 30 granted safe conduct to merchants "to buy and sell without any manner of evil tolts, by the old and rightful customs." It has been objected that the provision applied only to merchant strangers.[153] This is true and even Coke recognized the scope

wrong in saying Coke cited 9 Edw. 3, c. 21, though right in suggesting the irrelevance of that particular statute to Coke's argument.

149. *The Case of Monopolies,* 11 Co. Rep. 84b, 88a, 77 Eng. Rep. 1260, 1265 (K.B. 1602).
150. Coke annotated the 1216 edition of the Charter in the Second Part of his *Institutes.*
151. W. McKechnie, *Magna Carta* 322–23 (2d ed. 1958).
152. 2 *Inst.* *1–78.
153. See W. McKechnie, *supra* note 151, at 400.

of the article.[154] But if he was interested in trade free from arbitrary duties imposed by the King and not free trade, then the limited scope of article 30 would be irrelevant.

That Coke was interested in royal restraints is again suggested by his supporting citations. In the Third Part of his *Institutes,* he mentioned the petition of the House of Commons to Richard II against the special trading privileges granted to Yarmouth.[155] The petition urged that such privileges contravened a statute recently confirmed. The statute was 2 Rich. 2, c. 1 which in turn confirmed 9 Edw. 3, c. 1, the importance of which has just been noted. Coke also found a precedent from the reign of Philip and Mary. They had granted a charter to Southampton, making the town the sole port of entry for malmsey and allowing it to levy a treble duty. But in 1560 the grant was deemed by "all the justices of England" to be a "restriction of the liberty of the subject" and "against the laws and statutes of the realm"—namely Magna Carta, art. 30; 9 Edw. 3, c. 1; 25 Edw. 3, c. 2.[156]

The most controversial of Coke's examples was *Peache's* (or *Peeche's*) *Case,*[157] in which the Parliament of 1376 censured his patent for the exclusive right to sell sweet wines at retail in London. One critic has suggested that Peache was punished because of his connections with John of Gaunt and that he was a victim of political rivalries.[158] Another has suggested that Peache was really punished for the flagrant use he made of his privilege by charging extortionate prices.[159] Both observed that Parliament challenged the use Peache made of his privilege and not the King's right to grant the privilege. The decision in *The Case of Monopolies,* however, asserted that extortionate prices were by definition a necessary result of monopoly and Peache's case provided evidence to that effect. The political details of the fourteenth century were of no interest to common lawyers in the seventeenth. And these details aside, the case revealed once again the danger of abuse in arbitrary interventions by the Crown.

Coke's citations all referred to attempts by the Crown to act without Parliament. Had he wanted to make a generalized argument in favor of unregulated commerce, Coke might also have cited statutory regulations and monopolies

154. 2 *Inst.* *57.
155. 3 *Inst.* *181.
156. *Id.*
157. *Rotuli Parliamentorum,* 50 Edw. 3, No. 33 (1376). Coke was not the first to cite this case. It was cited during the debates over monopolies in 1601. See Mr. Laurence Hide's statement in the House of Commons, 2 *Tudor Economic Documents* 273 (R. H. Tawney & E. Power eds. 1924).
158. Letwin, *supra* note 73, at 355, 358.
159. Wagner, "Coke and the Rise of Economic Liberalism," 6 *Econ. Hist. Rev.* 30, 41 (1935).

having statutory sanction.[160] But he did not. And one can only conclude that "freedom of trade and traffic" meant little more than trade free from exclusive royal privileges; that Coke's meaning fully accorded with parliamentary usage. In the early seventeenth century, several bills for "free trade" were debated in the House of Commons.[161] Yet they too aimed only at broadening the membership of trade companies or abolishing royal patents of monopoly. Members who supported these bills never denied the efficacy of economic regulation. None saw any inconsistency when Coke introduced "A Bill for Free Trade"[162] in the same session he argued against the export of wool, or when he declared freedom to be the life of trade[163] in the same session he argued against the import of Spanish tobacco.

Both in Parliament and in court, "free trade" was far too narrow to permit a *laissez-faire* construction. It was a political slogan used by Coke in a political context in his report of *The Case of Monopolies.* Darcy had defended his privileges[164] as lawful emanations of the Crown prerogative to regulate foreign trade and generally to act *pro bono publico.* Neither Coke nor the King's Bench was prepared to deny the legitimacy of this prerogative.[165] But on the basis of common law doctrine they (rightfully) voided all royal patents of monopoly and not just Darcy's. This came perilously close to denying the Crown's right to grant patents altogether, hence Coke's elaborate attempt to justify the court's decision by demonstrating how frequently the Crown had misinterpreted the public interest[166] and how frequently royal actions had aroused protest. The "free trade" argument was used first to fill a constitutional no-man's land and later to justify Parliament's invasion of the royal prerogative.

160. Unlike industrial patents of monopoly, most municipal charters had received parliamentary endorsement, as had many of the trading corporations.

161. In May of 1606, Parliament legislated against the Spanish Company in an "Act to enable all his Majesty's loving subjects of England and Wales to trade freely into the dominions of Spain, Portugal and France." 4 Jac. 1, c. 9 (1606). In 1621, the trade of the Shrewsbury drapers was thrown open to all by an act "for the full liberty of buying and selling of Welsh clothes." In all cases, the sweeping rhetoric of free trade applied to very specific provisions.

162. This was the original title of the Statute of Monopolies.

163. 1 *Journals of the House of Commons* 589 (April 24, 1621).

164. And Coke, as his counsel, had presented his claims to the court in 1603.

165. In fact, no one challenged this prerogative. The problem was to define its scope. See M. Judson, *The Crisis of the Constitution,* especially ch. 1 (1949).

166. Technically, the Crown could still do no wrong; Coke and other critics of royal policy all attributed errors to faulty advice. This led them to claim parliamentary say over the choice of Councillors, although this was done not in the name of cabinet responsibility but of Parliament as the defender of the public interest. For Coke's belief (at least in the 1620's) that Parliament was "accomptable to a publique trust" see *id.* 256.

V

Provoked for twenty years by King James' flagrant disregard for the common law, the Parliament of 1624 finally enacted the declaratory Statute of Monopolies.[167] It was drafted principally by Coke who had also chaired the Committee on Grievances which exposed the need for legislative reform.[168] Except for a few political concessions, the statute did very nearly embody Coke's views at the most radical stage of his career. Yet it contradicts even the most considered aspects of the *laissez-faire* thesis. It reveals Coke's complete unfamiliarity with modern notions of competition and his willingness to sacrifice industrial progress to the needs of full employment, the selectivity of his opposition to monopolies and once again, the political cast of that opposition.

In the statute, Coke defined monopoly as "an institution or allowance by the King" and explicitly reserved to Parliament the right to grant exclusive privileges.[169] In addition, by drastically limiting the scope of his attack on monopolies, Coke by-passed a splendid opportunity to create more competitive conditions of trade. Section 1 of the statute seemed to void all institutions exercising exclusive control of any product or form of commerce,

> all monopolies and all commissions, grants, licenses, charters and letters patent heretofore made or granted or heretofore to be made or granted to any person or persons, bodies politic or corporate whatsoever, of or for the sole buying, selling, making, or using of anything within this realm.

The comprehensiveness of this provision, however, was limited by qualifying clauses. The Statute did not include printing, the production of saltpeter, gunpowder and other products deemed essential to the realm. Rights to the exclusive production of new processes or machines were likewise excepted, for the Statute recognized the legitimacy of a copyright patent.[170] Section 9 protected the "liberties" and customs of corporations so that it remained perfectly legal for a city like London to prevent "foreigners" from keeping any shop or

---

167. 21 Jac. 1, c. 3 (1624).

168. Coke's role in the monopoly controversy is best explained by Elizabeth Read Foster in "The Procedure of the House of Commons Against Patents and Monopolies, 1621–24," in *Conflict in Stuart England* 57–87 (W. Aiden & B. Henning eds. 1960) [reprinted here on p. 302].

169. Parliament did in fact make use of this right, as when in 1624 it incorporated the Sheffield cutlers. G. Clark, *The Wealth of England, 1496–1760,* at 122 (1947). Another example, and one which particularly demonstrates the political aspect of the monopoly controversy, is the granting by Parliament of Darcy's monopoly of playing cards to the Company of Card Players. See Letwin, *supra* note 73, at 367.

170. See pp. 220–23 *infra.*

using any trade within its limits.[171] Section 9 also excepted companies which enjoyed the exclusive privilege of trading with specific countries or in specific commodities. Since most foreign trade was controlled by corporations, this provision excluded a particularly large class of monopolies.

The same class of monopolies dealt with in section 9 had likewise been excluded from an act[172] framed by Commons in 1601, and Coke had to consider Parliament's wish to preserve what remained of the medieval corporate structure and even certain forms of trade privilege. "Landed" lords of the upper house thought statutory proscription of all corporations would constitute too great an infringement of the King's prerogative.[173] "Patriotic" commoners were often shareholders in trade companies and anxious to retain their privileges. Self-interest apart, they foresaw only chaos if all commerce were free. In 1586–1587, the privileges of the Merchant Adventurers had been revoked in an attempt to grant "libertye" to English and foreign strangers to sell cloth.[174] The experiment failed as did the attempt in 1604 to "free" the Levant trade from monopoly control.[175]

All these considerations plus the gravity of the trade crisis[176] in 1623 must have weighed on Coke as he formulated the Statute of Monopolies. But personally, he too seems to have believed the company system essential to the maintenance of an ordered trade. He and other stalwart critics of monopolies knew that in addition to exploiting exclusive rights to specific routes or products, companies created the very conditions essential to trade. The Crown at that time was unable to maintain fortresses or consuls or to protect merchants against confiscation. Companies had come to provide these services and without them most merchants would hardly venture forth.

For this reason and others,[177] Coke had approved Elizabeth's confirmation

---

171. Coke had upheld that principle in *The City of London's Case,* 8 Co. Rep. 12b, 77 Eng. Rep. 658 (K.B. 1609).

172. A. Friis, *Alderman Cockayne's Project* 149 (1917).

173. See Coke's report of a conference with the Lords in 1 *Journal of the House of Commons* 770 (April 19, 1624).

174. Gould, "The Crisis in the Export Trade, 1586–1587," 71 *Eng. Hist. Rev.* 212–22 (1956).

175. Durham, "The Relations of the Crown to Trade Under James I," 13 *Transactions of the Royal Historical Society* (n.s.) 205–6 (1899).

176. Because the debate on monopolies coincided with a trade crisis, the consequences of a sudden revocation of company privileges seemed particularly threatening. Both Coke and Sir Dudley Digges agreed that this course would only hinder trade. 1 *Journal of the House of Commons* 612 (May 7, 1621).

177. One consideration, often overlooked, arose in *Michelborne v. Michelborne,* 2 Brownl. & Golds. 296, 123 Eng. Rep. 952 (C.P. 1609), in which Coke held that merchants trading with infidel nations had to have a license from the King because of the danger of being converted from the Christian religion. Infidel nations were by definition "unfriendly" and it was therefore essential to provide some institutional guarantees of

of the charter of the Russia Company.[178] He had settled the charter of the Virginia Company[179] and approved that of the East India Company[180] as well as approving the Exeter Merchants' right to trade with France exclusive of all other merchants of Exeter.[181] It might perhaps be argued that Coke was then in the service of the Crown and therefore obliged to endorse the policy of corporate monopolies. Yet except for his later objection to the East India Company's export of bullion, Coke never retracted his support of these companies. He endorsed, unequivocally, corporations "erected for the Maintenance, Enlargement, or ordering of any Trade of Merchandize. . . ."[182]

Whether joint stock or regulated, virtually all those corporations were monopolies.[183] Their charters bestowed the exclusive right to trade with given countries or in given commodities or both. The Levant Company,[184] for example, had the sole right of trade with Turkey and Venice and the sole right to import currants and wines from Candia; the French, Spanish and East India Companies were all assigned territorial spheres. No competition existed among companies. And more important, no merchant not a member could trade without the permission of the company concerned.[185] If he did, he was liable to prosecution as an "interloper."

Though surprising in light of the *laissez-faire* thesis, Coke accepted this state of affairs and confined his criticism of trade companies to specific abuses. He inveighed against the charter and practices of the Merchant Adventurers[186]

---

the safety of traders. In addition, Coke and his contemporaries took into consideration whether or not a company was opening up a new trade route. If so, they did not question the need for corporate control.

178. His approval is cited in *The Great Case of Monopolies* (*East India Co. v. Sandys*), 10 Howell's State Trials 371, 547–48 (1684). That was the case in which the validity of the East India Company's charter was unsuccessfully challenged.

179. F. Maitland, *English Law and the Renaissance* 31 (1901).

180. *The Great Case of Monopolies,* 10 Howell's State Trials 371, 551 (1684).

181. *Id.* at 547.

182. Statute of Monopolies § 9, 21 Jac. 1, c. 3 (1623).

183. By far the greatest protest in Coke's day was directed against the joint stock companies. Even Adam Smith later attacked them, relying on the petitions of merchants who wanted to secure entrance into trade without the cost of purchasing shares. The cost of these shares and also the limited number of subscriptions were actually the real problem. For as W. R. Scott has shown, the shares were technically open to all. 1 W. Scott, *Joint Stock Companies to 1720,* 122, 442–53 (1912). With regard to the regulated companies, most criticism came from "outport" merchants, too far from the London-based companies to participate actively in their trade.

184. 2 E. Lipson, *The Economic History of England* 338 (1947). That was the charter of 1592.

185. *Id.* 222–25. Lipson aptly observes that "interlopers" were called "free traders." *Id.* 228.

186. Coke withdrew his support of the New Merchant Adventurers incorporated under Cockayne because the charter, drawn up for them by Bacon, bestowed the right to force and commit non-members without bail or appeal, and also because membership in the corporation was highly restricted. A. Friis, *supra* note 172, at 245. For his criticism of the Old Company see *id.,* app. D.

and he disapproved of most early experiments in joint stock finance.[187] But at no time did Coke express a desire for more competitive conditions of trade or attack the company system as such.[188] His great concern was for employment, not competition, and the companies Coke termed monopolies were simply those whose membership was too restrictive. At a meeting of the Privy Council in 1613, he denounced the Merchant Adventurers saying "a thing granted to a hundred is a monopoly if the rest is prohibited."[189] Eight years later, Coke again noted that their membership was grossly disproportionate to the size of the market[190] and his attack on the Spanish Company followed a similar line of reasoning.[191] Exclusiveness led to unemployment and disorder and generally hindered trade whereas the true function[192] of companies was good "order and government."

Again and again, Coke distinguished between trade regulation and trade restriction, and he did so not only with regard to companies but also corporate towns and boroughs and even guilds.[193] He objected when the Newbury Weavers made an ordinance that no person might use the art of weaving within the town unless he had been apprenticed with the town.[194] He objected when the Ipswich Taylors tried to prevent a qualified craftsman from practicing his trade until he had presented himself before them. These restraints, Coke said,

187. Though he demurred on particulars, Coke generally approved the Commons' attempt in 1604 to abolish joint stock companies. The attempt was made in April when the House voted on a bill "for all merchants to have free liberty of trade into all countries," a bill which was directed only against the joint stock companies. After 1604, the bills were even more particular in stipulating those companies which were to be reformed or abolished. Durham, *supra* note 175, at 204–8.

188. The most sweeping statement Coke made was when he noted that "New Corporations trading into foreign parts, and at home, which under the fair pretence of order and government, in conclusion tend to the hinderance of trade and traffique, and in the end produce monopolies." 2 *Inst.* *540. Yet implicit in that statement was a distinction between companies which were monopolies and those which were not—a distinction based on admission policy and unconcerned with the absence of competition among companies whose membership seemed sufficient.

189. B. M. Caesar Papers, Add. MS. 14027 *quoted* in A. Friis, *supra* note 172, app. D. at 459.

190. 1 W. Scott, *supra* note 183, at 221. This reference was to the company re-chartered after the failure of the Cockayne project.

191. After peace had been restored with Spain and trade had revived, the membership of the Company became relatively exclusive and it was precisely at that point, in 1606, that Parliament freed the trade of the Company by throwing it open to all merchants. Coke supported the legislation against the Company, as may be seen in 2 *Journal of House of Lords* 405 (April 1, 1607), 412 (April 12, 1607).

192. Section 9 of the Statute of Monopolies, 21 Jac. 1, c. 3 (1624), acknowledged the validity of those corporations "erected for the Maintenance, Enlargement, or Ordering of any Trade of Merchandize. . . ." See also note 114 *supra*.

193. See T. Travers, "Sir Edward Coke and Corporations" (unpublished paper, Yale University).

194. Norris v. Staps, Hobart 210, 80 Eng. Rep. 357 (K.B. 1616). The provision of the ordinance was far more restrictive than the Statute of Artificers and by creating unemployment in fact vitiated one of the purposes of that Statute. See text accompanying notes 216–17 *infra*, to the effect that by giving priority to national policy, Coke was enhancing central power and not contributing to the growth of *laissez-faire*.

were "against the liberty and freedom of the subject, . . . a means of extortion in drawing money from them, either by delay, or some other subtle device, or of oppression of young tradesmen, by the old and rich of the same trade. . . ."[195] At the same time, Coke firmly supported the right of guilds to make "ordinances for the good order and government of men of trades and mysteries. . . ."[196] Such ordinances might include stipulations of quality or fair wages or marketing time. In the case of municipal corporations, lawful ordinances or customs[197] might include one compelling any citizen, freeman, or stranger within London to bring any broadcloth they wished to sell before the inspectors of Blackwell Hall in order that they might inspect the quality of the cloth.[198] As he said in Commons,[199] "If a Corporation, for the better government of the Town, not contrary to the Law; but, if any sole Restraint, then gone [sic]."

The danger of "any sole Restraint" was arbitrary power and unemployment, considerations which underlay Coke's antagonism to royal patents of monopoly as well as to trade corporations. None of his contemporaries disputed the legitimacy of a copyright patent so there was nothing particularly modern about Coke's statutory provision. True, he would have preferred limiting the term to seven rather than fourteen years.[200] But he would not have altered the conditions of the grant, and the conditions differed greatly from those today. With few exceptions, improvements in a method of production could not be patented, for it was felt that the subject of a grant ought truly to be a "new manufacture." In the Third Part of his *Institutes,* Coke explained that "if the substance was *in esse* before, and a new addition thereunto, though that addition make the former more profitable, yet it is not a new manufacture in law."[201] If patents for improvements were sanctioned, then existing industries would be prejudicially affected, craftsmen would be displaced and

195. *The Tailors of Ipswich Case,* 11 Co. Rep. 53, 54, 77 Eng. Rep. 1218, 1220 (K.B. 1614).
196. *Id.*
197. Sometimes Coke sanctioned customs whose lawfulness he would not have recognized had their substance been made by grant. *The Chamberlain of London's Case,* 5 Co. Rep. 62b, 77 Eng. Rep. 150 (K.B. 1590).
198. *Id.* at 63, 77 Eng. Rep. at 151.
199. 1 *Journals of the House of Commons* 770 (1628).
200. Hulme, "The History of the Patent System Under the Prerogative and at Common Law," 12 *L.Q. Rev.* 141, 153 (1896). According to Hulme, the effect of the Statute of Monopolies was to confirm the practice of the Crown between 1561–1603 and the only innovation was the imposition of a statutory limitation on the term of a grant. But the Statute also disallowed the bestowal of privileges on those who imported rather than invented new processes.
201. 2 *Inst.* *184. See also 1 W. Hawkins, *A Treatise on the Pleas of the Crown* 628–29 (8th ed., 1824).

unemployment would result.[202] One with a "capitalist mentality" might find it difficult to understand this discouragement of initiative, but Coke's mentality was anything but capitalist.

Indeed, his outlook was fully rooted in Tudor precept, trained to balance deftly the needs of social harmony against innovation and to value innovation or improvement in terms of its contribution to the State. A desire for industrial self-sufficiency, not an individualistic ethic, had justified copyright patents in the first place and this remained Coke's criterion. When a contemporary proposed to introduce the manufacture of salt into England,[203] and when Zouch undertook to preserve England's forests by making glass from coal instead of wood,[204] Coke was more than willing to grant them exclusive rights of production. He was so enthusiastic as sometimes to be deceived by the claims of prospective patentees. Just as he had been deceived by Cockayne, so he was deceived by Zouch, and did not foresee that the higher cost of smelting glass with coal would raise prices, or that craftsmen skilled in the old methods of glass production would be kept from working.[205] These consequences—when apparent—were abhorrent to Coke, and in 1621 and in 1623 he condemned the patent which had since been transferred to Sir Robert Mansell, a court favorite. To save the bill,[206] he recommended the exception of the patent from the Statute of Monopolies. But the precise terms of its exception invited prosecution by the common law, and Coke explicitly urged[207] that the patent not be renewed at the end of its term.

Significantly, Coke withdrew his support when he realized the patent was not in fact being used to promote new methods of production. Legitimate copyright patents were one thing, arbitrary privileges, another. What Coke and his contemporaries found objectionable was the bestowal of monopolies on

---

202. Part of Coke's concern was for the poor generally. He insisted that "common right be done to all, as well poor as rich." 4 *Inst.* *183. And he decried those who "ground the face of the poor" by penal laws. 4 *Inst.* *41. As judge, he went out of his way to support hospitals and other charitable organizations. See, e.g., *The Case of Sutton's Hospital,* 10 Co. Rep. 23, 77 Eng. Rep. 960 (K.B. 1612). For Coke's support of the Poor Law, see 2 *Inst.* *729.

203. *Acts of the Privy Council, 1615–1616,* at 6, 7.

204. 1 *Journal of the House of Commons* 987. T. Mendenhall, *The Shrewsbury Drapers and the Welsh Wool Trade in the XVI and XVII Centuries* 168 n. 1 (1953), argues that Coke was inconsistent in his support of the glass patent of 1713.

205. Price, "English Patents of Monopoly," 1 *Harv. Econ. Studies* 70 (1913). Zouch and his partners did succeed in using the method, and technically Coke and the Committee on Grievances erred in condemning the patent as a "grievance in creation." 2 *Proceedings in the House of Commons, 1620–1621,* at 73 (May 14).

206. Price, *supra* note 205, at 76. For Coke's condemnation of the patent, see Foster, *supra* note 168, at 73.

207. 1 *Journal of the House of Commons* 696 (May 1, 1624).

court favorites, sycophants and others who knew nothing of the trade which they controlled and who injured craftsmen who did. They sought to remedy the ills which had developed in the administration of the patent system, but not to destroy the system itself.

Coke and his colleagues had been young men at the time Elizabeth initiated[208] the policy of granting exclusive rights of production to foreign craftsmen in order to encourage their immigration to England. They knew that England lagged behind her continental rivals in industrial skill, so much so that in 1562 the patent system was extended to "industrious" denizens who either imported or invented new processes. Thus far, Coke went along with both Tudor policy and practice. But in the 1580's, abuses crept into the system.[209] Licenses to sell as well as to manufacture commodities frequently accompanied patents. *Non obstante* clauses enabled monopolists to disregard statutory prohibitions on the import of certain items and become exclusive traders in those items.[210] More important, Elizabeth now conferred privileges to practice well-established trades. Craftsmen who had hitherto enjoyed the right to work found themselves unemployed or forced to pay a considerable sum to the patentee. Prices rose and often the quality of goods deteriorated.

As usual, matters became worse under James. Not only did he perpetuate his predecessor's abuses, he did so after the courts declared monopolies invalid,[211] and after he himself endorsed the court's decision.[212] He was prodigal in his bestowal of privileges, most of which went to court favorites. Making them the beneficiaries of lucrative privileges in no way enhanced their popularity. Resistance and evasion became so rife that James granted his patentees additional wide discretionary power to search and seize rival produce.[213] For all these reasons, Parliament determined to free trade of the restrictions imposed by monopolists. In 1597 and 1601, it protested the abuses of Elizabeth's patentees.[214] In 1604, it assumed the abuses to be a necessary corollary of the

208. There were earlier instances of Crown encouragement of new industries, but they were unsystematic and the privileges conferred were in the nature of safety and safe-passage to aliens.

209. Price, *supra* note 205, at 8–9.

210. For a good discussion of the royal dispensing power, see Birdsall, "*Non Obstante*—A Study of the Dispensing Power of English Kings," in *Essays in History and Political Theory in Honor of Charles Howard McIlwain* (1936).

211. The decision in *The Case of Monopolies* was handed down in 1602.

212. In 1610, James published his *Book of Bounty,* declaring monopolies to be void and contrary to public policy.

213. H. Fox, *Monopolies and Patents* 186–88 (1949).

214. For a fine discussion of the early parliamentary protest against monopolies, see J. Neale, *Elizabeth I and Her Parliaments, 1584–1601* at 352–62 (1966).

grant,[215] and for the next twenty years attempted to restrict the prerogative power of the King.

The chronological progression of the parliamentary protest, the limited scope of the Statute of Monopolies, the specific nature of the grievance against industrial patents, all suggest that had Elizabeth and James held to the original purpose of bestowing trade privileges, there would have been no complaints. Coke aimed neither at creating a "freer" economy nor at destroying its traditional corporate structure. He wanted, basically, to protect the rights of Englishmen[216] and to prevent individuals or institutions from pursuing policies inconsistent with the newly imposed national standards.[217]

With the Tudors there had begun a concerted movement toward uniformity. Coke admired that movement and supported the whole new structure of economic legislation. Loyalty to paternalist policy and also to the common law in fact prompted his opposition to certain monopolies. Historians may point to Coke's radical methods of protest and suggest the later importance of his seemingly modern rhetoric. But when they try to ascribe to Coke an anticipation of *laissez-faire,* they misinterpret profoundly the nature of his thought. For Coke was interested in full employment and not efficiency; just prices and not competition. Far from searching for new economic concepts, he drew upon the Commonwealth ideal, arguing consistently that "trade and traffique cannot be maintained or increased without order and government. . . ."[218]

215. This was implicit in the decision of *The Case of Monopolies.* See section III *supra.*

216. That is, the right to work, the right to property, and the right not to be subjected to abuses by privileged corporations.

217. Virtually all of the guild ordinances which Coke censured were more restrictive than the provisions of the Statute of Artificers; corporate exclusiveness hampered the general policy of full employment; the practice of forestalling raised prices and helped to create scarcity, thus destroying the balanced polity the Tudors tried to establish. As suggested throughout this article, Coke looked to corporate bodies to administer national policies but not to take the initiative, especially if it proved injurious.

218. *The Case of the City of London,* 8 Co. Rep. 121b, 125, 77 Eng. Rep. 658, 663 (K.B. 1609).

Sir Edward Coke, Ciceronianus: Classical Rhetoric and the Common Law Tradition

ALLEN D. BOYER

❧ ❧ ❧

And verily I suppose, if there might once happen some man, having an excellent
wit . . . exactly or deeply learned in the art of an orator, and also in the laws
of this realm . . . undoubtedly it should not be impossible for him to bring the
pleading and reasoning of the law, to the ancient form of noble orators.

SIR THOMAS ELYOT

John Selden, reflecting on the common law, called it "the English Janus."[1] The image of Janus is an apt one to consider when thinking of Sir Edward Coke, no less than when considering the law for which he served as apologist and prophet. The face we know best is that of the Elizabethan judge, with pointed beard and velvet cap and chain of office, who stares piercingly at us from the deepest alcove of the law library. Looking back at Coke, we see the first titan in the history of the modern common law, the earliest judge and jurisprudent whose works are still regularly cited by practicing lawyers.

But Coke has another aspect, one which it is harder to recover. From his Elizabethan vantage point he looks back into different centuries and a different mode of thought, into the heritage of classical rhetoric. The common-law tradition within which he worked derived much of its strength from the broader, older disciplines of argumentation and discourse. For the Elizabethans, rhetoric—called Ciceronian rhetoric, in honor of its most notable

"Sir Edward Coke, Ciceronianus: Classical Rhetoric and the Common Law Tradition" is reprinted from *International Journal for the Semiotics of Law* 10, no. 28 (1997): 3–36. © 1997 *International Journal for the Semiotics of Law,* reprinted with kind permission from Kluwer Academic Publishers.

1. John Selden, *Jani Anglorum Facies Altera* (1610).

practitioner—comprehended not only the craft of oratory, but also reasoning and the crafting of judgments.

As a methodology, Ciceronian rhetoric overlapped with logic. Because it was concerned with creating opinion and inspiring action, it was bound up with the determination and implementation of policy. It identified the refinement of speech with public-spiritedness, insisting that language was inextricably connected to the larger world. In short, rhetoric was what Sir Francis Bacon called it, the discipline that applied "reason to imagination for the better moving of the will."[2] To study Coke's work, in all its aspects, is to recognize the work of a lawyer steeped in such Ciceronian rhetoric.

Overview of Coke's Jurisprudence

Among jurisprudents of the common law, Coke remains an archetype of intransigence and reaction. He is generally remembered for obstinate defenses—for asserting the rights of the subject and the independence of the judiciary, but in a profoundly defensive posture. His epistemology has been considered medieval, in all this word's meanings.[3] He was a ferocious prosecutor, given to angry bombast and witness-badgering.[4] He helped to draft the witchcraft statute of 1604.[5] His interest in legal history, which was genuine, was marred by reckless assertions that the common law had not changed since the days of the Druids.[6] Coke's masterpiece, the *Commentary upon Littleton,* purports to

2. Sir Francis Bacon, *Works,* ed. James Spedding (1857), III, 409. Spelling and usage have generally been modernized throughout this article except in quotations from poetry.

3. E.g., the comment of Maitland, reported by Holdsworth: "Coke's books are the great dividing line, and we are hardly out of the Middle Ages till he has dogmatized its results." Sir William Holdsworth, *History of English Law* (Boston: Little, Brown & Co., 1945), V, 489.

4. Most notably, Sir Walter Ralegh, in 1603. See William Cobbett, *Cobbett's Complete Collection of State Trials* (1809), II, 1–32. Thirteen years later, following the murder of Sir Thomas Overbury, Coke both investigated and sat in judgment on Robert Kerr and Frances Howard, Earl and Countess of Somerset. So confident was Coke of his findings that he sent several defendants to the gallows while others were still awaiting trial. See David Lindley, *The Trials of Frances Howard: Fact and Fiction at the Court of King James* (London: Routledge, 1993), 145–92.

5. See Wallace Notestein, *A History of Witchcraft in England from 1558 to 1718* (1911; repr. New York: Gordon Press, 1974), 102–03.

6. E.g., Coke's Prefaces to the Third Part (1603) and Sixth Part (1607) of his *Reports.* The classic critique of Coke as an insular thinker remains J. G. A. Pocock, *The Ancient Constitution and the Feudal Law: A Study of English Historical Thought in the Seventeenth Century* (Cambridge: Cambridge University Press, 1987, 2d ed.), 30–58. This perspective has been refined and critiqued by Harold J. Berman, "The Origins of Historical Jurisprudence: Coke, Selden, Hale," *Yale Law Journal* 103 (1994), 1651–1738 and Glenn Burgess, *The Politics of the Ancient Constitution: An Introduction to English Political Thought, 1603–1642* (State College, Pennsylvania: Pennsylvania State University Press, 1992).

cover the law of estates, while rambling in fact across the entire common law.[7]
Overall, the general conception of Coke's character may be crystallized in a
remark of George Orwell:

> The hanging judge, that evil old man in scarlet robe and horsehair wig, whom
> nothing short of dynamite will ever teach what century he is living in, but who
> will at any rate interpret the law according to the books and will in no circum-
> stances take a money bribe, is one of the symbolic figures of English law.[8]

But (to extend and shift the Janus metaphor) there was another side to
Coke's jurisprudence: the immovable jurist was also an irresistible innovator. If
Coke warned against reform by statute, he wholeheartedly participated in judicial legislation. As counsel in *Slade's Case* (1597–1602), he helped broaden the
availability of assumpsit, opening the door to modern contract law.[9] His role
in *Calvin's Case* (1609) helped effectuate the union of England and Scotland
under one monarch.[10] He fought against the temporal power of the Church of
England, reining in the powers of church courts and the High Commission.[11]

Perhaps most important, Coke actively moved to shape the evolving common law, often giving a surreptitious kick in the direction he felt it should
go. On the border of jurisprudence and power politics, Coke's definition of
law as "artificial reason," the collective professional opinion of experienced
judges, asserted the authority of the judiciary.[12] Testing legal issues by the
judges' reason gave the judiciary a marvellously effective weapon for striking
down anything found "unreasonable": actions by government officials, manorial customs which weighed hard on copyhold tenants, restrictive municipal ordinances.[13] The assumptions inchoate in this process were articulated

---

7. See *infra,* at text accompanying nn. 80–85.

8. George Orwell, *A Collection of Essays* (San Diego, California: Harcourt Brace Jovanovich, 1946), 252.

9. *Slade's Case,* 4 Co. Rep. 92b, 75 E.R. 1074 (1597–1602).

10. *Calvin's Case,* 7 Co. Rep. 1, 77 E.R. 377 (1609) (Scots born after the accession of James VI to the English throne enjoyed rights of English subjects, while Scots born prior to James' accession remained aliens
under English law).

11. See *passim* Roland G. Usher, *The Rise and Fall of the High Commission* (Oxford: Oxford University
Press, 1913).

12. Able discussions of the concept have been provided by John U. Lewis, "Sir Edward Coke: His Theory
of 'Artificial Reason' as a Context for Modern Basic Legal Theory," *Law Quarterly Review* 84 (1968), 330–42
[reprinted here on p. 107]; Charles M. Gray, "Reason, Authority, and Imagination: The Jurisprudence of Sir
Edward Coke," in *Culture and Politics from Puritanism to the Enlightenment,* ed. P. Zagorin (Berkeley, California: University of California Press, 1980), 25–66. See also Allen D. Boyer, "'Understanding, Authority,
and Will': Sir Edward Coke and the Elizabethan Origins of Judicial Review," *Boston College Law Review* 39
(1997), 43–93.

13. E.g., the actions of lower government bodies. *Rook* v. *Withers,* 5 Co. Rep. 99b, 100a, 77 Eng. Rep.
209, 210 (1598) (Commissioners of Sewers' discretion bounded by "the rule of reason and law").

in 1610, when Coke wrote in *Bonham's Case* that "in many cases, the common law will control acts of parliament, and sometimes adjudge them to be utterly void."[14] This led inexorably to judicial review, and the judicial activism which such doctrines can foster is something which Coke himself seems to have foreseen.[15]

Following this vision of law, Coke resisted attempts by James I to take a personal hand in judging cases. In *Fuller's Case* (1607), Coke told the king that James, whatever his native intelligence and scholarly learning, nonetheless lacked the training to decide common-law issues. "True it was," Coke stated,

> [T]hat God had endowed His Majesty with excellent science, and great endowments of nature; but His Majesty was not learned in the laws of his realm of England, and causes which concern the life, or inheritance, or goods, or fortunes of his subjects, are not to be decided by natural reason, but by the artificial reason and judgment of law, which law is an act which requires long study and experience, before that a man can attain to the cognizance of it.[16]

Coke did not confuse his beliefs in the independence of the judiciary and the excellence of the common law with the belief that law can be separated from politics—that is, from policy choices. Rooted in the Ciceronian tradition are the methodology with which Coke worked, the faith in which he fought against royal interference, and the confidence with which he shaped the emerging law.

Coke's Place in the Rhetorical Tradition

Like all other Elizabethan lawyers—like all other shapers and educated consumers of Elizabethan culture—Coke was thoroughly steeped in classical learning. The books he valued show his involvement with classical rhetoric. When he catalogued his library, he listed the volumes dealing with the dis-

14. *Bonham's Case*, 8 Co. Rep. 113b, 118a, 77 Eng. Rep. 646, 652 (1610).

15. That Coke understood what his language might unleash is suggested by the fact that he wrote out this passage at least twice in his own hand. J. H. Baker, *Introduction to English Legal History* (London: Butterworths, 3d ed. 1990), 241. See further T. F. T. Plucknett, "*Bonham's Case* and Judicial Review," *Harvard Law Review* 40 (1926), 30–70 [reprinted here on p. 150]; Samuel Thorne, "Dr. Bonham's Case," *Law Quarterly Review* 54 (1938), 543–52; Charles M. Gray, "Bonham's Case Revisited," *Proceedings of the American Philosophical Society* 116 (1972), 35–58; James R. Stoner, *Common Law and Liberal Theory: The Origins of American Constitutionalism* (Lawrence, Kansas: University Press of Kansas, 1992), 13–68.

16. *Prohibitions del Roy*, 12 Co. Rep. 63, 65, 77 Eng. Rep. 1342, 1343 (1607). See further Roland G. Usher, "James I and Sir Edward Coke," *English Historical Review* 18 (1903), 664–75, 664.

course arts in the section immediately following his law books. "And seeing philosophy, rhetoric, grammar, logic and schoolbooks are handmaids to the knowledge of laws, they shall follow in the next place," he remarked.[17] His library was stocked with texts drawn from the rhetorical canon. Marcus Tullius Cicero was represented by a 15-volume octavo set of "Tullies Works," backed up with separate copies of "Tullies offices" and "Tullies Epistles." The twelve volumes of Quintilian's *Institutiones Oratoria* were bound in green and gilt. The collection was anchored in Aristotle (the *Topics, Rhetoric, Politics,* and *Ethics*) and reached to Erasmus (*De Copia, De Ratione Studii, Colloquia,* and *De Conscribendi Epistolae*). Mixed in were English logicians, whose works' presence suggest a conservative outlook: John Seton and John Argall.[18]

Coke's writings are liberally dotted with quotations from Latin writers: Juvenal, Cato, Sallust, Pliny, Horace, Seneca, Tacitus, Virgil, and Cicero.[19] He kept a commonplace book, the orator's essential reference, although it was packed with case reports rather than garlands of speech.[20] In construing Magna Carta, he found the occasion to trace a phrase to Cicero.[21] His speeches mark him as a thorough exponent of the Ciceronian school. "When Mr. Cuffe, secretary to the Earl of Essex, was arraigned, [Coke] would dispute with him in syllogisms," John Aubrey wrote.[22] At the trial of the Earl of Essex, the defendant contemptuously sought to break in on Coke's speech for the Crown: "Will your lordships give us our turn to speak, for he playeth the orator."[23] To clinch a point, Coke often relied on a volley of Latin tag-lines. This was a recognized rhetorical technique, the liberal application of *sententiae* to *exempla,* transposed by Coke from the rostrum to the printed page.[24]

At the arraignment of the Gunpowder Plotters, Coke offered a grim im-

---

17. W. O. Hassall, *A Catalogue of the Library of Sir Edward Coke* (New Haven, Connecticut: Yale Law Library, 1950), 59.

18. *Id.* at 59–63.

19. See John Marshall Gest, "The Writings of Sir Edward Coke," *Yale Law Journal* 18 (1909), 504–32, at 516–18.

20. See *infra,* at text accompanying n. 85.

21. "[W]here some have thought that *baro* is no Latin word," Coke wrote, "we find it in Tullies Epistles, *apud patronem, et alios barones te in maxima gratia posui.*" Sir Edward Coke, *The Second Part of the Institutes of the Laws of England* (1645), 5.

22. John Aubrey, *Aubrey's Brief Lives* (Harmondsworth, England: Penguin Classics, 1987), 163.

23. 1 *State Trials, supra* note 4, at 1339.

24. Thomas Hobbes, the protégé of Coke's arch-rival Francis Bacon, attacked him scathingly on this point. Hobbes wrote that Coke "endeavours by inserting Latin sentences, both in his text and in the margin, as if they were principles of the law of reason, without any authority of ancient lawyers, or any certainty of reason in themselves, to make men believe that they are the very grounds of the law of England." Thomas Hobbes, *A Dialogue Between a Philosopher and a Student of the Common Laws of England,* ed. J. Cropsey (University of Chicago Press, 1972), 96.

promptu apology for that most terribly English of punishments—hanging, drawing, and quartering.

> For first after a traitor hath had his just trial and is convicted and attainted, he shall have his judgment to be drawn to the place of execution from his prison as being not worthy any more to tread upon the face of the earth whereof he was made; also for that he has been retrograde to nature, therefore is he drawn backward at a horse-tail. For which cause also he shall be strangled, being hanged up by the neck between heaven and earth, as deemed unworthy of both, or either, as likewise, that the eyes of men may behold, and their hearts contemn him. Then he is to be cut down alive, and to have his privy parts cut off and burnt before his face as being unworthily begotten . . .[25]

So bloodthirsty a passage is obviously the work of a dedicated trial lawyer—and this grim drum-roll of cruelties bespeaks the terrible majesty which was the boast of English law—but, in fact, this bloody effusion reworks a classical theme. Coke draws on Cicero's explanation of the punishment reserved, by Roman courts, for parricides: being sewn into a sack and then thrown into a river. The founders of Rome, Cicero argued, had

> cut the culprit off and shut him out of the entire sphere of nature. By depriving him, at one single blow, of sky and sun and water and earth, they created a situation in which the murderer of the very person to whom he owed his life should in turn be deprived of all the elements which have given life to the world. [M]en condemned for this crime live, as long as they are allowed to go on living, without being able to breathe the air from the sky. They die without the earth coming into contact with their bones. They are tossed about by the sea without its cleansing waters ever reaching them. And, at the end, when they are cast up on the shore, even the rocks do not support their dead bodies to give them rest.[26]

As this shows, Coke's knowledge of the classics went beyond familiarity or quotation. The judge who fathered the modern common law knew Cicero well enough to steal from Cicero.

25. *Trial of Guy Fawkes and Others (The Gunpowder Plot)*, ed. Donald Carswell (1934; repr. Gryphon Books Notable Trials Library, 1991), 89–90.

26. Cicero, *Murder Trials* 65–66 (Harmondsworth, England: Penguin, 1975). David Seipp has suggested another possible source: that Coke may have drawn upon the papers relating to the English government's execution of Sir William Wallace, in which similar language occurs.

The Ciceronian Inheritance

"Rhetoric is the greatest barrier between us and our ancestors," C. S. Lewis wrote in his magisterial survey of English Renaissance prose and poetry.[27] Lewis spoke of the way in which the discipline of rhetoric dominated Renaissance thought, providing the vocabulary of cultural expression. Nowadays, the word "rhetoric" often carries a pejorative connotation. It commonly refers to verbal posturing through the use of phrases which are glib and disingenuous. In Coke's day, rhetoric was better regarded, accorded the same respect it had received from Cicero and Aristotle.

Rhetoric and Culture: The Orator's Role

Rhetoricians associated their art with the social and philosophical dimensions of the process of communication.[28] Oratory had created society, Cicero argued: cities would never have been built had not orators shown scattered peoples the value of social organizations.[29] This does not speak only to issues of social organization. Its cultural implications may be better seen by recognizing the identical claims asserted by modern-day semioticians. The mirror image of the rhetorician's belief that language creates culture by focusing the popular will is the semiotician's belief that society contains signs and patterns which can be read like a literary text. Both approach the significance of a thing (what it is, what it means) as a function of how that thing is signified (how language defines it). Umberto Eco, for example, has noted the existence of "strong homologies between linguistic devices and devices of power . . . [and] that the knowledge on which power is nourished is produced through linguistic means." Despite the adaptations necessary for a discussion of Barthes and Foucault, the immediate subjects of Eco's essay, this is the same claim Cicero made for the importance of oratory in organizing society.[30] To say that language ultimately nourishes power is to say that oratory leads to action.

27. C. S. Lewis, *English Literature in the Sixteenth Century Excluding Drama* (Oxford: Clarendon Press, 1954), 61.
28. As R. W. Southern has noted, the medieval grammarian "was interested in the meanings and derivations of words, in the relation between language and reality, and in the rules of eloquence." *The Making of the Middle Ages* (1953; New Haven: Yale University Press, 1975), 198.
29. Cicero, *De Inventione* i.ii.2.
30. Umberto Eco, *Travels in Hyperreality,* trans. W. Weaver (Orlando, Florida: Harcourt Brace Jovanovich, 1986), 254.

The full import of this is that rhetoric provides the medium of larger cultural patterns. The concepts which language allows to be expressed define the beliefs which can be held and the enterprises which can be undertaken.

The belief that rhetoric organized society—that is, enlightened and empowered—had its counterpart in the belief in the nobility of the orator. The classical orator was by definition a fluent speaker, but the tradition insisted that mere fluency was not enough. Fluency would not make a man an orator unless it were backed by intelligence and morality and urged a program whose wisdom could be grasped by the orator's listeners. For Cicero, the orator was a man who combined eloquence with wisdom.[31] For Quintilian, the orator was a man who combined eloquence and personal virtue.[32] Coke transposed such beliefs to the realm of legal studies. Urging his readers to emulate the example of past sages of the law, he wrote, "I never saw any man of a loose and lawless life attain to any sound and perfect knowledge of the said laws: and on the other side, I never saw any man of excellent judgment in these laws, but was withall (being taught by such a master) honest, faithful, and virtuous."[33]

The vision of the orator as a good man personalizes a belief in the soundness of society. Underpinning the theory of classical rhetoric is the assumption of an interplay between orator and society. Belief in the orator's power to teach and move presupposes that those who listen to the orator (the institutions before whom the pleader appears, the populace before whom the spokesman urges action) have the capacity to appreciate and the will to act. The social and political connections of classical rhetoric are overt—so direct, in fact, that they may be hidden in plain sight. The efficacy of rhetoric, conceptually and functionally, is shown in action taken by or through government.

Rhetoric's fortunes as a discipline correlate with the existence of governing institutions which are open to persuasion and which can be mobilized to action. If Demosthenes and Cicero were the archetypal orators, the classical republics in which they spoke were oratory's archetypal settings—a public sphere lost until the humanists reclaimed it.[34] The privileged status which

---

31. Cicero, *De Oratore* 3.56–90.

32. Quintilian, *Institutiones Oratoria,* Preface ("the perfect orator, who cannot exist unless he is above all a good man"). See further Quentin Skinner, "'Scientia Civilis' in Classical Rhetoric and in the Early Hobbes," in *Political Discourse in Early Modern Britain,* ed. Phillipson and Q. Skinner (Cambridge: Cambridge University Press, 1993), 67–93.

33. Preface to the Second Part of the *Reports* (1602). In the oratorical tradition, this looks back to the comments of Cicero and Quintilian. In terms of Coke's own thought, it forms an obvious underpinning of artificial reason. If the good lawyer is also honest, faithful, and virtuous, this suggests that it is sound policy to entrust the laws to such men.

34. Under the Roman Empire, rhetoric withered. The fragmentation which rhetoric endured during

rhetoric won in Tudor England foreshadows the vast changes which the seventeenth century would bring in the organization of English government. The discipline's resurgence suggests a growing community of interest, the emergence of a group whose training in self-expression had made them culturally and politically self-aware. Training in oratory, in the articulation of the individual voice, went hand-in-hand with the assertion of a culture's new-found identity.

Rhetoric and Logic

Rhetoric, the art of persuasion, drew heavily on logic, the science of analysis.[35] Renaissance theorists largely conflated the two. Thomas Wilson, the most important of England's early rhetoricians, wrote in 1553, in *The Art of Rhetoric:* "Every man should desire, and seek to have his Logic perfect, before he look to profit in rhetoric, considering the ground and confirmation of causes, is for the most part gathered out of logic."[36]

While rhetoricians worked within an ancient tradition, significantly, rhetoric taught a pragmatic, real-world orientation. Its links to logic reiterated the discipline's sense of engagement with life and action, because logic, as understood by Queen Elizabeth's subjects, was closely connected with the physical world. This was partly an inheritance from the medieval world, in which metaphysics had been an area monopolized by professional theologians. Warned away from such rarified realms, logicians had focused on the natural world — in particular, medicine and the physical sciences. As Walter Ong has observed, Aristotle was "the Newton or Einstein or Pasteur rather than the Hegel or John Henry Newman of the age" — respected as a philosopher because of the value of his work on the physical world.[37]

---

the Middle Ages largely reflects the fact that monasteries and tribal kingdoms offered little scope for the discourse arts. On the fragmentation of rhetoric during this epoch (the divorce of theory from practice, understanding from action, letter-writing from sermon-making and both of these from versifying, as the discipline shattered into balkanized specializations), see Brian Vickers, *In Defense of Rhetoric* (Oxford: Clarendon Press, 1988), 214–53.

35. See W. S. Howell, *Rhetoric and Logic in England 1500–1700* (Princeton: Princeton University Press, 1956), 17–20.

36. Thomas Wilson, *The Art of Rhetoric,* ed. Peter E. Medine (1553; State College, Pennsylvania: Pennsylvania State University Press, 1994), 145. Wilson noted further, "The places of logic give good occasion to find out plentiful matter." *Id.* at 49. See further Walter J. Ong, *Ramus: Method and the Decline of Dialogue* (Cambridge, Massachusetts: Harvard University Press 1958), 96–115.

37. Ong, *Ramus, supra* n. 36, at 143–45 (quotation at 144). In one notable instance, scholars requesting works by Thomas Aquinas asked not for the *Summa Theologica,* but rather for studies of astronomy and a

Following the same path, in the century before Coke, the great neo-Ciceronian Rudolph Agricola had sought to involve logic with the real world by emphasizing invention. From one angle, invention concerned itself only with generating viewpoints and ideas which a speaker could use. Agricola taught—and his disciples, including Thomas Wilson, reiterated—that devising material for discourse involved the generation of new ideas and insights.[38] In this engagement with other disciplines, logic lost most or all of any remaining self-absorption. Walter Ong has put the matter neatly:

> The medieval logical "technicalities" have been set aside in favour of the approach of the enlightened amateur, who was interested in logic in terms of psychology, miscellaneous metaphysical detail, practical pedagogy, and eloquence. The emphasis on practical pedagogy was one of the factors which produced the lawyers' logics of Hegenfort, Everard of Middleburg, Thomas Wilson (i.e., his *Arte of Rhetorique*), Johann Thomas Freige, Abraham Fraunce, and others (the twentieth-century equivalent of this sort of production might be something like *Logic for Business Men*). . . . By being integrated with "life" ("eloquence" is the sixteenth-century equivalent), formal logic has practically ceased to exist as an autonomous discipline. . . . By being made "practical," all logic has now become a kind of rhetoric.[39]

The Ciceronian identification of *eloquence, logic,* and *life* represents the same equation as the modern-day connection of *discourse, law,* and *society.* Both statements emphasize the social dimension of law and politics—maintain that assemblies and courts should make decisions which reflect (and shape) the consciousness of the communities they serve. If rhetoric privileged public-spiritedness, logic privileged practical application. The conflation of the two disciplines underlay the realism of the Elizabethan common law.

Rhetoric and the Common Law

The associations between rhetoric and the common law were particularly strong in Tudor England. There were long-standing affinities between the way

---

book on heavy engineering, *à la* Da Vinci: *How to Put up Aqueducts and How to Make Mechanical Devices for Military Operations.* See *id.* at 131–48, *esp.* 143–44, *and* Hanna H. Gray, "Renaissance Humanism: The Pursuit of Eloquence," *Journal of the History of Ideas* 24 (1963), 497–514.

38. Ong, *Ramus, supra* n. 36, at 121–26; Peter E. Medine, *Thomas Wilson* (Boston: Twayne, 1986), 36–40.

39. Ong, *Ramus, supra* n. 36, at 125.

in which rhetoricians understood their art and the models of pleading and proof followed by the bar. In the English Renaissance, under the influence of the humanist revival of classical learning, the link between rhetorical method and legal practice grew closer.

Rhetoric and the Tudor Curriculum

In Tudor England, every lawyer was a rhetorician first. The structure of learning made that inevitable. For as much as twelve hours a day, for approximately 36 weeks a year, and for a total four to six years, the schoolboys of Tudor England were drilled in grammar, rhetoric, and literature. Learning Latin and translating between Latin and English, the schoolboys memorized tropes and figures of speech, learned to identify them, practiced using them themselves. They were taught the three styles of rhetoric, the five parts of an oration. They mastered set compositions, following models, and learned to balance arguments, *pro* and *con,* in a thesis.[40]

In these circumstances, as C. S. Lewis observed, Elizabethan thinkers must be pictured

> growing up from boyhood in a world of "prettie epanorthosis," paranomasia, *isocolon* and *similer cadentia.* Nor were these, like many subjects in a modern school, things dear to the masters but mocked or languidly regarded by the parents. Your father, your grown-up brother, your admired elder schoolfellow all loved rhetoric. Therefore you loved it too. You adored sweet Tully and were as concerned about asyndeton and chiasmus as a modern schoolboy is about county cricketers or types of airplanes.[41]

William Shakespeare, trained in such an environment, knew and used approximately 200 figures of speech.[42] And the training which Edward Coke received at the Norwich Grammar School, where he enrolled in 1560 at the age of eight, seems to have followed a typically Elizabethan course of study.[43]

40. See Vickers, *In Defense of Rhetoric, supra* n. 34, at 258–83; Joel Altman, *The Tudor Play of Mind: Rhetorical Inquiry and the Development of Elizabethan Drama* (Berkeley, California: University of California Press, 1978), 43–53. The classic treatment of the Tudor curriculum remains T. W. Baldwin, *William Shakspere's Small Latine and Lesse Greeke* (Urbana, Illinois: University of Illinois Press, 1944).

41. C. S. Lewis, *English Literature, supra* n. 27, at 61.

42. Vickers, *In Defense of Rhetoric, supra* n. 34, at 283.

43. H. W. Saunders, *A History of the Norwich Grammar School* 150–51 (Norwich, England: Jarrold & Sons, 1932).

Notable among the texts used at Norwich (as throughout England) was the *Apthonii Progymnasmata*—the *Progymnasmata* of Apthonius of Tyre, a fourth-century grammarian. Translated from Greek to Latin by Agricola and Johannes Cataneus, and with further revisions by Reinhard Lorich, the *Progymnasmata* was the standard text from which Tudor schoolboys worked their way into the rhetorical tradition.[44]

The *Progymnasmata* prescribed a series of exercises. As these became more complex, the memorization of simple homilies shifted into issues of societal morality and public policy. In texts which taught schoolboys to deride and condemn evil, the rule of law was portrayed as a counterbalance to despotism. The *Progymnasmata* offered its pre-adolescent readers examples of speeches denouncing tyrants. They learned that despotism offended the commonwealth, in which "laws are established among us, and courts of justice are part of our political structure."[45]

This was highly politicized material—hardly the curriculum which a monarch who believed in his divine right to govern would have preferred. And from such grammar-school exercises, it was only a short step to the moots of fledgling lawyers. The Inns of Court might teach aspiring gentlemen the formal rules of the legal system. As for inculcating respect for the rule of law, however, the Inns could hardly improve on the work of the grammar schools.

The Commonplace Book as Pedagogical Methodology

Humanist learning centred on the commonplace book. A commonplace book is a journal in which an apprentice orator copies down material to be used in subsequent orations: aphorisms, examples, thoughts—anything which is notable, or which may persuade. Significantly, although a commonplace book is a notebook kept by a student, it is not simply a student journal. The commonplace book is an artifact of a distinctive methodology. It is as closely and specifically tied to humanist learning methods and classical rhetorical struc-

44. See Donald Lemen Clark, "The Rise and Fall of Progymnasmata in Sixteenth and Seventeenth Century Grammar Schools," *Speech Monographs* 19 (1952), 259–63, *and* Ray Nadeau, "*The Progymnasmata of Apthonius* in Translation," *Speech Monographs* 19 (1952), 264–285, 266.

45. Nadeau, "*The Progymnasmata of Apthonius* in Translation," *supra* n. 44, at 271. In one Tudor primer, Richard Rainold's *Foundacion of Rhetorike* (1563), a vernacular version of Apthonius, such generalized denunciations of tyranny appear to have been updated. The sample offered was "A Narration Historical upon King Richard the Third, the Cruel Tyrant." See Baldwin, 2 *William Shakspere's Small Latine and Lesse Greeke, supra* n. 40, at 44.

tures as the modern legal casebook is to the case method and the Socratic dialogue.[46]

Humanist teachers required that their pupils keep notebooks and write down in them phrases from the classical authors whom they were reading. The object was to collect a stock of phrases, of apt quotations—to break up pieces of classical literature into parts which the student could then reassemble into new structures.[47] Erasmus offered a whimsical metaphor. "And so the student, like the industrious bee, will fly about through all the authors' gardens and light on every small flower of rhetoric, everywhere collecting honey that he may carry off to his own hive."[48]

The student copied down *exempla*. To the rhetorician, *exemplum* meant *example* or *instance,* a similar incident: *pattern, model, precedent, case.*[49] The category was broadly defined: *exempla* could be fables, apologues, parables, proverbs, analogies, scenes from poetry, prose, or drama—any persuasive example or pithy remark, virtually anything that could be persuasively quoted. Modern examples might include any anecdote which begins, *As Sir Winston Churchill once remarked,* any story which opens, *A traveler came to a river,* and *The Chinese ideogram for crisis is made by combining the ideogram for danger with the ideogram for opportunity.*[50] At the same time, however, an *exemplum* could be considered a miniature case-study—Erasmus noted that "the *exemplum* pertains to the deeds of individual men" (as opposed to the parable, a generalized illustration).[51]

The student who learned to dissect writing into component elements ac-

---

46. The term *commonplace* translates *locus communis*—as defined by Cicero, a "general theme, applicable to many particular cases." This usage reflected the practice of garnering material as a general preparation for debate. To commonplace a work meant to taxonomize its contents, *i.e.,* to enter it by sections into a commonplace book. More loosely, this commonplacing process came to be synonymous with debating. Sir Francis Bacon used the word in this sense when he told King James that he "need not commonplace" the value of having work done by select committees. These developments are supplied in the *Oxford English Dictionary.*

47. R. R. Bolgar, *The Classical Heritage and Its Beneficiaries* 272 (Cambridge: Cambridge University Press, 1954). However, collecting phrases did not begin with the humanists. Quintilian, for example, had given the same advice to the apprentice orator: from worthwhile authors "must be gathered a stock of words, a variety of figures, and the art of composition . . . for it cannot be doubted that a great portion of art consists in imitation." Quintilian, *Institutiones Oratoria* 10.2.1.

48. Desiderius Erasmus, *On Copia of Words and Ideas [De Utraque Verborum ac Rerum Copia]* trans. Donald B. King and H. Davis Rix (Milwaukee, Wisconsin: Marquette University Press, 1963), 90. This work is hereafter cited as *De Copia.*

49. Lewis & Short, *A Latin[-English] Dictionary* (Oxford: Clarendon Press, 1879).

50. Citing *exempla,* Erasmus considered, was the most effective rhetorical device. Erasmus, *De Copia, supra* n. 48, at 67.

51. *Id.* at 76. The idea was nothing new. In relying on *exempla* to teach, humanism drew on an older tradition. *Exempla* had been used by the Church, since the High Middle Ages, to demonstrate aspects of doctrine or practice. Bolgar, *supra* n. 47, at 272.

quired thereby a store of phrases, "ornaments of speech."[52] But ornamentation did not mean non-structural encrustation, the application of superficial rhetorical flourishes. *Ornamentum* was the term applied, in classical Latin, to the gear a warrior carried on his battle-harness.[53] The rhetorician's commonplace book armed him for oral argument. In 1990, in New York City, a continuing legal education program on trial techniques billed itself, with litigators' machismo, as "Weapons for the Firefight." Four centuries later, the language was laden with more bravado, but the central point was exactly the same.

The humanist practice of collecting illustrations was matched by a practice of applying *sententiae* to *exempla*—that is, following the story by explicitly stating the moral. A skilful glossator could use for many different morals any of the *exempla* which he had collected. In a masterful passage, Erasmus showed how many different morals—complementary or even contradictory— one could draw from the death of Socrates.

> [T]he death of Socrates provides not only an *exemplum* that death should not be feared by the good man, since Socrates drank the hemlock with such a cheerful countenance, but also that virtue is liable to injury from envy and is not safe when surrounded by evil men. It also provides an *exemplum* that the study of philosophy is useless or even pernicious unless one conforms to the general mores.[54]

The idea of splitting up literature into its components goes hand-in-hand with the application of the moralizing comment. In fact, it demands it. The rhetorician is by turns both scavenger and *bricoleur,* shattering existing texts in order to reuse their materials. Each separate *exemplum* is a brick to be fitted into place. The glossing *sententiae* are the mortar which holds the structure together—which reshape those materials to new uses.[55]

The use of *sententiae* to draw the moral of a story has a modern echo in the language of the law. There is only one sense in which contemporary speakers of English continue to use the word *sentence* in the same way Renaissance humanists did, as an expression of moral judgment: when they speak of the societal

---

52. Erasmus, *De Copia, supra* n. 48, at 67.
53. See Vickers, *In Defense of Rhetoric, supra* n. 34, at 284.
54. Erasmus, *De Copia, supra* n. 48, at 90–91.
55. In his library at Holkham, Coke possessed at least three collections of *sententiae* and *exempla: Theologici loci Communes per Stephanum Szegedinum* (1599), Johan de Peckham's *Divinarum sententiarum collectarium* (1513), and Johan Piscator's *Aphorismi Doctrinae Christiane* (1615). Hassall, *supra* n. 17, at 3, 11, 12. He also owned two copies of the *Polyanthea Nova,* a collection of Latin proverbs and quotations organized by topic headings, and—late in his career—began indexing one of these copies himself. *Id.* at 5.

condemnation and judgment, the penal sentence, imposed by a judge upon a guilty defendant.

The legal commonplace book, as prepared by a Tudor student of the law, remained a document prepared to assist its maker in speaking copiously—eloquently, fluently, persuasively. As a methodology for learning, commonplacing carried on seamlessly from the grammar school to the Inns of Court. Law students' notebooks, Sir Thomas Elyot observed, would include "the places whereof they shall fetch their reasons, called of orators *loci communes*."[56] William Fulbecke, in the first systematic guide to learning the law, followed the humanist approach to learning, counselling students that "it is a profitable course under titles to digest the cases of the law."[57] Moreover, not only can it be shown that lawyers stored *ornamentum* in their commonplace books; it can also be shown that they extracted *ornamentum* for re-use. In 1608, when drafting his opinion in *Calvin's Case,* Lord Chancellor Ellesmere drew on a commonplace book from his early legal career, reaching back to quote materials he had written down at least four decades before.[58]

At the Inns of Court, professional training elaborated on the classical rhetoric which had previously been learned. In *The Book Named the Governor* (1531), Sir Thomas Elyot discussed legal training as the apex of a nobleman's education. His discussion makes clear the way in which rhetorical concepts had been woven into the fabric of legal training.

56. Sir Thomas Elyot, *The Book Named the Governor,* ed. John M. Major (1531: New York: Columbia University Teachers' College, 1969), 125.

57. William Fulbecke, *A Direction, or Preparative to the Study of the Lawe* 44 (1600).

A tentative review of law students' commonplace books from the Elizabethan and Stuart eras suggests that most students followed an alphabetical approach to topical organization. See, e.g., J. H. Baker, 2 *English Legal Manuscripts in the United States of America 1558–1902* (London: Selden Society, 1990), 35 (two commonplace books in the collection of Columbia Law School, covering respectively *Attornment to Estates* and *Herriott to Grant*). So common was the practice that Elizabethan legal commonplace books, when they arrive on the contemporary auction market, are frequently misdescribed as "handwritten legal encyclopaedias." Personal communication from Prof. Victor Tunkel, Selden Society secretary, June 15, 1994.

58. The material on which Ellesmere drew had been written down sometime between about 1557 and about 1571. This painstaking identification was made by Samuel Thorne. See [Thomas Egerton, Lord Ellesmere], *A Discourse upon the Statutes,* ed. Samuel Thorne (San Marino, California: Huntington Library, 1942), 92–100, esp. 98 n. 212.

Coke's personal notebooks, preserved in the British Library and at Cambridge University, follow a commonplace format. He provided headings at the tops of pages, often, as if expecting that one page might be enough space to exhaust a topic: *Pleadings, Office et officers, Parlement & Statutes, Waste, Devises.* British Library MS Harl. 6687-D, ff. 790ʳ, 803ʳ, 805ᵛ, 849ʳ, 871ʳ. However, as Coke continued to take notes, this framework was buried in a lode of commonplaced material: case reports, notes on statutes, extracts from records, and notes of personal accomplishments, including a description of the ceremonial collar Coke wore as Chief Justice. See J. H. Baker, "Coke's Note-Books and the Sources of His *Reports,*" *Cambridge Law Journal* 30 (1972), 59–86 [reprinted here on p. 357].

It is to be remembered that in the learning of the laws of this realm, there is at this day an exercise wherein is a manner, a shadow or figure of the ancient rhetoric. I mean the pleading used in court and Chancery called moots, where first a case is appointed to be mooted by certain young men containing some doubtful controversy, which is instead of the head of a declamation, called *thema.* The case being known, they which be appointed to moot, do examine the case, and investigate what they therein can espy which may make a contention, whereof may rise a question to be argued (and that of Tully is called *constitutio,* and of Quintilian *status causae*). Also they consider what pleas on every part ought to be made, and how the case may be reasoned: which is the first part of rhetoric, called *invention;* then appoint they how many pleas may be made for every part, and in what formality they should be set: which is the second part of rhetoric, called *disposition.*[59]

Elyot recognized that the method followed by students at the Inns followed the forms of classical rhetoric.[60] Beyond that, he identified specific elements of common-law pleading, the thrusts and parries that formed the stages of an action at law, as models built on the archetypes of rhetorical argumentation.

Moreover there seemeth to be, in the said pleadings, certain parts of an oration: that is to say, for *narrations, partitions, confirmations,* and *confutations* (named of some *reprehensions*), they have *declarations, bars, replications,* and *rejoinders.* Only they lack pleasant form of beginning, called in Latin *exordium;* nor it maketh

---

59. Sir Thomas Elyot, *supra* n. 56, at 124. On legal education at the Inns of Court in Coke's day, see generally Wilfrid R. Prest, *The Inns of Court Under Elizabeth I and the Early Stuarts 1590–1640* (London: Longmans, 1972), 115–173.

60. Coke felt it "necessary" that the would-be lawyer

come from one of the universities to the study of the common law, where he may learn the liberal arts, and especially logic, for that teacheth a man not only by just argument to conclude the matter in question, but to discern between truth and falsehood, and to use a good method in his study, and probably to speak to any legal question, and is defined thus, *dialectica est scientia probabiliter de quovis themate disserendi.*—Sir Edward Coke, *Commentary upon Littleton* 235a (1628).

Amplifying on the language of Abraham Fraunce, Peter Goodrich has suggested that, within the Inns of Court, "The lawyers hated the 'fine university men'; they explicitly denied that a good scholar could ever make a good lawyer. . . . Fraunce cites the legal scorn of university men who, in the opinion of those wise in the law, 'can better make new found verses of Amyntas' death, and popular discourses of ensigns, armoury, emblems, hieroglyphs and Italian impresses,' than apply their heads to the study of law which is hard, harsh, unpleasant, unsavoury, rude and barbarous." P. Goodrich, *Languages of Law: From Logics of Memory to Nomadic Masks* (London: Weidenfeld & Nicolson, 1990), 21. This puts matters too strongly. The attitude which Fraunce identified, rather than reflecting a general anti-intellectualism among the bar, should be seen as the disdain of the professional and the craftsman for the dilettante.

thereof no great matter—they that have studied rhetoric shall perceive what I mean.[61]

Legal pleading, in turn, reflected a return influence on other areas of literary culture. The close connection between legal terminology and poetic language—a connection due to the fact that both drew upon rhetoric—was reflected in George Puttenham's *The Arte of English Poesie* (1589). In order to define poetic figures of speech, Puttenham often found it helpful to use legal terms of art. In explaining *impartener,* a form of apostrophe, Puttenham summoned up a scene reminiscent of Year Book colloquies. This figure of speech was called *impartener,* Puttenham commented,

> because many times in pleading and persuading, we think it a very good policy
> to acquaint our judge or hearer or very adversary with some part of our counsel
> and advice, and to ask their opinion, as who would say they could not otherwise
> think of the matter than we do.[62]

On the border between rhetorical learning and legal practice, certain texts taught lawyers to apply the discourse arts to their courtroom work. Thomas Wilson's *Rule of Reason* (1551) and *Art of Rhetoric* (1553), the first treatment of logic and the first full treatment of Ciceronian rhetoric in the English language, were directed at the prototypical student at the Inns of Court—"the man of affairs who may not have had much Latin or Greek but who needed practical assistance in various forms of spoken discourse, including epistles, sermons and legal pleas."[63] And it seems that Wilson was successful in reaching his intended audience. Gabriel Harvey, the academic rhetorician who was Coke's contemporary, noted that *The Art of Rhetoric* had become "the daily bread of our common pleaders and discoursers."[64]

---

61. Sir Thomas Elyot, *supra* n. 56, at 124.

62. George Puttenham, *The Arte of English Poesie,* ed. Gladys Doidge Willcock and Alice Walker (1589; Cambridge: Cambridge University Press, 1936), 227. As a close relation of Sir James Dyer, Puttenham was a notably well-placed observer. Dotting his essay on poetry are numerous back-stage glimpses of the Elizabethan legal community, scenes which confirm the value lawyers placed on rhetoric. "I have come to the Lord Keeper Sir Nicholas Bacon," Puttenham noted, and "found him sitting in his gallery alone with the works of Quintilian before him, indeed he was a most eloquent man, and of rare learning and wisdom." *Id.* at 140.

63. Peter E. Medine, Introduction to Thomas Wilson, *The Art of Rhetoric, supra* n. 36, at 8.

64. Virginia F. Stern, *Gabriel Harvey: His Life, Marginalia, and Library* (Oxford: Oxford University Press, 1979), 239. See further William G. Crane, *Wit and Learning in the Renaissance* (New York: Columbia University Press, 1937); Richard J. Schoeck, "Lawyers and Rhetoric in Sixteenth-Century England," in *Renaissance Eloquence: Studies in the Theory and Practice of Medieval Rhetoric,* ed. J. J. Murphy (Berkeley, California: University of California Press, 1983), 274–91, 285–86.

In the next generation, Sir John Dodderidge, Coke's colleague on the King's Bench, carried such cross-disciplinary studies further. With *The Lawyer's Light* (1629), Dodderidge essayed nothing less than a book-length critique of legal doctrines in the light of rhetoric and logic. He wrote with much the same rigor with which modern writers have measured legal concepts by economic standards. Dodderidge reduced the arguments in *Shelley's Case* and *Calvin's Case* to syllogisms, analyzed the nature of rights of common according to material cause (yielding rights to commons in pasture, of estover, and of turbary) and by formal cause (which yielded commons rights appendant, appurtenant, and in gross). Written on a higher level than Wilson's books, *The Lawyer's Light* was also a popular success; the anonymous edition issued in Dodderidge's lifetime was expanded and reissued posthumously.

John Hawarde's reports of Star Chamber cases provide one illustration, involving an inquest in which Sir Thomas Egerton (later Lord Keeper and Lord Chancellor) sat as a commissioner, which shows how closely law and the discourse arts had come to be associated.

> [A]n article was interrogated [*i.e.* a question was asked] if such a one died seised of certain wastes. The plain people and ignorant deposed readily that he was seised and died seised. Whereupon I demanded and said, "Hear you me, Father, do you know what it is to be seised or to die seised?"; "Sir," saith he, "I know what I say, I care not for your chopping for logic"; whereupon I caused the clerk to write this his answer also as part of his examination; and then said his Commissioner, "Father you mean he was possessed and took the profits to the time of his death"; he answered, "Aye, Sir, Aye, God's blessing of your heart."[65]

The idea that lawyering meant logic-chopping had percolated down to the general Elizabethan population. Even plain people and ignorant expected it of the lawyers who crossed their paths.

The Lawyer as Rhetorician in Elizabethan England

Attorneys and rhetoricians were prone to flatter themselves by attributing to their arts the foundation of civilization. The order which rhetoric brought out of chaos was crystallized by law. Stephen Hawes, writing under Henry VIII,

---

65. John Hawarde, *Les Reportes del Cases in Camera Stellata 1593–1609,* ed. W. P. Baildon (1894), 116–17.

adopted these conjectures. If Cicero and Quintilian had written in fluid Latin, the vigorous rhyme of Hawes' *Pastime of Pleasure* echoed Chaucer and the Gawain Poet.

> Before the lawe / in a tumblying barge
> The people sayled / without parfytenes
> Throughe the world / all about at large
> They hadde none ordre / nor no stedfastnes
> Tyll rethorycyans / founde Iustyce doubtles
> Ordenynge kynges of ryghte hye dygnyte
> Of all comyns / to have the soverainte
> The barge to stere / with lawe and Iustyce
> Over the waves of this lyfe transytorye . . .[66]

Under Henry VIII, in the 1540's, a royal commission headed by Sir Nicholas Bacon examined the state of legal instruction then carried on by the Inns. Among the recommendations of this body was one which indicated the classical orientation of Tudor legal professionals. Throughout the academic year, Bacon and his fellows recommended,

> every Monday, Tuesday and Wednesday, (festival days only excepted) one of the excellent knowledge in the Latin and Greek tongue [should be appointed] to read some orator or book of rhetoric, or else some other author, which treateth of the government of a commonwealth, openly to all the company.[67]

Oratorical skills, such recommendations show, ranked with political studies as the heart of the legal curriculum. Indeed, the two were to be equated: books of oratory and rhetoric are interchangeable with books which deal with the government of the commonwealth.[68]

---

66. Stephen Hawes, *The Pastime of Pleasure* (1517), quoted in Brian Vickers, "The Power of Persuasion: Images of the Orator, Elyot to Shakespeare," in *Renaissance Eloquence: Studies in the Theory and Practice of Renaissance Rhetoric,* ed. J. J. Murphy (Berkeley, California: University of California Press, 1983), 411–35, 415.
Similarly, in the first English-language textbook on rhetoric, Leonard Cox's *Rhethoryke* (ca. 1530), the dedication spelled out the connection between grammar-school learning and the lawyers' art. Leonard Cox, *Rhethoryke, quoted in* W. S. Howell, *Logic and Rhetoric, supra* n. 35, at 90–91. It was his ability as a rhetorician and linguistic facility which first brought legal preferment to Sir Thomas More. See William Nelson, "Thomas More, Grammarian and Orator," *Publications of the Modern Language Association* 58 (1943), 337–52.
67. D. S. Bland, "Rhetoric and the Law Student in Sixteenth Century England," *Studies in Philology* 54 (1957), 498–508, 501, *citing* the report as published in *Fortescutus Illustratus* 539–46 (ed. Edward Waterhous 1663). The report is reprinted at D. S. Bland, "Henry VIII's Royal Commission on the Inns of Court," *Journal of the Society of Public Teachers of Law* 10 (1969), 178–94.
68. Lord Burghley, according to Sir Henry Peacham, "to his dying day would always carry Tully's

One may perhaps discount the flattering statements which lawyers and rhetoricians made about each other. If the lawyers claimed that in their hands rhetoric had created society—well, so too did the poets. But it is very important that the men who governed Elizabethan England, accustomed both to wielding political power and making legal judgments, had been schooled to connect rhetoric, law, and society. This meant that the language of rhetoric provided the languages of government and law; and particularly that there was a very close identification, through the common medium of rhetoric, between law and government.

One particular category of *exempla—judicia,* or judgments—may also have particular importance for Elizabethan lawyers' vision of law. Erasmus commented:

> *Judicia* . . . are also, as we have said, classified as *exempla.* And they are the *sententiae* of famous writers, of peoples, of wise men or renowned citizens. A great number of *judicia* can be collected from the celebrated poets of antiquity, and also from historians, from philosophers, and from private letters. . . . Likewise the apothegms of wise men are useful, of which type are the sayings of famous men reported by Plutarch. . . . [T]here are serious sayings, facetious sayings, and pointed sayings. To this class also belong proverbs, either those taken from authors, or popular sayings. For I do not see that public practices of people differ from *exempla* in any respect.[69]

A very similar passage in Thomas Wilson's *The Rule of Reason* makes clear the connection between legal reasoning and the rhetorical paradigm.

> All such testimonies may be called sentences of the sage, which are brought to confirm any thing, either taken out of old authors, or else such as have been used in this common life. As the sentences of noble men, the laws in any realm, quick

---

Offices about with him either in his bosom or his pocket." Sir Henry Peacham, *The Compleat Gentleman* 45 (1634), *quoted in* Conyers Read, *Mr. Secretary Cecil and Queen Elizabeth* (London: Jonathan Cape, 1962), 30. Puttenham considered that Burghley's training in the discourse arts might have been reflected in his statesmanship and eloquence. Puttenham, *supra* n. 62, at 140.

As John Baker notes, the idea of the commonwealth remained more an ideal to conjure by than a grounds for deciding cases. The gentlemen who hailed the idea of increasing the public weal were at pains to explain that they were not promoting social leveling or allotting new rights to the lower social classes. Nonetheless, the idea remains "[t]he most universal ethical and political concept of the English Renaissance," arguing "that human institutions should be concerned with the advancement of the common wealth, and that the promotion of private commodity or 'singular interest' at the expense of the public good was undesirable." J. H. Baker, Introduction to 2 *Reports of Sir John Spelman,* 94 Publications of the Selden Society (London, 1978), 34–36, 34.

69. Erasmus, *De Copia, supra* n. 48, at 80. "There are past deeds and past sayings for example," Erasmus remarked elsewhere, "and common customs of people are adduced in *exempla.*" *Id.* at 68.

sayings, proverbs, that either have been used before, or be now used. Histories of wise philosophers, the judgments of learned men, the common opinion of the multitude, old customs, ancient fashions, or any such like.[70]

This passage draws closely on Erasmus' discussion of *judicia,* but Wilson subtly shifts the emphasis. Erasmus spoke of serious sayings and public practices; Wilson emphasizes laws, judgments, common opinion, and old customs—the raw material with which the common-law judge worked.[71]

The ease of this transposition may explain the self-confidence of the common law's masters. From regarding public practice and common opinion as *judicia,* it is a short step to confirming custom with legal judgments. In a sentence Coke might have written, Wilson argued, "That is right by custom which long time hath confirmed, being partly grounded upon nature and partly upon reason."[72] The common wisdom which the rhetoricians claimed to express and the common law which the judges interpreted drew upon the same amalgam of popular beliefs and practices. Both claimed to express and confirm the cultural vocabulary of implicit understandings and societal routine.

Where such connections were drawn from rhetoric to political action and cultural identity, training students in rhetoric prepared them for political activity and cultural self-assertion. It is no coincidence that Thomas Wilson, after being the first to bring rhetoric and logic into the English vernacular, also prepared the first English translation of Demosthenes, and that he did so in the year of the Armada.[73] Invective leveled at Philip of Macedon was easily turned against another threatening tyrant, Philip of Spain.

The grammar-school students who copied out Cicero and Erasmus included the parliamentarians who would make the House of Commons an indispensable, permanent, and paramount political institution. They included the lawyers who would bring *habeas corpus* cases and write family settlements which tested the land-law's every limit—asserting and institutionalizing indi-

---

70. Thomas Wilson, *The Rule of Reason* Sig. M.5ᵛ–M.6ʳ (1551).

71. In an age where legal authority had not hardened into *stare decisis,* the authority on which a lawyer could draw was broad. To square an opinion with what Chief Justice Hody had said might be important. One could shore up an opinion just as serviceably, however, with an insight from literature which the community of the realm knew and respected. Virgil might be quoted on the right of the accused to be heard in his or her own defense. On the desirability of controlling extravagant housing, one might cite Sir Thomas More (not as Lord Chancellor, but as the translator of Euripides: *To build many houses and many to feed / To poverty that way doth lead*). More and Virgil counted as wise men or renowned citizens, and Coke would draw upon them more than once. See further Gest, *supra* n. 19, at 517–18.

72. Wilson, *The Art of Rhetoric, supra* n. 36, at 74–75.

73. See generally Medine, *Thomas Wilson, supra* n. 38.

viduals' rights over liberty and property. If Coke is considered as a latter-day orator, these lawyers (and the clients whose demands they met) were the populace whom he moved to action.

Coke's Achievement and the Ciceronian Tradition

Since Coke's day, it has been more important for lawyers to know the *Reports* and *Institutes* and the medieval common law as it appears there (whether accurately reported, mistaken, or rigorously misapplied) than to know the original Year Books. With this reverence for the law went an insistence on the independence of the judge. Coke repeatedly struck sparks in his dealings with James I, resisting his king's efforts to influence the bench, and claimed for judges a legal competence surpassing Parliament: the authority, based on the judges' training and wisdom, to review statutory law.

In both these areas can be traced the influence of the rhetorical tradition. Coke's institutional writings draw their structure from rhetorical models; the *Commentary upon Littleton* is a commonplace book, heroically amplified. The professional expertise which Coke felt privileged the judges to make and unmake law is modelled on the technical accomplishment which rhetoricians felt made their art superior.

The Case, the Exemplum, and the Commonplace Book

Very closely related to the realism of the common law was the concept of the case. As lawyers and clients demanded harder-and-faster guidance as to what was lawful and what was not, law-making moved from being a matter of clarifying doctrine to being the determination of concrete cases. Behind the lawyers' concept of the case can be identified the rhetoricians' *exemplum*—another instance of law's borrowing from the discourse arts.

Over the same centuries in which literary humanists collected *exempla,* the term *exemplum* was also developing a long, illustrious association with the common law. It figured in Roman jurisprudence,[74] and reached England in the time of the *Year Books,* received into Law French as *ensample,* which judges

---

74. See, e.g., *Justinian's Institutes,* 1, 2, 6 ("ad exemplum trahere").

used when speaking of single precedents.[75] Francis Bacon used *exempla* similarly, to describe occasional decisions which had not yet achieved the force of law. Bacon considered that *exempla* were sources to which courts might look when filling lacunae in existing law.[76]

To the rhetorician, *exempla* were cases, relevant and analogous instances. To the lawyer, *exempla* were opinions entitled to respect. The implicit connection is close, and sometimes the different meanings might be deliberately brought together. Consider the following example from Elizabeth's reign:

> Sempronius, a nobleman *sui juris,* loved Seja, a young woman similarly *sui juris,* and after a long courtship procured her consent to marriage; but because secretly he feared the prince (of whose family Seja was born) they contracted the marriage without witnesses, except for the sister of Sempronius (who died not long after); earnest was given to and from, an unknown priest was brought, carnal connection followed, and in the end a son was begotten abroad which was truly Sempronius's. When the fact was disclosed to the prince, Seja was cast into prison, because she had proceeded to the union with Sempronius without the prince's knowledge, and he also (being sent for) was placed under imprisonment; the case was committed to judges for examination; Sempronius and Seja made known the espousals and marriage which they alleged for their right. The judges reject all these things and proceed to a definitive sentence, the effect of which is that Sempronius and Seja have committed fornication against the laws of God and man, and that therefore they are to be punished with a just and fair penalty.

This reads like an extract from a commonplace book, some tale that Shakespeare might have borrowed from Plautus or Ovid. And the tale of Sempronius and Seja does come from a sort of commonplace book: the case notes of Chief Justice James Dyer. It reflects the facts of a clandestine love-affair conducted within the Tower of London by the Earl of Hertford and Lady Katherine Grey, both too close to the crown for the state to take no interest in such matters. Dyer noted that the case was so framed for submission "to the best civilians and canonists on this matter."[77] A law-case had been given the shape of a rhetorical *exemplum,* the better for its issues to be resolved.

Coke reported cases — eleven volumes of them, priding himself that he re-

75. See J. H. Baker, *Manual of Law French* (Aldershot, England: Scolar Press, 2d ed. 1990), 102.

76. Sir Francis Bacon, 5 *Works* at 92, *quoted in* Daniel Coquillette, *Francis Bacon* 245–46 (Edinburgh, Scotland: Edinburgh University Press, 1992).

77. J. H. Baker, 1 *Reports from the Lost Notebooks of Sir James Dyer* (London: Selden Society, 1994), 92 (Publications of the Selden Society 109).

ported the decisions of judges rather than the reflections of civilians. His language shows that he saw the law-case as a legal version of the rhetorical *exemplum*. In his preface to the Sixth Part of his *Reports,* he went so far as to claim divine sanction for this outlook:

> The reporting of particular cases or examples, is the most perspicuous course of teaching the right rule and reason of the law: for so did Almighty God himself, when he delivered by Moses his judicial laws, "exemplis docuit pro legibus," as it appeareth in Exodus, Leviticus, Numbers and Deuteronomy. And the glossographers of the rule of the civil law, do often reduce the rule into a case, for the more lively expressing and true application of the same.[78]

He later considered the point further: "And albeit it is truly said, that *Judicium est legibus & non exemplis:* And as the logician saith, *Exempla demonstrant, non probant;* yet undoubtedly it is a great contentment and a good conscience, especially in cases that concern the life and liberty of a man, to follow the precedent of grave and learned men."[79]

For Coke, the case had become the set of facts which the lawyers' arguments explored and on which the judges' wisdom focused. The eleven volumes in which he reported cases confirmed the law's shift (marked by the reports of Plowden and Dyer) from doctrine to jurisprudence—from an absorption with theory to an emphasis on decided cases. As books of case-reports became extant—as publishing made cases available for consultation, as standardized editions supplied lawyers with a common set of references—case law attained critical mass.

Coke's *Commentary upon Littleton* is known for its density of detail and unwieldy sprawl. As Holdsworth described it, *Coke upon Littleton* is "a legal encyclopaedia arranged on no plan except that suggested by the words and sentences of Littleton."[80] Ostensibly, the work only provides Coke's marginal glosses on the *Tenures* of Sir Thomas Littleton. However, the detail and range of Coke's line-by-line comments result in a study which sweeps across the entire common law. As J. H. Baker has written, Coke

> wrote like a helpful old wizard, eager to pass on all his secrets before he died, but not quite sure where to begin or end. The comment on the first section of *Littleton* provides a typical foretaste. The text itself is a definition of "fee simple";

---

78. Preface to the Sixth Part of the *Reports.*
79. Sir Edward Coke, *A Little Treatise of Baile and Mainprize* 29–30 (1635).
80. Sir William Holdsworth, *supra* n. 3, at 467.

but the commentary wanders through such disparate topics as etymology, alien
status, misnomer in grants, interest rates and usury, the precedence of earth over
the other elements, the correct Latin words for ponds, marshes, rushes, willows,
elders and boileries of salt, the Domesday Book, the eight parts of a deed, the
styles and titles of the kings of England, the ownership of the Isle of Man, and
the legal status of monsters and hermaphrodites.[81]

Not only does Coke's masterwork provide a torrent of material; it appears to
apply its learning with the all-encompassing, random nature of a flood. Corporations are discussed under the topic of descents, hermaphrodites under
tenants by the courtesy. The concept of the court of record holds as significant
a place in Coke's battle with Chancery as the concept of equal protection does
in American constitutional law.[82] Yet the *Commentary* first mentions "court
of record" in its discussion of villainage, without any indication that the term
means any more than the court in which villain status may be confessed.[83]

James Fitzjames Stephen commented that "a more disorderly mind than
Coke's . . . would be impossible to find."[84] With that trenchant, short-sighted
dismissal, Stephen's Benthamite sympathies led him astray. To fault the *Commentary upon Littleton* for a lack of order is to misunderstand its context and
purpose. For a truer reading, we must look back two centuries before Stephen,
to the antiquarian John Aubrey, whose long, sad experience with lawsuits led
him frequently through the Inns of Court. Aubrey repeated a lawyers' gripe
about Coke's work: that the bar "had expected from [Coke] a Commentary
upon Littleton's *Tenures;* and he left them his common-place book."[85]

This complaint points out what otherwise might be hidden in plain sight.
The *Commentary* is a commonplace book. And the *Commentary,* like other
commonplace books, does not pretend to present a normative schematization
of the topics dealt with in its pages. The commonplace book does not develop
or discuss; it records and cross-references. It is not a treatise; it is a close cousin
to the thesaurus and the data-base.

The practice of drawing morals, of applying *sententiae* to *exempla,* shaped
the structure of the commonplace book—or, better said, freed the common-

81. J. H. Baker, *Introduction to English Legal History, supra* n. 15, at 218.
82. Samuel Thorne, "Courts of Record and Sir Edward Coke," *University of Toronto Law Journal* 2
(1937), 24–29.
83. Sir Edward Coke, *Commentary upon Littleton, supra* n. 60, at 117b.
84. Sir James Fitzjames Stephen, *History of the Criminal Law of England* 2 (1883), 206.
85. Aubrey, *Brief Lives, supra* n. 22, at 163.

place book from the need for structure. Where a system of thought expects meaning to be provided by gloss, rather than uncovered in the text of the work, the structure of the work will provide no key to its meaning. In fact, there is no "structure"—no correlation between the work's organization and the way in which its contents are to be read. Holdsworth was exactly right; the *Commentary* is in fact, as it was intended to be, a legal encyclopedia arranged according to the phrases comprising Littleton's *Tenures.*

Artifice in Rhetoric and Law

Rhetoricians claimed a special privilege for their discipline, that the highest eloquence could be achieved only by mastery of its technical forms. Thomas Wilson wrote, "Many speak wisely which never read logic, but to speak wisely with an argument, and to know the very foundations of things: that can none do, except they have some skill in this art."[86] Put another way, the rhetoricians asserted that not only were their figures of argument the most persuasive form of discourse; they also claimed that the sophistication of their discipline made rhetorical discourse the only appropriate discourse for public life. Puttenham's comments are revealing:

> And though grave and wise counsellors in their consultations do not use much superfluous eloquence, and also in their judicial hearings do much mislike all scholastical rhetorics: yet in such a case as it may be (and as this Parliament was) if the Lord Chancellor of England or Archbishop of Canterbury himself were to speak, he ought to do it cunningly and eloquently, which can not be without the use of figures. . . .[87]

The "artificial logic" which distinguished the rhetoricians' discourses is closely and obviously related to the "artificial reason" which Coke acclaimed as the life of the common law. As expounded by Abraham Fraunce,

> Logic is an art, to distinguish artificial logic from natural reason. Artificial logic is gathered out of divers examples of natural reason, which is not any art of logic, but that ingraven gift and faculty of wit and reason shining in the particular discourses of several men, whereby they both invent, and orderly dispose. . . . This

---

86. Wilson, *The Rule of Reason, supra* n. 70, Sig. O.2^r–O.2^v.
87. Puttenham, *The Arte of English Poesie, supra* n. 62, at 139.

as it is to no man given in full perfection, so diverse have it in sundry measure.
... And then is the logic of art more certain than that of nature, because of many
particulars in nature, a general and infallible constitution of logic is put down in
art.[88]

This bears comparison with Coke's celebrated definition of law. "Reason is
the life of the law," Coke wrote,

> nay the common law itself is nothing else but reason, which is to be understood
> of an artificial perfection of reason gotten by long study, observation and experi-
> ence and not of every man's natural reason. . . . This legal reason *est summa ratio.*
> And therefore if all the reason that is dispersed into so many several heads were
> united into one, yet could he not make such a law as the law in England is; be-
> cause by many succession of ages it hath been fined and refined by an infinite
> number of grave and learned men, and by long experience grown to such a per-
> fection for the government of this Realm, as the old rule may be justly verified
> of it, *Neminem oportet esse sapientiorem legibus:* no man out of his own private
> reason ought to be wiser than the law, which is the perfection of reason.[89]

That both lawyers and rhetoricians stressed the artifice of their disciplines
shows a common emphasis on professional rigor (consistent with a robust self-
esteem). Both locate the individual talent within a professional tradition, and
insist that the individual perspective is constrained and bounded by professional consensus. Accomplishment is acquired by long study, the student's
self-familiarization with the community's outlooks and conventions, and no
single perspective should (or can) be considered to outweigh the common
agreement.[90]

Where rhetoric was privileged, the way was cleared for Coke's privileging

---

88. Abraham Fraunce, *The Lawiers Logike, exemplifying the praecepts of Logike by the practise of the common Lawe,* Sig. B.ii (1588).

As Peter Goodrich has noted, Fraunce sought to purify and remodel English law along lines drawn from
rhetoric and logic. See Goodrich, *supra* n. 60, at 15–52. Thus, it is particularly important that the words
and ideas of the reforming theoretician are so close to those of the Lord Chief Justice: the similarity reveals
how directly the common law already relied on the conceptual framework of the discourse arts.

89. Sir Edward Coke, *Commentary upon Littleton, supra* n. 60, at 97b.

90. Significantly, Coke was not the only common lawyer to call the law "artificial reason" or to describe
it in terms patterned on rhetoric. Sir John Dodderidge wrote that law

> is called reason; not for that every man can comprehend the same; but it is artificial reason; the
> reason of such, as by their wisdom, learning, and long experience are skilful in the affairs of men,
> and know what is fit and convenient to be held and observed for the appeasing of controversies
> and debates among men, still having an eye and due regard of justice, and a consideration of the
> commonwealth wherein they live.—Sir John Dodderidge, *The English Lawyer* (1631), 242.

of the judges' reason. The master's competence with the techniques of his discipline (in law as in rhetoric) provided an unanswerable claim to superior wisdom. Moreover, the rhetoricians' equation of eloquence with rhetorical accomplishment could be given a corollary: that no trained rhetorician need accept an argument which was not couched in the figures and conventions of rhetoric. To the extent that common lawyers carried over this perspective into law, it may have underlain resistance to changes and innovations which came from outside the common-law tradition.

This implicit belief lies at the heart of *Fuller's Case.* When Coke insisted that the judges could execute justice in a way that the king could not, due to their practice in "the artificial reason and judgment of law, which requires long study and experience before that a man can attain to the cognizance of it,"[91] he spoke in terms familiar to generations of pleaders and discoursers.

Two writers trained in the rhetorical tradition of Tudor England make it possible to describe Coke's place on the boundary between classical rhetoric and the common-law tradition. Sir John Elyot, considering law in the context of oratory, made an unwitting prophecy of what Coke was to achieve.

> And verily I suppose, if there might once happen some man, having an excellent wit . . . exactly or deeply learned in the art of an orator, and also in the laws of this realm . . . undoubtedly it should not be impossible for him to bring the pleading and reasoning of the law, to the ancient form of noble orators.[92]

Coke may have viewed his work in institutionalizing the common law as a challenge thrown out to the civil law, a legal regime which traced its ancestry more directly to the classical world. With the *Reports* and *Institutes,* he asserted a claim to be the true heir of Cicero and Quintilian. In his works, the common law was raised to the status of the law those noble orators had mastered.[93]

The other comment was an off-hand remark by Coke's brother judge Sir

---

91. *Prohibitions del Roy, supra* n. 16, 12 Co. Rep. at 65, 77 Eng. Rep. at 1343.
92. Sir Thomas Elyot, *supra* n. 56, at 125.
93. Richard Helgerson has perceptively written:
   The law-French cases [of the *Reports*] address a purely professional audience and insert them into a textual sequence that stretches from the yearbooks . . . down to the court reports of our own time. The prefaces, printed in both Latin and English but not in law French, speak to a broader English and even continental readership. . . . These were working books, books that every common lawyer needed to own and consult. But they were also ideal figurations of the legal community and the nation—books that told not only how the law functioned and what the courts had decided but also what England was and what part lawyers had in the making of its identity.—Richard Helgerson, *Forms of Nationhood: The Elizabethan Writing of England* (Chicago: University of Chicago Press, 1992), 86.

John Dodderidge. Toward the end of *The English Lawyer,* Dodderidge discussed the role invention played in the law. Dodderidge noted that Sergeant-at-Law Richard Morgan, in Edward VI's day, had distinguished two kinds of arguments. *"Il y sont deux principall choses sur que Arguments poiens este fait, s. nostre Maximes, & reason, le Mere de touts Leyes, &c."* Dodderidge elaborated:

> I think by the latter of these, the use of argumentation upon reasons drawn from the logical place of invention, are to be understood; as namely, to argue and reason in cases of debate, from the causes, effects, parts, consequents, mischiefs, and inconveniences, and such like . . . which kind or course of Argument is much used in ancient books, when as there were fewest books of reports extant.[94]

This shift, from argumentation to citation, was the juncture in which Coke appeared as Janus. As a pleader, Coke had imbibed the Ciceronian tradition. As a reporter, his work was instrumental in opening a new age for the common law. For rising generations of lawyers, an argument's validity would be judged not by general reason or plausibility, but by its consonance with precedent. Coke's *Reports* and *Institutes* provided a substitute for the fabric of invention.

Conclusion

The common law continues to draw on rhetoric in its assertion that decisions should be consonant with reason. In the "Grand Tradition" of the common law, Karl Llewellyn observed, justice is most effective where reason provides the template for decision-making: "Each rule with a singing reason apparent on its face, each rule a rule whose reason guides and even controls application according to the double maxim: *the rule follows where its reason leads; where the reason stops, there stops the rule."*[95] This outlook descends from the rhetorical tradition, which sees reason flowing through oratory into action. Llewellyn's call for rules which sing of reason is a modern embroidery of Cicero's ideal

---

94. John Dodderidge, *The English Lawyer, supra* n. 90, at 261. Morgan went on to become Chief Justice of Common Pleas under Mary Tudor. This quotation comes from his argument in the case of *Colthirst* v. *Bejushin,* 1 Plowd. 21, 75 Eng. Rep. 33 (1550), the decision which established the contingent remainder.

95. Karl N. Llewellyn, *The Bramble Bush: On Our Law and Its Study* (1930; Dobbs Ferry, New York: Oceana Press, 1960), 189. The reason of which Llewellyn speaks is never quite an abstract term. It may be better understood as the expert understandings of prior judges who have considered the issue; the harmony, synchronization, and internal coherence of the justice system; the sense a decision makes when tested against everyday practice. See further Karl N. Llewellyn, *The Common Law Tradition: Deciding Appeals* (Boston: Little, Brown, 1960), 36–37.

of uniting *oratio* with *ratio*. Indeed, Llewellyn argued that the law school curriculum should include the topic of "Spokesmanship."[96]

In the Elizabethan world—in the rhetorical context which Coke understood—to praise the orator and to value rhetoric (the methodology upon which the orator relied) was to praise courts which forthrightly weighed policy in making decisions.[97] To praise the orator for wisdom or morality, as Cicero and Quintilian had done, recognized that judicial decisions were never made in the abstract. Each involved real-world consequences which would be either good or bad, intelligent or unworkable. To speak of rhetoric's appeal to the emotions revealed an awareness that decision-making should take into account all those matters of intuition and conscience which influence emotion. To hail the orator's role in public life, to applaud oratory as a catalyst for action, was to recognize the perils of inaction.

Where rhetoric was connected with law and with social organization, jurisprudence could not be seen as a purely doctrinal matter; its sociological dimension had to be recognized. A judge trained in rhetoric was thoroughly prepared to weigh political and economic factors. Drawing morals was practice in making decisions. Preparing orations was practice in justifying decisions, in making right choices convincing. The active, constructive role which Coke pursued in his career as jurisprudent and judge can be described as a function of such rhetorical postulates. And this rhetorical inheritance remains very important to Anglo-American law: the idealized figure of the classical orator bears a striking resemblance to the idealized figure of the common-law judge.

96. This he envisioned as a capacity directly descended from the disciplines of classical rhetoric and medieval dialectic, but framed more broadly so as to inculcate a respect for the working of the legal system—a means of developing attorneys who in representing individual clients would display a judge's respect for "the rival goals of victory and reconciliation." Llewellyn, *The Bramble Bush, supra* n. 95, at 185–86.

97. This is not necessarily to idealize Coke, who made obstinacy and energy do double duty for subtler, finer qualities. Nor is it necessarily to bless the union of law and politics. In the generation after Coke, the English judiciary played an active role in enforcing the policies of Charles I, with disastrous results for both crown and bench. See W. J. Jones, *Politics and the Bench: The Judges and the Origins of the English Civil War* (London: George Allen & Unwin, 1971).

The Common Lawyers and
the Chancery: 1616

SIR JOHN BAKER

❧ ❧ ❧

Sixteen sixteen was a catastrophic year in the history of the English judicial system: a year, wrote Bacon,[1] "consecrate to justice." The story of the political, legal and personal controversies which reached a climax in that year is well known, for in some ways those controversies formed the first phase of the seventeenth century constitutional revolution.[2] But the story of the dispute between the common lawyers and the Chancery will bear telling in detail.[3] The viewpoint of Coke and his supporters has been glossed over by most writers on the subject, who have tended to accept Gardiner's statement that on the Chancery question "it has been universally admitted that Coke was in the wrong."[4] Yet it is clear that Coke's fears about the rule of law were shared by many of his brethren and his profession. The common law, because of its appearance of antiquity and continuity, commanded some popular support, whereas the newer systems, most of them worked by Civil lawyers, were often associated with unlimited royal prerogative and tyranny. In the first decade of his reign, King James I had evinced little sympathy for the common law in spite of his outward affirmations,[5] and it was widely rumored that he wished to replace it with the Civil Law;[6] the arguments over prohibitions and prerogative courts

"The Common Lawyers and the Chancery: 1616" is reprinted by permission of John H. Baker. Originally published in the *Irish Jurist,* new series 9 (1969): 368–92.

1. "A Memorial for His Majesty": J. Spedding, *Letters and Life of Francis Bacon* (1869), vol. 5, p. 349.
2. C. H. McIlwain, *Political Works of James I* (1918), p. xl.
3. This is not intended as a criticism of the article by J. P. Dawson, "Coke and Ellesmere disinterred: The Attack on the Chancery in 1616" (1941) 36 *Illinois Law Review* 127. The aim of the present study is to examine in greater detail the events as they happened, and contemporary reactions to them.
4. S. R. Gardiner, *History of England* (1883), vol. 3, p. 24.
5. See J. P. Kenyon, *The Stuart Constitution* (1966), p. 91.
6. James strongly denied the rumors on several occasions: *e.g.* speech in Parliament, 21 March, 1609,

were at least partly caused by the fear of Civil Law encroachments.[7] When barristers could be imprisoned for impugning the prerogative at the bar,[8] and the superior judges coerced into extra-judicial consultations with the King,[9] there was some cause for anxiety about the independence of the common law.

The difficulty in making a balanced judgment in hindsight arises largely from the fact that the Bacon-Ellesmere material is super-abundant, whereas anti-prerogative opinions were safer in the mind than on paper. This imbalance is reflected in Spedding's biased account of Bacon's part in the events of 1616. In restoring the balance, one manuscript in particular has been heavily drawn upon here: a volume of law reports written by Timothy Tourneur, a barrister of Gray's Inn.[10] In 1616 he was thirty years old and of five years' standing at the Bar, and although some of his views are strong they deserve respect because of his position. Tourneur was a Welsh judge under Charles I, out of office during the Interregnum, and near the end of his days, in 1669, one of the oldest serjeants at law ever created.[11]

The General Background

The story has been told in several ways. It is one aspect of the fall of Coke through his opposition to James I and the absolute prerogative.[12] Coke came

---

Political Works (ed. McIlwain), p. 310; *His Majesties Speach in the Starre Chamber the xx of June 1616*, sig. B4; *Cal. State Papers* (Dom. 1611–1618), p. 375. Evidently the rumor persisted.

7. See McIlwain, *op. cit.*, pp. xl–xli, lxxxvii–lxxxix; J. Simon, "Dr. Cowell" [1968] *Cambridge Law Journal* 260; R. Usher, *The Rise and Fall of the High Commission* (1968 Repr.), pp. 149–221.

8. *E.g.*, Nicholas Fuller (1607) and James Whitelocke (1613). Taswell-Langmead said of these cases, "James was careful to do what he could to repress the independence of the Bar": *English Constitutional History* (1880 ed.), p. 515 n. *Cf.* Plucknett's 11th ed. (1960), p. 352. James declared in 1616 that it was blasphemy to question his prerogative at the bar: speech in Council on 6 June, *Acts of the Privy Council 1615–1616* (1925), p. 602; *His Majesties Speach etc.*, sig. Dv, D3.

9. *Infra*, note 14.

10. Brit. Mus. MS. Add. 35957, from the Hardwicke collection. At the top of f. 1 the book claims to be *Liber Timothei Tourneur de Gr. Inne appr. in lege*, and there is internal evidence confirming that he was its author and not merely an owner. At f. 124*v* he records the birth of his daughter Susan Tourneur on 1 November, 1622, and he also reports events at Chester (f. 77*v*) and Ludlow (f. 124*v*), which was his home country. There is also some Gray's Inn material. The manuscript may be compared with a collection by Tourneur, MS. Ogden 29 in the library of University College, London. The latter includes an autobiographical memorandum (f. 116) and both have references to Branlingham's reports, which the writer has not met with elsewhere.

11. W. R. Williams, *Lives of the Welsh Judges* (1899), p. 38. He took the coif at 85, and was excused the procession on foot to Westminster: Edward Ward, *Notebook 1668–1678*, Lincoln's Inn MS. Misc. 500, f. 53*v*. He died in 1677.

12. *E.g.*, S. R. Gardiner, *History of England* (1883), vol. 3, pp. 1 *et seq.*

into frequent conflict with the King over the extent of the residuary or extraordinary jurisdiction of the Crown, and in 1608 he is supposed to have provoked
James to physical anger by denying the authority of the High Commission and
asserting that the King, being unlearned in the law, ought not to decide cases
in person.[13] To Coke, the King was under God and the law, which the King
construed to mean under God and the common law judges. The King believed
himself answerable to God alone, and that all judicial authority was received
through himself as God's vicegerent on Earth. The dispute came to a head in
1616 after several attempts by the King to stay argument in cases touching his
prerogative rights until the judges had consulted him. Coke resolutely resisted
such attempts to interfere with the judiciary,[14] and his conduct in the Privy
Council on June 6, 1616[15] resulted in his dismissal later in the year.

   Alternatively, the story has been told as the culmination of a long-standing
conflict between the common lawyers and the jurisdictions based on discretion, Civil Law, and prerogative.[16] Coke was ever vigilant to keep extraordinary
jurisdictions within their bounds, and while he was on the bench prohibitions
issued daily to the ecclesiastical courts, the Admiralty, Requests, and provincial conciliar or equity courts. His enemies represented his surveillance as an
encroachment on the prerogative itself,[17] though in fact the King stated openly
that he wished to preserve the jurisdictional *status quo*.[18] The Chancery was
the supreme "prerogative court," and its conflicts with the common law the
most serious of all.

   Thirdly, the events of 1616 are represented as the climax of the personal antagonism between Coke, conservative defender of the old common law, and
Lord Ellesmere, personification of the King in judgment and stout defender
of the royal prerogative. Coke's fall is seen to have been stage-managed by
Francis Bacon, the Attorney-General, anxious to take the Great Seal from the

   13. See R. G. Usher, "James I and Sir Edward Coke" (1903) 18 *English Historical Review* 664. On one
occasion the King said that the judges deserved to be hanged for disobeying his instruction, and that he
could question any of their judgments in person: *ibid.,* p. 673.
   14. *Peacham's Case* (1614) Spedding, *op. cit.,* vol. 5, pp. 90–128; *Case of Rege Inconsulto* (*Brownlow v.
Michel and Cox*) (1615) *Works of Bacon* (1859 ed.), vol. 7, pp. 683–725; 1 Rolle Rep. 188, 206, 228; 3 Bulstrode
32; Moore K.B. 842; *Somerset's Case* (1616) Spedding, *op. cit.,* vol. 5, p. 269, note.
   15. *Case of Commendams* (1616) *Acts of the Privy Council 1615–1616* (1925), pp. 595–609. There are many
copies of this in manuscript. For the proceedings at law see *Colt and Glover v. Bishop of Lichfield and Coventry*
(1614–1616) 1 Rolle Rep. 451, Hobbart 140, Moore K.B. 1262.
   16. *E.g.,* Dawson, *op. cit.,* pp. 128–32.
   17. See Bacon's list of "Innovations Introduced into the Laws and Government" (1616) Spedding, *op.
cit.,* vol. 6, pp. 90–93.
   18. Speech in Parliament 21 March, 1609, *Political Works* (ed. McIlwain), p. 312; *His Majesties Speach in
the Starre Chamber the xx of June 1616,* sig. D2.

moribund Ellesmere. There is some evidence that Bacon's advancement to be a Privy Councillor in 1616[19] was upon condition that he "exercise his power to disgrace the Lord Coke,"[20] a task which he discharged successfully. With these great guns aimed at Coke, questions of principle lost much of their significance.

Ellesmere and the Common Law

The dispute between Coke and Ellesmere was not about the need for equity in suitable cases, but about the finality of judgments at common law and the enlargement of Chancery jurisdiction at the expense of the law courts.[21] Coke never denied the need for a system of equity, though he sometimes adopted a restrictive view of its scope. He believed that the King's Bench was bound to watch all other courts to ensure that they did not exceed their powers; this was an established attitude long before Coke came to office.[22]

Interference with common law judgments had been a source of complaint for over a century.[23] One of the Lords' articles against Wolsey had charged that "the said Lord Cardinall hath examined divers and many matters in the Chancery after judgment thereof given at the common law, in subversion of your lawes."[24] There were two basic objections to such interference. Firstly, parties would try their luck at common law, and if unsuccessful could re-open the whole case in Chancery.[25] This was, in effect, an appeal from a judgment at law, a procedure regarded by many as unconstitutional. Secondly, and as a

19. He was sworn on 9 June, having obtained the favor through Villiers: Spedding, *op. cit.,* vol. 5, pp. 255, 260, 347–349. After this date he ceased to practice at the Bar: *ibid.,* p. 348; R. Hutton, *Diary vol. I,* Univ. Lib. Camb. MS. Add. 6862, f. 98.

20. MS. Add. 35957, f. 55: "*Et ceo advancement de Bacon ut audivi fuit sur certen purposes et condicions (come Shileton dit a moy) q'il exercisera son power a disgracer le Seignor Coke. . . .*" His informant was probably Richard Shilton of the Inner Temple, a favorite of Villiers, who became Attorney-General in 1625 (D.N.B.; Brit. Mus. MS. Lansd. 1118, f. 166). Coke had fallen foul of Villiers over a patent office in the King's Bench: see Gardiner, *op. cit.,* vol. 3, pp. 27–35. Bacon regarded Coke as a rival contender for the Seal: Spedding, *op. cit.,* p. 242.

21. The struggle has therefore been interpreted as a competition for judicial remuneration: D.E.C. Yale, *Lord Nottingham's Treatises* (1965), pp. 9–10; J. Simon, "Dr. Cowell" [1968] *Camb. L.J.* at p. 265.

22. W. J. Jones, *The Elizabethan Court of Chancery* (1967), pp. 463 *et seq.*

23. An early example is M.22 E.4, 37, *pl.* 6, *per* Hussey C.J.

24. Articles of 1 December, 1529, 4 *Inst.* 91, no. 20. *Cf.* no. 26. Coke had seen the original document (3 *Inst.* 124), which is now lost: A. F. Pollard, *Wolsey* (1929), p. 261, note 3.

25. MS. Add. 35957, f. 55v: "*Et ceo est ore usuall que quant le defendant al comon ley ad try son fortunes la et* stood out all the course of the law and in the end the matter adjudged against him then will he exhibite his bill in Chauncery and grownd yt upon poinctes of equitie for which he might have preferred his suite in Chauncery before the judgment *et issint dowble et infinite vexacion.*"

consequence, the value and finality of the judgment was lessened, and the law itself might have been subverted because litigants would bypass the law and commence their suits in Chancery.[26]

The answer of the Chancellor was that the suit in equity was not an appeal to correct the legal decision, but a means of correcting the corrupt conscience of a party who sought to avail himself of a judgment contrary to equity.[27] Whether or not the suit was an abuse of the Chancery or the law courts was a matter of conscience for the Chancellor, and not the King's Bench, to decide.[28]

In 1598 this question, having caused some bad feeling, was referred to all the judges of England assembled in the Exchequer Chamber.[29] Coke participated in the arguments, which went over all the grounds which were to be raised in 1616, and according to his report all the judges except Walmsley J. held that Chancery could not re-examine matters after judgment at law:

> It would be perilous to permit men after judgment and trial in law to surmise matter in equity and by this to put him who recovered to excessive charges. And by these means suits would be infinite and no one could be in peace for anything that the law had given him by judgment. But a contentious person, who had an unquiet spirit, might continually surmise matter in equity and so vex him who recovered endlessly; which would be a great inconvenience. And it is absurd that a court, which as to equity is not a court of record, should control judgments which are of record.[30]

The judges also ruled, according to Coke, that such a suit in Chancery was prohibited by the statutes of 4 Hen. 4, c. 23 and 27 Edw. 3, c. 1. The resolution was communicated to Lord Keeper Egerton by Popham C.J., who evidently made no protest at that time. Whether Coke's report is trustworthy is an open question since no independent report has so far come to light. Neither is it certain why Walmsley J. dissented from the resolution, because in 1600 he said of the Court of Requests:

26. 3 *Inst.* 124–25. See also S. F. C. Milsom, *Historical Foundations of the Common Law* (1969), p. 84.

27. *Earl of Oxford's Case* (1615) 1 Cha. Rep., pt. i, pp. 1–16. In *Throgmorton's Case* (note 29, *infra*), counsel argued *"que l'entention del plaintiff ne fuit a impeacher les ditz iudgmentes mes ore confessant les iudgmentes d'estre relieve pur matter in equitie."*

28. W. J. Jones, *op. cit.*, pp. 484–85.

29. *Finch v. Throgmorton* cited 3 *Inst.* 124, 4 *Inst.* 86, 3 Buls. 118, Cro. Jac. 344. A full report, in Coke's own hand, is to be found in Brit. Mus. MS. Harl. 6686, ff. 226*v*–29. The matter was referred to the judges because it was *"de graunde consequence, et semblable d'estre president a multes auters"* (*ibid.*, f. 227). Dawson traced the case in the Chancery Order Book, which confirms that Egerton consulted the judges: *op. cit.*, pp. 134–35.

30. *Ibid.*, f. 228 (translated). For Coke's attack on the Chancery on the ground that it was not a court of record, see S. E. Thorne in 2 *Toronto Law Journal* at p. 47.

We have been informed that they assume to call our judgments in question and to annihilate them and to order that the party release the judgments, or to imprison him. To which it was said by the whole court that it is good to lay informations on the statute of Edward III for calling the judgments in question where they have nothing to do with them.[31]

In 1606, in another case concerning the Court of Requests, Popham C.J. apparently asserted that a bill in equity might be preferred after a judgment at law, and Coke, standing at the bar, protested:

If this were the law then the statute of 4 H. 4, c. 23 would serve for little or nothing . . . And then also it would seem that all injunctions out of these courts of equity are idle, if they may as well decree it after judgment. And he said that it had been resolved accordingly by all the judges in a case in which he had been of counsel.[32]

Coke was appointed Chief Justice of the Common Pleas in June 1606, and as he began his crusade to uphold the supremacy of the common law, Egerton (created Lord Ellesmere in 1603) began to assert the supremacy of the Chancery over the courts of law in a dogmatic fashion. As Ellesmere grew older he became more obstinate and difficult and opposed to the common law.[33] He regarded himself as outside and above the rest of the judiciary.[34] In 1613, Fleming C.J. had written to the King complaining that the Chancellor was hearing suits which were determinable at law, and Ellesmere caused the King to be greatly offended, and persuaded him to hear his law officers "confute and reproach" the Chief Justices,[35] a humiliating technique to which he was to resort again in 1616. Sergeant Hutton witnessed that Ellesmere became more choleric and "in

31. *Smith's Case* (1600) Inner Temple MS. Barrington 6, f. 43v (translated). The reference to the statute of *praemunire* is interesting in the light of the events to come in 1616.

32. *Cardinall v. De la Broke* (1606) Inner Temple MS. Barrington 7, ff. 209v–10 (translated). The reporter ended "*Quere de cest matter.*" It would seem strange if Popham C.J. had forgotten the decision of 1598, but he died a year later and may have been amnesic.

33. Chamberlain to Carleton, 29 June, 1615, *Letters of John Chamberlain* (ed. McClure, 1939), vol. 1, p. 604 (ascribes defects to sourness of age). In an obituary letter Chamberlain says he "left but an indifferent name beeing accounted too sowre, severe and implacable, an ennemie to parlements and the common law, only to maintain his owne greatnes, and the exorbitant jurisdiction of his court of chauncerie": *ibid.*, vol. 2, p. 65.

34. E. Coke, "Poyntes dangerous et absurd affirme devant le Roy per Egerton Chancellor," copied (from Coke's *vade mecum*) in U.C.L. MS. Ogden 29 (*supra*, note 10), f. 569, no. 13.

35. *Ibid.*, no. 11. Coke, then Chief Justice of the Common Pleas, also submitted a written opinion that this precedent "*tend al subvercion del ley et justice.*" Egerton had promised the King not to exceed his jurisdiction (*infra*, note 109), and soon after receiving the Seal in 1596 had promised not to give "*ascun reliefe in equitie contrary a ascun positive ground in ley*" nor aid in any case "*ou ascun bon remedy d'estre ew per comon ley*": *Note,* Inner Temple MS. Petyt 561/5, f. 58v.

many things laboured to derogate from the common law and the judges,"[36] and Tourneur described him as "*acerrimus propugnator* of the Chauncerye and Starchamber, in a worde the bane of the law, yet not for any hate he bare yt but for the love he bare to his owne honor to greaten himself by the fall of others."[37] One lawyer went so far as to say he was "the greatest enemye to the common law that ever did bear office of state in this kingdome."[38]

The Proceedings of 1614–1616

Coke was translated to the King's Bench in October 1613 and was thus given more power to attack the prerogative courts. By this time the excesses of Ellesmere's Chancery were becoming intolerable to common lawyers. Ellesmere himself was a good lawyer and judge, but he was growing very old and relying more and more on his subordinates, and less and less on the judges assistant. The appointment of Sir Julius Caesar as Master of the Rolls in 1614 on the death of Sir Edward Phillips[39] exacerbated the lawyers. He was a Civil lawyer by training, ignorant of Chancery procedure, unwilling to accept advice, and unable to dispatch business efficiently.[40] The constitutional questions were approaching a climax, and the Chancery was, under Ellesmere, a bastion of the prerogative. In 1614 the House of Commons heard a bill to prevent judgments at common law from being questioned in other courts, "for the peace of the King's subjects," though it proceeded no further than its first reading.[41] In the same year Coke refused to obey a Chancery injunction to stay execution of a judgment in the King's Bench,[42] and also considered the possibility of sending

36. R. Hutton, *Diary vol. 1,* Univ. Lib. Camb. MS. Add. 6862, f. 126 (obituary): "*il fuit un home de grand et profound judgment, un eloquent speaker, et uncore in son daren temps il deveigne plus chollerick et oppose le jurisdiction del common ley et inlarge le jurisdiction del Chancery, et il in plusors choses a derogate del common ley et del judges.*"

37. M.S. Add. 35957, f. 81*v.* (obituary). He has some good things to say; like Hutton he acknowledges his profound judgment and pleasing tone of voice.

38. J. Whitelocke, *Liber Famelicus,* Camden Soc. (O.S.), vol. 70, p. 53. Whitelocke, a barrister of the Middle Temple, had been badly treated by Ellesmere for defending the Chancery jurisdiction against the Commissioners for the Office of Earl Marshal; *ibid.,* pp. 34–40; *supra,* note 8.

39. Phillips was a sergeant at law and respected by the lawyers. In *Wraynham's case* (1618) a man was punished by the Star Chamber for defaming Phillips (though dead) and Coke praised his memory very highly: Univ. Lib. Camb. MS. Dd. iii. 87, art. 7, f. 13.

40. Hutton, *op. cit.,* f. 89, wrote of his appointment "*pur le quel [office] in l'opinion de plusors sages del ley il fuit grandment unapt,*" Tourneur, *op. cit.* f. 79*v.,* says he was "*trop ignorant in le course del Chancery et nient hable a faire ascun despatch.*" See also E. Foss, *The Judges of England* (1857), vol. 6, p. 270.

41. Draft Bill, 3 June, 1614, in the House of Lords Library: H.M.C. *Third Report,* Appendix p. 15.

42. *Heath v. Ridley* (1614) 2 Bulstrode 194, Cro. Jac. 335.

prohibitions to the Chancery.[43] However, the vehicle of interference was not to be the prohibition, but the writ of *habeas corpus*. The use of this writ to examine the lawfulness of a committal by the Chancellor was established before Coke's time.[44] Some of the cases which came before the King's Bench were most unmeritorious, but a judge cannot prearrange cases on which to make a point of principle. Coke's duty, as he saw it, was to see that the law had been observed in cases which came before him, regardless of their merits.

Glanvill's Case

The first case in the series was, indeed, singularly lacking in merit. Richard Glanvill, an unscrupulous London jeweller, had in 1606 sold Francis Courtney a topaz which he misrepresented as a diamond, and thereby obtained an unduly high price. Glanvill's accomplice, Davies, pretended to be the servant of a goldsmith, Hampton, and took an obligation in Hampton's name for the price. Glanvill recovered this sum by using Hampton's name. Apparently judgment had been obtained without the privity of Courtney or the judges by the fraudulent method of paying an attorney to confess judgment out of term on Courtney's behalf. The judgment was affirmed on error, but pending the writ of error Courtney had preferred a bill in Chancery. Notwithstanding the judgment in error, the Master of the Rolls decreed a rescission of the sale, fixing a proper price for the stone, and ordered that Hampton should be procured to release the judgment at law.[45] It was the last part of the decree which became the basis of complaint, because the Chancery had not previously claimed the power to interfere with the judgment itself.[46]

Glanvill refused to obey the decree and was committed, in 1613. In Michaelmas Term 1614 he was removed into the King's Bench by *habeas corpus,* and his

43. *Wright's Case* (1614) Moore K.B. 836, 1 Rolle Rep. 71. There was some authority for this: Fitz. Abr. *Prohibition, pl.* 11 (13 Edw. 3); R. Compton, *L'Authoritie et Jurisdiction des Courts* (1594), pp. 56–57; *Note,* Cary 3.

44. M.22 E.4, 37, *pl.* 6, *per* Hussey C.J.; *Astwick's Case* (1567) Moore K.B. 839; *Humfrey v. Humfrey* (1577) Dalison 81, 3 Leonard 18, *per* Bendlowes sjt.; *Michell's Case* (1577) Moore K.B. 839; *Addis' Case* (1609) Cro. Jac. 219; *Anon.* (no date) Moore K.B. 916.

45. See "Richard Glanvill's Case 4° Jacobi," Brit. Mus. MS. Harl. 1767, f. 37; MS. Harl. 4265, f. 75v; "The state of the cause between Richard Glanvill citizen and goldsmith of London and Francis Courtney Esquire," Brit. Mus. MS. Lansd. 163, f. 122; and the law reports cited below.

46. *Cobb v. Nore* (1465), a very similar case, was relied on: the problem had then been referred to a special commission of the Chancellor and some judges. This, according to Coke, showed that the Chancellor could not deal with it of his own authority. The case had been discovered by Coke as counsel in *Throgmorton's Case:* Brit. Mus. MS. Harl. 6686, ff. 212v, 227v. Cf. 3 *Inst.* 124, 4 *Inst.* 86.

counsel prayed his discharge. The court of equity, said counsel, had imprisoned him for a matter of which he had two judgments at law. Coke exclaimed
"So long as I have this coif on my head I will not allow this,"[47] and expressed
his surprise that the Chancellor had gone back on his promise not to interfere
with judgments at law. Glanvill was bailed until Hilary Term when, because
the return gave no cause for the commitment, he was released.[48]

Lord Ellesmere joined battle by committing Glanvill again, on 7 May, 1615.
A new *habeas corpus* was sued out in Trinity Term, and this time the return
was: *quod commissus fuit prisone per mandatum Thome Domini Ellesmere Cancellarii Anglie.* The judges, following the precedents, held the return bad for
its generality.[49] According to Coke, this decision was the result of a conference with all the judges of England.[50] There one may leave Glanvill for the
moment, but it was by no means the end of his story.

It may have been unfortunate that the issue was raised in a case so devoid of
merit. Yet the question at issue was the validity of the return, and according to
all the judges at that time the King's Bench were entitled to ask not merely *who*
committed the prisoner but *why.* For this purpose, no judicial notice could be
taken of the merits.

Apsley and Ruswell

Two cases less deficient in merit were debated at the same time as *Glanvill's
Case.* Michael Apsley had been in the Fleet for seven years for contempt of
Chancery. Ruswell, who had refused to obey an illegal decree[51] had been committed on 30 May, 1614, *per consideratione curie Cancellarie Domini Regis pro
contemptu eidem Curie.* These two cases, and others,[52] came before the King's
Bench in Easter Term 1615. In each case the return was general. After an adjournment until Trinity Term, and several debates, privately in Coke's house
and in open court, Coke delivered the unanimous opinion of the judges that
the returns were bad. Ruswell's return was altered later in the Term so as to set

---

47. 1 Rolle Rep. 111.
48. *Ibid.,* 2 Bulstrode 302, Moore K.B. 838, Cro. Jac. 343.
49. 2 Bulstrode 302, 1 Rolle Rep. 218. *Cf.* the cases cited in note 42, *supra.*
50. MS. Add. 35957, f. 2*v.*
51. The decree was contrary to the Statute of Wills and was later reversed by Bacon: Rolle Abr. *Chancerie*
(S) 5. Yelverton, Att.-Gen., spoke strongly against the decree: MS. Add. 35957, f. 82.
52. 1 Rolle Rep. 193.

out the decree in detail. George Croke, who complained that his conduct was being watched,[53] argued that the matter was outside the Chancellor's jurisdiction. The case was adjourned because of a doubt,[54] and no more was heard of it until 1617 when hostilities were over.

Allen's Case

The line was drawn in the case of Allen, the archetype inhumane creditor. The matter arose out of the bankruptcy of one Edwards, whose lands were sold at a low price to Allen. Later the creditors entered into a composition agreement whereby Allen was to convey the land to two of the creditors, Smith and Wood, who would bind themselves to pay out ten shillings in the pound to all the others. Allen then repudiated the agreement and sued in Chancery for possession, which was decreed to him. He evicted Edwards' children "in frost and snowe" despite the undersheriff's tearful plea for compassion. When the parents died of plague *pendente lite* Lord Ellesmere re-opened the case, out of humanity, and assigned Sergeant Francis Moore to be of counsel for the children *in forma pauperis.* A new, and more just, decree was made and for refusing to perform it Allen was committed on 13 November, 1613. Apparently he had two judgments at law relating to the debts, but he had instituted the Chancery suit himself and had previously assented to the composition agreement.[55] It was difficult to find any ground for his *habeas corpus* application, and the King's Bench refused to deliver him.[56] These facts have been related because Allen re-appears a little later in the dispute.

These cases opened the way for the collision between Coke and Ellesmere. This collision occurred, but with less impact than might have been expected, in Michaelmas Term 1615 in an important case involving the Master of Magdalene College, Cambridge.

---

53. Brit. Mus. MS. Harl. 1691, f. 55v: "*del commencement que il parle en cest cause il ad estre watche: mes hors del son duty al court il voile parler.*" In the case of *Commendams,* the Bishop of Winchester had been watching for the Crown: *Acts of the Privy Council 1615–1616,* p. 596. And in the case of *Rege Inconsulto,* Secretary Winwood had sat below the judges in the King's Bench "*et come fuit report in le Sale le Secretary fuit enioyne per le Roy d'estre present al argument*": MS. Add. 35957, f. 37.
54. 1 Rolle Rep. 219. Coke is reported to have said, "*Cest returne induce nous al tryer le bill et answer et pur ceo portes ceux en court*": MS. Harl. 1691, f. 55v.
55. "Allen's Case in Chancery," Brit. Mus. MS. Harl. 1767, f. 39; MS. Harl. 4265, f. 78.
56. Moore K.B. 840.

The Earl of Oxford's Case

The Chancellor was well aware of the preceding events and in September had set the King's counsel to investigate precedents for him by delivering them a treatise with his own reasons in it.[57] The test case was to be *The Earl of Oxford's Case,* the last of the *habeas corpus* applications before 1616. Legal historians have attached much significance to this case. Perhaps they have given it too much significance, because it did not result in a final decision of the question.

The case concerned the power of the Chancery to interfere with the legal title to land, contrary to statute, on the basis that a person who built houses on another person's land ought to be compensated in equity. In 1613 an action of ejectment had been brought in the King's Bench to try the Earl's title to a lease of Covent Garden by Magdalene College. The title, which depended on certain statutes, was discussed by the judges with a great deal of erudition and in 1615 they decided against the plaintiff.[58] The plaintiff then preferred a bill in Chancery, and the defendant demurred on the ground that he had had judgment at law. Sir John Tindal, Master in Chancery, ordered him to make answer, and for refusing to do so he was in October 1615 committed to the Fleet. The plaintiff was allowed to proceed in default of answer. Lord Ellesmere took the opportunity to explain the nature of his jurisdiction and its relationship with the law in a judgment familiar to generations of law students.[59] The Chancery did not meddle with the judgment, said Lord Ellesmere, but with the "hard conscience of the party."

No doubt this was intended as a challenge to Coke. Coke was forced to accept it when the defendants, Dr. Googe[60] and the lessee Smith, came before the King's Bench on *habeas corpus.* The return stated that they had been committed to the Fleet by order of the Chancery for refusing to answer the bill, which was specified. Sergeant Bawtrey moved for their release, because the matter in the bill had already been determined at law and the Chancery suit

57. This had a wide circulation in manuscript. In the British Museum are at least nine copies. It was printed in 1641 as *The Privileges and Prerogatives of the High Court of Chancery.*

58. *The Case of Magdalene College (Warren v. Smith)* (1615) 11 Rep. 66, Cro. Jac. 364, 1 Rolle Rep. 151. Dodderidge J. later stated, "There never was any learned man (if he were an honest man) that was of another opinion than we were of, in the giving of this judgment (unless he was a time-server)": 3 Bulstrode 116.

59. *The Earl of Oxford's Case (Oxford and Smith v. Googe and Wood)* (1615) 1 Cha. Rep., pt. i, 1; White and Tudor, *Leading Cases in Equity* (1928 ed.) vol. 1, pp. 615–21. The date of committal is variously given as 22 October (*ibid.*), 31 October (1 Rolle Rep. 277) and 21 October (Brit. Mus. MS. Harl. 1767, f. 30*v;* MS. Harl. 4265, f. 68*v;* Univ. Lib. Camb. MS. Mm. i. 43, f. 466).

60. Barnaby Googe or Gouch, M.A., LL.D., Master of Magdalene College, Cambridge 1604–1626.

was contrary to the statute of 1403. Coke answered that if the matter did appear to be the same, the court would deliver the prisoners, because their committal would be contrary to statute and common law. Dodderidge J. agreed with Coke that "It would tend to the downfall of the common law, if judgments here given should be suffered to be called in question in courts of equity." There followed a debate as to whether the matter did appear to be the same, and the argument ended inconclusively. Coke told counsel, "It is better for you that we hear no more of it." The prisoners were bailed until the next term on sureties to attend *de die in diem,* but nothing more was done.[61]

The impression given by the reports is that Coke was unwilling to take a stand against Ellesmere on *habeas corpus.*[62] For one thing, the King had personally intervened to remonstrate with his two principal judges about their "disgraceful" disputes, and told them to refer cases of difficulty to himself.[63] And then the state trial of Somerset distracted both Coke and Ellesmere from pursuing their personal rivalries.[64] Possibly Coke would have preferred that the question were raised in such a way that it could be tried by jury, so that the judges took no personal responsibility for the result. Whatever the reason, no more was heard of *habeas corpus* to examine Chancery decrees.

The dispute began to move into the sphere of the criminal law. In *Dr. Googe's Case* Coke referred to the two statutes which were to figure largely in the arguments which followed, the 27 Edw. 3, st. 1, c. 1 and the 4 Hen. 4, c. 23. Both had been relied on in 1598 in *Throgmorton's Case.* Back in 1614 Coke had remarked, "It is much to be wondered that none will inform upon these laws in such cases against the party that procures such injunctions after judgments at common law . . . ,"[65] and he had dropped the same hint on other occasions.[66] The statute of 1403, though directed primarily at the Council, could be interpreted to support Coke's proposition in relation to the Chancery.[67] St. Germain, nearly a century earlier, had construed it to include the Chancery,

61. *Dr. Googe's Case* (1615) 1 Rolle Rep. 277, 3 Bulstrode 115.

62. Glanvill, whose word is not gospel, later said of the *habeas corpus* that "Lord Coke misliked it": *loc. cit.* in note 74, *infra.*

63. Winwood to Carleton, 13 July, 1616, *Cal. State Papers* (Dom. 1611–1618), p. 381.

64. Bacon to the King, 27 January 1616, Spedding, *op. cit.,* vol. 5, p. 236; "they will not square while those matters are in hand, so that there is *altum silencium* of that matter."

65. *Heath v. Rydley* (1614) 2 Bulstrode 194.

66. See *Trobervil v. Brent* (1611) 2 Brownlow & Golds. 97; *Wright v. Fowler* (1614) Moore K.B. 836, 1 Rolle Rep. 71, 2 Bulstrode 284; *Glanvill's Case* (1615) Moore K.B. 838.

67. The statute (4 Hen. 4, ch. 23) recited how parties had been brought before the King or his Council in subversion of the common law, and ordained "*q'apres juggement rendu en les courtes nostre seignur le Roy les parties et leur heirs soient en pees tanqe le juggement soit anientiz par atteinte ou par errour . . .*"

for it was better, he said, that an individual should occasionally suffer than that "great vexations and unjust expenses" should be incurred if the law had no end.[68] The statute of Edward III did not cover the case so clearly, for it was designed to restrain appeals to Rome.[69] But Ellesmere and Bacon both conceded that it included ecclesiastical courts since the Reformation, and stood upon the point that the Chancery did not meddle with judgments directly. In 1614 Sir Anthony Mildmay was convicted of *praemunire* for committing a party by authority of his office as a Commissioner of Sewers, contrary to a judgment at law.[70] Coke believed the same could be done with the Chancery, and he was not the first to hold this belief. In 1588 John Hele, a bencher of the Inner Temple, had been indicted on the statute for counselling a Chancery suit after a judgment at law. The indictment had been quashed for misnomer, but the judges endorsed it that the matter was good.[71] No doubt reliance was placed on the more doubtful statute because of the penalties contained in it, and the absence of a specific sanction in the statute of 1403. It could not be long before someone would take Coke's hint, and to the undoing of the common lawyers' case it was taken up by the least deserving characters.

The Indictments for Praemunire

The rogue Glanvill after his release by the King's Bench had incubated an enthusiasm for the common law which manifested itself in an irresponsible scheme to overthrow the Chancery. Fired with this nefarious ardor, he visited the Fleet prison and spread the news to the prisoners that they might all be freed if they brought *habeas corpus* as he had done.[72] He calumniated Elles-

68. *Doctor and Student,* book 1, ch. 18. *Accord.* R. Crompton, *L'Authoritie et Jurisdiction des Courts* (1594), pp. 41, 66, 67.

69. The relevant words of the 27 Edw. 3, st. 1, ch. 1, imposed the penalties of *praemunire* on all lieges of the King who *"suent en autri court a deffaire ou empescher les juggements renduz en la Court le Roi." "Autri court"* means "the court of another" and not "any other court." Chancery and King's Bench were both courts of the King.

70. *Mildmay's Case* (1614) 2 Bulstrode 197, Cro. Jac. 336.

71. *Hele's Case* (1588) 2 Leonard 115, 3 *Inst.* 124, Crompton, *op. cit.,* pp. 57–58. The Chancellor committed the counsel who drew the indictment to the Fleet and expressed his wonder at such a proceeding "to blemish and deface the authority of the court": C. Monro, *Acta Cancellariae* (1847), pp. 5–8.

72. "The Breviate of the Cause in the Starchamber between the King's Atturney pl. against Allen and Glanvill and Levesay def. 1616": Brit. Mus. MS. Add. 11574, at f. 43. This hitherto unnoticed document in the Caesar papers has been used in the present account, though it must be remembered that it is taken from the prosecutor's brief.

mere, saying that he lived on bribes and was in league with the Devil.[73] Worst of all, he fixed his attentions on the statute of *praemunire*. Why should he not indict the Chancellor and everyone who had persecuted him? The King would surely be grateful for the forfeiture of Ellesmere's estates, and there might be something in that for Glanvill. An indictment was drawn accordingly, but on reflection Glanvill decided it would be politic to proceed, at first, against lesser persons. He enlisted the help of Crown Office lawyers in drawing an indictment, according to Mildmay's precedent, by pretending that he had directions from Coke.[74] The defendants were Courtney, and his counsel and attorney. The bill was preferred in Michaelmas Term 1615, but the grand jury of Middlesex returned it *ignoramus.*

Undaunted, Glanvill enlisted the support of the infamous Allen, and a dishonest scrivener called Levesay. Perhaps he also made representations to the judges, for when the Middlesex grand jury appeared at the bar in Hilary Term 1616 a new article was given in charge by Sir John Croke: "If any man, after a judgment given, had drawn the said judgment to a new examination in any other court."[75] One of the grand jurors was Levesay, and on the last day of term (13 February) he delivered the bills of indictment to his fellows. This time Allen had also preferred a bill, against his Chancery opponents,[76] Sergeant Moore,[77] and Master Sir John Tindal.[78] The accounts of what took place in court are biased, but sufficient evidence was collected to indicate that Coke's behavior was decidedly partial.[79] Though pressed by Levesay, the jurors were unwilling to find the bills true. Coke grew angry. He remanded them two or three times and threatened to commit them, but they were adamant. The foreman insisted on returning *ignoramus,* at which Levesay protested that it

73. *Ibid.,* art. 2. This was the standard complaint of the aggrieved Chancery litigant, and cannot be taken seriously.

74. *Ibid.,* f. 44, art. 5. Glanvill confessed the indictment drawn against Ellesmere, but it was never preferred.

75. Bacon to the King, 21 February, 1616, Spedding, *op. cit.,* vol. 5, p. 251.

76. Smith and Wood. Bacon adds Alderman Bowles (Edwards' mortgagee), but he is not named in the Caesar MS.

77. Moore was "*un graund favorite de Egerton*" (MS. Add. 35957, f. 54*v*). One of the Chancellor's last acts was to try to secure for the sergeant a place as Baron of the Exchequer in 1617: Whitelock, *Liber Famelicus,* p. 54.

78. Tindal was shot in November by an unbalanced litigant.

79. The prosecution brief, preserved among the Ellesmere papers in the Huntington Library, California, (MSS. EL. 5971, 5973), has been published by Professor Thorne: "Praemunire and Sir Edward Coke" (1938) 2 *Huntington Library Quarterly* 85–88. This is presumably the document cited by Lord Campbell in his *Lives of the Lord Chancellors* (1848), vol. 2, pp. 257–58. There is a different summary in the Caesar Papers: MS. Add. 11574, f. 47. See also MS. Add. 35957, f. 54*v*: Spedding, *op. cit.,* vol. 5, p. 251.

was not a unanimous verdict. Coke therefore examined the jurors by the poll, one by one, and counted seventeen against two. The verdict of *ignoramus* was therefore accepted. Coke warned the sheriff to produce a wiser jury the next term, and is said to have told Glanvill and Allen to prepare themselves. Later the same day Coke threatened to foreclose any barrister from practice in the King's Bench if he put his hand to a bill after a judgment at law.[80]

Glanvill and Allen employed themselves in the Lent Vacation following to petition the Privy Council, stating that they had preferred bills of indictment for the King, and if the prosecutions had been successful the King's coffers would be greatly filled.[81] This appeal to the royal avarice was hardly tactful, and the two petitioners before long faced prosecution themselves. Glanvill's last fling was an action of false imprisonment against the Warden of the Fleet and his gaolers. The Warden was actually arrested by a sergeant-at-mace, but of course was promptly discharged by a *supersedeas* from the Chancery. Glanvill's campaign was not allowed to proceed any further.[82]

The Retaliation of Bacon and Ellesmere

These circumstances provided Bacon and Ellesmere with the opportunity they had been waiting for to settle the dispute, and perchance to disgrace Coke at the same time. Bacon complained to James of the "great and public affront" not only to the Chancellor himself ("at a time when he was thought to lie on dying, which was barbarous") but to the Court of Chancery, the court of the King's absolute power.[83] Though Bacon accounted the affair to be "a kind of sickness of my Lord Coke's," he confessed he could not implicate Coke in the prosecutions, and suggested that the real blame lay with the puisne judges.[84] He recommended the disgrace of any judge whose implication could be proved, the removal (but without disgrace) of Coke, and the reproof of all the judges on their knees in Council. The suggestion that an unfair advan-

---

80. *Goodwyn v. Gouldsmithe,* cited 2 *Huntington L.Q.* at p. 88.
81. Copies of both petitions in MS. Add. 11574, ff. 44, 46.
82. *Ibid.,* f. 45, art. 7.
83. Bacon to the King, 21 February, 1616, Spedding, *op. cit.,* vol. 5, pp. 249–254.
84. His caution seems to be political rather than genuine, since Coke's disgrace would have been dangerous in view of his popularity. The Ellesmere Papers reveal a clear attempt to implicate Coke. It was to be shown that he had browbeaten the jury, told them that Ellesmere was dead, and that he had been overheard saying to the other judges "wee must seeme to knowe nothing of this matter": 2 *Huntington Lib. Q.* 85, 87.

tage had been taken of a dying man was ludicrous. Ellesmere was very senile and prone to constant bouts of sickness, and many believed that he was apt to feign illness when it suited him.[85] If he could not defend his own actions, he was unfit to continue in office.[86] In any case, Bacon privately wrote that the matter would enliven the old Chancellor and "raise his spirits."[87]

Ellesmere made his own "greevous complaint" to the King, blaming Coke,[88] and asking for James' personal resolution of the following case:

> Whether upon apparent matter of equity, which the judges of the law by their place and oath cannot meddle with or relieve, (if a judgment be once passed at common law) the subject shall perish, or that the Chancery shall relieve him; and whether there be any statute of *praemunire* or other, to restrain this power in the Chancellor.[89]

The matter being thus presented to him, the King's course was inevitable. He decided to take advice. But whereas his predecessor would have taken the advice of her judges, James was prevailed upon to consult his own law officers, who had in any case been briefed by Ellesmere the previous year. Coke must have found this as galling as anything that happened in 1616—that the King should have acted on the advice of his counsel without conferring with the judges.[90] The King also ordered Glanvill and Allen to be prosecuted in the Star Chamber, which was done in Easter Term.[91] They were tortured, or rather clogged with irons,[92] to persuade them to answer interrogatories,[93] but Bacon failed to fix the authorship of the indictments on any particular judge. The Archbishop of Canterbury and others were appointed to take evidence con-

---

85. W. J. Jones, *op. cit.*, p. 93. When he absented himself at the time of Coke's removal, the rumor was that he was pretending to be ill: MS. Add. 35957, f. 62*v*; *Chamberlain Letters*, vol. 2, p. 35.

86. See *infra*, note 133.

87. Bacon to Villiers, 19 February, 1616, Spedding, *op. cit.*, vol. 5, p. 248.

88. MS. Add. 35957, f. 54*v*: "*Le Chancelor esteant a ceo temps (come le mond pense) in graund favour ove le Roy fait greevous complaint de ceo attempt al Roy. Et le matter fuit mult aggravate, ut audivi, vers Coke Chief Justice entant que le Court de Chauncery (come fuit urge) fuit le very Treasury del ancient prerogative del Corone et le mynte de novels prerogatives. Ee que (come fuit auxi urge ut audivi) le Seignior Coke in ceo matter affront principallment le prerogative.*"

89. Spedding, *op. cit.*, vol. 5, p. 350. *Cf.* alternative form of the question, *ibid.*, p. 389. Both forms were, of course, "leading" questions.

90. See his "Poyntes dangerous et absurd etc.," cited in note 34, *supra*, at f. 569. Coke complained openly about this practice in the *Case of Commendams: Acts of the Privy Council 1615–1616*, at p. 606.

91. *Att.-Gen. v. Glanvill, Allen and Levesey* (1616), copy of Star Chamber bill in MS. Add. 11574, f. 49.

92. See Yale, *op. cit.*, p. 26n. This was the *peine fort et dure* which was designed to induce accused persons to answer the charges against them.

93. *Att.-Gen. v. Glanvill et als.* (1616) Hobart 115. Their refusal was held tantamount to refusing to answer the bill.

cerning the *praemunire*,[94] probably with a view to inculpating Coke, but it seems that little they collected could be used against him.[95]

The King's counsel, acting on two commissions,[96] duly collected their precedents and arguments, and consulted other members of the Bar such as William Hakewill.[97] The content of the official report of the King's counsel is well known.[98] But in some ways more interesting is the florid dissertation by Anthony Ben of the Middle Temple,[99] preserved among the Caesar papers.[100] In his opinion on the *praemunire* proceedings he expatiated in wide terms on the need for equity as an adjunct to a legal system. "God forbid," he wrote,[101] "that we should think all justice is tyed to the common law, or that all that is done in equity is done against justice, because it is done in a diverse manner from law . . ." Equity served the same end as law:

> Justice is her plain song, as it is the plaine song of the lawe; the descant is many-fold, yet no other then such as the law also makes her musick of . . . Justice is the soule of the law and equity is the life of justice . . . why then should law and equity become now of a sodaine incompetible who have so long time bene found proffitable servauntes to the state, why should they now be presented to the world like Essau and Jacob wrastling for birthright?[102]

This is how posterity has tended to view the dispute, but the dispute was not about theory. Ben did not discuss the defects of the Chancery or of the Chancellor, for he was not retained to do so. The judges were not given the opportunity to state their case openly, and it may be that King James was not fully apprised of all the facts. Howbeit, the object was achieved, the reasons were collected, and a public decision was to be given.

94. *Calendar of State Papers* (1611–1618), p. 370 (4 June).

95. Spedding (*op. cit.,* vol. 5, p. 380) could not find any report. But the paper cited in note 79, *supra,* may have been their work. It was certainly used in the charges against Coke: *Acts of the P.C. 1616,* at pp. 645–646.

96. Dated 19 March and 27 March and transmitted through Ellesmere: see Spedding, *op. cit.,* vol. 5, pp. 386, 388.

97. Brit. Mus. MS. Lansd. 174, f. 226. Hakewill was a legal antiquary and Member of Parliament. (*D.N.B.*)

98. It is printed in Carey 117–133; 1 Cha. Rep. iii, 20–48; Spedding, *op. cit.,* vol. 5, pp. 385–95; *Collectanea Juridica,* vol. 1, pp. 35–53.

99. Ben was favored by Buckingham and the King. See Whitelocke, *Liber Famelicus,* p. 54: *Chamberlain Letters,* vol. 2, p. 134. He was made Recorder of London in 1617 and died in 1618.

100. "Mr. Antony Ben his discourse touching the premunire brought against Sergeant More and others for prosecution of a cause in Chancery after judgment given thereof at common lawe": Brit. Mus. MS. Lansd. 174 ff. 205–15.

101. *Ibid.,* f. 210*v.*

102. *Ibid.,* ff. 211*v,* 214*v*–15.

The King's Speech in the Star Chamber

James conceived it his divine duty to terminate the conflict between his courts, and he resolved to do so in the Star Chamber. It was the first time he had sat there. He had, he explained, spent seven years studying the law, and another seven waiting for a suitable opportunity.[103] So on 20 June, 1616 the Star Chamber was prepared with "great magnificence" and the King was escorted thither by the peers and judges, from King's Bridge, and made his entry, with Prince Charles and the officers of state, to deliver a speech to the assembly.[104]

He was there, he said, to perform his coronation oath concerning justice, and to discharge his duty as God's vicegerent: "As Kings are to accompt to God, so Judges unto God and Kings."[105] He proclaimed his respect for the common law and denied the rumors that he intended to introduce the Civil Law from Scotland.[106] Then he turned to address the judges. He wished to purge the law from two corruptions, uncertainty and novelty. The judicial office was *ius dicere,* not *ius dare.*[107] They might not encroach on the king's prerogative, nor invade other jurisdictions, "which is unfit, and an unlawfull thing."[108] The King was careful to explain that he expected all the courts, including the Chancery, to keep their ancient bounds. The Chancellor had no warrant but to proceed according to precedents: "these were the limits I gave unto him; beyond the same limits hee hath promised me he will never goe."[109] So far the King had been strictly impartial, but on the question of the *praemunire* he was firm and specific:

> I thought it an odious and inept speech, and it grieved me very much, that it should bee said in Westminster Hall, that a *premunire* lay against the Court of the Chancery and the officers there: how can the King grant a *premunire* against himself? It was a foolish, inept and presumptuous attempt, and fitter for the time of some unworthie King: understand me aright; I meane not, the Chancerie should exceed his limite; but on the other part, the King onely is to correct it, and none

103. *His Majesties Speach in the Starre Chamber the xx of June Anno 1616,* sig. B2. The speech is reproduced in C. H. McIlwain, *Political Works of James I* (1918), pp. 326–45.

104. W. Camden, *Annals of James I,* in *A Complete History of England* (1706), vol. 2, p. 646; MS. Add. 35957, f. 55.

105. *His Majesties Speach etc.,* sig. B1v.

106. *Ibid.,* sig. B4. See note 6, *supra.*

107. *Ibid.,* sig. C4. (the very words with which Bacon began his 56th essay, *Of Judicature*).

108. *Ibid.,* sig. D2.

109. *Ibid.,* sig. D4.

else. And therefore sitting here in seate of judgement, I declare and command, that no man hereafter presume to sue a *premunire* against the Chancery.[110]

The King then turned to the audience and charged them to be acquiescent in judgments, for "it is better for a King to maintain an unjust decree, than to question every decree and judgment, after the giving of sentence; for then suites shall never ende."[111] A clever twist, to make the faults of the Chancellor those of the litigants. Even so, these words were a weak royal confirmation of the spirit of the statute of 1403. The rest of the speech was given in the manner of the annual charge to the circuit judges.

To the moderate ear this speech was tolerant and balanced, not intended to introduce any novelty into the legal system, but to put a stop to the *praemunire* prosecutions. Sergeant Hutton thought it "a most gracious speech, full of religion and justice."[112] There was no public disgrace to the judges, as had been widely expected,[113] and the King's words were in no way derogatory of the law. The only part of the speech which might have given offence was the assertion that the Chancery was not subject to review by any other court. Tourneur, however, perceived another ominous evil creeping into the constitution, and noted a very angry reaction to the affair. Although his words were extempore he evidently intended them to be read and used by later generations.[114] "God forbid," were his feelings, "that the irregular power of Chancellors who respect nothing but their private ends should turn the common law of the land into contempt by making decrees after judgments at common law, against statute law and common law, upon causes of equity in being long before the judgment at law obtained . . ."

> And this is maintained by the high power of the Chancellors who persuade the King that they are solely the instruments of his prerogative, and insinuate with the King that his prerogative is transcendant to the common law. And thus in a

110. *Ibid.*, sig. D4–D4*v*.

111. *Ibid.*, sig. E4. He added, "Make not changes from court to court: for hee that changeth courts, shewes to mistrust the justnesse of the cause. Goe to the right place, and the court that is proper for your cause; change not thence, and submit yourselves to the judgment given there."

112. *Op. cit.*, f. 98. Camden said "he made a very fine speech . . . and gave the judges a gentle touch": *loc. cit.*, note 5, *supra*.

113. M.S. Add. 35957, f. 55*v*: "*Nul particuler disgrace fuit fait a ceo temps al ascun des judges come le common people a ceo temps expect, nec come spero unquam serra, car lour disgrace est tort al ley mesme.*" In the margin is added, "Disgrace of the judges and professors of lawes done to the lawe itself for without them the law is but a dead letter."

114. See *ibid.*, memorandum at end.

short time they will enthral the common law (which yields all due prerogative), and by consequence the liberty of the subjects of England will be taken away, and no law practised on them but prerogative, which will be such that no one will know the extent thereof. And thus the government in a little time will lie in the hands of a small number of favourites who will flatter the King to obtain their private ends, and notwithstanding the King shall be ever indigent. And if these breeding mischiefs are not redressed by Parliament the body will in a short time die in all the parts. But some say that no Parliament will be held again in England, *et tunc valeat antiqua libertas Anglie.*[115]

The Decree of 18 July, 1616

The royal pronouncement of 20 June did not end the matter. Perhaps it was thought that the Chancellor's authority was left in some doubt, and it seems Ellesmere wanted a specific direction in writing—"some formal manifesto with the reasons"[116]—which could be enrolled in the Chancery. A decree was drawn up accordingly, under the privy seal, which set out the complaints of the Chancellor and the opinions of the King's counsel, and ordered that:

> Our Chancellor or Keeper of the Great Seal for the time being shall not hereafter desist to give unto our subjects upon their several complaints now or hereafter to be made such relief in equity (notwithstanding any former proceedings at the common law against them) as shall stand with the true merits and justice of their cases, and with the former ancient and continued practice and precedency of our Chancery.[117]

This had the appearance of finality, and the victorious Chancery treated the decree as its charter of independence.[118] Yet the matter in it remained contentious. The judges had not been consulted and the King could not change the law spontaneously. Coke was in no position at the time to remonstrate since he was about to be suspended from the Council and from sitting as a judge. In

---

115. *Ibid.* (translated). Possibly this was written after the issue of the decree of 18 July (*infra*).

116. Spedding, *op. cit.*, vol. 5, p. 385.

117. *Ibid.*, pp. 385–95; Pat. 14 Jac. p. 6, m. 25; *Cal. State. Papers* (Dom. 1611–18), p. 384; Carey 186. The decree was widely circulated in manuscript. In the British Museum see MS. Harl. 1767, f. 49; MS. Harl. 4265, f. 83; MS. Lansd. 174, f. 119; MS. Lansd. 613, f. 47; MS. Lansd. 826, f. 2; MS. Stowe 298, f. 217*v*; MS. Stowe 415, f. 63; MS. Harg. 227, f. 583; MS. Harg. 249, f. 159; MS. Harg. 269, art. 6.

118. See Yale, *op. cit.*, p. 14, note (2).

his private papers he wrote that the decree had been "obtained by the importunity of the then Lord Chancellor being vehemently afraid: *sed judicandum est legibus,* and no president can prevail against an act of parliament."[119]

The decree certainly put a stop to *praemunire,* and *habeas corpus,* against the Chancery. But it was confined to the Chancery and was not extended to the other courts of equity.[120] And the judges continued to assert that the Chancellor could not meddle with a judgment at law as his proceedings were *in personam.*[121] By the time of the Interregnum the royal decree itself would be disputed.[122]

The decree was also a theoretical success for the prerogative notion of Chancery jurisdiction: the "precedency of our Chancery." But in practice it was detrimental, if not nearly disastrous, to the already overburdened equity jurisdiction. The Chancery was overloaded, and the pressure on the Chancellor far greater than Ellesmere could bear. It was observed that the Chancery was generally complained of at the time of the decree because its jurisdiction was "inlarged out of measure, and so suits become as yt were immortall."[123] Tourneur of course, was highly critical:

> Note that this term [Hilary 1617] I heard a Clerk of the Chancery affirm that there were 8,000 suits depending in court there, of which without doubt 7,900 are thrust into chambers and corners by reference to the Masters of the Court, and to the merchants and others in the country to arbitrate them or to make report of their opinions. Which shuffling of causes arose by reason of the great age of Egerton Chancellor who is now so decrepit that he cannot expedite business as in time past, and yet will not voluntarily resign to any other who might better order the Chancery.[124]

---

119. 3 *Inst.* 125. This was published posthumously.

120. *Calmady's Case* (1640) Cro. Car. 595.

121. Anon. (1627) Litt. Rep. 37: "*si judgment soit done in un accion al common ley, le Chancellour ne poet alter ou medle ove le judgment, mes il poet proceede versus le person pur corrupt conscience quia il prend advantage del ley encounter conscience." Tompson v. Hollingsworth* (1641) March N.R. 83; *Anon.* (1647) Style 27.

122. See W. S. Holdsworth, *History of English Law,* vol. 1 (1956 ed.), pp. 463–65, which is based on Hargrave's learned note to Swanston 22, in 36 E.R. at pp. 542–44. Sergeant Rolle wrote that "*un cause ne serra examine sur equitie en le court de Requests Chancerie ou auter court de equitie apres judgment at common ley*": *Abridgment de plusieurs Cases* (1668), vol. 1, p. 381, *Chancerie* (Y) 2.

123. Chamberlain to Carleton, 14 November, 1616, *Letters of Chamberlain,* vol. 2, p. 36.

124. MS. Add. 35957, f. 79*v.* He also said that the realm was greatly vexed by the inability of Ellesmere and Caesar to manage their places.

Exeunt Coke and Ellesmere

The lasting effect of these events could not be ascertained until the two principal characters left the stage. Fate arranged this to happen within the year.
The story of the removal of Coke and its significance in English constitutional
history is familiar. After Coke's censure, his dismissal was postponed by James
until Michaelmas Term, possibly because of Coke's great popularity.[125] When
Bacon and Ellesmere jogged the royal memory in October, they suggested
summary dismissal rather than a hearing in Council to which the rules of natural justice would apply.[126] Montague, the King's Sergeant, was to be the new
Chief. If the King were tired of a Chief Justice who put the rule of law first, he
would choose one who would put the King first. Anyway, it was thought Montague would pay more than the other contenders.[127] Coke's *supersedeas* was sent
in November by Sir George Coppin, Clerk of the Crown, and Coke received it
"with dejection and tears." Montague added to the injury by asking Coke for
his collar of SS., but Coke declined to part with it.[128] On 18 November Montague was made Chief Justice and the whole affair was calculated to humiliate
Coke as much as possible. Ellesmere, now Viscount Brackley, dragged himself from his sickbed to relish the opportunity of railing against his defeated
enemy in public. In addressing Montague he denounced his predecessor by
way of example, saying that it had been God's pleasure to cut down Coke and
set up Montague.[129] When the Chancellor rose to leave, the new Chief Justice
bowed obsequiously and

> required to be defended by his lordship, promising to attempt nothing rashly.
> Which submissive petition was noted as unworthy to proceede from a Chief Jus-
> tice. Also the chorus censured my Lord Chancellor of over much presumption
> thus taking upon him to schoole a Lord Chief Justice, which I heard some of the
> graver sort say had nott bin used in former tymes. This solempnity performed

125. See *Chamberlain Letters*, vol. 2, p. 11. Sergeant Hutton wrote, "*Dieu grant que il poit estre restore*":
op. cit., f. 105.

126. Spedding, *op. cit.,* vol. 6, pp. 76–82.

127. Sherburn to Carleton, 5 October, 1616, *Calendar of State Papers* (Dom. 1611–1618), p. 397.

128. C. D. Bowen, *The Lion and the Throne* (1957), pp. 325–336. The requisite warrants were sent to
the King by Bacon on 13 November: Spedding, *op. cit.,* vol. 6, p. 97. In his private papers Coke noted his
complaint that the discharge was worded in general terms "*pro diversis causis,*" whereas in fact there was no
cause: Brit. Mus. MS. Harl. 6687, f. 15*v*.

129. Moore K.B. 826; *Buccleuch Papers* (H.M.C. 1926), vol. 3, p. 196; Hutton, *op. cit.,* f. 112; MS. Add.
35957, f. 62*v*; S.P. 14/89, nos. 26–28; S.P.Misc. 12, f. 117; Brit. Mus. MS. Harl. 39, f. 281; Bodl. Lib. MS.
Ashm. 781, f. 119.

the old deathgreeved Chancellor departed, his deepe rooted malyce against the Lord Coke little satisfied with his breakefast.[130]

The next day Montague went in grand procession to Westminster Hall in his new robes, which was the final affront. It was obvious that the robes had been prepared before Coke's discharge, and all the ceremonies betrayed an indecent haste.[131]

At the time of this unsavory exhibition Brackley himself was growing into disfavor with the King, partly because his son had not been made Lord President of Wales.[132] The Chancellor was mentally ill, or senile, as well as bodily infirm,[133] and it was thought he was reluctant to give up the Great Seal.[134] One of Dudley Carleton's correspondents wrote that if the Chancellor recovered from his sickness there would be more bills preferred against him in the Star Chamber than had been preferred against Coke.[135]

As he lay dying he kept the Seal near him, and he wrote to the King that he was "an old man and did not use to putt off his cloathes before he went to bed."[136] Finally, after the Chancellor had refused to put the Seal to certain patents, the King paid him a visit on 3 March and personally relieved him of it.[137] Tourneur cynically wrote that this hastened Brackley's death "for wanting the smell of yellow waxe."[138] His retirement was indeed short-lived, and he departed this life on 15 March.

The Significance of the 1616 Decree

Montague was obviously not disposed to step into Coke's shoes and continue the opposition to Chancery, and he had publicly promised Brackley that he

130. MS. Add. 35957, f. 63. *Cf. Buccleuch Papers, loc. cit.*

131. Hutton, *op. cit.*, f. 122: "*Et fuit mult marvailed at que il voet vaer al Westminster le prochein jour cy hastement, intant que per common probability s'il n'ad provide ses robes devant main, il ne puissoit estre ready, et ne fuit politiquely handled.*"

132. Hutton, *op. cit.*, f. 126; MS. Add. 35957, f. 81*v*; Tate to Montague, 27 February, 1617, *Beaulieu Papers* (H.M.C. 1900), p. 93.

133. S.P. 14/87, no. 17; S.P. 14/90, no. 135.

134. He had earlier petitioned to be allowed to resign. Perhaps senility had made him unpredictable. See S.P. 14/87, nos. 17, 67; S.P. 14/90, nos. 105, 135; MS. Add. 35957, ff. 79*v*, 81*v*.

135. S.P. 14/90, no. 113.

136. Hutton, *op. cit.*, f. 126. *Cf. Letters of Chamberlain*, vol. 2, p. 9.

137. Camden wrote that the giving up of the seal had been voluntary and that the King took it with tears: *Annals of James I*, in *A Complete History of England*, (1706), vol. 2, p. 647. It is difficult to judge between the conflicting accounts.

138. MS. Add. 35957, f. 63, margin.

would not do so. Soon after his appointment he stayed execution in a King's Bench case because a suit had been commenced in Chancery after judgment at law.[139] Yet the King was desirous of avoiding a repetition of the personal clashes, and when he gave the Great Seal to Bacon he charged him not to repeat the faults of his predecessor. He was to "contain the jurisdiction of the court [of Chancery] within the true and due dimits, without swelling or excess,"[140] and not to extend the royal prerogative too far.[141] When Bacon took his seat in Chancery on 7 May, 1617 he made an announcement, emulating the Roman praetors, of the principles he would observe in exercising his judicial office.[142]

Firstly, he would supply, but not subvert, the law, and would try demurrers or pleas to the jurisdiction in person. Secondly, as to suing in Chancery after judgment at law, he referred to the King's decision of the previous year. But to meet the criticisms of the practice he would require such complainants to enter into good bonds to prove their suggestions,[143] "so that if he will be relieved against a judgment at common law upon matter of equity, he shall do it *tanquam in vinculis,* at his peril."[144] In drawing up regulations to give effect to this he was careful to acknowledge the spirit of the 1403 statute: "Decrees upon suites brought after judgment shall containe no words to make voyd or weaken the judgment, but shall onely correct the corrupt conscience of the party. . . ."[145] Thirdly, he would not grant injunctions to stay proceedings at law merely upon priority of suit,[146] or upon a mere complaint without evidence, nor would he alter possessions *pendente lite.* Fourthly, he would not act upon the report of a Master in Chancery without giving the party time to show cause against it. Finally, he said he would never be "so sovereign or

139. *Anon.* (Mich. 1616) Brit. Mus. MS. Harl. 1692, f. 61; *cf. Huet v. Conquest* (Mich. 1616) MS. Add. 35957, f. 66. Tourneur wrote in the margin "When Coke was gone they began to make Chancery orders" (in the King's Bench).

140. Spedding, *op. cit.,* vol. 6, p. 184. He had given the like direction to Egerton: *supra,* note 105.

141. Camden, *loc. cit.,* in note 137, *supra.* This report is not very explicit.

142. "The Effect of that which was spoken by the Lord Keeper . . . at the Taking of his Place in Chancery in Performance of the Charge his Majesty had given him when he Received the Seal": Spedding, *op. cit.,* vol. 6, pp. 182–193. This was widely circulated in manuscript.

143. This was the suggestion of the lawyers. Tourneur had the same year written that if this were done "*les subiectes trovera mult ease et les officers de Chauncery meyns profit*": MS. Add. 35957, f. 79v. See 15 Hen. 6, ch. 4 and 17 Ric. 2, ch. 6.

144. *Cf. Ordinances Made by Bacon* (pr. 1642), no. 33.

145. *Ibid.,* no. 34. *Cf.* note 117, *supra.*

146. This had been the practice at the end of the 16th century: *e.g. Bill v. Body* (1560) Cary 50, Dick. 1; *Crowder v. Robinson* (1577) Cha. Cas. 115. Bacon said "I do not mean to make it a horse-race who shall be first at Westminster Hall": *loc. cit.*

abundant in mine own sense" as to neglect the assistance of the common law judges in cases of difficulty.

The last promise was not made idly. Bacon, having achieved the ambition which was the cause of all his scheming, was genuinely anxious to restore peace. The day after his speech in Chancery he invited the judges to dinner and told them to account him one of their number—as their "foreman." Sitting with them after the meal he said

> He was firmly persuaded that the former discords and differences between the Chancery and other courts was but flesh and blood; and now the men were gone, the matter was gone; and for his part, as he would not suffer any the least diminution or derogation from the ancient and due power of the Chancery, so if any thing should be brought to them at any time touching the proceedings of the Chancery which did seem to them exorbitant or inordinate, that they should freely and friendly acquaint him with it, and they should soon agree.

At these words, Bacon saw "cheer and comfort in their faces."[147]

One of Bacon's first acts was to re-open the case of *Ruswell,* and to appoint Doddridge and Hutton JJ. as assistants. In the course of argument the judges, with Bacon's assent, laid down some general principles governing the relations between law and equity. Equity could not operate against a maxim of the law, which would be to make a new law, but could only relieve in cases of particular mischief.[148] And while equity could in particular instances relieve against a statute,[149] it would not directly "cross" a statute, as had been done in the case at bar.[150] Accordingly, Lord Ellesmere's decree was reversed. These deliberations were comforting to the common lawyers, but they also demonstrated that error in Chancery could only be tried in the Chancery itself, on a bill of review.[151] This may have been the point at which the judges amicably, for the time being, gave up the struggle to control the Chancellor's decisions. For the rest of Bacon's tenure of the Great Seal little is heard of the older wrangles.

Bacon's successor, the last clerical custodian of the Seal, was wise enough

---

147. Spedding, *op. cit.,* vol. 6, p. 198. The quotation has been transposed from the first to the third person here.

148. H. Rolle, *Abridgment de Plusieurs Cases* (1668), vol. 1, pp. 375–77, *Chancerie* (R) 1, 5, 8, 10, 11, 12, 13.

149. *Ibid.,* (S) 1, 3, 5, 6, 8. This had been at issue in the *Earl of Oxford's Case, supra.*

150. *Ibid.,* p. 379, (S) 5. Ellesmere's decree had been contrary to the Statute of Wills.

151. *Ibid.,* p. 382, *Chancerie* (Z) 1. Cf. *Sir George Reynell's Case* (1617), *ibid.,* (Z) 2.

to preserve the good relations with the law. Bishop Williams in his praetorian address of 1621 announced:

> I will never make any decree, that shall cross the grounds of the common or statute laws, for I hold by my place the custody not of mine own, but of the King's conscience; and it were most absurd to let the King's conscience be at enmity and opposition with his laws and statutes. This Court (as I conceive it) may be often occasion'd to open and confirm, but never to thwart, and oppose, the grounds of the laws. I will therefore omit no pains of mine own nor conference with the learned judges, to furnish myself with competency of knowledge, to keep my resolution in this point firm and inviolable.[152]

Thomas Coventry, who followed Williams as Lord Keeper, was a judge's son and a barrister, and he made efforts to continue the reforms of the Chancery. In his first year of office he cleared a backlog of two hundred cases, and earned the reputation of being a helpful and intelligent judge in equity.[153] An anonymous biographer commented on this good reputation:

> Where it falls into observation that this high place [Lord Keeper] is rarely well served but by men of law and persons of deepest judgment in the statute and common lawes of the land; whereby they may distinguish of cases whether they lye proper in that court to be relieved in equitie without intrenching on the jurisdiction of the kingdome, which is the inheritance of the subject.[154]

Bacon, Williams and Coventry succeeded in banishing that part of the rivalry which was governed by envy and the clash of forceful personalities. The remaining defects of the Chancery, and the reforms proposed during the Revolution, form the subject of another story which cannot be recounted here.

Conclusion

Maitland wrote of the affairs of 1616: "The victory of the Chancery was final and complete—and if we were to have a Court of equity at all, it was a neces-

---

152. J. Hackett, *Scrinia Reserata* (1693), part 1, p. 73. The same biographer affirms that "the counsel at the Bar were greatly contented with him"; *ibid.,* p. 76.

153. Anon., *The Character of Lord Keeper Coventry,* Brit. Mus. MS. Stowe 619, ff. 50*v*, 52; MS. Sloane 3075, f. 7. The latter copy seems to be nearer the original.

154. MS. Sloane 3075, f. 7*v*.

sary victory."[155] It is submitted that this is an exaggeration.[156] For one thing, it is doubtful whether the decree had any effect other than prohibiting the common law courts from reviewing Chancery decisions. And if Bacon, Williams and Coventry genuinely attempted to remedy the defects and seek the advice of judges assistant as in the past, the common law courts had no need for such a revisory power. In so far as the dispute was about interference with judgments, Bacon made it clear that he would not "subvert" the law, but only correct the conscience, and so the bone of contention was buried. To the minds of such contemporaries as Tourneur, the decree had greater political than juridical significance. This is certainly true of the events of 1616 as a whole. Pollock found in the wider implications of these occurrences the motivation of Selden's famous aphorism that "equity is a roguish thing":[157] "It is so because the measure of the Chancellor's foot may go too near to follow the measure of Charles I's foot, peradventure even Archbishop Laud's."[158] Another writer has proposed that but for the other events of that eventful year, the Chancery dispute would have been no more than a storm in a tea cup.[159]

It is easy to see a connection between the decree of 1616 and s. 25 of the Judicature Act, 1873.[160] There is more than a hint in some books that the common lawyers lost in the end. Sir Jocelyn Simon has conjured up the murmur of Coke turning in his grave as the clause was passed by the House of Commons without debate,[161] but it is doubtful whether Coke's remains would have been so exercised. Equity by its very nature prevails over law in appropriate circumstances, but the difficulties which had troubled Coke and his contemporaries had been practical problems of judicial comity and personality, rather than theoretical problems of conflicting notions of justice. The battle had been fought not so much between equity and law, as between the Chancellor and the common lawyers. As Bacon himself said, "When the men were gone, the

155. F. W. Maitland, *Constitutional History of England* (1908), p. 270. Potter went so far as to say that the decree "determined the continued right of the Chancery to exist": *Historical Introduction to English Law* (1958 ed.), p. 160.

156. Later writers have tended to make less of the decree: *e.g.* W. S. Holdsworth, *History of English Law* (1924), vol. 5, p. 236; Yale, *op. cit.*, p. 14; Jones, *op. cit.*, p. 473.

157. J. Selden, *Table Talk* (1927 ed.), p. 43.

158. F. Pollock, *Essays in Legal History* (1913), pp. 294–95.

159. Jones, *op. cit.*, p. 473.

160. 36 & 37 Vict., c. 66, s. 25 (11); now the Judicature Act 1925, s. 44. Maitland said the provision had little effect because there was no conflict between law and equity before the Act was passed: *Lectures on Equity* (1969 repr.), pp. 16–17. For the connection, see generally White and Tudor, *op. cit.;* Yale, *op. cit.,* p. 14; G. W. Keeton, *An Introduction to Equity* (1965 ed.), p. 43; J. Tiley, *Casebook on Equity and Succession* (1968), p. 20.

161. [1968] *Cambridge Law Journal* at p. 272.

matter was gone." The Judicature Acts in fact prevented the possibility of such troubles recurring, by fusing the administration of law and equity and abolishing common injunctions. Equity is now administered by the same judges who administer the common law, and the Lord Chancellor rarely, if ever, sits in equity. One is therefore tempted to conclude that in 1873 it was Coke's victory which became final and complete.

Note

Since the foregoing article was published, several further writings have appeared: G. W. Thomas, "James I, Equity and Lord Keeper Williams" (1976) 91 *Eng. Hist. Rev.* 506–28; C. M. Gray, "The Boundaries of the Equitable Function" (1976) 20 *A.J.L.H.* 192–226; L. A. Knafla, *Law and Politics in Jacobean England: The Tracts of Lord Chancellor Ellesmere* (1977), esp. pp. 123–81. These do not detract from the thesis advanced above. The title, however, is potentially misleading: it was not meant to imply that the conflict was with Civil lawyers, or that there was in 1616 a distinct Chancery bar.

The Crown and the Courts
in England, 1603–1625

W. J. JONES

❧ ❧ ❧

The attention traditionally paid to James I's dealings with courts, judges, and lawyers is not altogether without merit although writers no longer concentrate instinctively upon theories of divine right of kings and unlikely extensions of prerogatives. James was not an original thinker but he did have a practical and theoretical interest in various kinds of law. Often irritated by common lawyers, whom he once likened to wind instruments, he probably had doubts about their education and he certainly enjoyed jokes made at their expense. Unlike Elizabeth he became involved in legal and jurisdictional disputes. His difficulties with Sir Edward Coke are a fact, but the nature of their "confrontation" should not be distorted. Notions that the king was "opposed" by judges or common lawyers lack credibility. Indeed it can be suggested that both he and his son placed too much reliance upon common lawyers and the common law.

The pitfall which historians may traverse but not evade is provided by the rhetoric and grandiose statements of the age. Kings were gods, but then so were judges, although this might be explained away by reference to delegation. One inclines toward Plucknett's view that in deciding for the Crown judges who relied upon available historical evidence often spoiled the effect by "gratuitously introducing a good deal of dogma on divine right." An exercise of the prerogative, quite acceptable on strict legal grounds, might be defended on the more debatable ground of "absolute power."[1] An appeal by Lord Chancellor

"The Crown and the Courts in England, 1603–1625" is reprinted from Alan G. R. Smith, ed., *The Reign of James VI and I* (London: Macmillan, 1973). © Alan G. R. Smith, Jennifer M. Brown, Gordon Donaldson, S. G. E. Lythe, Christina Larner, John Bossy, Brian Dietz, Louis B. Wright, Menna Prestwich, W. J. Jones, G. C. F. Forster 1973. Reproduced with permission of W. J. Jones and Palgrave.

1. J. Hawarde, *Les Reportes del Cases in Camera Stellata*, ed. W. P. Baildon (1894), pp. 176–77; T. F. T. Plucknett, *A Concise History of the Common Law* (1956), pp. 50, 487.

Ellesmere to the law of God has been interpreted as "an elegant allusion rather than an integral part of his argument."[2] There was never any question that the highest law of the land, statute law, could only be made in Parliament, but it has been argued that James accepted this "grudgingly" and trouble arose because the prerogative "was supreme where the law had not insinuated itself."[3] Some judicial opinions must have worried the king, and Coke's assertion that "Magna Carta is such a fellow that he will have no sovereign" has been read as a blow against the prerogative.[4] Coke's constant stand on the sovereignty of law however has too often been interpreted as a rebuttal of James whereas it seems equally appropriate to view it as a constraint on the sovereignty of Parliament. In 1607, producing a stream of precedents to support the doctrine of naturalization by allegiance, he treated the arguments of Commons spokesmen with contempt. He can be grouped with Sir John Davies and others in that they emphasized the common law to the point of confining statute. It was, writes Dr. Hinton, "a plain contradiction of parliamentary legislative sovereignty . . . ; the effect of this was to elevate the status of the King in relation to the status of Parliament."[5]

There is a danger that the pendulum of interpretation might swing too far. Professor Kenyon's assessment of James reflects our current understanding: "he was careful always to operate within the framework of the common law; he never imprisoned anyone without trial, he never levied money from his subjects without authorization from Parliament or the courts of common law, he never promulgated law of his own accord, even if he believed he could, and he was certainly more moderate and 'constitutional' than Queen Elizabeth."[6] This is more to the point than many previous verdicts although the contrast drawn with respect to his predecessor needs justification. However something else needs to be said. With respect to the levy of money there was an increasing demand for the authorization of both Parliament and the courts. As an M.P. asked in 1610: "shall all other courts be at liberty . . . to dispute the law and shall this court [Parliament] be barred and tied not to dispute it? Is not the

2. D. E. C. Yale, Introduction to E. Hake, *EPIEKEIA* (New Haven 1953), p. xvi.

3. H. Hulme, "Charles I and the Constitution," in *Conflict in Stuart England*, ed. W. A. Aiken and B. D. Henning (1960), pp. 89, 93.

4. Christopher Hill, *Intellectual Origins of the English Revolution* (Oxford 1965), p. 246.

5. Gardiner commented that "the natural tendency of the judges was to put forward on every occasion the authority of the sovereign." S. R. Gardiner, *History of England*, I (1887), 335; R. W. K. Hinton, "The Decline of Parliamentary Government under Elizabeth I and the Early Stuarts," *Cambridge Historical Journal* (1957), p. 129; "English Constitutional Theories from Sir John Fortescue to Sir John Eliot," *English Historical Review* (1960), pp. 421, 422.

6. J. P. Kenyon, *The Stuart Constitution* (Cambridge 1966), p. 8.

King's prerogative disputable?"[7] He was referring to the Exchequer decision of 1606 with respect to impositions and the attempt to restrict parliamentary discussion of the same subject. Actually the prerogative—a legal exercise of royal authority—was hardly ever denied. At various times some wondered about its rightful exercise, perhaps thinking that favorites manipulated the situation to their own advantage, or questioning if some particular area was really within the prerogative. With respect to impositions, the point was made by Coke in 1614: "if it be a prerogative it is warranted by law, for the King hath no prerogative to impose that the law giveth him not power to do." Ellesmere expressed the same sentiment: "the King hath no prerogative but that that is warranted by law and the law hath given him."[8]

The ability of modern historians to recognize their ignorance about many of the forums and institutions which provide the essential context for an interpretation of the rights of Crown and subject has led to a new picture, one which is slowly being built out of minute details. We are becoming better acquainted with borough and manorial courts, petty and quarter sessions, and the general world of local officialdom. There is a good book on the Elizabethan Council in the Marches of Wales and its author has provided some telling papers on the early Stuart situation. Old books on the Council in the North—although supplemented by a modern pamphlet—and on the Palatine of Durham are hardly adequate. Ecclesiastical courts in the diocese of York have been surveyed by Dr. Marchant, who provides detail without avoiding debate.[9] The *Victoria County History* is valuable, articles proliferate and graduate theses multiply. However little has been put together. Insubstantial generalizations about the great courts have been shattered, but there is little to put in their place. Major works are expected on the Admiralty and the Star Chamber, the latter court already having been exposed by Professor Barnes.[10] My book on the Elizabethan Chancery deals with the administrative and political background to jurisdic-

---

7. Elizabeth R. Foster, *Proceedings in Parliament, 1610* (New Haven 1966), I, xvi.

8. HMC *Hastings,* IV, 256, 263.

9. P. Williams, *The Council in the Marches of Wales under Elizabeth I* (Cardiff, 1958); "The Activity of the Council in the Marches under the Early Stuarts," *Welsh History Review* (1961), pp. 133–60; "The Attack on the Council in the Marches, 1603–1642," *Transactions of the Honourable Society of Cymmrodorion* (1961); R. R. Reid, *The King's Council of the North* (1921); F. W. Brooks, *The Council in the North* (1963); G. T. Lapsley, *The County Palatine of Durham* (Cambridge, Mass. 1900); R. A. Marchant, *The Church under the Law* (Cambridge 1969); see also P. Tyler, introduction to R. G. Usher, *The Rise and Fall of the High Commission* (Oxford 1968).

10. T. G. Barnes, "Star Chamber Mythology," *American Journal of Legal History* (1961), pp. 1–11; "Due Process and Slow Process in the Late Elizabethan–Early Stuart Star Chamber," *American Journal of Legal History* (1962), pp. 221–49, 315–46.

tion and procedures, but much remains to be done on fees, rolls and writs. Certainly there is no warrant to suggest that we know very much about the Marian or Jacobean institution.[11] Our knowledge of Common Pleas and Exchequer is even more minimal. King's Bench provides almost as sad a picture, but here the gloom is parted by work such as Dr. Blatcher's piece on *latitat*. Much of England's legal heritage had become outmoded. This was inevitable, but lawyers and officials were unable to comprehend change. Their attempts at rectification, shrouded in traditional assumptions, must call to mind Plucknett's warning about the perennial trouble of casual reform which did not make a clean sweep of the past. This must be understood if we are to grasp the effort of King's Bench to free itself from medieval bonds. "Although the motive was self-interested and the means a fiction, those who employed the writ of *latitat* to achieve that end were serving the cause of necessary change." Dr. Blatcher has provided a classic exposition of the role played by resort to fiction.[12]

How then should future work be constructed? One possibility is provided by Dr. Blatcher's essay. Another is suggested by work done on the Court of Wards. Dr. Bell wrote a solid study of particular interest to the early Stuart period, but Professor Hurstfield's Elizabethan analysis is outstanding because it blends the institution into the realities of society.[13] A similar ambition should be applied to other areas. We cannot understand the history of criminal law without studying criminals and crimes, and it is hopeless to write about debt without studying debtors. A little has been said on equity but any serious study must collate work on the provincial councils, the palatine courts, the rewarding records of the Exchequer and many other tribunals. Equity would become synonymous with Chancery but this was not the situation in James's reign although that institution's preponderant role had been acknowledged. Above all it is pointless to write about the land law without studying the land and hence all that such a massive theme entails.

What is a court? Certainly it is not just a series of law reports or manuscript legal proceedings although too many works have been constructed upon this basis—as though a cow could be described in terms of its milk. Courts

11. W. J. Jones, *The Elizabethan Court of Chancery* (Oxford 1967).

12. Marjorie Blatcher, "Touching the Writ of Latitat: An Act 'of no great moment,'" in *Elizabethan Government and Society*, ed. S. T. Bindoff, Joel Hurstfield and C. H. Williams (1961), pp. 188–212; Plucknett, p. 130.

13. H. E. Bell, *An Introduction to the History and Records of the Court of Wards and Liveries* (Cambridge 1953); Joel Hurstfield, *The Queen's Wards* (1958).

were institutions with a physical location, departments, officials, records and rooms, all of which might be dispersed. There was a greater distance between the Chancery bench and its administrative heart, the Rolls in Chancery Lane, than there was between the benches of Chancery, Common Pleas and King's Bench, separated as they were by a few feet and some partitions in Westminster Hall. Coke's removal from Common Pleas to King's Bench meant that he had to walk a distance of perhaps eighty yards. Not surprisingly it was said that "there are not two such acres in all the country as the Exchange and Westminster Hall."[14] Yet the remarkable activity which this edifice housed represented only one aspect. Chancery was an institution which issued over 10,000 subpoenas annually in the early years of Elizabeth and twice that number in the last years of James—figures which can become insignificant when compared with the number of judicial writs it issued returnable to Common Pleas and King's Bench. Courts gave employment to elevated seniors, burdened hacks and service officials—the Exchequer at Chester had a carpenter and mason. The six clerks of Chancery had fine plate and table linen; the lowlier cursitors had a society which dined regularly, the meal followed by the reading of writs. Competition and selection for office, apparent at all levels, was just one element which confirmed that all institutions were part of the general political picture.[15]

Thomas Powell wrote about the "great courts at Westminster, to whose motion all other courts . . . are diurnally moved."[16] He was referring to the shadow of regulation which Chancery, Common Pleas, Exchequer, King's Bench and Star Chamber had thrown over minor, provincial and specialized jurisdictions. The eminence and power of these central and national courts was underlined by Coke's acknowledgment that there were different kinds of jurisdiction: "the bounds of all and every several courts being most necessary to be known."[17] A major theme of James's reign is to be discerned in principles of regulation and supervision adopted by judges of the major courts. Delivery by habeas corpus of those committed, injunctions and prohibitions were the major weapons. Process of this nature—really the standard means of communication between courts—was in exceptional demand, and we must

---

14. *The Life and Letters of Sir Henry Wotton,* ed. L. P. Smith (Oxford 1907), II, 490.

15. Add. MSS, 14822, f. 14; W. S. Holdsworth, *History of English Law,* I (1956), 423–24; "The Rights and Jurisdiction of the County Palatine of Chester," ed. J. B. Yates, *Chetham Misc.* (1856), p. 28; Jones, pp. 120–21, 159.

16. T. Powell, *The Attourney's Academy* (1623), subtitle.

17. Sir E. Coke, preface, *The Fourth Part of the Institutes of the Lawes of England* (1669).

not ignore the multitude of instances in which writs were refused or quashed. The judges of Westminster courts were clearly asserting their claim to decide the limits of other jurisdictions, but the real issue was that of finding lines of demarcation between all courts. There was debate between Common Pleas and King's Bench, between common law and ecclesiastical courts, between diocesan courts and the Arches. The hardest task of all was that of distinguishing between the proper jurisdictions of courts which exercised a similar procedure or which avowed a similar competence. Across this tangle swept the demands of great Westminster courts, aided by superior procedures and record requirements. Amid many issues, the arrogant assertion of these national courts is most obvious. Yet a sense of context is still all important. Common Pleas did deny the right of High Commission to define its own jurisdiction but it and other courts adopted the same attitude toward many tribunals. In 1598 the power of the Court of Requests to imprison was cut to pieces by the chief justice of the Common Pleas—it was said that an action of false imprisonment might be had—but in that same year the power of the Requests to commit to prison was vindicated against the lord mayor's court.[18] England was a network, a jig-saw puzzle, of courts constructed on different levels. At every stage there was a struggle to assert authority. Provincial courts, scrutinized from Westminster, were themselves supervising lesser units. The Exchequer at Chester demanded acceptance of its supremacy from the courts of the city of Chester and elsewhere in the palatinate. Despite resistance and complaints—Berwick, Beverley, Carlisle, Heddon, Hull and York struggled to avoid the mesh—the Council in the North established control over lesser courts from the Trent to the Scottish Border. There was trouble over the jurisdictional boundaries of the Tower and the City of London. Surrey J.P.s questioned London's authority over Southwark.[19] A myriad of examples could be given and perhaps the manorial courts were the most obvious victims of this process of regulation and record superiority. However the bigger courts—whether it was the Common Pleas surveying the nation or the Exchequer at Chester surveying the palatine—had no wish to embark upon a course of destruction. All jurisdictions, lay and ecclesiastical, provincial or specialized, were valued and often supported. Courts which claimed the power of supervision had neither the wish nor the ability to handle all kinds of suit. There was a

18. W. B. J. Allsebrook, "The Court of Requests in the Reign of Elizabeth" (London University M.A. thesis, 1937), pp. 156–57.
19. Reid, pp. 316–19; Brooks, pp. 26–29; *Acts of the Privy Council of England 1613–14*, pp. 219–21.

trend toward excluding small cases, personal actions and actions not involving title to land from Westminster. There are limits to the thesis that competition provides an explanation of the difficulties between courts, and it must be recognized that great courts did not want to be swamped by small cases which, if heard at Westminster, would entail costs, expenses and time out of all proportion to the matter in dispute. Local, provincial and specialized courts would still attract considerable business but in the long run their area of ability was defined and this invited extinction. Courts which could not change or expand in accordance with the fluctuating needs of society had little future even if they continued into the nineteenth century. Only the great courts of Westminster Hall, excepting Star Chamber which was felled amid curious political turmoil, adapted themselves. Tudor government had been based upon the centralization of authority and the decentralization of its administration. In later times both would be centralized and this was not always conducive to efficiency. One has only to look at the hideous monstrosity that was the eighteenth-century Chancery.

The great courts at Westminster had their differences, but they maintained a common front. The appearance of justices on the benches of Chancery and Star Chamber was only the most superficial expression of this accord. This does not imply that disputes can be taken lightly, and in the contest for fees Exchequer and King's Bench raids upon the lucrative area of Common Pleas civil jurisdiction has justifiably been called shabby.[20] There was none the less a trend toward deleting the possibility that different courts might offer different remedies. Initially Common Pleas played the most independent role; subsequently Chancery was to occasion difficulty; finally King's Bench seemed inclined to run a course of its own and Thomas Powell found that his pen was excluded from "meddling" in the crown office side of that court.[21] Definition was still the essential problem. The Westminster courts supervised other tribunals but it was wondered if they also should not be supervised. Those who asked this question looked to Crown or Parliament.

Judges were government employees active in administration. Justices of assize for example oversaw most aspects of local life and without them early Stuart government is inconceivable. A clear distinction between judicial and administrative authority would only be grasped in later years. Yet there was an apparent contradiction. It might make sense to place limits upon lesser and

20. J. P. Dawson, *The Oracles of the Law* (Ann Arbor, 1968), p. 48.
21. Powell, p. 168.

provincial jurisdictions, or for that matter the Privy Council, but this meant that the justices were regulating the structure of government as established under the Tudors. They were an integral part of the system and yet seemed to be assuming the role of a *deus ex machina*. They owed their exceptional position to the Crown, the fount of the law and the source of all their authority. The king appointed them, paid them and used them.[22] It is hardly surprising therefore that James, who was not enamored of ideas which drew too sharp a distinction between the personality and function of the sovereign, felt sometimes called upon to intervene. James being James was fascinated and puzzled by theoretical implications. Being the source of jurisdiction, he wondered how he could give a *praemunire* against himself.[23] He was after all the linchpin of justice and he represented the idea of enforceable arbitration. The practical justification for his interference—he was the most interested person—called in question the value of his attempts. His particular legal rights, or prerogatives, with respect to proceedings before the courts made him an unlikely arbitrator.[24]

No one is more rightly associated with the questioning of jurisdictions than Coke. Furthermore he was outstanding among the many lawyers who contributed to the current emphasis on historiography. Many myths were unearthed —Coke once described thirty-three martyr popes of a former Protestant Rome[25]—but he and others cannot be judged by modern ideas of historical scholarship. Even so it is clear that his reputation is no longer accorded its former respect. His *Reports* have been justifiably criticized,[26] but Coke, even at his most bombastic, might have been perplexed by some later dependence upon his authority. That he was headstrong was clear before he joined the bench as chief justice of the Common Pleas in 1606, but he was no more arrogant than others. Indeed he deserves sympathy in that he had to deal with Thomas Walmsley, a Common Pleas justice since 1589, and Peter Warburton, a justice since 1600. These Cheshire men, associates of Ellesmere, were

22. Involvement with the Crown has often been interpreted as a weakness, but such an approach pays too much attention to the notion of independence assumed by later generations. The performance and position of the judges would certainly raise questions during the reigns of James I's son and grandsons; it may have been the wrong kind of strength, but it certainly was not weakness.
23. *The Political Works of James I,* ed. C. H. McIlwain (New York 1918), pp. 334–35. On this occasion—it was 1616—James allowed his own sense of grievance to appear: "none of you but will confess you have a King of reasonable understanding, and willing to reform."
24. J. P. Cooper, "The Fall of the Stuart Monarchy," in *New Cambridge Modern History,* IV, ed. J. P. Cooper (Cambridge 1970), p. 539; Kenyon, pp. 103, 106.
25. Hawarde, p. 255.
26. Cf. Dawson, pp. 68–73.

renowned for their scathing tongues. Often they agreed, but when genuine points of legal difference arose the debate was fierce. During these years the Common Pleas bench was an exciting place. Similar difficulties doubtless afflicted the King's Bench, and for a time the number of justices in both courts was increased from four to five in the hope that ties could be avoided.[27] A necessary appreciation of personal and political circumstances helps to explain how great constitutional and legal issues came to be raised. There was also a struggle for influence and office which in the mid-period of the reign had its roots in the fragmented interests of those who opposed Howard dominance at Court. Coke's difficulties in 1616 are crucial to an understanding of the success of the new favorite, Villiers, and Bacon's story forms part of the same picture. Once political battle was joined however it was natural that dissension would prompt serious analysis and disagreement with respect to affairs of jurisdiction and judicial performance.

Amongst instruments of regulation, the writ of prohibition, issued to forbid inferior courts from further proceedings in a cause, is perhaps best known. It had long been used to restrain ecclesiastical courts, but in the second part of Elizabeth's reign it seemed to attract a novel demand. Initially High Commission and Requests were the most worried, but around the time of James's accession major provincial courts became targets. Prohibitions to the Council of the Marches of Wales had previously been rare, although English proceedings before the Council had of course been confined by Chancery to cases within the geographic boundaries of the Council's jurisdiction. This done, it was almost inevitable that these boundaries would be challenged. Disagreement over the status of the four Marcher shires was apparent in the 1597 Parliament, and it is possible that dissident border gentry were already making their voices heard. Under James, the matter was repeatedly before the House of Commons and it has been suggested that the king's personal intervention played some part in the Council's retrenchment of authority over these shires. Even so it was the early years of James which marked the greatest flow of prohibitions to the Council. The Council in the North experienced more or less the same thing. In the course of one term Common Pleas could issue over fifty prohibitions to York. In 1605, before Coke reached the bench, Archbishop Bancroft complained about "the over frequent and undue granting of prohibitions," and Sir Henry Townshend fumed over the issue of this writ to the

27. This experiment, inaugurated before Coke's appointment to the bench, ended early in the reign of Charles I.

chamberlain of Chester. In the second half of James's reign the pressure slackened and by 1617 the Welsh Council had recovered from a difficult decade. Prohibitions still issued, it would have been revolutionary if they had ceased, but many problems which had occasioned their grant had been resolved for the time being. Even so Wentworth, on becoming president of the Council in the North, would describe them in 1628 as "the bleeding evil."[28]

Courts and judges did not act in a vacuum. Prohibitions, like injunctions and other process, were only issued in response to individual request. It is not therefore surprising that the most serious complaint was that prohibitions were granted on surmise. However Bancroft's suggestion that prohibitions, although returnable elsewhere, should only be issued from Chancery was unrealistic. The archbishop subsequently tried to invoke royal power as a means to reform abuses in the use of writs but the judges retorted that "what the law doth warrant in cases of prohibitions to keep every jurisdiction in his true limits is not to be said an abuse, nor can be altered but by Parliament."[29] Far more serious was argument over the right of a court which did not have a suit before it or which did not claim jurisdiction to issue a prohibition. If this could not be done, it meant that the ability of a court such as Common Pleas to regulate other jurisdictions was seriously circumscribed. Common Pleas justices themselves were divided on the matter. Coke supported the issue of a prohibition against a court which did not have jurisdiction, but Walmsley said that this was only justifiable if some court had jurisdiction and the dispute, or something material to it, should already be "hanging" in Common Pleas.[30]

The difficulties of supervision were most apparent with respect to the hierarchy of ecclesiastical courts. These had authority over clergy and laity in matters of heresy, matrimony, morality, testaments, tithes and so on. Obscurity between spiritual and temporal jurisdictions was enhanced by the inadequacy of church legislation. Church courts, the troublesome canons of 1604 notwithstanding, had to rely mostly on old canon law and some statutes. Tudor Parliaments had allowed clerical marriage, governed clerical discipline and regulated degrees of consanguinity, tithes, grants of administration and other matters.

28. Williams, *Council in the Marches of Wales,* pp. 224–25; "Attack on the Council," pp. 3–6; "Activity of the Council," pp. 138–39; H. A. Lloyd, *The Gentry of South-West Wales, 1540–1640* (Cardiff 1968), pp. 167–73; Reid, pp. 316–19; HMC *Salisbury,* XVII, 466.

29. J. R. Tanner, *Constitutional Documents of the Reign of James I* (Cambridge 1930), p. 182; *State Trials,* II, 134.

30. Henry E. Huntingdon Library, Bridgewater and Ellesmere Manuscript, 2010.

Justices of the great courts viewed statute as just one of the lines of authority which enabled them to provide supervision. Thus it was declared that the opening of shops on Sunday was forbidden by statute and outside the scope of the High Commission. However the essence of supervision is to be found in the concern expressed by the justices that a proper order of doing things should be followed. A prohibition was issued because the plaintiff had sued for tithes in the wrong diocese. Above all there seems to have been much interest in maintaining a line of appeal from the archdeacon to the diocesan court and thence to the provincial court of the archbishop—the Arches for Canterbury or the chancery court for York. If licensed by the bishop, the Arches or its fellow could act as a court of first instance. Otherwise Common Pleas would grant a prohibition on the grounds that evasion of the diocesan court robbed men of their statutory right of appeal. The archdeacon should not remit cases to the archbishop; instead he should remit to the bishop and only the latter could remit to the archbishop. The principle was that all courts had a proper jurisdiction and procedure. Ecclesiastical tribunals, surveyed by the great central courts, were not alone in their predicament but they were singularly trapped within the enforced web of their own rules. It was the confinement of church courts within set limits, not the prohibitions debate as such, which in the long run sapped their strength.[31]

In granting or refusing a prohibition the justices sometimes explained their understanding of jurisdictions. The Welsh Council was authorized by its instructions to hold plea where there was no common law remedy but this did not allow it to poach on ecclesiastical courts and so a "prohibition may be granted to reduce that to its proper court." The Council was also rebuffed when, during a minority, it tried to take account of an administrator. This responsibility belonged to the ecclesiastical court. Coke had no objection to the High Commission exercising jurisdiction over polygamy and the Common Pleas refused to interfere in an accessory matter, as when an acquitted defendant was required to pay costs. Late in James's reign it was declared that a "legacy is a thing merely which is determinable in the spiritual court, and no other court may have conusance of that." Supervision of legacies was a matter of spiritual jurisdiction, but payment of the testator's debts concerned the temporal courts. Acquisition of business was always important, but the great courts were also nudging ecclesiastical tribunals into alignment with common

---

31. 1 Brownl., 44, 46; 2 Brownl., 1–3, 27–28, 38–39; Marchant, p. 113.

law rules. Coke once argued that if the spiritual court found itself faced with a collateral temporal issue there need be no difficulty so long as common law rules of evidence and law were used. Common Pleas later ruled that an executor should be able to prove a full administration by the same rules as those which applied in actions of debt.[32]

Some idea of the nature of supervision and other themes can be gained by a glance at the Courts of Admiralty and Requests. The Admiralty was valued: its proceedings were relatively speedy, its system of direct written examinations was advantageous, and it could employ commissions to examine abroad. The judges of this court had an unrivalled grasp of foreign agreements, contracts and techniques. Yet it lacked authority in some areas and hence the necessary aura of command. Early in Elizabeth's reign contracts made abroad became a matter of common law jurisdiction through the fiction of describing the place as being "in the parish of St. Mary-le-Bow in the ward of Cheap." In the reign of James the Admiralty's power to enforce appearance or to imprison was questioned. It was denied jurisdiction over offenses committed on land or over contracts made in England or abroad, irrespective of whether they were to be performed on the high seas. It was once declared that the Admiralty was only competent to handle contracts arising on the sea: otherwise "though it arise upon any continent, port or haven in the world out of the King's dominions . . . the courts of common law have unlimited power in causes transitory." If a bond was clearly made *super altum mare* the Admiralty had jurisdiction, but if these words were omitted a different situation would prevail. Some found this ridiculous, and they noted that contracts entered abroad were governed by the civil law. Coke responded by observing that there was nothing to prevent the justices from seeking the advice of civilians. It is fair to note that these experts were often invited to speak before the Common Pleas bench when Coke was chief justice. Certainly there was a struggle for business and there were particular complications, instanced by the Spanish ambassador's complaint against prohibitions and commissions of appeal granted after a decree for possession. Holdsworth suggested that Coke and his fellow justices were unscrupulous, but perhaps it is better to give them the benefit of the doubt and suppose that they were trying to make sense of a disordered situation. In the reign of Charles I a settlement, framed in a set of King's Bench resolu-

---

32. Win., 78, 103; 2 Brownl., 7; Edith G. Henderson, *Foundations of English Administrative Law* (Cambridge, Mass. 1963), pp. 121, 122.

tions, was achieved. There would still be difficulties, but the Admiralty would be singularly undisturbed by revolutionary episodes.[33]

The flow of prohibitions to the Court of Requests became noticeable in the 1580s, but Common Pleas also referred cases to it and the chief justice of that court warned against ignoring its injunctions. In the 1590s the number of prohibitions increased, "the like whereof is not remembered to have been done in former times." Denial of its right to stay suits before the great courts of Westminster or to issue injunctions after judgment was only natural and therefore not very significant. More serious was the claim that it could not imprison and that it could not take bonds with condition to appear. Its ambition to be a court of record was thus denied. Sir Julius Caesar would emerge as an indignant champion of this court, but in truth the number of prohibitions was small in comparison with the litigation entertained. Every so often there were gleams of encouragement. In 1599 Walmsley recommended a suit to the Requests: "God be thanked," it was noted, "that court which woundeth can heal some times." In retrospect the challenge posed by prohibitions appears to have been a flurry of shots which was not backed by any great will to direct a destructive charge. The authority of the court was damaged but it remained popular. Coke appreciated this and he advocated that it should be recognized by statute. Certainly the volume of business handled by the Requests could not be ignored, and in 1627 it was reported to have as many suits and clients as the Chancery. Envisaged by Chancery as a convenient disposal unit for small matters and poor plaintiffs, the Requests acquired the reputation of being an "alms basket" for the greater court.[34]

The commissioners of ecclesiastical causes are now seen as having their origin not in the royal supremacy so much as in the Crown's traditional duty to guard the Church. The commissioners—those at York enjoyed an active existence independent of Canterbury—enforced the Statutes of Supremacy and Uniformity, suppressed movements dangerous to the Church and handled ecclesiastical offenses. In 1613 they were empowered to enforce the rules of censorship. The High Commission was not unpopular and its disputed habits of

33. Coke, *Fourth Institute,* pp. 135–38; Holdsworth, 1, 550–58; 1 Brownl., 42; 2 Brownl., 16–17, 26–27, 30; W. J. Jones, "Ellesmere and Politics, 1603–1617," *Early Stuart Studies,* ed. H. S. Reinmuth (Minneapolis 1970), pp. 24–25; J. Campbell, *The Lives of the Chief Justices of England* (1849), p. 360; Allsebrook, pp. 70–71, 113, 152–59; Jones, *Chancery,* pp. 82, 382; Coke, *Fourth Institute,* pp. 97–98.

34. Citation not supplied in original article. On the Court of Requests, see I. S. Leadham, *Select Cases in the Court of Requests 1497–1569,* Selden Society, vol. 12 (1898), and Timothy Stretton, *Marriage Litigation in the Court of Requests* (Cambridge University Press, forthcoming 2004).

fining and imprisonment were as much an attraction to confident litigants as they were an offense to others. These powers, together with the *ex officio* oath, attracted most criticism. The issue however was whether Common Pleas and King's Bench had the right to supervise the procedural ability of the commissioners. In pointing out that a person could not be bound to appear in another court, the Common Pleas justices explained that they themselves for example could not take an obligation binding a man to appear before the Council in the North. With respect to appearance before the High Commission itself, the judges repeatedly said that the only proper procedure was citation—those arrested might have an action of false imprisonment—and the commissioners were constantly told that they could not impose "pecuniary or corporal" penalties. Above all there was a feeling that the High Commission often encroached on other jurisdictions. With respect to cases between party and party, Coke and Walmsley agreed that jurisdiction in the first instance lay with the ordinary ecclesiastical courts unless the matter was "enormous," but they differed on the meaning of this word. One man, sentenced before the ordinary for adultery, had refused maintenance to his wife, and consorted with two other women, fathering two bastards. Walmsley agreed with Serjeant Doddridge that the man was so "incorrigible" that the matter became "enormous," but Coke, Foster and Warburton did not see it this way.[35]

Imprisonment was the issue which more than any other exposed the possibility of debate over the royal authority. Bancroft, Coke and James conspired to open this Pandora's box. Walmsley accepted that the Statute of Supremacy did not give power to imprison, but he emphasized that the sovereign's discretion had been mentioned and he argued that the exercise of imprisonment across two decades could not be ignored. Coke disagreed: the "King is the supreme head by the common law, as to the coercive power, and . . . the letters patent of the King cannot give power to imprison where they cannot imprison by the common law."[36] Bancroft had complained about prohibitions before Coke became chief justice but the hardening attitude of Common Pleas prompted him to renew his efforts in 1607. This time he made reference to the king's right to hear cases personally, a theme which was to cause embarrassment as when Coke argued that although James had the right to sit on a bench he could not reassume the judicial power which had been delegated.

35. Tyler, p. xxiii; 2 Brownl., 14–16, 18–20, 37.
36. 2 Brownl., 18–20.

As a matter of academic debate points could be made for both positions, but Coke hit the nail on the head when he suggested that anyhow James lacked the proper expertise and learning.[37]

Westminster justices, confident that there was a proper jurisdiction for every court, would have been astounded by the suggestion that they were attacking the king's authority. Their reliance upon this authority was fundamental to the grant of prohibitions. Coke, in justification of the issue of a prohibition, said that the admiral and his officers "have without all colour encroached and intruded upon a right and prerogative due to the Crown." James however felt that he must intervene. He urged all courts to define their jurisdiction, and he encouraged Common Pleas and King's Bench to be less "prodigal" in granting prohibitions. He thought that this writ should be granted in open court and not by one judge or in the vacation. By no means opposed to prohibitions as such, he wanted to do all that he could to "keep every river within his own banks and channels." Conferences were arranged but the king muddled his role as arbitrator, as when he solicited opinions from the King's Bench justices to the effect that Common Pleas should only issue a prohibition when it was in "first possession." In March 1610 he spoke against both sides but he was most severe on the Common Pleas justices. The situation was not improved by objection to the High Commission in a Commons petition and by a brief from the lord admiral. There was the appearance of a truce but nothing had been settled, and in 1611 Walmsley provided Ellesmere with his own particular views.[38]

Bancroft's death provided an opportunity for compromise, and it was apparently hoped that new letters patent issued in 1611 would clarify the powers of the High Commission. Coke, already enraged by having had to present a defense of past prohibitions, was annoyed to find that he had been named in the Commission and that the justices of King's Bench unlike those of Common Pleas, had advance knowledge of it. In any case, the letters patent contained "divers points against the laws and statutes of England." The King's Bench justices were not very happy with the course of events even though they had not always agreed in the past with their colleagues of Common Pleas. During the ceremony of tending the oath, said Coke, "I stood, and would not sit as I was requested . . . and so by my example did all the rest of the Justices."[39]

37. Tanner, pp. 146–48, 186–87.
38. Coke, *Fourth Institute,* p. 136; *Political Works of James I,* pp. 312–13; Henry E. Huntingdon Library, Bridgewater and Ellesmere Manuscript, 2008, 2010; Kenyon, pp. 73–75.
39. Tanner, pp. 162–63.

The new letters patent named the lord chancellor, the chief justices, the chief baron, six justices and the attorney and solicitor generals. Earlier commissions had included leading judges and lawyers, but the real question was the degree to which these would participate. There were some changes in response to objection: jurisdiction over alimony disputes was barred, it was stipulated that at least five commissioners were necessary for a final sentence and there was provision for a commission of review. All this did nothing to dampen Coke's indignation. His opponents were happy to point out the former collaboration of common lawyers and they cited a warrant for arrest signed by Coke when he was attorney general. Argument continued, but a new period in the history of the Commission had been inaugurated and subsequent letters patent would both clarify and establish some aspects of its ability.[40]

With respect to both the High Commission and the ordinary ecclesiastical courts a change of emphasis can be discerned in the second half of the reign. This would appear to coincide with the refreshed confidence of the Council in the Marches of Wales. Plenty of prohibitions still issued, this was only natural, but, perhaps Coke's departure from the bench had something to do with the less acrimonious tone. It may also be suggested that the solution of problems and the formulation of rough sets of acceptable rules was also a factor. It is probable that some points had been conceded by the central justices, but flexibility was easier as the supreme power of supervision claimed by the Westminster courts came to be accepted.

Coke could still unite his fellow justices in 1611, but this did not erase antagonisms, and doubts were expressed as to the veracity of his reports and recollections. The undercurrent of criticism was apparent in 1612. After two men had been convicted by the High Commission, Abbott requested writs of *de haeretico comburendo*. Coke denied the legality of this proceeding. The archbishop, after consultation with James, asked Ellesmere to take the opinion of the judges, preferably those of the King's Bench. These had experience in capital cases and anyhow the king did not want Coke to be involved "lest by his singularity in opinion he should give stay to the business." Justice Williams took the opportunity to report that he and Baron Altham "did once very roundly let the Lord Coke know their minds, that he was not such a master of the law as he did take on him, to deliver what he list for law and to despise all other."[41]

---

40. Tyler, p. xxxiii; Henry E. Huntingdon Library, Bridgewater and Ellesmere Manuscript, 1988, 2013.
41. *The Egerton Papers,* ed. J. P. Collier (Camden Society 1840), pp. 446–48.

Coke probably guessed that his intractability was a factor which determined the king's behavior, and James knew that Coke did not command unanimous support even from his own bench. Hence during the height of the prohibitions dispute James had already begun to employ devious if legitimate practices in dividing the judges when he sought opinions. Coke was translated to King's Bench in the judicial reshuffle of 1613, and in 1614 he was admitted to the Council. In 1615 with Peacham's case and in 1616 with the case of Commendams James solicited separate opinions from the judges. In the latter instance he made it clear that he wished to participate in discussions. This time the judges refused, but in the end all save Coke recanted. The affair hastened Coke's dismissal. Coke and Ellesmere were in dispute over the jurisdictions of King's Bench and Chancery, and the chief justice had enraged the old lord chancellor by striking when the latter was mistakenly supposed to be at death's door. Attorney General Bacon, imbued with his own hopes, fanned the flames. That this was very much the stuff of politics does not diminish the genuine nature of debate over legal issues. Yet the dominant feature of the enmity between Coke and Ellesmere was that it revealed a rift among those who opposed the powerful Howard faction. Bacon's arbitration cruelly disguised his involvement with the rising star of George Villiers. Coke for his part had become saddled with the consequences of his aptitude for histrionics. In the trial of Somerset, the king's former favorite, he had seemed to invite too much exposure of the Court's dirty linen. Now, in his dispute with Ellesmere, he was trapped by his own reliance upon some dubious, perhaps fraudulent, litigants. His detractors moved in and his ability to blunt an attack upon his *Reports* had little immediate significance. Humiliating dismissal followed but he was still a man of consequence and he was by no means out of favor. In 1620 he was again offended when Montague, the graceless person who had replaced him on King's Bench, was made lord treasurer and in the following year he cannot have liked the selection of Williams as lord keeper of the great seal to succeed the fallen Bacon. Coke was over seventy by this time. Despite some petulant remarks by James, he never conceived himself to be a critic of Crown or prerogative.

It was a world of paradox.[42] There was a cry for reform but this always seemed to threaten vested interests. More officials were needed, but this meant more offices to sell. Established clerks were happy to increase the number of

---

42. The point is made by Cooper, p. 535.

their subordinates but they did not wish more of their own kind and status. They complained bitterly against new offices created by patent and the noise of their objection may have done something to encourage popular criticism of offices in general. On another level it is apparent that lawyers were associated with greed and incompetence, but even so their services were in constant demand. Attorneys, clerks and counsel were held responsible for all the ails of a system which rested upon the backs of laymen. Great courts established their authority on the basis of an expanding complexity of procedures which required expense and time. Chancery and Star Chamber spawned an extraordinary machinery of evidence. With respect to one set of Star Chamber depositions, Walmsley said that a man might just as well have paid four subsidies or provided twenty horses for defense of the realm.[43] The circumstances of debtors illustrate another aspect. Their treatment was recognized as a social wrong but every attempt to alleviate their burden or to avoid senseless imprisonment aroused objection. This was the quagmire which lured Bacon toward destruction. He fastened upon the notion that a minority of creditors might be coerced by the majority into allowing the debtor more time or even a composition. The idea was not new, but Bacon was exploiting the reaffirmation of chancery powers obtained in 1616. In 1621, amid a storm of parliamentary objection, he was cut down, and there was general criticism of administrative practices in Chancery and other great courts.

Some aspects of the Parliament of 1621 are only understandable if the performance of previous assemblies is appreciated. James's ministers had to find more money and patronage. Trade and the structure of office provided most opportunity to crown lawyers who were happy to employ conventional legality. The Crown forced the pace with respect to impositions, and James could confront Parliament with the judgment of the Exchequer in Bate's case. This was basic to Salisbury's extension of trade taxes in 1608, but the Crown did not rely solely upon the limited decision expressed in Bate's case. Opponents, who employed lawyers to construct a counter-argument, questioned the right to impose but they also tried to distinguish between different commodities or challenged the amount of the tax. In 1610 this issue helped to disrupt consideration of Salisbury's proposals with respect to feudal incidents. In 1614 dissent over impositions was even more important. The House of Lords refused a conference with the Commons. Coke and his fellow judges declined to pronounce

---

43. Hawarde, p. 54.

upon the legality of the tax. They had good reasons, but the episode underlined the fact that the judges as assistants to the Upper Chamber could only be of minimal help. This Parliament was dissolved without legislation being passed and so there was a problem about statutes which, it might be supposed, should have been renewed. An eventual solution was discerned in the theory that an assembly which failed to pass legislation was only a convention and not a parliament. It followed that statutes needing renewal continued in force until the next Parliament. There was embarrassment after the Parliament of 1621–22, which in mid-session passed a subsidy act and an act confirming the clerical subsidy but no other legislation—at times neither the justices nor the justices of the peace seemed to know what to do—but the Parliaments of 1624 and 1625 more or less cleaned up the mess. This little episode is important because it indicates that legitimate legal interpretations of Parliament were outmoded. Activity in the House of Commons made it impossible to interpret Parliament solely according to the established principles of traditional legal analysis. In terms of political reality, the Lower Chamber was a strident debating forum in which the grievances and ideas of the upper crust of society were presented.[44]

Traditional legal attitudes did not accord with the political role of the Commons but they were extremely relevant to the judicial revival of the Upper Chamber in 1621, one of the most striking occurrences of James's reign. The trials of Bacon and Mompesson are renowned, but in retrospect the most interesting factor was provided by a mass of petitions some of which invited supervision of proceedings in the great courts of law. The House of Lords, somewhat aided by Coke's explanations of its authority, seized the opportunity. By the end of the decade its specialized committee had developed recognized procedures and powers. Beneath the king the House of Lords made arrangements which matched its claim to be the summit of the legal structure.[45]

The reign of James was part of a period renowned for litigation, but often this means no more than that a great number of people were involved in the machinery of the law. In a large county, jury service could touch over a thousand men in a year.[46] The theme of dependence upon laymen is vital but so is the notion that distinctions between law and administration cannot be drawn

44. W. J. Jones, *Politics and the Bench* (1971), pp. 80–83.

45. Jessie L. Stoddart, "Constitutional Crisis and the House of Lords, 1621–1629," (University of California, Berkeley, Ph.D. thesis, 1966).

46. E. W. Ives, "The Law and the Lawyers," in *Shakespeare in His Own Age,* ed. Allardyce Nicoll (Cambridge 1965), p. 73.

too easily, and this was as true for the village as for great affairs of state. That there were many faults, acutely apparent to contemporaries, cannot be denied. The primitive nature of common law criminal proceedings was made more objectionable by the increasing severity of the criminal law. Civil procedures were protracted and sometimes destructive to parties with a good case. Obstreperous litigants were matched by fee-hunting attorneys, clerks, lawyers and solicitors. Disputes between courts, whether justified as part of a natural process of regulation or condemned as poaching, confused and embittered the citizen. The modern attitude toward case law can hardly be said to have existed, and Coke has been described as wandering at random over the cases in question.[47] Yet in the years that lay ahead a greater reliance on precedent, particularly when it seemed to buttress the financial claims of the Crown, aroused an even greater popular antagonism. Bate's case, as an M.P. had feared in 1614, did indeed become a precedent.[48] It was very easy to criticize the courts, their behavior and officials, but there was an insufficient appreciation of real problems and real endeavors. James merely had to suffer a constant ebb and flow of difficulty and grievance but the climax would come in the reign of Charles. Oliver Cromwell, really a "moderate" on this subject, would express the accumulated frustration of several decades. "There is one general grievance in the nation. It is the law. Not that the laws are a grievance; but there are laws that are. And the great grievance lies in the execution and administration."[49]

---

47. Dawson, pp. 72–73. Plucknett, p. 281.
48. T. L. Moir, *The Addled Parliament of 1614* (Oxford 1958), p. 95.
49. Cited D. Veale, *The Popular Movement for Law Reform, 1640–1660* (Oxford 1970), p. 1.

The Procedure of the House of Commons Against Patents and Monopolies, 1621–1624

ELIZABETH READ FOSTER

❦ ❦ ❦

In 1621 and 1624 the House of Commons conducted an exhaustive examination of the King's grants of monopolies and patents.[1] It was Sir Edward Coke, "Captain Coke" as James called him, "the darling of the Parliament," who presided over the investigation and steered it through precarious legal shoals. His careful work as chairman of the Committee for Grievances in both 1621 and 1624 adds a revealing chapter to a tempestuous life;[2] and the investigation as a whole gives many interesting clues to the intricacies of the political situation. It shows also the way in which the House of Commons attacked grievances, evolving new ways of procedure or stretching older ones to meet the new situations which arose.

"The Procedure of the House of Commons Against Patents and Monopolies, 1621–1624" is reprinted, by permission of New York University Press, from *Conflict in Stuart England: Essays in Honour of Wallace Notestein,* W. A. Aiken and B. D. Henning, eds. (New York: New York University Press, 1960).

1. The sources for the Parliament of 1624 parallel those of 1621. The most valuable of these are the manuscript accounts, which I have used through the courtesy of Wallace Notestein and Hartley Simpson. This collection consists of ten accounts of 1624: (1) the diary of Edward Nicholas, hereafter referred to as *Nicholas;* (2) the diary of John Pym, hereafter called *Pym;* (3) an anonymous diary (hereafter called *Gurney*) found among the Gurney papers at Keswick Hall, Norfolk, but since purchased by Harvard University; (4) the diary of Sir Walter Erle, hereafter called *Erle;* (5) the diary of Sir Thomas Holland, hereafter called *Holland;* (6) the diary of John Holles, hereafter called *Holles;* (7) D'Ewes's *Journal,* hereafter called *Harl. 159;* (8) an account of two meetings of the Committee of Courts of Justice in the *Book of Committees* (May 7th and May 10th, Lords MSS.; this is part of the same manuscript published in *Commons Debates 1621,* vol. VI; (9) the "Braye Manuscript" in the possession of Lord Braye at Stanford Hall (*Historical Manuscripts Commission,* Tenth Report, Appendix VI), a journal drawn up by John Brown who became Clerk of Parliament in 1640, almost identical with the *Commons Journal* with some few corrections and additions; (10) Rawlinson D723, a collection of "separates," February 19th–February 24th, with some account of February 23rd. In direct quotations I have modernized spelling.

2. David Harris Wilson, *The Privy Councillors in the House of Commons, 1604–1629,* Minneapolis, 1940 [Oxford, 1940], 153. *S. P. Venetian, 1621–1623,* XVII, 271. Patents and monopolies were investigated by other committees, such as the Committee on Trade; but the procedure followed was the same throughout.

A monopoly, to follow Coke's definition, was "an institution or allowance by the King by his grant, commission or otherwise, to any person or persons, bodies politic or corporate of or for the sole buying, selling, making, working or using of anything whereby any person or persons, bodies politic or corporate are sought to be restrained of any freedom or liberty that they had before, or hindered in their lawful trade."[3] The Commons had complained of monopoly grants to Elizabeth. In 1603, in the famous case of *Darcy* v. *Allen,* the judges had declared them illegal, a statement which James reaffirmed in his Book of Bounty. This proclamation issued in 1610 as a measure of fiscal reform outlined James's proposed policy with regard to patents and monopolies. It listed two categories of grants which the King would not issue: (1) "Things contrary to our Law," which were monopolies, and "grants of the benefit of any penal laws, or of power to dispense with the law, or compound for the forfeiture"; and (2) grants which the King reserved to his own use.[4] But still the Crown issued grants in increasing numbers. They included not only monopoly grants for new inventions, for the introduction of new industry, or for the control of other industries like saltpetre and the printing of books long recognized as essential to the common welfare, but also grants of commercial privileges which involved dispensing with existing statutes, licenses to perform functions belonging properly to the Government, and grants delegating to an individual the dispensing power of the Crown. In earlier times grants had been made by the Crown for the introduction of new industries, and the Crown itself had retained control of the industry. But by the end of the sixteenth century grants were made increasingly to private persons on their own application, and control had shifted from the Crown to the patentee, making possible grievous abuses.[5] The Privy Council had considered withdrawing some grants before Parliament met in 1621 to "sweeten" the Commons for the subsidy. But nothing had come of this plan, largely through the influence of Buckingham.[6] Redress through the courts was slow and apt to be dangerous and unavailing if the grants were backed by King and favorite.[7] The quashing of an indi-

---

3. Sir Edward Coke, *The Third Part of the Institutes of the Laws of England,* London, 1660, Chapter LXXXV, 181.

4. *Commons Debates 1621,* VII, Appendix B, 491–96.

5. W. S. Holdsworth, *A History of English Law,* Boston, 1924 [London, 1934], IV, 346–53. E. Wyndham Hulme, "The History of the Patent System Under the Prerogative and at Common Law," *Law Quarterly Review,* XII, 141–54.

6. James Spedding, ed., *The Letters and Life of Francis Bacon,* London, 1861–74, VII, 152. Willson, 43–45.

7. Little came of Elizabeth's promise to leave the patents to common law, and one case at least was stayed. *Holdsworth,* IV, 348. Glanville remarked in 1624 "that heretofore when a man would speak against

vidual grant, as was clear from the case of *Darcy* v. *Allen,* would hardly stem the flood. It was increasingly evident that the only real hope for relief was in Parliament.

There were many men in the House of Commons, as there had been in the past, to complain of these grants. The country gentry had been particularly offended by Sir Giles Mompesson's grant of licensing inns.[8] The representatives of the outports had long been trying to break the monopoly of the London companies, and were glad to take advantage of prevailing winds to advance their own barks.[9] The common lawyers, who were so important in the House, were outraged at the grant of the right of dispensing with penal statutes.[10] Special interest groups in many trades lobbied for their own freedoms under the general head of "grievances." Personal animosities and the current distrust of the policies of the King and of his Ministers and favorites sharpened the complaints against Bacon, who had passed on the legality of many patents,[11] and perhaps against Buckingham, whose men held many of the grants and whose powerful backing had foiled earlier efforts at reform.[12]

---

a patent of monopoly, it must be before a council table and there have a perpetual emparlance and could not have the trial of it by the common law, and this was the cause of the preferring of this Bill [the Bill of Monopolies]." *Nicholas,* f. 25*v.* (Folio references are to Nicholas's 1624 diary.) There were a number of complaints in 1621 that the proclamations accompanying patents took protests against the execution of the patent to the Star Chamber. Wallace Notestein, Frances Helen Relf, Hartley Simpson, eds., *Commons Debates 1621,* New Haven, 1935.

8. *Commons Debates 1621,* II, 109–10; V, 483–84. In 1624 Wentworth "desired course might be taken to prevent an abusive clause now usual in patents to command the justices to aid and assist them. They are to execute the laws of the kingdom and ought not to be made subject to every paltry patentee, which is a slavery makes men weary of the office of a justice of peace." *Pym,* ff. 81*v.*–82.

9. The Commons were partial to the outports and often applied the term "monopoly" to companies. Astrid Friis, *Alderman Cockayne's Project and the Cloth Trade,* London, 1927, 153 ff., 163–64. *Commons Debates 1621,* II, 217, and note 27. T. C. Mendenhall, *The Shrewsbury Drapers and the Welsh Wool Trade in the XVI and XVII Centuries,* London, 1953, Chapter VI.

10. For the decision of the judges in 1605 in the case of the grant of the power of dispensing with penal statutes, see Sir Edward Coke, *The Seventh Part of the Reports of Sir Edward Coke,* London, 1727, 36–37. The Book of Bounty, 1610, also declared such grants illegal. *Commons Debates 1621,* VII, Appendix B, 492. For protests in 1621 and 1624, see Edward Nicholas, *Proceedings of the House of Commons in 1620 and 1621,* Oxford, 1766, I, 63–65, 146–47; *Commons Debates 1621,* VI, 249; V, 35–36, 41–42, 258; IV, 79, 147–48. In 1624 the debate on the continuance and repeal of statutes again raised the question in connection with the Earl of Nottingham's patent. See the debate on May 22nd, 1624, *Erle,* ff. 189*v.*–190; *Nicholas,* ff. 216–216*v.; Gurney,* 235. Paul Birdsall, "'Non Obstante'—A Study of the Dispensing Power of English Kings" in *Essays in History and Political Theory in Honour of Charles Howard McIlwain,* Cambridge, Mass., 1936 [Oxford, 1936], is valuable. The protest at this time was not against the dispensing power which was generally conceded to be a prerogative right, but against its grant to others. A speech of Sandys's makes this especially clear: *Nicholas,* I, 200.

11. S. R. Gardiner, *History of England from the Accession of James I to the Outbreak of the Civil War, 1603–1642,* London, 1908, IV, 40, 46–50. *Nicholas,* I, 222–23.

12. For grants promoted or procured by Buckingham, see *Commons Debates 1621,* VII, 312, 367, 379, 391–92, 415–17, 461, 469–70; *Nicholas,* f. 31. For his procuring of the enrollment of grants, see *Commons*

There was much discontent, then, when the House assembled in 1621, and the Commons were ready to make the most of their historic position as "representatives of the realm." The decline of parliamentary government on the Continent, the precarious position of Protestantism, the failure of Court and Council to provide remedies, made them more than usually conscious of their own position and responsibilities.[13]

An awareness of public opinion runs through the debates of both sessions. In December 1621, although a message from the King about their privileges left the House dumbfounded, the House ordered Sir Edward Coke to give his report from the Committee of Grievances, "that the Town may take notice, that we are again proceeding with Businesses."[14] It was with their eyes on the "country" that the Commons fought for their privileges. As William Mallory remarked: "We are entrusted for our country. If we lose our privileges, we betray it; if we give way to this, we lose our privileges. . . . Let us not look upon ourselves only, but upon our posterity also. . . ."[15] Sir Henry Withrington reminded his colleagues of the imprisonment of Sir Edwin Sandys: "I have heard this business hath been questioned three times before my coming up. . . . They told me in the country you are as like to speak as any man, take heed, you see what is become of Sir Edwin Sandys; you are brave fellows whilst you are together, but what becomes of you when you are parted. . . ."[16]

The debate on the subsidy shows a similar concern for the "country." In 1621 there was a good deal of discussion as to whether redress of grievances, Bills and subsidy should go together. Sir George More and Sir Edward Coke, both old Parliament men, agreed that grievances and supply were their chief busi-

Debates 1621, VII, 311, 332, 340, 345, 348–49, 370, 379, 386–87, 390, 416–17, 429, 443, 458, 470. John Hacket, *Scrinia Reserata: A Memorial Offer'd to the Great Deservings of John Williams D.D.,* London, 1692, 49, comments on both Bacon's and Buckingham's part in monopoly grants. For the significance of the attack on patents in relation to Buckingham see Gardiner, IV, 45, 51–54, 85. *Cabala, sive Scrinia Sacra . . . ,* London, 1691, I, 2. *S. P. Venetian,* XVI, 767, 774, 789; XVII, 2, 40, 56, 84. Tillières to Puysieux, Paris Transcripts, *P.R.O.,* 3/54–55. See also the letters of Salvetti, the English representative of the Grand Duke of Tuscany, March 19th, March 26th, April 16th, April 23rd, May 21st, 1621. *Salvetti MSS.* 27962 A, I and II, *Salvetti MSS.* 27962 B. Willson, 43, 148, 292.

13. *S. P. Venetian,* XVI, 608, 631, 644.
14. *Nicholas,* II, 361.
15. *Commons Debates 1621,* II, 484. See also the debate on December 11th, 1621, *Commons Debates 1621,* VI, 232. Pollard feels that in the early seventeenth century, Parliament insisted on its privileges for its own sake and only later translated privileges into terms of responsibility to the constituencies. A. F. Pollard, *The Evolution of Parliament,* London, 1920, 178–79. While this may have been true for the eighteenth century (Pollard, 179–81), the evidence indicates that it is not for the early seventeenth. The House of Commons was conscious of public opinion and the fight for privileges was connected with the concept of themselves as "the representative body of the realm."
16. *Commons Debates 1621,* II, 485.

ness. "Grievances and supply like twins, as Jacob and Esau, should go hand in hand." "It will be a good encouragement to us to enable us to give a good account of our doings to our country for whom we are entrusted." When time grew short and it was apparent that Parliament would be adjourned before the grievances could all be prepared, Wentworth still fought for some Bills to go up to the King with the subsidy; for, "He that thinks country men have no understanding or that they will be fed with words shall find himself much deceived. . . ."[17] Part of these debates followed what the Members loved to call the "old parliamentary way" of bargaining subsidy for redress of grievances, a policy which they condemned roundly, but none the less astutely pursued just as they had under Elizabeth and in earlier times.[18] The Members of the Commons knew that the eyes of the country were upon them, that copies of their speeches circulated in manuscript or in printed form, that in ale-houses and in country seats talk was of Parliament matters.[19]

Both King and Commons felt that a member of the House of Commons should inform the sovereign of affairs in his own shire and borough. In 1624 each Member was asked to report on recusants in his particular district.[20] As Glanville and Coke put it, the Commons represented not themselves, as did the Lords, but their counties and boroughs. To the Commons, the King, "who would not have his subjects overburdened," referred the matter of subsidy "because we know the countries best."[21] Not only should a Member represent his "country" to the King, but carry news of State back home as well. A petition concerning a collection for the Queen of Bohemia was read in the House of Commons in 1624, so that it could be generally known.[22]

But the Members of the House of Commons believed that they represented more than their own "countries." They stood, too, for the nation. "Every man

17. *Ibid.,* 21–23; 163.
18. The link between subsidies and grievances is clear throughout the debates in 1621. In 1624 subsidies were promptly voted in a wave of enthusiasm for the proposed change in foreign policy, the break with Spain and the possibility of war with the old enemy. The bitterness of the debate on May 27th, 1624 reflected the Commons's regret at having acted so impetuously: ". . . if we had not agreed at the beginning of Parliament to give subsidies we should not in the end of it been put to these extremities by their Lordships. It were good we would find out and fall again into the old way of Parliament, which is now passed by. . . . It is our own faults, that we are thus used by them." *Nicholas,* ff. 231*v.*–232. For some interesting reflections on this point see Margaret Judson, *The Crisis of the Constitution,* New Brunswick, N.J., 1949, 72–75.
19. *Commons Debates for 1629,* ed. Wallace Notestein and Frances Relf, Minneapolis, 1921, v–lxiii. Wallace Notestein, *Winning of the Initiative,* London, 1924, 42–43. J. E. Neale, *Elizabeth I and Her Parliaments 1559–1581,* New York, 1952 [London, 1953], points out the propaganda possibilities of the subsidy preamble, pp. 124, 161.
20. *Commons Journal,* 754, 776.
21. *Holles,* f. 97; *Gurney,* 136–37 (1624).
22. *Nicholas,* f. 118; *Gurney,* 181–82.

that sits have three powers, one of himself, and the country, and the whole realm after his coming."[23] The whole of the House of Commons was greater than the sum of all its parts. It was more than an aggregation of local representatives, more than a body of informers, more than a group of messengers for the sovereign. It was the representative body of the realm. Because it was the representative body of the realm its privileges were important. Because it was the representative body of the realm it had its own peculiar function, as the Lords had theirs, and its own peculiar power.

From this concept, the Commons believed, proceeded not only their right but also their duty to inform the sovereign of grievances which afflicted his people. Grievances were no great matter to the Lords. "The great ones are not acquainted with the caterpillars that annoy us." Grievances, like the initiation of money bills, were the peculiar and important business of the Commons.[24] James himself recognized this ancient function of the Lower House in his opening speech in 1621, but he cautioned Members to consider only those grievances they brought with them from the country, not those which they found in town. The Speaker's conventional request for privileges on February 3rd included the plea that "they may have Liberty to prefer their grievances to his Majesty and expect Reformation from his Justice."[25] Coke elaborated this idea by maintaining that Parliaments should be summoned frequently to perform properly these essential duties. Members questioned his precedents but he defended his position with characteristic vigor.[26]

The Commons's function, they thought, was not only to consider and petition for redress of grievances and to present the griefs of their countries, but also to hear those griefs which men dared not present elsewhere. Parliament need fear neither prestige nor place. On April 26th, 1621 Sir John Jephson, Privy Councillor for Ireland, pictured the sorry state of Ireland to the House of Commons. Sir Edward Coke spoke in favor of an investigating committee, justifying first the Commons's jurisdiction over Irish affairs and secondly their consideration of such grievances. "None of these main grievances durst any man complain of out of Parliament that are here now." "All grievances are

23. *Holles*, ff. 29–29v. *Holland*, 2v. Coke has some interesting comments: Sir Edward Coke, *The Fourth Part of the Institutes of the Laws of England*, London, 1658, 2, 12, 14, 49.
24. Sir Edward Coke said in 1624: "The House, as they invited none, so neither could they refuse any that complained. The Members of the House were inquisitors of the realm, as coming from every part of it and being more sensible of grievances than the Lords in the Upper House were because they were once liable unto them." *Harl. 159*, f. 60v.; see also *Holles*, f. 29v.; *Holland*, f. 2v.
25. *Commons Debates 1621*, V, 431.
26. *Nicholas*, I, 134; *Commons Journal*, 551; *Commons Debates 1621*, V, 36.

not complained of out of Parliament. Who durst have spoken against those
great ones we have talked of freely?" Who, indeed, especially since the Irish
complaints were suspected to be a hit at Buckingham?[27] Much the same point
arose in 1624 in connection with the Earl Marshal's court, when the abuses
of the Heralds were discussed. "Those things," commented Sir Edward Coke,
who had reason to know, "that have great authority are safest to be dealt withal
by the Parliament."[28]

Parliament, too, was the place where men turned increasingly for redress
of grievances which could find no relief elsewhere. If the King and the Privy
Council would not withdraw monopolies, if the processes of law were piti-
ful means to fight the increasing swarm of parasites that plagued the land,
then the Commons would and could. By 1621 discontent was widespread and
protests against the patentees came in from many parts of the country. By
1621, also, the Commons had developed a committee system and a parliamentary procedure capable of handling a complicated investigation and of seizing
the initiative from King and Councillors who would rather have steered them
rapidly to supply and away from grievances. In 1621 and 1624 the House of
Commons had on its benches able men like Coke, Alford, Sandys, Wentworth,
Pym, Glanville and Noy, articulate, bold, learned and experienced in the affairs of Parliament and law, who could take the leadership left vacant by the
death of Salisbury and the negligence of a short-sighted King.[29]

On February 5th, 1621 Parliament's first day of actual business, the Members of the House of Commons fell to discussing the agenda for the session,
and quickly divided their business into four main parts to be further debated
at a committee of the whole House that afternoon: (1) the recurrent question
of liberties and privileges, (2) the desirability of petitioning the King to execute the laws against recusants, (3) supply, and (4) grievances. The committee
of the whole pursued these points in order, and it was not until February 19th
that the matter of grievances engaged its full attention.[30]

Noy opened the discussion. Monopolies and the grant of powers to dispense
with penal laws were, he said, the chief grounds of all grievances. Coke fol-

27. *Commons Debates 1621,* III, 91; V, 102; VI, 396.
28. *Holland,* II, f. 57v.; see also *Pym,* f. 81v. In 1624 the House suspected that petitioners were being
kept from Parliament. A committee was appointed "to inquire, who those men were that were deterred
from complaining to this House; and who did deter them." *Commons Journal,* 759–60; see also *Harl. 159,*
ff. 101v. ff.
29. Notestein, *Winning of the Initiative, passim.* Willson, 236 ff.
30. *Commons Debates 1621,* II, 24; VI, 249, note 1.

lowed with a long speech, declaring all monopolies, all grants of dispensation from penal laws directly void in law.[31] These two speeches, introducing the Commons's investigation, might well have served also as conclusion and summary, for they state effectively and fully the attitude toward grievances which the House was to follow during both the sessions of 1621 and 1624. There was throughout an emphasis on patents, on monopoly grants, on grants of dispensations from penal laws, as the major grievances and the basic cause of many other evils. There was, too, always the effort to show that such grants were illegal, that the King had been misinformed in allowing them. If the King's counsel had misled him it was the Commons's task to show him where the error lay, to make known their findings, and in the light of them to appeal from the King ill-informed to the King better-informed.

There was no lack of material for them to consider. Complaints against the patents and monopolies poured into the House from all sides, for the streams of discontent found many channels. Privy Councillors and Government officials who sat in the House as elected Members, brought grievances to the floor.[32] Other Members of the House of Commons, true to their character as informers and "general inquisitors," were eager with complaints. Some of them reflected local conditions, which the Members knew at first hand; some of them were "notorious and known grievances," like the patent of inns and alehouses, which would inevitably occur to the representative body of the realm. Sir Edward Coke spoke on February 22nd, 1621 of receiving "complaints out of his own country" against the patent of ale-house recognizances. Savage, Mallett and Mallory brought in examples of Sir John Townsend's execution of the patent of concealments; and William Salisbury, who represented Merioneth, raised the question of concealed subsidies in Wales. Some Members had probably compiled lists of patents to be considered beforehand. Noy had prepared his opening speech well. Sir Edward Coke had taken part in the committee of judges which considered withdrawal of some grants before Parliament met, and Hakewill remarked on March 22nd that there were "some Patents not yet named of greater consequence than any yet named."[33]

On February 21st Sir Edward Sackville moved that the House send for Mr. Sadler, Secretary to the Lord Privy Seal, who "hath a note of all the Monopolies and suchlike grants, whereof he is collector and receiveth all the Benefit which

---

31. *Nicholas,* I, 63; *Commons Debates 1621,* IV, 78; VI, 249–51.
32. *Commons Debates 1621,* VI, 251, 265; II, 123, 134. Willson, 248.
33. *Commons Debates 1621,* IV, 78, 183; VI, 249, 265. *Nicholas,* I, 63, 218–19.

comes to his Majesty." He could therefore inform the House what monopolies there were, and what the King got from them. The House agreed and Sadler later appeared, bringing his book. Crew moved on May 17th, 1621 that all grievances collected in the last Parliament be considered and presented to the King together with those of the present session. In 1624 a similar motion was made: that the Committee of Grievances should consider patents condemned or questioned by the last Parliament. Rich extended the motion to include the grievances of 1610, and it was so ordered.[34] Such wholesale methods brought a great many patents and monopolies to the floor. Individual Members added particular grievances from day to day.[35]

How often these Members of Parliament were moved by their own initiative to present grievances, and how often they spoke as the representatives of special interests, it is difficult to say. Plenty of men outside the House of Commons, for one reason or another, were anxious to bring special patents to the floor and sought Members of the House to do this for them.[36] In some instances the process is quite clear. Thus, on April 17th, 1621, Mallory presented a petition from the company of Armourers against the patent of arms.[37] In other cases there is no mention of the method by which the petition was presented, and it probably in many instances came directly into the House or the Committee of Grievances without the special sponsorship of a Member of the House.

The interests of many petitioners are quite apparent from the petition itself. Thus the grant of privileges for making starch to Vaughan and his associates put other starch-makers out of business, and subjected them to the oppressions of the patentees who seized their stock, and fined them. Lobbyists for the Shrewsbury Drapers, hoping for a share of the export trade, repeatedly attempted to bring the exclusive patent of the French Company under attack.[38] But whether private gentlemen spoke for others or spoke for themselves only further research can reveal. John Lambe's statement, though obviously biased

34. *Nicholas,* I, 73. *Commons Debates 1621,* II, 114; V, 303, note 8; III, 280. *Nicholas,* II, 87. *Commons Journal,* 718. *Nicholas,* f. 62. *Erle,* f. 66v.

35. *Nicholas,* I, 81. *Commons Journal,* 563, 575, 623, 718. *Commons Debates 1621,* V, 309; IV, 183, 196, 200; VI, 81; II, 122, 378. *Nicholas,* f. 21; *Holles,* f. 93v.

36. The Venetian Ambassador, for instance, was interested in opening up the trade in glass, raisins and muscatels, which had been closed by the grants to Mansell and to the Levant Company. He evidently encouraged opposition to both these grants. *S. P. Venetian,* XVII, 26; XVII, 59.

37. *Commons Debates 1621,* V, 330. *Commons Journal,* 578. *Nicholas,* I, 260–61.

38. *Commons Debates 1621,* VII, Appendix B, 513–15. Appendix B also contains other revealing petitions. *Mendenhall,* 180–87.

since he had been called into question by the Committee on Courts and was writing to the King, is interesting in this connection. "The Complainants are underhand set on and countenanced by greater persons in this county that, through me, aim at your Majesty's Ecclesiastical jurisdiction . . ."[39] Possibly there was more behind the petitions and the complaints of Members of the House against grievances of patents and monopolies than met the eye.

Privy Councillors, Government officials, Members of Parliament, private gentlemen, and "lobbying" interests, eagerly supplied the House with grievances. General debate on seemingly unrelated subjects brought forth still more. On February 6th, 1621, in the debate on "want of coin," Glanville analyzed the causes of the scarcity. His reasons were various, but among them appeared the patent of the East India Company to transport silver. Spencer added the patent of gold lace, and Alford moved that a select committee examine "all patents of that nature." On February 26th the same question was raised again. Herrick mentioned as one of the causes of the decay of money, the patent of gold wire. Sandys, Coke, Phelips and others, questioned the patent of tobacco. The consideration of the depression in the cloth trade likewise involved grants, and brought the patent of Staplers, and the patent of dyestuffs under discussion.[40]

Bills also brought patents and monopoly grants to the agenda. Some, like the Bill presented by the grocers against the apothecaries, the Act against the patent of Welsh butter, the Bill to ratify the charter of the Goldsmiths' Company, may be regarded as another method of petitioning the House. The Bill for sea-marks, reported on March 9th, 1621, led to the order that the Committee of Grievances consider patents of the lighthouses of Dungeness and Winterton Ness.[41]

Some Bills, on the other hand, were more general in scope, and raised a larger issue where individual patents emerged indirectly. Thus, the debates in 1624 on the Bill of Monopolies bred a host of proposed exceptions, among them the question of the subpoena office. This point was debated on April 19th, and Coke finally moved and the House resolved that all patents mentioned in the Bill be "seen and considered of, before anything be done."[42] On

39. *Commons Debates 1621,* VII, Appendix C, 606–9. See also Hacket, 191; Willson, 181–82.
40. *Commons Debates 1621,* II, 29–30, 140, note 20, 204, 214–15; IV, 19, 95–98; V, 159, 262–63, 469, 486–88, 524–29; VI, 10, 16, 456. *Nicholas,* II, 86–88. *Commons Journal,* 549.
41. *Nicholas,* f. 46; *Gurney,* p. 74; *Pym,* f. 17v.; Holland, ff. 78 ff. *Commons Journal,* 564. *Commons Debates 1621,* IV, 110; II, 204; VI, 456.
42. April 19th, 1624. *Commons Journal,* 771; Pym, ff. 71v. ff.

April 28th, 1624 Noy's report of the Bill for Continuance and Repeal of Statutes had a similar effect. "For either the law or the dispensation naught. And so
to have it presented to the King." Patents of dispensation were consequently
ordered in to the Committee of Grievances.[43]

The examination of patents and monopolies in 1621 and 1624 came to be
fairly stereotyped. A complaint, as we have seen, was presented either to the
House or to one of its standing committees—in the case of patents and monopoly grants usually either to the Committee of Grievances, of which Sir
Edward Coke was chairman, or to the Committee of Trade with Cranfield,
who was also a Privy Councillor, as its chairman. Once the complaint came on
to the agenda and had been accepted as worthy its consideration and proper to
its work,[44] the committee (or the sub-committee as the case may be) warned
the patentees to appear for a hearing and summoned witnesses on both sides.
Either, with permission, might appear with or by counsel;[45] and this practice
became so well established that several attorneys made it their special business
to plead cases before the House.[46] The patent in question was called in, and
any relevant documents necessary to a full investigation: the books and memoranda of the patentees, court records, or the accounts of Government officials.
Often special groups or individuals interested in the recall of the patent supplied written affidavits of its ill effects.

The House was, then, exercising two distinct powers: that of summoning
individuals to appear before it, and that of ordering in documents. Who could
be and was summoned? By far the largest group were the patentees and men
involved in some way in the complaints or petitions presented to the House.[47]
Among them came officers of the Crown, such as the Lieutenant of the Tower,

43. April 28th, 1624. *Commons Journal,* 693, 778. *Pym,* f. 82.
44. Sub-committees were appointed to receive petitions and sort them. (*Nicholas,* I, 115, 220, 278. *Commons Debates 1621,* IV, 146; II, 208, 274, note 3; V, 328–29. *Commons Journal,* 550, 572, 582.) Possibly they
rejected some. (*Commons Debates 1621,* IV, 146. *Commons Journal,* 550.) Sub-committees also prepared the
committee's work by investigating particular petitions. They acted as a fact-finding body which heard witnesses and complainants, and examined relevant documents, reporting their findings to the grand committee in cases where the committee did not undertake the investigation itself. (*Commons Debates 1621,* V, 319;
II, 291, note 2; III, 195; VI, 217, and in many other places.) The sub-committee to consider the Merchant
Adventurers' patent was granted the power of summons and the power to call in documents. (*Commons
Journal,* 598–99; *Commons Debates 1621,* III, 111.) There was a strong feeling in the House that all petitions
should be answered and those rejected so marked and returned. (*Commons Debates 1621,* II, 207–8; III, 22.
Nicholas, I, 279. *Commons Journal,* 582.)
45. For 1621, see *Commons Debates 1621,* I, Index, 180. For 1624 the examples are equally numerous:
Erle, ff. 81, 86v.–87v.; *Holland,* f. 82; Pym, ff. 49v. ff; *Nicholas,* ff. 221–221v., and elsewhere.
46. *Commons Debates 1621,* II, 50, note 23.
47. See, for example, *Commons Debates 1621,* V, 469, 476–77, 296, 245; VI, 451, 266, 271, 456–57, 79,
462–63; II, 112–13, 365; III, 441; IV, 92, 339; VI, 1624: *Pym,* f. 22v.; *Nicholas,* ff. 79–79v.; *Erle,* f. 92; *Nicholas,*
f. 172v.

and Gibbs of the Bedchamber. Officers of the Crown were likewise called as witnesses, as Sadler, Secretary to the Lord Privy Seal.[48] The Commons attempted to summon witnesses and parties on both sides, and in cases involving the royal interest, arranged to hear the King's counsel.[49] In some cases the House actually "sequestered" persons during the time of their examination.[50] It regarded refusal to obey a summons as "contempt," and dispatched the Serjeant to fetch offenders guilty of repeated refusal.[51]

Patentees were usually ordered to bring their patents with them and any proclamations or commissions issued in support of the patent. This practice the King protested at the end of the session of 1624. "You have a custom," he said, "(which I'll know whether it be agreeable to ancient usage or not) presently upon any complaint to send for the patent and to keep it with you . . . When once ye have a patent, ye take it upon you to keep it from my patentees. You have nothing to do but to read it and see that it agree with the patent and then deliver it back to the patentees. And if you do not so, I must take a course it be done."[52] "No court," replied Sir Edward Coke, the next day in the House of Commons, "doth judge on copies but on records, and therefore it is reason we should have the patents here brought to us."[53] There was more than the inevitable lawyer's defense in Coke's statement, and there was more than idle protest in the King's remark. The two together may show much of the significance of the Commons's procedure and of the investigation as a whole. But the point for the moment is that James's statement was quite accurate as to fact. The Commons did call in patents, and did keep them while they were under consideration, which, with the amount of business before the Committee of Grievances, usually meant that they kept them a long time. In fact, the orders for the return of patents at the end of the session of 1624 seem to indicate that for that session, at least, they kept them during the whole session and did not ever return those which were condemned.[54] The calling in of the actual patent

48. *Commons Debates 1621*, II, 114, 291, note 2; VI, 62, 278; IV, 192–93; *Nicholas*, I, 156; *Commons Journal*, 554, 574. Belasyse notes in his diary: "Blundell [patentee of pedlars] and Mompesson were called in person to answer, though they were the King's servants." *Commons Debates 1621*, V, 35. Mompesson was, of course, an M.P., but he doubtless would have been summoned, as others were, even without this special claim to jurisdiction.

49. *Commons Debates 1621*, III, 197. *Gurney*, 216; *Holland*, II, ff. 18*v.*–19, *Harl. 159*, ff. 109*v.*, 111.

50. *Commons Debates 1621*, II, 112–13; VI, 271. *Commons Journal*, 535–36.

51. *Commons Debates 1621*, III, 146; IV, 335. *Commons Journal*, 780.

52. *Harl. 159*, f. 35.

53. May 29th, 1624. *Nicholas*, ff. 244–46 for Coke's speech and the debate in the House.

54. *Commons Debates 1621*, V, 142–43. There was an interesting debate at the end of the session in 1624 on what to do with the patents in the House. Those which had not been "censured" were ordered to be given back to the patentees. Various suggestions were made about those which had been "condemned as

and its supporting proclamations and commissions was in effect, if the law be strictly read, a stay in the execution of the grant during the period of its consideration, for the patentees were not in possession of the legal authorization for their acts. The House also issued specific orders that patents should not be executed while they were under consideration, and that suits pending on them should be stayed.[55]

Account books and other documents relative to the patents and their execution, warrants, certificates and memoranda, were likewise ordered in, and in some cases these papers were seized.[56] In 1621 the King, possibly prompted by the company itself, attempted to withhold the books of the Merchant Adventurers from the Committee of Trade which had called for them. The House, partly at the instigation of the Cinque Ports, who held a brief against the company, raised the cry of breach of their liberties; but the question was pushed no further till 1624, when James compromised by allowing a committee of six to examine the books "and pick out what was material to the business."[57] To make its knowledge more complete the House, when necessary, searched court records and on occasion had them brought into the House.[58] Assuming, then, a sincere desire for a full investigation, the Commons had the necessary information at hand.

---

grievances." Wentworth thought that they should be endorsed, "condemned," or turned over to the King's Council, with the request that a *scire facias* be brought against them. Coke supported this last plan. The Chancellor of the Duchy was for marking them "condemned," and leaving them in the House, with the order that if the King's Council should send for them that they be delivered. *Nicholas,* ff. 244–46. Digges was against having an order in the matter; and Wentworth, according to another account, was of the same mind, moving that the Clerk should simply do as had been done before. It was finally resolved that there should be no order. *Erle,* ff. 199–199v.

55. For specific orders staying the execution of specific patents, see *Commons Debates 1621,* II, 133; VI, 8, 459–60; IV, 193; V, 321, 330. *Commons Journal,* 563, 565, 573–74, 578, 637. *Nicholas,* I, 88, 90, 261. For the debate on the stay of the execution of the patent of surveying sea coals in Newcastle, and the King's attempt to intervene, in 1624, see *Commons Journal,* 736; *Holles,* f. 100v.; *Erle,* ff. 82v.–83; *Holland,* ff. 52 ff.; *Erle,* ff. 192–192v.; *Gurney,* 241. For general orders on the stay of all patents condemned or under consideration, see *Commons Debates 1621,* VI, 464, 479. In both 1621 and 1624 there were breaches of the House's orders. *Commons Debates 1621,* IV, 335. *Nicholas,* II, 251, 306–7. *Commons Journal,* 652. *Nicholas,* II, 306–7. In 1624 there were even more cases; for in the three years since Parliament had last met many of the patents condemned in 1621 had been put in execution again in defiance of the Commons's order of June 2nd, 1621. *Commons Debates 1621,* VI, 479. The offending patentees were ordered to bring these patents in and attend the House for censure. *Holles,* f. 83; *Gurney,* 39–40; *Erle,* ff. 61–61v.

56. See, for example, *Commons Debates 1621,* VI, 456–57; V, 323; III, 2–3. *Commons Journal,* 573. In Michell's case a warrant was granted to search his study. *Commons Journal,* 540. *Commons Debates 1621,* II, 170; V, 28, 274. For a description of the type of papers the House of Commons had in this case see *Commons Journal,* 551.

57. *Commons Debates 1621,* III, 157–58, 246 ff.; IV, 339. Friis, 88, note 1. *Commons Journal,* 758. *Holles,* f. 125. For the report on the committee's search of the Book see *Erle,* ff. 139–139v.; *Holland,* II, ff. 22 ff.; *Pym,* ff. 64v.–65.

58. *Commons Debates 1621,* II, 481; VI, 480. *Nicholas,* II, 159.

The Commons were not only quite conscious of the type of investigation they were thus able to conduct, but also explicit as to its nature. They insisted first that all valid complaints should be fully examined, and that both sides to a dispute should be heard. Where there were complainers, there were also defenders; and both were entitled to a hearing.[59] Defendants were not allowed written copies of the charges, but on one occasion at least (though it was not the case of a patent) provision was made that the charges should be specific, for "no man is bound by the Law to answer to a general charge. . . . And therefore the honour and justice of the House to have the particulars set down."[60] The King complained that the very name of patent had become odious to the Commons; patentees charged that the cards were stacked against them, and that they were not fully heard; but whatever the political motives that played into the matter, the constitutional and legal framework for an impartial examination was adequate.[61]

Actual procedure varied, of course, with the individual patent. In general, however, it was fairly uniform. A date was assigned for the hearing on each patent, and announced in advance, that the parties might be warned to appear and their counsel be prepared. The chairman of the committee probably led the questioning, though members were free to make remarks or interject questions of their own.[62] There was much discussion in both 1621 and 1624 of the power of the House to administer an oath and to examine upon oath, but it did not do so.[63] There were other means at hand for enforcing truthful state-

59. There must be an examination: *Commons Debates 1621,* VI, 253; II, 214–15; *Commons Journal,* 540–41, 771, 773; *Pym,* ff. 77*v.*–78; *Nicholas,* ff. 168–69; *Holland,* II, f. 44; *Harl. 159,* ff. 106*v.* Both sides must be heard: *Commons Debates 1621,* V, 88 and note 9; II, 278; *Commons Journal,* 575; *Harl. 159,* ff. 109*v.*, 111. For records of examinations, indicating that both sides were heard, see *Commons Debates 1621,* V, 319, 123; *Nicholas,* f. 175*v.* There were some complaints that patentees had not been fully heard: *Commons Debates 1621,* II, 321; John Rushworth, *Historical Collections,* London, 1659, I, 147. Michell maintained that Coke's questioning of him had been sarcastic and had prejudiced the House: *Commons Debates 1621,* VII, 505; VI, 264, note 6; II, 125, note 39; 129, note 11; 167, note 25. The King maintained that the examination was cursory: "Your judgment is too quick in those matters." *Harl. 159,* f. 126.

60. *Nicholas* I, 147, 163; II, 82–83. *Commons Debates 1621,* VI, 359; III, 383; V, 171, 194.

61. Noy's speech on February 19th, 1621 set the tone of the whole attack on patents as an *investigation:* "Let these and all other in the like case who have done this against the King's mind [i.e., procured grants against the Book of Bounty] be called to give an 'account of their husbandry,' to be rewarded if they have done well, 'if ill, to be punished.'" *Commons Debates 1621,* IV, 78–79. The King protested that the Commons should not call in patents until they knew them to be grievous. *Commons Debates 1621,* VI, 388–89; Rushworth, *Collections,* I, 47. This, of course, invalidated an investigation such as Noy outlined before it had begun. However, since most of the grants called were condemned, the King's statement that the very name of a patent was objectionable to the House (*Harl. 159,* f. 35) may have been a good deal more realistic than Noy's. James was probably right that calling in a patent would lead to its condemnation, and therefore became in itself a brand of condemnation on it.

62. *Commons Debates 1621,* VI, 352; IV, 33.

63. The power to use an oath was flatly denied (*Commons Debates 1621,* II, 3, 283; III, 24; *Harl. 159,*

ments; for as we have already seen the House heard both parties to a dispute, it searched records and examined corroborative evidence both oral and written. It punished witnesses for untrue statements, and delinquents only added contempt of the House to their other sins if caught in a falsehood.[64]

The examination may, for the sake of clarity, be divided into two parts: the first concerned the nature of the grant itself, the type of grant and its provisions, to what alleged purpose granted, and to whom; the second concerned the consequences of the grant, how executed, and the actual effect of its execution. The nature of the grant was often discovered by a reading of the patent itself, and by questioning the patentees.[65] Their counsel, their opponents' counsel, and Members of the House, like Noy, Coke or the Solicitor, who were trained in the law, interpreted the provisions. The patentees and their counsel were likewise asked to whom the patent had been granted, who procured it and who shared in it.[66] Sources of information on the consequences of the grant, its execution and its effect, were wider. Again the provisions, proclamations and commissions of the patent itself were consulted; again the patentees and their counsel were questioned. But their answers were weighed with the great body of evidence brought in by their opponents. It was against the execution that complaints were most readily lodged. Painters and bookbinders, for example, testified that the patent of gold foliate had raised its price and that far from conserving bullion, as it had promised, had actually spent it. Fishmongers claimed that Wigmore's patent raised the price of fish, and they were enjoined by the committee to set down the price of fish before the patent, and the quantity of fish brought in before and since.[67]

---

f. 67) and as flatly asserted (*Commons Debates 1621*, III, 167, 181–82; VI, 400 ff.; IV, 312). There was some discussion of settling the point by Bill (*Commons Debates 1621*, II, 160 and note 15) or by the petition to the King on privileges (*Commons Debates 1621*, VI, 342). Procedure without oath was justified on the grounds that the House was the representative body of the realm "and therefore not to be presumed to be ignorant of the country." (Glanville: *Commons Debates 1621*, V, 46. Coke said: "We are judges here and have notice of all things in the commonwealth." *Commons Journal*, 557.) The power to administer an oath involved the whole question of the jurisdiction of the House, and much of the debate centered on this point, which was raised in the Floyd case and the procedure against Mompesson and Bennet. The question was raised in 1624 during the debate on the Subsidy Bill. Sandys said: ". . . heretofore it hath been debated on and inclined to be the opinion of this House that in such cases as this House hath power to give a final judgment in and end this House may administer an oath, but in such cases as this House doth not finally determine but transmit it over to the Lords the House did seem to doubt whether we had power or not to administer an oath, but did resolve nothing in it but made claim to have right and power to do it." *Nicholas*, f. 205; see also f. 225v., and Coke's statement, *Holland*, II, f. 87v.)

64. *Commons Debates 1621*, IV, 187; VI, 82; III, 249–54, 338. *Commons Journal*, 639.

65. For typical examples see *Commons Debates 1621*, V, 89–90, 478–79; IV, 200, 352–53; III, 63, 82–84; 195. *Nicholas*, I, 75–77, 115–17, 222, 295–96, 303, 320–24; *Nicholas*, II, 38–39. *Commons Journal*, 538. *Erle*, ff. 61v., 80v.

66. *Commons Journal*, 541. *Commons Debates 1621*, IV, 129; II, 172–73; V, 31–32, 275 ff.; VI, 34–35.

67. *Nicholas*, I, 294–95, 339–40. *Commons Debates 1621*, V, 88, 105–6.

Such testimony came, as we have suggested, from various sources. The committee had plenty of material to work on. Those who attacked grants and those who defended them both strove to make a strong case, and presented their evidence in many ways. Oral testimony came from patentees and their counsel, complainers, petitioners and their counsel, and witnesses presented or called on both sides.[68] Written testimony was admitted in petitions and certificates.[69] Collateral and corroborative evidence appeared in the patents themselves, in proclamations and commissions issued for their execution, in memoranda of patentees, in State documents and court records.[70]

Members of the House of Commons, though sometimes called as formal witnesses, also testified voluntarily and informally.[71] Many had their own special interests to serve in so doing, such as Sandys of the Virginia Company who attacked the patent of tobacco.[72] Others spoke from more general concern or class interest, such as the country gentlemen who pointed out that Mompesson's patent threatened the authority of justices of the peace. With the same Members of the House who sat as an investigating committee actively participating in gathering the case against the patentees, the King's charge of partiality was from the legal point of view quite justified.[73] Men like Sandys acted at once as witnesses and judges in their own case. Perhaps the House of Commons as a whole did much the same thing. Certainly though it acted within a framework of just procedure, it was also a political body, and the temper of that body was all too clear.

The political element in the investigation stands out perhaps most sharply in the proposed attack on the referees. The King had provided that all proposed grants be referred to certain of his Privy Councillors to be certified as legal and as "convenient" to his subjects.[74] The House of Commons in examining patents and monopoly grants called for the names of these referees.[75] It was natural, of course, that a fact-finding body should pursue this policy; but

68. *Commons Journal*, 543. *Commons Debates 1621*, V, 278; VI, 26; IV, 121–22; II, 195–97, 255 ff. *Nicholas*, I, 339–40, 360–63. *Nicholas*, II, 39–40.

69. Nicholas I, 156, 360–63. *Commons Debates 1621*, VI, 83 and note 4; VII, 508–11; II, 261; IV, 288. *Commons Journal*, 602. *Erle*, ff. 183v–184.

70. *Commons Debates 1621*, II, 166–67; IV, 140, 192–93; VI, 456–57; V, 311.

71. *Commons Debates 1621*, VI, 259–62; IV, 108; III, 82–83, 193–94. *Nicholas*, I, 218–19, 295–96, 321–24, 360–63. *Nicholas*, II, 36–38. *Erle*, ff. 61v.–62. *Nicholas*, ff. 81v.–82v.

72. *Commons Debates 1621*, V, 262, 524–29.

73. *Harl. 159*, f. 35.

74. William Hyde Price, *The English Patents of Monopolies*, Boston, 1906, 25–26. *Commons Debates 1621*, VII, 491–92.

75. *Commons Debates 1621*, VI, 259–62, 7, 269, 27, 57; II, 234–44, 250–51; V, 323, 311, 59; III, 42–43, 63, 102–4, 195. *Nicholas*, I, 146–47, 294–95, 305. *Commons Journal*, 541.

the House had other motives as well. The whole attack on the royal grants was carefully couched in terms of respect for the King and the prerogative. Naming the referee shifted responsibility for grievous grants from the King, as James, his Councillors and the Commons all vigorously insisted.[76] Referees were also convenient scapegoats for patentees themselves. Some professed to know very little about the certification of the grants they held, but others sought refuge from the Commons's attack in the fact that the King's counsel had approved their projects. Thus, winds blew upon the referees from both sides. It was suggested in the House that they be called to account for their misdeeds, and punished. Their names were brought out in nearly every patent examination, but nothing ever came of the plans for dealing with them.[77]

Stronger currents may have been blowing. The complete omission of the referees' names in the conference with the Lords on Mompesson's patents, despite instruction from the Commons to the contrary, seems suspicious. Members of the Commons's committee were directly charged with having faltered from fear.[78] Perhaps there was more at stake than individual patentees or individual grants. The Lord Chancellor's name appears again and again as referee, and the Lord Chancellor's impeachment came in 1621. Buckingham's name, though rarely mentioned in the House, could easily have been spelled out as one of the greatest of all "procurers"; and the drive against Buckingham was gathering force even now.

The attack on referees involved other issues as well. On March 21st, 1621 Coke reported Flood's patent of engrossing wills from the Committee of Grievances. In the debate that followed, Noy criticized the patent vigorously, declaring it to be against the law and liberty of the people. He brushed aside Flood's defense that it had been certified by two great men (Bacon and Yelverton): "I say if the certificates of two men shall make a law, we need not a Parliament. In some records I find that certain men made ordinance (5 E.2 New Ordinances) of which many might be good, but they were questioned

76. *Commons Debates 1621,* IV, 19, 78, 99, 158; II, 84–90, 108, 150; V, 480. *Nicholas,* I, 17, 63–64, 89. *Commons Journal,* 583–89, 555. The King saved himself from blame by placing responsibility on the referees. F. H. Relf, ed., *Notes of the Debates in the House of Lords, 1621, 1625, 1628,* Camden Society, London, 1929, 12–15. In 1624 he spoke of "my judges and Council without whom I have done nothing, and if there be in any patent any clause or thing that is not fit, they are on fault for it and not I." *Nicholas,* ff. 243–243v.

77. *Commons Debates 1621,* VI, 269; IV, 99, 188; VII, 501; II, 161, 252–53, 147; V, 291, 25; III, 68. *Nicholas,* I, 196, 147–48, 309–10. 1624: *Holles,* f. 100v.; *Erle,* ff. 82v.–83; *Holland,* ff. 52 ff.; *Nicholas,* ff. 79v.–80; *Gurney,* 115. This was the debate on the patent of surveying sea coals in Newcastle. Sir John Saville accused Coke of being "too tender to men of his coat" and "he would have the referees questioned." *Holles,* f. 100v.

78. *Commons Journal,* 540–41, 546. Norman Egbert McClure, *The Letters of John Chamberlain,* Philadelphia, 1929, II, 351–52.

at the Parliament at York where it was declared that they were made against the royalty and liberty of the realm. (15 E.2 *Revocatio novarum Ordinationum*.) For laws cannot be made but by a general consent which cannot be had but in a Parliament."[79] Noy here posed the question which James himself had raised and was to raise again in 1624. It was a question implied in the whole attack on the referees, for the attack on referees, however much personalities played into it and political issues, was an attack on the legality of the King's grants.

How far, actually, did the Commons go, and to what purpose had been all their investigation, their calling of witnesses, their search of records and their examination of patentees and their papers? The committees acted as fact-finding bodies, but they did not rest content with this role. Throughout the examinations there was discussion. Lawyers and laymen alike commented on the facts discovered, laymen expounding the inconveniences which followed from the grants in question, the dangers to the commonweal, and lawyers interpreting those inconveniences in legal terms. Having investigated and debated, the committee summed up its findings in a "judgment" of the patent, voting it to be "inconvenient" or a "grievance in creation," or a "grievance in execution," or both. The decision of the committee was reported back to the House, usually by its chairman, who also carried the chief responsibility of defending its stand in the debate which followed. In every case of which we have record the House confirmed the report of its committee, and the patent then stood officially "condemned."

The legal reasons which the House of Commons and its committees found for condemning patents and grants they had examined were various and drawn from many sources. One of the simplest cases against a royal grant was that it was a monopoly. Monopolies were in general conceded to be illegal. They were held to run counter to the ruling principle at common law, which, as interpreted in the early seventeenth century, guaranteed freedom of enterprise.[80] Exceptions were made in two instances: when the monopoly was for a new invention, or when it was necessary for the good of the State. The term "in-

---

79. *Commons Debates 1621*, II, 254.

80. Sir Edward Coke, *The Second Part of the Institute of the Laws of England*, London, 1642, commentary on Magna Carta, *c.* 29. Sir Edward Coke, *The Eleventh Part of the Reports of Sir Edward Coke*, London, 1727, 86–88. D. O. Wagner, "Coke and the Rise of Economic Liberalism," *Economic History Review*, VI, 30–44. Eli F. Heckscher, *Mercantilism*, London, 1935, I, 269 ff. Edward S. Mason, "Monopoly in Law and Economics," *Yale Law Journal*, XLVII, 34–39. Friis, 459. *Commons Debates 1621*, V, 105–6. *Nicholas*, f. 132v. It was, however, generally conceded that both King and Parliament had the right to restrict this freedom for the good of the Commonwealth. The exceptions in the law which were consistently made for chartered companies might be explained in these terms.

vention" included both originator and importer. It did not necessarily include improver.[81] The second exception admitted the power of the King or Parliament to restrict freedom of enterprise and the liberties of the subject for the good of the State.[82]

Mansell's patent for the sole manufacture and sale of glass was a monopoly involving both these exceptions. It had been granted as a privilege for what purported to be a new process of glass-making, which was also to be of benefit to the commonwealth by using less wood for fuel than the old process. To upset such a grant legally it was necessary to refute both these claims, and it was precisely this which the Commons undertook to do in 1621. The making of glass was not, they determined from the evidence they had heard, a new invention. Far from promoting the general welfare, the patent was detrimental to it. It did not conserve wood; and it created the three conditions which the judges in 1603 had found to be incident to a monopoly:[83] it raised prices, lowered quality and displaced workmen from their lawful trades. The Commons thus established their case, to their own satisfaction, and voted the patent a grievance in creation.[84]

A second ground against a royal grant was that it authorized a subject to dispense with a penal law. Such transference of prerogative power to an individual was, according to common law precedent, illegal. Blundell's patent of pedlars was found, according to the evidence accepted by the House of Commons, to grant the patentee power to dispense with the Statute of 39 Eliz. concerning rogues and vagabonds; and it was consequently judged to be against the law and a grievance in creation.[85] Mompesson's patent for the licensing of inns was found to empower the patentees to dispense with the Statutes of 13 Rich. II and 4 H. IV, and was judged to be against the law and a grievance in creation.[86]

The execution of patents was likewise condemned on the ground either that the provision for execution was in itself illegal or that illegal acts were committed in carrying out the provisions. The difficulty arose because the

81. E. W. Hulme, "The History of the Patent System Under the Prerogative and at Common Law," *Law Quarterly Review,* XII, 141–54; XVL, 44–56. "On the History of Patent Law in the Seventeenth and Eighteenth Centuries," *Law Quarterly Review,* XVIII, 280–88.

82. *Wagner,* 31.

83. Coke, *Reports,* XI, 86–87. The existence of these incidents was not necessary to establish the fact of monopoly, though their presence could, according to Coke's statements in the House of Commons in 1621 and 1624, void it. *Commons Debates 1621,* V, 105–6, 121–22; III, 195. *Holles,* f. 118.

84. *Nicholas,* II, 73.

85. *Nicholas,* I, 146–47. *Commons Debates 1621,* V, 35–36; IV, 147–48; II, 250.

86. *Commons Debates 1621,* II, 180–83.

patentees were entrusted with the enforcement of their own grants, and, in some instances, empowered by a commission or proclamation to seize the goods of offenders, to compound with them or to fine and imprison.[87] Petitioners maintained that the patentees of gold foliate threatened those who complained about the quality of the product, sued one who made better foliate than they, imprisoned him and seized his goods, only releasing him on condition that he would work for them.[88] The Commons heartily condemned such means of enforcement. "No proclamation ought to go out for any private cause,"[89] Coke said. Imprisonment and seizure of goods by virtue of a patent were unlawful. Hence, patents executed in this way were illegal, and a grievance in execution.

The line between the execution of a patent and the patent itself was not always clearly drawn, nor were the Commons wholly consistent in making this distinction. But the essential point is that they considered both execution and patent in legal terms and condemned them on legal grounds. Patents were condemned in creation because the grant itself had been issued contrary to the King's intentions,[90] because it ran counter to precedent,[91] because it was contrary to various aspects of the common law. They were condemned in execution if illegal acts were committed in their enforcement, or if the provision for enforcement was in itself illegal and tended to the subversion of justice.[92]

In declaring it to be illegal the Commons made their strongest case against

87. For examples see *Commons Debates 1621,* V, 586–88; IV, 95–96; II, 134, 176; VII, 513–14, 442–43.

88. *Nicholas,* I, 339–40.

89. *Commons Debates 1621,* II, 112–13. See also *ibid.,* II, 118–21, 193, 413–14; IV, 66, 71, 90; V, 48, 483–84; VI, 284. *Nicholas,* f. 114.

90. The Commons argued in good English fashion that the King, having declared in the Book of Bounty that he would not issue certain types of grants, would not issue them contrary to his own declaration. When such grants were found to exist it was clear that the procurers had misinformed the King as to their nature. (See, for example, *Commons Debates 1621,* II, 145, 250, 253–54.) This doctrine was applied by the Commons in 1621 and 1624 not only to the King's intentions as expressed in the Book of Bounty, but also to his intentions as expressed in the particular grant under consideration. The same point had been made by the Judges in the decision in the case of *Darcy* v. *Allen:* "The Queen was deceived in her grant; for the Queen as by the preamble appears, intended it to be for the weal public, and it will be employed for the private gain of the patentees, and for the prejudice of the weal public . . ." Coke, *Reports,* XI, 87. It was common practice for procurers of patents to promise benefit to the commonwealth. Sir Edward Coke said: "Projectors like watermen, look one way and row another; they pretend public profit, intend private." *Commons Debates 1621,* V, 76. For other examples of this point, and for patents thus condemned, see *Commons Debates 1621,* II, 78, 193; IV, 288–99; V, 41, 483–84.

91. Monopolies were, for instance, shown to be illegal by common law precedent. *Commons Debates 1621,* VI, 249–51; IV, 79–81, 258; II, 228–29; III, 2; V, 74. *Commons Journal,* 697. This point was so well established that in some instances it sufficed to say that a grant was a monopoly; its illegality followed. *Harl. 159,* ff. 97v.–98, 106.

92. Noy and Coke classified the grounds on which patents were condemned by the House, *Nicholas,* I, 63–66; *Commons Debates 1621,* IV, 78–81; VI, 249–51; V, 258; III, 44, 280.

a patent. But when they could not clearly do this they might judge it "inconvenient," either in creation or execution, or both. They defined as "inconvenient" a grant which, though clearly obnoxious or injurious to the commonwealth, could not be proved definitely illegal. The distinction was not, however, always clear; and the Commons themselves were only too eager to blur the line between grants which were inconvenient and those which were illegal. "Inconvenience" might mean various things. The King had a right to make certain grants; but if these infringed the right and inheritance of the subject they could be condemned. The question, then, whether a patent was illegal or inconvenient was the question whether the actual rights of the subject had been infringed, or merely the best interests of the commonwealth impaired.[93] The Commons, in considering these matters of inconvenience and illegality, were essentially concerned with defining the rights of the subject, and their definition obviously tended to be quite broad. The King protested the procedure in 1621 and again in 1624. "I am sure you will not take upon you to be judge of my seal. It is not enough for me if some of your doctors of law stand up and say this patent is against the law. I must for the law rely upon my learned counsel and upon my judges, whether the patent be in itself good by law or not. But if there fall out any inconvenience in the execution of it, you may complain of it. . . ."[94]

The Commons had, in fact, evolved out of the old private Bill procedure a method of investigation and of passing judgment very like a court procedure.[95] There is some evidence that patentees feared the House of Commons.[96] By answering its summons and pleading their cases before it they tacitly acknowledged its jurisdiction. In some instances they even surrendered their patents;[97] and the House attempted to enforce its judgment by punishing "projectors"[98] and cancelling patents.[99]

93. *Commons Debates 1621*, V, 32, 277; IV, 189.

94. *Harl. 159*, f. 35.

95. Hearings were also held on private Bills, parties appeared by counsel, and witnesses were examined. This procedure has long been recognized as judicial or semi-judicial in character. Charles Howard McIlwain, *The High Court of Parliament*, New Haven, 1910 [Oxford, 1934], 125, 219–23; Pollard, *The Evolution of Parliament*, 118.

96. *Commons Debates 1621*, IV, 92, 203–4; II, 272; V, 292; VI, 26; VII, 312. *Commons Journal*, 577.

97. *Commons Debates 1621*, V, 521, 267; VI, 271–72.

98. There was some debate on how to punish patentees. *Commons Debates 1621*, II, 113–14, 131; VI, 265. *Commons Journal*, 651. *Nicholas*, f. 212v. Those "projectors" actually punished were Members of the House and were "sequestered" from the House or expelled. *Commons Journal*, 536, 566–67. *Commons Debates 1621*, V, 315; II, 255; VI, 460–61; III, 130; IV, 289; VI, 125. *Nicholas*, II, 3, 182. *Gurney*, 170; *Holland*, ff. 78 ff.

99. *Commons Debates 1621*, V, 263, 308; III, 2–3. The remark of a Member of the House of Commons during the debate on monopolies in 1601 is interesting in this connection: "Let us do generously and bravely,

The House of Commons claimed and was generally recognized to be a court with jurisdiction over its own Members, over its privileges and over offences against the House.[100] It claimed sole jurisdiction in these areas, though it had still to gain its point with the King as the arrest of Members bore witness. But it was also reaching out for wider powers, as is clear from its handling of impeachment cases and the famous Floyd affair.[101] In the impeachment of Mompesson and Michell the Commons insisted that the charges they sent up to the Lords be fully proved, and that the judgment be based upon the charges presented. They were raising their role from mere informers to partakers in the act of judicature itself.[102]

In the consideration of patents and monopolies they took an even clearer stand. They investigated facts, pronounced a judgment and made some efforts to execute that judgment. Patents and monopolies could not be construed as offences against the House. For their jurisdiction in this field the Commons relied on the idea that grievances were the special province of the representatives of the realm.[103]

Rightly or wrongly the Commons laid claim to power to investigate and condemn the King's patents. But, as in Floyd's case, they did not insist on all the logical implications of their claims. Sir Edward Coke protested the King's criticism of the procedure of condemning patents. Coke asserted the Commons's right to call in and examine the original patents. But even Coke recommended in 1624 that the condemned patents be turned over to the King's Council "with a request that they may be proceeded against."[104]

---

like Parliament men, and ourselves send for them and their patents, and cancel them before their faces, arraign them as in times past, at the Bar, and send them to the Tower." Quoted in Edward P. Cheyney, *A History of England from the Defeat of the Armada to the Death of Elizabeth*, New York, 1926 [London, 1926], II, 299–300. The Long Parliament "called in" and "cancelled" a large number of monopoly patents. Price, 46.

100. The King conceded this in 1621: *Commons Debates 1621*, III, 134; VII, 626; *Nicholas*, II, 294. The Lords likewise conceded it: *Commons Debates 1621*, III, 183; VI, 401; IV, 313.

101. *Commons Debates 1621*, III, 122–28, 134–52, 163–68, 173–84, 191–92, 205, 208–9, 231, 237–39, 272; VI, 128; V, 134, 364; IV, 296.

102. *Commons Debates 1621 passim* for the debates on the Mompesson case and those of Sir John Bennet, Lambe and Craddock. Mompesson's patents were the chief complaint against him. These were examined by the House of Commons and declared to be grievances. In 1624 Phelips made an important speech, protesting that the Lords had not censured Cranfield "upon every particular of their charge." *Harl. 159*, f. 116v.; *Erle*, ff. 183–183v. See also *Erle*, ff. 186v.–187 for a similar protest in another case. McIlwain, *The High Court of Parliament*, 190–94, discusses the struggle of the Commons to take part in the actual judgment.

103. *Commons Debates 1621*, III, 140, 167; IV, 77, 292, 405. The King in his message about Floyd asked whether the House of Commons "hath a power of judicature in such matters as do not concern our own [the Commons's] privileges and Members or a public grievance of the kingdom." *Commons Debates 1621*, IV, 290.

104. *Nicholas*, ff. 244–46; *Erle*, ff. 199–199v.

Neither he nor the other Members of the House were willing to leave the patents to the Commons's condemnation alone. When, then, by vote of the House a patent stood officially condemned as an "inconvenience" or "grievance" in the explicit and legal sense of the word,[105] the House of Commons proceeded in several ways. In some cases it drew up a special Bill to deal with a special patent, like the Bill to regulate lighthouses,[106] thus remedying the situation in the conventional parliamentary way.

The larger group of patents was included in a general petition of grievances presented to the King at the end of the session of 1624 by the House of Commons without the assistance of the House of Lords. This, too, was the old parliamentary way, but the petition had been drawn up with special care. It included only those "grievances" investigated by the Commons and shown to be "grievances" in the technical sense of the word—"grievances" because they were against the law and infringed the rights of the subject.[107] The Commons were consistent throughout. They had based their condemnation of patents on common law precedent. They petitioned the King on the same basis. Their petition of grievances in 1624 was far more than a petition of grace. It was more nearly the kind of petition they were to use in 1628. It was more nearly a petition of right.[108]

As the King protested the Commons's procedure against his grants, so, too, could he protest and with justice the great Statute of Monopolies which emerged from the sessions of 1624 as Parliament's third method of dealing with the King's grants. The Statute of Monopolies was, as Dr. McIlwain has

---

105. The term "grievance" was used in 1621 and 1624 in two distinct ways. It was loosely applied to actions or grants whether they were investigated or not in the sense of complaint. *Commons Debates 1621,* V, 475: the patent of inns is a "grievance fit to be examined and redressed." It was also used in a second more technical sense; and in this sense it was only appropriate after a grant had been investigated and discovered for certain definite legal reasons to be a *grievance* in a certain, definite legal way: in creation, in execution or in both. In this second sense it was used in contradistinction to "inconvenient" and acquired the specific meaning of illegal.

106. *Commons Debates 1621,* III, 7; VII, 218 ff. For similar Bills see *Commons Debates 1621,* IV, 253; V, 95; *Holland,* f. 82; *Pym,* ff. 49v. ff.; *Nicholas,* ff. 217–217v.; *Harl. 159,* f. 120. Bills were also drawn up which affected or voided patents not previously condemned: *Commons Debates 1621,* V, 469; VII, 77–80, 108 ff.; V, 270; III, 148; VII, 259.

107. I am speaking here only of that part of the petition which concerned patents and monopolies. For the petition see *Harl. 159,* ff. 35v. ff. and *S. P. Domestic, 1623–1625,* CLXV/53. A committee of thirty took the petition to the King, and the Solicitor spoke. *Commons Journal,* 714. *Erle,* ff. 198–198v. For the King's remarks on this occasion see *Harl. 159,* f. 35; *Nicholas,* ff. 243–243v. Charles answered the petition in 1625.

108. Coke: "A petition of right is when we petition that grievances may be suppressed . . ." *Commons Debates 1621,* III, 367. ". . . there is a petition of grace (as to have insufficient justices put out) and a petition of right (to have grievances suppressed)." *Commons Debates 1621,* II, 413–14. Coke also made the point that a petition of right required an answer. *Commons Debates 1621,* II, 495–96.

sagely pointed out, the first statutory invasion of the prerogative.[109] But it is significant of the House of Commons's political thought, of its medieval inheritance and of its legal personnel, that it was framed as a declaratory Act. The purpose of the Statute was not to introduce new law but simply to fix what the Commons regarded as the proper interpretation of the common law in its application to patents and monopolies. It declared what the law was in general, as they had declared it in the particular instances raised by the patents they condemned.[110] As a declaratory Act the Statute, though certainly it limited the prerogative, cannot accurately be described as an attack upon it. It affected the prerogative because it gave a statutory definition to the subject's interest in royal grants, and thus set a statutory limit to the area in which the prerogative operated.

The preparation of the Bill of Monopolies in 1621 and 1624 was regarded by the Commons as not only important but, like a money Bill, their own particular province. They felt slighted in 1621 when the Lords rejected their Bill and proposed a conference to draw a new one. "The Lords have no inconvenience by monopolies, but the poor cedars and shrubs have danger of it."[111] Parliament was adjourned before the two Houses could agree. In 1624 the Commons tried again and this time sent their Bill to the Lords with special recommendation and a large delegation of Members, "for the Speaker saith a good Bill in Queen Elizabeth's time miscarried in the Upper House, because they supposed it was not much favoured below, having no more attendance."[112] The Lords, after conference with the Commons, raised seventeen exceptions. In addition, Coke reported, they "will not consent to have the Bill to touch or concern all, but only those that are hereafter to be granted, not those patents which are in present execution, but to reserve them for their time only and to make sure against any in future. . . ." The Commons were disappointed, but, as Coke advised, willing to compromise to save the Bill.[113] Thus altered, it finally passed both Houses, and, accepted by the King at the end of the session, became law.[114]

---

109. Charles Howard McIlwain, *Constitutionalism, Ancient and Modern*, Ithaca, New York [Oxford, 1940], 1940, 138.

110. There were other general Bills drawn to void patents or to make certain types of grants illegal in the future—for instance, the Bill of Concealments, *Commons Journal*, 533; *Nicholas*, I, 135–36. For others see: *Commons Journal*, 569; *Commons Debates 1621*, IV, 183, 231; III, 18; V, 113.

111. *Commons Journal*, 661, 663, 664; *Nicholas*, II, 302–3; *Commons Debates 1621*, II, 508–9, 521–22; VI, 230, 237.

112. *Gurney*, 114; *Nicholas*, f. 77v.; *Holles*, f. 100; *Pym*, f. 28v.

113. *Gurney*, 238. *Commons Journal*, 696; *Nicholas*, f. 188v.; *Holland*, II, f. 69v.; *Pym*, f. 86.

114. *Commons Journal*, 793–94.

To summarize, then, the House of Commons in 1621 and 1624 undertook the investigation of patents and monopolies because there was no adequate remedy elsewhere. Less and less, men turned to the Privy Council for redress of grievances, partly because the very men who sat there had obtained or passed the grants and partly because the Privy Council seemed less and less to represent the public interest. Progress in the courts was slow. Thus circumstances added stature to the House of Commons's traditional role as petitioners for redress of grievances. The development of their procedure, the evolution of the committee system, the emergence of sound leadership, equipped the Commons to meet their new responsibilities effectively. Out of the old private Bill procedure and the methods used in the Committee of Elections, they evolved an interesting technique of investigation and judgment. They even made some attempt to execute their judgments. But at the same time they realized that their action could not stand alone, that only the King, the Council or the courts could finally void a royal grant.

To this end they prepared their petition of grievances. In the petition they included only those grants which had been investigated and condemned. Sir Edward Coke felt that a patent so condemned in Parliament could not be asked for again. This was the significance of the Commons's procedure against it. This was the significance of their petition to the King.[115] It was, they hoped, a compelling statement, for it came from the representative body of the realm. Grievances were, they thought, their special business. The petition assumed added importance when the Lords so amended the Bill of Monopolies that it would not void past grants. Thus all the methods which the Commons had used against patents and monopolies had their place: investigation and condemnation, the passing of Bills to void individual grants, petition (to withdraw condemned patents), and the passing of the Statute of Monopolies which prohibited such grants in the future and provided that they should be tried in the common law courts.

The Privy Council withdrew a large number of grants after Parliament adjourned.[116] The great Statute of Monopolies had been passed. So far the efforts

115. The petition was also a device for saving time. In 1621, toward the end of the session, Coke moved "that since there are so many Grievances here in the House complained of . . . as that we cannot make Laws against them all, that we should have a Petition made to the King, beseeching his Majesty to be pleased by a Proclamation or otherwise to decry or make void the same. . . ." *Nicholas,* II, 248.

116. Many of the patents condemned by the House of Commons in 1621 were revoked by proclamation on July 10th, 1621. For this proclamation, its preparation by the Privy Council and the Privy Council's consideration of the Commons's action against grants, see *Commons Debates 1621,* III, 416, note 25, and the

of the House of Commons were successful. They had, moreover, evolved a technique of investigation of royal administration which would prove valuable in years to come. The revival of impeachment, which stemmed directly from the monopoly investigation, was to be used again with telling effect; and the "country" could not be unaware that when other remedies had failed the Commons had forced redress of grievances.

---

references there cited. For some further examples of the Privy Council's consideration of grants condemned by the Commons see *Commons Debates 1621*, Appendix B; *Acts of the Privy Council, 1621–1623*, London, 1932, 408; *Acts of the Privy Council, 1623–1625*, London, 1933, 238, 247, 256, 491.

The Origins of the Petition
of Right Reconsidered

❧ ❧ ❧

Whatever their differing interpretations of the prehistory of the Civil War, historians of early Stuart England have long recognized the unsolved problems raised by the parliament of 1628.[1] Did Charles I abuse the legal procedures of King's Bench in the five knights' case in order to defy the spirit of English "due process" legislation? In starting the chain of events which led to the petition, who were the innovators? Why did the house of commons pass resolutions which were an absolute denial of Charles I's right of discretionary imprisonment *in any circumstances?* And why did M.P.s endure the ugliest parliamentary scenes before 1640 in their desire to secure an explanatory document in the spirit of their resolutions? In view of the wealth of literature on the petition, it is perhaps surprising that these issues have never been satisfactorily addressed.[2]

"The Origins of the Petition of Right Reconsidered" is reprinted, by permission of J. A. Guy and Cambridge University Press, from *Historical Journal* 25, no. 2 (1982): 289–312. © 1982 Cambridge University Press.

1. I am most grateful to Miss Sheila Lambert, Professor G. R. Elton, Professor Conrad Russell and Mr. Peter Salt for most valuable comments on an earlier version of this paper.

2. For discussion of the issues raised in 1628 see especially S. R. Gardiner, *History of England from the Accession of James I to the Outbreak of the Civil War, 1603–1642* (London, 1886), VI, 213–326; F. H. Relf, *The Petition of Right* (Minneapolis, 1917); M. A. Judson, *The Crisis of the Constitution, 1603–1645* (New Brunswick, 1949), pp. 240–69; M. F. S. Hervey, *The Life, Correspondence and Collections of Thomas Howard, Earl of Arundel* (Cambridge, 1921), pp. 260–64, 279–80; I. H. C. Fraser, "Sir Robert Heath" (University of Bristol M. Litt. thesis, 1954), pp. 93–127; E. R. Adair, "The Petition of Right," *History,* V (1921), 99–103; S. Reed Brett, *John Pym* (London, 1940), pp. 89–102; H. Hulme, *The Life of Sir John Eliot, 1592–1632* (London, 1957), pp. 184–229; see also his article, "Opinion in the House of Commons on the Proposal for a Petition of Right, 6 May 1628," *English Historical Review,* L (1935), 302–6; C. V. Wedgwood, *Thomas Wentworth, First Earl of Strafford, 1593–1641* (London, 1961), pp. 61–71; W. J. Jones, *Politics and the Bench* (London, 1971), pp. 70–75; C. Thompson, "The Origins of the Politics of the Parliamentary Middle Group, 1625–1629," *Transactions of the Royal Historical Society,* 5th series, XXII (1972), 71–86; E. R. Foster, "The Painful Labour of Mr. Elsyng," *Transactions of the American Philosophical Society,* new series, LXII, part 8 (1972), 27–35; see also her article, "Petitions and the Petition of Right," *Journal of British Studies,* XIV (1974), 21–45; J. H. Hexter, "Power Struggle, Parliament and Liberty in Early Stuart England," *Journal of Modern History,* L (1978), 1–50; S. D. White, *Sir Edward Coke and the Grievances of the Commonwealth, 1621–1628*

The five knights' case was the first link in the chain of events leading to the petition, but no previous writer has looked at the King's Bench records of this litigation.[3] The reluctance of scholars to study the official records of parliament, as opposed to commons' diaries, has also obstructed progress in the matter of the petition's origins.[4] The purpose of this article is to reconsider the whole question of the petition's background, demonstrating the extent to which it was the discovery of the Crown's own apparent duplicities in 1628 which created the explosive situation in which the petition was born.[5]

(Chapel Hill, 1979), pp. 213–76; C. S. R. Russell, *Parliaments and English Politics, 1621–1629* (Oxford, 1979), pp. 323–89; see also his articles, "Parliamentary History in Perspective, 1604–1629," *History,* LXI (1976), 1–27, and "The Parliamentary Career of John Pym, 1621–1629" in *The English Commonwealth, 1547–1640* (ed. P. Clark et al.; Leicester, 1979), pp. 147–65; D. Hirst, "Parliament, Law and War in the 1620s," *Historical Journal,* XXIII, 2 (1980), 455–61. *Faction and Parliament* (ed. K. Sharpe; Oxford, 1978) contains three essays bearing on 1628: D. Hirst, "Court, Country and Politics before 1629"; J. N. Ball, "Sir John Eliot and Parliament, 1624–1629"; and K. Sharpe, "The Earl of Arundel, His Circle and the Opposition to the Duke of Buckingham, 1618–1628."

3. Most writers rely on Relf, *Petition of Right,* pp. 1–19. Her account is, however, marred by large errors of fact owing to failure to consult the proper King's Bench sources. The idea that the King's Bench records should be exhaustively searched for traces of the decision in the five knights' case was suggested to me by Professor J. H. Hexter. I am grateful to Mr. Hexter both for his idea and encouragement. An advance copy of the forthcoming appendix to *Commons Debates 1628* on the five knights' case by Mrs. Maija J. Cole of the Yale Centre for Parliamentary History was kindly sent to me by the author. I am grateful to Mrs. Cole for permission to read her appendix before writing this paper.

4. For a summary of the preferred methodology see G. R. Elton, "Studying the history of parliament," and the same author's "A reply," both in *Studies in Tudor and Stuart Politics and Government* (Cambridge, 1974), II, 3–18. Essential to an understanding of the records and workings of parliament are M. F. Bond, *Guide to the Records of Parliament* (London, 1971); his article, "Clerks of the Parliament, 1509–1953," *English Historical Review* LXXIII (1968), 78–85; S. Lambert, "The Clerks and Records of the House of Commons, 1600–1640," *Bulletin of the Institute of Historical Research,* XLIII (1970), 215–31; see also her masterly survey, "Procedure in the House of Commons in the Early Stuart Period," *E.H.R.* XCV (1980), 753–81. For 1628, the official commons' Journal and unofficial diaries have been published by the Yale Centre under the title *Commons Debates 1628* (ed. R. C. Johnson, M. F. Keeler et al.; New Haven, 1977–79; hereafter cited as *CD 1628*).

5. The official sources upon which this paper is based are (1) Public Record Office, King's Bench records: KB 21/9 (rule book, unfoliated); KB 145/15/3 (*Recorda* files, Michaelmas and Hilary terms 1627–28); KB 29/276 (controllment roll); KB 27/1558–61 (*coram rege* rolls, *Rex* side). All references to MSS in this paper are to documents in the P.R.O., unless otherwise stated. (2) Journals at the House of Lords Record Office: *Journals of the House of Lords* (London, 1864–), III; Journal of the house of commons for 1628 (MS 18), printed in *CD 1628*. (3) "Scribbled books" and draft journals of the house of lords in 1628 at H.L.R.O. and elsewhere (see below). The "scribbled books" were the original central record of proceedings in the house of lords, written at the table during sittings of the house. The draft journals represented the intermediate stage which existed in the seventeenth century between the "scribbled books" and the final Journals. Despite the inclination of historians to neglect these records in favour of the printed *Journals,* both sources contain much invaluable information not preserved in the Journals, e.g. membership of committees, reports of proceedings at conferences between the houses, and (for 1621–28) summaries of actual speeches; they also express more accurately than the Journals the precise order and format in which business was taken. In this paper, the "scribbled books" and draft journals are preferred to the printed *Journals.* Four "scribbled books" are extant for 1628: H.L.R.O., Minutes of Proceedings in the House of Lords ("Manuscript Minutes"), vol. 5 covers the period 17 March–20 Oct. (hereafter cited as MM, vol. 5); British Library, Additional MS 40091 covers 17 March–26 June; Inner Temple, Petyt MS 538.7 covers 17 March–30 April; Bodleian Library, Rawlinson MS A. 106 covers 1–31 May. These MSS have been haphazardly edited by F. H. Relf, *Notes of*

I

The starting point is the five knights' case, the litigation which was the fundamental point of reference in 1628 on discretionary imprisonment. In turn, the efforts of lords and commons to resolve the question of discretionary imprisonment resulted in the petition of right. Other issues were tackled by the petition, namely forced loans, billeting and martial law, but discretionary imprisonment was the one which dominated parliamentary proceedings prior to the petition. It was also the subject which Charles I knew most closely touched his prerogative. Hitherto, the source of the five knights' case has been the reporter's notes which were in circulation after the hearing, a version of which was printed in *State Trials*.[6] However, the notes of a reporter are an unofficial source for a King's Bench action, in the same way that parliamentary diaries are unofficial (and sometimes inadequate) sources for parliamentary history. The whole gamut of King's Bench records is extant, justifying a reappraisal of this *cause célèbre*.[7] The five knights were Sir Thomas Darnel, Sir John Corbet, Sir Walter Erle, Sir John Heveningham and Sir Edmund Hampden, who were among those imprisoned for refusing to contribute to the forced loan of 1626–27. All five decided to attempt legal redress in King's Bench, and each sought a writ of *habeas corpus* on petition from gaol. Writs were awarded on 3 November 1627, commanding the wardens of the respective gaols to produce their prisoners personally in King's Bench and return the cause of detention of each for examination by the judges. The writs were meant to be returned on 8 November, but none was received back on time because the wardens were unable to enter the cause of imprisonment without consulting the privy council.[8] To circumvent this problem, the day of return was extended by the judges to the 10th — but still nothing happened. The attorney-general, Sir Robert Heath, then intervened *ex officio* to order an award of an *alias habeas*

---

the Debates in the House of Lords (Camden Society; 3rd series; 1929). She chose as her main texts the Petyt and Rawlinson MSS; in footnotes were added extracts from MM, vol. 5 (cited by Relf as "B"), and B.L., Add. MS 40091 (cited by Relf as "A"). The main texts are good enough to be used here from Relf's edition, provided it is realized that there are substantial *lacunae;* the footnotes from MM, vol. 5 and B.L., Add. MS 40091 are a fraction of those important sources, and MM, vol. 5 (which throws valuable light on the origins of the petition) is used here from the original MS. I am most grateful to Mr. D. S. Mansfield for the loan of four microfilms. Two draft journals are extant for the house of lords in 1628: H.L.R.O., Braye MS 14 covers the period 17 March–30 April; H.L.R.O., Braye MS 15 covers 1 May–26 June.

6. *A Complete Collection of State Trials* (ed. T. B. Howell), III, 59.

7. See above n. 5 for KB references.

8. KB 21/9 (Mich., 3 Car. I).

in Darnel's case alone, the new writ being returnable on the 13th.[9] Evidently Heath was anxious to proceed with a test case. He was confident of Charles's position, since the privy council had decided on the 7th what form of return it wanted made to writs of *habeas corpus*. At a meeting at Whitehall, Lord Keeper Coventry, the earls of Manchester and Suffolk, Sir John Coke, Sir Humphrey May, Neile, Laud and others had agreed that the gaolers should return that both the initial commitment and continued detention of the five knights was "by his majesty's special commandment."[10] This form of words was a direct response to the prisoners' presumed strategy. In order to avoid any mention of the forced loan and possible review by the court of its legality, the government shifted the argument on to the far stronger ground of Charles's prerogative.

Darnel was led into King's Bench on 13 November 1627, when the warden of the Fleet returned that he "was and is committed by his majesty's special commandment." This form of return took Darnel unprepared; his counsel played for time and the outcome was an adjournment. In fact, Darnel decided to quit the arena, leaving his companions to fight on.[11] The other four petitioned King's Bench again and secured writs of *alias habeas* on 15 November, returnable two days later. This time there were no delays. The writs were returned, bearing the same formula as in Darnel's case, and legal argument began on the 22nd.[12] Sir John Bramston appeared as counsel for Heveningham, William Noy for Erle, John Selden for Hampden and Sir Henry Calthorp for Corbet. Heath spoke for the Crown, formally defending the return in Heveningham's case as an example of all the returns on the 26th. He pleaded that the response "by his majesty's special commandment" was positive and sufficient in law, being a valid cause of imprisonment and not the "cause of the cause." He argued that Charles's power of discretionary imprisonment was upheld by strict law and precedents on record in King's Bench, and that those so imprisoned were not bailable. Finally, he asked that the defendants be remanded in custody.[13] When Heath had finished, Chief Justice Hyde promised a deci-

9. Ibid.

10. *Acts of the Privy Council of England, 1627–1628* (London, 1940), p. 131. It is not without interest that Manwaring's controversial sermon on apostolical obedience, licensed for the press as propaganda for the forced loan of 1626–27, appeared with the inscription "by his majesty's special command"; see H. R. Trevor-Roper, *Archbishop Laud, 1573–1645* (2nd edn.; London, 1962), p. 80.

11. KB 21/9 (Mich., 3 Car. I).

12. KB 145/15/3 (Hilary, 3 Car. I); KB 21/9 (Mich., 3 Car. I). The writs are on the Hilary file, because they were kept out until the beginning of March 1628 in connection with the special entry planned by Sir Robert Heath, for which see below, pp. 336–37.

13. SP 16/85/53 (full report of the five knights' case in Heath's hand).

sion within twenty-four hours, and he duly pronounced the court's resolution on the 27th. It is on this crucial matter of the decision that the King's Bench records must be quoted. The entry reads, "Ordinatum est quod defendentes remittuntur separalibus prisonis ubicunque antea fuerunt salvo custodiendo quousque, etc."[14] Unlike the printed report, the record explains first the basis on which the defendants were remanded in custody: "quousque, etc.," or to expand the King's Bench abbreviation, "quousque secundum legem deliberati fuerint" — "until they have been delivered according to law." Secondly, the form and location of the record, which was entered in the rule book of King's Bench, proves that the decision in the five knights' case was a "rule of court" and not a final judgment, the difference being that "rules" resolved procedural matters and "judgments" settled substantive ones. In the five knights' case, the rule of 27 November 1627 settled no more than that the defendants were to be refused bail. They were to be remanded pending the filing, hearing and judgment of substantive charges, or until such time as their counsel obtained new writs of *alias habeas* to enable their pleas to be reheard. But the practical effect of the court's ruling was firmly negative. On the one hand, Charles I did not intend to file substantive charges against the appellants, because he declined to expose the forced loan to judicial review. On the other, there was little point in seeking further writs of *alias habeas* in political actions at this time, because a rule of King's Bench would not be changed unless new factual grounds were produced to show that bail could be granted, which could never happen until the returns to writs of *alias habeas* were amended by the Crown to reveal the "cause of the cause" of detention.[15]

14. KB 21/9 (Mich., 3 Car. I). The rule book also establishes that the date of the decision was 27 November 1627 (*dies Martis proxime post quindenam Sancti Martini*). The chronology of the case given in *State Trials* is typically inaccurate.

15. The technical legal status of the rule of King's Bench in the five knights' case was that of an interlocutory order in the nature of a *curia advisari vult*, by which is meant that nothing had been adjudged, and the court reserved its right to rehear the matter upon further advice. (See the interpretations in parliament in 1628 of Solicitor-general Shelton and the King's Bench judges, *CD 1628*, II, 155, 159, 162; Relf, *Notes of Debates*, pp. 100, 105, 112.) But such advice could only come from the Crown in the five knights' case, because the prisoners had been detained *per speciale mandatum domini regis*. Furthermore, the advice could only be "known" by King's Bench when received in proper form, either as an amended return in response to a new writ of *alias habeas*, or (possibly) in the form of letters close under Charles's sign manual addressed to the judges. In other words, the cards were stacked wholly in favor of the Crown, provided substantive charges were never filed against the prisoners, and provided Charles and the privy council stuck to *per speciale mandatum domini regis* as the form of their return to any future writs of *alias habeas*. Without knowledge of the "cause of the cause," the King's Bench judges could never have bailed the five knights, not least because to have done so in a case of detention *per speciale mandatum domini regis* would have been to have judged the imprisonment "a wrong done by the King" (Relf, *Notes of Debates*, p. 100). John Selden stressed the negative practical effect of the rule in the five knights' case on 28 March 1628, when he told the

The practical effect of the decision in the five knights' case, in view of Charles I's refusal to file substantive charges, was thus to give the Crown the apparent right to detain the four prisoners until such time as Charles decided to let them go free. It was not the first time in English history that this issue had arisen. It was aired in King's Bench in 1526, after Cardinal Wolsey had committed one William Hurne to gaol on a warrant signed by himself and others.[16] It was treated in Serjeant Browne's case in 1540, when the judges resolved in Star Chamber that "the king can send a man to prison. And his discretion is not to be argued about. . . . But whether the cause for which he sent him to prison is lawful or not may be determined by the law; the statute of Magna Carta is *nullus liber homo capiatur etc. nec super eum mittemus etc.,* from which it appears that the king cannot treat his subject contrary to the law."[17] On the other hand, the Elizabethan judges explained in 1592 that "if any person be committed by her Majesty's commandment from her person, or by order from the Council Board, or if any one or two of her Council commit one for high treason, such persons so in the case before committed may not be delivered by any of her courts without due trial by the law, and judgment of acquittal had."[18] The decision of 1592 acknowledged that the special command of the monarch or the authority of the privy council as a body was a sufficient warrant both to commit suspects to gaol and to prevent King's Bench from discharging them either absolutely or on bail. Even so, the Elizabethan judges seem to have had the trial of substantive charges in mind as the proper outcome, and what they were saying was no more than that bail must be refused to dangerous men prior to trial, rather than that persons so committed could be arbitrarily imprisoned. Furthermore, they expressly said that a cause of imprisonment should be certified to King's Bench in *habeas corpus* proceedings;

---

commons with reference to rules of court *quousque, etc.,* "The course of an officer is to enter *quousque, etc.,* that is till they be delivered by law, and 'tis all the judgment that can be" (*CD 1628,* II, 174, 180). This was not strictly true, but it reflected Selden's frustration with the return *per speciale mandatum domini regis.* In fact, Selden had not tried to obtain a new writ of *alias habeas* in the case of his client Sir Edmund Hampden. He could have obtained such a writ on 28 November 1627, prior to the end of Michaelmas term, but evidently had not thought this worthwhile. The judges pointed out in the upper house that new writs could have been requested (Relf, *Notes of Debates,* pp. 100, 102, 107; see also below, p. 343).

16. KB 145/10/19.

17. *The Reports of Sir John Spelman* (ed. J. H. Baker; 2 vols., London, 1977–79), I, 183–84. Unfortunately, it is not clear from Spelman's report whether the cause in question had to be specific, or whether it could be general (i.e., *per speciale mandatum domini regis*).

18. *CD 1628,* I, 106. Some M.P.s in 1628 thought that this decision of 34 Elizabeth "made for the liberty of the subject" (ibid. II, 229, 233). However, their assumption was that the cause of imprisonment to be expressed in *habeas corpus* proceedings was to be specific, not general. In fact, the judges in 1592 had been ambiguous on this point (see also Gardiner, *History of England, 1603–1642,* VI, 244–45).

however, the judges could in law know only what was certified to them by way of return to a writ of *habeas corpus*. For example, they could never "know" that the "cause of the cause" of a prisoner's commitment was refusal to pay a forced loan, rather than, as in the case of Guy Fawkes, an intent to blow up the parliament house while it was in session. We should note that English judges had to give decisions on their "legal" rather than personal knowledge in the interests of strict justice and professional ethics. If Chief Justice Hyde and his colleagues had allowed themselves to "know" what everyone else in London knew in 1627, namely that the five knights were in prison for refusing to lend money to the Crown, they would have allowed bail without prejudice to the issue.[19] But this was inadmissible. Far from obtaining redress, then, the five knights had beamed a searchlight on to a minor loophole which had become a political weapon in the hands of Charles I. Nevertheless, we must understand that although the King's Bench judges had ruled that the knights must remain locked up, they had not explicitly approved Charles's alleged right of discretionary imprisonment for reasons of state. The judges had decided that the imprisoned gentlemen could not be released on bail—nothing more or less. The distinction matters, because the *legal* effect of the decision in the five knights' case turned out to be very different from the apparent expectations of the Crown.

II

A precedent cannot be stronger than it appears on record; the form of bureaucratic enrollment is crucial, and it transpired that the legal value to Charles of the decision in the five knights' case was substantially reduced by a quirk of King's Bench book-keeping. Rarely are minor archival details the stuff of which history is made, but this was so in the wake of the King's Bench hearing. The records of the court consisted of rolls and files, together with such working tools of the trade as the appearance book and rule book. The convention was that a precedent was not on record unless enrolled on the *coram rege* or controlment roll. It might just be accepted if available from one of the various series of King's Bench files, but very few persons knew their way around the mass

19. The judges' dependence on their legal "knowledge" was emphasized by Justice Whitlocke when speaking to the house of lords on 14 April 1628; Relf, *Notes of Debates*, p. 100.

of files even in the seventeenth century. Quite categorically an entry in a rule book—being on paper not parchment—was not "on record" and could not subsequently be cited as a source of legal knowledge. The King's Bench records are fully extant for 1627–28, and we shall shortly see that Sir Robert Heath was the first of Charles's men to discover that the one complete official entry of the decision of 27 November 1627 was in the rule book.[20] The course of the court was that the four writs of *alias habeas* returned on 17 November had been placed with the court's *Recorda,* the file series representing the appellate jurisdiction of King's Bench.[21] Following the decision of the 27th, Mr. Keeling as secondary clerk of the Crown had written *remittitur* both on the face of the writs themselves and also beside four existing memoranda concerning their return already entered on the controlment roll in accordance with normal practice.[22] The four memoranda recited that the cause of imprisonment in each case was *per speciale mandatum domini regis*—"by his majesty's special commandment." Hence the final record of the controlment roll—nothing at all was entered on the *coram rege* roll—was that, after receipt of the return "by his majesty's special commandment" to each of the four writs of *alias habeas,* the four defendants had been remanded in custody (*remittitur*). The writer has closely examined the early Caroline controlment rolls, together with the rule books and *Recorda* files, and it is an archival fact that whether or not the rule of court in *habeas corpus* cases was *remittitur* or *remittitur quousque, etc.,* in either case the entry on the controlment roll and on the face of the relevant writ was *remittitur* alone, even though *remittitur* was also the standard entry used when defendants were returned to gaol *without formal resolution of the question of bail.*[23] This discrepancy had no legal significance: as Justice Whitlocke later confirmed in evidence to the house of lords, "Much spoken of the form of entry between *remittitur* and *remittitur quousque,* but no difference."[24] However, it followed that, if the terms *remittitur* and *remittitur quousque, etc.* were

20. See below, pp. 336–37.

21. KB 145/15/3 (Hilary, 3 Car. I). For a description of the King's Bench files see C. A. F. Meekings, "King's Bench Files," in *Legal Records and the Historian* (ed. J. H. Baker; London, 1978), pp. 97–139.

22. KB 29/276, ro. 80.

23. Justice Doddridge later explained that there was some clerical laxity in this matter (Relf, *Notes of Debates,* p. 107). The rules representing the adjournments of Darnel's case (13 Nov. 1627) and those of the other four knights on 22 Nov. 1627 were *remittitur* (KB 21/9 [Mich., 3 Car. I]).

24. Relf, *Notes of Debates,* p. 101. John Selden was not correct when he told the commons on 28 March 1628 that *remittitur quousque, etc.* was substantively different from *remittitur* in King's Bench practice (*CD 1628,* II, 174, 180, 183); what he meant was that *remittitur quousque, etc.* in the five knights' case was in practical terms final, because the knights would not obtain release from gaol without the consent of the Crown (see above, n. 15).

interchangeable, it was impossible for the Crown ever to prove in the after-
math of a rule of court that a prisoner's application for bail had been refused.
The rule book could clarify this point, but that document was not on record,
the rationale behind this situation being that rules of court (from which there
was no appeal in error to the house of lords) must never be allowed to decide
substantive matters. The evolutionary process of King's Bench had expressly
provided that rules left prisoners "where they were found" in strict law. As
Heath soon realized, the Crown could not prove that its alleged right of discretionary imprisonment for a matter of state had been given judicial sanction
on 27 November 1627. Only by feloniously perverting one of the "final" entries
on the controlment roll for this day to show that the substantive issue of discretionary imprisonment had been *adjudged* in its favor could the Crown do
this. To the horror of both lords and commons in 1628, it was exactly such an
act of archival perversion which Heath next attempted.

III

Charles I decided to release all the imprisoned loan refusers at the end of
December 1627. A month or so later he conceded that a parliament was the
proper way to supply the necessities of war. But almost as soon as parliament
met on 17 March 1628, it became locked into debates on English liberties.
Grievances ranged from the forced loan, billeting, impressment of soldiers
and martial law, to impositions and Arminianism, but the central issue was
discretionary imprisonment in the wake of the five knights' case. The matter
was raised in the house of commons on 27 March, when Sir Richard Shelton,
solicitor-general, gave an interpretation of the decision of 27 November 1627.[25]
Next day John Selden dropped a bombshell. As Hampden's former counsel in
King's Bench, he had visited the Crown office to check the entries on the controlment roll. He reported that although Shelton had said that the decision
was *remittitur quousque, etc.,* the roll had nothing but *remittitur.* As we now
know, the solicitor had been well informed, but Selden had located the government's archival problem. Selden quickly won the round on points, securing
the naming of a select committee to query each legal reference cited in the
five knights' case.[26] After visiting the Crown office, the committee reported

25. *CD 1628,* II, 146–52.
26. *CD 1628,* II, 173–74, 176, 180–81.

on 31 March that the controlment roll entries, as Selden had claimed, were indeed *remittitur* alone. But a horrific discovery had been made in the Crown office, one which was to influence the whole course of events in 1628. Solicitor Shelton had shown the select committee a copy of an alleged "judgment" in Sir John Heveningham's case, which he believed had been entered on the roll. The new entry was shocking, because in addition to recording that Sir John had been remanded in custody on 27 November 1627, it stated, too, that the words "by his majesty's special commandment" had been reviewed by King's Bench and *adjudged* to be a definitive return to a writ of *habeas corpus* despite no mention of any specific cause of detention. In other words, the new document, if entered on the controlment roll, would have perverted the existing rule of court in Heveningham's case into a binding precedent on record, settling the substantive issue of discretionary imprisonment for unknown causes permanently in favour of the Crown.[27] By 1 April 1628, Selden had unearthed the full story in the Crown office. Sir Robert Heath had learned at the end of 1627 that the one complete official entry of the decision in the five knights' case was in the rule book. He had then requested Mr. Keeling to make a special entry on the controlment roll. Keeling had replied that such an entry was foreign to King's Bench practice, but that he would obey if the judges consented. Heath had drafted the special entry, of which Selden had now obtained a copy, and Keeling had approached the judges, who immediately refused to condone constitutional innovation and "would not assent to any special entry." Keeling procrastinated, but Heath kept up the pressure throughout Hilary term 1628. Heath "divers times sent to him, and told him there was no remedy, but he must draw it."

> And a week before the parliament the Attorney called to him for it, and told him he must enter it, and not long since the Attorney called to him for it again to be delivered to the Attorney, and thereupon . . . yet he gave it to Mr. Attorney as he drew it, but never heard more of it since. And as touching the entry in the rolls, he said he wondered that there was no entry, but there is an entry to be made and it useth to be made before this time.[28]

27. *CD 1628*, II, 211–12.
28. *CD 1628*, II, 229. Keeling's evidence requires explanation. When he said, "He wondered that there was no entry," he must have meant either that there was no special entry, or that there was no entry on the *coram rege* roll, since Selden had already found *remittitur* entered on the controlment roll. His remark that an entry "useth to be made before this time" refers to the fact that it was wholly improper to add to or alter the legal records of a superior court after the rolls had been sewn up at the end of the law term. The five knights' case had been heard in Michaelmas term 1627, and entries arising from it should have been on record by the beginning of Hilary term 1628.

Selden's news of the draft "judgment" was greeted with trepidation in the commons. Apart from himself, at least two others of the house's acknowledged leaders in 1628 immediately appreciated the enormity of what had been attempted by the Crown. Sir Robert Phelips said on 31 March that if what was alleged was true, "It takes away all qualification. It determines the question against us for ever and ever. I hope that it was the draft but of some man that desired to strike us all from our liberties."[29] Sir Edward Coke declared that, "As for the intended judgment, I fear (were it not for this parliament) it had been entered. . . . This draft of the judgment will sting us."[30] Selden concurred that, "I do so very believe that this order had been recorded but for the parliament, as I do believe that it will be recorded yet so soon as the parliament arises, *if it be not prevented*."[31] Selden, then, together with Phelips and Coke made it dramatically plain to M.P.s that a felonious act had been attempted by the Crown in the wake of the five knights' case in order to obtain a precedent on record for Charles's alleged right of discretionary imprisonment for reasons of state.[32] In addition, Selden believed that remedial action was necessary to prevent the entry of the draft "judgment" upon the roll at the end of the session. The full impact of the arguments of Selden, Coke and Phelips on the minds of ordinary M.P.s cannot be accurately gauged from the diary accounts, but the chain of events can be clearly reconstructed. The lawyers' concern was reciprocated by Sir John Eliot and Sir Thomas Wentworth: Eliot who echoed, "Had not this parliament been, I think it had been entered ere now"; Wentworth who mused, "The more I hear, the more I find the circumstances considerable."[33] It was indeed Eliot who realized on hearing Sir Edward Coke's speech that he had at home none other than former Chief Justice Anderson's report of the key decision of the Elizabethan judges made in 1592, which Anderson's son, William, had recently lent him. William had refused the forced loan in 1627, and had sent his father's manuscript to Eliot to make it "visible to our eyes."[34] Eliot now saw for the first time the overriding significance of obtaining Anderson's own volume, and he brought it into the chamber on the morning of 1 April, when it was read to M.P.s and compared with the copy of Heath's

29. *CD 1628,* II, 212.

30. *CD 1628,* II, 213, 218, 221.

31. *CD 1628,* II, 219 (my italics).

32. To wilfully raze, remove, avoid, vacate or constructively pervert the legal records of the superior courts was a felony by 8 Henry VI, c. 12.

33. *CD 1628,* II, 213, 232.

34. *CD 1628,* II, 213, 219, 229, 230.

draft "judgment" already secured by Selden.[35] The text of Anderson's report was by no means as explicit as Phelips and Coke triumphantly asserted, but it served to convince M.P.s that the house was entitled to condemn Heath's special "judgment" as illegal before another entry was made on the controlment roll, because Anderson had noted that although those imprisoned by the monarch or privy council could not be bailed by King's Bench or another court prior to trial of substantive charges, nevertheless a cause of commitment ought to be certified to the judges in *habeas corpus* proceedings.[36] No *specific* cause of commitment had been returned in the five knights' case, and on the strength of Anderson's report the commons' lawyers persuaded a committee of the whole to formulate four resolutions on 1 April, which were unanimously accepted by the full house two days later.[37] Resolution one proclaimed that discretionary imprisonment for causes unknown to the law was illegal. Next the writ of *habeas corpus* was said to be one of right, not grace. The third resolution affirmed that it was illegal for defendants in *habeas corpus* proceedings to be remanded in custody if no specific cause of legal detention was returned to the court. Finally, the fourth condemned non-parliamentary taxation.[38] As such, the resolutions amounted to a dogmatic summary of subjects' rights as enshrined in English "due process" legislation since 1225, the 1484 statute of benevolences and the judges' decision of 1592.[39] In other words, what Selden's discovery of the Crown's draft "judgment" had done between 31 March and 3 April was to galvanize the house of commons into unanimously deciding to commit itself to formal denials of Charles I's right either to imprison subjects for unknown causes or to raise forced loans, the denials being applicable to Charles's position *in any circumstances.* In turn, these denials of Charles's alleged rights became crucial to the debates of 1628, because they were eventually adapted as the proposed basis of remedial legislation designed to overthrow the Crown's presumed assumption that discretionary action for reasons of state was both legal and justifiable.[40]

Nevertheless, everything depended on exactly what procedure the commons decided to follow, because resolutions of the lower house, however eloquent, had no binding force whatsoever beyond the limits of the chamber ex-

35. *CD 1628,* II, 229–41.
36. *CD 1628,* I, 106; II, 229–30, 232–33, 235–36. See also above, n. 18.
37. *CD 1628,* II, 231, 238–39, 276.
38. *CD 1628,* II, 231, 276.
39. *CD 1628,* I, 106, 128, 133.
40. See below, p. 349.

cept (possibly) upon members of the house, and even then only if, in fact, they resolved something touching the behavior or activities of members.[41] What happened on 3 April was that a select committee of M.P.s, led by privy councillors, was appointed to recommend "what is next fit." The committee advised that a meeting with the lords be requested to consider joint action on the commons' resolutions, and the result was indeed a conference between the houses on 7 April, when the commons' spokesmen presented legal arguments in support of the resolutions.[42] Starting with the *lex terrae* clause of Magna Carta in its statutory form of 1225, Sir Dudley Digges and others attacked the Crown's stand in the five knights' case.[43] Selden then exposed the Crown's attempt to pervert the King's Bench records, Heath's special "judgment" was read to the lords and Selden glossed that its purpose was to put a new principle of English law on record that "no man could ever be enlarged from imprisonment that stood committed by any such an absolute command." This was an innovation. If entered on the controlment roll, the "judgment," in Selden's view, would stand perpetually in flat contradiction of existing English law "to the utter subversion of the chiefest liberty and right, belonging to every free man of this kingdom."[44]

IV

The final link in the chain of events connecting the five knights' case, Heath's attempt to enroll a special "judgment" and the petition of right was forged after 28 April 1628, when the commons declined to abandon their debates on subjects' liberties without first obtaining a guarantee of explanatory legislation in the spirit of their resolutions of 3 April. The commons had good reason to expect reforming legislation in the wake of their four resolutions, because Charles I himself expressly promised on 4 April that he would permit this. Delivering a royal message exhorting M.P.s to vote speedy and sufficient supply, Sir John Coke, secretary of state, assured the house that "we shall enjoy our rights and liberties with as much freedom and security . . . as in any age here-

41. Selden's claim that the resolutions were "resolutions of law, and no man can make question of them" (26 April 1628) was tendentious; *CD 1628,* III, 96. I am grateful to Professor Elton for advice on this point.
42. *CD 1628,* II, 277, 296.
43. *CD 1628,* II, 332–42, 356–58.
44. *CD 1628,* II, 342–56.

tofore under the best of our kings. And whether you shall think fit to secure yourselves herein by way of bill or otherwise . . . he [the king] promiseth and assureth you that he will give way unto it."[45] But the question became, what form should the remedial bill take? In order to understand why the commons aimed to foreclose on the Crown's right of discretionary imprisonment for reasons of state after 28 April, despite heavy pressure to the contrary from both the Crown and the peers, it is necessary to consider the work of the house of lords from 9 to 25 April. The lords did everything to clarify exactly what had been decided by the five knights' case and what had been attempted afterward by the attorney-general, because their reaction to the conference of 7 April was to adopt procedure by parliamentary judicature.[46] On 9 April, the peers decided to summon Heath "to answer these Allegations now spoken on behalf of the Subject."[47] Three days later it was agreed that each of the judges should attend the upper house to explain the matter of fact of the decision in the five knights' case.[48] In debating procedure, Lord Saye and Sele said that the commons had a formal right of reply to Heath before "we think of proceeding to Judgment," and Bishop Harsnett, one of a middle group of lords led by the earls of Arundel and Bristol, asked for a second conference between the houses "before we proceed to judgement in this great cause."[49] When Chief Justice Hyde temporarily declined on 14 April to discuss the five knights' case without express royal warrant, the earl of Devonshire retorted, "We here in this Court may call any judge whatsoever in matter of fact which they have formerly made."[50] Lord Saye "wondered that there should be any question whether this Court might not call to account any court whatsoever," because a writ of error lay from King's Bench to the lords.[51] Buckingham tried to protect Hyde on the grounds that writs of error were not allowed in criminal

45. *CD 1628,* II, 297, 302–3.

46. On the background to parliamentary judicature in early Stuart England, see L. O. Pike, *A Constitutional History of the House of Lords* (London, 1894), pp. 279–304. C. G. C. Tite's analysis of *Impeachment and Parliamentary Judicature in Early Stuart England* (London, 1974) is somewhat undermined by his failure to notice that the tract *Of the Judicature in Parliaments,* published as Selden's work in 1681, was in fact written by Henry Elsyng senior (see Foster, "The Painful Labour of Mr. Elsyng," pp. 42–46).

47. MM, vol. 5, fo. 27ᵛ.

48. MM, vol. 5, fo. 32ᵛ.

49. MM, vol. 5, fo. 32ᵛ. The existence and importance of a middle group in the parliamentary events of the period 1625–29 was discovered by C. Thompson (see his article, "The Origins of the Politics of the Parliamentary Middle Group"). The history of a later group was delineated by J. H. Hexter in *The Reign of King Pym* (Cambridge, Mass., 1941), pp. 31–99, and V. Pearl, "Oliver St. John and the 'Middle Group' in the Long Parliament, August 1643–May 1644," *English Historical Review* LXXXI (1966), 490–519.

50. MM, vol. 5, fo. 33ᵛ.

51. MM, vol. 5, fo. 33ᵛ.

cases without express warrant under the king's sign manual, but the duke was overruled.[52] In particular, the attention of peers focused on Selden's revelations concerning the King's Bench records. Heath had confirmed the story of the special "judgment" in his appearance before the lords on 12 April, when he "confessed that he gave direction for the drawing up of the judgement in the King's Bench against the gentlemen imprisoned upon the loan."[53] He admitted that the special entry in Sir John Heveningham's case "came forth now by misfortune," whereupon Buckingham defended his client at the expense of his king by disclosing that Heath *had been rebuked by Charles I* for failing to enter the "judgment" on the controlment roll.[54] Nevertheless, the legal issues turned solely on the matter of fact to be presented by the judges. Given on 14 and 15 April, their submissions lucidly resolved five fundamental points. First, there had been no "judgment" in the five knights' case but only a rule of court.[55] Secondly, the rule was not a precedent for Charles's alleged right of discretionary imprisonment for reasons of state. Thirdly, the question of bail was always a matter for the decision of King's Bench, each case being taken on its merits. Fourthly, the decision in the five knights' case had been dictated by the technical question of legal "knowledge." Finally, permission had been refused for the addition of Heath's special entry to the controlment roll.[56]

When the full implications of the judges' words had been digested, it was

52. MM, vol. 5, fo. 34; Relf, *Notes of Debates,* pp. 99–100. Buckingham's argument was, in any case, bad, because the five knights had not committed a crime.

53. MM, vol. 5, fo. 32.

54. Relf, *Notes of Debates,* p. 93. The precise reason why Buckingham decided to make this astonishing leak at this point is elusive, but it is not likely to have been an accident. In the event, the significance of his statement was almost completely obscured in an outbreak of friction between the two houses over the alleged claim by the earl of Suffolk on 12 April 1628 that "Mr. Selden had razed a record and did deserve to be hanged" and that "Mr. Selden went about to divide the King and his people" (*CD 1628,* II, 508–9, 514–16). Suffolk denied in the upper house on 17 April that he had spoken these words, maintaining that he had misunderstood Attorney-general Heath to say that the record of the five knights' case had been razed, and "that I [Suffolk] conceived that Selden had razed a record in putting out of material matter, and therefore *if he had done so* he had deserved to be hanged" (MM, vol. 5, fo. 42; Relf, *Notes of Debates,* pp. 115–16). Suffolk added, "If offended in this, it is because I was mistaken," to which the earl of Berkshire replied, "*Humanum est errare.* He is sorry for it, but the word 'if' extenuates it" (Relf, *Notes of Debates,* p. 116). On 17 April the commons exhorted the lords to charge Suffolk at the bar of the upper house "and that they will proceed against him in justice" (*CD 1628,* II, 516). The lords ignored this request. That Suffolk was in error is confirmed by the fact that neither the controlment nor *coram rege* rolls for 1627–28 have been razed. It is possible to speculate that a space had been left on the controlment roll for Heath's special entry (KB 29/276), because membrane 88 is followed immediately by membrane 90, but such spaces (or "windows") as the absent membrane 89 were not unusual on the King's Bench rolls, since the membranes were numbered before the beginning of the term to which they pertained, and not all membranes so numbered were subsequently used by the clerks.

55. MM, vol. 5, fos. 33–38; Relf, *Notes of Debates,* pp. 100–101, 104–7, 111–12. For the exact technical status of the rule of 27 November 1627, see above, n. 15.

56. MM, vol. 5, fos. 34–38; Braye MS 14, fos. 69ᵛ–72; Relf, *Notes of Debates,* pp. 100–102, 104–9.

obvious that the lords did not need to proceed further as a court. The King's Bench rule of 27 November 1627 was not a binding precedent on record. The imprisoned loan refusers had been refused bail, but there had been nothing to prevent counsel for the appellants from obtaining new writs of *alias habeas* if they had wished, a process which, however futile in the face of the Crown's refusal to specify the "cause of the cause," could theoretically have continued *ad infinitum.*[57] It was the *practical abuse* of the law by the Crown which had defied the spirit of the *lex terrae* clause of Magna Carta. The judges were vindicated: they could neither "know" the "cause of the cause" in proceedings on a writ of *habeas corpus,* nor "know" whether or not the Crown had declined to file substantive charges against the prisoners. In short, the King's Bench judges had acted correctly (if ingenuously) within the existing legal framework. But the peers now saw plainly that the Crown's action and subsequent attempt to pervert the legal records had created an explosive situation, because the commons had been galvanized into formulating a political manifesto, namely resolutions which were an absolute denial of Charles's right of discretionary imprisonment *in any circumstances.* The question was, could the commons be persuaded to relax their view? To this end, the earls of Arundel and Bristol threw the weight of the middle group of lords in favor of accommodation with the lower house.[58] Both the commons and Sir Robert Heath were invited to attend a second conference on 16 and 17 April, at which the commons were told the true status of the decision in the five knights' case and assured that the rule of 27 November 1627 was not a precedent on record.[59] Then, in an effort to begin again as if nothing had happened, Heath delivered a conciliatory statement on Charles's behalf. He confirmed that Magna Carta was still valid, although it was "as fully made for the king as the subject," he agreed that the king could not imprison any subject except *per legem terrae;* lastly, he conceded that the King's Bench judges had done nothing substantive in the five knights' case. There followed an emotional effort to thrash out on both sides the meaning of the *lex terrae* clause of Magna Carta and of the statutes

---

57. See above, p. 332 and n. 15; Relf, *Notes of Debates,* p. 100. Justice Whitlocke answered the objection that a man "might be kept in prison *durante vita*" on a rule of court *quousque, etc.* by explaining that new writs of *alias habeas* might be sued out to rehear the case. To the extent that a man imprisoned *per speciale mandatum domini regis* would never secure bail against the wishes of the Crown, however many writs of *alias habeas* were sued (see above n. 15), his explanation was ingenuous, even dissembling, but it was *correct in strict law.* The moral obligation lay with the Crown to behave within the spirit of English "due process" legislation.

58. MM, vol. 5, fos. 38–39^v.

59. MM, vol. 5, fos. 39^v–46^v; *CD 1628,* II, 490–503, 524–38.

and precedents previously cited. *But the work done by the lords to confirm that the decision in the five knights' case could never have been legally employed as a precedent for discretionary imprisonment for reasons of state had served to cast in a sinister light Heath's earlier attempt to pervert the King's Bench records in order to obtain exactly such a precedent.* As a result, the commons' spokesmen put the bit between their teeth, and the debates of 16–17 April had the opposite effect to that intended, because they led to polarization on the disputed points of legal interpretation. Heath argued that, "If *lex terrae* be taken for due process of law, then none can be imprisoned for felony before indictment." Reasons of state dictated, rather, that dangerous men like Guy Fawkes be locked up prior to trial *per legem terrae,* and the king must not be expected to set down the particular cause. "It is to be intended it is for some matter of state not to be revealed." To this the commons' spokesmen retorted, "It can be no prejudice to the King by reason of matter of state; for if it be for suspicion of treason, misprision of treason, or felony, it may be by general words expressed, *vizt., pro suspicione proditionis, etc.* If it be for any contempt, or any other thing, the particular cause must be shown."[60]

On 21 and 22 April, the lords debated in the privacy of the upper house what their response, if any, should now be to the commons' resolutions of 3 April. Following the unhappy second conference, the chief sticking point was less the decision in the five knights' case than the *lex terrae* clause of Magna Carta. If Magna Carta was valid, could Charles I or the privy council legally imprison subjects "without present cause shown"? Since Secretary-of-state Conway refused to condone anything which limited the king's power or the privy council's, a basic principle was agreed by peers that "a commitment by the king or his council is good for point of authority. And if the cause of the commitment be just, then the commitment is good for the matter."[61] Of course, everything hinged on the means by which the "justice" of the cause was to be ascertained, and on this subject there was disagreement. However, the lords cannot be criticized for trying to plumb the depths of the legal labyrinth without prejudice either to royal prerogative or the liberty of the subject. They began to work out more precise ideas on 22 April, when Saye at last conceded that proper allowance had to be made for discretionary power in times of emergency, though such power was not "to rule the law nor leave a gap."[62] In the ensuing debate,

---

60. *Journals of the House of Lords,* III, 746–47, 753–63; *CD 1628,* II, 527–33; MM, vol. 5, fos. 44^v–48.
61. Braye MS 14, fo. 92^v.
62. Relf, *Notes of Debates,* p. 124. Saye's idea that an expression on record of subjects' liberties should be

Dorset, who opposed the commons' resolutions, stood adamant that the king could imprison for reasons of state and was to be trusted: "If he abuse it, *habet deum ultorem.*"[63] But Saye argued that the question was "whether that trust shall prevent the ordinary common law?"[64] Lord Weston defended the *status quo:* "The law, standing as it doth, preserveth the prerogative and the subject's liberty."[65] His speech was a godsend to Buckingham, who moved to curtail the proceedings by forcing a vote. However, the duke was outfooted by the combined efforts of Bristol, Arundel, Saye, Clare and Bishop Harsnett.[66] Having won this minor victory, Bristol reformulated the case for accommodation and another conference with the commons, an approach which was accepted despite isolated objections. But rather than risk further polarization between Sir Robert Heath and the commons' spokesmen over interpretation of the legal issues, the peers resolved that the new negotiations would be conducted "without dispute." Instead, terms of proposed compromise were to be drafted by a select committee and simply handed to the commons' representatives as a basis for future discussion.[67]

The lords named a committee of eighteen to draw up their terms on 23 April.[68] Those peers selected included Saye, Warwick and Devonshire among the commons' allies, and Arundel, Bristol, Clare, Harsnett and Williams from the middle group, forces which comfortably outnumbered anything which Buckingham and Dorset could muster as opponents of the commons' resolutions.[69] The committee met a delegation of thirty-six M.P.s, who were told that "the lords do concur with them in their desire of the just liberties of the subject." However, the committee's spokesman, Archbishop Abbot, emphasized that "they do find it fit and necessary to preserve the just preroga-

---

understood not to prevent emergency action by the Crown is important in judging whether the supporters of the petition of right were seeking to curtail the prerogative or not. The middle group followed Saye, who argued on 21 May 1628 that, since there was nothing in the petition beyond what concerned subjects' rights, a saving clause for the king's prerogative was not necessary (ibid. p. 189). It was the hardline members of the commons, Sir Edward Coke, Eliot and Coryton, who feared that anything less than an absolute denial of discretionary imprisonment for unknown causes would be ineffective. Thompson, "Origins of the Politics of the Parliamentary Middle Group," pp. 84–85; J. N. Ball, "The Petition of Right in the English Parliament of 1628," in *Album Emile Lousse,* IV (Louvain, 1964), 50. This point requires research beyond the scope of the present paper, for which see Dr. Ball's thesis, "The Parliamentary Career of Sir John Eliot, 1624–1629," Cambridge Ph.D., 1953.

63. Relf, *Notes of Debates,* p. 130.
64. MM, vol. 5, fo. 51.
65. MM, vol. 5, fo. 51^v.
66. MM, vol. 5, fo. 52; Relf, *Notes of Debates,* pp. 131–34.
67. MM, vol. 5, fo. 52^v.
68. MM, vol. 5, fo. 53^v.
69. MM, vol. 5, fo. 54.

tive of the king also."[70] The commons' delegation reported back to the whole house, and was next day formally reappointed to receive the lords' propositions.[71] On 25 April the lords' committee concluded its own deliberations, and a copy of its propositions was duly presented to the commons' representatives in the painted chamber.[72] The first three proposals invited Charles I to confirm Magna Carta and six other statutes forming the basis of "due process" in England, and to declare that "every free subject of this realm has a fundamental propriety in his goods and a fundamental liberty in his person." The fourth and fifth propositions stressed the illegality of forced loans and identified the problem of the "cause of the cause" raised in the five knights' case as the true source of current controversy. In addition, proposition five explicitly conceded the commons' interpretation of the judicial decision of 1592, namely that substantive charges should be brought against subjects committed to prison for reasons of state within a reasonable time. On the other hand, the fifth proposition defined Charles's prerogative as "intrinsical to his sovereignty," upheld his right to imprison for reasons of state and tacitly acknowledged that the decision in the five knights' case had been correct within the existing framework of English legal institutions.[73]

V

The commons began to debate the lords' propositions on 26 April. Noy, Pym, Digges and Sir Thomas Wentworth favored the first three, but no one could accept the olive branch tendered by the last two proposals on the grounds that Charles's power of discretionary imprisonment was defended.[74] It was becoming clear that the Crown's earlier attempt to pervert the King's Bench records was about to backfire on Charles, because the commons refused to relax their absolute denial of Charles's right to imprison for unknown causes despite the peers' assurance that the decision in the five knights' case was not a precedent for discretionary imprisonment for reasons of state. At face value, the lords' propositions fairly encapsulated the "just meridian" between civil

70. MM, vol. 5, fo. 54ᵛ; Braye MS 14, fo. 96.
71. *CD 1628,* III, 60–62.
72. MM, vol. 5, fos. 54ᵛ–56ᵛ; Braye MS 14, fos. 98ᵛ–100.
73. Braye MS 14, fos. 100–101; *CD 1628,* III, 74–75.
74. *CD 1628,* III, 94–119.

liberties and royal prerogative which peers had sought since the first conference on 7 April. But in the soured atmosphere of 1628, Sir Edward Coke and Selden were overtly hostile to all five of the lords' proposals. They held the first three to be irrelevant to the issues, since they did not explicitly define whether the king had emergency powers beyond the reach of Magna Carta. Sir Edward read that part of the fourth proposal which mentioned cases "within the cognizance of the common law" to mean that other cases were rightly triable by martial law, while everyone opposed the ambiguities of proposition five, with its reference to the prerogative as an "intrinsical" aspect of sovereignty. Coke added that an "intrinsical" prerogative was unbounded by law; it was entrusted to Charles by God "and then it is due *jure divino,* and then no law can take it away." If so, Charles I had a discretionary power of imprisonment, something Sir Edward had come to think was contrary to Magna Carta.[75] Yet M.P.s still wished to avoid a head-on collision between the houses over royal prerogative and the right to decide disputed points of law. In particular, John Pym took a pragmatic view: "First apprehensions are seldom serious. We are now to consider if we shall yield to a conference."[76] However, no conference was permitted to take place. When the commons reassembled on 28 April, they were quickly summoned to the upper house to hear Lord Keeper Coventry read a royal address. After noting the setbacks to the war effort caused by the commons' earlier decision to hold up the subsidy bill in committee while grievances were discussed, Coventry informed the houses that Magna Carta and the six other statutes were valid, that subjects would be maintained in "the just freedom of their persons and safety of their estates," that Charles intended to govern according to the laws of England, and that "you shall find as much security in his Majesty's royal word and promise as in the strength of any law."[77]

This intervention was perhaps the best move open to Charles at the end of April 1628, when most of the fleet gathered to raise the siege of La Rochelle and defend the English coast was still anchored at Plymouth without supplies. At a stroke, the king reduced the disputed legal issues to a question of trust in his royal word which could not be challenged without impugning his honour and good intentions, and Charles's clarification of his position certainly sat-

75. *CD 1628,* III, 94–96. Cf. Russell, *Parliaments and English Politics,* pp. 353–54.
76. *CD 1628,* III, 97.
77. *CD 1628,* III, 125.

isfied the lords, who dropped all further reference to their propositions until the petition of right was submitted to them on 8 May.[78] But Coventry's address boomeranged in the commons for three reasons. First, Charles's demand that M.P.s rely on his promise to respect the rule of law in future was heavily undermined by Heath's felonious quest for a precedent for discretionary imprisonment for reasons of state. Secondly, M.P.s had learned so much about the events of the previous two years by 28 April that they declined to curtail their debates without drafting remedial legislation. The commons rejoiced in Charles's promise to defend liberty and property, but the king had done nothing to indicate that his *interpretation* of English law now corresponded to theirs. Thirdly, members recalled at this point that Charles had *already* promised that he would permit remedy of grievances by bill.[79] On 4 April 1628 he had informed the lower house that "whether you shall think fit to secure yourselves herein by way of bill or otherwise . . . he promiseth and assureth you that he will give way unto it."[80] A select committee was thus appointed on 28 April to frame a reforming bill, and a draft tackling the issues of discretionary imprisonment, non-parliamentary taxation and billeting was laid before the commons next day. After a preamble reciting the medieval statutes alleged by the commons to have been violated by Charles's government, the first enacting clause confirmed these acts and declared that all judgments, awards and rules of court "given or to be given to the contrary shall be void." Thereafter the commons' resolutions of 3 April were to be enacted, together with a clause against billeting.[81]

The terms of this bill provoked some agony in the commons, since Sir Nathaniel Rich, Pym, Digges and Sir Thomas Wentworth preferred not to imperil the legislative enterprise by including the resolutions of 3 April until these were fully endorsed by the lords. The critics were adamant, though, that they did not wish to relax the *meaning* of the resolutions; their point was exactly that if the resolutions were already based on existing law as reported by Chief Justice Anderson, then it was better tactically just to confirm these same laws and to outlaw breaches of them since 1625.[82] As Sir Benjamin Rudyard echoed

---

78. The bishop of Exeter, Joseph Hall, sent a letter to the commons on 28 April in which he exhorted them to accept Charles's word alone. H.L.R.O., Braye MS 89, fo. 91; *CD 1628*, III, 125 n. 26.
79. *CD 1628*, III, 128.
80. *CD 1628*, II, 297; see above, pp. 340–41.
81. *CD 1628*, III, 123–24, 149; Relf, *Petition of Right*, appendix B.
82. *CD 1628*, III, 149–68, 172–73, 175–82, 187–88.

on 30 April, "We too much flatter ourselves if we believe the Lords, that they approve of what we have done." No draft was viable if it could not be expected to command the support of the upper house.[83] But Rudyard was overruled by Phelips and Eliot, who now said that the king's goodness was eclipsed only by the "interposition of officers."[84] Even so, the commons remained united by a basic desire for reforming legislation, and on the third day of the debate (1 May), Sir Thomas Wentworth proposed that the select committee's draft be replaced by a watered-down bill which would have confirmed Magna Carta and the six other statutes without addition, would have omitted any denial of Charles's right to imprison for reasons of state, but would have prescribed immediate bail in *habeas corpus* proceedings for persons deprived of liberty for causes unknown to the law.[85] However, before M.P.s could express an opinion on Wentworth's interesting suggestion, Secretary-of-state Coke brought a brusque message from Charles. The king "would know whether we will rest on his royal word or no, declared to us by the Lord Keeper; which if we do, he assures us it shall be really performed."[86]

Charles's message poisoned the atmosphere completely. He had indicated that his government's interpretation of English law must be deemed valid on the basis of his verbal promise alone, despite the fact that he had previously offered the prospect of reforming legislation and notwithstanding the Crown's attempt to obtain a precedent for discretionary imprisonment for reasons of state by means of a felonious act. His message also implied that if the commons continued any further with bill procedure, their action would not only be read as an infringement of royal prerogative, it would be taken to mean, too, that they did not trust Charles. The commons were thus trapped between Scylla and Charybdis: to abandon hope of remedial legislation after six weeks' work was to go home empty-handed to their constituents, while to seek a tangible outcome was to fail in their duty to Charles. In any case, since Charles had unquestionably promised on 4 April that the commons *could* proceed by bill, Secretary Coke was obliged to gloss that if a bill, after all, were to contain "no enlargement of former laws, it will pass."[87] However, a majority of M.P.s repudiated the idea of bare confirmation, not because they explicitly mistrusted

83. *CD 1628*, III, 172.
84. *CD 1628*, III, 173.
85. *CD 1628*, III, 188.
86. *CD 1628*, III, 188–89.
87. *CD 1628*, III, 191–92.

Charles's future intentions at this stage,[88] but rather because Secretary Coke
had himself made repeated and embarrassing admissions since 22 March that
illegal courses had indeed been followed during the war preparations of 1626–
27.[89] Not even Charles's councillors could deny in 1628 that illegal acts had
been committed which could not be redressed by due process of existing law
(*lex terrae*). Yet neither his own confessions nor the wide apprehension created
since 1 April that Charles's government had effectively renounced its commitment to the rule of law by attempting to pervert the King's Bench records
prevented Secretary Coke from telling the commons on 1 May that it was still
his duty as a minister to commit men to prison for reasons of state, though
not to commit "without a just cause"—whatever that meant.[90] As a result,
Eliot's previous remarks on the "interposition" of Charles's councillors were
now reinforced by Sir Thomas Wentworth: "We are accountable to a public
trust, and therefore, since there has been a public violation by his ministers,
nothing will satisfy but a public amends."[91] But Charles sent in reply an even
more abrasive message next day to say that while he fully intended to "rec-
tify what has been or may be found amiss" on subjects' liberties, he would
not permit "new explanations, interpretations, exposition, or additions in any
sort" to existing law. He would not allow encroachment, as he saw it, on royal
prerogative. Furthermore, parliament was to be prorogued on 13 May.[92]

VI

We turn to the immediate situation in which the petition of right was born. On
3 May, the house of commons approved the text of a formal answer to Charles's
messages, which was read to the king and premier peers two days later by the
Speaker, Sir John Finch, in the banqueting house at Whitehall.[93] The Speaker
assured Charles that the house was "as full of trust and confidence in your royal
word and promises as ever House of Commons reposed in any of their best
kings"; but, since illegal acts had been committed by ministers, nothing short

88. *CD 1628,* III, 210–12, 215–16, 219–21, 224, 225, 227–28, 229, 234–35, 237, 239, 240–41, 247, 248–49, 253–54, 271–73.
89. *CD 1628,* II, 65; III, 201, 203. See also Hirst, "Parliament, Law and War in the 1620s," p. 460.
90. *CD 1628,* III, 189.
91. *CD 1628,* III, 211.
92. *CD 1628,* III, 212–13.
93. *CD 1628,* III, 253–54.

of a public remedy would "raise the dejected hearts of your loving subjects to a cheerful supply of your Majesty." The commons then appealed to Charles's original promise of a bill, protesting that it was not their intention to make inroads on his sovereignty and prerogative, and that they had no wish to strain or reinterpret existing English law. All that was sought was an explanation of the true meaning of *lex terrae,* combined with "some moderate provision for execution and performance."[94] But it was in vain. Charles conferred with the peers, after which Coventry turned to deliver the *coup de grâce.* If the commons trusted the king, why did they need explanatory legislation? Charles was willing to confirm Magna Carta and the six other statutes in legislative form, but without paraphrase, additions or explanations. If the commons pressed the point, they must be "accountable to God and your country for the ill success of this meeting." Coventry then reiterated that parliament was to be prorogued the following week.[95]

The lord keeper's speech was the obituary of reforming legislation on subjects' liberties. When M.P.s gathered on 6 May, no one except William Coryton, an embittered loan refuser and enemy of Buckingham, thought it right to pursue an explanatory bill against Charles's expressed wishes.[96] There remained the possibility of accepting a bare confirmation of Magna Carta and the other statutes. John Hoskins favored "wiping the rust" off Magna Carta, but his view was opposed. In particular, the grave and learned Edward Littleton drove home the point that, since the existing laws were already acknowledged to be valid, bare confirmation would, in fact, serve to efface the commons' resolutions of 3 April.[97] Since all M.P.s were eager to do nothing that might make matters worse, the idea of bare confirmation could not gain consensus. In any case, Sir Roger North, who described himself as a "mere country" member, knew that bare confirmation would not satisfy the constituencies: "When we come down and be asked what is done, and we shall say we have a confirmation of the laws, they will ask us when they were repealed, and *lex terrae* is an unfolded riddle still." With the end of the session in sight, North ventilated the approaching prospect of another parliament from which most M.P.s would return empty-handed to their localities. Even so, he took loyal satisfaction from Charles's promises, wishing "no other law than the King's

94. *CD 1628,* III, 254.
95. *CD 1628,* III, 254.
96. *CD 1628,* III, 269.
97. *CD 1628,* III, 269–70, 275–76, 280–81.

word."[98] At this point Sir Nathaniel Rich rose to object that Charles had given no specific redress: "Let us first determine whether the satisfaction given by his Majesty be sufficient or no. It is twofold. He promises he will govern us by his laws, or the confirmation of the laws. We have nothing thereby but shells and shadows. The King and Council *did commit men against the law.*"[99] Rich then argued that the issue of trust in the king, the most sensitive issue conceivable in early Stuart England, was fundamentally distinct from that of legal interpretation, which was the true cause of the present friction. What Charles had done by his messages, Rich asserted, was to reduce disputed legal issues to the more basic question of trust as a primitive form of parliamentary guillotine. However, Rich did not think that legal points could be settled in this way, and cited an example. If a man owed money to another, the exact amount of which was not mutually agreed, the fact that trust existed between the parties was not an adequate solution of their business problem. For trust to be efficacious, the "point of trust" had to be defined. Thus if Charles declared that forced loans, billeting and discretionary imprisonment were against the law, he would immediately be trusted.[100]

It is easy to see why Secretary Coke expressed horror at the drift of this debate. The big fear, shared by Wentworth, Littleton and John Glanville, was that a vote might take place on the question of trust. But Pandora's box began to close as speakers focused on Rich's defense that trust was distinct from specific redress.[101] Pym, Eliot, Goodwin and Seymour supported the argument that reliance on Charles's promises was an illogical solution, because the disputed legal points upon which the administration of justice depended remained unexplained.[102] M.P.s thus skirted the issue of trust, on the grounds that good intentions were an insufficient guarantee of a true understanding of *lex terrae.* Pym encapsulated the matter when he said that Charles's word would be sufficient, "if we knew what the King's sense and meaning is." The authorities believed that law was on their side; the privy council acted in good faith. Pym said he was more concerned that Charles had neither outlawed imprisonment for refusing loans nor forbidden reliance on reasons of state for the future. "If the King knew the law, that he ought not to commit without cause, he would

98. *CD 1628,* III, 269–70, 275.
99. *CD 1628,* III, 270.
100. *CD 1628,* III, 270, 275, 276.
101. *CD 1628,* III, 270–72.
102. *CD 1628,* III, 271–72, 276–77, 281–83.

not."[103] The question was, how were the commons to convert Charles to their view of "the law"? This was indeed the dilemma, summarized by Peter Ball. "The question is not whether the laws be in force or no, but for the meaning of them. What is *lex terrae?* We all agree what it is, but have the Lords and the judges so agreed?"[104] Ball was, in fact, the first M.P. to admit specifically that the lords' decision to offer negotiations on the basis of their own propositions meant in reality that the definition of *lex terrae* enshrined in the commons' resolutions of 3 April was contentious. "Say this question come again into Westminster Hall, can the judges take notice of our resolutions?"[105] Here Ball stated the essence. The truth was that Selden and the commons' lawyers had failed to vindicate the interpretation of English law they had evolved on 1 April; the four resolutions were worthless unless translated into legislative form. M.P.s were now going round in circles, undoubtedly because they were no longer working within an accepted procedural framework. Charles's messages had successfully interrupted the consultative process between the two houses: the commons were isolated. In particular, the king's insistence that his verbal promise was sufficient put the commons at a dangerous disadvantage. The implication was that anyone seeking reforming legislation did not trust him, an innuendo which had to be neutralized. As Sir Edward Coke explained, "For any not to rely on the King it is not fit, trust in him is all the confidence we have under God."[106]

In these circumstances, Sir Edward's idea that the parliamentary solution was to proceed by petition of right showed a unique ability to cast invention out of necessity. For whatever the precise status of the petition as first conceived in his own brain, Coke had identified the sole escape-route by which the commons could avoid the threatened prorogation, restore communications with the lords and join with them in handing Charles an explanatory document to which an answer was expected.[107] His proposal was supported by Glanville, Littleton, Wentworth, Pym, Eliot, Phelips, Rich, Hoby and others, and a drafting committee was quickly appointed.[108] As before, the grievances to be addressed were discretionary imprisonment, non-parliamentary taxation

103. *CD 1628,* III, 271, 276, 281–82.
104. *CD 1628,* III, 270–71.
105. *CD 1628,* III, 271.
106. *CD 1628,* III, 271–72 (where the reading of MSS 8–12 seems to make best sense).
107. For the background to petitioning and the petition of right as a formal document, see Mrs. Foster's article, "Petitions and the Petition of Right," pp. 21–45.
108. *CD 1628,* III, 272–73, 277–78, 282–84, 286–87, 290–91, 293–94, 296.

and billeting.[109] But while Coke's idea commanded enthusiastic acclaim, it was none the less seriously defective from the commons' point of view. M.P.s had chosen bill procedure in the first place because they wanted reforming *legislation*—not a manifesto "wrapped up in a parliament roll."[110] Unless Coke's idea could offer a firm guarantee of legislation foreclosing on Charles's alleged right of discretionary imprisonment for causes unknown to the law, its adoption would nullify the whole constitutional approach of the commons' leaders. For neither the casuistry of Sir Nathaniel Rich nor the protestations of Wentworth, Littleton and Glanville could disguise that what was at stake in 1628 was the need to obtain results. The illegal acts of Charles's reign—the earl of Arundel's imprisonment, the forced loan, compulsory billeting and the use of martial law in cases involving civilians—had culminated in the Crown's felonious attempt to pervert the record of the five knights' case. As Pym inquired, what had Charles done to prevent such illegal acts in future?[111] What lay in store for subjects whose sovereign adhered to the letter, if not the spirit of existing "due process" legislation? Secretary Coke affirmed that a royal promise "binds the King further than the law can. First, it binds his affections, which is the greatest bond between king and subjects, and it binds his judgement also, nay, his honour."[112] Yet by insisting that his verbal promise was sufficient, Charles had, in fact, reneged on his promise of 4 April to allow reforming legislation. Coryton was alone in thinking it possible to make distrust of Charles an explicit issue prior to the petition of right, but the ideological position of the commons had been clearly signalled by their resolutions of 3 April, which were an expression of utter horror at the Crown's relapse into lawless rule as manifested by its designs on the King's Bench records. Despite Heath's fair words and the lords' efforts at accommodation, the commons had repeatedly refused to relax these resolutions—naturally, since if the Crown wished to legalize discretionary imprisonment for reasons of state *it must originally have intended to practice it*. Why, then, did the commons agree to proceed by peti-

---

109. *CD 1628*, III, 273, 278.

110. Cf. *CD 1628*, III, 98 (26 April 1628). Sir Thomas Wentworth had said, "Neither do I think it fit to go in a petition of right, for that is wrapped up in a parliament roll." The precise legal status of the petition is discussed (not entirely satisfactorily) by Mrs. Foster in "The Painful Labour of Mr. Elsyng," pp. 28–29, 31–32, 33–35; see also her article, "Printing the Petition of Right," *Huntington Library Quarterly,* XXXVIII, 1 (1974), 81–83.

111. See above, pp. 352–53. It was the *scale* of Charles's dubious operations in 1626–27 which may well have been at the forefront of M.P.s' minds on 6 May 1628: the imprisonment of so many gentlemen, pillars of their communities, in such a doubtful way. This point was drawn to my attention by Professor Derek Hirst, to whom I am grateful.

112. *CD 1628*, III, 268, 274.

tion of right? The truth was that Charles's exploitation of the issue of trust had obliged the commons' leaders to resort to compromise after all. The unanimity of support for Sir Edward Coke's proposal must otherwise be inexplicable: everyone except Coryton and William Hakewill chose to forget on 6 May that procedure by petition of right had failed to interest M.P.s during the debate on the lords' propositions ten days before *because it could not guarantee legislation.*[113] As Coryton objected (with Hakewill's scholarly aid), legislation had not been made by means of petition and answer since the fifteenth century. Just what use was a petition of right if it could never become law?[114] But this crucial objection was brushed aside: the threat of a broken parliament, doubly heinous in time of war, seems to have been too close on 6 May for the commons' leaders to listen to unwelcome home truths. Charles I had eliminated bill procedure from the equation; the commons, if they were not to concede total defeat, had no choice but to snatch at an option of primarily cosmetic value.

VII

To sum up. Reappraisal of the five knights' case establishes that Charles I had abused the legal procedures of King's Bench in order to defy the spirit of English "due process" legislation. The Crown's action was exposed in parliament in 1628, and the house of commons passed resolutions which were an absolute denial of the Crown's alleged right to imprison for reasons of state. These resolutions were opposed on behalf of the Crown by Sir Robert Heath, who upheld Charles's power to imprison for causes unknown to the law. Despite the moderating efforts of the upper house, the views of Heath and the commons' spokesmen became polarized, and the commons declined, if possible, to allow the disputed points to be settled by default in favor of the Crown. In starting this chain of events, Charles and Heath were the innovators. Heath, who Buckingham admitted was acting under pressure from Charles, had originally attempted to pervert the record of the decision in the five knights' case in order to legalize Charles's claim to practice discretionary imprisonment for

---

113. *CD 1628*, III, 98, 102–3, 108, 111.

114. *CD 1628*, III, 273, 278, 284. The petition was given statutory authority in 1641 by the act against Ship Money (17 Charles I, c. 14). I am grateful to Conrad Russell for this reference. I am preparing another paper on the legal authority of the petition in 1628 and 1629.

reasons of state. Furthermore, the lords verified correctly that the decision in the five knights' case could never have been legally employed as a precedent for such imprisonment, with the result that the Crown's acts and intentions appeared in an unfavorable light. In the interests of compromise and unity, the lords assumed responsibility for trying to resolve the disputed legal points themselves, but their propositions were unacceptable to the commons on the grounds that they acknowledged Charles's ultimate right of discretionary imprisonment in times of emergency. The truth was that the revelation of Heath's attempt to pervert the King's Bench records had sown fears that Charles's government had repudiated its commitment to the rule of law. Hence the commons' lawyers would not agree that Charles had ever had the right to practice discretionary imprisonment in defiance of English "due process" legislation. When Charles then stepped in to curtail the consultative process between the houses, he managed to isolate the commons but failed to quash their desire for reforming legislation. The petition of right was born when Charles reneged on his promise of 4 April. In approving the idea of the petition, the commons espoused the one remaining parliamentary method by which an explanatory document in the spirit of their resolutions might be devised. However, the decision to abandon bill procedure in favor of the petition was a major setback in terms of what had gone before, and future historical inquiry will need to examine how far the petition, in fact, marked the victory of politics over principle.

Coke's Note-Books and the Sources of His *Reports*

SIR JOHN BAKER

☙ ☙ ☙

Four hundred years ago this April, Edward Coke of Trinity College, Cambridge, was admitted to the Inner Temple, an event momentous not merely in the history of the Inn but also in the history of the common law. For it was in 1572 that young Coke began to attend the courts and to observe the decisions there,[1] to listen to Bendlowes and Plowden and Dyer as they opened for him the secrets of jurisprudence. He was to continue his attendance at Westminster Hall for forty-four years, and from 1579 to record all the important cases which came to his notice. It is, therefore, an auspicious moment to remember Coke's achievement as a reporter of cases, a matter of particular interest in "that famous University of Cambridge, *alma mea mater*," to whose legal offspring Coke's literary works were especially addressed.[2]

It is unnecessary to sing the praises of Coke's *Reports* as sources of law and history. For all their quaint defects they "will last to be admired by the judicious posterity whilst fame hath a trumpet left her, and any breath to blow therein."[3] In view of their undiminished importance, the almost complete absence of original textual studies is somewhat remarkable. In the latest edition

---

"Coke's Note-Books and the Sources of His *Reports*" is reprinted by permission of John H. Baker. Originally published in *Cambridge Law Journal* 30 (1972): 59–86.

1. In Co.Litt. 384, 385, is cited a Common Pleas case of 1572 which Coke himself "heard and observed." The earliest case he reports at length in print is *Vernon's Case* (1572) 4 Rep. 1. For other observations between 1572 and 1579, see note 49, *infra*. Coke was twenty years old in 1572.

2. Co.Litt., preface. Coke was admitted to Trinity College in September 1567, and went down at the end of 1570. He was admitted to Clifford's Inn on 21 January 1571, and to the Inner Temple on 24 April 1572. (Memoranda in MS.Harl. 6687.) There is no record of his taking the B.A. degree. An Edward Coke of the Inner Temple graduated B.A. in 1600 from St. Catharine's Hall, but this was Sir Edward's eldest son. Sir Edward proceeded M.A. in 1597 by special grace, and was elected High Steward of the University in 1614. (*Ibid.; Venn.*)

3. T. Fuller, *History of the Worthies of England* (1662), p. 251.

of the *Reports,* published as long ago as 1826,[4] Mr. J. H. Thomas attempted to sever the personal comment and digression from the actual resolutions of the courts; but his only guide was his own instinct, corroborated where possible from other contemporary reports. Then, exactly thirty years ago, Professor Plucknett set himself the task of trying to discover the sources of, and the plan behind, the *Reports.*[5] He brought to the problem his usual insight and attention to detail, but confessed that the irregularity in composition was "deeply puzzling" and concluded that the reports had not been taken in the customary manner:

> The first glance at Coke is enough to show that the set of reports as a whole does not come from a chronologically arranged register like Plowden's, and does not reproduce a single series of cases noted down as they occurred. Indeed, no single series of any sort, chronological or systematical, seems to explain the present arrangement of the reports.

To solve the puzzle, Plucknett postulated that some of the cases had been taken from a commonplace book arranged by subject, and others from "collections made by other hands than his." He also posed, but left unanswered, the question whether the reports were contemporary, or were written up from memory, or from the writings of others, at the time of publication. Plucknett squeezed the last drop of evidence from the printed volumes themselves, but could not find the answer therein. He omitted to take into account the many short reports to be found in the *Institutes,* and because of war-time conditions he made no attempt to trace relevant manuscripts.[6] Further investigation was inhibited by the fact that no manuscripts of Coke's reports remained in his library at Holkham Hall, Norfolk; and it was thought that as a result of the confiscation of Coke's papers the original reports had long been lost.[7]

The new evidence began to emerge when the writer's attention was caught by MS.Harl. 6686 in the British Museum. It soon became apparent that, although no one seemed to have noticed the fact since 1715, the volume con-

---

4. By J. H. Thomas and J. F. Fraser, in six volumes. Citations below are from this edition, always referring to the old foliation.

5. "The Genesis of Coke's Reports" (1942) 27 *Cornell Law Quarterly* 190.

6. *Ibid.,* esp. pp. 200, 203, 208, 212.

7. See W. O. Hassall, *A Catalogue of the Library of Sir Edward Coke* (1950), pp. vi–vii: "The manuscripts of Coke's own *Reports* apparently already were lost in 1634, for they do not appear." It can now be shown that they do appear, but anonymously. The MSS. were probably confiscated in 1634, and they never returned to Holkham: see pp. 377–79, *infra.*

tained an extensive and valuable collection of reports in Coke's own hand, including not only early versions of reports which were later printed, but also many cases not in print at all. Comparison with MS.Harl. 6687, which bears Coke's signature, confirmed the authorship; and Dr. W. O. Hassall's edition of Coke's own library catalogue (compiled *c.* 1634) revealed that both volumes had once belonged to Coke. The discovery at Cambridge of a further volume of reports in Coke's hand (MS.Ii.v. 21²), which answered to the description of another volume in the Holkham catalogue, confirmed the suspicion that the anonymous chronological series of reports listed there was Coke's own personal collection. It appears from the descriptions made *c.* 1634 that the complete series occupied seven notebooks. Of these seven, four are still lost. Fortunately they are the least important volumes in the series; but it would be valuable to find them, and for this reason descriptions will now be given of all seven. To avoid confusion with the numbered parts of the printed *Reports,* the notebooks have here been lettered in chronological sequence from A to G.

MANUSCRIPT A: 1579–1588

The first manuscript in the series is now part of MS.Harl. 6687.[8] The careless script in which the volume is written, and the mass of corrections, additions, interlineations and annotations which cover its pages, are consistent only with its being a private notebook, and the autograph work of its author. The identity of that author is revealed by the signature "Edward Coke" and sixteen leaves of autobiographical memoranda at the front of the volume. Included in the volume is an interleaved copy of Littleton's *Tenures,* and this naturally led observers to the conclusion that the manuscript insertions contained the draft of *Coke upon Littleton.* Mr. R. Nares described the manuscript in 1804 as "the original observations and enlargements of the L.C. Justice Coke [on *Littleton*] in his own hand-writing," and pointed out that "this very curious and valuable book has till lately escaped the notice of the editors and commentators upon Lord Coke's writings."[9] The volume is now labelled *Coke upon Littleton Autograph.*

In spite of Nares' comments, advertised to the learned world in the printed catalogue of the Harleian collection, the only part of the volume which has

---

8. For its provenance, see pp. 379–80, *infra.*
9. *Catalogue of the Harleian Manuscripts,* Vol. III (1808), p. 384.

attracted any further attention (and that over a century ago) is the autobiographical section at the beginning. The Commissioners on the Public Records
drew attention to this part in 1812,[10] and an anonymous contributor to the
Penny Cyclopaedia hailed it as the long lost *Vade Mecum* mentioned in Fuller's
Worthies.[11] It was published in 1840 in an antiquarian journal.[12] The editor,
John Bruce, described the remainder as comprising "the germ and substance
of Coke's celebrated commentary" on *Littleton*. He had obviously not read
it. Such descriptions deterred anyone from deciphering the difficult script in
which the greater part of the volume is written. Since the printed *Coke upon
Littleton* was prepared for the press by the author, there seemed little value in
poring over the preliminary draft from which it was supposedly printed.

In fact the manuscript bears no resemblance to the printed *Commentary
upon Littleton*. It has all the appearance of having been Coke's constant companion in his legal studies, and is more like a commonplace book than a continuous text or comment. As a work of reference its usefulness expired with
its author. The printed *Commentary,* on the other hand, was the fruit of the
author's retirement and truly his *magnum opus.* Its publication during Coke's
lifetime removed the contemporary value of the manuscript, and it is uncertain
whether it survived.[13]

When it was presented to Harley the volume had been a massive octavo of
over 900 leaves, which by 1800 were in danger of falling apart. Shortly after
that date the librarian of the British Museum caused the book to be disbound
and rebound in four separate volumes. In this process the original order seems
to have been lost. The volumes are now foliated continuously throughout in
red ink, but the original foliation in black ink enables the constituent parts
to be reconstructed from the confusion. It appears that, besides the printed
Littleton, there are no less than five separately foliated items. It is not improb-
able that originally these had been separate, or in smaller volumes. Apart from

---

10. *Report from the Commissioners etc.,* 8 June 1812, p. 78.
11. Fuller, *op. cit.,* note 3, *supra,* p. 251; copied *verbatim* in D. Lloyd, *State-Worthies* (1670 ed.), p. 824;
Penny Cyclopaedia, Vol. VII, p. 332. Isaac Disraeli had hoped that the *Vade Mecum* might be recovered (*Curiosities of Literature* [1st ed., 1817], Vol. III, p. 170), but either he was unaware of or unconvinced by this
identification when he wrote in 1849 that "this precious memorial may still be disinterred": *Curiosities etc.*
(14th ed.), Vol. II, p. 576. For Fuller's description, see p. 376, *infra.*
12. J. B., "Sir Edward Coke's Vade Mecum" (1840) VI *Collectanea Topographica et Genealogica,* 108–122.
For the identification of J. B. as Bruce, see E. Foss, *Judges of England* (1870), p. 179.
13. Sir Thomas Phillipps owned a manuscript (MS.Phill. 2628) described as "Coke's comments on
Lyttleton." This was sold at Sotheby's in 1903 for one shilling (Phillipps sale, 29 April, lot 599). It is not described in the catalogue, and the purchaser, Dobell, was a bookseller. The present Mr. Dobell has no record
of its resale. I am grateful to Dr. A. L. Munby, Librarian of King's College, for tracing this sale for me.

the separate foliation, the signs of constant use suggest that they would not have held together as a unit while Coke was active. They were, however, bound together before Coke's death, perhaps when he had finished with them, or at the beginning of his retirement. They were "covered with a rich embroidery wrought by his own daughter,"[14] and were thus described in the library catalogue prepared shortly before Coke's death:

> Littleton mixed not onely with booke cases and many titles of the lawe inter-
> mixed therewith, but with many reports of cases in the raigne of Queene Eliza:
> before the 32. yeare of the same Q: with a Cover of Crimson Sattine curiouslie
> imbrodred with gold silver and silke and over that a Cover of Crimson damaske.
> in 8°.[15]

If only this description had been more widely known in the nineteenth century, the truth would have been revealed before now. The component parts are as follows:[16]

(i) Littleton's *Tenures* in French (1572 ed.—note the date): S.T.C. 15741. With some marginal notes by Coke. (Begins in Vol. *A*, f. *187*, and continues in Vols. *B* and *C*.)

(ii) Commonplace book, prefaced by personal memoranda; with Coke's signature. 121 ff. (Vol. *A*, ff. *17–186*.)

(iii) Another commonplace book; including the "booke cases" (Year Books), and a long section on uses. Probably an early study companion. 145 ff. (Vol. *D*, ff. *756–906*.)

(iv) A third commonplace book; begins with notes on estates, and includes extracts from *Plowden* and other reports. 284 ff. (Vol. *A*, ff. *189–243*; Vol. *B*, ff. *245–291, 340–496*; Vol. *D*, ff. *498–704*.)

(v) Reports of cases, 21 Eliz.1–Mich. 26 & 27 Eliz.1. (Hil. 27 Eliz.1 missing.) The first cases are from *Bendlowes*, but by f. *304* Coke has begun his own series. 55 ff. Eight leaves now missing near the end. (Vol. *B*, ff. *293–339*; table at f. *339*.)

(vi) Reports of cases, Pas. 27 Eliz.1–Mich. 30 & 31 Eliz.1. A continuation of the last. 48 ff. (Vol. *D*, ff. *708–755*.)

---

14. R. Nares, *op. cit.,* note 9, *supra.* The embroidered covers were thrown away when the volume was rebound.

15. *Catalogue of the Library of Sir Edward Coke* (W. O. Hassall, ed., 1950), p. 29, no. 369. (Hereinafter cited as the *Holkham Catalogue.*) The original is Holkham MS. 748B, and is signed by Coke in several places.

16. References are to the modern foliation in red.

The last two parts are those which we have together designated MS. A. Although separately foliated, they were continuous; the missing term is matched by eight missing leaves at the end of the book numbered (v). Their identification as the first part of Coke's original manuscript reports is corroborated by Coke's own statement that he began reporting in the twenty-second year of the Queen,[17] which is where the more substantial reports begin.

MANUSCRIPT B: 1588–91

The series continued in a smaller volume, which has become separated from its partners and apparently lost. It may have been with MSS. A and C when these were presented to Lord Harley in 1715,[18] but it has not been traced in the Harleian collection. Coke referred to this as his *"petit livre de reports,"*[19] and it was thus described in his lifetime:

> A little booke covered with blewe velvett cont: reports of 31. 32. and 33 Eliza: cont' alsoe a table to the reports of the Cheife Justice, and lastlie a table or repertorie of records and acts of parliament, which the Cheife Justice called his Vade Mecum. in 8°.[20]

The volume presumably started in the latter part of Michaelmas Term 1588, and began with a *"fort bon case."*[19] It contained a report of the great case of *Finch* v. *Throgmorton* (1591) on f. 34.[21] The reports probably occupied little more than fifty leaves.[22] Its main contents could be reconstructed from the printed reports, but it is almost certain that (like MSS. A and C) it contained cases never printed, and it would be useful to find it.

---

17. 1 Rep., preface, p. xxviii.

18. Wanley, the librarian, noted the receipt of the gift on 6 August 1715, and said "Those *three* which are in covers of velvet etc. are supposed to be of the Hand of the Lord Chief Justice Sir Edward Coke": *The Diary of Humfrey Wanley* (C. E. and R. C. Wright, eds., 1966), p. 13. (My italics.) The third book ought to be MS.B, unless either MS.Harl. 6686 or 6687 was then in two parts; but there is no other reference to their being divided in this way.

19. MS.C, f. 567v: *"vide fort bone case in mes reportes Mich. 30 et 31 Eliz. regine fol. 1 in le petit livre de reportes."* This does not refer to MS. A, so Michaelmas Term must have been divided between MSS. A and B.

20. *Holkham Catalogue*, p. 27, no. 336. It is there listed separately from MSS.C–G.

21. Cited in MS.C, f. 99. There should also be a report of *Herlakenden's case* under Trin. 31 Eliz. (cited MS.C, f. 22v); of *Thetford's case* on f. 22v (cited MS.C, 20); of *Daubeney* v. *Gore* on f. 25 (cited MS.A, f. 306v); and a case of slander on f. 27 (cited MS.A, f. 325v).

22. There was a case of Pas. 33 Eliz. on f. 44 (cited MS.A, f. 331), and there was only one later term (Trin. 33 Eliz.).

MANUSCRIPT C: 1591–1606

The next manuscript, which continues the chronological series from Michael-mas Term 33 & 34 Eliz. 1 to Trinity Term 4 Jac. 1, was presented to Harley with MS. A, and is now MS. Harl. 6686. Although it was attributed to Coke in 1715, this had been forgotten by the end of the century, when it was described as "A thick octavo, containing precedents and cases in law from the 33 Eliz. until 5 [*sic*] James 1. 713 leaves, very closely written in a small hand."[23] The "small hand" is clearly Coke's, and the volume answers to the description in Coke's library catalogue: "One booke of reports covered with black velvett in 8°. beginning with Pasche 33 Eliz: and ending Tr: 4° Jac: regis and cont' 713. leaves."[24] The velvet covers were lost when the book was rebound *c.* 1805; the new binding is labelled "Law Precedents."

The manuscript is inscribed by Coke "*liber primus.*" The inference is that Coke regarded the earlier reports as youthful experiments, and that he had now taken seriously to reporting as a public service. Perhaps by now he had publication in mind. His report of *Shelley's Case* had already enjoyed a wide circulation in manuscript,[25] and by the time he had filled up MS. C he had published the first five parts of the *Reports.* The volume is far more substantial than its predecessors. Whereas MS. A covered ten years in about one hundred leaves, MS. C covers fifteen years in over seven hundred leaves. It contains the core of the *Reports*—more than one half of all the printed cases—and many more besides.

MANUSCRIPT D: 1606–1608

The manuscript here designated D, which Coke would have called his *liber secundus,* was described in 1634 as: "Another booke of reports beginning Pasche 4° Jac: regis and endinge Mich: 6° Jac: regis and cont' 81 leaves, with a redd guilded closure in 4°."[26] Clearly it was nowhere near so substantial a volume as MS. C. It probably contained *Calvin's Case,* the last six cases in Part VI (ff. 56–80), and the last five in Part VII (ff. 38–45). The residue was separated after

23. *Loc. cit.,* note 9, *supra.* "5" is an error for "4."
24. *Holkham Catalogue,* p. 22, no. 293. The volume begins with a single case entered in Easter Term 33 Eliz. I (*Elmer* v. *Thacker:* see Co.Litt. 355*b*), and this would account for the date here. The "*liber primus*" commences, however, on f. 7 (originally f. 1), in Michaelmas Term.
25. See p. 370, *infra.*
26. *Holkham Catalogue,* p. 22, no. 294.

Coke's death and later published from a copy as ff. 1–65 of Part XII. Since this volume passed into circulation after Coke's death, it is doubtful whether the original manuscript would contain any cases not already to be found in the collections associated with Part XII. But it would be satisfying to find it, and to have Coke's original and private versions of the important cases which he himself published from it.

MANUSCRIPT E: 1608–1611

The fifth volume in the series (or the third, counting MS. C as *liber primus*) was described as: "Another booke of reports beginninge Mich. 6° Jacobi regis and ending Pasche 8° eiusdem regis, and cont' 111. leaves, bound in redd leather in fol:" [27]

In 1658 this very volume was displayed to the profession by Henry Twyford the law publisher, at his shop in the Temple.[28] At some time in the next forty years it came into the possession of John Moore, Bishop of Norwich and later of Ely; by which time its identity had been forgotten.[29] Moore's library, fortunately, was purchased by King George I and presented to Cambridge University in 1715. (It seems to be pure coincidence that MSS. A and C were acquired by Harley in the same year.) The oblivion into which MS. E had fallen was not dispelled when Professor Abdy carelessly described it, in the 1858 printed catalogue, as "Law Reports . . . some of the cases are in Coke, Croke, Ley, and Moore."[30] The volume has now lost its red leather binding, and has been bound behind another work with which it has no connection. But it is in the same distinctive hand as MSS. A and C, with all the author's interlineations and corrections. The reports collate exactly with the printed cases in Part XIII, and the number of leaves and the period covered are exactly as described in the *Holkham Catalogue*. Moreover, the book is inscribed "*Liber tertius*" on f. 1, and is dated 4 November 1608, presumably the date of commencement. This date alone is inconsistent with the volume being anything but Coke's contemporary notebook, and it shows that the Michaelmas Term was divided between MSS. D and E at the beginning of November.

---

27. *Ibid.*, no. 295.
28. See p. 381, *infra*.
29. It was described by Bernard as "Reports in the reign of King James 1. fol.": *Librorum MSS. D.D. Johannis Mori Episcopi Norvicensis Catalogus*, p. 375, no. 542, in E. Bernard, *Catalogi MSS. Angliae* (1697).
30. *Catalogue of Manuscripts in the Library of the University of Cambridge,* Vol. III (1858), p. 486. The shelf-mark is Ii.v.21².

The volume is slender beside MS.C, although it is written on larger paper and contains nearly ninety entries, including such famous cases as *Crogate's, Dr. Bancroft's,* and *Dr. Bonham's.*[31] It accounts for all the printed cases from the period covered, except for a few cases of Michaelmas Term 1608 which were presumably noted (in MS.D) before 4 November. It is the source of nearly every case in Part VIII, and of the whole of Part XIII.

MANUSCRIPTS F AND G: 1611–1616

The series was completed by two notebooks, overlapping in date, which are both lost. One of them (MS.G) was a mere twenty-six leaves, with cases between Hilary Term 1614 and Hilary Term 1616. The other must have contained most of the remaining cases used by Coke in his later volumes, and the residue which appeared in Part XII: in other words, Part VIII, ff. 144–end, Part IX, ff. 242–end, the whole of Part X, Part XI (excepting three earlier cases),[32] and Part XII, ff. 65–end. This latter volume contained 222 leaves, and was bound in vellum.[33]

Coke's Method

Coke began his long series of reports in the traditional manner by collecting cases out of the reports of his immediate predecessors: in his case, from Plowden, Dyer, Broke, and from the manuscript reports of Sergeant Bendlowes which Coke borrowed about the time he was called to the Bar in 1578.[34] Soon after this date he was himself noting down decisions which he had heard given at Westminster or which he heard about in the Temple. He had soon caught the eyes of the older lawyers, and so it is no surprise to find him noting what he had been told by old Plowden,[35] or the Solicitor-General,[36] or a friendly

---

31. At ff. 9v–10, 42, 90v–95v.
32. *The Case of Monopolies,* MS.C, ff. 571v–74; *Auditor Curle's Case,* MS.E, f. 84; *Earl of Devonshire's Case,* which was probably in MS.D.
33. *Holkham Catalogue,* p. 22, nos. 296 and 297.
34. MS.A, f. 292: *Ex libro Bendlowes servientis ad legem.* It is not known how widely these circulated before the sergeant's death in 1584. Coke later had two copies at Holkham: *Holkham Catalogue,* p. 26, no. 330, and p. 28, no. 349.
35. MS.A, f. 327v: "*Nota in mesme cestui terme* [M. 1583] *Plowden dit a moy. . . .*" Plowden died the following year. *Cf.* 3 Rep. 79.
36. MS.A, f. 318 (H. 1583): "*Egerton Sollicitor dit a moy. . . .*"

serjeant,[37] or by Wray C.J. *"veniendo de* Westminster."[38] The chronological arrangement of the notes, with a flourish of red ink at the start of each new term (in MS. A), and continuous headlines indicating the term and year, show that Coke wrote all this down contemporaneously. The notebooks were also used as a commonplace, in which Coke would write personal memoranda,[39] obituaries,[40] notes on the royal prerogative and on administrative practices,[41] historical notes from ancient records,[42] notes on the meaning of statutes,[43] particularly of recusants,[44] and numerous notes of things Popham C.J. had told him.[45]

Nevertheless, a significant number of reports do not appear in their proper chronological places. This is because Coke continued throughout his career to enter into his notebooks details of earlier cases which he had come across in writing or which he had heard cited in court. He entered such cases under the term in which he learned of them, usually citing the plea roll. This fact provides a touchstone for separating the cases written down as they were decided from those which were probably collected by hearsay. No such indication is given in the printed versions. Thus *Thoroughgood's Case,* decided in 1584, appears under Trinity Term 1598 with the explanation: "In this same term I saw a record in the Common Bench, Trin. 26 Eliz., Filmer, Essex. . . ."[46] This case is followed by notes of *Manser's Case, Goddard's Case,* and *Wiseman's Case,* all apparently

37. *Ibid.*, ff. 317*v* ("*Nota que Gawdy serieant dit a moy veniendo de Westminster. . . .*"), 725 ("*Nota Serieant Walmesley dit a moy. . . .*").

38. *Ibid.*, f. 712 (M. 1585).

39. MS. C, ff. 34–35 (appointed Solicitor-General), ff. 86–87*v* (appointed Attorney-General). On the flyleaf of MS. A is a note, presumably scribbled when Coke was made Chief Justice: "Choller of SS. con' 53 SS. and knotes, foure percullis & two roses."

40. MS. C, f. 54 (Manwood, different from 3 Rep. 26): *cf.* 6 Rep. 75 (Popham); 9 Rep. 14–15 (Dyer), 121–122 (Lord Sanchar); 10 Rep. 34 (Fleming).

41. See MS. C, ff. 57*v*–58 (tithes), 69*v* (fees of the Clerk of the Market, 1 July 1593), 88*v* (letters patent), 112 (debt to the Crown), 257*v* ("Concerning the mynte"), 261 ("Concerning the stalling of debts due to her majestie"), 327*v* (forests), 461*v* (fines on original writs), 503*v* (Green Wax). Notes on Parliament: *ibid.*, ff. 56, 209–210, 576*v*. Notes on purveyance: *ibid.*, ff. 606*v*–9, 649*v*–51*v*, 682*v*–86, 688–94*v*.

42. See MS. C, ff. 69*v* (fine before eight justices, 1453), 118*v* (ancient Welsh custom that females did not inherit, 1430), 119 (Rolls Chapel, and attorneys), 123 (grant of swan-mark), 123*v* (Priory of St. John's, 1352), 124 (London customs concerning widows), 124*v* (record of 1229 showing that younger sons inherited before daughters of elder sons), 143–44 and 147–48*v* (record of 1298 proving that lands held by grand sergeanty were forfeited for alienation without license), 207*v* (*Cobb* v. *Nore*, 1465), 271*v* (degradation of duke, 1477), 373 (creation of Prince of Wales by Edward I), 446 (removal of Swillington A.-G. for misdemeanors, *c.* 1526). Some of the records were copied by a secretary.

43. See MS. C, ff. 57, 65, 81, 89, 145*v*, 255, 284*v*, 320*v*, 403*v*, 418, 459*v*–61*v*, 505, 554*v*, 562, 609*v*.

44. See MS. C, ff. 68*v*, 81*v*–82, 84*v*–85, 99, 125*v*.

45. *E.g.*, MS. C, ff. 93, 109, 135*v*, 158, 159, 171, 203, 274, 306, 307, 308, 317*v*, 396*v*, 446, 563. *Cf.* ff. 81, 82*v* (Egerton), 135 (Anderson).

46. *Ibid.*, f. 300*v*. See 2 Rep. 1–16.

extracted from the rolls of 26 and 27 Eliz. 1, with notes of the argument added. Coke later printed these cases at the beginning of Part II, though in a different order, giving no indication that they were other than his own report. It is possible, of course, that Coke recalled having been present; but the fact that he made no note for fifteen years suggests otherwise. His interest may have been aroused by research in the plea rolls, after which he made inquiries of the counsel and judges involved, or borrowed a report. Sometimes Coke noted that he had "seen" an earlier case, which probably meant he had seen a report or record.[47] Sometimes, especially in the *Institutes,* he mentioned cases which he had "heard" or "observed";[48] most of these date from the period 1572–79, and probably Coke was using another report of a case which he remembered from his student days but which he had not himself reported.

REPORTS CITED BY COKE

Plucknett suggested that Coke had taken some of his cases from Sir Christopher Wray's reports, citing a passage in Part IV where a reference is made to something which was "said and reported by Wray C.J."[49] It is submitted that this plainly refers to an oral report by Wray, and not a written report. Elsewhere Coke relates what he *heard* Wray "report" in the King's Bench,[50] and the word "report" often indicated citations in open court.

To what extent Coke did draw upon other identifiable reports is not easy to judge from the notebooks themselves, because Coke did not always state his source. He possessed, and frequently cited from, Sergeant Bendlowes' reports.[51] He owned a copy of part of Justice Spilman's reports, and sometimes cited from it.[52] He had access to a manuscript of "Keilwey" before it was pub-

47. *E.g.,* MS.A, f. 732*v* (T. 1584, seen M. 1587); MS.C, ff. 29*v* (M. 1588, seen H. 1592), 40*v* (H. 1591, seen M. 1592), 68 (H. 1590, seen P. 1593), 112 (M. 1576, seen H. 1595), 133*v* (1583, seen H. 1596), 192 (T. 1562, seen P. 1597), 230 (H. 1593, seen M. 1597), 266 (T. 1585, seen H. 1598), 268 (M. 1588, seen H. 1598), 300 (T. 1584, seen T. 1598), 348 (M. 1594, seen T. 1599), 355*v* (M. 1590, seen T. 1599), 558*v* (M. 1574, seen P. 1603). Several of these appear in the printed *Reports* without any indication that they were second-hand. Most of them were decided in Coke's own time.
48. MS.C, f. 21; 11 Rep. 48, 60; Co.Litt. 31*v*, 59*v*, 77, 210, 211, 221*v*, 249, 269, 270*v*, 311, 317, 318*v*, 365*v*, 384, 385; 2 Inst. 313 ("in my time"), 502. Only two of these fall outside the period 14–21 Eliz., and they are both in the notebooks (Co.Litt. 210 = MS.A, f. 308; Co.Litt. 270*v* = MS.C, f. 239*v*).
49. 27 *Cornell Law Quarterly* at p. 212; 4 Rep. 63.
50. 4 Inst. 324. Apparently Wray did compile reports, which appear to be cited in MS.Lansd. 1084, ff. 36*v*, 81 (*cf.* f. 93: "*come Wrai dit a moy*").
51. Note 34, *supra;* cited in MS.A, f. 292, MS.C, ff. 38, 177, 192*v*, 1 Rep. 26, 96, 176, 2 Rep. 49, 3 Rep. 91, 4 Rep. 51, 88, 95. (Later citations may be from the printed edition of 1602.) Many MS. versions are known.
52. *Holkham Catalogue,* p. 26, no. 326; cited in MS.C, f. 568, 6 Rep. 62, 63, Co.Litt. 130, 146, 229*v*, 2

lished in 1602.[53] He had access to some of Justice Dalison's reports which were not in print.[54] He had seen a manuscript by Plowden, in which there was a report of *Sir John Baker's Case* superior to that in *Dyer*.[55] By 1610 at least he had acquired a manuscript said to be in Dyer's handwriting,[56] containing numerous cases not in print, from which Coke often made citations.[57] Coke also cited "Periam," by folio, presumably reports by Chief Baron Peryam (d. 1604);[58] and also "Wyndam," presumably by Francis Wyndham J. (d. 1592).[59] His library catalogue lists three books of reports by "Thurston," and three anonymous volumes of reports.[60] Apart from the allegation that he used the reports of Bridgeman in composing some of his own printed reports,[61] which it is difficult as yet to check, there is little reason to think that Coke actually borrowed many primary reports from these sources. Most of the sources were too old. When he did refer to them he did so by name, and he was more meticulous than most writers in noting references to his authorities. The fact that the unattributed reports are scattered throughout the notebooks suggests that they came from a variety of sources, probably verbal as well as literary. It should not be thought, in any case, that these reports are numer-

Inst. 49, 50, 493, 636, 3 Inst. 9, 17, 30, 126, 4 Inst. 59, Cro.Jac. 152. Spilman's original MS. was still in the possession of his family in Coke's time, but it is now lost; the best copy, though it contains many errors, is in MS.Hargr. 388.

53. See MS.C, ff. 138 ("*extra librum Keylwey*"), 245v ("*ex libro Kelywaye*"). John Croke, who published the reports in 1602, was a bencher of the Inner Temple; it is likely that Coke saw his manuscript.

54. See Golds. 153.

55. MS.C, f. 170; "*Nota in mesme cestui terme ieo viewe le case . . . report per mounsieur Plowden.*" It is not in the printed book. Coke cites the same case in 7 Rep. 8 "as I myself have seen."

56. Exeter Coll. Oxford MS. 128, f. 149v (cited by G. D. G. Hall, 69 L.Q.R. 208n): "This cause is found in a manuscript written altogether with the hand of my Lord Dyer remayninge in the Custody of my lord Cooke." *Cf.* 10 Rep.pref., p. xxxiv: "the very original whereof, written with his own hand, I have." See *Holkham Catalogue*, p. 23, no. 302: "Foure bookes of the Collection of cases by the Lord Dier in fol: whereof two are written with his owne proper hand." See also 9 Rep. 15, 11 Rep. 77, 3 Buls. 49. The MSS. are no longer at Holkham. *Cf.* Inner Temple MS.Petyt 511.13, ff. 34–70; MS.Hargr. 26, ff. 166v–74.

57. See Co.Litt. 9, 13, 58v, 148v; 2 Inst. 61, 657, 682; 3 Inst. 17, 24, 61, 112, 126, 127, 172, 182; 4 Inst. 61, 240.

58. MS.C, ff. 81, 124. Peryam was alive at the time of the citations, so Coke must have borrowed them from the author.

59. MS.A, ff. 305v, 711v, 722, 741v.

60. *Holkham Catalogue*, p. 28, nos. 347–48: "Thurstone 3 books of reports in fol: and one other . . . Two other Ms: of reports in fol:" Thurston is probably John Thurston, Reader of the Inner Temple in 1560. Coke may have been referring to his reports when he showed in court a report of the sergeants' case of 1555 "reported by an ancient and learned bencher of the Inner Temple" (10 Rep. 128).

61. Lost MS. report of *Lloyd* v. *Gregory*, cited by Ellis J. in 1 Mod. 205, in which: "Jones . . . denied the case of *Hunt* v. *Singleton* [3 Rep. 60]. He said, that himself and Sir Rowland Wainscott [Wandesford] reported it, and that nothing was said of that point, but that Lord Coke followed the report of Bridgeman, who was three or four years their puisne, and that he mistook the case." There is no reference to Bridgeman's reports in Coke's manuscript: MS.C, f. 349v.

ous in relation to the collection as a whole; and there is certainly no doubt as to the authorship of the longer reports, where all the argument is noted in detail.

One obvious contrast between the notebooks and the printed reports is that the former are more intimate and personal, and less polished. They are full of "*ieo argue*" and "*moy semble*": a continuous record of Coke's professional career. In MS. A he usually noted when he was retained of counsel, and it seems he was engaged in most of the important cases noted. Even when all else escaped Coke's notice, he would record his own argument: as he did with *Slade's Case*. It was only natural that a reporter who himself played a leading role in the cases reported should remember his own arguments and citations more clearly than those of the other side. Of the one-sidedness of Coke's reports there is contemporary, if biased, corroboration by at least two sources.[62] Moreover, once Coke was in busy practice he could hardly have been present throughout the hearing of many cases in which he was not personally engaged; this fact alone divides the reports into those in which Coke was involved, and therefore probably had a formed opinion, and those which he presumably heard about by the relation of friends. Most of the "*graund*" cases, however, attracted Coke's personal attendance.

The change in character of the reports in the notebooks suggests that most of the later reports were original. In his earlier years, before he was at the center of legal life, Coke was more dependent on hearsay; though he took care to note what was not his own. In 1583 he wrote in the margin against cases cited in court: "*ex auditu.*"[63] Elsewhere he copied a report shown to him and ended: "*Quod nota ex relatione aliorum, ideo vide recorda in banco communi*";[64] a mere report was not enough without checking the record. Toward 1600, and even more so after, it becomes clear that Coke's personal experience was sufficient to account for most of the material. By this time he had publication in mind and "*nota lecteur*" is frequently found in the manuscript. The majority of cases in MS. C, and the great majority in MS. E, are contemporary. The evidence confirms that Coke was unwilling to trust to memory, and re-

---

62. Bacon and Ellesmere. See J. Spedding (ed.), *Letters and Life of Bacon*, Vol. V (1869), pp. 86 ("too much *de proprio*"), 399 ("many exorbitant and extravagant opinions"); Vol. VI (1872), pp. 65 ("some peremptory and extrajudicial resolutions more than are warranted"), 87 ("scattering and sowing his own conceits"). See also Brit.Mus.MS.Add. 14030, f. 91; MS.Harg. 254. Anderson C.J. said of the report of *Shelley's Case*: "*rien de ceo fuit parle en le Court ne la monstre*" (1 And. 71).
63. MS. A, f. 327. Cf. *ibid.*, f. 714v: "*come fuit dit a moy.*"
64. *Ibid.*, f. 732 (1587).

garded an "orderly observation in writing" as the most essential requisite to the knowledge of the common law.[65]

The Published Reports

Coke tells us that he had lent his reports to friends before they were printed, and in this way they had become partly public in the last decade of the sixteenth century.[66] No complete copy of the earlier reports is known, and only a few partial copies have been discovered. The first general publication by Coke was his *Report of Shelley's Case,* completed in January 1582 and dedicated to Lord Buckhurst. This enjoyed a wide circulation in manuscript.[67] It was the case in which Coke made his name, only two years after his call to the Bar, and the report was primarily a record of his own speech for the plaintiff. Of immense value to the profession, it was not without value as publicity for Coke, although in the manuscript version he tactfully attributed his speech to "an utter barrister of the Inner Temple." The report was evidently written in order to be published; it is not in MS.A, and all the known versions are in English.

By 1600 Coke had covered over one thousand pages of his *Vade Mecum* with reports, and in that year he published his first selection in print.[68] This first volume contained, naturally, the cream of his collection, including the report of *Shelley's Case* translated into French. The preface to that case was adapted and extended to form the "Preface to the Reader." All the cases in the volume are from MS.C, except *Pelham's Case* (which was probably in MS.B), *Corbet's, Albany's,* and *Chudleigh's Cases.*[69] Coke expressly states that his re-

---

65. See 1 Rep.pref., p. xxvii: "I allow not of those that make memory their storehouse, for at their greatest need they shall want of their store. . . ." See also 7 Rep.pref., p. iv, quoted below.

66. *Ibid.,* p. xxviii. In MS.Lansd. 1084, f. 42*v,* are two cases "*report per Cooke,*" which must refer to the MS; one is in MS.A, f. 308, the other in MS.C, f. 119*v.* The most extensive copy discovered so far is Camb.U.L. MS.Gg.v. 4, ff. 37–50, 63*v*–68*v,* which begins "*Cases escrie ex Libro Cooke que il mesme collect 22 et 23 Eliz. in Bancke le roy.*" It contains a selection of over fifty cases from MS.A, ff. 305–32 (1580–84). The copy was certainly made in Coke's lifetime, but it cannot be accurately dated since the Cambridge MS. is itself a copy of the copy.

67. *A Report of the Judgment and Part of the Arguments of Shelleys Case* (2 Jan. 1581/82), Holkham MS. 251; MS.Lansd. 1072, ff. 107–20; MS.Harl. 443, ff. 1–9; MS.Hargr. 373, f. 56; Camb.U.L.MS.Dd.xiii. 24, ff. 52*v*–58: Lincoln's Inn MS. Misc. 361, ff. (i), 1–11; MS. at Longleat House. The dedication is signed by Coke, and the signature is copied in each case by the transcriber.

68. S.T.C. 5493. The publisher was Thomas Wight.

69. The references in MS.C are: f. 271*v* (*Buckhurst's Case*), ff. 42*v*–45 (*Porter's Case*), ff. 384–400 (*Alton Woods' Case*), ff. 41–42 (*Capel's Case*), ff. 236*v*–37 (*Archer's Case*), f. 237 (*Bredon's Case*), f. 90*v* (*Mayowe's*

port of *Corbet's Case* was "a summary report only of the principal reasons and causes of their judgment." A good proportion of it was taken up with reports of two other cases, cited by Anderson C.J., both of which were fully reported in MS.C.[70] Coke himself was of counsel in *Chudleigh's Case,* though he admits that he did not hear some of the arguments of counsel.[71] Of his report he says:

> All which arguments of the judges and barons I heard, except only that of Justice Beamond, and therefore what I shall say of that, I shall say by credible relation of others; but my intent is not to report any of their arguments at large, and in the same form as they were delivered by them, but to make such a summary collection of the effect and substance of them all, as the matter (it being the first case which was adjudged, and being of great importance), will permit.[72]

Clearly this report was not typical of the collection as a whole.

The *Second Part,* published in 1602, is more typical, and is more nearly contemporaneous with the cases it contains. Coke now abandoned the division according to the courts in which the cases were decided, and put them in more or less chronological order. Nearly all of them were either decided or shown to Coke between 1594 and 1601, and noted in MS.C. And of the many cases cited within cases, over half were from MS.C. Two principal cases have not been traced, but they were probably in MS.B. The *Third Part,* published the same year, follows the same scheme. Apart from *Cuppledike's Case,* on f. 5,[73] the cases are in strict chronological order, beginning with four from MS.A. Again, over half the "cases within cases" are from the *Vade Mecum.*

After an interval of two years, the *Fourth Part* appeared. The plan this time was different. Most of Coke's longer cases had already been printed, and Coke now began to distill from his *Vade Mecum* the less substantial cases. The volume was longer, and there were more cases in it than there had been in all the

---

Case), ff. 323*v*–27 (*Rector of Chedington's Case*), ff. 400*v*–402 (*Digges's Case*), ff. 298–300 (*Mildmay's Case*). There is not the space to give references to the cases in the later parts discussed below.

70. *Germin* v. *Arscot* (ff. 128*v*–33), *Cholmley* v. *Humble* (ff. 228*v*–30).

71. 1 Rep. 121. See Wallace's comment: *The Reporters* (1882 ed.), p. 176.

72. 1 Rep. 132. Coke's version may profitably be compared with other good MS. reports: *e.g.,* MS.Harg. 26, ff. 176*v*–86, MS.Lansd. 1072, f. 201, Camb.U.L. MS.Hh.ii. 1, ff. 102*v*–6, MS.Ii.v. 12, ff. 81–85. Coke's must have been one of the best, for a contemporary collector wrote "*Icy fuit le case Chudley que ieo aie interlesse quia est report per Mr. Attorney coment soit icy excellment report*" (MS.Ee.iii. 2, f. 34*v*). And another wrote "*Vide cest case in Mounser Cokes Reportes en print en un excellent manner*" (MS.Harg. 26, f. 176*v*). See also 1 And. 309, Poph. 70.

73. From MS.C, ff. 486*v*–89.

first three parts. Instead of arranging it wholly in chronological order, Coke divided the first part by subjects. After f. 48 the order is chronological, with a few cases from MSS. A and B, and sixteen cases drawn strictly in order from MS. C. The cases grouped by subject were taken from the same collections, and not from any other book arranged by subject as Plucknett guessed. A similar pattern was reproduced in the *Fifth Part* (1605). Of nearly the same length, it contained 120 cases. All but a small handful of the cases reported have been traced in MSS. A and C. It begins with a separately foliated report of *Cawdrey's Case,* which originated in MS. C; then follows a subject arrangement, which fades as the number of cases on each subject reduces, until f. 70, after which the chronological order is resumed in two sequences. The first sequence ends with *Semayne's Case,* Michaelmas Term, 1604, and the second with a case of Easter Term, 1605. It looks as though Coke had made a selection late in 1604, and had then been through his notebook again the next year to extend the collection by some forty folios.

The *Sixth Part* (1607) was the first to contain cases of later date than MS. C. This may account for some of the pre-1605 cases which have not been found in MS. C; they might have been shown to Coke after 1605, and recorded in MS. D. In ff. 1–56 are forty-one cases, of which all but six are from MS. C and none from MS. A. The remaining eleven cases must have been in MS. D. With three exceptions, the arrangement after f. 11 is chronological.

The following year was published the *Seventh Part,* prompted, according to its author, by the determination of *Calvin's Case:* "the greatest case that ever was argued in the hall of Westminster."[74] Coke's original note of this case was probably in MS. D, though it is evident from the following significant passage that he entirely rewrote the case for the press:

> This great case (for that memory is *infida et labilis*) while the matter was recent and fresh in mind, and almost yet sounding in the ear, I set down in writing, out of my short observations which I had taken of the effect of every argument (as my manner is, and ever hath been), a summary memorial of the principal authorities and reasons of the resolutions of that case, for my own private solace and instruction. . . . Now when I had ended it for my private use, I was by commandment to begin again (a matter of no small labour and difficulty) for the public. For certainly, that succinct method and collection that will serve for the

74. 7 Rep.pref., p. iv.

private memorial or repertory, especially of him that knew and heard all, will nothing become a public report for the present and all posterity.[75]

The report of this case occupies over one third of the volume, which is the shortest of all eleven parts. The remainder is in roughly chronological order, beginning with a case from MS. A and ending (ff. 38–45) with cases presumably from MS.D.

The *Eighth Part* was printed in 1611, by which time Coke's notes had reached MS.F. He felt it "more painful than any of the other have been to me."[76] It began with the great *Prince's Case,* which is not in MS.C where it belongs. All the cases (except three) between ff. 32 and 138 are from MS.E, including the Elizabethan cases. The remaining cases were presumably from MS.F, except for four of the cases in the final section of cases in the Court of Wards.

The *Ninth Part* (1613) is almost entirely based on the lost MS.F, and so little can be said of its construction. It appears on its face to contain far more comment and digression than the earlier volumes. The *Tenth Part* (1614) contained one case from MS.C, three cases on sewers from MS.E, and the remainder (8–11 James I) must have come from MS.F. In the preface, Coke explained his reasons for publishing each case; a novel departure, perhaps occasioned by criticisms which were being levelled at him.

Coke published his eleventh and last volume of cases "in the tempest of many other important and pressing business"[77] in the latter part of 1615. It contains eighteen cases between Trinity Term 10 James 1 and Trinity Term 13 James 1, presumably from MS.F, with the addition of the *Case of Monopolies* from MS.C, and two others.

Of the manuscript versions which Coke prepared for the press, and the very useful and entertaining prefaces, no trace seems to have remained. The absence of any reference to them among Coke's papers at the time of his death suggests that they may not have been preserved.

CHANGES MADE BEFORE PUBLICATION

Coke took a good deal of trouble preparing his reports for publication.[78] He distinguished between private and public reports, and pressed on with the

---

75. *Ibid.,* pp. iv–v. There is a short note in MS.C, f. 570*v* (H. 1603) on the status of *post-nati.*
76. 8 Rep.pref., p. xxxi.
77. 11 Rep.pref., p. x. He "therefore could not polish them as [he] desired": *ibid.,* p. xi.
78. See 10 Rep.pref., pp. iv, xxii; 11 Rep.pref., p. xi.

eleven volumes for fear that if he left the material unedited at his death someone would publish them in their imperfect state.[79] He considered it his duty
to select for publication only such cases as were "leading cases for the public quiet"[80] and to pass over arguments which were "not worthy to be moved
at the bar, nor remembered at the bench."[81] He also claimed as the right of
every reporter "to reduce the sum and effect of all to such a method, as, upon
consideration had of all the arguments, the reporter himself thinketh to be
fittest and clearest for the right understanding of the true reasons and causes
of the judgments and resolutions of the case in question."[82] Yet most of the
comment which it might have been thought that Coke added while editing a
case for the press is to be found in the *Vade Mecum*. A detailed textual study
will be necessary before it can be said how far Coke altered his reports for the
press, and why.

The most obvious interpolations in the printed volumes are the transcripts
from the records, which in the earlier parts occupy much space. The records in
the first volume were considered so important that in 1601 they were analyzed
and digested in a small book by Richard Cary.[83] The extent to which Coke
relied on the plea rolls as sources of law is evident from all his writings, and
particularly from his *Booke of Entries* (1614). Coke included a few reports in
the *Booke of Entries*,[84] some of which were taken from the *Vade Mecum*. He
also printed a remarkable report of two cases of 1579, written in law French
and enrolled in the Exchequer at the command of the barons to avoid erro-
neous interpretations by posterity of the differing judgments they had given.[85]
It seems impossible that Coke could have done all this work in person, but,
with or without clerical assistance, he clearly had a command of the contents
of all the plea rolls of the reign of Elizabeth I and the first fourteen years of
James I. It would be interesting to know how Coke acquired his mastery of
these cumbrous records.

The smaller textual alterations to the reports themselves are not unworthy

79. 8 Rep.pref., p. xxxii. The fear was perhaps aroused by the posthumous publication of Dyer's notebook in 1585: see 10 Rep.pref., p. xxxiv.
80. 9 Rep.pref., p. xi. See also the apologies in 10 Rep.pref.
81. *Case of Sutton's Hospital,* 10 Rep. at p. 24.
82. *Calvin's Case,* 8 Rep. at p. 4.
83. *Le necessarie vse & fruit de les Pleadings conteine en le lieur de le tresreuerend Edward Coke* (1601):
S.T.C. 4719. Cary did the work in the "last sommers vacation" and dedicated it to Anderson C.J.
84. Preface, sig. *Av:* "Here shall you find Presidents adjudged upon Demurrer . . . which being never
reported, here is for thy better Light (Studious Reader) a short touch given of the reasons and causes whereupon they were adjudged." There are about 22 such reports.
85. *Imber* v. *Wilking, op. cit.,* ff. 380–81, 383–84v.

of the legal historian's attention. Not only is the first person abandoned—*ieo* becomes "Coke"—but, either to enhance his own authority or to avoid embarrassment to others, Coke omitted many personal details in the printed reports. He does not say that he was told about a case by Anderson C.J.[86] or Popham C.J.[87] or that he was "shown a report."[88] He does not always say when he was of counsel, as he does in the notebook, and does not always make it clear that what he reports is his own speech. Sometimes judicial identities are obscured. Thus the sole dissentient in *Shelley's Case,* anonymous in the printed book, is named in the manuscript as Mead J. It was no secret that Walmsley J. was an habitual dissenter, and Coke records his dissent in *Chudleigh's Case;*[89] but he omits to tell us that he dissented in *Pinnel's Case,*[90] and thereby perhaps unwittingly anticipated modern criticisms of that decision. We also find that the famous "Mischief Rule," related by Coke as the resolution of the Court of Exchequer in *Heydon's Case,* began life in a dictum of Manwood C.B.:

> And he said that he did not take any certain ground for the construction of statutes, be they penal or beneficial, restrictive or enlarging of the common law, but only to consider the mischief which was before the statute and the remedy which the parliament intended to provide, and upon this to make construction to repress the mischief and to advance the remedy according to the intent of parliament.[91]

Presumably the contemporary note, written by Coke in 1584, is more historically accurate than the revised version of 1602; but it is easy to sympathize with Coke's desire to present such an attractive statement as a "resolution." Of course, Manwood C.B. may have been speaking on behalf of the court; but, if this were a resolution of the court, one would not expect other reporters of the case to miss it altogether.[92]

This is not the place to multiply examples; these few instances should be suf-

---

86. *Case of Market-Overt* (1596) 5 Rep. 83, MS.C, f. 35. Anderson reported the case himself: 1 And. 344.
87. *E.g., Wild's Case* (1599) 6 Rep. 16, MS.C, f. 328; *Vaughan's Case* (1596) 10 Rep. 114, MS.C, f. 157v. *Cf.* 4 Inst. 240, 297: "Of the report of Popham." (Was this a written report?)
88. *E.g., Thoroughgood's Case,* 2 Rep. 9, MS.C, f. 300v; *Beckwith's Case,* 2 Rep. 56, MS.C, f. 266; *Henstead's Case,* 5 Rep. 10, MS.C, f. 348; *Knight's Case,* 5 Rep. 54, MS.C, f. 268; *Chamberlain of London's Case,* 5 Rep. 62, MS.C, f. 355v.
89. 1 Rep. 132.
90. 5 Rep. 117, MS.C, f. 548v. Coke also omits to mention that Walmsley J. dissented in *Calvin's Case.*
91. MS.A, f. 333 (translated). *Cf.* 3 Rep. 7, 11 Rep. 73. The sentiment was not entirely new: see Camb.U.L.MS.Gg.v. 2, f. 132, *per* Periam J. (1582): "*Cest statute coment que soit penal serra prise liberally pur restrain' le mischief que les fesors intend de restrainer.*"
92. 1 Leo. 4, 4 Leo. 117, Sav. 66, Moo. 128.

ficient to demonstrate the value of comparing the notebooks with the printed cases.[93]

The Cases Not Printed in Parts I–XI of the *Reports*

It is well known that the *Reports* were prominent among the works and doings of Coke which were attacked at the time of his downfall in 1616, and that as a result Coke never published a further volume of reports after that date.[94] But he took with him in his retirement all that "formerly he had written, even thirty books with his own hand, most pleasing himself with a Manual, which he called his *Vade mecum,* from whence at one view he took a prospect of his life pass'd, having noted therein most remarkables."[95] We may now with reasonable confidence identify this "Manual" or *Vade Mecum* with the seven volumes described above,[96] and discard the nineteenth century interpretation which supposed the "remarkables" to have been purely personal autobiography.[97] It was truly the most extensive collection of reports written since the Year Books, covering nearly thirty years without intermission and occupying over 2,500 pages[98] of closely written notes. From it Coke had already filled eleven printed volumes, surpassing in number and influence, if not in length, all the collected editions of the Year Books. There was still a plentiful store remaining.

The extent to which Coke continued to use this material in his writings after 1616 has been overlooked. Plucknett even said that the whole of Coke's intellectual equipment was to be found in the Year Books.[99] But Coke drew heavily on all the recent material he could lay his hands on, particularly on the later plea rolls and his own manual. In the *Institutes,* written for the most part

93. Anyone who wishes to find the original of the renowned statement on judicial review in *Dr. Bonham's Case* will find it in MS.E, f. 93v. But he will be disappointed. No substantial alterations were made.

94. See note 62, *supra*. Even in 1633 the Council had the *Reports* under scrutiny: see memoranda of Council business, S.P.16/248/15, f. 52v: "In March 1632/33 Mr. Attor: was ordered to examin Sr Edw: Cokes reportes." Dr. Louis Knafla of the University of Calgary is editing Ellesmere's criticisms of the *Reports* for publication.

95. T. Fuller, *The Worthies of England* (1662), p. 251.

96. This is confirmed by Tourneur, who copied reports from "Lo. Cokes vade mecum": Univ.Coll. London, MS.Ogden 29, f. 569. See note 121, *infra*.

97. See note 11, *supra*.

98. MSS.A, C, D, E and F contained 1,241 leaves. MS.B probably contained about 50 leaves: note 22, *supra*. Only one term (T. 1593) is intermitted in the extant MSS.

99. *Concise History of the Common Law* (5th ed., 1956), p. 282.

before 1628,[100] over three hundred references may be found to cases decided in Coke's time, for which no report is cited. A preliminary search shows that about half of these are reported in the extant volumes of the *Vade Mecum*.[101] The remainder may be accounted for as having come from the lost volumes, or as having been taken directly from the records. Clearly by the time of his death in 1634 Coke had put his laborious collections to good use. Whether he would have continued with his published reports, if given the opportunity, is a matter for speculation; certainly there was enough material. Many of the leading cases relied on in the *Institutes* were never published in full, though Coke probably set out in the text most of what he considered worth recording. No doubt he preferred the institutional medium, since he could digress more freely and indulge his passion for giving instruction without the risk of censure for exceeding the duties of a reporter. The most substantial omissions were the great cases of state and matters touching the prerogative, which for various reasons Coke kept to himself. It was well known before Coke's death that he had an unequalled store of such material, and Charles I was worried that it might be put to bad use. In 1631 the King ordered inquiries to be made after Coke's health:

> and if hee bee in any present danger that care may bee taken to seal upe his study (if hee dies) where such papers are as use may bee made of them (haveing passed thourow so many great places in the state) for his majesties service and som supressed that may disserve him.[102]

Months before Coke's death a commission issued under the royal Sign Manual to Sir Francis Windebank authorizing him "to repaire to the house or place of abode of the said Sir Edward Coke, and there to seize and take into your charge, and bring away all such papers and manuscripts as yow shall think

---

100. Co.Litt. (1st ed., 1628), preface. In 3 Inst. 47 is reference to a case of 1630 "since these Institutes." The last part was completed between 1631, when it was in progress (see note 102, *infra*), and April 1633, when the MS. had been seized and the original notes sent to Pepys for safe keeping (see note 104, *infra*). It was suppressed by the King.

101. *Cf.* 4 Inst. *proeme:* "I have published nothing herein but that which is grounded . . . especially upon the resolution of the Judges of later times upon mature deliberation in many cases never published before; wherewith I was well acquainted, and which I observed and set down in writing, while it was fresh in memory."

102. S.P.16/183/18, f. 29: letter from the Earl of Holland to Lord Dorchester, the King's Principal Secretary, 24 Jan. 1630/31. The recipient was to write to the Lord Keeper that the book which Coke was working on should not "come forth." *Cf.* letter of Thomas Barrington (1631?), cited H.M.C. VII Rep., p. 548: "Sir Edw. Coke hath his papers seized by reason of a report that he is about a book concerning Magna Charta, and is likely to incur some trouble."

fitt."[103] This commission was executed a few days before Coke's death in September 1634. A large trunk was taken from John Pepys, Coke's private secretary, and brought to the King at Bagshot. The King "poked and stirred in the dusty relics of a life," and found, *inter alia,* a smaller trunk sent to Pepys on 17 April 1633 containing:

> One greate book of statutes called the buckskin book. three other books composed by him vizt. the pleas of the Crowne. the Jurisdiction of Courtes & the exposicion upon Magna Carta & other ancient statutes, which last is imperfect for that which was finished was taken away.[104]

Windebank also found a collection of state papers, with Coke's notes on all the great treason trials in which he had been engaged, in buckram bags.[105] Then, in December, Windebank authorized a clerk of the Council, called Nicholas, to break into Coke's study in the Inner Temple and to seize any papers "as you shall conceave in any sort to concerne his majesties service, or as may in any wise be behoofull or prejudiciall to the same."[106] The remainder of the books and papers were to be delivered to Sir Robert Coke, son and heir of Sir Edward.[107] The books seized by Nicholas included "A booke *in folio* intitled with Sir Edward Coke's own hand a Booke of Notes of my Arguments at the Barre, when I was Solicitor Attornie and before."[108] This precious volume has not been recovered; it would be of the utmost value if it could be identified.

None of the inventories mention the *Vade Mecum,* but Roger Coke (Sir Edward's grandson), who must have had further information, said that among the papers seized were:

---

103. S.P.16/272/62, f. 121: 26 July.

104. "A note of such thinges as were found in a Trunk of Sr. Edw: Coke taken from Pepys his servant. This trunk was brought to Bagshot by his Majesties comandment, & there broken up by his Majesty: 9: Septem: 1634:" Lambeth Palace MS. 943, ff. 369, 375. Most of the papers were of little consequence. The quotation is from C. D. Bowen, *The Lion and the Throne* (1957), p. 461.

105. *Ibid.,* f. 371: "A catalogue of Sr. Edward Cookes papers that by warrant from the Councell were brought to Whitehall. . . ." They included "a great buckrom bagg of the pouder treason." Mrs. Bowen presumed these came from the Temple: *The Lion and the Throne* (1957), p. 460.

106. S.P. 16/278/10: 4 December. The study had apparently been sealed on Windebank's orders. The same study had been ransacked 14 years earlier by Sir Robert Cotton and Sir Thomas Wilson, while Coke was in the Tower: Holkham MS. 727, Biography of Coke, cited H.M.C. IX Rep., p. 373.

107. S.P. 16/278/28: 9 December.

108. "A Note of the bookes & papers brought out of Sr. Edward Coke study from ye Temple remayning in ye Box": S.P. 16/278/35 (my italics). The books were delivered to Windebank on 10 December. The only other reports were "A Manuscript in folio intitled Le Case de Proxis" and "Another Manuscript in folio intitled Reports of Cases in Ireland" (Davies?).

Sir Edward Coke's Comment upon Littleton, and the History of his Life be-
fore it, written with his own Hand, his Comment upon Magna Charta &c. the
Pleas of the Crown, and Jurisdiction of Courts, and his 11th and 12th Reports in
Manuscript, and I think 51 other Manuscripts.[109]

The first item is obviously MS.A, and the distorted mention of the reports
probably refers to the remainder of the manual. It is almost certain that these
were among the papers seized, because if they had been handed to Sir Robert
Coke in 1634 they would have returned to Holkham. The precise fate of the
collection after this is unclear. Some of the manuscripts came into the hands
of Coke's executors.[110] Others (probably including the third and fourth *Institutes*) came into the hands of Finch C.J., who passed them on to his successor,
Littleton C.J.[111] Others were apparently dispersed. The *Vade Mecum* probably
passed into private hands at this time, because it was not recognized for what
it was. Toward the end of 1640 Sir Robert Coke petitioned the House of Commons for the return of the papers, hoping to make some profit by their publication. By 1641 the three remaining parts of the *Institutes* had been returned,
and the heir was desired to publish them with the protection of copyright
granted by Parliament.[112] They were published in 1642 and 1644.[113] None of
the volumes of the *Vade Mecum* was returned to Sir Robert.

THE TWELFTH AND THIRTEENTH PARTS

The exact history of the manual will probably never be known. It is safe to
assume, however, that at an early stage MSS.A–C were separated from the
later volumes. They may well have fallen into the possession of the Wyndhams of Norfolk and Somerset. Ann Wyndham, sister of Sir Hugh (Justice of
the Common Pleas, d. 1684) and Sir Wadham (Justice of the King's Bench,
d. 1668), was the mother of Sir George Strode, sergeant at law, whose daughter presented the volumes to Harley in 1715.[114] The Wyndhams were closely

109. *A Detection of the Court and State of England* (1697 ed.), p. 253.

110. H.C.J., Vol. II, p. 85: 13 February 1640/41.

111. *Ibid.,* p. 69: 18 January 1640/41. In C.U.L.MS.Ee.iv. 7, a commonplace book of Parliamentary
matters written by Edward Littleton, there are several references to "Coke MS. pl Cor." (ff. 13–15), and a
reference to "Coke MS. jurisdn. of Courtes" (f. 9).

112. *Ibid.,* pp. 45, 80, 470, 554; 2 Inst. (1642), f. 745v; Roger Coke, *op. cit.,* pp. 253, 279.

113. The history of the printing of the *Third Institute* in 1644 is now known from an important document
discovered by W. A. Atkinson: "The Printing of Coke's Institutes" (1926) 162 *Law Times* 435.

114. *The Diary of Humfrey Wanley* (C. E. & R. C. Wright, eds., 1966), Vol. I, pp. 13–14. The identifica-

connected with the Cokes, and Sir Hugh had married a daughter of Coke's friend Fleming C.J.

The later volumes, however, passed into general circulation and were avidly copied by legal collectors. This explains all the mystery which has hitherto surrounded the texts of the two posthumous parts of Coke's reports. None of the manuscript copies collates exactly with any other, because each copyist made different omissions and took his copies in different sequences. Some of the copies were taken directly from Coke's manual, others at second or third hand. One common feature, however, is that the cases usually fall into chronological groups which correspond exactly to the periods covered by each of the volumes of the *Vade Mecum*. None of the copies contains a single case from MSS.A–C.

A copy in the Hargrave collection, said to be taken from the autograph,[115] contains cases solely from MS.F. Another, in the University Library Cambridge, is taken solely from MS.D.[116] Two extant copies contain cases from MSS.D and F only.[117] The copy which belonged to Sir Matthew Hale was taken from MSS.D and F, with only ten cases from MS.E.[118] Most of the copies, however, combine material from all three (or four) volumes.[119] In Serjeant Maynard's copy the cases are arranged in chronological order throughout;[120] but in the other copies the notebooks were used out of order. Thus Timothy Tourneur's copy begins with MS.F, continues with MS.D, and ends

tion of the donor, Madam Thynne, seems beyond dispute. She was by 1715 the widow of Thomas Thynne, Viscount Weymouth, the owner of Longleat; but it is unlikely that the volumes were removed from Serjeant Thynne's collection, which is still preserved at Longleat. She was, however, the *heir* of Sergeant Strode, who died in 1701: see H. W. Woolrych, *Lives of Eminent Serjeants at Law* (1869), Vol. I, pp. 436–40.

115. MS.Harg. 34, ff. 108–30: "*Ceux Reportes et cases ensuant sont escrie hors del Reportes Sir Edw: Cooke que sont escrie ove son maine demesne.*" It is 12 Rep. 69–110, with omissions.

116. MS.Ll.iv. 9, ff. 1–111: "Lo. Cookes Reportes." It is 12 Rep. 6–64, with some variations. See also the four small leaves bound in MS.Ll.iii. 10, ff. 178–81, with copies of the *Case of Prohibitions* (12 Rep. 76), *Ashley's Case* (12 Rep. 90), and the *Case of Proclamations* (12 Rep. 74). These seem to be from an early copy, and are bound with readings given in the summer of 1634.

117. (1) Brit.Mus.MS.Add. 35956: "*Decisiones Judiciales.*" Corresponds roughly with 12 Rep. 71–84, 88–end, with omissions. (2) Lincoln's Inn, MS.Misc. 162. Corresponds with 12 Rep. 69–end, 1–15, 65–68.

118. MS.Lansd. 601, signed "Math.Hale" on f. 3. Umfreville said that Hale had entitled the volume "*Collectanea Edwardi Coke.*" He noted that the last ten cases were not in Part XII, but did not look as far as Part XIII, where they are all to be found. The cases from MS.D correspond with 12 Rep. 6–35.

119. This information is deduced from a knowledge of the contents of MS.E, and of the periods covered by MSS.D and F. It is not possible to take MS.G into account since it overlapped with MS.F. There are probably more MS. copies which we have overlooked. The Harvard Law School has a copy, apparently from MSS.D, E and F, corresponding to 12 Rep. 6 *et seq.*

120. Lincoln's Inn, MS.Mayn. 80: "The Lord Cookes 12th Reportes," 103 ff. Note at f. (97): "*Le Senr. Coke eit reporte que cest terme il veyast . . . ceux recordes.*" The volume also contains eight cases of prohibition from the "Reporte del Mr. Rolls" (Rolle?).

with MS.E.[121] John Bradshaw's copy, in the Inner Temple library, was formerly attributed to Coke himself on the basis of comparison with MS.Harl. 6687; but the hand is quite different, and some of the marginal notes (in a second hand) were written after Coke's death.[122] It begins with MS.E, continues with MS.F, and ends with MS.D. The same order is observed in the copy which Sergeant Pheasant transcribed in 1644 from the exemplar lent to him by Bramston C.J.[123] Yet another copy, from the library of Robert Paynell of Gray's Inn, begins with cases from MSS.D and F, some of them transposed, and ends with MS.E, including some cases not printed.[124]

Until the discovery of MS.E the textual problem raised by these widely divergent copies was insoluble. It is now quite easy to see how the copies derive from Coke's original, which was in form quite different from any of them. The copyists naturally left out what Coke himself had printed, and they also left out in varying degrees what they did not consider useful. When the *Twelfth Part* was published in 1658,[125] one of the incomplete copies was followed, containing cases from MSS.D and F only. Hence the jump at f. 65 from 6 James 1 to 8 James 1. Lawyers possessing more complete copies realized at once that the stock was not exhausted, and in the following year one J. G. published "some remains of [Coke's], under his own hand-writing, which have not yet appeared to the world"; known ever since as the *Thirteenth Part*.[126] All the cases in this book are in MS.E, and none are from elsewhere; it is possible,

121. Univ.Coll. London, MS.Ogden 29, ff. 439–569. Note at f. 569: "Soe farre of Lo. Cokes *vade mecum hoc libro: le residue vous troveres al fine de mes Reports del Eschequer in auter liver commenceant ove Widdrington Reports et finiant ove Reports del Eschequer 5 Car."* Tourneur's is probably a direct copy, including the *"Poyntes dangerous et absurd . . ."* from MS.E, f. 47v.

122. MS.Add. 21, presented in 1898 by H. D. Greene K.C. The marginal notes refer to *"Le Snr. Coke"* whereas Coke himself used the first person. On f. 140 is a note dated 1635, and on ff. 104v–5 are notes from a parchment register in the Tower lent to the writer by Mr. Collett on 30 January 1635/36. The annotator was probably Bradshaw, who was called to the Bar in 1627; his signature appears near the front of the book. The dates seem to indicate an early copy. Dr. Conway Davies attributed the notes to Coke himself: see Esther S. Cope, "Sir Edward Coke and Proclamations: a New Manuscript" (1971) 15 *A.J.L.H.* 317. This cannot be accepted.

123. MS.Lansd. 1079, ff. 1–123: *"Reports per Snr. Coke. 12a. pars. Liber Justice Phesant."* Corresponds roughly to 13 Rep. 1–71, 12 Rep. 69–135, 1–63. At the end the copyist wrote: *"Touts les cases devant fueront de Reports Snr. Coke, et jeo eux ay hors de un copy, que Sir John Brampstone, jades Cheif Justice d'Bank le Roy, lende a moy. Anno 1644. Pet: Phesaunt."*

124. MS.Harl. 4815: *"La Douzieme Part des Reports de Sir Edward Coke . . . Ne unques Publie in Printe."* This seems to derive from more than one copy, since there are several sequences and some duplication. For Paynell's ownership, see *The Diary of Humfrey Wanley* (C. E. & R. C. Wright, eds., 1966), Vol. I, p. 122.

125. *The Twelfth Part of the Reports of Sir Edward Coke, Kt., of divers resolutions and judgments . . . most of them very famous, being of the King's especiall reference, from the Council Table, concerning the prerogative . . .* (1658).

126. *Certain Select Cases in Law, reported by Sir Edward Coke . . . Translated out of a Manuscript written with his own Hand* (1659), sig. A.2.

therefore, that Coke's original was used, as the publishers keenly asserted.[127] There are, however, a few omissions in the printed version. There is nothing "spurious" about the volume, as Winfield suggested;[128] it is an accurate copy by the standards of the day, and fairly typical of Coke's unpolished and unsorted notes. Both the posthumous parts, being published after the statute of 1649, were translated from the manuscripts into English.

THE UNPUBLISHED RESIDUE

The two posthumous volumes published in 1658 and 1659 exhausted the greater part of the residue of MSS.D–F which Coke had not printed himself. Perhaps a dozen cases could be found which were not published, but none of them seems to be of great interest. The one item of value in MS.E which escaped the press is the roughly scribbled "*Poyntes Dangerous et Absurd affirme devant le Roy per Egerton Chancellor,*"[129] which throws some additional light on the dispute between Coke and Ellesmere.

It has been generally, and no doubt correctly, assumed that the reason why Coke did not himself publish the constitutional cases in MSS.D–F was that it would have been impossible, or at least impolitic, for him to have done so. Certainly he left a rich residue to be culled over after his death and published when the political climate was appropriate. The same is true, though to a lesser degree, of the earlier volumes of the *Vade Mecum.* But, because of the accident that these were separated and hidden soon after Coke's death, this part of the residue never saw the light of day.

The treason cases cited in the *Third Institute* have aroused not a little interest, since they appear inconsistent with Coke's traditional image as a persecutor of suspected traitors.[130] We now have the source of these cases, and can read Coke's original accounts of *Ninian Menville's,* the *Earl of Devonshire's, Francis Dacre's, Dr. Lopes', O'Cullen's, Da Gama's, Bradshaw's,* and *Lord Cobham's* cases.[131] More important than these is an extensive account of the Earl

---

127. *Ibid.,* sig. A.2*v:* "If any should doubt of the truth of these reports of Sir Edward Coke, they may see the originall Manuscript in French, written with his own hand, at Henry Twyford's shop in Vine-Court Middle Temple."

128. *Chief Sources of English Legal History* (1925), p. 189.

129. MS.E, f. 47*v*. Also occurs in the Tourneur and Bradshaw copies.

130. See G. P. Bodet, "Sir Edward Coke's Third Institute: A Primer for Treason Defendants" (1970) 20 *Univ. Toronto L.J.* 469.

131. MS.A, f. 336; MS.C, ff. 75*v*–78, 78*v*–79, 82*v*–85*v*, 127, 153, 194–95*v*, 246–48 (notes on treason), 562*v*–68*v*. There is also a brief note on Mary, Queen of Scots at ff. 82*v*–83, *in margine*.

of Essex's failure to put down the rebels and end the *"lingering guerres"* in Northern Ireland, and of his trial and sentence at York House for disobeying instructions and returning to England without permission. Coke makes some critical comments, and notes in particular that he was sentenced for contempt of the Council notwithstanding that his original commission was the widest and most absolute ever issued in war or peace.[132] There is also a full account of the trial of Essex, with the Earl of Southampton, for treason in 1601. This ends with a note of his decapitation on Tower Green and a remembrance of the recent "wofull examples" of traitors: "so that six dukes, two marquesses, ten earls and seven lords have been attainted of treason within our memory."[133] The same volume contains brief notes on the trial of Thomas Wynter, Guy Faux and others for the gunpowder treason, and on the trial of Abbingdon for receiving Henry Garnet, the jesuit, one of the gunpowder conspirators.[134] The notes are not concerned with the evidence, but with the legal problems of venue. Another interesting treason case is virtually unknown. Some apprentices had been whipped and pilloried by order of the Star Chamber, and afterwards (in 1595) a band of their fellow apprentices conspired to release them, to whip the Lord Mayor of London to death, and to sack the City. This was held to be treason within the statute of 13 Eliz. 1, c. 1, as an intent to levy war.[135]

Also of constitutional interest are the substantial reports of the suit against the executors of Sir Walter Mildmay, Chancellor of the Exchequer, concerning the royal treasure;[136] the *Earl of Derby's Case* concerning the Isle of Man;[137] *Sir Moyle Finch's Case* concerning the jurisdiction of the Chancery;[138] *Lord Zouch's Case* concerning the authority of the President and Council of Wales, following a conflict with the King's Bench over Magna Carta c. 29 and the liberty of the subject;[139] *Blofield* v. *Havers,* a case of *non procedendo rege inconsulto;*[140] and several notes on Parliament, the prerogative, and of the license given to Sir Walter Ralegh.[141] The report of *Doughtey's Case,* concerning the offices of

---

132. MS.C, ff. 408*v*–10.

133. *Ibid.,* ff. 438*v*–41*v* (translated).

134. *Ibid.,* ff. 682, 686*v*–88.

135. *Ibid.,* ff. 114–15*v*.

136. *R.* v. *Cary and Doddington* (1597), *ibid.,* ff. 214*v*–22.

137. *Ibid.,* ff. 274, 279–84. *Cf.* 4 Inst. 284.

138. *Throckmorton* v. *Finch* (1598) MS.C, ff. 222*v*–27. See 4 Inst. 86; "The Common Lawyers and the Chancery" (1969) 4 *Irish Jurist* (N.S.) 368 at pp. 371–72. See also *Hyde* v. *Cormet* (1594) MS.C, ff. 104*v*–5, on the jurisdiction of the Star Chamber.

139. MS.C, ff. 600–605, 617. *Cf.* 4 Inst. 242.

140. MS.C, ff. 47*v*–49. *Cf.* 2 Inst. 269; Vin.Abr. *Rege Inconsulto* (A) 9.

141. MS.C, ff. 55*v*–56*v*, 75, 95, 209–10, 376*v*, 629*v*.

Constable and Marshal, reveals that the appeal was brought against Sir Francis Drake himself for the death of Doughtey "*in son grand voiage per la mere,*" and that the Queen refused to create the officers "*considerant le veritie et circumstances de ceo.*"[142] The details of this remarkable interference with the course of justice do not, needless to say, appear in the *Institutes.*

The emotional element which one expects in Coke's writings is furnished by the full accounts of his elevation by Queen Elizabeth to the two law offices. He relates how on 14 June 1592 he was summoned to Greenwich and rebuked by the Queen for being of counsel in *Paget's, Englefield's,* and other cases, to defraud her of her escheats. Coke writes that he was

> so wholly appalled and dismayed (and being surprised with an incomparable greife that so gracious a prince should in any sort suspect my loialtye and inward duty and allegiance to her highnes, and feling a wonderfull naturall feare and love which god hath grafted in a subjectes hart towardes his naturell soveraigne) that my harte shaked within my body and all the partes of my body trembled so as I neyther could marke the conclusion of her speeche nor make any aunswere at all, nor untill myne eyes gushed out with teares could be reduced to perfect memory. . . .

The Queen, perceiving Coke's "exceeding griefe and anguish of mynde" then spoke gently to him, and after he had made a "sobbing" and "trobled" speech, informed him that she had appointed him to be her Solicitor-General. The tone of Coke's reply may be imagined.[143] When Coke succeeded Egerton as Attorney-General, he was also unable to control his emotions, and his "chekes were watered with teares" at the Queen's kindness.[144]

The more colorful material is only a small part of the unpublished residue of MSS. A and C, which mostly concerns private law. Many of the cases were woven into the fabric of the *Reports* and *Institutes,* and many of them are reported elsewhere. It is, nevertheless, valuable to have Coke's own selections and comments; and particularly valuable to have his unpolished, but full, accounts of such cases as *Collard* v. *Collard,*[145] *Germin* v. *Arscott,*[146] *Harvye* v.

---

142. MS. A, ff. 311*v*, 330. *Cf.* 3 Inst. 48.
143. MS. C, ff. 34–35.
144. *Ibid.,* ff. 86–87*v*.
145. *Ibid.,* ff. 102*v*–4, 186. For other reports, see Vin. Abr. *Uses* (O.2) 1.
146. MS. C, ff. 128*v*–33. Coke summarized the case at 1 Rep. 85, and it was fully reported in 1 And. 186. See also Vin. Abr. *Condition* (Z) 26.

Facye,[147] *John Littleton's Case*,[148] *Atkyns* v. *Longvile*,[149] and so on. If these names are unfamiliar, it is only because Coke did not publish their cases at length. There are also dozens of cases, more briefly reported, of which no other printed report exists. That the notebooks are a mine worth working there can be no doubt.

It is difficult to resist the comparison of Coke with his eminent contemporaries Bacon and Shakespeare; what they were to philosophy and literature, Coke was to the common law.[150] Yet his works have received less editorial attention than a minor poet can usually expect, and his unpublished works have been completely forgotten. It is more than three centuries since the *Thirteenth Part* of the *Reports* was published. The time must now be ripe for the *Fourteenth*.

Note

To save others from repeating fruitless inquiries, a brief mention must be made of two spurious "Coke" manuscripts.

(1) G. P. Macdonnell, at the end of his biography of Coke in the *Dictionary of National Biography*, refers to "a law commonplace book, 2 vols., supposed to be by Coke, in the Bishop's Library, Norwich, No. 462." This very misleading citation is presumably a careless allusion to the catalogue of the library of John Moore, Bishop of Norwich, printed by Bernard in 1697: "A Law Commonplace Book believ'd to be made by the Lord Chief Justice Cooke and to be written with his own hand. 4to. 2 vols."[151] The volumes were in the Bishop's personal library, not in the Library of the Bishops of Norwich, and they are now in the University Library Cambridge: shelf-marks Hh.iv. 4–5. They contain abridged Year Book cases in a neat law hand, inscribed in a later hand on f. 1 "MSS. Edwardi Coke Mil' &c. 2 Voll." They belonged to Anthony Ireby (of Lincoln's Inn) in 1694. They are certainly not in Coke's handwriting,

---

147. MS.C, ff. 173*v*–78: "*Nota cest case duit aver estre report.*" Coke noted the case briefly in 3 Rep. 91. See also 2 And. 109; Poph. 61; Univ.Lib.Camb. MS.Ee.iii. 45, ff. 54*v*–68*v*.

148. MS.C, ff. 508*v*–25*v*. Coke noted the case at 9 Rep. 15. The only printed report is the brief note in Moo. 746.

149. MS.C, ff. 620–25*v*. The only printed reports are very brief: Moo. 934, Cro.Jac. 50.

150. So says W. S. Holdsworth, *Some Makers of English Law* (1938), p. 132. *Cf.* J. M. Gest, "The Writings of Sir Edward Coke" (1909) 18 *Yale Law Journal* 504.

151. *Librorum MSS. D.D. Johannis Mori Episcopi Norvicensis Catalogus*, p. 373, no. 461 (not 462).

and they are in no way remarkable. The note on f. 1 is probably a bookseller's puff.

(2) Mrs. C. D. Bowen includes in her bibliography of Coke's works: "Autograph MS., *Reports in the King's Bench, 15th–19th Years of the Reign of James I.* Carson Collection on Growth of the Common Law, Philadelphia Free Library. Folio, 97 leaves, in the handwriting of Sir Edward Coke."[152] These dates are, of course, inconsistent with the account given above. But the manuscript (shelfmark LC. 14/48) is not in Coke's handwriting and has no connection with his *Reports.* The false identification was probably made by a bookseller.[153]

---

152. *The Lion and the Throne* (1957), p. 483. The reference further down the page to MS.Harl. 1572 should be to MS. Harl. 6687.

153. The writer is grateful to Mr. Howard J. Heaney, Librarian of the Rare Book Department, Free Library of Philadelphia, for the latter suggestion and for sending photocopies of specimen leaves.

Index

❦ ❦ ❦

Abbot, George (archbishop of Canterbury), 345–46
Abridgment (Brook), 165
activism. *See* judicial activism; reform
Adams, John, 25, 64 n. 60, 180
Adams, Samuel, 25
Addled Parliament, x
Admiralty. *See* Court of Admiralty
Adoption Act of 1950, 119
advisory opinions, 13–14
Agricola, Rudolph, 233
agricultural land use, 197–98, 198 n. 72
alias habeas, 332, 343
allegiance owed the state
    Calvin's Case and Coke, 90–97, 106
    categories of, 92, 101–2
    and common law, 87, 97, 103
    defined, 91, 101
    God and, 86, 99, 102
    natural *v.* legal, 95, 100–102, 103–4
    nature of, 86
    oaths, 86, 91–93, 104
    and personal *v.* political capacity of king, 93–97, 100
    and possession of crown, 96, 98–100, 103, 105
    and treason, 94
    William and Mary, 97–105
Allen's Case, 263, 269
American law, Coke's influence on, 24–25, 66, 67, 107, 178–83
Anderson, Chief Justice Edmund, 4, 9, 77, 338–39
Annuitie 41 (*Annuitie* 11), 156
antitrust theory, 186
apprenticeships, 200–201, 202–3
Apsley, Michael, 262–63

Apsley and Ruswell's Case, 262–63
Apthonius of Tyre, 235
Apthonii Progymnasmata, 235
Aquinas, St. Thomas, 112, 117, 232 n. 37
Aristotle, 232
art, law as, 121, 125–26
Arte of English Poesie, The (Puttenham), 240
artificial reason. *See* reason, artificial
Art of Rhetoric, The (Wilson), 232, 240
assumpsit
    Coke and considerations, 77 n. 35, 191–92
    and contract claims, vii, 71, 191
    against executors, 79
    in King's Bench *v.* Common Pleas, 70–71, 73–74, 77–79, 81
    need for a reason or consideration, 76–77, 80–81
    non assumpsit, 77, 79 n. 45
    in *Slade's Case,* 70, 74–85, 226
    special *assumpsit,* 76 n. 30, 81, 82–83, 83 n. 65
Aston's Case (1585), 72 n. 9
Atkins, Henry, 135
attorneys-general, 7–8
Aubrey, John, 228, 248

Bacon, Sir Francis
    and *Bonham's Case,* 147
    in Chancery, 277
    on Chancery and common law conflict, 280–81
    and Coke, xii, 9, 15, 35–37, 48–49, 167, 256–57, 268–69, 275
    on Coke, 4, 369 n. 62
    on Coke's *Reports,* 43, 49, 53 n. 41
    and common law judges, 278
    De Augmentis, 49

Bacon, Sir Francis (*continued*)
  on debtors, 299
  exempla, use of, 246
  impeached, 36
  Instauratio Magna, Coke's comments on,
    43
  on judges as reporters of law, 48–49
  Maxims, regula xix, 164
  on monopolies, 187 n. 4
  and patents, 304
  on rhetoric, 225
  Rules and Decisions, 43
  and writing English law, 37–39, 38 n.
    16–17, 40–42, 47, 48
Bacon, Sir Nicholas, 242
"bad man" theory of law, 120
Bagg's Case (1615), x
bail, in five knights' case, 332, 333–34, 342,
  343, 343 n. 57
Baker, J. H., 29, 30, 60, 247–48
Baker v. Herbert (1911), 119
Ball, Peter, 353
Bancroft, Richard (archbishop of
  Canterbury), 139–40, 145, 290, 295
Barber-Surgeon's Company, 134, 136, 147
Baron v. Boys (1608), 199–200
Bate's Case, 299, 301
Bawtrey, Sergeant, 264
Ben, Anthony, 270
Bereford, Chief Justice, 155
Berkeley, Justice, 169
Bill of Monopolies, 311, 325
Bill of Rights, 171
Blackburn, Justice, 175
Black Death, 209
Blackstone, William, 60–61, 66–67, 176
body politic ideal, 197 n. 67, 211
Bonham, Thomas, 133–36, 138, 147–48, 152
Bonham's Case
  Archbishop of Canterbury intercedes,
    139–40
  Coke, authorities cited by, 154–66
  Coke's argument, 141–46, 153–54
  Coke's argument, reception of, 166–77
  common law and acts of Parliament, xi,
    107–8, 115, 227
  Common Pleas, 135–36, 137–41

  courts control of acts of Parliament, 25
  in King's Bench, 137, 138
  political and institutional context, 127
  reports on, 151–52
  See also London College of Physicians
Booke of Entries (Coke), 374
Book Named the Governor (Elyot), 238–39
Book of Entries (Rastell), 75
Bowman v. Middleton (1792), 183
Brackley, Viscount. *See* Ellesmere, Thomas
  Egerton, Lord Chancellor
Bracton, Henry de, 13, 26, 46, 113–14
Bramston, Sir John, 331
Bretnor, Thomas, 147
Bridgman, Orlando, 6
Britton, John (bishop), 92
Brook's *Abridgment,* 165
Browne, Sergeant, 333
Brownlow's report of *Bonham's Case,* 151
Buckingham, George Villiers, 1st Duke of
  and Bacon, 298
  brother wed to Coke's daughter, 16, 54,
    194 n. 45
  Coke and, 257 n. 20
  in five knights' case, 341–42, 342 n. 54, 345
  and patents, 303, 304, 318
  wars, xii

Caesar, Sir Julius, 19, 260, 294
Calthorp, Sir Henry, 331
Calvin's Case (1608)
  Coke and allegiance, 90–97, 106
  Coke's report of, 372–73
  Coke's role in, 226
  natural and legal allegiance, 102, 104
  nature of rights of common, 241
  rights of Scottish subjects, ix
Cambridge University, 3, 145, 153, 357, 364
Camden, William, 56–57
canon law, 157–58
capitalism, 186, 188, 204
Cary, Richard, 374
case, concept of, 245–47
case law, 301
Case of Commendams (1616), x, 15, 53
Case of Monopolies (1602), 201, 206 n. 116,
  208, 212, 214

Case of the Archbishop of York, 205 n. 111
Case of the Sale of Barley (1505), 72
certiorari, 173
Cessavit, 155
Chamberlain, John, x
Chancery
    Allen's Case, 263, 269
    Apsley and Ruswell's Case, 262–63
    Bacon in, 277
    and Coke, 192, 260–61, 267–68
    and common law courts, 257–60, 272–74,
        276–77, 280
    decree on jurisdiction of, 273–74, 276–79
    Earl of Oxford's Case, 264–66
    Glanvill's Case, 261–62, 266–68, 269
    and King's Bench, ix
    praemunire, 271–72
    and royal prerogative, 256, 260–61, 274,
        277
    subpoenas issued, 286
Chandelor v. Lopus (1603), 84 n. 67
Charge speech (Coke), 189
Charles I
    and Coke, xii, 377–79
    Coke's papers seized, xiii, 18, 56, 377–79
    discretionary imprisonment, 331, 336–40,
        343, 346, 354
    five knights' case felony, 336, 354
    forced loans, 330, 331, 331 n. 10, 332, 336
    and judges, 15–16
    law, abuse of (illegal acts), 343, 350–51,
        354
    and Parliament, 18
    policies of, 253 n. 97
    and publication of Coke's *Institutes,* 56
    and reforming legislation, 340–41, 348,
        349–50, 354
    and royal prerogative, 350
    trust, 347–48, 350, 352, 353, 355
Chudleigh's Case (1594)
    Coke and, 375
    Coke's argument, vii, 371
    nature of law, 109
    perpetuities, 5
church courts. *See* ecclesiastical courts
Cicero, 229
Ciceronian rhetoric, 224–25, 230

City of London v. Wood (1701), 171–72
civilization and rhetoric, 241–42, 243
civil law, English
    compared to common law, 39, 251
    contracts entered abroad, 293–94
    education in, 27
    and royal prerogative, 254–55
    uncertainty in, 59–60
civil law, European, 30
civil law, Roman
    as common law of Europe, 26–27, 28–32
    as model for writing English law, 29, 32,
        37–40, 48, 68
    power of emperor, 55, 57
    See also Institutes (Justinian)
Clifford's Inn, 3
cloth manufacturing and trade, 195–97, 206,
    217, 219, 311
Clowes, William, 133
Cockayne, Alderman, 196
Code (Justinian), 37
Coke, Richard, 137
Coke, Roger, 378–79
Coke, Sir Edward
    on allegiance to king, 90–97
    arrest of, xii, 17, 54
    on Bacon's *Instauratio Magna,* 43
    birth, vii
    on Chancery, 258, 259
    common law influenced by, xiii–xiv, 22,
        50, 87, 89, 107–8, 226–27
    criticism of, 168–69, 298
    death of, xiii, 18
    economic implications of his work,
        186–88, 223
    on education, 239 n. 60
    education of, vii, 2–4, 227–28, 234–35,
        357, 357 n. 2
    enemies, 12, 16
    family, vii, x–xi, 2, 9, 16, 54, 194 n. 45,
        357 n. 2, 378
    historical importance, 18–22, 50, 65–69,
        107, 111–12, 184, 224, 225–27, 357
    indexing proverbs, 237 n. 55
    influence on American law, 24–25, 66, 67,
        107, 178–83
    as innovator, 226

Coke, Sir Edward (*continued*)
  on James I's qualifications as judge, ix, 13,
    227, 295–96
  on judiciary, role of, 12–13, 48–49
  and jurisdiction, 289
  on king's power to imprison, 295, 338
  on legal innovation's perils, 46–47
  and legal system abuses, xi–xii
  library, 42–43, 59, 227–28, 237 n. 55, 358,
    359, 368
  marriage of daughter, x–xi, 16, 54,
    194 n. 45
  marriages, 9
  motto, 1–2
  papers seized, xiii, 18, 56, 377–79
  past-mindedness, 22, 93
  personal traits, 2, 189, 221 n. 202, 226
  as a political theorist, 20
  poor, concern for, 221 n. 202
  on reason and the law, xi, 13, 61–64,
    88–89, 110–20, 123–24, 250
  on reform of law, 46–49
  religion, 188, 188 n. 13
  reputation, 5, 9, 18
  rhetoric and, 224–53
  on trusting the king, 353
  wealth, 189
Coke, Sir Edward: career and appointments,
    vii–viii, 4–10, 188
  attorney-general, 7–8, 384
  and Bacon, xii, 9, 15, 35–37, 48–49,
    256–57, 268–69, 275
  and Charles I, xii, 18, 56, 377–79
  Common Pleas, viii, 2, 9–12, 15
  Common Pleas, removal from, 14
  Crown's relationship with, ix, x, 9–10
  Earl of Oxford's Case, 264–66
  and Elizabeth I, 6–7, 384
  and Ellesmere, ix, 12, 275–76, 298, 382
  experience at the bar, 10–11
  five knights' case, 338, 340, 349, 350, 352
  House of Commons, xi–xiii, 6, 16–17, 54
  House of Commons investigation of
    monopolies and patents, 302, 308–9,
    312, 313, 318, 321, 323, 326
  and James I, x, xii, 2, 12–13, 16–17, 53,
    62–63, 194 n. 45, 255–56, 275

  judicial activism, 16
  King's Bench, ix, 14–15, 168, 260, 298
  King's Bench, removal from, x, 15, 43,
    194 n. 45, 275
  Petition of Right, 18, 21–22, 54, 353, 354,
    355
  Privy Council, 15, 16, 298
  Privy Council, removal from, 53, 54
  Privy Council, returned to, 54, 194 n. 45
  as prosecutor in state trials, 8–9
  raising revenues for James I, 16–17
  and writing of English law, 33, 42, 46–48,
    52, 65, 67–68
Coke, Sir Edward: works of
  overview, xiii, 1, 33
  spurious manuscripts, 385–86
  unpublished works, 382–85
  —— *Booke of Entries,* 374
  —— *Charge* speech, 189
  —— *Coke on Littleton (Commentary upon
    Littleton, First Institute)*
  American regard for, 66, 67, 178
  Baker on, 247–48
  as a commonplace book, 248–49
  content of, 61
  "High Court of Parliament," 17
  Holdsworth on, 247
  importance of, xiii, 23, 58
  organization of, 58, 60–61, 60 n. 54, 110,
    247–49
  perspective on the law, 60, 110–11
  and property law, 22
  publication of, 54, 56
  sale of manuscript, 360 n. 13
  Thomas's rearrangement of, 66–67
  —— *Institutes of the Laws of England*
  allegiance and treason, 96–97, 382–83
  commentary on civil law, 59–60
  Elizabeth I praised, 52
  ideology of, 68
  importance of, 69
  influence on American law, 24–25, 107,
    178
  organization of, 54–55, 56–57, 60–61, 64
  precedent cited in, 60
  publication of, 54, 56
  representing the order of the state, 65 n. 62

scope of, xiii, 23–24, 65 n. 62
writing of, 376–77
and the writing of English law, 67–68
—— note-books and commonplace books
Coke upon Littleton Autograph, 359–62
format/organization of, 238 n. 58, 361–62,
    366–67
manuscripts of, 358–65
and rhetoric, 228
and seizure of Coke's papers, 358
style of, 369
—— *Report of Shelley's Case,* 370
—— *Reports*
Bacon on, 43, 49, 53 n. 41
cases not in parts I–XI, 376–82
Coke's method of writing, 365–70, 373–75
content of, 47, 49–50, 50–51
Egerton on, 49
function of, 44–45, 50, 251 n. 93
importance of, xiii, 24, 69, 150, 251 n. 93,
    357–58
James I's order to revise, 53, 168
law-case as *exemplum,* 247
in note-books of Coke, 362, 363, 366–70,
    374–76
organization of, 358, 370–73
prefaces to, 49–50, 374 n. 84
publication of, 370–73
selection of cases, 373–76
sources of cases, 367–69
twelfth and thirteenth parts, 379–82
and the writing of English law, 43, 67
—— *Vade Mecum,* 360, 370, 371, 376, 377,
379
Coke, Sir Robert, 378, 379
Coke on Littleton. See under Coke, Sir
    Edward: works of
Colgate v. Bacheler (1601), 204
College of Physicians. *See* London College
    of Physicians
Colthirst v. Bejushin (1550), 5
Colt v. Glover (1616), x
Commentaries on the Laws of England
    (Blackstone), 66–67, 177
commerce. *See* trade
commercial law, 192
Committee of Grievances, 310, 312, 313

Committee of Trade, 314
common law courts
    and acts of Parliament, 25, 128, 156, 167
    Bonham prosecuted in, 137
    and the Chancery, 257–60, 272–74,
        276–77, 280
    commercial litigation, 193
    and custom, 244
    jurisdiction of, 144, 192–93
    principal courts, 27–28
    and royal patents, 205
common law in American colonies, 24–25,
    178–79, 180–81
common law in Europe, 26–27, 28–32
common law of England
    and allegiance, 87, 97, 103
    Coke on Littleton and, 56
    Coke's influence on, xiii–xiv, 22, 50, 87,
        89, 107–8, 226–27
    contributions of civilians to, 39 n. 22
    defined by Coke, xi, 88–89, 116
    estates, rules governing, 5
    as fundamental, 184, 185
    and God's law, 114
    and James I, 216, 254–55, 282, 283
    and judging one's own case, 154
    and liberty, 31, 273
    Littleton's *Tenures,* 56–57
    medicine, practice of, 130
    and monopolies/patents, 319, 321, 324, 325
    and natural law, 115–16
    and Parliament, xi, 107–8, 111, 115, 143,
        146–47, 154, 168, 227
    and reason, 61–65, 108, 179 n. 97, 252–53
    reform efforts, 26–28, 31–32, 37–42
    reports, importance of, 48–49, 51–52
    and rhetoric, 233–34, 244, 245–49
    and Roman civil law, 26–27, 28–30,
        37–40, 48, 68
    and royal patents, 205, 208
    and royal prerogative, 36, 54, 55, 111, 170,
        171, 272–73
    source of, 26, 41, 68–69, 88
    statute law and, 111
    and trade restraints, 210
    See also English law
common-law pleading, 239–40

commonplace, defined, 236 n. 46
commonplace books
    case and *exemplum*, 245–49
    Coke on Littleton as, 248–49
    Coke's own, 228, 238 n. 58, 358, 360, 361
    in Tudor education, 235–41
Common Pleas. *See* Court of Common
    Pleas
common sense, 119
commonwealth, idea of, 243 n. 68
company system, 217–19
composition, education in, 236–37, 236 n. 47
Coningsby, Justice, 73
constitution
    and allegiance to monarch, 103
    and *Bonham's Case,* 148
    as check on legislation, 183
    and Coke, 67–68, 275, 382
    "constitution" defined, 88 n. 10
    doctrine of "ancient constitution," 88–89
    unwritten, 183 n. 124
    written, 185
constitutional crisis of 1689, 97
constitutionalism, 20–21
constitutional revolution, 254
contingent remainders, 5, 6
contracts
    in Admiralty Court, 293–94
    assumpsit and *indebitatus assumpsit,* 70–85
    defined, 80
    enforcement of, 191, 192
    entered abroad, 293–94
    inferring agreement from conduct, 83–85
    and loans, 83
    prohibiting practice of a trade, 204
    purely executory contracts, 71
    in restraint of trade, 204
    sale of specific goods, 81
    See also Slade's Case (1602)
conveyancing, 5–6
"Cook's Case," 4
Copper v. Gederings, 155, 163
Coppin, Sir George, 275
copyright patents, 216, 220, 221
Corbet's Case, 371
corporate bodies as judge and party, 141, 144
corporations, 217–20

Corpus Juris (Justinian), 37–38, 41
Coryton, William, 351, 354
cosmopolitanism, 28, 29, 30, 43, 65
Council of the Marches of Wales, 14, 290,
    297
Court of Admiralty
    handling contracts, 293–94
    jurisdiction of, 192–93
Court of Common Pleas
    Bonham's Case, 135–36, 137–41
    Coke as chief justice, viii, 2, 9–12, 15
    and the High Commission, 295
    indebitatus assumpsit, 70–71, 74, 77–79, 81
    jurisdiction of, 11–12, 78, 136, 291
    prohibitions, 296
Court of Exchequer Chamber
    Calvin's Case, 90–97
    and Common Pleas, 71
    "Mischief Rule," 375
    in *Slade's Case,* 78–79
Court of High Commission
    power and jurisdiction of, viii, 296
    supervision of, 294–95
    See also ecclesiastical courts
Court of King's Bench
    Bonham's Case, 137, 138
    and Chancery, ix
    Coke as chief justice, viii, ix, x, 14–15, 43,
        168, 194 n. 45, 260, 275, 298
    five knights' case, 329, 329 n. 3, 332 n. 15,
        343
    five knights' case records, 334–40, 343,
        344, 355–56
    and the High Commission, 295
    indebitatus assumpsit, 70–71, 73–75,
        77–79, 81
    jurisdiction, 10, 15, 257
    power over judgments of other courts,
        ix, x
Court of Requests, 287, 294
courts
    complexity and expense, 299
    defined, 285–86
    House of Commons as, 322–23
    James I and jurisdiction, 296
    jurisdiction of, 286–90 (*see also under
        specific courts*)

Parliament as a high court, 17, 113, 114

records, 337 n. 28, 342 n. 54

records perverted in five knights' case, 334–40, 343, 350, 355–56

regulation and supervision of, 286–90, 297

rules of court *v.* judgments, 332, 336, 338

See also common law courts; ecclesiastical courts; Star Chamber

Coventry, Thomas, 279

Cowell, John, 39, 41, 42, 58 n. 49

Coxe, Brinton, 158, 170

criminal law, 23, 264–66, 301

Croke, George, 263

Croke, Sir John, 267

Cromwell, Lord Edward, vii

Cromwell, Oliver, 301

Cromwell, Thomas, 32

Cromwellian legislation, 27 n. 2

Crown

  advisory opinions elicited from judges, 13–14

  allegiance owed to (*see* allegiance owed the state)

  authority of and the issue of jurisdictions, 296

  as birthright, 95

  and the church, 294

  Coke and, ix, x, 9–10

  Coke and Charles I, xii, 18, 56, 377–79

  Coke and Elizabeth I, 6–7, 384

  Coke and James I, ix, x, xii, 2, 12–13, 16–17, 53, 62–63, 227, 255–56, 275, 295–96

  in Coke's *Institutes,* 68

  divine right of kings, 111, 282–83

  due process legislation, 343 n. 57

  finances, 187

  forced loans, 330, 331, 331 n. 10, 332

  and God, 63, 86, 99, 102, 256, 271

  and judges' authority, 256, 289

  and the law, 2, 13, 36–37, 48, 62–65, 64 n. 61, 108, 111, 114, 151, 153, 170, 256, 343–46

  law, abuse of (illegal acts), 343, 350–51, 354

  and Parliament, 65 n. 62

  paternalistic duty of, 140–41, 153

  personal *v.* political capacity of, 93–94, 97, 100

  power of, 2, 21–22, 105, 271

  power of, limiting, 58

  power of judicature, 14, 256, 295–96

  power over legislation, 65 n. 62, 170

  powers concerning clergy, 15

  power to change law, 31, 48

  power to imprison, 295, 330, 331, 333, 336–40, 343–46, 354, 355–56

  power to regulate trade, 194–95, 205, 212–13, 214–15, 217–18 n. 177, 320

  succession, 99

  trade privileges bestowed by, 205

  trust in, 347–48, 350, 352, 353, 355

  as unable to do wrong, 215 n. 166

  writing the law, 38–39, 38 n. 17, 40–41, 48

  See also royal patents; royal prerogative; *specific* monarchs

cultural implications of rhetoric, 230–32

Cushing, John, 180

customs duties, 194

Darcy v. Allen (1603), 303, 304

Davenant v. Hurdis (1598), 206–7, 208

Davies, Sir John, 51, 58–59

Day v. Savadge (1614), 167, 175

De Augmentis (Bacon), 49

debate, 236 n. 46

debts

  Allen's Case, 263

  Case of the Sale of Barley (1505), 72

  to the Crown, 213

  Edwards v. Burre, 77

  Gill v. Harewood, 76

  Hodge v. Vavisour, 84

  Norwood v. Read (1558), 84, 85

  partial payment of, 192 n. 30

  Pickering v. Thoroughgood, 72–73, 74

  Pinchon's Case, 71, 83, 84

  Slade's Case, 70, 74–85, 191

  treatment of debtors, 299

  Whorwood v. Gybbons, 77

"defactoism," 96, 105

De Laudibus Legum Angliae (Fortescue), 31

democracy, 89

De Officio Regis (Wycliffe), 31

Despenser, Hugh, 94, 95
Devereux, Robert. *See* Essex, Robert
    Devereux, 2nd Earl of
Dialogue Between Pole and Lupset (Starkey),
    26, 27
Dialogue Between the Doctor and the Student
    (St. Germain), 116
Digest (Justinian), 37–38
Digges, Sir Dudley, 340
*Discourse Touching the Reformation of the
    Laws of England* (Cromwell), 32
divine right of kings, 111, 282–83
Dodderidge, Sir John, 241, 250 n. 90, 252,
    265, 278
Donoghue v. Stevenson (1932), 119
Doughtey's Case, 383–84
Downes, Theophilius, 103, 104–5
Dr. Google's Case, 264–66
Drake, Sir Francis, 384
Duchess of Hamilton's Case (1712), 175
due process, 108, 213, 328, 339, 343 n. 57, 355
Duke of Norfolk's Case (1681), 6
Dyer, James, 246, 368
Dyer's Case (1414), 204 n. 105

Earl of Oxford's Case, 264–66
East India Company, 195, 218, 311
ecclesiastical courts
    and the Chancery, 266
    jurisdiction of, 295
    prohibition, 11–12
    supervision of, 291–93, 294–95
    survey of, 284
    See also Court of High Commission
Eco, Umberto, 230
economic liberalism, 20, 186, 204
economics
    Coke and capitalist doctrine, 20
    Coke raising revenue for James I, 16
    Coke's protectionist bias, 195 n. 48,
        196 n. 59
    fines imposed to raise revenue, 16
    implications of Coke's work, 186–88,
        223
    and royal authority, 194–95
    Tudor policies, 197
    See also trade

education
    Coke on universities, 145
    humanistic learning, 235–38
    in Latin, 2
    of lawyers, 3–4, 27, 49 n. 36, 234–41,
        239 n. 60, 242, 242 n. 66, 244–45
    medical knowledge, 143
    of physicians, 129–30
    in rhetoric, 234–41
    in Tudor England, 234–41
    in writing, 236–37, 236 n. 47
Edwards v. Burre (1578), 77
Egerton, Thomas. *See* Ellesmere, Thomas
    Egerton, Lord Chancellor
Eliot, Sir John, 338
Elizabeth I
    attorneys-general, 7
    and Coke, 6–7, 384
    and judges, 52
    royal patents, 222, 303 n. 7
Ellesmere, Thomas Egerton, Lord
    Chancellor
    Allen's Case, 263
    authority of, 273
    and *Bonham's Case,* 136, 147, 169
    Chancery and common law, 256–60
    and Coke, ix, 12, 275–76, 298, 382
    on Coke, 369 n. 62
    Coke and Glanvill and Allen, 269
    on Coke's *Reports,* 49, 53
    death of, 276
    fitness for office, 269, 274
    offices held by, 7
    on royal prerogative, 284
Elton, G. R., 27 n. 2
Elyot, Sir Thomas, 224, 238–39, 251
employment. *See* trades (professions)
enclosure laws, 197–98
English law
    "aesthetic" feel for, 121, 125–26
    antiquity and sources of, 45–46
    Bacon's role in writing of, 37–42
    as barbaric, 26, 32, 58 n. 49, 59–60
    Coke's defense of, 68–69
    Coke's importance to, 50, 65, 107
    Coke's role in writing of, 33, 42, 52, 65,
        67–68

Coke's views of reform, 46–48
commentaries on, 59–60
consistency, 115
contrasted with European law, 28–30, 31, 33–34
and "generosity," 124
James I's plans for reform, 40–41
and the king's power, 58
need for writing of, 32, 34, 41, 43, 65
Parliament writing, 113
plans for writing of, 35–42
reporting unwritten law, 42–52
and Roman civil law, 26–27, 28–32, 37–40, 44, 48, 65, 68
shift from doctrine to jurisprudence, 29, 60
superiority of, 41, 49, 52, 88
See also civil law; common law; law; legislation
English Law and the Renaissance (Maitland), 27
English Lawyer, The (Dodderidge), 250 n. 90, 252
equity, 192, 257, 258, 270, 278, 280, 281, 285
Erasmus, 236, 243, 244
Essex, Robert Devereux, 2nd Earl of, viii, 8, 228, 383
estates. *See* real property
Europe
and Roman law, 26–27, 28–32, 38 n. 16
writing of national law, 38 n. 16
Exchequer Chamber. *See* Court of Exchequer Chamber
exempla
and lawyers' concept of the case, 245–47
and lawyers' vision of the law, 243
use of in rhetoric, 236–37

Fibrosa Case (1942), 118
Finch, Henry, 39, 41, 63
Finch, Sir John, 350
Finch v. Throgmorton, 362
fines imposed to raise revenue, 16
Fitzherbert, Sir Anthony, 155, 160
Fitzjames, Chief Justice, 73
five knights' case
    bail, 332, 333–34, 342, 343, 343 n. 57

Charles I's refusal to file substantive charges, 332–33
Heath's special "judgment," 338–39, 342
judges knowing "cause of the cause" of imprisonment, 334, 343
names of knights, 330
Petition of Right resulting from, 350–56
and precedent, 334–40, 343
propositions debated, 346–50
records, attempt to pervert, 334–40, 343, 350, 355–56
reforming legislation debated, 340–46, 348, 349–50, 351
rule of court *v.* judgment, 332, 336, 338
significance of, 328–29
Fleming, Thomas, 13–14, 138–39, 259
Floyd's Case, 323
food supply, 195 n. 48, 198–200, 198 n. 73
forestalling and engrossing, 198–200, 198 n. 73, 210, 211–12
Fortescue, Sir John, 31
Fraunce, Abraham, 39, 239 n. 60, 249–50
free trade, 147, 200, 210–11, 212–13, 214–15, 319
Frowyke, Chief Justice, 166
Fulbecke, William, 238
Fuller, Rev. Thomas, 19
Fuller's Case (1607), viii, 227, 251

Galen, 141–42
Gardiner, S. R., 254
Gawdy, Francis, 9
George I, 364
Germain, Saint, 116
Gerrard, Gilbert, 7
Giddings v. Browne (1865), 178
Gill v. Harewood (1587), 76
Glanvil, Sergeant, 169–70
Glanvill, Richard, 261–62, 266–68
Glanvill's Case, 261–62, 266–68, 269
glassmaking, 320
God
    divine right of kings, 111, 282–83
    and the king, 63, 86, 99, 102, 256, 271
    and the law, 113, 114, 116, 181, 247, 256
    and power, 87 n. 4
Godden v. Hales, 165, 169, 170, 184

Goodrich, Peter, 239 n. 60
Google (Gooch), Barnaby, 264
government
    England as a mixed monarchy, 21, 89
    and judges, 289
    law as source of power, 108
    and the political nation, 86 n. 1, 87, 89
    and rhetoric, 231–32, 242, 243
    See also allegiance owed the state; Crown
Grand Junction Canal Co. v. Dimes (1849),
    175
Graunde Abridgement (Fitzherbert), 155–60
Gray, Charles, 128–29, 143
Grey, Lady Katherine, 246
Gridley, Jeremiah, 64 n. 60
grievance, defined, 324 n. 105
guilds, 205–7, 206 n. 114, 220
Gunpowder Plot, viii, 8, 228–29, 383

habeas corpus, 264, 265, 266, 274, 333–34,
    335, 339
Hale, Sir Matthew, 110
Harbert's Case (1586), 114
Harleian Manuscripts, 359–65
Harsnett, Bishop, 341
Harvey, Gabriel, 240
Hatton, Lady Elizabeth (wife of Coke), 9
Hawarde, John, 241
Hawes, Stephen, 214–42
Heath, Sir Robert, 330–31, 335, 336, 337, 339,
    343, 355–56
Hele, John, 266
Helgerson, Richard, 251 n. 93
Henry VIII
    attorneys-general, 7
    London College of Physicians, 129, 141,
        152
Hertford, Earl of, 246
Heveningham, Sir John, 337
Heydon's Case, 375
High Commission. *See* Court of High
    Commission
"High Court of Parliament," 17, 113, 114
Hill, Christopher, 188
Hinton, Dr., 283
Hobart, Attorney General, 138
Hobart, Sir Henry, 167

Hobbes, Thomas, 19, 62, 109, 110, 113, 115,
    228 n. 24
Hodge v. Vavisour (1617), 84
Holdsworth, William, xiii–xiv
Holland, Lord, 56
Holt, Lord Chief Justice, 172
Hoskins, John, 351
House of Commons
    Coke's career in, xi–xiii, 16–18, 54
    as a court, 322–23
    as debating forum, 300
    function of, 306–8, 326
    impeachments, xi
    jurisdiction of, 316 n. 63, 323
    members as representatives of districts
        and nation, 305 n. 15, 306–7
    methods of petitioning, 311
    powers of, 312–13, 315–16, 315 n. 63, 323
    privileges and responsibilities, 305, 305 n.
        15, 307
    See also Parliament
House of Commons' investigations of
        monopolies and patents
    Bill of Monopolies, 311, 325
    calling in actual patents, 313–14, 315 n. 65,
        323
    Coke's definition of monopolies, 216,
        303
    Coke's role in, 302, 308–9, 312, 313, 318,
        321, 323, 326
    James I's reaction, 313, 314, 315, 315 n. 65,
        318
    legal reasons for condemning patents and
        grants, 319–22
    members' special interests, 310–11, 317
    petition of grievances, 326, 326 n. 115
    political element, 317–19
    procedure for examination of patents,
        312–17, 312 n. 44, 322, 324
    referees, 317–19
    specific complaints, 309–12
    subsidies and grievances, 305–9, 306 n. 18,
        323, 324 n. 105
House of Lords
    Bill of Monopolies, 325
    five knights' case, 329 n. 5, 340–46, 353
    See also Parliament

Howard, Frances, 225 n. 4
humanistic learning, 235–38
humanists, 31, 52, 60, 68, 234
Hutchinson, Thomas, 179–80
Hutton, Sergeant, 259–60, 272, 278
Hyde, Chief Justice, 331–32, 341

imitation and composition, 236 n. 47
impeachments
    of Bacon, 36
    Coke and, xi
    of judges, 16
    of Mompesson and Michell, 323
    and monopoly investigations, 327
    by Parliament, xi, 17
"impossibility" and validity of laws, 123–24,
    158–59, 161, 172, 176
imprisonment
    common law and king, 295
    discretionary, 330, 331, 333, 336–40, 343,
        344, 346, 354
    and the Magna Carta, 344–46
    parliamentary resolution on, 339
indebitatus assumpsit, 70–85
industry. *See* manufacturing; monopolies;
    trade (commerce)
"infidel nations," 217–18 n. 177
inheritance, 366 n. 42
Inner Temple, 3–4, 189
Innocent III, 157 n. 27
Inns of Chancery, 3
Inns of Court, 3–4, 49 n. 36, 238, 239 n. 60,
    242
Instauratio Magna (Bacon), 43
Institutes (Justinian), 37–38, 39, 48, 55,
    56–57, 67
    See also civil law, Roman
Institutes of English Law (Cowell), 39
Institutes of the Laws of England. See under
    Coke, Sir Edward: works of
Instruments of Government, 169
Interpreter, The (Cowell), 39
inventions, patents for, 220–21, 222, 319–20
Ipswich Taylors, 219
Ireland, 307–8
Irish Reports (Davies), 51, 58–59

James I
    absolute sovereignty claimed, 40–41
    and *Bonham's Case*, 147
    and Coke, x, xii, 2, 12–13, 16–17, 53,
        62–63, 255–56, 275
    Coke on qualifications of James as a
        judge, ix, 13, 227, 295–96
    and common law, 216, 254–55, 282, 283
    conspiracy against, 8
    and judges, x, 41, 53, 282, 298
    judges, opinion of, 13, 64 n. 61
    jurisdiction of courts, 296
    legal education, 271
    on making law, 40–41
    patent investigation protested, 313, 314,
        315, 315 n. 65, 318
    patents, 222, 302–3
    on power of the king in judicature, 14,
        256, 295–96
    raising revenues, 16–17
    reason and the law, 62–63
    and reforming law, 46–48
    in Star Chamber in 1616, 15, 271–73
    and writing English law, 38 n. 17, 40, 48
James II, 90, 97, 101
Janus, 224
Jefferson, Thomas, 24–25, 66, 67
Jenkins, Roger, 131–32
Jephson, Sir John, 307
joint stock companies, 218 n. 183, 219
journals. *See* commonplace books; scribbled
    books
judges
    and acts of Parliament, 114
    allusions to divine right, 282–83
    authority of, 256, 289–90
    Bacon and, 278
    changing the law, 118
    and Charles I, 15–16
    Coke's view of the role of, 12–13
    Crown eliciting advisory opinions from,
        13–14
    decisions based on "legal" not personal
        knowledge, 334
    and Elizabeth I, 52
    independence of, 245
    and James I, x, 41, 53, 282, 298

judges (*continued*)
James I's view of, 13, 64 n. 61
reason, artificial, 251
reason and the law, 62 n. 57, 64 n. 61
reasoning, special nature of, 144, 144 n. 57
as reporters of law, 48–49
source of wisdom, 247
judging one's own case, 141, 144, 163, 167, 172, 173, 175
judgments *v.* rules of court, 332, 336, 338
judicature, power of the king in, 14, 256, 295–96
Judicature Acts, 280–81
judicia (judgments), 243
judicial activism, 11, 16, 227
judicial freedom and royal prerogative, 36
judicial integrity, 14
judicial review of legislation, xi, 108, 114, 127, 128, 167, 171–77, 180–83, 226–27
Juring Anglican Tories, 99, 99 n. 57, 101, 105, 106
jurisprudence replacing doctrine, 29, 60
jury service, 300–301
justice
and common law, 270
and reasonableness, 120, 252–53
in Tudor education, 235
Justice (icon), 2
Justinian, 32, 37, 40, 48, 55–56
Institutes, 37–38, 39, 48, 55, 56–57, 67

Keeling, secondary clerk of the Crown, 335, 337
Kenyon, Lord Chief Justice, 173–74
Kerr, Robert (Carr) (Earl of Somerset), 225 n. 4
Kingsmill, Justice, 166
kings of England. *See* Crown; *specific kings*
King v. Inhabitants of Cumberland, The (1795), 173
Kiralfy, Dr., 81

labor. *See* trades (professions)
laissez-faire, 187–88, 187 n. 2, 197, 211, 215, 216
Lambe, John, 310–11
land. *See* real property
land tenure, 57–58, 191, 197–98, 198 n. 72

language creating culture, 230–32
Latin, 2, 228
Latin maxims, 22–23
law
and alternative remedies in a single state of affairs, 72, 77, 82
antiquity of, 30, 30 n. 6, 45–46, 60, 62, 88, 150–51
canon law, 157–58
case law, 301
Charles I's promise to respect, 348
codification of, 27 n. 2
Coke on sovereignty of, 283
Coke's perspective on, 60, 110–20
command theories of, 109–10
commercial law, 192
and commonplace books, 238–39
criminal law, 23, 264–66, 301
defined, 109, 112, 119–20, 250
defined by Coke, xi, 108–9, 110, 111, 112, 114–15, 117, 119–20, 226
and events abroad, 124
function of, 21, 117
and grammar school education, 235, 242 n. 66
"impossible"/unfair to expect, 123–24, 158–59, 161, 172, 176
influence of Coke on future, 21, 117
integrity of, and the Crown, 17
invention, role of, 252
and the king (sovereign will), 2, 13, 36–37, 40–41, 48, 62, 108, 111, 114, 119–20, 153, 170
and liberty, 18
Littleton's perspective on, 60
as made rather than declared custom, 109, 113, 114
natural law, 115–16
nature of, 110, 117
obligation to obey, 117, 120
perils of innovation, 46
as product of reason *v.* will, 110
property law, 22 (*see also* real property)
and reason, xi, 61–65, 107–20, 226 (*see also* reason, artificial)
reporting, importance of, 48–49, 51–52
respect for rule of, 235

and rhetoric, 224–30, 233–34, 238–39,
    243, 249–52
role of adjudication and precedent, 11
a sense of "what fits," 121–23
social dimension of, 233
source of, xi, 38
as source of power, 108
writing of (*see under* English law)
See also civil law; common law; English
    law; legislation
Law, or a Discourse Thereof (Finch), 39
lawyers
    approach to Coke's *Reports,* 50
    as artists, 121
    Coke on, 68–69
    education of, 3–4, 27, 49 n. 36, 234–41,
        242, 244–45
    "logic-chopping," 241
    qualities of, 231 n. 33
    reason and the law, 62 n. 57, 63–64
    and rhetoric, 241–45
    in Rome, 55–66
Lawyer's Light, The (Dodderidge), 241
legacies, 292
legal authority, 244 n. 71
legal history
    Coke on common law, 225
    in Coke's *Reports,* 49–50
    contracts, 70–85
    and immemorability of law, 88–89
    publications on the courts, 284–85
    and writing the law, 30–31, 33–34
    See also civil law, Roman
legal obligation, 117, 120
legal terminology, 240
legal theory
    and Coke's "artificial reason," 107–20
    Coke's place in, 117–18
    in the Middle Ages, 116
    and monopolies, 188
legislation
    common law controlling, xi, 107–8, 115,
        143, 146–47, 154, 168, 227
    courts controlling, 25, 128, 156, 167, 172,
        173 n. 72
    due process, 328, 339, 343 n. 57, 355
    enforcing full employment, 209

ignoring statutes, 163–64, 174
judicial review of, xi, 108, 114, 127, 128,
    167, 171–77, 180–83
and the king, 65 n. 62
making a man judge in his own case, 167,
    172
Parliament dissolved without passing
    legislation, 300
reconciling with custom, 116
rights and the Magna Carta, 179, 180, 181
and royal prerogative, 164–65, 166, 187
written constitutions as check on, 183
See also specific statutes
Leigh v. Kent (1789), 174
Leslie, Charles, 105
letters patent. *See* royal patents
Letwin, William L., 205 n. 111
Levant Company, 218
Levellers, 19
Lévy-Ullman, 110
Lewis, C. S., 230, 234
liberty
    association with property, xii
    and common law, 31, 273
    defense of in *Coke on Littleton,* 58
    law and the king, 31, 65 n. 62
    and supremacy of law, 18
    See also Petition of Right; rights
Littleton, Edward, 351
Littleton, Sir Thomas
    motto, 1
    Tenures, xiii, 49 n. 36, 60, 126
Llewellyn, Karl, 252–53
loans, forced (1626–27), 330, 331, 331 n. 10,
    332, 339
Locke, John, 20, 109
logic and rhetoric, 224–25, 232–33, 240,
    249–50
London College of Physicians
    authority of, 127, 129–32, 133, 136, 138,
        141–44, 145–46, 149, 152
    Bonham attempts to join, 134–35
    founding of, 129, 141, 152
    prosecution of Jenkins and Read, 131–32
    prosecution of Perin, 147
    See also Bonham's Case
Lord Sheffield v. Ratcliffe (1615), 167–68

Lovelace v. Lovelace (1558), 5
loyalty. *See* allegiance owed the state
loyalty oaths, 86, 91–93

Magna Carta
  acts made against as void, 25
  Coke on, xii
  estates of Crown debtors, 213
  legislation and rights, 179, 180, 181
  lex terrae clause, 340, 343–46, 351, 353
  and power of the Crown, xii, 21–22, 213,
    214, 333
  in *Second Institutes,* 23
Maitland, F. W., 27, 28–30, 116, 225 n. 3,
  279–80
Mallory, William, 305, 310
malpractice, 142, 143
Mansfield, Lord, 118
manufacturing
  cloth manufacturing and trade, 195–97,
    206, 217, 219, 311
  encouraging immigration, 222
  glassmaking, 320
  and patents, 220–22, 309–12
  starch-making, 310
  See also trade (commerce)
Manwood, Chief Baron, 375
Marbury v. Madison (1803), 183
maxim, defined, 61
Maxims, regula, xix (Bacon), 164
maxims for lawyers, 22–23
Merchant Adventurers Company, 196, 217,
  218, 312 n. 44, 314
Merchant Taylors, 206
Merchant Taylors' ordinance, 201, 207
Mildmay, Sir Anthony, 266, 383
Milsom, 76
minstrels, 131
"Mischief Rule," 375
Mompesson, Sir Giles, 304, 320, 323 n. 102
monarchy, mixed, 21, 89
monopolies
  Bacon on, 187 n. 4
  bestowal on court favorites, 221–22
  Bill of Monopolies, 311, 325
  Case of Monopolies, 201, 206 n. 116, 208,
    212, 214

Coke and Bacon, xi–xii
  Coke in *Bonham's Case,* 146, 148
  Coke's opposition to, 186, 189, 201,
    205–10, 216
  and common law, 319, 321, 324, 325
  corporations as, 218, 219
  defined, 205, 211, 216, 303
  and employment, 209, 219
  for inventions, 220–21, 222, 319–20
  as judge and party, 144
  and prices, 214
  and public benefit, 320, 321 n. 90
  results of granting, 320
  royal grants of privilege, 212
  specific complaints against, 309–12
  Statute of Monopolies, 187 n. 3, 216–17,
    221, 324–25, 326
  trade restraints as, 210
  See also House of Commons investigations
    of monopolies and patents; royal
    patents
Montague, Sergeant, 275–78
Moore, Francis, 206, 207, 263, 267
Moore, John (bishop of Norwich), 364
morals in rhetoric, 237, 248–49
More, Sir Thomas, 244 n. 71
Morgan, Richard, 252
Morison, Richard, 32

Nares, R, 359
natural law, 115–16
Newbury Weavers, 219
Nichols v. Nichols (1576), 114
Nomotechnia (Finch), 39, 63
Non-Jurors, 98–99, 98 n. 55, 102–3, 105, 106
North, Lord Keeper, 60
North, Sir Roger, 351
Norwood v. Read (1558), 84, 85
Noy, William, 315 n. 61, 318–19, 331

oaths
  of allegiance, 92–93
  ex officio oaths, viii
  House of Commons' power to administer,
    315–16, 315 n. 63
  loyalty oaths, 86, 91–92
  purpose of, 104

of supremacy, 92
   See also allegiance owed the state
Omychund v. Barker (1744), 118
Ong, Walter, 232, 233
open markets, 210, 211
oration. *See* rhetoric
ornamentum, 237, 238
Orwell, George, 226
Otis, James, 25
Overbury, Sir Thomas, 225 n. 4

Paine, Mrs., 137
paper money, 181–82
Parish of Great Charte v. Parish of Kennington
   (1742), 175
Parliament
   authority over American colonies, 25
   and Charles I, 18, 350–53 (*See also* five
      knights' case)
   and common law, 111
   dissolved without passing legislation,
      300
   as a "high court," 17, 113, 114
   impeaching judges, 16
   and the king, 65 n. 62, 94 n. 38
   legal interpretations of, 300
   limited by law, 151
   power of, 18, 166, 283, 320
   resolutions and proposals resulting from
      five knights' case, 339–47, 353
   rights of, 89
   rights of subjects debated, 336
   role in preserving liberties, 17
   sovereignty of, 184
   trade regulations, 197, 320
   trade taxes, 299–300
   writing law, 113
   See also House of Commons; House of
      Lords
Parliament, acts of. *See* legislation
parole contracts, 70
Pastime of Pleasure (Hawes), 242
Paston, Bridget (wife of Coke), 9
patents, royal. *See* royal patents
patents for inventions, 220–21, 222, 319–20
Paxton's Case (1761), 179
Peacham, Rev. Edmund, 14

Peacham's Case (1615), 15
Peach's (Peeche's) Case (1376), 214
penal statutes, 46–47, 304, 308, 320
Pepys, John, 377 n. 100, 378
Percy, Henry, 165
Periam, Justice, 77–78
Perin, George, 147
perpetuities: Coke's cases, 5–6
Petition of Right
   Coke and, 18, 21–22, 54, 353, 354, 355
   Coke's definition of, 324 n. 108
   committee to draw up terms, 345–46
   effect on reforming legislation, 353, 354–55
   events leading to, 328–40, 350–53
   grievances addressed in, 353–54
   House of Commons debate, 346–50
   House of Lords debate, 340–46
   issues tackled by, 330
   reasons for, xii–xiii, 355–56
   and subjects' liberties, 344–45 n. 62
Phillips, Sir Edward, 260
physicians. *See* Bonham's Case; London
   College of Physicians
Pickering v. Thoroughgood (1533), 72–73, 74
Pinchon's Case (1612), 71, 83, 84
Pinnel's Case, 375
pleading, 239–40
Plowden's reports, 44
Plucknett, T. F. T., 282, 358
Pocock, J. G. A., 33, 88, 89
Poeton, Edward, 148
poetry, 32, 68, 240
political nation, 86 n. 1, 87, 89
Pollard, A. F., 305 n. 15
Pollock, Sir Frederick, 118–19, 155–56
Popham, Chief Justice John, 7, 84, 131,
   132–33, 207, 259
Port, Justice, 74
Portman, Justice, 73
Pound, Dean, 107
Powell, Thomas, 286, 288
power
   based on possession of crown, 105
   and God, 87 n. 4
   in government of England, 21–22
   in government of Rome, 55
   law as source of, 108

power (*continued*)
  of oratory, 230–31
  See also under Crown
Powys, Sir Thomas, 170, 175
praemunire, 15, 266–68, 270, 271–72, 274,
  289
precedent
  in *Bonham's Case,* 154–66
  in *Calvin's Case,* 91
  in Coke's *Institutes,* 60
  Coke's view of, 11
  in five knights' case, 334–40, 343
  foundation of, 10
  judging argument's validity by, 252
  and legal change, 11
  and loyalty to king, 86
  and "perfect reason," 114
  reliance on, 301
  and royal prerogative, 114
  as source of common law, 26
prerogative. *See* royal prerogative
price regulation, 198–200, 205, 209–10, 211,
  214
Prince's Case (1606), ix
*Prior of Castle Acre v. the Dean of
  St. Stephen's,* 166
private law, 57
Privy Council, 15, 16, 53, 54, 294 n. 45, 298,
  326
Proclamation Case (1611), 108
Proctor's Case (1614), 10 n. 11
Progymnasmata (Apthonius of Tyre), 235
prohibitions, 11–12, 13, 256, 290–92, 294–97
property
  association with liberty, xii
  Charles I's promise to respect, 348
  See also real property
property law in *Coke on Littleton,* 22
property rights, 113
prosopopeia, 48
Puritans, viii, 188, 188 n. 13
Puttenham, George, 240, 243 n. 68, 249
Pym, John, on king and law, 352–53

Quintillian, 231, 236 n. 47
quotations. *See exempla*

Ralegh (Raleigh), Sir Walter, viii, 8, 383
Rastell's *Book of Entries,* 75
Ratcliff's Case (1592), 114
Read, Simon, 131, 132
Readings, 4
real property
  and the art of law, 125–26
  in *Coke on Littleton,* 58
  Crown debtors, 213
  disseisins, 122–24
  enclosure laws, 197–98
  and the king, 65 n. 62
  Littleton, 126
  and perpetuities, 5–6
reason
  Coke's use of the term, 115–17
  and common law, 179 n. 97, 252–53
  and fundamental law, 151
  and justice, 252–53
  king's reason and the law, 62 n. 57,
    64 n. 61
  and the law, xi, 61–65, 107–8, 110–20,
    176, 250 (*see also* reason, artificial)
  laws regulating craftsmen, 207
  "perfect reason," 112
  and the rhetorical paradigm, 244
reason, artificial
  Coke and "impossibility," 123–24
  Coke and modern legal theory, 107–20
  Coke's argument *ab utile,* 125–26
  Coke's definition of, 61–62, 88–89, 115, 250
  Dodderidge on, 250 n. 90
  and generosity, 124
  and James I, 13, 227
  and judicial review, 226
  as the life of the law, 61–65, 250
  and oratorical tradition, 231 n. 33
  rhetoricians' artificial logic, 249–50
  and a sense of "what fits," 121–23
reasonableness, defined, 118–20
reform
  Coke on reform of English law, 46–48
  of English common law, 26–28, 31–32, 37,
    41
  expected from five knights' case, 340–41,
    348–50, 351, 354–55

fiscal (1610), 303
    by judicial action *v.* legislation, xi
    judicial activism, 11, 16, 227
    reports as writing law, 48
    and vested interests, 298–99
Reformation, 160
religion
    Coke and, 188
    Crown's powers concerning clergy, 15
    Elizabeth I and Parliament, 6
    and English monarchism, 1, 99
    a man's trade as his life, 208 n. 129
    prosecutions, viii, 8
    trade with "infidel nations," 217–18 n. 177
    See also ecclesiastical courts; God
religious house lands, 160–62
religious house seals, 156–58
rent service, 161–62
reporting law, importance of, 48–49, 51–52
Report of Shelley's Case (Coke), 370
Reports (Coke). *See under* Coke, Sir Edward: works of
reports by writers other than Coke, 367–69
reports published by Plowden, 44, 368
Restoration, 169
Revolution of 1688, 171
rhetoric
    Bacon on, 225
    and civilization, 241–42, 243
    Coke's place in tradition of, 227–29
    and common law, 233–34, 244, 245–49
    and commonplace books, 235–41
    cultural implications of, 230–32
    education in, 234–41
    exempla, use of, 236–37, 243, 245–47
    and government, 231–32, 243
    importance of for Elizabethans, 224–25
    law and artifice, 249–52
    and lawyers, 241–45
    and legal reasoning, 244
    and legal terminology, 240
    and logic, 224–25, 232–33, 240, 249–50
    in the Middle Ages, 232 n. 34
    orator, defined, 231
    power of, 231
Rich, Sir Nathaniel, 352

Ridley, Sir Thomas, 39
rights
    and acts of Parliament, 179, 180
    Charles I's promise to respect, 348
    and civil wars, 186
    Coke in five knights' case, 340–41
    and common law in America, 179
    debated in Parliament, 336
    Dodderidge on, 241
    to employment, 207
    freedom of trade, 212
    and imprisonment, 336
    and the Magna Carta, 179, 180, 181
    of Parliament, 89
    of the poor, 221 n. 202
    to practice a trade, 144, 148, 200–201,
        202–3, 207, 208 n. 129
    preservation of, 17
    property, 113
    resolutions and proposals resulting from
        five knights' case, 339–47, 353
    and royal patents, 322, 324
    and royal prerogative, 344–45 n. 62, 345,
        347
    of Scottish subjects, ix, 91 n. 17, 226 n. 10
    and threat to the rule of law, xii
    tillage and tenurial, 198 n. 72
    and trade restraints, 220, 223
    trial by jury, 181
    See also liberty; Petition of Right
Robin et al. v. Hardaway et al. (1772), 181
Rogers v. Perry (1613), 204
Roman Catholics, 8
Roman law. *See* civil law, Roman
Rowles v. Mason (1612), 111
royal patents
    in *Bonham's Case,* 144, 146
    and Coke's definition of monopolies, 216,
        303
    for court favorites, 221–22
    Elizabeth I, 222, 303 n. 7
    enforcement of, 321
    inconvenient *v.* illegal, 322, 324
    James I, 222, 302–3, 313, 314, 315, 315 n. 65
    limits to, 213, 303
    and monopolies, 205, 208, 215, 220

royal patents (*continued*)
  and prices of goods, 316
  and public benefit, 320, 321 n. 90
  and rights of subjects, 322, 324
  specific complaints against, 309–12
  staying execution of, 314
  See also House of Commons investigations
    of monopolies and patents; monopolies
royal prerogative
  antiprerogative opinions, 255
  and antiquity of English law, 46
  and the Bill of Rights, 171
  and the Chancery, 256, 260–61, 274, 277
  Charles I on, 350
  Coke on, xii, 42, 111, 116, 255–56, 284
  and Coke's definition of law, 114
  and common law, 36, 54, 55, 111, 170, 171,
    272–73, 284
  dispensing with statutes, 164–65
  Ellesmere on, 284
  and High Commission's powers, viii
  imprisonment, 330, 331, 333, 336–40, 343,
    344, 346, 354
  James I on, 271
  judges defending, 282–83
  and judicial freedom, 36
  as the law, 170
  law as source of power in government, 108
  monopolies, 187, 215
  and rights, 344–45 n. 62, 345, 347
  and statute law, 283
  and statutes conflicting with, 160–62
  statutory invasion of, 325
  transfer to an individual, 320
  and tyranny, 254–55
  and writing the law, 39
  See also Crown
Rudyard, Benjamin, 348–49
rule book, 334–36
rule of court *v.* judgment, 332, 336, 338
Rule of Reason (Wilson), 240, 243–44
Rules and Decisions (Bacon), 43
Russell, Conrad, xii
Russel v. Russel (1783), 174
Russia Company, 218
Ruswell's case, 262–63, 278

Sackville, Sir Edward, 309
Sadler, Secretary to the Lord Privy Seal,
    309–10
Salisbury, William, 309
Sandys, Sir Edwin, 195, 305
Saye, Lord, 341, 344
Scotland, rights of subjects in, ix, 91 n. 17,
    226 n. 10
scribbled books, 329 n. 5
Scrope, Henry, Ninth Baron, 6
seals, keeping of, 156–58
Selden, John
  on Coke, 55
  on common law, 224
  on English law, 29
  five knights' case, 331, 332–33 n. 15, 336–38,
    342 n. 54
self-incrimination, viii
sententiae, 237–38, 243
Septennial Acts of 1730, 108
sergeants-at-law, 7
Settled Land Act of 1882, 6
settlement of landed estates, 5–6, 6 n. 9
Shakespeare, William, 234
Sharswood, George, 66, 67
Shelley's Case (1581), vii, 5, 241, 363, 370, 375
Shelton, Sir Richard, 336
Sheriff of Northumberland's Case, 164, 165,
    170
Sherlock, William, 98–99, 101–2
Shilton, Richard, 257 n. 20
Shrewsbury Drapers, 310
Simon, Sir Jocelyn, 280
Slade's Case (1602)
  alternative remedies, 72, 77, 82
  changing the law, 79–85
  Coke's argument, vii, 79 n. 47, 82–83, 85
  Coke's reporting of, 369
  and contract laws, 226
  enforcement of contracts, 191
  indebitatus assumpsit, 70–85
slavery, 181
Smith, Adam, 211–12 n. 144, 218 n. 183
Smith, Sir Thomas, 124
"social contract," 109
social dimension of law and politics, 233

society and oratory, 230–32
Socrates, death of, 237
Somerset, Robert Carr (Kerr), Earl of, 15, 298
sovereign power of the king, 21–22
Spelman, Justice, 73, 74, 74 n. 17
Spenser, Edmund, 31
Stamp Act, 179–80
Standard Oil Co. v. United States (1911), 186 n. 1
Star Chamber
    expense of depositions, 299
    James I sitting in 1616, 15, 271–73
    jurisdiction, 10–11
Starkey, Thomas, 26–27, 28, 31–32
state, allegiance to. *See* allegiance owed the state
statute law, 40, 111, 283
Statute of 1552, 199
Statute of Artificers, 200–201, 202, 219 n. 194
Statute of Carlisle, 156
Statute of Frauds, 174
Statute of Labourers, 209
Statute of Monopolies, 187 n. 3, 216–17, 221, 324–25, 326
Statute of Supremacy, 295
Statute of Treason, 96, 105
Statute of Uses, vii, 113
statutes. *See* legislation
Stephen, James Fitzjames, 248
Stewart v. Lawton (1823), 174
Strowd's Case (1575), 162
Surgeon's Case (1370), 82
Symonds, Justice, 178

taxation
    customs duties, 194
    loans, forced (1626–27), 330, 331, 331 n. 10, 332, 339
    nonparliamentary, 339
    of trade, 299–300
tenancy
    agricultural land, 197–98, 198 n. 72
    in Littleton and *Coke on Littleton,* 57–58
Tenures (Littleton), xiii, 49 n. 36, 56, 57

text law, 40
Thomas, J. H., 66–67, 358
Thorne, Samuel E., 23, 128
Thoroughgood's Case (1584), 366
Throgmorton's Case, 265
Thurston, John, 368 n. 61
Tindal, Sir John, 264, 267
tobacco, 195, 311
Tooley's (Tolley's) Case (1613), 202, 203
Tories, 66, 67, 99
Tourneur, Timothy, 255, 272, 274, 276
Towers v. Barnett (1786), 118
Townshend, Sir Henry, 290–91, 309
trade (commerce)
    Coke's interest in, 190–93, 223
    commercial law, 192
    commercial litigation, 193
    company system, 217
    contracts restraining, 204
    and the Crown, 194–95, 205, 212–13
    domestic commerce, 197–203
    due process, 213
    in foods, 195 n. 48
    foreign commerce, 194–97, 199, 215, 217, 218, 310, 311
    forestalling and engrossing, 198–200, 198 n. 73, 210
    free trade, 147, 200, 210–11, 212–13, 214–15, 319
    with "infidel nations," 217–18 n. 177
    price regulation, 198–200, 205, 209–10, 211, 214
    and public good, 207, 211
    regulation, power of, 320
    regulation and restriction, defined, 206 n. 114, 219
    taxation of, 299–300
    Tudor economic policies, 197
    See also manufacturing; monopolies
trade crisis, 217
trade depression, 195
trade privileges, 187 n. 3
trades (professions)
    contracts prohibiting practice of, 204
    guilds, 205–7, 206 n. 114, 220
    labor shortage, 209

trades (professions) (*continued*)
   monopolies and unemployment, 209, 219
   reason and laws regulating, 207
   right to practice a trade, 144, 148,
      200–201, 202–3, 207, 208 n. 129
   statutes affecting, 209
trading companies, 190
treason
   cases in *Third Institute,* 382–83
   Coke on, 65 n. 62, 96, 229
   Coke's arrest for, 54
   Coke's prosecutions, viii
   Essex, trial of, viii, 8, 228, 383
   Gunpowder Plot, viii, 8, 228–29, 383
   king's power to imprison for, 333
   and nature of allegiance to king, 94
   punishment for, 229
   Statute of Treason, 96, 105
   and William and Mary, 97–105
Tregor's Case, 154
Trevett v. Weeden, 170, 181–82
trial by jury, 181
True Law of Free Monarchies (James I), 40
tyranny, 46, 235, 254–55
Tyrringham's Case (1584), 198 n. 72

United States. *See* American law, Coke's
   influence on
Unwin, George, 187

Vade Mecum (Coke), 360, 370, 371, 376, 377,
   379
Variation of Trusts Act of 1958, 119
Varnum, Major-General, 181–82
View of the Civil and Ecclesiastical Law
   (Ridley), 39
Villiers, George. *See* Buckingham, George
   Villiers, 1st Duke of
Villiers, Sir John, 54, 194 n. 45

Vindication (pamphlet), 101
Virgil, 244 n. 71
Virginia Company, 190, 195, 218

Wade v. Braunch (1596), 72 n. 9
Wagner, Donald O., 188, 212
Walmesley, Justice Thomas, 140, 145, 146,
   153, 258–59, 289–90, 294, 375
war
   civil wars, 186, 187 n. 5
   and forced loans, 336
   with France and Spain, xii
   illegal courses preparing for, 350
   with Spain, 17–18
Warburton, Justice Peter, 140, 289–90
Welsh Council, 292
Wentworth, Sir Thomas, 338, 350
Whigs, 66, 67, 97
Whitby, Daniel, 98, 99–100
Whitelocke, Justice, 260 n. 38
Whitlocke, Justice, 335
Whorwood v. Gybbons (1587), 77
Willes, Justice, 175–76
William and Mary, 90, 97–106
Williams (bishop), 279
Williams, Justice, 297
Wilson, Thomas, 232, 233, 240, 243–44, 249
Wimbish v. Tailbois (1550), 113
Windebank, Sir Francis, 377, 378
Withrington, Henry, 305
Wolsey, Cardinal Thomas, 333
Wray, Justice, 77
Wright, Lord, 118
writing, education in, 236–37
Wycliffe, John, 31
Wyndhams of Norfolk and Somerset,
   379–80

Year Books, 22, 27, 44, 245

This book is set in Adobe Garamond, a modern adaptation by
Robert Slimbach of the typeface originally cut around 1540 by the
French typographer and printer Claude Garamond. The Garamond
face, with its small lowercase height and restrained contrast between
thick and thin strokes, is a classic "old-style" face and has long been
one of the most influential and widely used typefaces.

Printed on paper that is acid-free and meets the requirements of the
American National Standard for Permanence of Paper for
Printed Library Materials, z39.48-1992. ⊚

Book design by Sandra Strother Hudson
Athens, Georgia
Typography by Tseng Information Systems
Durham, North Carolina
Printed and bound by Worzalla Publishing Company
Stevens Point, Wisconsin